THE
# BIBLIOGRAPHY
OF
# HUMAN BEHAVIOR

# THE
# BIBLIOGRAPHY
## OF
# HUMAN BEHAVIOR

## HIRAM CATON,
### Editor-in-Chief

Frank K. Salter
and J.M.G. van der Dennen,
Associate Editors

Bibliographies and Indexes in Anthropology, Number 7

**GREENWOOD PRESS**
Westport, Connecticut • London

**Library of Congress Cataloging-in-Publication Data**

The bibliography of human behavior / editor-in-chief, Hiram Caton
; associate editors, Frank K. Salter and J.M.G. van der Dennen.
p. cm.—(Bibliographies and indexes in anthropology, ISSN
0742-6884 ; no. 7)
Includes index.
ISBN 0-313-27897-0 (alk. paper)
1. Psychology—Bibliography. 2. Human behavior—Bibliography.
3. Behavior evolution—Bibliography. I. Hiram Caton. II. Series.
Z7201.C37 1993
[BF121]
016.15—dc20 93-3066

British Library Cataloguing in Publication Data is available.

Library of Congress Catalog Card Number: 93-3066
ISBN: 0-313-27897-0
ISSN: 0742-6884

First published in 1993

Greenwood Press, 88 Post Road West, Westport, CT 06881
An imprint of Greenwood Publishing Group, Inc.

Printed in the United States of America

The paper used in this book complies with the
Permanent Paper Standard issued by the National
Information Standards Organization (Z39.48-1984).

10 9 8 7 6 5 4 3 2 1

# Contents

# Preface

This bibliography is meant to facilitate access to the literature on human behavior and psychology based on the biological sciences. The decision to spread the net widely was prompted partly by the need for a guide to the traffic across disciplinary boundaries, and partly by the proliferation of new applications from basic disciplines to once remote subjects.

The intention has been to select the best and the latest from an eligible literature of about 60,000 titles. About 80 percent of our entries were published after 1979. The editors have nevertheless been mindful of classics. Charles Darwin, needless to say, is a vital if ambiguous force in contemporary research, but Romanes, Lashley, Spearman, Yerkes, Lorenz, and other major contributors are included in the title lists.

The criteria for inclusion were the attributes of the good scientific article: novelty and adequacy of concepts and data, methodological soundness or innovation, significance of the findings, and suggestiveness toward further research. Concept formation and criticism, especially where evolutionary ideas or mind-brain relations are involved, inspires a sizable speculative literature. It is represented here, together with the critical debates that seem to be its leaven.

Various procedures have been used to identify publications having the desired features. The principal method was to develop bibliographies of specific fields in collaboration with professional associations or research centers. Their contributions have varied in kind and degree, but in aggregate they have been essential to the validity of our title lists.

For fields in which such collaboration was not established, the editors relied primarily on the consensual ranking of journals. Articles appearing in leading specialist journals were deemed to be more eligible for inclusion than articles appearing elsewhere. For books and edited volumes, reviews appearing in journals specializing in reviews have been a guide; the standing of a series or a publisher were also taken to be indicative as was the standing of individuals, research centers, and laboratories. In addition, we obtained from a number of investigators their own nominations of their best publications.

Estimates of standing were not derived from a formal methodology. This presents no difficulty with respect to professional associations, which the bibliographer may assume to represent the considered judgment of a particular field. More refined title selection uses bibliometric methods. This option was not pursued because we doubted that the quality enhancement so obtained would be cost-effective.

Standard on-line and printed bibliographies have been used for title searches, but they are of limited value. We found that the most effective means of compiling title lists was to examine publications directly on the library shelf. On-line systems were however indispensable for title verification. They were accessed through AARNet, which links Australian research institutions with on-line data bases world-wide. The Harvard University HOLLIS system and the University of Melbourne library were the sources most often tapped for title verification.

We have elected to classify titles by discipline, and in a few cases by sub-field topic. This approach anchors our lists in the research mainstreams from which they spring. The disadvantage is that so much research crosses disciplinary boundaries. It is possible for a study of an emotion to be assignable to psychiatry because of a morbidity element, to neurology because of a neural reference, and to endocrinology because of a hormone reference. Thus our sub-field file, Sexuality, is based primarily on endocrinology, but there is substantial in-put from studies of personal and cultural experience of sexual expression. Some of these investigations are conducted by endocrinologists, but ethologists, sociobiologists, sexologists, and psychiatrists also contribute. Again, Parenting is anchored in inclusive fitness investigations and studies of attachment, but other fields also figure. The moral is that the disciplinary origin of a title does not determine its location in our lists. The indexes have been compiled to provide additional paths through these ambiguities.

The most heterogeneous file is History and Philosophy; the most promiscuous subject is evolutionary theory. The simple solution to the latter problem was to establish an Evolutionary Theory title list. However, much evolutionary theory has no direct bearing on human behavior, whereas some disciplines, such as sociobiology, engage substantially in evolutionary theory, or a branch of it. In this predicament, we have classified evolutionary theory titles that bear substantially on philosophical or paradigm issues in the History and Philosophy list. Other general evolutionary theory has been assigned to Human Evolution, unless there is a subject angle that directs it to another list, such as Sociobiology or Behavior Genetics. Numerous general evolutionary theory titles have been included not because of their application to human behavior but because they influence the orientation of empirical investigation.

The history of ideas territory covered is the domain of Charles Darwin and successors. No effort has been made to represent the history of the behavioral sciences, although a sufficient number of such titles are included to provide indications of the literature. As for the man and his theory, the bibliography tracks the outpouring of studies over the past decade that have substantially revised the view that prevailed at the time of the Darwin centenary. It is now believed that Darwin's dependence on the natural theology of William Paley reaches to the core of his "long argument" for the origin of species by natural selection. On this view, Darwin accepted Paley's zoological demonstrations of adaptation as the evidence of a central directing agency, while changing the agency from God to natural selection. The personal motivation for this shift, it now seems, was its aptness for resolving the problem of evil by making adversity and extinction integral to the life process. Historians have also revised the belief in the triumph of Darwinism, by the end of the nineteenth century, by detailing numerous criticisms from a diversity of biologists.

The ferment of ideas has been abundant in the past two decades. The extinctions controversy of the Seventies featured, among other things, a replay of the contention between Uniformitarians and Catastrophists. The now general acceptance of some major and many minor asteroid collisions seems to have shifted the balance, for the time being, to the Catastrophists (Raup 1986).

The consensus that Homo evolved in a savannah environment was challenged in the Eighties by revival of Alister Hardy's proposal that many details of human adaptation point to an aquatic phase of human evolution (Roede 1991). Meanwhile the rival chronologies of recent evolution, based on paleobiology and molecular methods, respectively, have enriched evolutionary thought by adding exact laboratory methods to the traditional morphological approach to phylogeny.

At the Darwin centenary, the central thesis of neo-Darwinism was characterized as the belief that evolutionary change derives from small genetic changes under selection pressure. This thesis has been contested during the period covered by this bibliography. In 1982 the *Journal of Social and Biological Structures* published a manifesto proclaiming the successor to neo-Darwinism, Constructional Biology. At about the same time, an exponent of punctuated equilibrium avowed that neo-Darwinism "is effectively dead, despite its persistence as textbook orthodoxy." The 1984 Ho and Saunders volume, *Beyond Neo-Darwinism*, and the 1985 Depew and Weber edited volume, *Evolution at a Crossroads: The New Biology and the New Philosophy of Science,* were further signs of conceptual trends and empirical breakthroughs that include the discovery of somatic hypermutation, an apparent Lamarckian inheritance mechanism.

This ferment, important as it may be, has not substantially influenced the great body of our titles, whose orientation is unambiguously neo-Darwinian. The enormous surge of innovative ethological and sociobiological studies throwing very new light on human behavior is proof against premature epitaphs. No doubt fractal mathematics, by describing previously unexplored nonlinear phenomenon, has promoted catastrophist research simply by providing an alternative to the equiprobability rule invoked so widely in physics and genetics. Physicists have long since accepted wave and particle interpretations of radiation. Perhaps a similar acknowledgement of "complementarity" awaits the evolutionary sciences.

A number of titles on cosmology and physical theory have been included in the History and Philosophy list. This is traditional, since theories of life on earth have always comprised a sublunary cosmology inviting linkage to the stellar universe. But since many of these studies expound cosmology using nonlinear models, their inclusion is particularly apposite.

While most of the titles are anchored in biologically oriented studies of human behavior, there are exceptions. The largest cohort are animal, especially primate studies, elucidating behaviors occurring also in humans. The Prehistory file however lists numerous archaeological investigations that are only loosely related to paleobiology or to cultural evolution. Their inclusion is dictated by the need to represent Prehistory as a field. Although some social psychologists began to connect with psychobiology, ethology, and sociobiology in the Eighties, a substantial number of non-biologically oriented titles have been included.

The study of cultural evolution is experiencing a revival after a period of relative obscurity as a sub-field of prehistory and anthropology. In the last century cultural evolution was the central idea of grand sociology in the manner of Spencer, Mill, Comte, and Marx. The current revival is driven from diverse directions; population genetics, economic history, and evolutionary psychology are prominent. The revival does not at the moment seem to form a coherent subject. The focus of our list is technological and economic expansion, since artifacts and techniques are clearly units of cultural change, whatever else might also be units. Some recent economic studies that take techniques as units of change interpret them in the mathematical idiom of population genetics. An interpretation of technological change as a nonlinear phenomenon has not come to our attention.

Critical to the understanding of cultural evolution is not only what drives it forward but what holds it in a steady state, or sends it into retrograde. The history of disease is likely to be an important factor in this story. The outward expansion of Europe from 1300 transmitted European diseases to New World and Oceanic peoples who had no immunity. The high morbidity and mortality rates among natives resulting from European contact may illustrate the principle of independent simultaneous causes in the establishment of cultural dominance.

Scientific film is a distinctive methodology for data collection and preservation of non-recurrent data. Our investigation of film archives quickly revealed that the number of archives alone would defeat an attempt to describe their contents in a synoptic fashion; a bibliography devoted specifically to behavioral and ethnographic film would be required. We mention here but two sources for which there is published documentation listed in the Bibliography file. In 1957 Carleton Gajdusek made the first of numerous expeditions to Papua New Guinea and neighboring islands to document his studies of disease patterns in primitive cultures. He established a film archive at the National Institute of Neurological Diseases and Blindness; for its description together with an analysis of the methodologies of film studies and film archiving, see Sorenson and Gajdusek, 1966. A second archive is the Institute for Scientific Film, Göttingen, Germany. The archive covers biology, ethnology, medicine, history, psychology, technology, and natural sciences. Archive holdings are described in two publications, *Publikationen zu wissenschaftlichen Filmen* and *Encyclopaedia Cinematographica*. The Max Planck Center for Human Ethology, under its Director Professor Irenäus Eibl-Eibesfeldt, pioneered the ethological film. Over 130 films made by Max Planck scientists in the course of their five-site, twenty year longitudinal studies are incorporated into the Göttingen archive; see Galle, 1980-. Many countries maintain similar archives, and there are major holdings in the Pitt Rivers Museum, Oxford, the Peabody Museum, Harvard, and the Smithsonian Institution, to mention a few.

Film methodologies for the study of animal and human movement have developed in tandem with technologies of visual data analysis. Film studies of human facial expression, which commenced with the Ekman and Friesen (1977) Facial Action Coding System of still photographs, have progressed through computer coding and analysis of video to the new technology of computer-generated facial images. Leonard and colleagues (Leonard 1991) have automated computer coding by using artificial intelligence techniques for digitizing facial signals.

There are a number of other exclusions in addition to film. The exclusion of book reviews prompts misgivings, since they are an important medium of evaluation and of shop talk. Hopefully the inclusion of review articles (indicated as such in the Subject Index) and of open peer review articles is some compensation. With fewer misgivings we have excluded theses, conference papers and communications to newsletters. A list of newsletters would have been relevant, but it is among the ornaments that the project's limited budget could not afford.

Another exclusion is applied research, with the exception of some clinically-related research. Five years hence this exclusion will not be viable. Clinics are utilizing genetics, neurology, and endocrinology. Impacts are spreading to education, law and justice, public health, insurance, family policy, multicultural policy, economics, and politics, inclusive of the gender equality question. This phenomenon signals that the Era of Biology has arrived in the domain of public policy.

A related exclusion is policy and ethical studies of technological impacts. Although the editors have in hand some 500 titles in this area, they have not been included because they were not collected systematically and because their inclusion would tilt the bibliography in the direction of applications.

The Politics list is brief because linkages between political behavior and the evolutionary sciences are still weakly developed, notwithstanding some important contributions. Articles appearing in

*Politics and the Life Sciences* deal in the main with policy questions. That journal sponsors a bibliography of biopolitical and policy publications (Somit and Peterson 1990).

This bibliography has a history. One of us has compiled a 100,000 title bibliography on war, aggression and violence. The other two commenced their title collection over a decade ago as political scientists seeking illumination from science colleagues. The rewards of this activity resemble the rewards of the naturalist: one becomes attuned to slight differences and celebrates novel specimens. There is also the reward of tracking the large changes that occur in decade increments. The level of sophistication reached during the Eighties may be measured by reading the interpretations of the evolutionary sciences emanating from the Fifties. Social scientists could derive little more than general ideas and no method to speak of. Today biological methods and hypotheses are pursued in all fields of social science, while the advance of behavioral medicine and other applications in leisure and design are gradually replacing cultural and philosophical interpretations of the body by a naturalistic view.

In offering this bibliography, we acknowledge its imperfections. Significant publications have been omitted from want of sufficient acquaintance with certain fields. Quite a few have been omitted because the project's budget would not support the cost of their verification. It is hoped nevertheless that it will be a useful tool for the promotion of research.

# Acknowledgments

The bibliography has been assisted by numerous colleagues and organizations. The sponsoring professional associations were the Australian Society for Human Biology, the International Society for Human Ethology, the European Sociobiology Society, the Politics and Life Sciences Association, and the Association for Behavior Analysis. Their officers and interested members were vital to establishing the project's cross-disciplinary and international reach. Those especially instrumental in the early phase of the project were Randy Nesse, then President of Human Behavior and Evolution Society, Roger D. Masters, Albert Somit, Jan Wind, Frans X. Plooij, Gail Zivin, and Vincent S.E. Falger. In the middle phase of the project, Edward K. Morris, then President of the Association for Behavior Analysis, offered the Association's support, which soon took the form of Henry D. Schlinger, Jr., the compiler of the Behavior Analysis title list.

The Director and staff of the Max-Planck Center for Human Ethology have been closely involved in the project for over two years. Their assistance, advice, and encouragement have been vital. Thanks particularly to Karl Grammer for assistance in compiling the human ethology title list, and to Christine Enhuber, Johanna Uher, and Gottfried Hohmann for assistance with proof-reading.

Over a dozen journal and newsletter editors responded to our request to publish an announcement of the project. Their support is appreciated.

For funding we thank the Max-Planck Center for Human Ethology and the University Research Grants fund at Griffith University. Grants from the Pioneer Fund Inc. for another project greatly relieved pressures against our limited resources for this one. The Faculty of Humanities provided funds for the first two years of the project and support facilities throughout. The Polemological Institute, University of Groningen, also provided support facilities.

The Australian Research Council declined to consider our application for funds. It is be hoped that the bibliography's publication will in some small way prompt the Council's grant committee to acknowledge human behavioral biology as valid research fields.

The project's editorial consultants are Henry D. Schlinger, Jr., Department of Psychology, Western New England College, behavior analysis; Elizabeth Kandel-Englander, Westfield State College; parenting and related psychology; Randolph M. Nesse, M.D., Department of Psychiatry, University of Michigan Medical Center, psychiatry and related psychology; and N. G. Martin, Queensland Institute for Medical Research, behavioral genetics and related psychology.

The project's programmers were Kas Somers and Robert Howlett. Diane McGowan and Kas Somers entered most of the titles. Lee Hutchinson transferred the titles and indexes from the data base into word processing files. Our thanks to all these persons.

# 1

# Human Evolution

1 Alberch, P. 1982. The generative and regulatory role of development in evolution. In *Environmental Adaptation and Evolution.* Edited by Mossakowski, D, G Roth. Stuttgart: Gustav Fisher.

2 Alcock, J. 1978. Evolution and human violence. In *War: A Historical, Political and Social Study.* Edited by Farrer, LL Pp. 21-27. Santa Barbara: ABC-Clio.

3 Alexander, R D. 1974. The evolution of social behavior. *Annual Review of Ecological Systems* 5: 325-383.

4 Alexander, R D, K M Noonan. 1979. Concealment of ovulation, parental care, and human social evolution. In *Evolutionary Biology and Human Social Behavior.* Edited by Chagnon, N A, W Irons. Pp. 436-461. North Scituate, MA: Duxbury.

5 Alexander, R D, D W Tinkle, eds. 1981. *Natural Selection and Social Behavior: Recent Research and New Theory.* New York: Chiron Press.

6 Alexander, R D. 1990. *How Did Humans Evolve? Reflections on the Uniquely Unique Species.* Ann Arbor: Museum of Natural History Monograph 1.

7 Alland, A. 1973. *Evolution and Human Behavior: An Introduction to Darwinian Anthropology.* 2nd ed. New York: Doubleday.

8 Andrews, P. 1985. Improved timing of hominoid evolution with a DNA clock. *Nature* 314: 498-499.

9 Angel, J L. 1973. Paleogeology, paleodemography and health. In *Population, Ecology and Social Evolution.* Edited by Polgar, S. Pp. 167-190. Chicago: Aldine.

10 Armstrong, E, D Falk, eds. 1982. *Primate Brain Evolution: Methods and Concepts.* New York: Plenum.

11 Atchley, WR, DS Woodruff, eds. 1981. *Evolution and Speciation: Essays in Honour of M.J.D. White.* Cambridge: Cambridge University Press.

12 Bar-Yosef, O, ed. 1988. *L'homme de Néandertal: La pensée.* Liège: ERAUL.

13 Bell, G. 1982. *The Masterpiece of Nature: The Evolution and Genetics of Sexuality.* Berkeley: University of California Press.

14 Bendall, DS, ed. 1983. *Evolution from Molecules to Men.* Cambridge: Cambridge University Press.

15 Berge, C, R Orban-Segebarth, P Schmid. 1984. Obstetrical interpretation of the australopithecine pelvic cavity. *Journal of Human Evolution* 13: 573-581.

16 Bigelow, RS. 1972. The evolution of cooperation, aggression and self-control. In *Nebraska Symposium on Motivation.* Edited by Cole, J K, D D Jensen. Pp. 1-57. Lincoln: University of Nebraska Press.

17 Birdsell, JB. 1972. *Human Evolution: An Introduction to the New Physical Anthropology.* Chicago: Rand McNally.

18 Blum, HF. 1968. *Time's Arrow and Evolution.* 3rd ed. Princeton: Princeton University Press.

19 Blumenberg, B. 1985. Population characteristics of extinct hominid endocranial volume. *American Journal of Physical Anthropology* 68: 263-279.

20 Blumenschine, R J. 1987. Characteristics of an early hominid scavenging niche. *Current Anthropology* 28: 383-391.

21 Bock, W J. 1981. Functional-adaptive analysis in evolutionary classification. *American Zoologist* 21: 5-20.

22 Boesch, C, H Boesch. 1983. Optimisation of nut-cracking with natural hammers by wild chimpanzees. *Behaviour* 13: 265-86.

23 Boesch, C, H Boesch. 1984. Possible causes of sex differences in the use of natural hammers by wild chimpanzees. *Journal of Human Evolution* 13: 415-40.

24 Borgia, G. 1980. Human aggression as a biological adaption. In *The Evolution of Human Social Behavior.* Edited by Lockard, J. Pp. 165-91. New York: Elsevier.

25 Brace, C L, A Montagu. 1977. *Human Evolution: An Introduction to Biological Anthropology.* 2nd ed. New York: Macmillan.

26 Brauer, G. 1984. The 'Afro-European sapiens hypothesis', and hominid evolution in East Asia during the late Middle Pleistocene and Upper Pleistocene. *Forschung Institut Senckenberg* 69: 145-65.

27 Brauer, G. 1984. A craniological approach to the origin of anatomically modern H. sapiens in Africa and implications for the

appearance of modern Europeans. In *The Origins of Modern Humans.* Edited by Smith, F H, F Spencer. Pp. 327-410. New York: Alan R. Liss.

28 Bromage, T G, M C Dean. 1985. Reevaluation of the age at death of immature fossil hominids. *Nature* 311: 252-257.

29 Brown, F, J Harris, R Leakey, A Walker. 1985. Early Homo erectus skeleton from west Lake Turkana, Kenya. *Nature* 316: 788-792.

30 Bull, J J. 1983. *Evolution of Sex Determining Mechanisms.* Menlo Park, CA: Benjamin-Cummings.

31 Bunn, H T. 1981. Archaeological evidence of meat-eating by Plio-Pleistocene hominids from Koobi Fora and Olduvai Gorge. *Nature* 291: 574-577.

32 Bunn, H T. 1983. Evidence on the diet and subsistence patterns of Plio-Pleistocene hominids at Koobi Fora, Kenya and Olduvai Gorge, Tanzania. In *Animals and Archaeology, Vol 1, Hunters and Their Prey, British Archeological Report 163.* Edited by Clutton-Brock, J, C Grigson. Pp. 21-30. London: British Archaeological Reports.

33 Bunn, H T, E Kroll. 1986. Systematic butchery by Plio/Pleistocene hominids at Olduvai Gorge, Tanzania. *Current Anthropology* 25: 431-442.

34 Butzer, K W. 1977. Environment, culture, and human evolution. *American Scientist* 65: 572-584.

35 Byrne, R W, A Whiten. 1988. *Machiavellian Intelligence: Social Expertise and the Evolution of Intelligence in Monkeys, Apes, and Man.* London: Oxford University Press.

36 Calvin, W H. 1982. Did throwing stones shape hominid brain evolution? *Ethology and Sociobiology* 3: 115-24.

37 Campbell, B G. 1982. *Humankind Emerging.* Boston: Little, Brown.

38 Cann, R L, M Stoneking, A C Wilson. 1987. Mitochondrial DNA and human evolution. *Nature* 325: 31-35.

39 Carey, J W, A T Steegman. 1981. Human nasal protrusion, latitude, and climate. *American Journal of Physical Anthropology* 56: 313-319.

40 Charnov, E L. 1978. Evolution of eusocial behavior: Offspring choice or parental parasitism? *Journal of Theoretical Biology* 75: 451-465.

41 Charnov, E L. 1982. *The Theory of Sex Allocation.* Princeton: Princeton University Press.

42 Chavaillon, J. 1976. Evidence for the technical practices of early Pleistocene hominids, Shungura Formation, Lower Omo Valley, Ethiopia. In *Earliest Man and Environments in the Lake Rudolf Basin.* Edited by Coopens, V, F Howell, G Isaac, R Leakey. Pp. 565-573. Chicago: University of Chicago Press.

43 Cherfas, J. 1983. Trees have made man upright. *New Scientist* 97: 172-178.

44 Chevalier-Skolnikoff, S. 1976. The ontogeny of primate intelligence and its implications for communicative potential: A preliminary report. In *Origins and Evolution of Language and Speech.* Edited by Harnad, S R, H D Steklis, J Lancaster. New York: New York Academy of Sciences.

45 Ciochon, R L, R S Corruccini, eds. 1983. *New Interpretations of Ape and Human Ancestry.* New York: Plenum.

46 Clark, J. 1976. African origins of man the toolmaker. In *Human Origins.* Edited by Isaacs, G, E McCown. Pp. 1-53. Menlo Park, CA.: Benjamin-Cummings.

47 Clark, G A. 1989. Alternative models of Pleistocene biocultural evolution: A response to Foley. *Antiquity* 63: 153-62.

48 Clarke, J D, H Kurashina. 1979. Hominid occupation of the east-central highlands of Ethiopia in the Plio-Pleistocene. *Nature* 282: 33-39.

49 Coon, C S. 1954. *The History of Man.* New York: Knopf.

50 Coon, C S. 1962. *The Origin of Races.* New York: Knopf.

51 Coon, C S. 1965. *The Living Races of Man.* New York: Knopf.

52 Coppens, Y, F C Howell, G L Isaac, R E F Leakey. 1976. *Earliest Man in the Lake Rudolf Basin.* Chicago: University of Chicago Press.

53 Corballis, M C. 1991. *The Lop-Sided Ape: Laterality and Human Evolution.* New York: Oxford University Press.

54 Cracraft, J, N Eldredge, eds. 1979. *Phylogenetic Analysis and Paleontology.* New York: Colombia University Press.

55 Crook, J H. 1980. *The Evolution of Human Consciousness.* New York: Oxford University Press.

56 Cunningham, J. 1990. *Sexual Dimorphism in the Animal Kingdom: A Theory of the Evolution of Secondary Sexual Characters.* London: Adam and Charles Black.

57 Dahlberg, F, ed. 1981. *Woman the Gatherer.* New Haven: Yale University Press.

58 Daly, M, M Wilson. 1978. *Sex, Evolution and Behavior.* North Scituate, MA: Duxbury.

59 Darlington, C D. 1960. Cousin marriage and the evolution of the breeding system in man. *Heredity* 14: 297-332.

60 Darlington, C D. 1969. *The Evolution of Man and Society.* London: Lowe and Brydone.

61 Dawkins, R. 1986. *The Blind Watchmaker.* New York: Norton.

62 Day, M H. 1982. The homo erectus pelvis: Punctuation of gradualism? In *L'Homo erectus et la place de l'Homme de Tautavel parmi les hominides fossiles.* Edited by de Lumley, H. Pp. 411-421. Paris: C.N.R.S.

63 Day, M H. 1986. *Guide to Fossil Man.* 4th ed. London: Cassell.

64 Day, M. 1989. Fossil man: The hard evidence. In *Human Origins.* Edited by Durant, J R. Pp. 9-26. Oxford: Clarendon Press.

65 Dean, M C, C B Stringer, T G Bromage. 1986. Age at death of the Neanderthal child from Devil's Tower, Gibraltar and the implications for studies of general growth and development in Neanderthals. *American Journal of Physical Anthropology* 70: 301-309.

66 Delluc, B, G Delluc. 1981. Les plus anciens dessins de l'homme. *La Recherche* 118: 14-22.

67 Delson, E, ed. 1985. *Ancestors: The Hard Evidence.* New York: Alan R. Liss.

68 DeRousseau, C J, ed. 1990. *Primate Life Histories and Evolution.* New York: Wiley-Liss.

69 Diamond, J. 1991. *The Rise and Fall of the Third Chimpanzee.* London: Radius.

70 Dobzhansky, T. 1966. An essay on religion, death, and evolutionary adaptation. *Zygon* 1: 317-331.

71 Dobzhansky, T. 1970. *Mankind Evolving.* New York: Bantam Books.

72 Doolittle, W F, C Sapienza. 1980. Selfish genes, the phenotype paradigm and genome evolution. *Nature* 284: 601-3.

73 Dover, G A, R B Flavell, eds. 1982. *Genome Evolution.* London: Academic Press.

74 Durant, J R, ed. 1989. *Human Origins.* Oxford: Clarendon Press.

75 Dyson, F. 1985. *The Origins of Life.* Cambridge: Cambridge University Press.

76 Ehrlich, P, A Ehrlich. 1981. *Extinction: The Causes and Consequences of the Disappearance of Species.* New York: Random House.

77 Eisely, L. 1957. *The Immense Journey.* New York: Random House.

78 Eldredge, N, S J Gould. 1972. Punctuated equilibria: An alternative to phyletic gradualism. In *Models in Paleobiology.* Edited by Schropf, T. Pp. 82-115. San Francisco: Freeman.

79 Eldredge, N, I Tattersall. 1977. Evolutionary models, phylogenetic reconstruction, and another look at hominid phylogeny. In *Historical Biogeography, Plate Tectonics and the Changing Environment.* Edited by Gray, J, A J Boucet. Corvallis: Oregon State University Press.

80 Eldredge, N, J Crancraft. 1980. *Phylogenetic Patterns and the Evolutionary Process: Method and Theory in Comparative Biology.* New York: Columbia University Press.

81 Eldredge, N, I Tattersall. 1982. *The Myths of Human Evolution.* New York: Columbia University Press.

82 Eldredge, N. 1989. *Macroevolutionary Dynamics: Species, Niches, and Adaptive Peaks.* New York: McGraw Hill.

83 Eldredge, N. 1991. *Fossils: The Evolution and Extinction of Species.* Wantirna South, Vic: Houghton Mifflin 1991.

84 Else, J G, P Lee, eds. 1986. *Primate Evolution.* Cambridge: Cambridge University Press.

85 Else, J, P Lee, eds. 1986. *Primate Ontogeny, Cognition and Social Behaviour.* Cambridge: Cambridge University Press.

86 Etkin, W. 1985. Evolution of the human mind and emergence of tribal culture: A mentalist approach. *Perspectives in Biology and Medicine* 28: 498-525.

87 Falk, D. 1975. Comparative anatomy of the larynx in man and chimpanzee: Implications for language in Neanderthal Man. *American Journal of Physical Anthropology* 43: 123-132.

88 Falk, D. 1980. Hominid brain evolution: The approach from paleoneurology. *Yearbook of Physical Anthropology* 23: 93-107.

89 Falk, D. 1985. Hadar AL 162-28 endocast as evidence that brain enlargement preceded cortical reorganization in hominid evolution. *Nature* 313: 45-47.

90 Falk, D. 1987. Hominid paleoneurology. *Annual Review of Anthropology* 16: 13-30.

91 Falk, D. 1990. Brain evolution in Homo: The radiator theory. *Behavioral and Brain Sciences* 13: 333-343.

92 Feldman, M W. 1986. On speciation and linguistic divergence. In *Language Transmission and Change*. Edited by Wang, W S Y. Oxford: Blackwell.

93 Foley, R. 1984. Early man and the red queen: Topical African community evolution and hominid adaptation. In *Hominid Evolution and Community Ecology: Prehistoric Human Adaptation in Biological Perspective*. Edited by Foley, R. Pp. 85-110. London: Academic Press.

94 Foley, R, ed. 1984. *Hominid Evolution and Community Ecology: Prehistoric Human Adaptation in Biological Perspective*. London: Academic Press.

95 Foley, R. 1989. The search for early man. *Archaeology* 42: 26-32.

96 Gamble, C. 1985. Early man as complex hunter. *Nature* 316: 485-486.

97 Garn, S M. 1961. *Human Races*. Springfield, MA: Charles C. Thomas.

98 Geiger, G. 1990. *Evolutionary Instability: Logical and Material Aspects of a Unified Theory of Biosocial Evolution*. Berlin: Springer.

99 Ghiselin, M T. 1974. *The Economy of Nature and the Evolution of Sex*. Berkeley: University of California Press.

100 Ghiselin, M. 1982. The intellectual path to natural selection. *New Scientist* 94: 156-159.

101 Gingerich, P D. 1984. Primate evolution: Evidence from the fossil record, comparative morphology, and molecular biology. *Yearbook of Physical Anthropology* 27: 57-72.

102 Glucksmann, A. 1981. *Sexual Dimorphism in Human and Mammalian Biology and Pathology*. London: Academic Press.

103 Godfrey, L, K H Jacobs. 1981. Gradual, autocatalytic and punctuational models of hominid brain evolution: A cautionary tale. *Journal of Human Evolution* 10: 254-272.

104 Goldschmidt, R B. 1952. Evolution as viewed by one geneticist. *American Scientist* 40: 84-98.

105 Gomberg, D N, B M Latimer. 1984. Observations on the transverse tarsal joint of A. afarensis, and some comments on the

interpretation of behavior from morphology. *American Journal of Physical Anthropology* 63: 164-167.

106 Goodall, J. 1976. Continuities between chimpanzees and human behavior. In *Human Origins: Louis Leakey and the East African Evidence.* Edited by Isaac, G L, E R McCown. Pp. 81-95. Menlo Park, CA: Benjamin-Cummings.

107 Goodman, M, R E Tashian, J H Tashian, eds. 1981. *Molecular Anthropology: Genes and Proteins in the Evolutionary Ascent of Primates.* New York: Plenum.

108 Goodman, M, ed. 1982. *Macromolecular Sequences in Systematic and Evolutionary Biology.* New York: Plenum.

109 Gottlieb, G. 1984. Evolutionary trends and evolutionary origins: Relevance to theory in comparative psychology. *Psychological Review* 91: 448-56.

110 Gould, S J. 1977. *Ontogeny and Phylogeny.* Cambridge: Harvard University Press.

111 Gould, S J, D M Raup, J J Jepkowski, T J M Schopf, D S Simberloff. 1977. The shape of evolution: A comparison of real and random clades. *Paleobiology* 3: 23-40.

112 Gould, S J. 1980. *The Panda's Thumb: More Reflections on Natural History.* New York: Norton.

113 Gould, S J, G G Simpson. 1980. Palaeontology and the modern synthesis. In *The Evolutionary Synthesis.* Edited by Mayr, E, W B Provine. Pp. 153-172. Cambridge: Harvard University Press.

114 Gould, S J. 1980. Is a new and general theory of evolution emerging? *Paleobiology* 6: 199-230.

115 Gould, S J. 1982. Darwinism and the expansion of evolutionary theory. *Science* 216: 380-387.

116 Gould, S J. 1983. The hardening of the modern synthesis. In *Dimensions of Darwinism.* Edited by Grene, M. Cambridge: Cambridge University Press.

117 Gould, S J. 1984. Toward the vindication of punctuational change. In *Catastrophes and Earth History.* Edited by Berggren, W A, J A Van Couvering. Pp. 9-34. Princeton: Princeton University Press.

118 Gould, S J. 1986. Punctuated equilibrium at the third stage. *Systematic Zoology* 35: 143-148.

119 Gowlett, J A J, J W K Harris, D Walton, B A Wood. 1981. Early archaelogical sites, hominid remains and traces of fire from Chesowanja. *Nature* 294: 125-29.

120 Greenwood, P J, P H Harvey, M Slatkin, eds. 1985. *Evolution: Essays in Honour of John Maynard Smith.* Cambridge: Cambridge University Press.

121 Gribbin, J, J Cherfas. 1982. *The Monkey Puzzle: Reshaping the Evolutionary Tree.* New York: Pantheon.

122 Groves, C P. 1989. *A Theory of Human and Primate Evolution.* Oxford: Clarendon Press.

123 Guilmet, G. 1977. The evolution of tool-using and tool-making behaviour. *Man* 12: 33-47.

124 Hahn, M E, C Jensen, B C Dudek. 1979. *Development and Evolution of Brain Size: Behavioral Implications.* New York: Academic Press.

125 Hall, R L, H S Sharp, eds. 1978. *Wolf and Man: Evolution in Parallel.* New York: Academic Press.

126 Hamilton, W D. 1964. The genetical evolution of social behavior. *Journal of Theoretical Biology* 7: 1-52.

127 Harding, R S O, G Teleki, eds. 1981. *Omnivorous Primates: Gathering and Hunting in Human Evolution.* New York: Columbia University Press.

128 Harper, A B. 1980. Origins and divergence of Aleuts, Eskimos and American Indians. *Annals of Human Biology* 7: 547-554.

129 Hasegawa, T, M Hiraiwa, T Nishida, H Takasaki. 1983. New evidence on scavenging behavior in wild chimpanzees. *Current Anthropology* 24: 231-232.

130 Hasegawa, M, T Yano. 1984. Phylogeny and classification of Hominoidea as inferred from DNA sequence data. *Proc. Japan. Acad.* 60: 389-92.

131 Hecht, M K, P C Goody, B M Hecht, eds. 1977. *Major Patterns of Vertebrate Evolution.* New York: Plenum.

132 Hecht, M K, B Wallace, G T Prance, eds. 1983. *Evolutionary Biology.* New York: Plenum.

133 Hewes, G W. 1964. Hominid bipedalism: Independent evidence for the food carrying theory. *Science* 146: 416-418.

134 Hewett-Emmett, D, C N Cook, N A Barnicot. 1975. Old World monkey haemoglobins: Deciphering phylogeny from complex patterns of molecular evolution. In *Molecular Anthropology: Genes and Proteins in the Evolutionary Ascent of Primates.* Edited by Goodman, M, R E Tashian, J H Tashian. Pp. 257-276. New York: Plenum.

135 Hicks, R E, M Kinsbourne. 1976. On the genesis of human handedness: A review. *Journal of Motor Behavior* 8: 257-266.

136 Hill, A. 1983. Hyaenas and early hominids. *British Archaeological Reports International Series* 163: 87-92.

137 Hill, A P. 1984. Hyaenas and hominids: Taphonomy and hypothesis testing. In *Hominid Evolution and Community Ecology.* Edited by Foley, R. Pp. 111-124. New York: Academic Press.

138 Hofman, M A. 1984. On the presumed co-evolution of brain size and longevity in hominids. *Human Evolution* 13: 271-276.

139 Holloway, R L. 1967. The evolution of the human brain: Some notes towards a synthesis between neural structure and the evolution of complex behavior. *Current Anthropology* 12: 3-19.

140 Holloway, R L. 1970. Neural parameters, hunting, and the evolution of the human brain. In *The Primate Brain.* Edited by Noback, C R, W Montagna. Pp. 299-310. New York: Appleton-Century-Crofts.

141 Holloway, R L. 1976. Paleoneurological evidence for language origins. In *Origins and Evolution of Language and Speech.* Edited by Harnad, S, H Steklis, J Lancaster. Pp. 330-348. New York: New York Academy of Sciences.

142 Holloway, R L. 1981. Culture, symbols, and human brain evolution: A Synthesis. *Dialectical Anthropology* 5: 287-303.

143 Holloway, R L. 1982. Revisiting the South African Taung Australopithecine endocast: The position of the lunate sulcus as determined by the stereoplotting technique. *American Journal of Physical Anthropology* 56: 43-58.

144 Holloway, R L. 1983. Human brain evolution: A search for units, models and synthesis. *Canadian Journal of Anthropology* 3: 215-230.

145 Holloway, R L. 1983. Cerebral brain endocast pattern of Australopiethecus afarensis hominid. *Nature* 303: 420-422.

146 Hooff, J A R A M v. 1972. A comparative approach to the phylogeny of laughter and smiling. In *Non-Verbal Communication.* Edited by Hinde, R A. Pp. 209-238. Cambridge: Cambridge University Press.

147 Howells, W W. 1980. Homo erectus who, when and where: A survey. *Yearbook of Physical Anthropology* 23: 1-23.

148 Hrdy, S B. 1981. *The Woman That Never Evolved* Cambridge: Cambridge University Press.

149 Hubert, E. 1931. *Evolution of Facial Musculature and Facial Expression*. London: Oxford University Press.

150 Hublin, J, A-M Tillier, eds. 1984. *Aux origines de la diversité humaine*. Paris: Presses Universitaires de France.

151 Huxley, J S. 1942. *Evolution: The Modern Synthesis*. London: Allen & Unwin.

152 Isaac, G, E McCown. 1976. *Human Origins*. Menlo Park, CA: Benjamin-Cummings.

153 Isaac, G. 1976. The activities of early African hominids: A review of archeological evidence from the time span two and a half to one million years age. In *Human Origins*. Edited by Isaac, G, E McCown. Pp. 483-514. Menlo Park, CA: Benjamin-Cummings.

154 Isaac, G. 1976. Stages of cultural elaboration in the Pleistocene: Possible archeological indicators of the development of language capabilities. In *Origins and Evolution of Language and Speech*. Edited by Harnad, S, H Steklis, J Lancaster. Pp. 275-288. New York: New York Academy of Sciences.

155 Isaac, G. 1978. The food-sharing behavior of protohuman hominids. *Scientific American* 238: 90-108.

156 Isaac, G. 1980. Aspects of human evolution. In *Evolution from Molecules to Men*. Edited by Bendall, D S. Pp. 509-543. Cambridge: Cambridge University Press.

157 Isaac, G. 1980. Casting the net wide: A review of archaeological evidence for early hominid land-use and ecological relations. In *Current Arguments on Early Man*. Edited by Königsson, L K. Pp. 114-134. New York: Pergamon.

158 Isaac, G, D C Crader. 1981. To what extent were early hominids carnivorous? An archaeological perspective. In *Omnivorous Primates: Gathering and Hunting in Human Evolution*. Edited by Harding, R, G Telecki. Pp. 37-103. New York: Columbia University.

159 Isaac, G. 1983. Bones in contention: Competing explanations for the juxtaposition of Early Pleistocene artifacts and faunal remains. In *Animals and Archaeology*. Edited by Clutton-Brock, J, C Grigson. Pp. 3-19. London: British Archaeological Reports.

160 Isaac, G. 1989. Cutting and carrying: Archaeology and the emergence of the genus Homo. In *Human Origins*. Edited by Durant, J R. Pp. 106-122. Oxford: Clarendon Press.

161 Issac, G L. 1984. The archaeology of human origins: Studies of the Lower Pleistocene in East Africa 1971-1981. *Advances in World Archaeology* 3: 1-87.

162 Itzkoff, S W. 1983. *The Form of Man: The Evolutionary Origins of Human Intelligence.* Ashfield, MA: Paideia.

163 Itzkoff, S W. 1985. *The Triumph of the Intelligent: The Creation of Homo sapiens sapiens.* Ashfield, MA: Paideia.

164 Jeffreys, A J. 1989. Molecular biology and human evolution. In *Human Origins.* Edited by Durant, J R. Pp. 27-52. Oxford: Clarendon Press.

165 Jelinek, J. 1980. European Homo erectus and the origin of Homo sapiens. In *Current Argument on Early Man.* Edited by Konigsson, L-K. Oxford: Pergamon Press.

166 Jerison, H J. 1973. Evolution of the Brain and Intelligence. *New York* Academic Press:

167 Jerison, H J. 1976. Paleoneurology and the evolution of mind. *Scientific American* 234: 90-101.

168 Jerison, H J. 1976. The paleoneurology of language. *Annals of the New York Academy of Sciences* 280: 370-382.

169 Jerison, H J. 1979. The evolution of diversity in brain size. In *Development and Evolution of Brain Size.* Edited by Hahn, M E, C Jensen, B C Dudek. Pp. 29-57. New York: Academic Press.

170 Johanson, D C, T D White. 1979. A systematic assessment of early African hominids. *Science* 203: 321-30.

171 Johanson, D, M A Ede. 1981. *Lucy: The Beginnings of Humankind.* New York: Simon and Schuster.

172 Jolly, C J, ed. 1978. *Early Hominids of Africa.* London: Duckworth.

173 Jontach, E, C H Waddington, eds. 1976. *Evolution and Consciousness.* Reading, MA: Addison-Wesley.

174 Joysey, K A, A E Friday, eds. 1982. *Problems of Phylogenetic Reconstruction.* London: Academic Press.

175 Jungers, W L. 1982. Lucy's limbs: Skeletal allometry and locomotion in Australopithecus afarensis. *Nature* 297: 676-678.

176 Karlin, S, S Lessard. 1986. *Sex Ratio Evolution.* Princeton: Princeton University Press.

177 Karlin, S, E Nevo, eds. 1986. *Evolutionary Processes and Theory.* Orlando, FL: Academic Press.

178 Keith, A. 1948. *A New Theory of Human Evolution.* London: Watts.

179 King, G. 1975. Socioterritorial units among carnivores and early hominids. *Journal of Anthropological Research* 31: 69-87.

180 King, M C, A C Wilson. 1975. Evolution at two levels in humans and chimpanzees. *Science* 188: 107-116.

181 King, G. 1980. Alternative uses of primates and carnivores in the reconstruction of early hominid behavior. *Ethology and Sociobiology* 1: 99-110.

182 King, G E, H D Steklis. 1984. New evidence for the craniocervical killing bite in primates. *Journal of Human Evolution* 13: 469-482.

183 Kinzey, W, ed. 1987. *The Evolution of Human Behavior: Primate Models.* Albany: SUNY Press.

184 Kitahara-Frisch, J. 1978. Stone tools as indicators of linguistic abilities in early man. *Annual of the Japanese Association of Philosophy of Science* 5: 101-109.

185 Kleiman, D G, J R Malcom. 1981. The evolution of male parental investment in mammals. In *Parental Care in Mammals.* Edited by Gubernick, D J, P H Klopfer. New York: Plenum.

186 Kortlandt, A. 1980. How many early hominids have defended themselves against large predators and food competitors? *Journal of Human Evolution* 9: 79-112.

187 Kortlandt, A. 1986. The use of stone tools by wild-living chimpanzees and earliest hominids. *Journal of Human Evolution* 15: 72-132.

188 Königsson, L-K, ed. 1980. *Current Argument on Early Man.* Oxford: Per-gamon.

189 Kramer, A. 1986. Hominid-pongid distinctiveness in the Miocene-Pliocene fossil record: The Lothagam mandible. *American Journal of Physical Anthropology* 70: 457-473.

190 Kurland, J A, S J Beckerman. 1985. Optimal foraging and hominid evolution: Labor and reciprocity. *American Anthropologist* 87: 73-93.

191 Laitman, J T. 1985. Evolution of the hominid upper respiratory tract: The fossil evidence. In *Hominid Evolution: Past Present and Future.* Edited by Tobias, P V. New York: Alan R. Liss.

192 Lancaster, J B. 1975. *Primate Behavior and the Emergence of Human Culture.* New York: Holt, Rinehart and Winston.

193 Lancaster, J B, C S Lancaster. 1983. Parental investment: The hominid adaptation. In *How Humans Adapt: A Biocultural Odyssey.*

Edited by Ortner, D. Pp. 33-66. Washington, D.C.: Smithsonian Institution Press.

194 Langdon, J H. 1986. *Functional Morphology of the Miocene Hominoid Foot: Contributions to Primatology.* New York: Karger.

195 Larsen, C, R M Matter. 1985. *Human Origins: The Fossil Record.* Prospect Heights, Il: Waveland Press.

196 Latimer, B M. 1983. The anterior foot skeleton of Australopithecus afarensis. *American Journal of Physical Anthropology* 60: 217.

197 Leakey, M D. 1966. A review of the Olduwan culture from Olduvai Gorge, Tanzania. *Nature* 210: 462-466.

198 Leakey, M D. 1971. *Olduvai Gorge: Excavations in Beds I and II, 1960-1963 Vol 3.* London: Cambridge University Press.

199 Leakey, R E, R Lewin. 1977. *Origins.* New York: Dutton.

200 Leakey, R E. 1981. *The Making of Mankind.* London: Michael Joseph.

201 Leaky, R E F, A C Walker. 1985. Homo erectus unearthed *National Geographic* 168: 624-629.

202 Leroi-Gourhan, A. 1982. *The Dawn of European Art.* Cambridge: Cambridge University Press.

203 Leutenegger, W. 1982. Encephalization and obstetrics in primates with particular reference to human evolution. In *Primate Brain Evolution: Methods and Concepts.* Edited by Armstrong, E, D Falk. Pp. 85-95. New York: Plenum.

204 Lewin, R E. 1984. *Human Evolution: An Illustrated Introduction.* New York: Freeman.

205 Lockard, J S, C E Fahrenbruch, J L Smith, C J Morgan. 1977. Smiling and laughter: Different phyletic origins? *Bulletin of Psychonomic Society* 10: 183-186.

206 Lockard, J S, ed. 1980. *The Evolution of Human Social Behavior.* New York: Elsevier.

207 Lovejoy, C O. 1981. The Australopithecines. *Science* 211: 341-350.

208 Lovejoy, C O. 1982. Diaphyseal biomechanics of the locomotor skeleton of Tautavel man with comments on the evolution of skeletal changes in Late Pleistocene man. In *L'Homo erectus et la place de l'homme de Tautavel parmi les hominides fossiles.* Edited by de Lumley, H. Pp. 447-470. Paris: C.N.R.S.

209 Lowenstein, J M, A Zihlman. 1984. Human evolution and molecular biology. *Perspectives in Biology and Medicine* 27: 611-622.

210 Lumsden, C J, E O Wilson. 1981. *Genes, Mind, and Culture.* Cambridge: Harvard University Press.

211 Lumsden, C J, E O Wilson. 1983. *Promethean Fire: Reflections on the Origin of Mind.* Cambridge: Harvard University Press.

212 MacLean, P D. 1985. Brain evolution relating to family, play and the separation call. *Archives of General Psychiatry* 42: 405-417.

213 MacLean, P D. 1990. *The Triune Brain in Evolution.* New York: Plenum.

214 MacNeilage, P F, M G Studdert-Kennedy, B Lindblom. 1987. Primate handedness reconsidered *Behavioral and Brain Science* 10: 247-303.

215 MacNeilage, P. 1987. The evolution of hemispheric specialisation for manual function and language. In *Higher Brain Functions: Recent Explorations of the Brain's Emergent Properties.* Edited by Wise, S. Pp. 285-309. New York: Wiley.

216 Markl, H, M Feldman, eds. 1980. *Evolution of Social Behavior: Hypotheses and Empirical Tests.* Weinheim: Verlag Chemie.

217 Marks, A E. 1983. Changing care reduction strategies: A technological shift from the middle to the upper Paleolithic in the southern Levant. In *The Mousterian Legacy: Human Biocultural Change in the Upper Pleistocene.* Edited by Trinkaus, E. Pp. 13-34. London: British Archaeological Reports (International Series).

218 Marshack, A. 1988. The Neanderthals and their human capacity for symbolic thought: Cognitive and problem-solving aspects of Mousterian symbol. In *L'homme de Néandertal: La pensée.* Edited by Bar-Yosef, O. Liège: ERAUL.

219 Martin, R D. 1990. *Primate Origins and Evolution: A Phylogenetic Reconstruction.* Princeton: Princeton University Press.

220 Marzke, M W, M S Shackley. 1986. Tools and the morphology of hominid hands. *American Journal of Physical Anthropology* 69: 237.

221 Maynard Smith, J. 1976. Group selection. *Quarterly Review of Biology* 51: 277-283.

222 Maynard Smith, J. 1977. *Processes of Organic Evolution.* Englewood Cliffs, N.J.: Prentice-Hall.

223 Maynard Smith, J. 1978. *The Evolution of Sex.* Cambridge: Cambridge University Press.

224 Maynard Smith, J. 1982. *Evolution and the Theory of Games.* Cambridge: Cambrdige University Press.

225 Maynard Smith, J, ed. 1983. *Evolution Now: A Century After Darwin.* San Francisco: Freeman.

226 Mayo, O. 1983. *Natural Selection and Its Constraints.* London: Academic Press.

227 Mayr, E. 1963. *Animal Species and Evolution.* Cambridge: Harvard University Press.

228 Mayr, E. 1976. *Evolution and the Diversity of Life.* Cambridge: Harvard University Press.

229 Mayr, E, W B Provine, eds. 1980. *The Evolutionary Synthesis.* Cambridge: Harvard University Press.

230 McGrew, W C, C E Tutin, P J Baldwin. 1979. Chimpanzees, tools, and termites: Cross-cultural comparisons of Senegal, Tanzania, and Rio Muni. *Man* 14: 185-214.

231 McHenry, H M. 1982. The pattern of human evolution: Studies on bipedalism, mastication, and encephalization. *Annual Review of Anthropology* 11: 151-173.

232 Mehlman, M J. 1984. Archaic Homo sapiens at Lake Eyasi, Tanzania: Recent misrepresentations. *Human Evolution* 13: 487-502.

233 Melhen, S L W. 1981. *The Evolution of Love.* Oxford: Freeman.

234 Mellars, P, ed. 1989. *The Human Revolution: Behavioural and Biological Perspectives on the Origins of Modern Humans.* Edinburgh: Edinburgh University Press.

235 Milner, R. 1990. *Encyclopedia of Evolution: Humanity's Search for Its Origins.* New York: Facts on File.

236 Morgan, E. 1982. *The Aquatic Ape: A Theory of Human Evolution.* London: Stein and Day.

237 Morgan, E. 1984. The aquatic hypothesis. *New Scientist* 102: 11-13.

238 Morgan, E, M Verhaegen. 1986. In the beginning was the water. *New Scientist* 104: 27-28.

239 Motulsky, A R. 1960. Metabolic polymorphisms and the role of infectious diseases in human evolution. *Human Biology* 32: 28-62.

240 Napier, J. 1962. The evolution of the hand. *Scientific American* 207: 56-62.

241 Nelson, H, R Jurmain. 1985. *Introduction to Physical Anthropology.* St. Paul, MI: West Publishing.

242 Nishida, T, S Uehara. 1982. Natural history of a tool using behavior by wild chimpanzees in feeding on wood boring ants. *Journal of Human Evolution* 11: 73-99.

243 Nottebohm, F. 1976. Vocal tract and brain: A search for evolutionary bottlenecks. *Annals of the New York Academy of Science* 280: 643-649.

244 O'Brien, E M. 1981. The projectile capabilities of an Acheulean handaxe from Olorgesaile. *Current Anthropology* 22: 76-79.

245 O'Brien, E M. 1984. What was the Acheulean hand ax? *Natural History* 93: 20-23.

246 Orgel, L E, F H C Crick. 1980. Selfish DNA: The ultimate parasite. *Nature* 284: 604-607.

247 Otte, M, ed. 1988. *L'homme de Néandertal: Actes du Colloque International.* Liège: ERAUL.

248 Oxnard, C. 1973. *Form and Pattern in Human Evolution: Some Mathematical, Physical, and Engineering Approaches.* Chicago: University of Chicago Press.

249 Oxnard, C. 1983. *The Order of Man.* New Haven: Yale University Press.

250 Parker, S T, K R Gibson. 1979. A developmental model for the evolution of language and intelligence in early hominids. *Behavorial and Brain Sciences* 2: 367-408.

251 Parker, S T. 1985. A social-technological model for the evolution of language. *Current Anthropology* 26: 617-39.

252 Passingham, R. 1982. *The Human Primate.* Oxford: Freeman.

253 Petterson, M. 1978. Acceleration in evolution before human times. *Journal of Social and Biological Structures* 1: 201-206.

254 Pilbeam, D, S J Gould. 1974. Size and scaling in human evolution. *Science* 186: 892-901.

255 Pilbeam, D, J R Vaisnys. 1975. Hypothesis testing in paleoanthropology. In *Paleoanthropology: Morphology and Paleoecology.* Edited by Tuttle, R H. Pp. 3-14. The Hague: Mouton.

256 Pilbeam, D. 1983. Hominoid evolution and hominid origins. In *Recent Advances in the Evolution of the Primates.* Edited by Chagas, C. Pp. 43-61. Rome: Pontificae Academiae Scientiarum Scripta Varia 50.

257 Pitt, R. 1978. Warfare and hominid brain evolution. *Journal of Theoretical Biology* 72: 551-575.

258 Plotkin, H C, F J Olding-Smee. 1981. A multiple-level model of evolution and its implications for sociobiology. *Behavioral and Brain Sciences* 4: 225-268.

259 Poirier, F E. 1987. *Understanding Human Evolution.* Englewood Cliffs, N.J.: Prentice-Hall.

260 Pollard, J W, ed. 1984. *Evolutionary Theory: Paths into the Future.* New York: Wiley.

261 Pope, G G, J E Cronin. 1984. The Asian Hominidae. *Journal of Human Evolution* 13: 377-396.

262 Post, P W, F Daniels, R T Binfold. 1975. Cold injury and the evolution of white skin. *Human Biology* 47: 65-80.

263 Potts, R, P Shipman. 1981. Cutmarks made by stone tools on bones from Olduvai Gorge, Tanzania. *Nature* 291: 577-580.

264 Potts, R. 1983. Homes bases and early hominids. *American Scientist* 72: 338-347.

265 Premack, D. 1976. Mechanisms of intelligence: Preconditions for language. *Annuals of the New York Academy of Sciences* 280: 544-561.

266 Premack, D. 1986. *Gavagai!, or The Future History of the Animal Language Controversy.* Cambridge: M.I.T. Press.

267 Radinsky, L G. 1979. *The Fossil Record of Primate Brain Evolution. 49th James Arthur Lecture.* Washington: American Museum of Natural History.

268 Radovcic, J. 1985. Neanderthals and their contemporaries. In *Ancestors: The Hard Evidence.* Edited by Delson, E. Pp. 310-18. New York: Alan R. Liss.

269 Rak, Y. 1983. *The Australopithecine Face.* New York: Academic Press.

270 Rancour-Laferrierre, D. 1985. *Signs of the Flesh: An Essay on the Evolution of Hominid Sexuality.* New York: Aldine.

271 Raup, D M. 1979. Size of the Permo-Triassic bottleneck and its evolutionary implications. *Science* 206: 1501-1503.

272 Reader, J. 1981. *Missing Links: The Hunt for Earliest Man.* London: Collins.

273 Reichs, K J, ed. 1983. *Hominid Origins: Inquiries Past and Present.* Washington: University Press of the Americas.

274 Reid, R G B. 1985. *Evolutionary Theory: The Unfinished Synthesis.* Ithaca: Cornell University Press.

275 Reynolds, P C. 1981. *On the Evolution of Human Behavior: The Argument from Animals to Men.* Berkeley: University of California Press.

276 Richards, G. 1987. *Human Evolution.* London: Routledge.

277 Ridley, M. 1983. *The Explanation of Organic Diversity.* Oxford: Clarendon Press.

278 Ridley, M. 1985. *The Problems of Evolution.* Oxford: Oxford University Press.

279 Ridley, M. 1986. *Evolution and Classification: The Reformation of Cladism.* London: Longmans.

280 Riel, L A. 1980. Fitness, uncertainty, and the role of diversification in evolution and behavior. *American Naturalist* 115: 623-638.

281 Rightmire, G P. 1985. The tempo of change in the evolution of mid-pleistocene homo. In *Ancestors: The Hard Evidence.* Edited by Delson, E. Pp. 255-264. New York: Alan R. Liss.

282 Rightmire, G P. 1990. *The Evolution of Homo Erectus: Comparative Anatomical Studies of an Extinct Human Species.* New York: Cambridge University Press.

283 Robinson, J T. 1972. *Early Hominid Posture and Locomotion.* Chicago: University of Chicago Press.

284 Roebroeks, W, J Kolen, E Rensink. 1988. Planning depth, anticipation, and the organization of Middle Palaeolithic technology: The "archaic natives" meet Eve's descendants. *Helinium* 28: 17-34.

285 Roede, M, ed. 1991. *The Aquatic Ape Revisited: Fact or Fiction? The First Scientific Evaluation of a Controversial Theory of Human Evolution.* London: Souvenir.

286 Ronen, A, ed. 1980. *The Transition from Lower to Middle Palaeolithic and the Origin of Modern Man.* International Series 151. Oxford: British Archaeological Reports.

287 Roper, M K. 1969. A survey of the evidence of intrahuman killing in the Pleistocene. *Current Anthropology* 10: 427-459.

288 Rosenblatt, J, B Komisaruk. 1977. *Reproductive Behavior and Evolution.* New York: Plenum.

289 Ross, P E. 1992. Eloquent remains. *Scientific American* 266: 72-81.

290 Salzano, R M, S M Callegari-Jacques. 1988. *South American Indians: A Case Study in Evolution.* Oxford: Clarendon Press.

291 Schopf, T J M, ed. 1972. *Models in Paleobiology.* San Francisco: Freeman.

292 Schwartz, J H. 1984. The evolutionary relationships of man and orangutan. *Nature* 308: 52-54.

293 Scott, A F, et al. 1984. The sequence of the gorilla fetal globin genes: Evidence for multiple gene conversions in human evolution. *Molecular Biology and Evolution* 1: 371-89.

294 Senut, B, C Tardieu. 1985. Functional aspects of Plio-Pleistocene hominid limb bones: Implications for taxonomy and phylogeny. In *Ancestors: The Hard Evidence.* Edited by Delson, E. Pp. 193-201. New York: Alan R. Liss.

295 Sept, J M. 1992. Was there no place like home? A new perspective on early hominid archaeological sites from the mapping of chimpanzee nests. *Current Anthropology* 33: 187-207.

296 Shea, J. 1989. A functional study of the lithic industries associated with hominid fossils in the Kebara and Qafzeh caves, Israel. In *The Human Revolution: Behavioural and Biological Perspectives on the Origins of Modern Humans.* Edited by Mellars, P, C Stringer. Edinburgh: Edinburgh University Press.

297 Shipman, P, J Rose. 1983. Evidence of butchery and hominid activities at Torralba and Ambrona: An evaluation using microscopic techniques. *Journal of Archaelogical Science* 10: 465-474.

298 Shipman, P. 1983. Early hominid lifestyle: Hunting and gathering or foraging and scavenging? In *Animals and Archaeology.* Edited by Clutton-Brock, J, C Grigson. Pp. 31-50. London: British Archaeological Reports.

299 Shipman, P, J Rose. 1983. Early hominid hunting, butchering, and carcass-processing behaviors: Approachers to the fossil record. *Journal of Anthropological Archaeology* 2: 57-98.

300 Shipman, P. 1986. Baffling limb on the family tree. *Discover* September: 87-93.

301 Shipman, P. 1986. Scavenging or hunting in early hominids: Theoretical framework and tests. *American Anthropologist* 88: 27-43.

302 Sibley, C G, J E Ahlquist. 1984. The phylogeny of the hominoid primates as indicated by DNA-DNA hybridization. *Journal of Molecular Evolution* 20: 2-15.

303 Simons, E L. 1976. The fossil record of primate phylogeny. In *Molecular Anthropology, Genes and Proteins in the Evolutionary Ascent of the Primates.* Edited by Goodman, M, R E Tashian. Pp. 35-62. New York: Plenum.

304 Slobodkin, T B. 1968. Toward a predictive theory of evolution. In *Population Biology and Evolution.* Edited by Lewontin, R C. Pp. 187-205. Syracuse: Syracuse University Press.

305 Sloman, L. 1976. The role of neurosis in phylogenetic adaptation, with particular reference to early man. *American Journal of Phychiatry* 133: 543-547.

306 Sloman, L, M Konstamtareas, D W Dunham. 1979. The adaptive role of maladaptive neurosis. *Biological Psychiatry* 14: 961-971.

307 Smith, F H, F Spencer, eds. 1984. *The Origins of Modern Humans: A World Survey of the Fossil Evidence.* New York: Alan R. Liss.

308 Smith, F, E Trinkaus. 1984. Modern human origins in central Europe: A case of continuity. In *Aux origines de la diversité humaine.* Edited by Hublin, J, A-M Tillier. Paris: Presses Universitaires de France.

309 Smith, F H. 1984. Fossil hominids from the Upper Pleistocene of Central Europe and the origin of modern Europeans. In *The Origins of Modern Humans.* Edited by Smith, F H, F Spencer. Pp. 137-209. New York: Alan R. Liss.

310 Sober, E. 1984. *The Nature of Selection.* Cambridge: M.I.T. Press.

311 Spencer, F. 1984. The Neandertals and their evolutionary significance: A brief historical survey. In *The Origins of Modern Humans: A World Survey of the Fossil Evidence.* Edited by Smith, F, F Spencer. Pp. 137-210. New York: Alan R. Liss.

312 Sperber, G. 1990. *From Apes to Angels: Essays in Anthropology in Honor of Phillip V. Tobias.* New York: Wiley-Liss.

313 Stahl, A B. 1984. Hominid dietary selection before fire. *Current Anthropology* 25: 151-168.

314 Stanley, S M. 1979. *Macroevolution: Pattern and Process.* San Francisco: Freeman.

315 Stanley, S M. 1981. *The New Evolutionary Timetable: Fossils, Genes, and the Origin of Species.* New York: Basic Books.

316 Steegman, A T. 1970. Cold adaptation and the human face. *American Journal of Physical Anthropology* 32: 243-250.

317 Steklis, H B, S R Harnad, J Lancaster. 1976. *Origins and Evolution of Language and Speech.* New York: New York Academy of Sciences.

318 Steklis, H D. 1985. Primate communication, comparative neurology, and the origin of language reexamined *Journal of Human Evolution* 14: 157-73.

319 Stern, J T, R L Susman. 1983. The locomotor anatomy of Australopithecus afarensis. *American Journal of Physical Anthropology* 60: 279-317.

320 Stini, W A, ed. 1979. *Physiological and Morphological Adaptation and Evolution.* Mouton: The Hague.

321 Stoneking, M, R Cann. 1989. African origins of human mitochondrial DNA. In *The Human Revolution: Behavioural and Biological Perspectives on the Origins of Modern Humans.* Edited by Mellars, P, C Stringer. Edinburgh: Edinburgh University Press.

322 Stringer, C B, R Burleigh. 1981. The Neanderthal problem and the prospects for direct dating of Neanderthal remains. *Bulletin of the British Museum of Natural History (Geology)* 35: 225-241.

323 Stringer, C B. 1983. *Aspects of Human Evolution.* London: Academic Press.

324 Stringer, C B. 1984. The definition of Homo erectus and the existence of the species in Africa and Europe. *Forschung Institut Senckenberg* 69:

325 Stringer, C B, J J Hublin, B V Vandermeersch. 1984. The origin of anatomically modern humans in western Europe. In *The Origins of Modern Humans.* Edited by Smith, F H, F Spencer. Pp. 51-135. New York: Alan R. Liss.

326 Stringer, C B. 1985. Middle Pleistocene hominid variability and the origin of the late Pleistocene humans. In *Ancestors: The Hard Evidence.* Edited by Delson, E. Pp. 289-295. New York: Alan R. Liss.

327 Stringer, C B, P Andrews. 1988. Genetic and fossil evidence for the origin of modern humans. *Science* 239: 1263-1268.

328 Stringer, C B. 1989. Homo sapiens: Single or multiple origin? In *Human Origins.* Edited by Durant, J R. Pp. 63-80. Oxford: Clarendon Press.

329 Stuart, A J. 1982. *Pleistocene Vertebrates of the British Isles.* London: Longman.

330 Studdert, R C. 1983. *Selection: The Stress Theory of Evolution.* Smithtown, NY: Exposition Press.

331 Sugiyama, J, J Koman. 1979. Tool using and making behavior in wild chimpanzees at Bossou, Guinea. *Primates* 20: 513-524.

332 Susman, R L, J T Stern, W L Jungers. 1984. Arboreality and bipedality in the Hadar Hominids. *Folia Primatologica* 43: 113-156.

333 Suzuki, H, F Takai. 1970. *The Amud Man and his Cave Site.* Tokyo: University of Tokyo.

334 Suzuki, A. 1975. The origin of hominid hunting: A primatological perspective. In *Socioecology and Psychology of Primates.* Edited by Tuttle, R H. Pp. 259-278. The Hague: Mouton.

335 Tanner, N M. 1981. *On Becoming Human: A Model of the Transition from Ape to Man and the Reconstruction of Early Human Social Life.* Cambridge: Cambridge University Press.

336 Tattersall, I. 1992. Evolution comes to life. *Scientific American* 267: 62-69.

337 Templeton, A R. 1982. Genetic architectures of speciation. In *Mechanisms of Speciation.* Edited by Barigozzi, C. Pp. 105-121. New York: Alan R. Liss.

338 Thoday, A. 1975. Non-Darwinian "evolution" and biological progress. *Nature* 255: 675-677.

339 Thompson, E. 1975. *Human Evolutionary Trees.* New York: Cambridge University Press.

340 Thompson, P R. 1976. A behavioral model for Australopithecus africanus. *Journal of Human Evolution* 5: 547-558.

341 Thorne, A. 1989. *Man on the Rim: The Peopling of the Pacific.* Sydney: Angus & Robertson.

342 Thorne, A G, M H Wolpoff. 1992. The multiregional evolution of humans. *Scientific American* 266: 28-33.

343 Tobias, P V. 1971. *The Brain in Hominid Evolution.* New York: Columbia University Press.

344 Tobias, P V. 1981. The emergence of man in Africa and beyond. *Philosophical Transactions of the Royal Society (London)* B292: 43-56.

345 Tobias, P V, ed. 1985. *Hominid Evolution: Past, Present and Future.* New York: Alan R. Liss.

346 Tobias, P V. 1988. The brain of Homo habilis: A new level of organization in cerebral evolution. *Journal of Human Evolution* 16: 741-61.

347 Toth, N. 1985. The Oldowan reassessed: A close look at early stone artifacts. *Journal of Archaeological Science* 12: 101-120.

348 Toth, N, D Clark, G Ligabue. 1992. The last stone ax makers. *Scientific American* 267: 66-71.

349 Trinkaus, E, W W Howells. 1979. The Neanderthals. *Scientific American* 241: 118-133.

350 Trinkaus, E. 1982. Evolutionary continuity among archaic Homo sapiens. In *The Transition from Lower to Middle Palaeolithic and the Origins of Modern Man.* Edited by Ronen, B. Pp. 301-314. Oxford: British Archaeological Reports International Series.

351 Trinkaus, E. 1983. Human Biocultural Change in the Upper Pleistocene. In *The Mousterian Legacy.* Edited by Trinkaus, E. Pp. 165-200. London: British Archaeological Reports.

352 Trinkaus, E, ed. 1983. *The Mousterian Legacy.* London: British Archaeological Reports.

353 Trinkaus, E. 1983. *The Shanidar Neanderthals.* New York: Academic Press.

354 Trinkaus, E, F H Smith. 1985. The fate of the Neanderthals. In *Ancestors: The Hard Evidence.* Edited by Delson, E. Pp. 325-333. New York: Alan R. Liss.

355 Trinkaus, E. 1986. The Neanderthals and modern human origins. *Annual Review of Anthropology* 15: 193-218.

356 Trinkaus, E. 1987. Bodies, brawn, brains and noses: Human ancestors and human predation. In *The Evoltution of Human Hunting.* Edited by Nitecki, M H, D V Nitecki. Pp. 107-147. New York: Plenum.

357 Trinkaus, E, ed. 1989. *The Emergence of Modern Humans: Biocultural Adaptations in the Later Pleistocene.* Cambridge: Cambridge University Press.

358 Tuttle, R H. 1975. *Paleoanthropology: Morphology and Paleoecology.* The Hague: Mouton.

359 Tuttle, R H, ed. 1975. *Socioecology and Psychology of Primates.* The Hague: Mouton.

360 Tuttle, R H. 1975. Knuckle-walking and knuckle-walkers: A commentary on some recent perspectives on hominoid evolution. In *Primate Functional Morphology and Evolution.* Edited by Tuttle, R H. Pp. 203-212. The Hague: Mouton.

361 Tuttle, R H. 1981. Evolution of hominid bipedalism and prehensile capacities. *Philosopical Transactions of the Royal Society (London)* B292: 89-94.

362 Tuttle, R H. 1985. Ape footprints and Laetoli impressions: A respone to the SUNY claims. In *Hominid Evolution: Past, Present and Future*. Edited by Tobais, P V. Pp. 129-133. New York: Liss.

363 Ullrich, H. 1986. Manipulations of human corpses, mortuary practice, and burial rites in Palaeolithic times. *Anthropos* 23: 227-36.

364 Vaina, L M, ed. 1987. *Matters of Intelligence*. Dortrecht: Riedel.

365 van den Berghe, P L. 1983. Human inbreeding avoidance: Culture in nature. *Behavioral and Brain Sciences* 6: 91-102.

366 van den Berghe, P L. 1986. La culture dans la nature. *Revue Europienne des Sciences Sociales* 24: 69-77.

367 van Gelder, R G. 1978. The voice of the missing link. In *Early Hominids of Africa*. Edited by Jolly, C J. Pp. 431-439. London: Duckworth.

368 Verhaegen, M. 1985. The aquatic ape theory: Evidence and a possible scenario. *Medical Hypotheses* 16: 17-32.

369 Verhaegen, M. 1987. Origin of human bipedalism. *Nature* 325: 305-306.

370 Verhaegen, M. 1988. Aquatic ape theory and speech origins: A hypothesis. *Speculations in Science and Technology* 11: 165-171.

371 Verhaegen, M. 1991. Aquatic features in fossil hominids? In *The Aquatic Ape Revisited* Edited by Roede, M. London: Souvenir.

372 Vilensky, J A, v H G.W., A R Damasia. 1982. The limbic system and human evolution. *Journal of Human Evolution* 11: 447-460.

373 Vining, D R. 1981. Group selection via genocide. *Mankind Quarterly* 21: 27-41.

374 Walker, A. 1981. Dietary hypotheses and human evolution. *Philosophical Transactions of the Royal Society (London)* 292: 57-64.

375 Walker, A, M R Zimmerman, R E F Leakey. 1982. A possible case of hypervitaminosis A in Homo erectus. *Nature* 296: 248-250.

376 Walker, D N. 1982. Cultural modification of bone from Pronghorn (Antilocapra americana) and other small mammals. In *The Agate Basin Site*. Edited by Frsion, G C, D J Standford. Pp. 270-274. New York: Academic Press.

377 Walker, A. 1984. Extinction in hominid evolution. In *Extinctions*. Edited by Bitecki, M H. Pp. 153-190. Chicago: University of Chicago Press.

378 Walker, A, R E Leakey, J M Harris, F H Brown. 1986. 2.5 Myr Australopithecus boisei from West of Lake Turkana, Kenya. *Nature* 322: 517-522.

379 Washburn, S L. 1960. Tools and human evolution. *Scientific American* 203: 62-75.

380 Washburn, S L. 1962. *Social Life of Early Man.* London: Methuen.

381 Washburn, S L. 1964. *Classification and Human Evolution.* London: Methuen.

382 Washburn, S L, P Jay, eds. 1968. *Perspectives on Human Evolution.* New York: Holt, Rinehart and Winston.

383 Washburn, S L, C Lancaster. 1968. The Evolution of Hunting. In *Man the Hunter.* Edited by De Vore, R L, I De Vore. Pp. 293-303. Chicago: Aldine.

384 Washburn, S, E McCown, eds. 1978. *Human Evolution: Biosocial Perspectives.* Menlo Park, CA: Benjamin-Cummings.

385 Washburn, S, S Moore. 1980. *Ape into Human: A Study of Human Evolution.* Boston: Little, Brown.

386 Wasser, S K, ed. 1983. *Female Vertebrates.* New York: Academic Press.

387 Weiner, J S. 1971. *The Natural History of Man.* New York: Universe Books.

388 Welden, C W, W L Slauson. 1986. The intensity of competition versus its importance: An overlooked distinction and some implications. *Quarterly Review of Biology* 61: 23-44.

389 Wenke, R J. 1980. *Patterns in Prehistory: Mankind's First Three Million Years.* New York: Oxford University Press.

390 Wheeler, P E. 1984. The evolution of bipedality and loss of functional body hair in hominids. *Journal of Human Evolution* 13: 91-98.

391 White, T D, D C Johanson, W H Kimbel. 1981. Australopithecus africanus: Its phyletic position reconsidered *South African Journal of Science* 77: 445-70.

392 Whitesides, G H. 1985. Nutcracking by wind chimpanzees in Sierra Leone, west Africa. *Primates* 26: 91-94.

393 Wienberg, J, R Stanyon, A Jauch, T Cremer. 1992. Homologies in human and Mucaca fuscata chromosomes revealed by in situ

suppression hybridization with human chromosome specific DNA libraries. *Chromosoma* 101: 265-270.

394 Williams, G C. 1966. *Adaptation and Natural Selection.* Princeton: Princeton University Press.

395 Williams, G C. 1975. *Sex and Evolution.* Princeton: Princeton University Press.

396 Wilson, P J. 1980. *Man The Promising Primate.* New Haven: Yale University.

397 Wilson, A C, R C Cann. 1992. The recent African genesis of humans. *Scientific American* 266: 22-27.

398 Wolpoff, M H. 1980. *Paleoanthropology.* New York: Knopf.

399 Wolpoff, M H, X Z Wu, A G Thorne. 1984. Modern Homo sapiens origins: A general theory of hominid evolution involving the fossil evidence from East Asia. In *The Origins of Modern Humans.* Edited by Smith, F H, F Spencer. Pp. 485-516. New York: Alan R. Liss.

400 Wolpoff, M. 1989. Multiregional evolution: The fossil alternative to Eden. In *The Human Revolution: Behavioural and Biological Perspectives on the Origins of Modern Humans.* Edited by Mellars, P, C Stringer. Edinburgh: Edinburgh University Press.

401 Wood, B A. 1978. *Human Evolution.* New York: Wiley.

402 Wood, B A. 1985. Early Homo in Kenya, and its systematic relationships. In *Ancestors: The Hard Evidence.* Edited by Delson, E. Pp. 206-214. New York: Alan R. Liss.

403 Wood, B A, L B Martin, P Andrews, eds. 1986. *Major Topics in Primate and Human Evolution.* Cambridge: Cambridge University Press.

404 Wynn, T. 1979. The intelligence of later Acheulean hominids. *Man* 14: 371-391.

405 Wynn, T. 1981. The intelligence of Olduwan hominids. *Journal of Human Evolution* 10: 529-541.

406 Yunis, J J, J R Sawyer, K Dunham. 1980. The striking resemblance of high-resolution G-banded chromosomes of man and chimpanzees. *Science* 208: 1145-1148.

407 Yunis, J J, O Prakash. 1982. The origin of man: A chromosomal pictorial legacy. *Science* 215: 1525-30.

408 Zeuner, F E. 1959. *The Pleistocence Period: Its Climate, Chronology and Faunal Successions.* London: Hutchinson.

409 Zihlman, A L, J E Cronin, D L Cramer, V M Sarich. 1978. Pygmy chimpanzee as a possible prototype for the common ancestor of humans, chimpanzees and gorillas. *Nature* 275: 744-746.

410 Zihlman, A L. 1983. A behavioral reconstruction of Australopithecus. In *Hominid Origins. Inquiries Past and Present.* Edited by Reichs, K J. Pp. 207-38. Washington: University Press of the Americas.

411 Zihlman, A L, J M Lowenstein. 1983. Ramapithecus and Pan paniscus: Significance for human origins. In *New Interpretations of Ape and Human Ancestry.* Edited by Ciochon, R L, R S Corruccini. Pp. 677-94. New York: Plenum.

412 Zihlman, A L. 1989. Common ancestors and uncommon apes. In *Human Origins.* Edited by Durant, J R. Pp. 81-105. Oxford: Clarendon Press.

413 Zubrow, E. 1989. The demographic modelling of Neanderthal extinction. In *The Human Revolution: Behavioural and Biological Perspectives on the Origins of Modern Humans.* Edited by Mellars, P, C Stringer. Edinburgh: Edinburgh University Press.

# 2

# Prehistory

414 Abramova, Z A. 1980. Concerning the cultural contacts between Asia and America in the Late Paleolithic. In *Early Native Americans*. Edited by Browman, D L. Pp. 133-139. The Hauge: Mouton.

415 Adovasio, J M, R C Carlisle. 1984. An Indian hunters' camp for 20000 years. *Scientific American* 250: 104-108.

416 Adovasio, J M, et al. 1985. Paleoenvironmental reconstruction at Meadowcroft Rockshelter, Washington County, Pennsylvania. In *Environments and Extinctions: Man in Late Glacial North America* Edited by Mead, J I, D J Meltzer. Pp. 73-110. Orono: Center for the Study of Early Man, University of Maine.

417 Agrawal, D P, R Dodia, M Seth. 1990. South Asian climate and environment at c. 18000 BP. In *The World at 18000 BP: High Latitudes*. Edited by Gamble, C, O Soffer. Pp. 231-236. London: Unwin Hyman.

418 Akazawa, T. 1982. Cultural Change in Prehistoric Japan: The Receptivity Process of Rice Culture. *The Japanese Archipelago, Advances in World Archaeology I, 151-211*.

419 Allen, W. 1972. Ecology, techniques, and settlement patterns. In *Man, Settlement, and Urbanism*. Edited by Ucko, P, R Tringham, G W Dimbleby. Pp. 48-71. London: Duckworth.

420 Allen, J, J Golson, R Jones, eds. 1977. *Sundra and Sahul: Prehistoric Studies in South-east Asia, Melanesia and Australia*. New York: Academic Press.

421 Allen, H. 1990. Environmental history in southwestern New South Wales during the Late Pleistocene. In *The World at 18000 BP: High Latitudes*. Edited by Gamble, C, O Soffer. Pp. 296-321. London: Unwin Hyman.

422 Allsworth-Jones, P. 1989. The Szeletian and the stratigraphic succession in Central Europe and adjacent areas: Main trends, recent results, and problems for solution. In *The Human Revolution: Behavioural and Biological Perspectives on the Origins of Modern Humans*. Edited by Mellars, P. Edinburgh: Edinburgh University Press.

423 Altuna, J. 1984. Bases de subsitencia de origen animal en el yacimeiento. In *El Yacimiento Prehistorico de la Cueva de Ekain*. Edited by Altuna, J, J Merino. Pp. 211-280. San Sebastian: Sociedad de Estudios Vascos.

424 Altuna, J. 1985. Bases de subsitencia de los pobladores de Erralla: macromamiferos. *Munibe* 37: 87-117.

425 Altuna, J. 1986. The mammalian faunas from the prehistoric site of La Riera. In *La Riera Cave*. Edited by Straus, L, G Clarke. Pp. 237-274,4211-479. Tempe, Arizona: Anthropological Research Papers, 36.

426 Ammerman, A J, L L Cavalli-Sforza. 1985. *The Neolithic Transition and the Genetics of Populations in Europe*. Princeton: Princeton University Press.

427 Anderson, D D. 1980. Continuity and change in the prehistoric record from North Alaska. *Senri Ethnological Studies* 4: 233-251.

428 Anon. 1983. *Prehistoric Times. Readings from the Scientific American*. San Francisco: Freeman.

429 Arambourou, R, L Straus, C Normand. 1986. Recherches de pre-histoire dans les Landes en 1985. *Bulletin de la Societé de Borda* 111: 121-140.

430 Bahn, P. 1982. *Pyrenean Prehistory: A Palaeoeconomic Survey of the French Sites*. Wiltshire: Aris & Phillips.

431 Bahn, P, J Vertut. 1988. *Images of the Ice Age*. Leicester: Windward.

432 Bailey, G N, ed. 1983. *Hunter-Gatherer Economy in Prehistory: A European Perspective*. Cambridge: Cambridge University Press.

433 Bailey, G N, P Callow. 1986. *Stone Age Prehistory*. Cambridge: Cambridge University Press.

434 Baker, H. 1970. *Plants and Civilization*. 2nd ed. London: Macmillan.

435 Bar-Yosef, O. 1980. Prehistory of the Levant. *Annual Review of Anthropology* 9: 101-133.

436 Bar-Yosef, O, M E Kislev. 1989. Early farming communities in the Jordan Valley. In *The Evolution of Plant Exploitation: Concepts and Processes*. Edited by Harris, D R, G C Hillman. Pp. 632-642. London: Unwin Hyman.

437 Bar-Yosef, O. 1990. The Last Glacial Maximum in the Mediterranean Levant. In *The World at 18000 BP: High Latitudes*. Edited by Gamble, C, O Soffer. Pp. 58-77. London: Unwin Hyman.

438 Barker, G, C Gamble, eds. 1985. *Beyond Domestication in Prehistoric Europe: Investigations in Subsistence, Archaeology and Social Complexity*. London: Academic Press.

439 Behrensmeyer, A K. 1985. Taphonomy and the paleo-eco-

logic reconstruction of hominid habits in the Koobi Fora Formation. In *L'environment des Hominides au PlioPleistocene.* Edited by Coppens, Y. Pp. 309-324. Paris: Masson.

440 Behrensmeyer, A K. 1987. Taphonomy and hunting. In *The Evolution of Human Hunting.* Edited by Nitecki, M H, D V Nitecki. Pp. 423-450. New York: Plenum.

441 Bellwood, P. 1978. *Man's Conquest of the Pacific: The Prehistory of Southeast Asia and Oceania.* Auckland: Collins.

442 Bellwood, P. 1990. From Late Pleistocene to Early Holocene in Sundaland. In *The World at 18000 BP: High Latitudes.* Edited by Gamble, C, O Soffer. Pp. 255-263. London: Unwin Hyman.

443 Bender, B. 1975. *Farming in Prehistory: From Hunter-Gatherer to Food-Producer.* New York: St. Martins Press.

444 Berger, R, H E Suess, eds. 1979. *Radiocarbon Dating.* Berkeley: University of California Press.

445 Binford, L R. 1977. *Theory Building in Archaeology.* New York: Academic Press.

446 Binford, L R. 1981. *Bones: Ancient Men and Modern Myths.* London: Academic Press.

447 Binford, L R. 1982. The archaeology of place. *Journal of Anthropological Archaeology* 1: 5-31.

448 Binford, L R. 1983. *In Pursuit of the Past: Decoding the Archaeological Record.* New York: Thames and Hudson.

449 Binford, L R. 1984. Butchering, sharing, and the archaeological record. *Journal of Anthropological Archaeology* 3: 235-257.

450 Binford, L R. 1985. Human ancestors: Changing views of their behavior. *Journal of Archaelogical Anthropology* 4: 292-327.

451 Binford, L R, C K Ho. 1985. Taphonomy at a distance: Zhoukoudian, the cave home of Beijing man? *Current Anthropology* 26: 413-422.

452 Binford, L R, N M Stone. 1986. Zhoukoudian: A closer look. *Current Anthropology* 27: 453-475.

453 Bintleff, J L, W van Zeist, eds. 1982. *Palaeoclimates, Palaeoenvironments and Human Communities in the Eastern Mediterranean Region in Later Prehistory.* Oxford: B.A.R. International Series.

454 Bisson, M S. 1982. Trade and tribute: Archaeological evidence for the origin of states in south central AfriCA *Cahiers d'études africaines*

22: 87-88; 343-361.

455 Bonavia, D, A Grobman. 1989. Andean maize: Its origins and domestication. In *The Evolution of Plant Exploitation: Concepts and Processes*. Edited by Harris, D R, G C Hillman. Pp. 456-470. London: Unwin Hyman.

456 Bonnichsen, R. 1979. *Pleistocene Bone Technology in the Beringian Refugium*. Mercury Series, Paper No. 89. Ottawa: Archaeological Survey of Canada.

457 Bonnichsen, R, D Young. 1980. Early technological repertoires: Bone to stone. *Canadian Journal of Anthropology* 1: 123-128.

458 Bordaz, J. 1970. *Tools of the Old and New Stone Age*. Newton Abbot: Davis and Charles.

459 Boserup, E. 1965. *The Conditions of Agricultural Growth*. Chicago: Aldine.

460 Bowen, D Q. 1978. *Quaternary Geology*. Oxford: Pergamon Press.

461 Bradley, B, G C Frison. 1987. Projectile points and specialized bifaces from the Horner site. In *The Horner Site: The Type Site of the Cody Cultural Complex*. Edited by Frison, G C, L C Todd. Orlando: Academic Press.

462 Braidwood, R J. 1960. The Agricultural Revolution. *Scientific American* 203: 131-148.

463 Braidwood, R J. 1975. *Prehistoric Men*. 8th ed. Glenview, IL: Scott, Foresman.

464 Brain, C K. 1981. *The Hunters or the Hunted? An Introduction to African Cave Taphonomy*. Chicago: University of Chicago Press.

465 Brain, C K. 1982. The Swartkrans site: Stratigraphy of the fossil hominids and a reconstruction of the environment of early Homo. In *L'Homo erectus et la place de l'homme de Tautavel parmi les hominides fossiles*. Edited by de Lumley, H. Pp. 676-706. Paris: C.N.R.S.

466 Braun, D P, S Plog. 1982. Evolution of "tribal" social networks: Theory and prehistoric North American evidence. *American Antiquity* 47: 504-525.

467 Brice, W, ed. 1978. *The Environmental History of the Near and Middle East since the Last Ice Age*. London: Academic Press.

468 Brumfield, E. 1976. Regional growth in the eastern valley of Mexico: A test of the "population pressure" hypothesis. In *The Early Mesoamerican Village*. Edited by Flannery, K. Pp. 234-248. New York: Academic Press.

469 Brumfield, E M, T K Earle, eds. 1987. *Specialization, Exchange, and Complex Societies.* Cambridge: Cambridge University Press.

470 Brumley, J H. 1984. The Laidlaw Site: An Aboriginal Antelope Trap from Southeastern Alberta. In *Archaeological Survey of Alberta, Occasional Paper No. 23.* Edited by Burley, D. Edmonton: Alberta.

471 Bryan, A L. 1980. The stemmed point tradition: An early technological tradition in western North America. In *Anthropological Papers in Memory of Earl H. Swanson, Jr.* Edited by Harten, L B, C N Warren, D R Touhy. Pp. 77-107. Pocatello: Idaho State Museum of Natural History.

472 Bryan, A L. 1986. Paleoamerican prehistory as seen from South AmeriCA In *New Evidence for the Pleistocene Peopling of the Americas.* Edited by Bryan, A L. Pp. 77-107. Center for the Study of Early Man, Orono: University of Maine.

473 Bulmer, S. 1989. Gardens in the south: Diversity and change in prehistoric Maori agriculture. In *The Evolution of Plant Exploitation: Concepts and Processes.* Edited by Harris, D R, G C Hillman. Pp. 688-705. London: Unwin Hyman.

474 Butler, A. 1989. Cryptic anatomical characters as evidence of early cultivation in the grain legumes (pulses). In *The Evolution of Plant Exploitation: Concepts and Processes.* Edited by Harris, D R, G C Hillman. Pp. 390-407. London: Unwin Hyman.

475 Butzer, K W, ed. 1971. *Environment and Archaeology: An Ecological Approach to Prehistory.* 2nd ed. Chicago: Aldine.

476 Butzer, K W. 1982. *Archaeology as Human Ecology: Method and Theory for a Contextual Approach.* Cambridge: Cambridge University Press.

477 Byrd, B, A Garrard. 1990. The last glacial maximum in the Jordanian desert. In *The World at 18000 BP: High Latitudes.* Edited by Gamble, C, O Soffer. Pp. 78-98. London: Unwin Hyman.

478 Campbell, B. 1983. *Human Ecology: The History of Our Place in Nature from Prehistory to the Present.* London: Heineman.

479 Cane, S. 1989. Australian Aboriginal seed grinding and its archaeological record: A case study from the Western Desert. In *The Evolution of Plant Exploitation: Concepts and Processes.* Edited by Harris, D, G Hillman. Pp. 99-119. London: Unwin Hyman.

480 Champion, T C. 1982. Fortification, ranking and subsistence. In *Ranking, Resource and Exchange.* Edited by Renfrew, C, S Shennan. Pp. 61-66. Cambridge: Cambridge University Press.

481 Champion, T C, C S Gamble, S J Shennan, A Whittle. 1984. *Prehistoric Europe.* London: Academic Press.

482 Chang, T T. 1989. Domestication and the spread of the cultivated rices. In *The Evolution of Plant Exploitation: Concepts and Processes*. Edited by Harris, D R, G C Hillman. Pp. 408-417. London: Unwin Hyman.

483 Chapman, R. 1982. The emergence of formal disposal areas and the "problem" of the megalithic tombs in prehistoric Europe. In *The Archaeology of Death*. Edited by Chapman, R, I Kinnes, K Randsborg. Pp. 71-82. Cambridge: Cambridge University Press.

484 Chase, P, H Dibble. 1987. Middle Paleolithic symbolism: a review of current evidence and interpretations. *Journal of Anthropological Archaeology* 6: 263-96.

485 Chase, P. 1989. How different was Middle Paleolithic subsistence? A zooarchaeological perspective on the Middle to Upper Paleolithic transition. In *The Human Revolution: Behavioural and Biological Perspectives on the Origins of Modern Humans*. Edited by Mellars, P, C Stringer. Edinburgh: Edinburgh University Press.

486 Chase, A. 1989. Domestication and domiculture in northern Australia: A social perspective. In *The Evolution of Plant Exploitation: Concepts and Processes*. Edited by Harris, D R, G C Hillman. Pp. 42-54. London: Unwin Hyman.

487 Chikwendu, V E, C E A Okezie. 1989. Factors responsible for the ennoblement of African yams: Inferences from experiments in yam domestication. In *The Evolution of Plant Exploitation: Concepts and Processes*. Edited by Harris, D, G Hillman. Pp. 344-357. London: Unwin Hyman.

488 Childe, V G. 1958. *The Pre-History of European Society*. London: Cassell.

489 Clark, D W, A M Clark. 1980. Paleo-Indians and fluted points: Subarctic alternatives. *Plains Anthropologist* 28: 283-292.

490 Clark, D W. 1981. Archaeology of the Batza Tena obsidian source, west-central Alaska. *Anthropological Papers of the University of Alaska* 15: 1-21.

491 Clark, G, S Yi. 1983. Niche-width variation in Cantabrian archaeofaunas: A diachronic study. In *Animals and archaeology: Hunters and their prey*. Edited by Clutton-Brock, J, C Grigson. British Archaeological Reports International Series 163.

492 Clark, J D, S A Brandt, eds. 1984. *From Hunters to Farmers. The Causes and Consequences of Food Production in* Africa  Berkeley: University of California Press.

493 Clarke, J D. 1983. The significance of culture change in the early later Pleistocene in nothern and southern Africa. In *The Mousterian Legacy: Human Biocultural Change in the Upper Pleistocene*. Edited

by Trinkaus, E. Pp. 1-12. Oxford: British Archaeological Reports International Series 164.

494 Close, A, F Wendorf. 1990. North Africa at 18000 BP. In *The World at 18000 BP: High Latitudes*. Edited by Gamble, C, O Soffer. Pp. 41-57. London: Unwin Hyman.

495 Clutton-Brock, J. 1981. *Domesticated Animals in Early Times*. Austin: University of Texas Press.

496 Cohen, M N. 1977. *The Food Crisis in Prehistory: Overpopulation and the Origins of Agriculture*. New Haven: Yale University Press.

497 Cohen, M N, G J Armelagos. 1984. *Paleopathology at the Origins of Agriculture*. London: Academic Press.

498 Collins, D. 1976. *The Human Revolution: From Ape to Artist*. Oxford: Phaidon.

499 Conkey, M. 1983. On the origins of Paleolithic art: A review and some critical thoughts. In *The Mousterian Legacy: Human Biocultural Change in the Upper Pleistocene*. Edited by Trinkaus, E. Pp. 201-219. Oxford: British Archaeological Reports International Series 164.

500 Cook, J, C B Stringer, A P Currant, H P Schwarcz, A G Wintle. 1982. A review of the chronology of the European Middle Pleistocene hominid record. *Yrbk Phys. Anthrop.* 25: 19-65.

501 Costantini, L. 1989. Plant exploitation at Grotta dell'Uzzo, Sicily: new evidence for the transition from Mesolithic to Neolithic subsistence in southern Europe. In *The Evolution of Plant Exploitation: Concepts and Processes*. Edited by Harris, D R, G C Hillman. Pp. 197-206. London: Unwin Hyman.

502 Curtis, G H. 1981. Establishing a relevant time-scale in anthropological and archaeological research. *Philosopical Transactions of the Royal Society (London)* B. 292: 7-20.

503 Davidson, I. 1983. Site variability and prehistoric economy in Levante. In *Hunter-Gatherer Economy in Prehistory*. Edited by Bailey, G. Pp. 79-95. Cambridge: Cambridge University Press.

504 Deacon, J. 1984. Later Stone Age people and their descendants in southern AfriCA In *Southern African Prehistory and Paleoenvironments*. Edited by Klein, R G. Pp. 221-328. Rottterdam: A.A. Balkema.

505 Deacon, J. 1984. *The Later Stone Age of Southernmost AfricA* London: British Archaelogical Reports International Series.

506 Deacon, J. 1990. Changes in the archaeological record in South Africa at 18000 BP. In *The World at 18000 BP: High Latitudes*. Edited by Gamble, C, O Soffer. Pp. 170-188. London: Unwin Hyman.

507 Dennell, R. 1983. *European Economic Prehistory: A New Approach.* London: Academic Press.

508 Dibble, H, A Montet-White, eds. 1988. *The Pleistocene Prehistory of Western Eurasia.* Philadelphia: University of Pennsylvania Press.

509 Dove, M. 1989. The transition from stone to steel in the prehistoric swidden agricultural technology of the Kantu' of Kalimantan, Indonesia. In *The Evolution of Plant Exploitation: Concepts and Processes.* Edited by Harris, D R, G C Hillman. Pp. 667-677. London: Unwin Hyman.

510 Drennan, R D. 1976. Religion and Social Evolution in Formative MesoameriCA In *The Early Mesoamerican Village.* Edited by Flannery, K V. Pp. 345-369. New York: Academic Press.

511 Dumond, D E. 1980. A chronology of nativet alaskan subsistence systems. *Senri Ethnological Series* 4: 23-47.

512 Dunnell, R C. 1980. Evolutionary theory and archaeology. In *Advances in Archaeological Theory and Method.* Edited by Schiffer, M B. Pp. 35-99. London: Academic Press.

513 Earle, T K, J Erickson. 1977. *Exchange Systems in Prehistory.* New York: Academic Press.

514 Earle, T K. 1980. *Modelling Change in Prehistoric Subsistence Economics.* New York: Academic Press.

515 Edwards, P. 1990. Kebaran occupation at the last glacial maximum in Wadi al-Hammeh, Jordan Valley. In *The World at 18000 BP: High Latitudes.* Edited by Gamble, C, O Soffer. Pp. 97-120. London: Unwin Hyman.

516 Fagan, B M. 1983. *People of the Earth: An Introduction to World Prehistory.* 4th ed. Boston: Little, Brown.

517 Falk, D. 1983. Cerebral cortices of East African early hominids. *Science* 221: 1072-1074.

518 Falk, D. 1985. Apples, oranges, and the lunate sulcus. *American Journal of Physical Anthropology* 67: 313-315.

519 Fentress, M. 1982. From Jhelum to Yamuna: City and settlement in the second and third millenium B.C. In *Harappan Civilization.* Edited by Possehl, G. Pp. 245-260. Warminster: Aris and Phillips.

520 Fisher, D C. 1984. Taphonomic analysis of late Pleistocene mastodon occurrences: Evidence of butchery by North American Paleo-Indians. *Paleobiology* 10: 338-357.

521 Fisher, D C. 1984. Mastodon butchery by North American Paleo-Indians. *Nature* 308: 271-272.

522 Fisher, D C. 1987. Mastodon procurement by Paleoindians of the Great Lakes region: Hunting or scavenging? In *The Evolution of Human Hunting.* Edited by Nitecki, M, D Nitecki. Pp. 309-423. New York: Plenum.

523 Fladmark, K R. 1983. Times and places: Environmental correlates of mid- to late-Wisconsinan human population expansion in North America. In *Early Man in the New World.* Edited by Shulter, R, Jr. Pp. 13-41. Beverly Hills: Sage Publications.

524 Flannery, K, ed. 1976. *The Early Mesoamerican Village.* New York: Academic Press.

525 Foley, R. 1982. A reconsideration of the role of predation on large mammals in tropic hunter-gatherer adaptations. *Man* 17: 393-402.

526 Forde, C D. 1934. *Habitat, Economy and Society: A Geographical Introduction to Ethnology.* London: Methuen.

527 Frayer, D W. 1984. Biological and cultural change in the European late Pleistocene and early Holocene. In *The Origins of Modern Humans.* Edited by Smith, F H, F Spencer. Pp. 211-250. New York: Alan R. Liss.

528 Freeman, L G, Jr. 1981. The fat of the land: Notes on Paleolithic diet in Iberia. In *Omnivorous Primates: Gathering and Hunting in Human Evolution.* Edited by Harding, R S O, G Telecki. Pp. 104-165. New York: Columbia University Press.

529 Frison, G. 1978. *Prehistoric Hunters of the High Plains.* New York: Academic Press.

530 Frison, G. 1982. Paleo-Indian winter subsistence strategies on the High Plains. In *Plains Indian Studies: A Collection of Essays in Honor of John C. Ewers and Waldo R. Wedel.* Washington: Smithsonian Contributions to Anthropology No. 30.

531 Frison, G C, C Graig. 1982. Bone, antler, and ivory artifacts and manufacture technology. In *The Agate Basin Site.* Edited by Frison, G C, D J Stanford. Pp. 157-173. New York: Academic Press.

532 Frison, G. 1984. The Carter/Kerr-McGee Paleoindian site: Cultural resource management and archaeological research. *American Antiquity* 49: 288-314.

533 Frison, G. 1985. Prehistoric and early historic mountain sheep procurement in the central Rocky Mountains. *Archaeological Survey of Alberta: Occasional Paper* 26: 267-276.

534 Frison, G, R L Andrews, J M Adovasio, R C Carlisle, R Edgar. 1986. A late paleoindian animal tapping net from Northern Wyoming. *American Antiquity* 51: 352-361.

535 Frison, G, L C Todd. 1986. *The Colby Mammoth Site: Taphonomy and Archaeology of a Clovis Kill in Northern Wyoming.* Albequerque: University of New Mexico Press.

536 Frison, G. 1987. Prehistoric, plains-mountain, large-mammal communal hunting strategies. In *The Evolution of Human Hunting.* Edited by Nitecki, M, D Nitecki. Pp. 177-225. New York: Plenum.

537 Frison, G. 1987. The tool assemblage, unspecialized bifaces, and stone flaking material sources for the Horner site. In *The Horner Site: The Type Site of the Cody Cultural Complex.* Edited by Frison, G, L C Todd. Orlando: Academic Press.

538 Gallagher, J P. 1989. Agricultural intensification and ridged-field cultivation in the prehistoric upper Midwest of North America  In *The Evolution of Plant Exploitation: Concepts and Processes.* Edited by Harris, D R, G C Hillman. Pp. 572-584. London: Unwin Hyman.

539 Gamble, G C. 1982. Interaction and alliance in Paleolithic society. *Man*  17: 92-107.

540 Gamble, C S. 1983. Culture and society in the Upper Palaeolithic of Europe. In *Hunter-gather economy in prehistory: A European perspective.* Edited by Bailey, G N. Pp. 201-11. Cambridge: Cambridge University Press.

541 Gamble, C S. 1986. *The Palaeolithic Settlement of Europe.* Cambridge: Cambridge University Press.

542 Gamble, C, O Soffer, eds. 1990. *The World at 18000 BP: Low latitudes.* London: Unwin Hyman.

543 Garland, E B, J W Cogswell. 1985. The Powers mastodon site. *Michigan Archives*  31: 3-39.

544 Geraads, D. 1985. La fauna des gisements de Melka-Kunture (Ethiopie). In *L'Envirouement des hominides au Plio-Pleistocene.* Pp. 165-174. Paris: Masson.

545 Gibson, M. 1972. Population shift and the rise of Mesopotamian civilization. In *The Explanation of Cultural Change: Models in Prehistory.* Edited by Renfrew, C. London: Duckworth.

546 Gilbert, R I, J H Mielke, eds. 1985. *The Analysis of Prehistoric Diets.* London: Academic.

547 Gilman, A. 1981. The Development of Social Stratification in Bronze Age Europe. *Current Anthropology* 22: 1-23.

548 Golson, J. 1989. The origins and development of New Guinea agriculture. In *The Evolution of Plant Exploitation: Concepts and Processes.* Edited by Harris, D R, G C Hillman. Pp. 678-688. London: Unwin Hyman.

549 Gordon, B. 1986. Of men and reindeer herds in French Magdalenian prehistory. In *The Pleistocene Perspective*. Edited by Simon, A. Pp. 297-318. London: Allen and Unwin.

550 Gramly, R M. 1984. Kill sites, killing ground and fluted points at the Vail site. *Archaeology of Eastern North America* 12: 110-121.

551 Grayson, D K. 1984. Nineteenth Century Explanations of Pleistocene Extinctions: A Review and Analysis. In *Quaternary Extinctions: A Prehistoric Revolution*. Edited by Martin, P S, R G Klein. Pp. 5-39. Tucson: University of Arizona Press.

552 Groube, L. 1989. The taming of the rain forests: A model for Late Pleistocene forest exploitation in New Guinea. In *The Evolution of Plant Exploitation: Concepts and Processes*. Edited by Harris, D R, G C Hillman. Pp. 292-305. London: Unwin Hyman.

553 Guilbert, G, ed. 1981. *Hill-fort Studies: Essays for A.H.A. Hogg*. Leicester: Leicester University Press.

554 Guthrie, R D. 1982. Mammals of the mammoth steppe as paleoenvironmental indicators. In *Paleoecology of Beringia*. Edited by Hopkins, D M, J V Matthews, C Schweger, S B Young. Pp. 307-326. New York: Academic Press.

555 Guthrie, R D. 1983. Osseous projectile points: Biological considerations affecting raw material selection and design among Paleolithic and Paleoindian peoples. *British Archaeological Reports International Series* 163: 110-121.

556 Guthrie, R D. 1985. Woolly arguments against the mammoth steppe: A new look at the paleonological data. *Quarterly Review of Archaeology* 6: 9-16.

557 Hannus, L A. 1983. Of mammoths, men and ice: Making it on the margins. *Geological Society of America* 15: 590.

558 Harlan, J R. 1989. The tropical African cereals. In *The Evolution of Plant Exploitation: Concepts and Processes*. Edited by Harris, D R, G C Hillman. Pp. 335-343. London: Unwin Hyman.

559 Harlan, J R. 1989. Wild-grass seed harvesting in the Sahara and Sub-Sahara of AfriCA In *The Evolution of Plant Exploitation: Concepts and Processes*. Edited by Harris, D R, G C Hillman. Pp. 79-98. London: Unwin Hyman.

560 Harris, D R, G C Hillman, eds. 1989. *Foraging and Farming: The Evolution of Plant Exploitation*. London: Unwin Hyman.

561 Harris, D R. 1989. An evolutionary continuum of people-plant interaction. In *The Evolution of Plant Exploitation: Concepts and Processes*. Edited by Harris, D R, G C Hillman. Pp. 11-26. London: Unwin Hyman.

562 Harrison, P D, B L Turner, eds. 1978. *Pre-Historic Mayan Agriculture*. Albuquerque: University of New Mexico Press.

563 Harrison, R J. 1985. The 'Policultivo Ganadero', or the secondary products revolution in Spanish agriculture, 5000-1000 B.C. *Proceedings of the Prehistoric Society* 51: 75-102.

564 Harrold, F B. 1980. A comparative analysis of Eurasian Palaeolithic burials. *World Archaeology* 12: 195-211.

565 Hassan, F. 1973. On Mechanisms of Population Growth During the Neolithic. *Current Anthropology* 14: 535-542.

566 Hassan, F A. 1981. *Demographic Archaeology*. London: Academic Press.

567 Haviland, W A. 1979. *Human Evolution and Prehistory*. New York: Holt, Rinehart & Winston.

568 Hawkes, J G. 1989. The domestication of roots and tubers in the American tropics. In *The Evolution of Plant Exploitation: Concepts and Processes*. Edited by Harris, D R, G C Hillman. Pp. 481-503. London: Unwin Hyman.

569 Hayden, B, A Cannon. 1984. *The structure of material systems: Ethnoarchaeology in the Maya Highlands*. SAA Papers No. 3. Washington, DC: Society for American Archaeology.

570 Hayden, B. 1986. Resources, rivalry, and reproduction: The influence of basic resource characteristics on reproductive behavior. In *Culture and Reproduction*. Edited by Handwerker, P. Pp. 176-195. Boulder: Westview Press.

571 Hayden, B, M Deal, A Cannon, J Casey. 1986. Ecological determinants of women's status among hunter/gatherers. *Human Evolution* 1: 449-473.

572 Hayden, B. 1990. Nimrods, piscators, pluckers, and planters: The origins of domestication. *Journal of Anthropological Archaeology* 9: 31-69.

573 Hayden, B, R Gargett. 1990. Big man, big heart?: A Mesoamerican view of the emergence of complex society. *Ancient Mesoamerica* 1: 3-20.

574 Haynes, C V. 1982. Were Clovis progenitors in Beringia? In *Paleoecology of Beringia*. Edited by Hopkins, M, J V Matthews, C E Schweger Jr., S B Young. New York: Academic Press.

575 Heiser, C B. 1989. Domestication of Cucurbitacaea: Cucurbita and Lagenaria. In *The Evolution of Plant Exploitation: Concepts and Processes*. Edited by Harris, D R, G C Hillman. Pp. 471-480. London: Unwin Hyman.

576 Helms, M W. 1979. *Ancient Panama: Chiefs in Search of Power.* Austin: University of Texas Press.

577 Higgs, E S, ed. 1972. *Papers in Economic Prehistory.* New York: Cambridge University Press.

578 Higgs, E S, ed. 1974. *Palaeoeconomy.* New York: Cambridge University Press.

579 Higham, C, B Maloney. 1989. Coastal adaptation, sedentism, and domestication: A model for socio-economic intensification in prehistoric Southeast Asia. In *The Evolution of Plant Exploitation: Concepts and Processes.* Edited by Harris, D, G Hillman. Pp. 650-666. London: Unwin Hyman.

580 Hill, J, ed. 1977. *Explanation of Prehistoric Change.* Albuquerque: University of New Mexico.

581 Hill, A P, A K Behrensmeyer. 1984. Disarticulation patterns of some modern East African mammals. *Paleobiology* 10: 366-376.

582 Hill, A P. 1985. Natural disarticulation and bison butchery. *American Antiquity* 50: 141-145.

583 Hill, H, J Evans. 1989. Crops of the Pacific: New evidence from the chemical analysis of organic residues in pottery. In *The Evolution of Plant Exploitation: Concepts and Processes.* Edited by Harris, D R, G C Hillman. Pp. 418-425. London: Unwin Hyman.

584 Hillman, G C. 1989. Late Palaeolithic plant foods from Wadi Kubbaniya in Upper Egypt: Dietary diversity, infant weaning, and seasonality in a riverine environment. In *The Evolution of Plant Exploitation: Concepts and Processes.* Edited by Harris, D R, G C Hillman. Pp. 207-239. London: Unwin Hyman.

585 Hillman, G, S Colledge, D Harris. 1989. Plant-food economy during the Epipalaeolithic period at Tell Abu Hureyra, Syria: Dietary diversity, seasonality, and modes of exploitation. In *The Evolution of Plant Exploitation: Concepts and Processes.* Edited by Harris, D R, G C Hillman. Pp. 240-268. London: Unwin Hyman.

586 Hodder, I. 1979. Economic and social stress and material cultural patterning. *American Antiquity* 44: 446-454.

587 Hodder, I. 1982. *Symbolic and Structural Archaeology.* Cambridge: Cambridge University Press.

588 Hoffecker, J E, C A Wolf, eds. 1988. *The Early Upper Paleolithic: Evidence from Europe and the Near East.* British Archaeological Reports International Series 437.

589 Holl, A. 1985. Background to the Ghana Empire: Archaeological investigations on the transition to statehood in the Dhar Tichitt Region

(Mauritania). *Journal of Anthropological Archaeology* 4: 73-115.

590 Hopkins, D M, J V Matthews Jr., Schweger, S B Young, eds. 1982. *Paleoecology of Beringia*. New York: Academic Press.

591 Huckell, B B. 1982. The Denver elephant project: A report on experimentation with thrusting spears. *Plains Anthropologist* 27-97: 217-224.

592 Hughes, O L, et al. 1981. Upper pleistocene stratigraphy, paleoecology, and archaeology of the norther Yukon interior, Eastern Beringia, 1. Bonnet Plume Basin. *Arctic Anthropology* 34: 329-365.

593 Huss-Ashmore, R, A H Goodman, G J Armelagos. 1982. Nutritional Inference from Palaeopathology. In *Advances in Archaeological Method and Theory*. Edited by Schiffer, M B. Pp. 395-474. New York: Academic Press.

594 Hutterer, K L. 1976. An evolutionary approach to the southeast asian cultural sequence. *Current Anthropology* 17: 221-242.

595 Ingold, T. 1980. *Hunters, Pastoralists and Ranchers*. Cambridge: Cambridge University Press.

596 Irving, W N. 1982. Pleistocene cultures in Old Crow Basin: Interim report. In *Peopling of the New World*. Edited by Ericson, J E, R E Taylor, R Berger. Pp. 69-79. Los Altos: Ballena Press.

597 Jennings, J D, ed. 1979. *The Prehistory of Polynesia*. Cambridge: Harvard University Press.

598 Johns, T. 1989. A chemical-ecological model of root and tuber domestication in the Andes. In *The Evolution of Plant Exploitation: Concepts and Processes*. Edited by Harris, D R, G C Hillman. Pp. 504-522. London: Unwin Hyman.

599 Johnson, E. 1982. Paleo-Indian bone expediency tools: Lubbock Lake and bonefire shelter. *Canadian Journal of Anthropology* 2: 145-157.

600 Jones, R, B Meehan. 1989. Plant foods of the Gidjingali: Ethnographic and archaeological perspectives from northern Australia on tuber and seed exploitation. In *The Evolution of Plant Exploitation: Concepts and Processes*. Edited by Harris, D R, G C Hillman. Pp. 120-135. London: Unwin Hyman.

601 Kajale, M D. 1989. Mesolithic exploitation of wild plants in Sri Lanka: archaeobotanical study at the cave site of Beli-Lena. In *The Evolution of Plant Exploitation: Concepts and Processes*. Edited by Harris, D R, G C Hillman. Pp. 269-281. London: Unwin Hyman.

602 Kirk, R L. 1981. *Aboriginal Man Adapting: The Human Biology of Australian Aborigines*. Clarendon Press.

603 Klein, R G. 1973. *Ice-age Hunters of the Ukraine.* Chicago, IL: University of Chicago Press.

604 Klein, R G. 1978. Stone Age predation on large African bovids. *Journal of Archaeological Science* 5: 195-217.

605 Klein, R G. 1983. The Stone Age prehistory of southern Africa *Annual Review of Anthropology* 12: 25-48.

606 Klein, R G. 1984. Mammalian extinctions and stone age people in AfriCA In *Quaternary Extinctions: A Prehistoric Revolution.* Edited by Martin, P S, R G Klein. Pp. 553-573. Tuscon: University of Arizona Press.

607 Klein, R G, K Cruz-Uribe. 1984. *The Analysis of Animal Bones from Archaeological Sites.* Chicago: University of Chicago Press.

608 Klein, R. 1987. Reconstructing how early people exploited animals: Problems and prospects. In *The Evolution of Human Hunting.* Edited by Nitecki, M H, D V Nitecki. Pp. 11-47. New York: Plenum.

609 Kowalewski, S A, R E Blanton, G Feinman, L Finsten. 1983. Boundaries, scale, and internal organization. *Journal of Anthropological Archaeology* 2: 32-56.

610 Kozlowski, S K. 1975. *Cultural Differentiation of Europe from 10th to 5th Millennium B.C.* Warsaw: Warsaw University Press.

611 Kristiansen, K. 1982. The formation of tribal systems in later European prehistory; northern Europe 4000-500 B.C. In *Theory and Explanation in Archaeology: The Southampton Conference.* Edited by Renfrew, C, M J Rowlands, B A Segraves. Pp. 241-280. New York: Academic Press.

612 Kroll, E M, G L Isaac. 1984. Configurations of artifacts and bones at early Pleistocene sites in East Africa. In *Instrasite Spatial Analysis in Archaeology.* Edited by Hietala, H J. Pp. 4-31. Cambridge: Cambridge University Press.

613 Ladizinsky, G. 1989. Origin and domestication of the Southwest Asian grain legumes. In *The Evolution of Plant Exploitation: Concepts and Processes.* Edited by Harris, D R, G C Hillman. Pp. 374-389. London: Unwin Hyman.

614 Lamb, H H. 1982. *Climate, History and the Modern World.* London: Methuen.

615 Lamberg-Karlovsky, C C. 1975. *Third Millenium Models of Exchange and Modes of Production in Ancient Civilization and Trade.* Albuquerque: University of New Mexico Press.

616 Lowenstein, J M, A L Zihlman. 1984. Human evolution and molecular biology. *Persp. Biol. Med.* 27: 611-22.

617 Mackie, E. 1977. *The Megalith Builders*. Oxford: Phaidon.

618 Madeyska, T. 1990. The distribution of human settlement in the extra-tropical Old World: 24000-15000 BP. In *The World at 18000 BP: High Latitudes*. Edited by Gamble, C, O Soffer. Pp. 24-40. London: Unwin Hyman.

619 Markey, T L. 1989. The spread of agriculture in western Europe: Indo-European and (non-)pre-Indo-European linguistic evidence. In *The Evolution of Plant Exploitation: Concepts and Processes*. Edited by Harris, D R, G C Hillman. Pp. 585-606. London: Unwin Hyman.

620 Marks, S A. 1982. Arguing from the present to the past: A contemporary case study of human predation on African buffalo. In *Paleoecology of Beringia*. Edited by Hopkins, D M, J V Matthews, C Schweger, S B Young. Pp. 409-423. New York: Academic Press.

621 Marshack, A. 1972. *The Roots of Civilization*. New York: McGraw-Hill.

622 Martin, P S, R G Klein. 1982. *Pleistocene Extinctions*. Tucson: University of Arizona Press.

623 Martin, P S, R G Klein, eds. 1984. *Quaternary Extinctions: A Prehistoric Revolution*. Tucson: University of Arizona Press.

624 Mason, R J. 1962. *The Prehistory of the Transvaal*. Johannesburg: Witwatersrand University Press.

625 Megaw, J V S, ed. 1977. *Hunters, Gatherers and First Farmers beyond Europe: An Archaeological Survey*. Leicester: Leicester University Press.

626 Mellars, P. 1975. Ungulate populations, economic patterns and the mesolithic landscape. In *The Effect of Man on the Landscape: The Highland Zone*. Edited by Evans, J G, S Limbrey, H Cleere. Pp. 49-56. London: Council for British Archaeology Research Report 11.

627 Mellars, P, ed. 1979. *The Early Postglacial Settlement of Northern Europe: An Ecological Perspective*. Pittsburgh: University of Pittsburgh Press.

628 Meltzer, D J, J I Mead. 1983. The timing of late Pleistocene mammalian extinctions in North AmeriCA *Quaternary Research* 19: 130-135.

629 Michael, H N. 1984. Absolute chronologies of Late Pleistocene and Early Holocene cultures of northeastern Asia. *Arctic Anthropology* 21: 1-68.

630 Miller, S J. 1983. Osteo-Archaeology of the mammoth-bison assemblage at Owl Cave, the Wasden Site, Idaho. In *Carnivores, Human Scavengers and Predators: A Question of Bone Technology*. Edited

by LeMoine, G M, A S MacEachern. Pp. 39-53. Calgary: University of Calgary Archaeological Association.

631 Minnis, P E. 1985. *Social Adaptations to Food Stress: A Prehistoric Southwestern Example.* Chicago: University of Chicago Press.

632 Mitchell, P. 1990. A palaeoecological model for archaeological site distribution in southern Africa during the Upper Pleniglacial and Late Glacial. In *The World at 18000 BP: High Latitudes.* Edited by Gamble, C, O Soffer. Pp. 189-205. London: Unwin Hyman.

633 Mithen, S J. 1988. Looking and learning: Upper Palaeolithic art and information gathering. *World Archaeology: New Directions in Palaeolithic Archaeology* 19: 297-327.

634 Moore, A M T. 1979. A pre-Neolithic farmers' village on the Euphrates. *Scientific American* 241: 50-58.

635 Moore, A M T. 1989. The transition from foraging to farming in Southwest Asia: present problems and future directions. In *The Evolution of Plant Exploitation: Concepts and Processes.* Edited by Harris, D R, G C Hillman. Pp. 620-631. London: Unwin Hyman.

636 Morlan, R E. 1980. Taphonomy and archaeology in the Upper Pleistocene of the Northern Yukon Territory: A glimpse of the peopling of the New World. *Archaeological Survey of Canada Paper* 94: 1-380.

637 Morlan, R E, J Cinq-Mars. 1982. Ancient Beringians: Human occupation in the late Pleistocene of Alaska and the Yukon Territory. In *Paleoecology of Beringia.* Edited by Hopkins, D M, J V Matthews Jr., Schweger, S B Young. Pp. 353-381. New York: Academic Press.

638 Morlan, R E. 1986. Pleistocene archaeology in Old Crow Basin: A critical reappraisal. In *New Evidence for the Pleistocene Peopling of the Americas.* Edited by Bryan, A L. Pp. 27-48. Orono, ME: Center for the Study of Early Man, University of Maine.

639 Morlan, R E. 1986. Review of "Environments and Extinctions: Man in Late Glacial North America". *Zooarchaeological Research News* 5: 10-16.

640 Nissen, H J. 1972. The city wall of Uruk. In *The Explanation of Cultural Change: Models in Prehistory.* Edited by Renfrew, C. London: Duckworth.

641 Nitecki, M H. 1987. The idea of human hunting. In *The Evolution of Human Hunting.* Edited by Nitecki, M H, D V Nitecki. Pp. 1-11. New York: Plenum.

642 Ortner, D, ed. 1983. *How humans adapt: A biocultural odyssey.* Washington, D.C.: Smithsonian Institution Press.

643 Parkington, J. 1990. A view from the south: Southern Africa before, during, and after the last glacial maximum. In *The World at 18000 BP: High Latitudes*. Edited by Gamble, C, O Soffer. Pp. 214-230. London: Unwin Hyman.

644 Pfeiffer, J E. 1977. *The Emergence of Society: A Prehistory of the Establishment*. New York: McGraw-Hill.

645 Pfeiffer, J E. 1982. *The Creative Explosion*. New York: Harper & Row.

646 Piggott, S. 1965. *Ancient Europe*. Chicago: Aldine Press.

647 Pires-Ferreira, J W, K V Flannery. 1976. Interregional exchange networks. In *The Early Mesoamerican Village*. Edited by Flannery, K V. Pp. 280-283. New York: Academic Press.

648 Pires-Ferreira, J W, K V Flannery. 1976. Ethnographic models for formative exchange. In *The Early Mesoamerican Village*. Edited by Flannery, K V. Pp. 286-292. New York: Academic Press.

649 Pires-Ferreira, J W. 1976. Obsidian exchange in formative mesoamerica. In *The Early Mesoamerican Village*. Edited by Flannery, K V. Pp. 292-306. New York: Academic Press.

650 Price, T D, J A Brown, eds. 1985. *Prehistoric Hunter-Gatherers. The Emergence of Cultural Complexity*. London: Academic Press.

651 Prichard, J E, ed. 1955. *Ancient Near Eastern Texts*. Princeton: Princeton University Press.

652 Pyramarn, K. 1989. New evidence on plant exploitation and environment during the Hoabinhian (Late Stone Age) from Ban Kao Caves, Thailand. In *The Evolution of Plant Exploitation: Concepts and Processes*. Edited by Harris, D R, G C Hillman. Pp. 282-291. London: Unwin Hyman.

653 Quilter, J, T Stocker. 1983. Subsistence economies and the origins of Anean complex societies. *American Anthropologist* 85: 545-562.

654 Raikes, R. 1964. The end of ancient cities in the Indus. *American Anthropologist* 66: 284-299.

655 Rathje, W L. 1971. The origin and development of lowland classic Maya civilization. *American Antiquity* 36: 275-85.

656 Redman, C L, M J Berman, E V Curtin, W T Laughorne, N M Versaggi, J C Wauser, eds. 1978. *Social Archaeology: Beyond Subsistence and Dating*. New York: Academic Press.

657 Reed, C A. 1959. Animal domestication in the prehistoric near east. *Science* 130: 1629-1639.

658 Reed, C A, eds. 1977. *Origins of Agriculture.* The Hague: Mouton.

659 Reeves, K O K. 1978. Head-Smashed-In: 5500 years of bison jumping in the Alberta Plains. *Plains Anthropologist Memoir* 14: 151-174.

660 Renfrew, C, eds. 1973. *The Explanation of Culture Change: Models in Prehistory.* London: Duckworth.

661 Renfrew, C. 1975. *Beyond a Subsistence Economy: The Evolution of Social Organization in Prehistoric Europe.* Cambridge: M.I.T. Press.

662 Renfrew, C, S J Shennan, eds. 1982. *Ranking, Resource and Exchange: Aspects of the Archaeology of Early European Society.* Cambridge: Cambridge University Press.

663 Rightmire, G P. 1984. Homo sapiens in sub-Saharan Africa In *The Origins of Modern humans.* Edited by Smith, F H, F Spencer. Pp. 295-325. New York: Alan Liss.

664 Rindos, D. 1984. *The Origins of Agriculture: An Evolutionary Perspective.* New York: Academic Press.

665 Roe, D A. 1981. *The Lower and Middle Palaeolithic Period in Britain.* London: Routledge and Kegan Paul.

666 Rogers, R A. 1985. Glacial geography and native North American languages. *Quaternary Research* 23: 130-137.

667 Ronen, A. 1982. *The Transition from Lower to Middle Palaeolithic and the Origin of Modern Man.* London: British Archaeological Reports International Series 151.

668 Roux, G. 1980. *Ancient Iraq.* 2nd ed. London: Penguin.

669 Rukang, W, J W Olsen, eds. 1985. *Palaeoanthropology and Palaeolithic Archaeology in the People's Republic of China.* Sydney: Academic Press.

670 Sabloff, J A. 1971. The collapse of classic Maya civilization. In *Patient Earth.* Edited by Harte, J, R Socolow. New York: Holt, Rinehart, Winston.

671 Sacchi, D. 1983. Les industries mésolithiques en Languedoc occidental et en Roussillon du 7ème au 6ème millénaire avant l'ère selon la chronologie du radiocarbonne. *Archaelogia Interregionalis, Université de Varsovie* 1983: 57-70.

672 Sacchi, D. 1986. *Le Paléolithique supérieur du Languedoc occidental et du Roussillon.* Gallia-Prehistoire. Paris: C.N.R.S.

673 Sacchi, D. 1989. Les plus anciennes traces du peuplement humain en Pays de Sault: La Cauna de Belvis, Aude. In *Pays de Sault, espace, peuplement, populations.* Pp. 73-100. Toulouse: C.N.R.S.

674 Sahlins, M D. 1968. *Tribesmen.* New York: Prentice-Hall.

675 Sahlins, M D. 1972. *Stone Age Economics.* Chicago: Aldine.

676 Sanders, W T, B J Price. 1968. *Mesoamerica: The Evolution of a Civilization.* New York: Random House.

677 Sanders, W T, J R Parsons, R S Santley. 1979. *The Basis of Mexico: The Ecological Processes in the Evolution of a Civilization.* New York: Academic Press.

678 Sanoja, M. 1989. From foraging to food production in northeastern Venezuela and the Caribbean. In *The Evolution of Plant Exploitation: Concepts and Processes.* Edited by Harris, D R, G C Hillman. Pp. 523-537. London: Unwin Hyman.

679 Saunders, J J. 1980. A model for man-mammoth relationships in late Pleistocene North America. *Canadian Journal of Anthropology* 1: 87-98.

680 Scarre, C, ed. 1983. *Ancient France, 6000-2000 B.C.: Neolithic Societies and their Landscapes.* Edinburgh: Edinburgh University Press.

681 Schiffer, M B, ed. 1980. *Advances in Archaeological Theory and Method.* London: Academic Press.

682 Schweitzer, F R, M L Wilson. 1982. Byneskranskop 1: A late Quaternary living site in the southern Cape Province, South AfriCA *Annals of the South African Museum* 88: 1-203.

683 Scott, K. 1980. Two Hunting Episodes of Middle Paleolithic Age at La Cotte de Saint-Brelade Jersey (Channel Islands). *World Archaeology* 12: 137-152.

684 Sharma, G R, V D Misra, D Mandal, B B Misra, J Pal. 1980. *Beginnings of Agriculture.* Allahabad: University of Allahabad.

685 Shennan, S. 1986. Central Europe in the third millenium B.C.: An evolutionary trajectory for the beginning of the European Bronze Age. *Journal of Anthropological Archaeology* 5: 115-146.

686 Sherratt, A G. 1981. Plough and pastoralism: Aspects of the secondary products revolution. In *Patterns of the Past: Studies in Honour of David Clarke.* Edited by Hodder, I, G Isaac, N Hammond. Pp. 261-305. Cambridge: Cambridge University Press.

687 Shipek, F C. 1989. An example of intensive plant husbandry: The Kumeyaay of southern California. In *The Evolution of Plant Exploita-*

*tion: Concepts and Processes.* Edited by Harris, D R, G C Hillman. Pp. 159-170. London: Unwin Hyman.

688 Simek, J, L Snyder. 1988. Patterns of change in Upper Paleolithic archaeofaunal diversity. In *The Pleistocene Prehistory of Western Eurasia.* Edited by Dibble, H, A Montet-White. Pp. 321-31. Philadelphia: University of Pennsylvania Press.

689 Singer, R, J Wymer. 1982. *The Middle Stone Age at Klasies River Mouth in South AfriCA* Chicago: University of Chicago Press.

690 Smith, M A. 1989. Seed gathering in inland Australia: Current evidence from seed-grinders on the antiquity of the ethnohistorical pattern of exploitation. In *The Evolution of Plant Exploitation: Concepts and Processes.* Edited by Harris, D R, G C Hillman. Pp. 305-317. London: Unwin Hyman.

691 Soffer, O. 1985. *The Upper Paleolithic of the Central Russian Plain.* New York: Academic Press.

692 Soffer, O, C Gamble, eds. 1990. *The World at 18000 BP: High Latitudes.* London: Unwin Hyman.

693 Speth, J D. 1983. *Bison Kills and Bone Counts. Decision Making by Ancient Hunters.* Chicagao: University of Chicago Press.

694 Spiess, A E. 1984. Arctic garbage and New England Paleo-Indians: The single occupation option. *Archaeology of Eastern North America* 12: 280-285.

695 Spooner, B. 1972. Population Growth: Anthropological Implications. In Cambridge: M.I.T. Press.

696 Stanford, S C. 1971. Invention, adoption and imposition : The evidence for the hillforts. In *The Iron Age and Its Hillforts.* Edited by Jesson, M, D Hill. Pp. 41-52. Southampton: Southampton University Archaeological Society.

697 Stanford, D J. 1979. Bison kill by Ice Age hunters. *National Geographic* 155: 114-119.

698 Stanford, D, R Bonnichsen, R E Morlan. 1981. The Ginsberg experiment: Modern and prehistoric evidence of a bone-flaking technology. *Science* 212: 438-440.

699 Stanford, D. 1984. The Jones-Miller site: A study of Hell Gap bison procurement and processing. *National Geographic Research Reports* 16: 615-635.

700 Starling, N J. 1985. Social change in the later neolithic of central Europe. *Antiquity* 59: 30-38.

701 Starling, N J. 1985. Colonization and Succession: The Earlier

Neolithic of Central Europe. *Proceedings of the Prehistoric Society* 51: 41-57.

702 Steponaitis, V P. 1981. Settlement hierarchies and political complexity in nonmarket societies: The formative period of the Valley of Mexico. *American Anthropologist* 83: 320-363.

703 Stoliar, A D. 1978. On the genesis of depictive activity and its role in the formation of consciousness. *Soviet Anthropology and Archaeology* 17: 3-33.

704 Straus, L G. 1977. Of deerslayers and mountain men: Palaeolithic faunal exploitation in cantabrian Spain. In *For Theory Building in Archaeology*. Edited by Binford, L R. Pp. 41-76. New York: Academic Press.

705 Straus, L, G Clark, J Altuna, J Oratea. 1980. Ice-Age subsistence in northern Spain. *Scientific American* 242: 142-152.

706 Straus, L G. 1982. Carnivores and cave sites in Cantabria Spain. *Journal of Anthropological Research* 38: 75-96.

707 Straus, L G. 1983. From the Mousterian to Magdalenian: Cultural evolution viewed from Vasco-Cantabrian Spain and Pyrenean France. In *The Mousterian Legacy: Human Biocultural Change in the Upper Pleistocene*. Edited by Trinkaus, E. Pp. 73-112. Oxford: British Archaeological Reports International Series 164.

708 Straus, L G. 1985. Stone age prehistory of northern Spain. *Science* 230: 501-507.

709 Straus, L. 1985. Le Magdalenien final de l'Abri Dufaure: Un aperçu de la chronologie et de la saison d'habitation humaine. *Bulletin de la Société Prehistorique de l'Ariege* 40: 169-184.

710 Straus, L G. 1986. The end of the Paleolithic in Cantabrian Spain and Gascony. In *The end of the Paleolithic in the Old World*. Edited by Straus, L. British Archaeological Reports International Series 284.

711 Straus, L G, ed. 1986. *The End of the Paleolithic in the Old World*. British Archaeological Reports International Series 284.

712 Straus, L. 1986. Late Wurm adaptive systems in Cantabrian Spain: The case of eastern Asturia. *Journal of Anthropoligical Archaeology* 5: 330-368.

713 Straus, L G. 1987. Hunting in late Upper Paleolithic Western Europe. In *The Evolution of Human Hunting*. Edited by Nitecki, M H, D V Nitecki. Pp. 147-177. New York: Plenum.

714 Straus, L G, C Heller. 1988. Explorations of the twilight zone: The Early Upper Paleolithic of Cantabria and Gascony. In *The Early Upper*

*Paleolithic.* Edited by Hoffecker, J, C Wolf. British Archaeological Reports International Series 437.

715 Stringer, C B. 1981. Towards a solution to the Neanderthal problem. *Journal of Human Evolution* 11: 431-438.

716 Struever, S. 1971. *Prehistoric Agriculture.* Garden City: Natural History Press.

717 Szathmary, E. 1985. Peopling of North America: Clues from genetic studies. In *Out of Asia: Peopling the Americas and the Pacific.* Edited by Kirk, R, E Szathmary. Pp. 79-104. Canberra: Australian National University.

718 Tabutin, D. 1984. La fecondité et la mortalité dans les recensements africains des 25 dernieres années. *Population* 39: 295-312.

719 Tax, S, L G Freeman, eds. 1977. *Horizons of Anthropology.* 2nd ed. Chicago: Aldine Press.

720 Terrell, J. 1986. Causal pathways and causal processes: Studying the evolutionary prehistory of human diversity in language, customs, and biology. *Journal of Anthropological Archaeology* 5: 187-198.

721 Thapar, B. 1982. The Harappan civilisation: Some reflections on its subsistence and resources and their exploitation, in Harappan Civilisation. In Edited by Possehl, G. Pp. 3-14. Wiltshire: Aris and Phillips.

722 Todd, L C. 1987. Analysis of kill-butchery bonebeds and interpretation of Paleoindian hunting. In *The Evolution of Human Hunting.* Edited by Nitecki, M H, D V Nitecki. Pp. 225-267. New York: Plenum Press.

723 Torrence, R. 1986. *Production and Exchange of Stone Tools: Prehistoric Obsidian in the Aegean.* Cambridge: Cambridge University Press.

724 Tosi, M. 1979. The Proto-Urban Culture of Eastern Iran and the Indus Civilisation, in South Asian Archaeology 1977. In Edited by Taddei, M. Pp. 149-172. Naples: Instituto Universitario Orientale.

725 Trinkaus, E, ed. 1983. *The Mousterian Legacy: Human Biocultural Change in the Upper Pleistocene.* Oxford: British Archaeological Reports International Series 164.

726 Troels-Smith, J. 1982. *The Rise of Civilization in India and Pakistan.* Cambridge: Cambridge University Press.

727 Trump, D H. 1980. *The Prehistory of the Mediterranean.* New Haven: Yale University Press.

728 Ucko, P J, G W Dimbleby, eds. 1969. *The Domestication and Exploitation of Plants and Animals.* London: Duckworth.

729 Ucko, P, R Tringham, G W Dimbleby, eds. 1972. *Man, Settlement, and Urbanism.* London: Duckworth.

730 Vandermeersch, B. 1976. *Les sépultures néandertaliennes.* Nice: Colloque XII, UISPP Congress.

731 Vencl, S L. 1984. War and warfare in archaeology. *Journal of Anthropological Archaeology* 3: 116-132.

732 Villa, P. 1983. Terra Amata and the Middle Pleistocene archaelogical record of southern France. *University of California Publications in Anthropology* 13: 1-103.

733 Voigt, E A. 1983. Mapungubwe: And archaeozoological interpretation of an Iron Age community. *Transvaal Museum Monograph* 1: 1-203.

734 Volman, T P. 1984. Early prehistory of southern Africa. In *Southern African Prehistory and Pale-environments.* Edited by Klein, R G. Pp. 169-221. Rotterdam: A.A. BalkeMA

735 Walker, N. 1990. Zimbabwe at 18000 BP. In *The World at 18000 BP: High Latitudes.* Edited by Gamble, C, O Soffer. Pp. 206-213. London: Unwin Hyman.

736 Waterbolk, H T. 1977. Walled Enclosures of the Iron Age in the North of the Netherlands. *Palaeohistoria* 19: 97-173.

737 Watson, P J. 1989. Early plant cultivation in the Eastern Woodlands of North America. In *The Evolution of Plant Exploitation: Concepts and Processes.* Edited by Harris, D R, G C Hillman. Pp. 555-571. London: Unwin Hyman.

738 West, F H. 1982. Making points with points. *Quarterly Review of Archaeology* 3: 6-7.

739 Whalen, M E. 1976. Zoning within an early formative community in the valley of Oaxaca. In *The Early Mesoamerican Village.* Edited by Flannery, K V. Pp. 75-79. New York: Academic Press.

740 Wheat, J B. 1978. Olsen-Chubbuck and Jurgens sites: Four aspects of Paleo-Indian economy. In *Bison Procurement and Utilization.* Edited by Davis, L B, M Wilson. Pp. 84-89. n.p.: Plains Anthropologist Memoir.

741 White, J P, J O'Connell. 1982. *A Prehistory of Australia, New Guinea, and Sahul.* Sydney: Academic Press.

742 White, R. 1982. Rethinking the Middle/Upper Paleolithic transition. *Current Anthropology* 23: 169-92.

743 White, R. 1983. Changing land-use patterns across the Middle/Upper Paleolithic transition: The complex case of the Perigord. In

*The Mousterian Legacy: Human Biocultural Change in the Upper Pleistocene.* Edited by Trinkaus, E. Pp. 113-122. Oxford: British Archaeological Reports International Series 164.

744 White, R. 1989. Visual thinking in the Ice Age. *Scientific American* 261: 92-99.

745 Wilkes, G. 1989. Maize: domestication, racial evolution, and spread. In *The Evolution of Plant Exploitation: Concepts and Processes.* Edited by Harris, D R, G C Hillman. Pp. 440-455. London: Unwin Hyman.

746 Willey, G R. 1962. The early great styles and the rise of the pre-Columbian civilizations. *American Anthropologist* 64: 1-14.

747 Williams, R C, et al. 1985. GM allotypes in native Americans: Evidence for three distinct migrations across the Bering Land Bridge. *American Journal of Physical Anthropology* 66: 1-19.

748 Wilson, D J. 1983. The origins and development of complex prehispanic society in the lower Santa Valley, Peru: Implication for Theories of State Origins. *Journal of Anthropological Archaeology* 2: 209-276.

749 Wing, E, A B Brown. 1979. *Paleonutrition: Method and Theory in Prehistory Foodways.* New York: Academic Press.

750 Winter, M C. 1976. The Archeological Household Cluster in the Valley of OaxaCA In *The Early Mesoamerican Village.* Edited by Flannery, K V. Pp. 25-31. New York: Academic Press.

751 Wobst, H H. 1976. Locational relationships in palaeolithic society. *Journal of Human Evolution* 5: 49-58.

752 Wobst, H. 1990. Minitime and megaspace in the Palaeolithic at 18K and otherwise. In *The World at 18000 BP: High Latitudes.* Edited by Gamble, C, O Soffer. Pp. 322-334. London: Unwin Hyman.

753 Wolley, C L. 1965. *The Sumerians.* New York: Norton.

754 Wolpoff, M H. 1980. *Palaeoanthropology.* New york: Knopf.

755 Yadin, Y. 1964. *The Art of Warfare in Biblical Lands.* London: Weidenfeld.

756 Yanushevich, Z V. 1989. Agricultural evolution north of the Black Sea from the Neolithic to the Iron Age. In *The Evolution of Plant Exploitation: Concepts and Processes.* Edited by Harris, D R, G C Hillman. Pp. 607-619. London: Unwin Hyman.

757 Zhimin, A. 1989. Prehistoric agriculture in China. In *The Evolution of Plant Exploitation: Concepts and Processes.* Edited by Harris, D R, G C Hillman. Pp. 643-649. London: Unwin Hyman.

758 Zohary, D. 1989. Domestication of the Southwest Asian Neolithic crop assemblage of cereals, pulses, and flax: The evidence from the living plants. In *The Evolution of Plant Exploitation: Concepts and Processes*. Edited by Harris, D R, G C Hillman. Pp. 358-373. London: Unwin Hyman.

# 3

# Population and Human Biology

759 Adelstein, M E, J G Pivall. 1971. *Ecocide and Population*. New York: St. Martin's.

760 Ager, J W, F P Shea, S J Agronow. 1982. Method discontinuance in teenage women: Implications for teen contraceptive programs. In *Pregnancy in Adolescence: Needs, Problems, and Management*. Edited by Stuart, I R, C F Wells. New York: Van Nostrand Reinhold.

761 Ahmad, S. 1985. Factors affecting fertility in four Muslim populations: A multivariate analysis. *Journal of Biosocial Science* 17: 305-316.

762 Allman, J. 1978. *Women's Status and Fertility in the Muslim World*. New York: Praeger.

763 Altmann, S A, J Altmann. 1979. Demographic constraints on behavior and social organization. In *Primate Ecology and Human Origins*. Edited by Bernstein, I S, E O Smith. Pp. 47-63. New York: Garland Publishing.

764 Altmann, J. 1986. Adolescent pregnancies in non-human primates: An ecological and developmental perspective. In *School-Age Pregnancy and Parenthood: Biosocial Dimensions*. Edited by Lancaster, J B, B A Hamburg. Pp. 247-262. New York: Aldine.

765 Amundsen, D W, C J Diers. 1969. The age of menarche in classical Greece and Rome. *Human Biology* 41: 125-132.

766 Amundsen, D W, C J Diers. 1973. The age of menarche in medieval Europe. *Human Biology* 45: 363-370.

767 Anderson, R M, R M May. 1982. *Population Biology of Infectious Diseases*. Berlin: Springer.

768 Anderson, P. 1983. The reproductive role of the human breast. *Current Anthropology* 24: 25-46.

769 Anderson, R M. 1984. Verterbrate populations, pathogens and the immune system. In *Population and Biology*. Edited by Keyfitz, N. Pp. 249-68. Liège: Editions Ordina.

770 Anon. 1983. *1983 World Population Data Sheet.* Washington, DC: Population Reference Bureau.

771 Appadurai, A, X Zhao. 1986. Sex preference, fertility, and family planning in China. *Population and Development Review* 12: 221-246.

772 Apter, D. 1980. Serum steroids and pituitary hormones in female puberty: A partly longitudinal study. *Clinical Endocrinology* 12: 107-120.

773 Aschoff, J, ed 1981. *Biological Rhythms.* New York: Plenum.

774 Axelrod, J, T D Reisine. 1984. Stress hormones: Their interaction and regulation. *Science* 224: 452-59.

775 Bailey, S. 1982. Absolute and relative sex differences in body composition. In *Sexual Dimorphism in Homo Sapiens.* Edited by Hall, R. Pp. 363-390. New York: Praeger.

776 Baker, P T, J M Hanna, T S Baker. 1986. *The Changing Samoans: Behaviour and Health in Transition.* New York: Oxford University Press.

777 Baldwin, W. 1984. *Adolescent Childbearing Today and Tomorrow. Statement to U.S. Senate Human Resources Committee.* Washington, D.C.: National Institute of Child Health and Human Development.

778 Barkow, J H, N Burley. 1980. Human fertility, evolutionary biology, and the demographic transition. *Ethology and Sociobiology* 1: 163-180.

779 Battin, D A, R P Marrs, P M Fleiss, D R Mishell. 1985. Effect of suckling on serum prolactin, luteinizing hormone, follicle-stimulating hormone, and estradiol during prolonged lactation. *Obstetrics and Gynecology* 65: 785-8.

780 Bennet, K A. 1979. *Fundamentals of Biological Anthropology.* Dubuque, IO: W.C. Brown.

781 Birdsell, J B. 1978. Spacing mechanisms and adaptive behaviour among Australian aborigines. In *Population Control and Social Behaviour.* Edited by Ebling, F J, D M Stoddart. Pp. 213-34. London: Institute of Biology.

782 Bloom, D. 1982. What's happening to the age at first birth in the United States? *Demography* 19: 351-370.

783 Bloom, D, J Trussel. 1984. What are the determinants of delayed childbearing and permanent childlessness in the United States? *Demography* 21: 591-612.

784 Blum, R H. 1969. A history of alcohol. In *Society and Drugs: Social and Cultural Observations.* Edited by Blum, R H, *et al.* Pp. 25-42. San Francisco: Jossey-Bass.

785 Blum, R H. 1969. A history of Opium. In *Society and Drugs: Social and Cultural Observations.* Edited by Blum, R H, et al. Pp. 25-42. San Francisco: Jossey-Bass.

786 Blurton-Jones, N, V Reynolds, eds. 1978. *Human Behaviour and Adaptation.* London: Taylor and Francis.

787 Bonfield, L, R Smith, K Wrightson, eds. 1986. *The World We Have Gained: Histories of Population and Social Structure.* Oxford: Blackwell.

788 Bongaarts, J. 1980. Does malnutrition affect fecundity? *Science* 208: 564-569.

789 Bongaarts, J, R Potter. 1983. *Fertility, Biology and Behaviour.* London: Academic Press.

790 Boorman, S, P Pevitt. 1973. Group selection on the boundary of a stable population. *Theoretical Population Biology* 4: 85-128.

791 Bornstein, M H. 1989. Sensitive periods in development: Structural characteristics and causal interpretations. *Psychological Bulletin* 105: 179-97.

792 Boserup, E. 1968. Shifts in the determinants of fertility in the developing world: Environmental, technical, economic and cultural factors. In *The State of Population Theory: Forward from Malthus.* Edited by Coleman, D, R Schofield. Pp. 239-55. Oxford: Blackwell.

793 Boyce, A J. 1984. *Migration and Mobility: Biosocial Aspects of Human Movement.* London: Taylor and Francis.

794 Boyden, S V. 1970. *The Impact of Civilisation on the Biology of Man.* Toronto: University of Toronto Press.

795 Brittain, A W, W T Morrill, J A Kurland. 1988. Parental choice and infant mortality in a West Indian population. *Human Biology* 60: 679-92.

796 Broer, M R, R Zernicke. 1979. *Efficiency of Human Movement.* 4th ed Philadelphia: Saunders.

797 Brooks-Gunn, J, A C Petersen, eds. 1983. *Girls at Puberty: Biological and Psychosocial Perspectives.* New York: Plenum.

798 Brothwell, D, A T Sandison, eds. 1967. *Diseases in Antiquity: A Survey of the Disease, Injuries and Surgery of Early Populations.* Springfield, MA: Charles C. Thomas.

799 Brothwell, D, ed. 1977. *Biosocial Man: Studies Related to the Interaction of Biological and Cultural Factors in Human Populations.* London: The Eugenics Society.

800 Brown, J B, P Harrisson, M Smith. 1978. Oestrogen and pregnanediol excretion through childhood, menarche, and first ovulation. *Journal of Biosocial Science* 5: 43-62.

801 Brown, P J. 1991. Culture and the evolution of obesity. *Human Nature* 2: 31-57.

802 Brudevoll, J E, K Liestol, L Walloe. 1979. Menarcheal age in Oslo during the last 140 years. *Annals of Human Biology* 6: 407-416.

803 Bulatao, R A, R D Lee, eds. 1983. *Determinants of Fertility in Developing Countries.* New York: Academic Press.

804 Bullough, V L. 1981. Age at menarche: A misunderstanding. *Science* 213: 365-366.

805 Bulmer, M G. 1970. *The Biology of Twinning in Man.* Oxford: Clarendon Press.

806 Burch, T K, ed 1980. *Demographic Behavior: Interdisciplinary Perspectives on Decision-making.* AAAS Symposium 45. Boulder: Westview Press.

807 Cain, M. 1982. Perspectives on family and fertility in developing countries. *Population Studies* 36: 159-175.

808 Cain, M. 1983. Fertility as an adjustment to risk. *Population and Development Review* 9: 688-702.

809 Caldwell, J C. 1980. Mass education as a determinant of the timing of fertility decline. *Population and Development Review* 6: 225-255.

810 Caldwell, J C. 1982. *Theory of Fertility Decline.* New York: Academic Press.

811 Caldwell, J. 1983. Direct economic costs and benefits of children. In *Determinants of Fertility in Developing Countries*. Edited by Bulatao, R, R Lee. New York: Academic Press.

812 Calot, G, C Blayo. 1982. Recent Course of Fertility in Western Europe. *Population Studies* 36: 349-372.

813 Calow, P. 1979. The cost of reproduction: A physiological approach. *Biology Reviews* 54: 23-40.

814 Carael, M. 1981. Child-spacing, ecology and nutrition in the Kivu province of Zaire. In *Child-spacing in Tropical Africa: Traditions and Change*. Edited by Page, H J, R Lesthaeghe. Pp. 275-86. London: Academic Press.

815 Carrier, D R. 1984. The energetic paradox of human running and hominid evolution. *Current Anthropology* 25: 483-495.

816 Carter, D R, W E Caler, D M Spengler, V H Frankel. 1981. Fatigue behavior of adult cortical bone: The influence of mean strain and strain range. *Acta Orthopedica Scandanavia* 52: 481-490.

817 Chahnazarian, A. 1988. Determinants of the sex ratio at birth: Review of recent literature. *Social Biology* 35: 214-235.

818 Chakraborty, R, R Weiss, P P Majumder, L C Strong, J Herson. 1984. A method to detect excess risk of disease in structured data: Cancer in relatives of retinoblastoma patients. *Genetic Epidemiology* 1: 229-244.

819 Chakraborty, R, E J E Szathmary, eds. 1985. *Diseases of Complex Etiology in Small Populations: Ethnic Differences and Research Approaches*. Progress in Clinical and Biological Research. New York: Alan R. Liss.

820 Chamie, J. 1981. *Religion and Fertility: Arab-Christian-Muslim Differentials*. Cambridge: Cambridge University Press.

821 Charlesworth, B. 1980. *Evolution in Age-Structured Populations*. Cambridge: Cambridge University Press.

822 Chen, L C, E Huq, S D'Souza. 1981. Sex bias in the family allocation of food and health care in rural Bangladesh. *Population and Development Review* 7: 55-70.

823 Cherlin, A J. 1981. Explaining the postwar baby boom. *Items* 35: 57-63.

824 Christiansen, F B, M W Feldman. 1985. *Population Genetics.* Palo Alto, CA: Blackwell.

825 Cicchetti, D, W Grove, eds. 1963. *Festschrift for Paul E. Meehl.* Cambridge: Cambridge University Press.

826 Clark, P, A E Stark, R J Walsh. 1981. A twin study of skin reflectance. *Annual of Human Biology.* 8: 529-541.

827 Clarke, J I, P Curson, S L Kayastha, P Nag, eds. 1989. *Population and Disaster.* Oxford: Blackwell.

828 Cohen, M. 1980. Speculations on the evolution of density measurement and population in Homo sapiens. In *Biosocial Mechanisms of Population Regulation.* Edited by Cohen, M N, R S Malpass, H G Klein. Pp. 275-304. New Haven: Yale University Press.

829 Coleman, D. 1986. Population regulation: A long-range view. In *The State of Population Theory: Forward from Malthus.* Edited by Schofield, R, D Coleman. Pp. 14-41. Oxford: Blackwell.

830 Coleman, D, R Schofield, eds. 1986. *The State of Population Theory: Forward from Malthus.* Oxford: Blackwell.

831 Cowlishaw, G. 1981. The determinants of fertility among Australian aboriginies. *Mankind* 13: 37-55.

832 Crawford, M H, J H Mielke. 1983. *Current Developments in Anthropological Genetics: Ecology and Population Structure.* New York: Plenum.

833 Crognier, E. 1977. Assortative mating for physical features in an African population from Chad. *Journal of Human Evolution* 6: 105-14.

834 D'Souza, S, L C Chen. 1980. Sex differentials and mortality in rural Bangladesh. *Population and Development Review* 6: 257-270.

835 Daly, M. 1979. Why don't male mammals lactate? *Journal of Theoretical Biology* 78: 325-45.

836 Davis, J H, M S Bernstam, R Ricardo-Campbell. 1986. Below-replacement fertility in industrial societies: Causes, consequences, policies. *Population and Development Review* 12: 111-36.

837 Day, L H, A T Day. 1984. Fertility and "life chances" - A comparison among nineteen countries of controlled fertility. *International Journal of Comparative Sociology* 25: 197-225.

838 Day, L. 1984. *Analysing Population Trends: Differential Fertility in a Pluralistic Society.* London: Croom Helm.

839 De Vries, J. 1985. Population and economy of the pre-industrial Netherlands. *Journal of Interdisciplinary History* 15: 661-82.

840 Diez-Noguera, A, T Cambras, eds. 1992. *Chronobiology and Chronomedicine: Basic Research and Applications.* Frankfurt: Peter Lang.

841 Diggory, P, S Teper. 1987. *Natural Human Fertility: Social and Biological Mechanisms.* London: Macmillan.

842 Donaldson, L. 1991. *Fertility Transition: The Social Dynamics of Population Change.* Oxford: Blackwell.

843 Dragastin, S, G H Elder. 1975. *Adolescence and the Life Cycle.* New York: Wiley.

844 Dumond, D E. 1975. The limitation of human population. *Science* 187: 713-20.

845 Dyke, B, W Morrill, eds. 1980. *Geneological Demography.* New York: Academic Press.

846 Dyson-Hudson, R, M A Little. 1983. *Rethinking Human Adaption: Biological and Cultural Models.* Boulderlo.: Westview Press.

847 Easterlin, R. 1980. *Birth and Fortune: The Impact of Numbers on Personal Welfare.* New York: Basic Books.

848 Eberstadt, N, ed 1981. *Fertility Decline in Less Developed Countries.* New York: Praeger.

849 Ebling, F J, D M Stoddart, eds. 1978. *Population Control and Social Behaviour.* London: Institute of Biology.

850 Ehrlich, P. 1977. *Ecoscience: Population, Resources, Environment.* San Francisco: Freeman.

851 Ellison, P. 1981. Prediction of age at menarche from annual height increments. *American Journal of Physical Anthropology* 55: 71-75.

852 Ellison, P. 1981. Threshold hypotheses, developmental age, and menstrual function. *American Journal of Physical Anthropology* 54: 337-340.

853 Ellison, P, N R Peacock, C Lager. 1989. Ecology and ovarian function among Lese women of the Ituri Forest, Zaire. *American Journal of Physical Anthropology* 78: 519-526.

854 Ellison, P. 1990. Human ovarian function and reproductive ecology: New hypotheses. *American Anthropologist* 92: 933-952.

855 Elster, A B, E R McAnarney. 1980. Medical and psychosocial risks of pregnancy and childbearing during adolescence. *Pediatric Annals* 9: 89-94.

856 Erhlich, P, A Ehrlich. 1972. *Population, Resources, Environment.* San Francisco: Freeman.

857 Eveleth, P B, J M Tanner. 1976. *Worldwide Variation in Human Growth.* Cambridge: Cambridge University Press.

858 Eveleth, P. 1986. Timing of menarche: Secular trend and population differences. In *School-Age Pregnancy and Parenthood: Biosocial Dimensions.* Edited by Lancaster, J B, B A Hamburg. Pp. 39-52. New York: Aldine.

859 Field, T, A Sostek, eds. 1982. *Infants Born at Risk: Perceptual and Physiological Processes.* New York: Grune & Stratton.

860 Field, T, J Demsey, H H Shuman. 1982. Five-year follow-up of preterm respiratory distress syndrome and postterm postmaturity syndrome in infants. In *Infants Born at Risk: Physiological and Perceptual Development.* Edited by Field, T, A Sostek. New York: Grune & Stratton.

861 Fitzsimons, J T. 1979. *The Physiology of Thirst and Sodium Appetite.* Cambridge: Cambridge University Press.

862 Ford, K, S Huffman. 1988. Nutrition, infant feeding and post-partum amenorrhea in rural Bangladesh. *Journal of Biosocial Science* 20: 461-469.

863 Foster, A, J Menken, A Chowdhurry, J Trussell. 1986. Female reproductive development: A hazards model analysis. *Social Biology* 33: 183-198.

864 Frankenhaeuser, M. 1984. Psychoneuroendocrine approaches to the study of stressful person-environment transactions. In *Selye's Guide to Stress Research.* Edited by Selye, H. Pp. 46-70. New York: Van Nostrand Reinhold.

865 Freedman, J L. 1973. The effects of population density on humans. In *Psychological Perspectives on Population*. Edited by Fawcett, J T. Pp. 209-238. New York: Basic Books.

866 Freedman, R. 1979. Theories of fertility decline: A reappraisal. In *World Population and Development: Challenges and Prospects*. Edited by Hauser, P M. Pp. 63-79. Syracuse: Syracuse University Press.

867 Freedman, J C. 1980. Human reactions to population density. In *Biosocial Mechanisms of Population Regulation*. Edited by Cohen, M N, R S Malpass, H G Klein. Pp. 189-308. New Haven: Yale University Press.

868 Freedman, R, D Freedman, A Thornton. 1980. Changes in fertility expectations and preferences between 1962 and 1977: Their relation to final parity. *Demography* 17: 365-378.

869 Friedlaender, S, W Howells, J Rhoads, eds. 1987. *The Solomon Islands Project: A Long Term Study of Health, Human Biology, and Culture Change*. Oxford: Clarendon Press.

870 Frisancho, A R, P T Baker. 1970. Altitude and growth: A study of the pattern of physical growth of a high altitude Peruvian Quechua population. *American Journal of Physical Anthropology* 32: 279-292.

871 Frisancho, A R. 1981. *Human Adaptation*. Ann Arbor: University of Michigan Press.

872 Frisancho, A R, J Matos, L A Bollettino. 1984. Influence of growth status and placental function on birth weight of infants born to young still-growing teenagers. *American Journal of Clinical Nutrition* 40: 801-807.

873 Frisch, R E, R Revelle. 1970. Height and weight at menarche and a hypothesis of critical body weights and adolescent events. *Science* 169: 397-399.

874 Frisch, R E, R Revelle, S Cook. 1973. Components of weight and the initiation of the adolescent growth spurt in girls: Estimated total water, lean body weight and fat. *Human Biology* 45: 469-483.

875 Frisch, R E, J W McArthur. 1974. Menstrual cycles: Fatness as a determinant of minimum weight for height necessary for their maintenance and onset. *Science* 185: 949-951.

876 Frisch, R E. 1976. Critical metabolic mass and the age at menarche. *Annals of Human Biology* 3: 489-491.

877 Frisch, R E. 1978. Population, food intake and fertility. *Science* 199: 22-30.

878 Frisch, R E, G Wyshak, L Vincent. 1980. Delayed menarche and amenorrhea in ballet dancers. *New England Journal of Medicine* 303: 17-19.

879 Frisch, R E. 1982. Malnutrition and fertility. *Science* 215: 1272-1273.

880 Frisch, R E. 1984. Body fat, puberty and fertility. *Biological Reviews* 59: 161-188.

881 Frisch, R E. 1987. Body fat, menarche, fitness and fertility. *Human Reproduction* 2: 521-533.

882 Frisch, R E. 1988. Fatness and fertility. *Scientific American* 258: 88-95.

883 Fritz, M A. 1988. Inadequate luteal function and recurrent abortion: Diagnosis and treatment of luteal phase deficiency. *Seminars in Reproduction Endocrinology* 6: 129-143.

884 Garn, S M. 1961. *Human Races.* Springfield, MA: Charles C. Thomas.

885 Garn, S, S Pesick, A Petzold. 1986. The biology of teenage pregnancy: The mother and the child. In *School-Age Pregnancy and Parenthood: Biosocial Dimensions.* Edited by Lancaster, J B, B A Hamburg. Pp. 77-94. New York: Aldine.

886 Garn, S M. 1986. *Prenatal Antecedents of Postnatal Growth.* Ann Arbor: University of Michigan Press.

887 Gergen, K L. 1967. The significance of skin color in human relations. *Daedalus* 96: 390-406.

888 Ghesquiere, J, R D Martin, F Newcombe, eds. 1985. *Human Sexual Dimorphism.* London: Taylor and Francis.

889 Glass, D V, D E C Eversley. 1965. *Population in History: Essays in Historical Demography.* Chicago: Aldine.

890 Goldman, N, C F Westhoff, L E Paul. 1987. Variations in natural fertility: The effect of lactation and other determinants. *Population Studies* 41: 127-146.

891 Golub, S, ed 1983. *Menarche.* New York: D.C. Heath.

892 Golub, S, ed 1983. *Menarche: The Transition from Girl to Woman*. Lexington, MA: D. C. Heath.

893 Goody, J. 1976. *Production and Reproduction*. New York: Cambridge University Press.

894 Gorsuch, R L, M K Key. 1974. Abnormalities of pregnancy as a function of anxiety and life stress. *Psychosomatic Medicine* 36: 352-362.

895 Graham, S B. 1985. Running and menstrual dysfunction: Recent medical discoveries provide new insights into the human division of labor by sex. *American Anthropologist* 87: 878-882.

896 Green, B B, J R Daling, N S Weiss, J M Liff, T Koepsell. 1986. Exercise as a risk factor for infertility with ovulatory dysfunction. *American Journal of Public Health* 76: 1432-1436.

897 Gross, R T, P M Duke. 1980. The effect of early versus late physical maturation on adolescent behavior. *Pediatric Clinics of North America* 27: 71-77.

898 Grumbach, M M, G D Grave, F E Mayer, eds. 1974. *Control of the Onset of Puberty*. New York: Wiley.

899 Guttentag, M, P Secord. 1983. *Too Many Women? The Sex Ratio Question*. Beverly Hills, CA: Sage.

900 Hall, R, ed 1982. *Sexual Dimorphism in Homo Sapiens*. New York: Praeger.

901 Hallam, H E. 1985. Age at first marriage and age at death in the Lincolnshire Fenland 1252-1478. *Population Studies* 39: 55-70.

902 Hallam, S J. 1989. Plant usage and management in Southwest Australian Aboriginal societies. In *The Evolution of Plant Exploitation: Concepts and Processes*. Edited by Harris, D R, G C Hillman. Pp. 136-151. London: Unwin Hyman.

903 Hamburg, D A. 1982. *Health and Behavior: Frontiers of Research in Biobehavioral Sciences*. Washington, D.C.: National Academy of Sciences.

904 Hamburg, B. 1986. Subsets of adolescent mothers: Developmental, biomedical, and psychosocial issues. In *School-Age Pregnancy and Parenthood: Biosocial Dimensions*. Edited by Lancaster, J B, B A Hamburg. Pp. 115-46. New York: Aldine.

905 Handwerker, W P. 1983. The first demographic transition: An analysis of subsistence choices and reproductive consequences. *American Anthropologist* 85: 5-27.

906 Handwerker, W P. 1986. *Culture and Reproduction: An Anthropological Critique of Demographic Transition Theory.* Boulderlo.: Westview Press.

907 Harburg, E, L Gleibermann, F Ozgoren. 1978. Skin color, ethnicity and blood pressure. *American Journal of Public Health* 68: 1177-88.

908 Harburg, E, L Gleibermann, J Harburg. 1982. Blood pressure and skin color: Maupitip, French Polynesia. *Human Biology* 54: 283-298.

909 Harkness, J, K Gijsbers. 1989. Pain and stress during childbirth and time of day. *Ethology and Sociobiology* 10: 255-262.

910 Harrison, G A, C F Huchemann, M A S Moore. 1969. The effects of altitudinal variation in Ethiopian populations. *Philosophical Transactions of the Royal Society (London).* 256: 147-182.

911 Harrison, G A, A J Boyce. 1972. *The Structure of Human Populations.* Oxford: Clarendon Press.

912 Harrison, G A. 1973. Differences in human pigmentation: Measurement, geographic variation and causes. *Journal of Investigative Dermatology.* 60: 418-26.

913 Harrison, G A, J B Gibson. 1976. *Man in Urban Environments.* Oxford: Oxford University Press.

914 Harrison, G A, J B Gibson, R W Hiorns. 1976. Assortative mating for psychometric, personality and anthropometric variation in a group of Oxfordshire villages. *Journal of Biosocial Science* 8: 145-53.

915 Harrison, G A, ed 1977. *Population Structure and Human Variation.* New York: Cambridge University Press.

916 Harrison, G. 1978. *Mosquitoes, Malaria, and Man: A History of the Hostilities since 1880.* New York: Dutton.

917 Harrison, G A, C D Palmer, D A Jenner, V Reynolds. 1981. Association between rates of urinary catecholamine excretion and aspects of lifestyle among adult women in some Oxfordshire villages. *Human Biology* 54: 617-33.

918 Harrison, G A, J M Tanner, D R Pilbeam, P T Baker. 1988. *Human Biology: An Introduction to Human Evolution, Variation, Growth, and Adaptability.* Oxford: Oxford University Press.

919 Harrison, G A, J Waterlow, eds. 1990. *Diet and Disease in Traditional and Developing Societies.* New York: Cambridge University Press.

920 Hassan, F. 1981. *Demographic Archeology.* New York: Academic Press.

921 Hauser, P, ed 1979. *World Population and Development: Challenges and Prospects.* Syracuse: Syracuse University Press.

922 Hayden, B. 1981. Subsistence and ecological adaptations of modern hunter/gatherers. In *Omnivorous Primates: Gathering and Hunding in Human Evolution.* Edited by Harding, R S O, G Teleki. Pp. 321-44. New York: Columbia University.

923 Heinsohn, G, O Steiger. 1979. The economic theory of fertility: An alternative approach for an economic determination of procreation. *Metroeconomica* 31: 271-98.

924 Hinkle, L E, W C Loring, eds. 1977. *The Effect of the Man-Made Environment on Health and Disease.* Atlanta: Center for Disease Control.

925 Hoff, C, W Wertelecki, S Zansky, E Reyes, J Dutt, A Stumpe. 1985. Earlier maturation of pregnant black and white adolescents. *American Journal of Diseases of Children* 139: 981-986.

926 Hofferth, S. 1984. Long-term economic consequences for women of delayed childbearing and reduced family size. *Demography* 21: 141-155.

927 Hogan, D P. 1987. Demographic trends in human fertility. In *Parenting Across the Life Span: Biosocial Dimensions.* Edited by Lancaster, J, J Altmann, A Rossi, L Sherrod. Pp. 315-50. New York: Aldine.

928 Hohn, C, R Mackensen, eds. 1982. *Determinants of Fertility Trends: Theories Re-examined* Liège: Editions Ordina.

929 Howell, N. 1968. Feedbacks and buffers in relation to scarcity and abundance: Studies of hunter-gatherer populations. In *The State of Population Theory: Forward from Malthus.* Edited by Coleman, D, R Schofield. Pp. 156-187. Oxford: Blackwell.

930 Howell, N. 1980. Demographic behavior of hunter-gatherers: Evidence for density dependent population control. In *Demographic Behavior: Interdisciplinary Perspectives on Decision-making, AAAS Symposium 45*. Edited by Burch, T K. Boulder: Westview Press.

931 Howie, P W, A S McNeilly. 1982. Effect of breast feeding patterns on human birth intervals. *Journal of Reproduction and Fertility* 65: 545-557.

932 Howie, P W, A S McNeilly, M J Houston, A Cook, H Boyle. 1982. Fertility after childbirth: Infant feeding patterns, basal PRL levels and post-partum ovulation. *Clinical Endocrinology* 17: 315-322.

933 Howlett, T A. 1987. Hormonal responses to exercise and training: A short review. *Clinical Endocrinology* 26: 723-742.

934 Hunn, E S. 1981. On the relative contribution of men and women to subsistence among hunter gatherers of the Columbian Plateau: A comparision with ethnolographic atlas summaries. *Journal of Ethnobiology* 1: 124-34.

935 Huss-Ashmore, R. 1980. Fat and fertility: Demographic implications of differential fat storage. *Yearbook of Physical Anthropology* 23: 65-91.

936 Issacs, H R. 1967. Group identity and political change: The role of color and physical characteristics. *Daedalus* 96: 353-375.

937 James, W. 1985. Sex ratio, dominance status, and maternal hormonal levels at the time of conception. *Journal of Theoretical Biology* 114:505-10.

938 James, W. 1987. The human sex ratio. Part 1: A review of the literature. *Human Biology* 59: 721-752.

939 James, W. 1987. The human sex ratio. Part 2: A hypothesis and a program of research. *Human Biology* 59: 873-900.

940 James, W. 1989. The norm for perceived husband superiority: A cause of human assortative marriage. *Social Biology* 36: 271-8.

941 James, W. 1990. Seasonal variation in human births. *Journal of Biosocial Science* 22: 113-119.

942 Johnson, N E, S Lean. 1985. Relative income, race, and fertility. *Population Studies* 39: 99-112.

943 Johnston, F E. 1974. Control of age at menarche. *Human Biology* 46: 159-171.

944 Jorm, A F, P A Jacomb. 1989. The informant questionnaire on cognitive decline in the elderly (IQCODE): Socio-demographic correlates, reliability, validity and some norms. *Psychological Medicine* 19: 1015-1022.

945 Kennedy, K I, R Rivera, A S McNeilly. 1989. Consensus statement on the use of breastfeeding as a family planning method. *Contraception* 39: 477-496.

946 Kessler, R C, J D McLeod. 1984. Sex differences in vulnerability to undesirable life events. *American Sociological Review* 49: 620-631.

947 Keyfitz, N. 1982. The limits of population forecasting. *Population and Development Review* 7: 579-594.

948 Keyfitz, N, ed 1984. *Biology and Demography*. Liège: Editions Ordina.

949 Keyfitz, N, ed 1984. *Population and Biology*. Liège: Editions Ordina.

950 King, J C. 1982. *On the Biology of Race*. Berkeley: University of California Press.

951 Kirkwood, T B L, R Holliday. 1979. The evolution of ageing and longevity. *Proceedings of Royal Society* 205: 531-46.

952 Kitagawa, E M, P M Hauser. 1973. *Differential Mortality in the United States: A Study in Socioeconomic Epidemiology*. Cambridge: Harvard University Press.

953 Knobil, E. 1980. The neuroendocrine control of the menstrual cycle. *Recent Progress in Hormone Research* 36: 53-88.

954 Knodel, J E. 1988. *Demographic Behavior in the Past: A Study of Fourteen German Village Populations in the Eighteenth and Nineteenth Centuries*. Cambridge: Cambridge University Press.

955 Knuth, U A, H P G Schneider. 1982. Influence of body weight on prolactin, estradiol and gonadrotropin levels in obese and underweight women. *Hormone Metabolism Research* 14: 142-46.

956 Koester, L S, H Papousek, M Papousek. 1989. Patterns of rhythmic stimulation by mothers with three-month-olds: A cross-modal comparison. *International Journal of Behavioral Development* 12: 143-54.

957 Konner, M J, C Worthman. 1980. Nursing frequency, gonadal function and birth spacing among !Kung hunter-gatherers. *Science* 207: 788-91.

958 Kunitz, S J. 1968. Mortality since Malthus. In *The State of Population Theory: Forward from Malthus*. Edited by Coleman, D, R Schofield. Pp. 279-302. Oxford: Blackwell.

959 Laska-Mierzejewska, T, H Milicer, H Piechaczek. 1982. Age at menarche and its secular trend in urban and rural girls in Poland. *Human Biology* 9: 227-33.

960 Lasker, G W. 1986. The significance for genetic population structure of repeating pairs of surnames in marriages. *Human Biology* 58: 421-25.

961 Laughlin, C D, I Brady, eds. 1978. *Extinction and Survival in Human Populations*. New York: Columbia University Press.

962 Le Magnen, J. 1985. *Hunger*. Cambridge: Cambridge University Press.

963 Lee, R B. 1980. Lactation, ovulation, infanticide and woman's work: A study of hunter-gatherer population in regulation. In *Biosocial Mechanism of Population Regulation*. Edited by Cohen, M N, et al. New Haven: Yale University Press.

964 Lee, R, R Bulatao, eds. 1982. *Fertility Determinants in Developing Countries*. New York: National Academy of Sciences Press.

965 Lee, R D, R A Bulatao. 1983. The demand for children: A critical essay. In *Determinants of Fertility in Developing Countries*. Edited by Bulatao, R A, R D Lee. Pp. 233-287. New York: National Academy of Sciences Press.

966 Leistol, K E. 1980. Menarcheal age and spontaneous abortion: A causal connection? *American Journal of Epidemiology* 111: 753-758.

967 Lejarraga, H, F Sanchirico, M Cusminsky. 1980. Age at menarche in urban Argentinian girls. *Annals of Human Biology* 7: 579-582.

968 Lemarchand-Beraud, T, M-M Zufferey, M Reymond, I Rey. 1982. Maturation of the hypothalamo-pituitary-ovarian axis in adolescent girls. *Journal of Clinical Endocrinology and Metabolism* 54: 241-246.

969 Lenton, E A, R Sulaiman, O Sobowale, I D Cooke. 1988. The human menstrual cycle: Plasma concentrations of Prolactin, LH, FSH,

Oestradiol and Progesterone in conceiving and non-conceiving women. *Journal of Reproduction and Fertility* 65: 131-139.

970 Leslie, P W, P H Fry. 1989. Extreme seasonality of births among nomadic Turkana pastoralists. *American Journal of Physical Anthropology* 79: 103-15.

971 Lester, B M, C T E Coll, C Sepkoski. 1982. A cross cultural study of teenage pregnancy and neonatal behavior. In *Infants Born at Risk: Perceptual and Physiological Processes*. Edited by Field, T, A Sostek. New York: Grune & Stratton.

972 Lesthaeghe, R. 1968. On the adaptation of sub-Saharan systems of reproduction. In *The State of Population Theory: Forward from Malthus*. Edited by Coleman, D, R Schofield. Pp. 212-38. Oxford: Blackwell.

973 Lesthaeghe, R. 1980. On the social control of human reproduction. *Population and Development Review* 6: 527-48.

974 Lesthaeghe, R. 1984. *Fertility and Its Proximate Determinants in Sub-Saharan Africa: The Record of the 1960s and 70s*. Liège: IUSSP.

975 Leutenegger, W. 1982. Sexual dimorphism in nonhuman primates. In *Sexual Dimorphism in Homo Sapiens*. Edited by Hall, R. Pp. 11-36. New York: Praeger.

976 Levine, D. 1987. *Reproducing Families: The Political Economy of English Population History*. New York: Cambridge University Press.

977 Levinson, D. 1983. Physical punishment of children and wifebeating in crosscultural perspective. In *International Perspectives on Family Violence*. Edited by Gelles, R J, C P Cornell. Lexington, MA: Lexington.

978 Lewontin, R, ed 1968. *Population Biology and Evolution*. Syracuse: Syracuse University Press.

979 Lindburg, D G. 1982. Primate obstetrics: The biology of birth. *American Journal of Primatology, Suppl.* 1: 193-199.

980 Lindemann, C. 1974. *Birth Control and Unmarried Young Women*. New York: Springer.

981 Lindert, P H. 1983. The changing economic costs and benefits of having children. In *Determinants of Fertility in Developing Countries*. Edited by Bulatao, R A, R D Lee. Pp. 364-68.

982 Lopez, A D, L T Ruzicka. 1983. *Sex Differential in Mortality: Trends, Determinants, and Consequences.* Canberra: Australian National University Press.

983 Lorimer, F. 1954. *Culture and Human Fertility.* Paris: UNESCO.

984 Low, W D, L S Kung, J C Y Leong. 1982. Secular trend in sexual maturation of Chinese girls. *Human Biology* 54: 539-51.

985 Loza, S F. 1981. *Egypt: Studies on Determinants of Fertility Behaviour II.* Liège: IUSSP.

986 Lunn, P G, S Austin, R G Whitehead. 1984. The effect of improved nutrition on plasma prolactin concentrations and postpartum infertility in lactating Gambian women. *American Journal of Clinical Nutrition* 39: 227-35.

987 MacFarlane, A. 1976. *Resources and Population: A Study of the Gurungs of Nepal.* Cambridge Cambridge: Cambridge University Press.

988 MacFarlane, A. 1986. *Marriage and Love in England: Modes of Reproduction 1300-1840.* Oxford: Oxford University Press.

989 Malina, R M. 1983. Menarche in athletes: A systhesis and hypothesis. *Annals of Human Biology* 10: 1-24.

990 Manniche, E. 1983. Age at menarche: Nicolai Edvard Ravn's data on 3385 women in mid-19th century Denmark. *Annals of Human Biology* 10: 79-82.

991 Marshall, W A, J M Tanner. 1969. Variations in pattern of pubertal changes in girls. *Archives of Diseases in Childhood* 44: 291-303.

992 Marshall, W A. 1974. Interrelationships of skeletal maturation, sexual development and somatic growth in man. *Annals of Human Biology* 1:29-40.

993 Marshall, W A, Y de Limongi. 1976. Skeletal maturity and the prediction of age at menarche. *Annals of Human Biology* 3: 235-243.

994 Marshall, W A. 1978. The relationship of puberty to other maturity indicators and body composition in man. *Journal of Reproduction and Fertility* 52: 437-443.

995 Mason, K. 1983. Norms relating to the desire for children. In *Determinants of Fertility in Developing Countries.* Edited by Bulatao,

R A, R D Lee. Pp. 388-428. New York: National Academy of Sciences Press.

996 Maynard Smith, J, J Hofbauder. 1987. The "battle of the sexes": A genetic model. *Population Biology* 32: 1-14.

997 McAnarney, E R, G Strickle, eds. 1981. *Pregnancy in the Teenager: Biological Aspects*. New York: Alan R. Liss.

998 McAnarney, E R. 1983. *Premature Adolescent Pregnancy and Parenthood*. New York: Grune & Stratton.

999 McClintock, M. 1981. Social control of the ovarian cycle and the function of estrous synchrony. *American Zoologist* 21: 243-256.

1000 McCown, E R. 1982. Sex differences: The female as baseline for species description. In *Sexual Dimorphism in Homo Sapiens*. Edited by Hall, R. Pp. 37-84. New York: Praeger.

1001 McEvedy, C, R Jones. 1978. *Atlas of World Population History*. Harmondsworth: Penguin.

1002 McFalls, J A, M H McFalls. 1984. *Disease and Fertility*. New York: Academic Press.

1003 McGaugh, J L, J G March, S B Kiesler. 1981. *Aging: Biology and Behavior*. New York: Academic Press.

1004 McKeown, T. 1976. *The Modern Rise of Population*. London: Academic Press.

1005 McKeown, T. 1991. *The Origins of Human Disease*. Oxford: Blackwell.

1006 McLaren, A. 1990. *A History of Contraception from Antiquity to the Present Day*. Oxford: Blackwell.

1007 McNeely, M J, M R Soules. 1988. The diagnosis of luteal phase deficiency: A critical review. *Fertility and Sterility* 50: 1-15.

1008 McNeill, W H. 1976. *Plagues and Peoples*. Garden City, N.Y.: Doubleday.

1009 McNeilly, A S, P W Howie, M J Houston, A Cook, H Boyle. 1982. Fertility after childbirth: Adequacy of post-partum luteal phases. *Clinical Endocrinology* 17: 609-615.

1010 Mellars, P, C Stringer, eds. 1989. *The Human Revolution: Behavioural and Biological Perspectives on the Origins of Modern Humans*. Edinburgh: Edinburgh University Press.

1011 Menken, J, J Trussell, S Watkins. 1981. The nutrition-fertility link: An evaluation of the evidence. *Journal of Interdisciplinary History* 9: 425-441.

1012 Menken, J, J Trussell, U Larsen. 1986. Age and infertility. *Science* 233: 1389-1394.

1013 Miller, A. 1991. *Working Dazed: Why Drugs Pervade the Workplace and What Can Be Done About It*. Wesport, CT: Greenwood Press.

1014 Mohr, J C. 1978. *Abortion in America: The Origins and Evolution of National Policy, 1800-1900*. New York: Oxford University Press.

1015 Moos, R H. 1976. *The Human Context: Environmental Determinants of Behaviour*. New York: Wiley.

1016 Mori, O, M Tokuhashi. 1956. Meausurement by age group of the color and gloss of the skin of healthy Japanese. *Journal of the Anthropological Society of Japan* 65: 1-19.

1017 Mosk, C. 1985. *Patriarchy and Fertility: Japan and Sweden, 1880-1960*. New York: Academic Press.

1018 Naeye, R L, E C Peters. 1982. Working during pregnancy: Effects on the fetus. *Pediatrics* 69: 724-727.

1019 Nag, M. 1962. *Factors Affecting Human Fertility in Nonindustrial Societies*. New Haven: Yale University Press.

1020 Nag, M. 1975. Marriage and kinship in relation to human fertility. In *Population and Social Organization*. Edited by Nag, M. Pp. 11-54. The hague: Mouton.

1021 Nag, M, ed 1975. *Population and Social Organization*. The Hague: Mouton.

1022 Nag, M. 1981. Economic value and costs of children in relation to human fertility. In *Fertility Decline in Less Developed Countries*. Edited by Eberstadt, N. Pp. 274-294. New York: Praeger.

1023 Neftolin, F, E Butz. 1981. Sexual dimorphism. *Science* 211: 1263-1324.

1024 Nelson, H, R Jurmain. 1985. *Introduction to Physical Anthropology*. St. Paul: West Publishing.

1025 Nerlove, S B, J M Roberts, R E Klein, C Yarbrough, J P Habicht. 1974. Natural indicators of cognitive development: An observational study of rural Guatemalan children. *Ethos* 2: 265-295.

1026 Newman, R W. 1970. Why man is such a sweaty and thirsty naked animal: A speculative review. *Human Biology* 42: 12-27.

1027 Nijhuis, J G, eds. 1992. *Fetal Behaviour: Developmental and Perinatal Aspects*. Oxford: Oxford University Press.

1028 Noble, C, et al. 1978. *Human Variation: The Biopsychology of Age, Race and Sex*. New York: Academic Press.

1029 Nugent, J B. 1985. The old-age security motive for fertility. *Population and Development Review* 11: 75-97.

1030 Nurse, G T, J S Weiner, T Jenkins, eds. 1985. *The Peoples of Southern Africa and Their Affinities*. Oxford: Clarendon Press.

1031 Ojeda, S R, W W Andrews, J O Advis, S S White. 1980. Recent advances in the endocrinology of puberty. *Endocrine Review* 1: 228-257.

1032 Ortner, D, ed 1983. *How Humans Adapt: A Biocultural Odyssey*. Washington, D.C.: Smithsonian Institution Press.

1033 Osbourne, T, C Noble, N Weyl, eds. 1978. *Human Variation: The Biopsychology of Age, Race and Sex*. New York: Academic Press.

1034 Page, H J, R Lesthaeghe, eds. 1981. *Child-spacing in Tropical Africa: Traditions and Change*. London: Academic Press.

1035 Page, H J, O Adegbola. 1981. Child-spacing and fertility in Lagos. In *Child-spacing in Tropical Africa: Traditions and Change*. Edited by Page, H J, R Lesthaeghe. Pp. 151-72. London: Academic Press.

1036 Parizkova, J. 1977. *Body Fat and Physical Fitness*. The Hague: Nijhoff.

1037 Peacock, N. 1986. Women athletes: A model for hunter-gatherer fertility? *AnthroQuest* 34: 5-6.

1038 Peacock, N. 1990. Comparative and cross-cultural approaches to the study of human female reproductive failure. In *Primate Life*

*Histories and Evolution.* Edited by DeRousseau, C J. New York: Wiley-Liss.

1039 Pearsall, D M. 1989. Adaptation of prehistoric hunter-gatherers to the high Andes: The changing role of plant resources. In *The Evolution of Plant Exploitation: Concepts and Processes.* Edited by Harris, D R, G C Hillman. Pp. 318-34. London: Unwin Hyman.

1040 Petersen, A C, B Taylor. 1980. The biological approach to adolescence: Biological change and psychological adaptation. In *Handbook of Adolescent Psychology.* Edited by Adelson, J. New York: Wiley.

1041 Petersen, A C. 1983. Menarche: Meaning of measures and measuring meaning. In *Menarche.* Edited by Golub, S. New York: D.C. Heath.

1042 Petersen, A, L Crockett. 1986. Pubertal development and its relation to cognitive and psychosocial development in adolescent girls: Implications for parenting. In *School-Age Pregnancy and Parenthood: Biosocial Dimensions.* Edited by Lancaster, J B, B A Hamburg. Pp. 147-76. New York: Aldine.

1043 Piazza, A, S Readine, G Zei, A Morani, L L Cavalli-Sforza. 1987. Migration rates of human populations from surname distributions. *Nature* 329: 714-16.

1044 Pickersgill, B. 1989. Cytological and genetical evidence on the domestication and diffusion of crops within the Americas. In *The Evolution of Plant Exploitation: Concepts and Processes.* Edited by Harris, D, G Hillman. Pp. 426-39. London: Unwin Hyman.

1045 Pinto-Cisternas, J, M C Castelli, L Pineda. 1985. The use of surnames in the study of population structure. *Human Biology* 57: 353-63.

1046 Pintor, C, A R Genazzani, R Pugoni, G Carboni, A Faedda, E Pisano, R Orani, G D'Ambrogio, R Corda. 1980. Effect of weight loss on adrenal androgen plasma levels in obese prepubertal girls. In *Adrenal Androgens.* Edited by Genazzani, A R, J H Thijssen, P K Siiteri. Pp. 259-67. New York: Raven Press.

1047 Piperno, D R. 1989. Non-affluent foragers: Resource availability, seasonal shortages, and the emergence of agriculture in Panamanian tropical forests. In *The Evolution of Plant Exploitation: Concepts and Processes.* Edited by Harris, D R, G C Hillman. Pp. 538-54. London: Unwin Hyman.

1048 Pirke, K M, U Schweiger, W Lemmel, J C Krieg, M Berger. 1985. The influence of dieting on the menstrual cycle of healthy young women. *Journal of Clinical Endocrinology and Metabolism* 60: 1174-79.

1049 Pirke, K M, U Schweiger, T Strowitzki, R J Tuschi, G Laessle, A Broocks, B Huber, R Middendorf. 1989. Dieting causes menstrual irregularities in normal weight young women through impairment of episodic luteinizing hormone secretion. *Fertility and Sterility* 51: 263-68.

1050 Plooij, F X, H H C Van de Rijt-Plooij. 1989. Vulnerable periods during infancy: Hierarchically reorganized systems control, stress, and disease. *Ethology and Sociobiology* 10: 279-96.

1051 Potter, R G, Jr., M L New, J B Wyon, J E Gordon. 1965. A fertility differential in eleven Punjab villages. *Milbank Memorial Fund Quarterly* 43: 185-201.

1052 Prentice, A M, R G Whitehead, S B Roberts, A A Paul. 1981. Long-term energy balance in child-bearing Gambian women. *American Journal of Clinical Nutrition* 34: 2790-99.

1053 Prentice, A M, R G Whitehead. 1987. The energetics of human reproduction. *Symposium of the Zoological Society of London* 57: 275-304.

1054 Preston, S H. 1982. *Biological and Social Aspects of Mortality and the Length of Life.* Liège: Editions Ordina.

1055 Quinton, P M. 1983. Sweating and its disorders. *Annual Review of Medicine* 34: 429-52.

1056 Raleigh, M J, G J Brammer. 1982. Sociopharmacology. *Annual Review of Pharmacology and Toxicology* 22: 643-661.

1057 Raleigh, M J, M T McGuire, G L Brammer, A Yuwiler. 1984. Social and environmental influences on blood serotonin concentrations in monkeys. *Archives of General Psychiatry* 41: 405-10.

1058 Reiter, E O, M M Grumbach. 1982. Neuroendocrine control mechanisms and the onset of puberty. *Annual Review of Physiology* 44: 595-613.

1059 Reiter, E O. 1986. The Neuroendocrine regulation of pubertal onset. In *School-Age Pregnancy and Parenthood: Biosocial Dimensions.* Edited by Lancaster, J B, B A Hamburg. Pp. 53-76. New York: Aldine.

1060 Retherford, R D. 1985. A theory of marital fertility transition. *Population Studies* 39: 249-296.

1061 Riley, V, ed 1972. *Pigmentation: Its Genesis and Biologic Control.* New York: Appleton-Century-Crofts.

1062 Roberts, D F, D P S Kahlon. 1972. Skin pigmentation and assortative mating in Sikhs. *Biosocial Science* 4: 61-100.

1063 Rose, M R. 1990. *Evolutionary Biology of Aging.* New York: Oxford University Press.

1064 Saw, S H. 1986. A decade of fertility below replacement level in Singapore. *Journal of Biosocial Science* 18: 395-401.

1065 Sawin, D, et al., eds. 1980. *Current Perspectives on Psychosocial Risks during Pregnancy and Early Infancy.* New York: Bruner/Mazel.

1066 Schiefenhövel, W. 1984. Preferential female infanticide and other mechanisms regulating population size among the Eipo. In *Population and Biology.* Edited by Keytitz, N. Pp. 169-92. Liège: Editions Ordina.

1067 Schoenmaeckers, R, I H Shah, R Lesthaeghe, O Tambashe. 1981. The child-spacing tradition and the postpartum taboo in tropical Africa: Anthropological evidence. In *Child-spacing in Tropical Africa: Traditions and Change.* Edited by Page, H J, R Lesthaeghe. Pp. 25-71. London: Academic Press.

1068 Schofield, R, D Coleman. 1986. Introduction: The state of population theory. In *The State of Population Theory: Forward from Malthus.* Edited by Coleman, D, R Schofield. Pp. 1-13. Oxford: Blackwell.

1069 Scott, E C, F E Johnston. 1985. Science, nutrition, fat, and policy: Tests of the critical fat hypothesis. *Current Anthropology* 26: 463-73.

1070 Scrimshaw, S C M. 1982. Infanticide as deliberate fertility regulation. In *Fertility Determinants in Developing Countries.* Edited by Lee, R, R Bulatao. New York: National Academy of Sciences Press.

1071 Scrimshaw, S C M. 1984. Infanticide in human populations: Societal and individual concerns. In *Infanticide.* Edited by Hausfater, G, S Blaffer Hrdy. Pp. 439-62. New York: Aldine.

1072 Short, R V. 1979. Sexual selection and its component parts, somatic and genital selection, as illustrated by man and the great apes. *Advances in the Study of Behavior* 9: 131-58.

1073 Short, R V. 1979. When a conception fails to become a pregnancy. In *Maternal Recognition of Pregnancy.* Pp. 377-394. London: Ciba Foundations.

1074 Short, R. 1983. Biological basis for the contraceptive effects of breast feeding. In *Neuroendocrine Aspects of Reproduction.* Edited by Norman, R. New York: Academic Press.

1075 Simons, J. 1982. Reproductive behaviour as religious practice. In *Determinants of Fertility Trends: Theories Re-examined* Edited by Hohn, C, R Mackensen. Pp. 131-45. Liège: Editions Ordina.

1076 Singer, S F, ed 1971. *Is There an Optimal Level of Populations?* New York: McGraw-Hill.

1077 Small, M F. 1981. Body, fat, rank, and nutritional status in a captive group of rhesus monkeys. *International Journal of Primatology* 2: 91-95.

1078 Smith, R M. 1981. Fertility, economy, and household formation in England over three centuries. *Population and Development Review* 7: 595-622.

1079 Smith, R M. 1984. Transfer incomes, risk and security: The Roles of the family and the collectivity in recent theories of fertility change. In *The State of Population Theory: Forward from Malthus.* Edited by Coleman, D, R Schofield. Pp. 188-211. Oxford: Blackwell.

1080 Soderberg, G. 1986. *Kinesiology: Application to Pathological Motion.* London: Williams & Wilkins.

1081 Sohal, R S, L S Birbaum, R G Cutter, eds. 1985. *Molecular Biology of Aging: Gene Stability and Gene Expression.* New York: Raven.

1082 Stahl, A B. 1989. Plant-food processing: Implications for dietary quality. In *The Evolution of Plant Exploitation: Concepts and Processes.* Edited by Harris, D R, G C Hillman. Pp. 171-195. London: Unwin Hyman.

1083 Stein, Z, M Susser. 1975. Fertility, fecundity, famine: Food rations in the Dutch Famine 1944/1945 have a causal relation to fertility, and probably to fecundity. *Human Biology* 47: 131-154.

1084 Stini, W A, ed 1979. *Physiological and Morphological Adaptation and Evolution.* The Hague: Mouton.

1085 Stini, W A. 1979. Adaptive strategies of human populations under nutritional stress. In *Physiological and Morphological Adaptation and Evolution.* Edited by Stini, W A. Pp. 387-407. The Hague: Mouton.

1086 Stini, W A. 1982. Sexual dimorphism and nutrient reserves. In *Sexual Dimorphism in Homo Sapiens.* Edited by Hall, R. Pp. 391-419. New York: Praeger.

1087 Stoddart, D M. 1985. Is incense a pheromone? *Interdisciplinry Science Reviews* 10: 237-247.

1088 Stoddart, D M. 1990. *The Scented Ape: The Biology and Culture of Human Odour.* New York: Cambridge University Press.

1089 Sugar, M. 1979. *Female Adolescent Development.* New York: Brunner/Mazel.

1090 Swedlund, A C. 1988. Mating distance and historical population structure: A review. In *Human Mating Patterns.* Edited by Mascie-Taylor, C G N, A J Boyce. Pp. 15-30. New York: Cambridge University Press.

1091 Teitelbaum, M S. 1976. Some genetic implications of population policies. In *Eugenics Then and Now.* Edited by Bajema, C J. Pp. 321-331. Stroudsburg, Pa.: Dowden, Hutchinson and Ross.

1092 Teitelbaum, M S. 1985. *The British Fertility Decline.* Princeton: Princeton University Press.

1093 Tills, D, A C Kopec, R E Tills. 1983. *The Distribution of Human Blood Groups and Other Polymorphisms.* Oxford: Oxford University Press.

1094 Tilly, C, ed 1978. *Historical Studies of Changing Fertility.* Princeton: Princeton University Press.

1095 Towe, A, E Luschei, eds. 1981. *Motor Coordination.* New York: Plenum.

1096 Trivers, R L, D E Willard. 1973. Natural selection of parental ability to vary the sex ratio of offspring. *Science* 179: 90-92.

1097 Trussell, J. 1978. Menarche and fatness: Reexamination of the critical body composition hypothesis. *Science* 200: 1506-9.

1098 Trussell, J. 1980. Statistical flaws in evidence for the Frisch hypothesis that fatness triggers menarche. *Human Biology* 52: 711-720.

1099 Tsunoda, T. 1985. *The Japanese Brain.* Tokyo: Taishukan.

1100 Turke, P. 1989. Evolution and the demand for children. *Population and Development Review* 15: 61-90.

1101 van den Berghe, P L, P Frost. 1986. Skin color preference, sexual dimorphism, and sexual selection: A case of gene-culture co-evolution? *Ethnic and Racial Studies* 9: 87-113.

1102 Vining, D R. 1982. On the possibility of the reemergence of a dysgenic trend with respect to intelligence. *American Fertility Differentials* 6: 241-264.

1103 Vining, D R. 1983. Fertility differentials and the status of nations: A apeculative essay on Japan and the West. *Mankind Quarterly* 22: 311-353.

1104 Vining, D R. 1983. Dysgenic fertility and welfare: An elementary test. *Personality and Individual Differences* 4: 313-318.

1105 Wahren, J, P Felig, G Ahlborg, L Jorfeldt. 1971. Glucose metabolism during leg exercise in man. *Journal of Clinical Investigation* 50: 2715-2725.

1106 Ward, R H. 1983. Genetic and sociocultural components of high blood pressure. *American Journal of Physical Anthropology* 62: 91-105.

1107 Warren, M P. 1981. Physical and biological aspects of puberty. In *Girls at Puberty: Biological and Psychosocial Perspectives.* Edited by Brooks-Gunn, J, A C Peterson. New York: Plenum.

1108 Warren, M P. 1981. Physical and biological aspects of puberty. In *Girls at Puberty: Biological and Psychosocial Perspectives.* Edited by Brooks-Gunn, J, A C Peterson. New York: Plenum.

1109 Warwick, D P. 1983. *Bitter Pills: Population Policies and Their Implementation in Eight Developing Countries.* Cambridge: Cambridge University Press.

1110 Wasser, S K, D P Barash. 1983. Reproductive suppression among female mammals : Implications for biomedicine and sexual selection theory. *Quarterly Review of Biology* 58: 513-538.

1111 Watts, E S, J A Gavan. 1982. Postnatal growth of nonhuman primates: The problem of the adolescent spurt. *Human Biology* 54: 53-70.

1112 Watts, E. 1985. Adolescent growth and development of monkeys, apes and humans. In *Nonhuman Primate Models for Growth and Development.* Edited by Watts, S. New York: Alan R. Liss.

1113 Weiner, J S, J A Lourie. 1969. *Human Biology: A Guide to Field Methods.* Oxford: Blackwell.

1114 Westhoff, C. 1974. The populations of the developed countries. *Scientific American* 232:

1115 Westhoff, C, N Ryder. 1977. *The Contraceptive Revolution.* Princeton: Princeton University Press.

1116 Westhoff, C F. 1983. Fertility decline in the west: Causes and prospects. *Population and Development Review* 9: 99-105.

1117 Westhoff, C F. 1986. Fertility in the United States. *Science* 234: 554-59.

1118 White, J C. 1989. Ethnoecological observations on wild and cultivated rice and yams in northeastern Thailand. In *The Evolution of Plant Exploitation: Concepts and Processes.* Edited by Harris, D R, G C Hillman. Pp. 152-58. London: Unwin Hyman.

1119 Whiting, J W M, V K Burbank, M S Ratner. 1986. The duration of maidenhood across cultures. In *School-Age Pregnancy and Parenthood: Biosocial Dimensions.* Edited by Lancaster, J B, B A Hamburg. Pp. 273-302. New York: Aldine.

1120 Wilkinson, G S, C T Nagoshi, R C Johnson, K A Honbo. 1989. Perinatal mortality and sex ratios in Hawaii. *Ethology and Sociobiology* 101: 1435-1448.

1121 Wilson, D S. 1979. *The Natural Selection of Populations and Communities.* Menlo Park, CA: Benjamin-Cummings.

1122 Wilson, C. 1986. The proximate determinants of marital fertility in England 1600-1799. In *The World We Have Gained: Histories of Population and Social Structure.* Edited by Bonfield, L, R M Smith, K Wrightson. Pp. 203-30. Oxford: Blackwell.

1123 Wohrmann, K, V Loeschcke, eds. 1984. *Population Biology and Evolution.* Berlin: Springer.

1124 Wood, J W, M Weinstein. 1988. A model of age-specific fecundability. *Population Studies* 42: 85-113.

1125 Woods, G I, C W Smith. 1983. The decline of marital fertility in the late 19th century; the case of England and Wales. *Population Studies* 37: 207-25.

1126 Woodson, R H, N G Blurton Jones, E da Costa Woodson, S Pollack, M Evans. 1979. Fetal mediators of the relationship between increased pregnancy and labour blood pressure and newborn irritability. *Early Human Development* 3: 127-39.

1127 Wrigley, E A. 1978. Fertility strategy for the individual and the group. In *Historical Studies of Changing Fertility*. Edited by Tilly, C. Pp. 135-54. Princeton, N.J.: Princeton University Press.

1128 Wrigley, E A, R S Schofield. 1981. *The Population History of England 1541-1871: A Reconstruction*. London: Edward Arnold.

1129 Wrong, D. 1980. *Class Fertility Trends in Western Nations*. New York: Arno.

1130 Wunsch, G J. 1984. Theories, models and knowledge: The logic of demographic discovery. *Genus* 40: 1-18.

1131 Wyshak, G, R E Frisch. 1982. Evidence for a secular trend in age of menarche. *New England Journal of Medicine* 306: 1033-35.

1132 Yen, S S C. 1984. Opiates and reproduction: Studies in women. In *Opioid Modulation of Endocrine Function*. Edited by Delitala, G, M Motta, M Serio. Pp. 191-209. New York: Raven Press.

1133 Yen, D E. 1989. The domestication of environment. In *The Evolution of Plant Exploitation: Concepts and Processes*. Edited by Harris, D R, G C Hillman. Pp. 55-78. London: Unwin Hyman.

1134 Zajonc, R B, G B Markus. 1975. Birth order and intellectual development. *Psychological Review* 82: 74-83.

# 4

# Cultural Evolution

1135 Abernathy, V. 1979. *Population Pressure and Cultural Adjustment.* New York: Human Sciences Press.

1136 Adams, R M. 1965. *Land Behind Baghdad.* Chicago: University of Chicago Press.

1137 Adams, R M. 1966. *The Evolution of Urban Society.* Chicago: Aldine Press.

1138 Adams, R M, H J Nissen. 1972. *The Uruk Countryside.* Chicago: University of Chicago Press.

1139 Adams, R M. 1981. *Heartland of Cities: Surveys of Ancient Settlement and Land Use in the Central Flood Plain of the Euphrates.* Chicago: University of Chicago Press.

1140 Adams, R N. 1988. *The Eight Day: Social Evolution as the Self-Organization of Energy.* Austin: University of Texas Press.

1141 Aitchison, L. 1960. *A History of Metals.* London: Macdonald.

1142 Alland, A. 1967. *Evolution and Human Behavior.* Garden City, NY: Natural History Press.

1143 Alland, A. 1970. *Adaptation in Cultural Evolution: An Approach to Medical Anthropology.* New York: Columbia University Press.

1144 Ames, K. 1981. The evolution of social ranking on the northwest coast of North America. *American Antiquity* 46: 789-805.

1145 Ames, K. 1985. Hierarchies, stress, and logistical strategies among hunter gatherers in northwestern North America. In *Prehistoric Hunter Gatherers.* Edited by Price, D, J Brown. Pp. 155-180. Orlando, FL: Academic Press.

1146 Anati, E. 1983. *Gli Elementi Fondamentali della Cultura.* Milan: Jaca Books.

1147 Ayres, C. 1962. *The Theory of Economic Progress.* 2nd ed New York: Schocken Books.

1148 Bach, W, J Pankrath, W Kellogg, eds. 1979. *Man's Impact on Climate.* Amsterdam: Elsevier.

86  *The Bibliography of Human Behavior*

1149 Balch, S H. 1989. Metaevolution and biocultural history. *Journal of Social and Biological Structures* 12: 303-318.

1150 Bargatzky, T. 1984. Culture, environment, and the ills of adaptationism. *Current Anthropology* 25: 399-415.

1151 Bargatzky, T. 1984. Supra-system evolution and the mature state. In *The Dynamics of the Early State.* Edited by Claessen, H J M. Leiden: Brill.

1152 Bargatzky, T. 1987. Upward evolution, suprasystem dominance, and the mature state. In *Early State Dynamics.* Edited by Claessen, H J M, P van de Velde. Leiden: É.J. Brill.

1153 Bargatzky, T. 1988. Evolution, sequential hierarchy, and areal integration: The case of traditional Samoan society. In *State and Society: The Emergence and Development of Social Hierarchy and Political Centralization.* Edited by Gledhill, J, B Bender, M T Larsen. Pp. 43-56. London: Unwin Hyman.

1154 Barnett, H G. 1953. *Innovation: The Basis of Social Change.* New York: McGraw-Hill.

1155 Basalla, G. 1988. *The Evolution of Technology.* Cambridge: Cambridge University Press.

1156 Beals, K, A J Kelso. 1975. Genetic variables and cultural evolution. *American Anthropologist* 77: 566-579.

1157 Becker, G S, K M Murphy, R Tamura. 1990. Human capital, fertility and economic growth. *Journal of Political Economy* 98: S12-S22.

1158 Beniger, J. 1986. *The Control Revolution.* Cambridge: Harvard University Press.

1159 Bennett, J W. 1976. *The Ecological Transition: Cultural Anthropology and Human Adaptation.* New York: Pergamon.

1160 Berrien, F K. 1968. *General and Social Systems.* New Brunswick, NJ: Rutgers University Press.

1161 Bintliff, J, ed. 1984. *Social Evolution.* Bradford: Bradford University Press.

1162 Bock, K E. 1978. Theories of progress, development, and evolution. In *A History of Sociological Analysis.* Edited by Bottomore, T, R Nisbet. Pp. 39-79. New York: Basic Books.

1163 Boehm, C. 1982. A fresh outlook on cultural selection. *American Anthropologist* 84: 105-124.

1164 Boserup, E. 1981. *Population and Technology.* Oxford: Blackwell.

1165 Boulding, K E. 1970. *A Primer of Social Dynamics: History as Dialectics and Development.* New York: Free Press.

1166 Boulding, K E. 1978. *Ecodynamics: A New Theory of Societal Evolution.* London: Sage Publications.

1167 Boulding, K. 1981. *Evolutionary Economics.* Beverly Hills, CA: Sage.

1168 Boulding, K. 1983. Technology in the evolutionary process. In *The Trouble with Technology.* Edited by McDonald, S, D M Lamberton, T Mandeville. Pp. 4-10. New York: St Martin's Press.

1169 Boyd, R, P J Richerson. 1983. Why is culture adaptive? *Quarterly Review of Biology* 58: 209-214.

1170 Boyd, R, P J Richerson. 1985. *Culture and the Evolutionary Process.* Chicago: University of Chicago Press.

1171 Boyd, R, P J Richerson. 1985. The cultural transmission of acquired variation: Effects on genetic fitness. *Journal of Theoretical Biology* 100: 567-596.

1172 Boyden, S V, ed. 1970. *The Impact of Civilisation on the Biology of Man.* Canberra: Australian National University Press.

1173 Braudel, F. 1977. *Afterthoughts on Material Civilization and Capitalism.* Baltimore: Johns Hopkins.

1174 Bremer, S J, D J Singer, U Luterbacher. 1973. The population density and war proneness of European nations,1816-1965. *Comparative Political Studies* 6: 329-348.

1175 Burns, T R, H Flam. 1987. *The Shaping of Social Organization: Social Rule Systems Theory with Applications.* London: Sage.

1176 Campbell, J K. 1964. *Honour, Family, and Patronage.* Oxford: Clarendon Press.

1177 Canican, F. 1965. *Economics and Prestige in a Maya Community.* Stanford, CA: Stanford University Press.

1178 Carefoot, G L, E R Sprott. 1969. *Famine on the Wind: Plant Diseases and Human History.* Montreal: McGill-Queens University Press.

1179 Carne, J C, M J Kirton. 1982. Styles of creativity: A test score correlations between the Kirton Adaption Innovation Inventory and the Myers-Briggs Type Indicatior. *Psychological Reports* 50: 31-36.

1180 Carneiro, R L. 1968. Cultural adaptation. In *International Encyclopedia of the Social Sciences*. Pp. 551-554.

1181 Carneiro, R L. 1970. The theory of the origin of the state. *Science* 169: 733-738.

1182 Carneiro, R L. 1972. From autonomous villages to the state: A numerical estimation. In *Population Growth: Anthropological Implications*. Edited by Spooner, B. Pp. 64-77. Cambridge: M.I.T. Press.

1183 Carneiro, R L. 1978. Political expansion as an expression of the principle of competitive exclusion. In *Origins of the State: The Anthropology of Political Evolution*. Edited by Cohen, R, E R Service. Pp. 205-223. Philadelphia: Institute for the Study of Human Issues.

1184 Carneiro, R L. 1981. The chiefdom: precursor of the state. In *Transition to Statehood in the New World*. Edited by Jones, G D, R R Kautz. Pp. 37-79. Cambridge: Cambridge University Press.

1185 Carneiro, R L. 1987. Further reflections on resource concentration and its role in the rise of the state. In *Studies in the Neolithic and Urban Revolutions*. Edited by Manzanilla, L. Pp. 245-260. Oxford: Bar International Series.

1186 Carneiro, R L. 1988. The circumscription theory: Challenge and response. *American Behavioral Scientist* 31: 497-511.

1187 Caton, H. 1988. *The Politics of Progress: The Origins and Development of the Commercial Republic 1600-1835.* Gainesville: University Presses of Florida.

1188 Cavalli-Sforza, L L, M W Feldman. 1973. Models for cultural inheritance: I. Group mean and within-group variation. *Theoretical Population Biology* 4: 42-53.

1189 Cavalli-Sforza, L L, M W Feldman. 1981. *Cultural Transmission and Evolution: A Quantitative Approach.* Princeton: Princeton University Press.

1190 Chao, K. 1986. *Man and Land in chinese History: An Economic Analysis.* Stanford: Stanford University Press.

1191 Childe, V G. 1951. *Social Evolution.* New York: H. Schuman.

1192 Childe, V G. 1965 [1936]. *Man Makes Himself.* 4th ed London: Watts & Company.

1193 Claessen, H J M, P Skalnik, eds. 1981. *The Study of the State.* The Hague: Mouton.

1194 Claessen, H J M. 1984. The internal dynamics of early states. *Current Anthropology* 25: 365-379.

1195 Claessen, H J M, P van de Velde, M E Smith, eds 1985. *Development and Decline: The Evolution of Sociopolitical Organizations*. South Hadley, MA: Bergin & Garvey.

1196 Claessen, H J M, P van de Velde, eds. 1987. *Early State Dynamics*. Leiden: Brill.

1197 Clark, N, C Juna. 1987. *Long-Run Economics: An Evolutionary Approach to Economic Growth*. London: Pinter.

1198 Clark, G, J Lindly. 1989. The case for continuity: Observations on the biocultural transition in Europe and Western Asia. In *The Human Revolution: Behavioural and Biological Perspectives on the Origins of Modern Humans*. Edited by Mellars, P, C Stringer. Edinburgh: Edinburgh University Press.

1199 Clarke, J I, P Curson, S L Kayastha, P Nag, eds. 1989. *Population and Disaster*. Oxford: Blackwell.

1200 Cohen, R. 1962. The strategy of social evolution. *Anthropologica* 4: 321-348.

1201 Cohen, Y A. 1968. Culture as adaptation. In *Man in Adaptation: The Cultural Present*. Edited by Cohen, Y A. Pp. 40-60. Chicago: Aldine.

1202 Cohen, Y A, ed. 1968. *Man in Adaptation: The Cultural Present*. Chicago: Aldine.

1203 Cohen, R. 1978. State origins: A reappraisal. In *The Early State*. Edited by Claessen, H J M, P Skalnik. The Hague: Mouton.

1204 Cohen, M N. 1981. The ecological basis for New World state formation: General and local model building. In *Transition to Statehood in the New World*. Edited by Jones, G D, R R Kautz. Pp. 105-122. Cambridge: Cambridge University Press.

1205 Cohen, R M. 1984. Warfare and state formation: Wars make states and states make wars. In *Warfare, Culture, and Environment*. Edited by Ferguson, R B. Pp. 329-358. New York: Academic Press.

1206 Colander, D, A W Coats, eds. 1989. *The Spread of Economic Ideas*. Cambridge: Cambridge University Press.

1207 Colinvaux, P. 1983. *The Fates of Nations: A Biological Theory of History*. Harmonsworth: Penguin.

1208 Conkey, M W. 1985. Ritual communication, social elaboration, and the variable trajectories of Paleolithic material culture. In *Prehistoric Hunter-Gatherers: The Emergence of Cultural Complexity*. Edited by Price, T D, J A Brown. Pp. 299-323. London: Academic.

1209 Cooper, R, M Foster. 1971. Sociotechnical systems. *American Psychologist* 26: 467-474.

1210 Corluy, R. 1984. The Wilson-Lumsden model of the coevolutionary process of genes and culture. *Journal of Human Evolution* 13: 41-48.

1211 Corning, P A. 1983. *Politics and the Evolutionary Process.* New York: Harper and Row.

1212 Corning, P A. 1983. *The Synergism Hypothesis: A Theory of Progressive Evolution.* New York: McGraw-Hill.

1213 Crosby, A W. 1972. *The Columbian Exchange: Biological and Cultural Consequences of 1492.* Westport, CT: Greenwood.

1214 Crosby, A W. 1986. *Ecological Imperialism: The Biological Expansion of Europe, 900-1900.* New York: Cambridge University Press.

1215 Darirty, W A, Jr. 1980. The Boserup theory of agricultural growth: A model for anthropological economics. *Journal of Development Economics* 7: 137-157.

1216 Darlington, C D. 1963. Psychology, genetics and the process of history. *British Journal of Psychology* 54: 293-298.

1217 Darlington, C D. 1969. *The Evolution of Man and Society.* London: Allen and Unwin.

1218 Davis, D E. 1985. Hereditary emblems: Material culture in the context of social change. *Journal of Anthropological Archaeology* 4: 149-176.

1219 De Winter, K W. 1984. Biological and cultural evolution: Different manifestations of the same principle. A systems-theoretical approach. *Journal of Human Evolution* 13: 61-70.

1220 Dewalt, B R. 1975. Changes in the cargo systems of Mesoamerica. *Anthropological Quarterly* 48: 87-105.

1221 Diener, P. 1980. Quantum adjustment, macroevolution, and the social field: Some comments on evolution and culture. *Current Anthropology* 21: 423-43.

1222 Diener, P, D Nonini, E E Robkin. 1980. Ecology and evolution in cultural anthropology. *Man* 15: 1-31.

1223 Dietz, T, T R Burns, F H Buttel. 1990. Evolutionary theory in sociology: An examination of current thinking. *Sociological Forum* 5: 155-172.

1224 Dimbleby, G W. 1972. The impact of early man on his environment. In *Population and Pollution.* Edited by Cox, P R, J Peel. Pp. 7-13. London: Academic Press.

1225 Dirks, R. 1980. Social responses during severe food shortages and famine. *Current Anthropology* 21: 21-44.

1226 Dobzhansky, T, E Boesinger. 1983. *Human Culture: A Moment in Evolution.* New York: Columbia University Press.

1227 Dodgshon, R. 1987. *The European Past: Social Evolution and Spatial Order.* New York: Macmillan.

1228 Donaldson, L. 1991. *Fertility Transition: The Social Dynamics of Population Change.* Oxford: Blackwell.

1229 Dostal, W. 1974. Theorie des öko-kulturellen Interaktionssystems. *Anthropos* 69: 409-44.

1230 Dostal, W, L Reisinger. 1981. Ein Modell des öko-kulturellen Interadaptationssystems. *Zeitschrift für Ethnologie* 106: 43-50.

1231 Dupre, J. 1987. Evolution of a mesh between principles of the mind and regularities of the world. In *The Latest on the Best.* Edited by Dupre, J. Cambridge: M.I.T. Press.

1232 Durham, W H. 1976. The adaptive significance of cultural behavior. *Human Ecology* 4: 89-121.

1233 Durham, W H. 1987. *Coevolution: Genes, Culture, and Human Diversity.* Stanford: Stanford University Press.

1234 Dyson-Hudson, R, E A Smith. 1978. Human territoriality: An ecological reassessment. *American Anthropologist* 80: 21-41.

1235 Earle, T K, ed. 1984. *On the Evolution of Complex Societies: Essays in Honor of Harry Hoijer.* Malibu, CA: Undena Publications.

1236 Earle, T K. 1989. *Economic and Social Organization of a Complex Chiefdom.* Anthropological Papers. Ann Arbor: University of Michigan Museum of Anthropology.

1237 Eaton, S B, M J Konner. 1985. Paleolithic nutrition: A consideration of its nature and current implications. *New England Journal of Medicine* 312: 283-289.

1238 Einzig, P. 1966. *Primitive Money.* Oxford: Pergamon.

1239 Elias, N. 1982. *State Formation and Civilization.* Oxford: Blackwell.

1240 Elster, J. 1983. *Explaining Technical Change: A Case Study in the Philosophy of Science.* Cambridge: Cambridge University Press.

1241 Fenner, F. 1970. The effects of changing social organization on the infectious diseases of man. In *The Impact of Civilisation on the Biology of Man.* Edited by Boyden, S V. Canberra: Australian National University Press.

1242 Ferguson, R B, ed. 1984. *Warfare, Culture, and Environment.* New York: Academic Press.

1243 Flannery, K V. 1972. The cultural evolution of civilizations. *Annual Review of Ecology and Systematics* 3: 399-426.

1244 Flannery, K. 1976. Interregional religious networks. In *The Early Mesoamerican Village.* Pp. 329-368. New York: Academic Press.
1245 Flinn, M V, R D Alexander. 1982. Culture theory: The developing synthesis from biology. *Human Ecology* 10: 383-400.

1246 Foster, J. 1987. *Evolutionary Macoeconomics.* London: Allen and Unwin.

1247 Frankfort, H. 1951. *The Birth of Civilization in the Near East.* Bloomington: University of Indiana Press.

1248 Freedman, D G. 1984. Village fissioning, human diversity, and ethnocentrism. *Political Psychology* 5: 629-634.

1249 Frick, F S. 1985. *The Formation of the State in Ancient Israel.* Sheffield: Almond.

1250 Fried, M H. 1967. *The Evolution of Political Society: An Essay in Political Anthropology.* New York: Random House.

1251 Fried, M, M Harris, R Murphy, eds. 1967. *War.* Garden City, N.Y.: Natural History Press.

1252 Friedman, J, M J Rowlands, eds. 1977. *The Evolution of Social Systems.* London: Duckworth.

1253 Friedman, J, M J Rowlands. 1977. Notes towards an epigenetic model of civilization. In *The Evolution of Social Systems.* Edited by Friedman, J, M J Rowlands. Pp. 201-276. London: Duckworth.

1254 Futia, C A. 1980. Schumpeterian competition. *Quarterly Journal of Economics* 94: 675-695.

1255 Garn, S M, ed. 1964. *Culture and the Direction of Human Evolution.* Detroit: Wayne State University Press.

1256 Gehlen, A. 1980. *Man in the Age of Technology.* New York: Columbia University Press.

1257 Geiger, G. 1983. On the dynamics of evolutionary discontinuities. *Mathematical Biosciences* 67: 59-79.

1258 Geiger, G. 1985. The concept of evolution and early state formation. *Politics and the Life Sciences* 3: 163-171.

1259 Geiger, G. 1985. Autocatalysis in cultural ecology: Model ecosystems and the dynamics of biocultural coevolution. *Biosystems* 17: 259-272.

1260 Geiger, G. 1988. On the evolutionary origins and function of political power. *Journal of Social and Biological Structures* 11: 235-250.

1261 Gellner, E. 1988. *Plough, Sword and Book: The Structure of Human History*. Chicago: University of Chicago Press.

1262 Gerard, R W, C Kluckhohn, A Rapoport. 1956. Biological and cultural evolution: Some analogies and exploration. *Behavioral Science* 1: 6-34.

1263 Gilman, A. 1981. The development of social stratification in Bronze Age Europe. *Current Anthropology* 22: 1-8, 17-23.

1264 Ginzberg, E, ed. 1964. *Technology and Social Change*. New York: Columbia University Press.

1265 Gledhill, J, B Bender, M T Larsen, eds. 1988. *State and Society: The Emergence and Development of Social Hierarchy and Political Centralization*. London: Unwin Hyman.

1266 Goldsmith, R E. 1984. Personality characteristics associated with adaption-innovation. *Journal of Psychology* 117: 159-165.

1267 Goldsmith, R E. 1985. A factorial compostition of the KAI inventory. *Educational and Psychological Measurement* 45: 245-250.

1268 Goldsmith, R E. 1986. Personality and adaptive-innovative problem solving. *Journal of Personality and Social Behaviour* 1: 95-106.

1269 Goldsmith, R E. 1986. Adaptation-innovation and cognitive complexity. *Journal of Psychology* 119: 461-467.

1270 Goody, J. 1977. Population and polity in the Voltaic region. In *The Evolution of Social Systems*. Edited by Friedman, J, M J Rowlands. Pp. 535-545. London: Duckworth.

1271 Gottlieb, G. 1992. *Individual Development and Evolution. The Genesis of Novel Behavior*. New York: Oxford University Press.

1272 Gottschalk, L, L C MacKinney, E H Pritchard. 1969. *The Foundations of the Modern World 1300-1775*. London: Allen & Unwin.

1273 Graber, R. 1988. A mathematical interpretation of circumscription applied to the westward expansion. *American Behavioral Scientist* 31: 459-71.

1274 Graber, R. 1989. Cultural evolution and the introversion of aggression. *Connecticut Review* 11: 105-113.

1275 Gregory, D, R Martin, G Smith, eds. 1990. *Rethinking Human Geography*. New York: Macmillan.

1276 Grigg, D B. 1980. *Population Growth and Agrarian Change: A Historical Perspective*. Cambridge: Cambridge University Press.

1277 Gruter, M, P Bohannan, eds. 1983. *Law, Biology and Culture: The Evolution of Law*. Santa Barbara: Ross-Erickson.

1278 Guha, A. 1981. *An Evolutionary View of Economic Growth*. Oxford: Clarendon Press.

1279 Haas, M. 1968. Social change and national aggressiveness, 1900-1960. In *Quantitative International Politics: Insights and Evidence*. Edited by Singer, J D. New York: Free Press.

1280 Haas, J. 1982. *The Evolution of the Prehistoric State*. New York: Columbia University Press.

1281 Haas, J, ed. 1990. *The Anthropology of War*. New York: Cambridge University Press.

1282 Hage, J, R Dewar. 1973. Elite values versus organizational structure predicting innovation. *Administrative Science Quarterly* 18: 279-290.

1283 Haken, H. 1980. Synergetics: Are cooperative phenomena governed by universal principles? *Naturwissenschaften* 67: 121-128.

1284 Hallpike, C R. 1979. *The Foundations of Primitive Thought*. Oxford: Clarendon Press.

1285 Hallpike, C R. 1985. Social and biological evolution 1: Darwinism and social evolution. *Journal of Social and Biological Structures* 8: 129-146.

1286 Hallpike, C R. 1986. Social and biological evolution II: Some basic principles of social evolution. *Journal of Social and Biological Structures* 9: 5-31.

1287 Hallpike, C R. 1987. *The Principles of Social Evolution*. New York: Oxford University Press.

1288 Handwerker, W P. 1989. The origins and evolution of culture. *American Anthropologist* 91: 313-326.

1289 Harré, R. 1954. *Pomp and Pestilence: Infectious Disease, Its Origins and Conquest.* London: Victor Gollancz.

1290 Hardin, G. 1986. Cultural carrying capacity: A biological approach to human problems. *BioScience* 36: 599-606.

1291 Hareven, T K. 1982. *Family Time and Industrial Time.* Cambridge: Cambridge University Press.

1292 Harris, M. 1979. *Cultural Materialism: The Struggle for the Science of Culture.* New York: Random House.

1293 Hass, J. 1982. *The Evolution of the Prehistoric State.* New York: Columbia University Press.

1294 Hassan, F A. 1975. Determination of the size, density, and growth rate of hunting-gathering populations. In *Population, Ecology, and Social Evolution.* Edited by Polgar, S. Pp. 27-52. The Hague: Mouton.

1295 Hausen, K, R Rürup, eds. 1975. *Moderne Technik Geschichte.* Köln: Kiepenheuer & Witsch.

1296 Hayden, B. 1981. Research and development in the stone age: Technological transitions among hunter/gatherers. *Current Anthropology* 2: 519-548.

1297 Headrick, D. 1981. *The Tools of Empire: Technology and European Imperialism in the Nineteenth Century.* New York: Oxford University Press.

1298 Headrick, D R. 1988. *The Tentacles of Progress.* New York: Oxford University Press.

1299 Heertje, A. 1983. Can we explain technical change? In *The Trouble with Technology.* Edited by McDonald, S, D M Lamberton, T Mandeville. Pp. 37-49. New York: St. Martin's Press.

1300 Heiser, C. 1973. *Seed to Civilization: The Story of Man's Food.* San Francisco: Freeman.

1301 Hermann, A, W Dettmering, eds. 1989-. *Technik und Kultur.* Dusseldorf: VDI-Verlag.

1302 Hickson, D J, D S Pugh, D C Pheysey. 1969. Operations technology and organization structure: An empirical reappraisal. *Administrative Science Quarterly* 14: 378-397.

1303 Hill, J. 1978. The origin of socio-cultural evolution. *Journal of Social and Biological Structures* 1: 377-386.

1304 Hill, J. 1989. Concepts as units of cultural replication. *Journal of Social and Biological Structures* 12: 343-355.

1305 Hindle, B. 1981. *Emulation and Invention.* New York: New York University Press.

1306 Hirsch, F. 1976. *Social Limits to Growth.* Cambrige: Harvard University Press.

1307 Hockett, C F, R Ascher. 1964. The human revolution. *Current Anthropology* 5: 135-68.

1308 Hodder, I. 1990. *The Domestication of Europe: Structure and Contingency in Neolithic Societies.* Oxford: Blackwell.

1309 Hofstede, G. 1984. *Culture's Consequences: International Differences in Work-Related Values.* Beverly Hills, CA: Sage.

1310 Hopkins, D R. 1983. *Princes and Peasants: Smallpox in History.* Chicago: University of Chiago Press.

1311 Hornell, J. 1946. *Water Transport: Origins and Early Evolution.* Cambridge: Cambridge University Press.

1312 Hudson, H, R W Burhoe, eds. 1962. *Evolution and Man's Progress.* New York: Columbia University Press.

1313 Hughes, J D. 1975. *Ecology in Ancient Civilizations.* Albuquerque: University of New Mexico Press.

1314 Hughes, J D, J V Thirgood. 1982. Deforestation in ancient Greece and Rome: A cause of collapse. *Ecologist* 12: 196-209.

1315 Hughes, J R T. 1986. *The Vital Few.* 2nd ed New York: Oxford University Press.

1316 Hughes, T P. 1987. The evolution of large technological systems. In *The Social Construction of Technological Systems.* Edited by Bijker, W E, T P Hughes, T J Pinch. Pp. 51-82. Cambridge: M.I.T. Press.

1317 Hull, D L. 1988. *Science as Progress.* Chicago: University of Chicago Press.

1318 Hunt, R G. 1970. Technology and organization. *Academy of Management Journal* 13: 235-252.

1319 Hutterer, K L. 1976. An evolutionary approach to the Southeast Asian cultural sequence. *Current Anthropology* 17: 221-242.

1320 Isaksen, S G, ed. 1987. *Frontiers of Creativity.* Buffalo, NY: Brearly.

1321 Jochim, M A. 1981. *Strategies for Survival: Cultural Behavior in an Ecological Context.* New York: Academic Press.

1322 Johnson, G A. 1982. Organisational structure and scalar stress. In *Theory and Explanation in Archaeology*. Edited by Renfrew, C, et al. New York: Academic Press.

1323 Johnson, G A. 1983. Decision-making organization and pastoral nomad camp size. *Human Ecology* 11: 175-199.

1324 Johnson, A, T K Earle. 1991. *The Evolution of the Non-Industrial Economy*. Stanford: Stanford University Press.

1325 Jones, G D, R R Kautz. 1981. *Transition to Statehood in the New World*. Cambridge: Cambridge University Press.

1326 Jones, E L. 1987. *The European Miracle: Environments, Economies, and Geopolitics in the History of Europe and Asia*. 2nd ed Cambridge: Cambridge University Press.

1327 Jones, E L. 1988. *Growth Recurring: Economic Change in World History*. Oxford: Clarendon Press.

1328 Kaplan, D, R A Manners. 1972. *Culture Theory*. Englewood Cliffs: Prentice-Hall.

1329 Kapp, E. 1877 [1978]. *Grundlinien einer Philosophie der Technik. Zur Entstehungsgeschichte der Cultur aus neuen Geschichtspunkten*. Dusseldorf: Stern-Verlag Janssen.

1330 Kaufman, H. 1985. *Time, Chance and Organizations: Natural Selection in a Perilous Environment*. Chatham: Chatham House.

1331 Keesing, R M. 1974. Theories of culture. *Annual Review of Anthropology* 3: 73-97.

1332 Keesing, R M. 1985. Killers, big men, and priests on Malaita: Reflections on a troika system. *Ethnology* 24: 237-252.

1333 Keller, R T, W W Holland. 1978. A cross-validation study of the Kirton Adaption: Innovation inventory in three research and development organizations. *Applied Psychological Measurement* 2: 563-570.

1334 Kiggundu, M N. 1983. Task interdependence and job design: Test of a theory. *Organizational Behaviour and Human Performance* 31: 145-172.

1335 Kirch, P V. 1984. *The Evolution of the Polynesian Chiefdoms*. Cambridge: Cambridge University Press.

1336 Kirch, P V. 1988. Circumscription theory and sociopolitical evolution in Polynesia. *American Behavioral Scientist* 31: 416-427.

1337 Kirton, M J. 1978. Adaptors and innovators in culture clash. *Current Anthropology* 19: 611-612.

1338 Kirton, M J. 1984. Adaptors and innovators: Why new initiatives get blocked *Long Range Planning* 17: 137-143.

1339 Kirton, K J. 1985. Adaptors, innovators and paradigm consistency. *Psychological Reports* 57: 487-490.

1340 Kirton, K J. 1987. *Kirton Adaption-Innovation Inventory (KAI).* 2nd ed Hatfield, U.K.: Occupational Research Centre.

1341 Kirton, M J, R McCarthy. 1988. Cognitive climate and organizations. *Journal of Occupational Psychology* 61: 175-184.

1342 Kluckhohn, C. 1952. Universal categories of culture. In *Anthropology Today: An Encyclopedic Inventory.* Edited by Kroeber, A L. Pp. 507-523. Chicago: University of Chicago Press.

1343 Kodama, F. 1991. *Analyzing Japanese High Technologies: The Techno-Paradigm Shift.* New York: Pinter.

1344 Kort, F. 1983. An evolutionary-neurobiological explanation of political behavior and the Lumsden-Wilson "thousand-year rule". *Journal of Social and Biological Structures* 6: 219-230.

1345 Kroeber, A L, ed. 1952. *Anthropology Today: An Encyclopedic Inventory.* Chicago: University of Chicago Press.

1346 Kuran, T. 1988. The tenacious past: Theories of personal and collective conservatism. *Journal of Economic Behavior and Organization* 10: 143-171.

1347 Kuznets, S. 1965. *Economic Growth and Structure.* New York: Norton.

1348 Landes, D. 1983. *Revolution in Time: Clocks and the Making of the Modern World.* Cambridge: Harvard University Press.

1349 Langer, W L. 1964. The black death. *Scientific American* 210: 114-121.

1350 Langrish, J, et al. 1972. *Wealth from Knowledge: Studies of Innovation in Industry.* London: Macmillan.

1351 Langton, J. 1979. Darwinism and the behavioral theory of sociocultural evolution: Analysis. *American Journal of Sociology* 85: 288-309.

1352 Laslett, P. 1971. *The World We Have Lost.* London: Methuen.

1353 Latham, M C. 1975. Nutrition and infection in national development. *Science* 188: 561-565.

1354 Le Goff, J. 1980. *Time, Work and Culture in the Middle Ages.* Chicago: University of Chicago Press.

1355 Lerner, D. 1958. *The Passing of Traditional Society.* Glenco, IL: Free Press.

1356 Lewis, W A. 1955. *A Theory of Economic Growth.* London: Allen & Unwin.

1357 Lewis, H S. 1981. *The Study of the State.* Edited by Claessen, H J M, P Skalnik. The Hague: Mouton.

1358 Lewis, H S. 1981. Warfare and the origin of the state. In *The Study of the State.* Edited by Claessen, H J M, P Skalnik. The Hague: Mouton.

1359 Lilley, S. 1965. *Men, Machines and History: The Story of Tools and Machines in Relation to Social Progress.* 2nd ed London: Lawrence & Wishart.

1360 Lilley, S. 1970. *Technological Progress and the Industrial Revolution 1700-1914.* London:

1361 Lindstrom, L. 1984. Doctor, lawyer, wise man, priest: Big-men and knowledge in Melanesia. *Man* 19: 291-309.

1362 Linton, R. 1936. *The Study of Man.* New York: Appleton Century Crofts.

1363 Linton, R, ed. 1945. *The Science of Man in the World Crisis.* New York: Columbia University Press.

1364 Lopreato, J. 1984. *Human Nature and Biocultural Evolution.* Boston: Unwin Hyman.

1365 Lopreato, J. 1986. Notes on human nature and biocultural evolution. *Revue Européenne des Sciences Sociales* 24: 97-123.

1366 Lopreato, J, M L Maniscalco. 1990. *Evoluzione e Natura Umana.* Soveria Mannelli, CZ: Rubbettino.

1367 Lorenz, K. 1974. *Civilised Man's Eight Deadly Sins.* London: Methuen.

1368 Lumsden, C. 1983. Cultural evolution and the devolution of tabula rasa. *Journal of Social and Biological Structures* 6: 101-114.

1369 Lumsden, C J, E O Wilson. 1985. The relation between biological and cultural evolution. *Journal of Social and Biological Structures* 8: 343-359.

1370 Mackinnon, D W. 1978. *In Search of Human Effectiveness: Identifying and Developing Creativity.* Buffalo, NY: Brearly.

1371 MacNeish, R S. 1964. The origins of the new world civilisation. *Scientific American* 211: 29-37.

1372 Mair, L. 1977. *Primitive Government: A State of Traditional Political Systems in Eastern Africa.* 2nd ed Bloomington: Indiana University Press.

1373 Maittal, S. 1982. *Minds, Markets and Money: Psychological Foundations of Economic Behavior.* New York: Basic Books.

1374 Masters, R D. 1986. Why bureaucracy? In *Biology and Bureaucracy.* Edited by White, E, J Losco. Pp. 149-192. Washington, D.C.: University Press of America.

1375 Mathias, P, J A Davis, eds. 1991. *Innovation and Technology in Europe: From the Eighteenth-Century to the Present.* Oxford: Blackwell.

1376 Maynard, S J, N Warren. 1982. Models of cultural and genetic change. *Evolution* 36: 620-627.

1377 Mazrui, A. 1968. From social Darwinism to current theories of modernization. *World Politics* 21: 69-83.

1378 McNeill, W H. 1963. *The Rise of the West: A History of the Human Community.* Chicago: University of Chicago Press.

1379 McNeill, W H. 1976. *Plagues and Peoples.* New York: Doubleday.

1380 McNeill, W H, R S Adams. 1978. *Human Migrations: Patterns and Policies.* Bloomington: University of Indiana Press.

1381 Merton, R K, ed. 1957. *Bureaucratic Structure and Personality in Social Theory and Social Structure.* New York: Free Press.

1382 Messick, S. 1976. *Individuality in Learning: Implications of Cognitive Styles and Creativity for Human Development.* San Francisco: Jossey-Bass.

1383 Messick, S. 1984. The nature of cognitive styles: Problems and promise in educational practice. *Educational Psychologist* 19: 59-74.

1384 Midgley, D F, G R Dowling. 1978. Innovativeness: The concept and its measurement. *Journal of Consumer Research* 4: 229-242.

1385 Millaart, J. 1975. The origins and development of cities in the Near East. In *Janus: Essays in Ancient and Modern Studies.* Edited by Orlin, L L. Ann Arbor, MI: Center for Coordination of Ancient and Modern Studies.

1386 Mohr, L B. 1971. Organizational technology and organizational structure. *Administrative Science Quarterly* 16: 444-457.

1387 Mokyr, J, ed. 1985. *The Economics of the Industrial Revolution.* Totowa, NJ: Rowman and Allanheld.

1388 Mokyr, J. 1990. *The Lever of Riches: Technological Creativity and Economic Progress.* Oxford: Oxford University Press.

1389 Mokyr, J. 1990. *Twenty Five Centuries of Technological Change: An Historical Survey.* Chur, Switzerland: Harwood.

1390 Mulkay, M S. 1972. *The Social Process of Innovation.* London: Macmillan.

1391 Mulligan, G, W Martin. 1980. Adaptors, innovators and the KAI. *Psychological Reports* 46: 883-892.

1392 Mumford, L. 1966. *The City in History.* Harmondsworth: Penguin.

1393 Mundinger, P C. 1980. Animal cultures and a general theory of cultural evolution. *Ethology and Sociobiology* 1: 183-223.

1394 Murdoch, G P, et al, eds. 1950. *Outline of Cultural Materials.* New Haven: Human Relations Area Files.

1395 Murdock, G P. 1968. The common denominator of cultures. In *Perspectives on Human Evolution I.* Edited by Washburn, S L, P Jay. Pp. 230-257. New York: Holt, Rinehart and Winston.

1396 Naroll, R, R Wirsing. 1976. Borrowing versus migration as selection factors in cultural evolution. *Journal of Conflict Resolution* 20: 187-212.

1397 Naroll, R, W Divale. 1976. Natural selection in cultural evolution: Warfare versus peaceful diffusion. *American Ethnologist* 3: 97-128.

1398 Narr, K. 1956. Early food-producing populations. In *Man's Role in Changing the Face of the Earth.* Edited by Thomas, W. Chicago: University of Chicago Press.

1399 Neel, J V. 1983. Some base lines for human evolution and the genetic implications of recent cultural developments. In *How Humans Adapt: A Biocultural Odyssey.* Edited by Ortner, D J. Pp. 67-93. Washington, D.C.: Smithsonian Institution Press.

1400 Nelson, R R, S Winter. 1982. *An Evolutionary Theory of Economic Change.* Cambridge, MA: Belknap.

1401 Nelson, R R. 1987. *Understanding Technical Change as an Evolutionary Process.* Amsterdam: North Holland.

1402 Netting, R M. 1972. Sacred power and centralization: Aspects of political adaptation in Africa. In *Population Growth.* Edited by Spooner, B. Cambridge: M.I.T. Press.

1403 Nettleship, M A, R Dalegivens, A Nettleship, eds. 1975. *War: Its Causes and Correlates.* The Hauge: Morton.

1404 Newman, L, ed. 1989. *Hunger in History: Food Shortage, Poverty and Deprivation.* Oxford: Blackwell.

1405 North, D C, R P Thomas. 1973. *The Rise of the Western World.* Cambridge: Cambridge University Press.

1406 Nystrom, H. 1979. *Creativity and Innovation.* Chichester: Wiley.

1407 O'Grady, R T. 1986. Historical process, evolutionary explanations, and problems with teleology. *Canadian Journal of Zoology* 64: 1010-1020.

1408 Oakley, K P. 1954. Skill as a human possession. In *A History of Technology.* Edited by Singer, C, E Holmyard. London: Clarendon Press.

1409 Oakley, K P. 1958. *Man the Tool-Maker.* 4th ed London: British Museum.

1410 Ogburn, W F. 1922. *Social Change.* New York: Huebsch.

1411 Olson, M. 1982. *The Rise and Decline of Nations: Economic Growth, Stagflation and Social Rigidities.* New Haven: Yale University Press.

1412 Ortner, D J, ed. 1983. *How Humans Adapt: A Biocultural Odyssey.* Washington D.C.: Smithsonian Institution Press.

1413 Oswalt, W. 1973. *Habitat and Technology.* New York: Holt, Rinehart and Winston.

1414 Oxenham, J. 1980. *Literacy: Reading, Writing and Social Organization.* London: Routledge.

1415 Pacey, A. 1983. *The Culture of Technology.* Cambridge: M.I.T. Press.

1416 Pacey, A. 1990. *Technology in World Civilization: A Thousand-year History.* Oxford: Blackwell.

1417 Parker, J E S. 1978. *The Economics of Innovation: The National and Multinational Enterprise in Technological Change.* 2nd ed London: Longman.

1418 Parsons, T. 1966. *Societies: Evolutionary and Comparative Perspectives.* Englewood Cliffs, NJ: Prentice-Hall.

1419 Persson, K. 1988. *Pre-industrial Economic Growth: Social organization and Technological Progress in Europe.* Oxford: Blackwell.

1420 Pfeiffer, J E. 1982. *The Creative Explosion: An Inquiry into the Origins of Art and Religion.* New York: Harper & Row.

1421 Phillips, C S, Jr. 1971. The revival of cultural evolution in social science theory. *Journal of Developing Areas* 5: 337-370.

1422 Phillipson, D W. 1979. Migration, ethnic differentiation and state formation in the Iron Age of Bantu Africa. In *Space, Hierarchy and Society.* Edited by Burnham, B C, J Kingsbury. Pp. 205-214. Oxford: British Archaeological Reports.

1423 Piddock, S. 1965. The Potlatch system of the Southern Kwakiutl: A new perspective. *Southwestern Journal of Anthropology* 21: 244-264.

1424 Polanyi, K, H Pearson, C Arensberg, eds. 1957. *Trade and Market in the Early Empires.* New York: Free Press.

1425 Price, T D, J A Brown, eds. 1985. *Prehistoric Hunter-Gatherers: The Emergence of Cultural Complexity.* Orlando: Academic Press.

1426 Pulliam, H R, C Dunford. 1980. *Programmed to Learn: An Essay on the Evolution of Culture.* New York: Columbia University Press.

1427 Rae, J. 1967. The invention of invention. In *Technology in Western Civilization. Vol. 1.* Edited by Kranzberg, M, C W Pursell Jr. Pp. 325-336. New York: Oxford University Press.

1428 Rappaport, R A. 1971. The sacred in human evolution. *Annual Review of Ecology and Systematics* 2: 23-44.

1429 Rappoport, A. 1967. Mathematical, volutionary, and psychological approaches to the study of total societies. In *The Study of Total Societies.* Edited by Klausner, S Z. New York: Anchor.

1430 Rasmussen, W D. 1982. The mechanization of agriculture. *Scientific American* 247: 49-61.

1431 Reed, C, ed. 1977. *The Origins of Agriculture.* The Hague: Mouton.

1432 Renfrew, C, et al, eds. 1982. *Theory and Explanation in Archaeology.* New York: Academic Press.

1433 Reynolds, V. 1973. *Ethology of social change.* Edited by Renfrew, C. The Explanation of Cultural Change: Models in Prehistory. London: Duckworth.

1434 Reynolds, V. 1984. The relationship between biological and cultural evolution. *Journal of Human Evolution* 13: 71-79.

1435 Richerson, P J, R Boyd. 1989. A Darwinian theory for the evolution of symbolic cultural traits. In *The Relevance of Culture*. Edited by Freilich, M. South Hadley, MA: Bergen and Garvey.

1436 Richter, M N. 1982. *Technology and Social Complexity*. Albany, NY: SUNY Press.

1437 Rindos, D. 1984. *The Origins of Agriculture: An Evolutionary Perspective*. New York: Academic Press.

1438 Rindos, D. 1986. The evolution of the capacity for culture. *Current Anthropology* 27: 315-332.

1439 Robertson, I T. 1985. Human information-processing strategies and style. *Behaviour and Information Technology* 4: 19-29.

1440 Rogers, E M, F F Shoemaker. 1971. *Communication of Innovations: A Cross-Cultural Approach*. 2nd ed New York: The Free Press.

1441 Rogers, E M. 1983. *Diffusion of Innovations*. 3rd ed New York: The Free Press.

1442 Roper, M K. 1975. Evidence of warfare in the Near East from 10000-4300 B.C. In *Wars, Its Causes and Correlates*. Edited by Nettleship, M A, R Dalegivens, A Nettleship. Pp. 299-343. The Hauge: Mouton.

1443 Roscoe, P B. 1988. From big-men to the state: A processual approach to circumscription theory. *American Behavioral Scientist* 31: 472-483.

1444 Rosenberg, N. 1976. *Perspectives on Technology*. Cambridge: Cambridge University Press.

1445 Rosenberg, N. 1982. *Inside the Black Box: Technology and Economics*. Cambridge: Cambridge University Press.

1446 Rosenberg, N, L E Birdzell. 1986. *How the West Grew Rich: The Economic Transformation of the Industrial World*. New York: Basic Books.

1447 Rostow, W W. 1960. *The Stages of Economic Growth*. Cambridge: Cambridge University Press.

1448 Rostow, W W. 1964. *The Economics of Take-Off into Sustained Growth*. London: Macmillan.

1449 Rostow, W W. 1975. *How it All Began*. New York: McGraw-Hill.

1450 Ruttan, V. 1971. Usher and Schumpeter on invention, innovation and technological change. In *The Economics of Technological Change: Selected Readings*. Edited by Rosenberg, N. Pp. 73-85. Harmonsworth: Penguin.

1451 Sabloff, J A, Lamberg-Karlovsky, eds. 1975. *Ancient Civilization and Trade.* Albuquerque: University of New Mexico Press.

1452 Sahal, D. 1981. *Patterns of Technological Innovation.* Reading, MA: Addison Wesley.

1453 Sahlins, M. 1958. *Social Stratification in Polynesia.* Seattle: University of Washington Press.

1454 Sahlins, M. 1963. Poor man, rich man, big man, chief: Political types in Polynesia and Melanisia. *Comparative Studies in Society and History* 5: 285-303.

1455 Salins, M, E Service. 1960. *Evolution and Culture.* Ann Arbor: University of Michigan Press.

1456 Sanders, W T, J R Parsons, R S Santley. 1979. *The Basis of Mexico: The Ecological Processes in the Evolution of a Civilization.* New York: Academic Press.

1457 Sanderson, S K. 1990. *Social Evolutionism: A Critical History.* Oxford: Blackwell.

1458 Schacht, R M. 1988. Circumscription theory: A critical review. *American Behavioral Scientist* 31: 438-448.

1459 Schelling, T. 1978. *Micromotives and Macrobehavior.* New York: Norton.

1460 Schneider, B. 1985. Organizational behaviour. *Annual Review of Psychology* 36: 573-611.

1461 Schomookler, A B. 1984. *The Parable of the Tribes: The Problem of Power in Social Evolution.* Berkeley: University of California Press.

1462 Schumpeter, J A. 1934. *The Theory of Capitalist Development.* Cambridge: Harvard University Press.

1463 Scott, J P. 1989. *The Evolution of Social Systems.* New York: Gordon and Breach Science Publishers.

1464 Semenov, S A. 1964. *Prehistoric Technology.* London: Cory, Adams.

1465 Service, E R. 1962. *Primitive Social Organization.* New York: Random House.

1466 Service, E R. 1972. *The Origins of the State and Civilization: The Process of Cultural Evolution.* Origins of the State. New York: Norton.

1467 Service, E R. 1978. Classical and Modern Theories of the Origin of Government. In *Origins of the State*. Edited by Service, E R, R Cohen. Washington: Institute for the Study of Human Issues.

1468 Sherratt, A G. 1984. Social evolution: Europe in the later neolithic and copper ages. In *Social Evolution*. Edited by Bintliff, J. Pp. 123-134. Bradford: Bradford University Press.

1469 Sillitoe, P. 1978. Big men and war in New Guinea. *Man* 13: 252-271.

1470 Simmel, G. 1969. The metropolis and mental life. In *Classic Essays on the Culture of Cities*. Pp. 47-60. New York: Appleton-Century-Crofts.

1471 Singer, C, E Holmyard, eds. 1954. *A History of Technology*. Oxford: Clarendon Press.

1472 Sjoberg, G. 1965. The origin and evolution of cities. *Scientific American* 213: 55-63.

1473 Smith, A D. 1988. *The Ethnic Origins of Nations*. Oxford: Blackwell.

1474 Spengler, O. 1932. *Man and Technics*. London: Allen and Unwin.

1475 Spicer, E H. 1971. Persistent cultural systems: A comparative study of identity systems that can adapt to contrasting environments. *Science* 174: 795-800.

1476 Spielman, K A. 1986. Interdependence among egalitarian societies. *Journal of Anthropological Archaeology* 5: 279-312.

1477 Spindler, G D. 1973. The transmission of culture. In *Culture in Process*. Edited by Beals, A R, G D Spindler, L Spindler. New York: Holt, Rinehart & Winston.

1478 Spindler, L L. 1977. *Culture Change and Modernization*. Prospect Heights, IL: Waveland Press.

1479 Spuhler, J N, ed. 1959. *The Evolution of Man's Capacity for Culture*. Detroit: Wayne State University Press.

1480 Stavrianos, L S. 1975. *The World Since 1500: A Global History*. Englewoood Cliffs, NJ: Prentice-Hall.

1481 Steward, J H. 1949. Cultural causality and law: A trial formulation of the development of early civilizations. *American Anthropologist* 51: 1-27.

1482 Steward, J H. 1952. Evolution and process. In *Anthropology Today: An Encycloopedic Inventory*. Edited by Kroeber, A L. Pp. 313-327. Chicago: University of Chicago Press.

1483 Steward, J. 1955. *Theory of Culture Change: The Methodology of Multilinear Evolution*. Urbana: University of Illinois Press.

1484 Steward, J H, D B Shimkin. 1962. Some mechanisms of sociocultural evolution. In *Evolution and Man's Progress*. Edited by Hoagland, H, R W Burhoe. Pp. 67-87. New York: Columbia University Press.

1485 Stoneman, P. 1983. *The Economic Analysis of Technological Change*. Oxford: Oxford University Press.

1486 Streufert, S, R W Swezey. 1986. *Complexity, Managers and Organisations*. New York: Academic Press.

1487 Thoden van Velsen, H. 1973. Robinson Crusoe and Friday: Strength and weakness of the big man paradigm. *Man* 8: 592-612.

1488 Thomas, W L, ed. 1956. *Man's Role in Changing the Face of the Earth*. Chicago: University of Chicago Press.

1489 Todd, E. 1985. *The Explanation of Ideology: Family Structures and Social Systems*. Oxford: Blackwell.

1490 Todd, E. 1987. *The Causes of Progress: Culture, Authority and Change*. Oxford: Blackwell.

1491 Tylor, E B. 1865. *Researches into the Early History of Mankind and the Development of Civilization*. London: Murray.

1492 Tylor, E B. 1899. *Anthropology: An Introduction to the Study of Man and Civilization*. London: Appleton.

1493 Upham, S, ed. 1990. *The Evolution of Political Systems: Sociopolitics in Small-Scale Sedentary Societies*. New York: Cambridge University Press.

1494 Van Crefeld, M. 1989. *Technology and War*. New York: Free Press.

1495 van der Dennen, J. 1990. Origin and evolution of 'primitive' warfare. In *Sociobiology and Conflict: Evolutionary perspectives on Competition, Cooperation, Violence and Warfare*. Edited by van der Dennen, J, V Falger. London: Chapman & Hall.

1496 van der Leeuw, S E. 1981. Information flows, flow structures, and the explanation of change in human institutions. In *Archaeological Approaches to the Study of Complexity*. Edited by van der Leeuw, S E. Pp. 230-312. Amsterdam: University of Amsterdam, Albert Egges van Giffen Institute for Prehistory.

1497 van der Leeuw, S, R Torrence, eds. 1989. *What's New?: A Closer Look at the Process of Innovation.* London: Unwin Hyman.

1498 van Parijs, P. 1981. *Evolutionary Explanation in the Social Sciences: An Emerging paradigm.* Totowa, NJ: Rowman and Little-field.

1499 Volti, R. 1988. *Society and Technological Change.* New York: St. Martin's Press.

1500 Webb, M C. 1985. The state of the art on state origins? *Reviews in Anthropology* 11: 170-281.

1501 Webb, M C. 1988. The first states: How—or in what sense—did "circumscription" circumscribe? *American Behavioral Scientist* 31: 449-458.

1502 Webster, D. 1975. Warfare and the evolution of the state: A reconsideration. *American Antiquity* 40: 464-470.

1503 White, L. 1949. *The Science of Culture.* New York: Farrar, Strauss.

1504 White, L. 1959. *The Evolution of Culture.* New York: McGraw-Hill.

1505 White, L. 1962. *Medieval Technology and Social Change.* Oxford: Oxford University Press.

1506 White, L. 1972. The expansion of technology, 500-1500. In *The Fontana Economic History of Europe, Vol 1, The Middle Ages.* Edited by Cipolla, C M. Pp. 143-174. London: Collins.

1507 White, L. 1978. *Medieval Religion and Technology.* Berkeley, CA: University of California Press.

1508 Whitehouse, R. 1977. *The First Cities.* Oxford: Phaidon.

1509 Wiet, G, V Elisseeff, P Wolff, J Navdov. 1975. *The Great Medieval Civilizations.* History of Mankind: Cultural and Scientific Development. London: Allen & Unwin.

1510 Wilkinson, R. 1973. *Poverty and Progress: An Ecological Perspective on Economic Development.* New York: Praeger.

1511 Wilson, D J. 1983. The origins and development of complex pre-Hispanic society in the lower Santa Valley, Peru: Implications for theories of state origins. *Journal of Anthropological Archaeology* 2: 209-276.

1512 Winner, L. 1977. *Autonomous Technology: Technics Out of Control as a Theme in Political Thought.* Cambridge: M.I.T. Press.

1513 Wittfogel, K. 1957. *Oriental Despotism: A Comparative Study of Total Power.* New Haven, CT: Yale University Press.

1514 Wright, H T, G A Johnson. 1975. Population, exchange, and early state formation in southwestern Iran. *American Anthropologist* 77: 267-289.

1515 Wright, H T. 1977. Recent research on the origin of state. *Annual Review of Anthropology* 6: 379-397.

1516 Wrigley, E A. 1988. *People, Cities and Wealth: The Transformation of Traditional Society.* Oxford: Blackwell.

1517 Wyatt, G. 1986. *The Economics of Invention: A Study of the Determinants of Inventive Activity.* New York: St. Martin's Press.

1518 Zinsser, H. 1935. *Rats, Lice, and History.* London: Routledge.

# 5

# Sociobiology

1519 Abernathy, V. 1978. Female hierarchy: An evolutionary perspective. In *Female Hierarchies*. Edited by Tiger, L, T Fowler. Pp. 123-134. Chicago: Beresford Book Service.

1520 Alexander, R D. 1974. Evolution of social behavior. *Annual Review of Ecological Systems* 5: 325-383.

1521 Alexander, R D. 1975. The search for a general theory of behavior. *Behavioral Science* 20: 77-100.

1522 Alexander, R D. 1978. Natural selection and societal laws. In *Morals, Science and Society*. Edited by Engelhardt, T, D Callahan. Hastings-on-Hudson, N.Y.: The Hastings Center.

1523 Alexander, R D, G Borgia. 1978. Group selection, altruism, and the levels of organization of life. *Annual Review of Ecology and Systematics* 9: 449-474.

1524 Alexander, R D. 1979. *Darwinism and Human Affairs*. Seattle: University of Washington Press.

1525 Alexander, R D, et al. 1979. Sexual dimorphisms and breeding systems in pinnipeds, ungulates, primates, and humans. In *Evolutionary Biology and Human Social Behavior*. Edited by Chagnon, N, W Irons. Pp. 402-435. North Scituate, MA: Duxbury.

1526 Alexander, R D. 1986. Ostracism and indirect reciprocity: The reproductive significance of humor. *Ethology and Sociobiology* 7: 253-270.

1527 Alexander, R D. 1987. *The Biology of Moral Systems*. Hawthorne, N.Y.: Aldine.

1528 Alexander, R D. 1990. Epigenetic rules and Darwinian algorithms: The adaptive study of learning and development. *Ethology and Sociobiology* 11: 241-303.

1529 Altmann, J. 1979. Age-cohorts as paternal sibships. *Behavioral Ecology and Sociobiology* 6: 161-169.

1530 Anderton, D, R Emigh. 1989. Polygynous fertility: Sexual competition versus progeny. *American Journal of Sociology* 94: 832-855.

1531 Aoki, K. 1983. A quantitative genetic model of reciprocal altruism: A condition for group selection to prevail. *Proceedings of the National Academy of Sciences, U.S.A.* 80: 4065-4068.

1532 Aoki, K. 1984. A quantitative genetic model of two-policy games between relatives. *Journal of Theoretical Biology* 109: 111-126.

1533 Aoki, K, K Nozawa. 1984. Average coefficient of relationship within troops of the Japanese monkey and other primate species with reference to the possibility of group selection. *Primates* 25: 171-184.

1534 Aoki, K. 1986. A stochastic model of gene-culture coevolution suggested by the "culture historical hypothesis" for the evolution of adult lactose absorption in humans. *Proceedings of the National Academy of Sciences, U.S.A.* 83: 2929-2933.

1535 Aoki, K. 1987. Gene-culture waves of advance. *Journal of Mathematical Biology* 25: 453-464.

1536 Aoki, K, M W Feldman. 1987. Toward a theory for the evolution of cultural communication: Coevolution of signal transmission and reception. *Proceedings of the National Academy of Sciences, U.S.A.* 84: 7164-7168.

1537 Aoki, K, M W Feldman. 1989. Pleiotropy and preadaptation in the evolution of human language capacity. *Theoretical Population Biology* 35: 181-194.

1538 Aoki, K. 1990. A shifting balance type model for the origin of cultural transmission. In *Population Biology of Genes and Molecules*. Edited by Takahata, N, J F Crow. Pp. 123-137. Tokyo: Baifukan.

1539 Archer, J. 1986. Animal sociobiology and comparative psychology: A review. *Current Psychological Research and Reviews* 5: 48-61.

1540 Archer, J. 1991. Human sociobiology: Basic concepts and limitations. *Journal of Social Issues* 47: 11-26.

1541 Axelrod, R. 1981. The emergence of cooperation among egoists. *American Political Science Review* 75: 306-318.

1542 Axelrod, R. 1984. *The Evolution of Cooperation.* New York: Basic Books.

1543 Axelrod, R. 1986. An evolutionary approach to norms. *American Political Science Review* 80: 1095-1111.

1544 Axelrod, R. 1987. Laws of life: How standards of behavior evolve. *The Sciences* 17: 44-51.

1545 Bachmann, C, H Kummer. 1980. Male assessment of female choice in hamadryas baboons. *Behavioral Ecology and Sociobiology* 6: 315-321.

1546 Badcock, C R. 1986. *The Problem of Altruism: Freudian-Darwinian Solutions.* Oxford: Blackwell.

1547 Baer, D, D L McEachron. 1982. A review of selected sociobiological principles: Application to hominid evolution. I. Development of group social structure. *Journal of Social and Biological Structures* 5: 69-90.

1548 Barash, D. 1975. Marmot alarm calling and the question of altruistic behavior. *American Midland Naturalist* 94: 468-470.

1549 Barash, D. 1980. Human reproductive strategies: A sociobiological overview. In *The Evolution of Social Behavior.* Edited by Lockard, J S. Pp. 143-164. New York: Elsevier.

1550 Barash, D. 1982. *Sociobiology and Behavior.* 2nd ed. New York: Elsevier.

1551 Barash, D. 1986. *The Hare and the Tortoise: Culture, Biology and Human Nature.* London: Penguin.

1552 Barkow, J. 1984. The distance between genes and culture. *Journal of Anthropological Research* 40: 367-379.

1553 Barkow, J. 1989. The elastic between genes and culture. *Ethology and Sociobiology* 10: 111-129.

1554 Barkow, J H. 1989. *Darwin, Sex, and Status: Biological Approaches to Mind and Culture.* Toronto: University of Toronto Press.

1555 Barkow, J, L Cosmides, J Tooby. 1990. *The Adapted Mind: Evolutionary Psychology and the Generation of Culture.* New York: Oxford University Press.

1556 Barlow, G W, J Silverberg, eds. 1980. *Sociobiology: Beyond Nature/Nurture? Reports, Definitions and Debate. AAAS Selected Symposium 35.* Boulder: Westview Press.

1557 Barlow, G W. 1991. Nature-nurture and the debates surrounding ethology and sociobiology. *American Zoologist* 31: 286-296.

1558 Beall, C, M Goldstein. 1981. Tibetan fraternal polyandry: A test of sociobiology theory. *American Anthropologist* 83: 5-12.

1559 Becker, G. 1981. *A Treatise on the Family.* Cambridge: Harvard University Press.

1560 Beckstrom, J H. 1985. *Sociobiology and the Law: The Biology of Altruism in the Courtroom of the Future.* Chicago: University of Illinois Press.

1561 Beckstrom, J H. 1987. The use of legal opinions to test sociobiological theory: Contract law regarding reciprocal relationships in a household. *Ethology and Sociobiology* 8: 221-229.

1562 Bernardi, B. 1986. *Age Class Systems: Social Institutions and Polities Based on Age.* Cambridge: Cambridge University Press.

1563 Bernstein, H, H C Byerly, F A Hopf, R E Michod. 1984. Origin of sex. *Journal of Theoretical Biology* 110: 323-351.

1564 Bertram, B C R. 1976. Kin selection in lions and in evolution. In *Growing Points in Ethnology.* Edited by Bateson, P P G, R A Hinde. Pp. 281-301. London: Cambridge University Press.

1565 Bertram, B C R. 1978. Living in groups: Predators and prey. In *Behavioral Ecology: An Evolutionary Approach.* Edited by Davis, N B, J R Krebs. Oxford: Blackwell.

1566 Bertram, B C R, et al., eds. 1981. *Current Problems in Sociobiology.* Cambridge: Cambridge University Press.

1567 Betzig, L. 1986. *Despotism and Differential Reproduction: A Darwinian View of History.* Chicago: Aldine.

1568 Betzig, L. 1986. Vaulting, leaping, skipping, and trudging ambition. *Quarterly Review of Biology* 61: 517-521.

1569 Betzig, L, P W Turke. 1986. Parental investment by sex on Ifaluk. *Ethology and Sociobiology* 7: 29-38.

1570 Betzig, L L, M Borgerhoff Mulder, P Turke, eds. 1988. *Human Reproductive Behavior: A Darwinian Perspective.* Cambridge: Cambridge University Press.

1571 Bischoff, N. 1972. Biological foundations of the incest taboo. *Social Science Information* 6: 7-63.

1572 Blaustein, A R, et al. 1991. Kin recognition in veretbrates: What do we really know about adaptive value? *Animal Behaviour* 41: 1079-1083.

1573 Blurton Jones, N. 1986. Bushman birth spacing: A test for optimal interbirth intervals. *Ethology and Sociobiology* 7: 91-106.

1574 Blurton Jones, N. 1987. Bushman birth spacing: Direct tests of some simple predictions. *Ethology and Sociobiology* 8: 183-204.

1575 Blurton Jones, N, K Hawkes, J F O'Connell. 1989. Modeling and measuring costs of children in two foraging societies. In *Comparative*

*Socioecology of Mammals and Man.* Edited by Standen, V, R Foley. London: Blackwell.

1576 Blurton Jones, N. 1990. Three sensible paradigms for research on evolution and human behavior. *Ethology and Sociobiology* 11: 353-360.

1577 Bonfield, L. 1986. Normative rules and property transmission: Reflections on the link between marriage and inheritance in early modern England. In *The World We Have Gained: Histories of Population and Social Structure.* Edited by Bonfield, L, R M Smith, K Wrightson. Pp. 155-176. Oxford: Blackwell.

1578 Boone, J L. 1986. Parental investment and elite family structure in preindustrial states: A case study of late medieval-early modern Portuguese genealogies. *American Anthropologist* 88: 859-878.

1579 Boone, J L. 1987. Parental investment, social subordination, and population processes among the 15th and 16th century Portuguese nobility. In *Human Reproductive Behavior: A Darwinian Perspective.* Edited by Betzig, L L, M Borgerhoff Mulder, P W Turke. Cambridge: Cambridge University Press.

1580 Borgerhoff Mulder, M. 1985. Polygyny threshold: A kipsigis case study. *National Geographic Research Reports* 21: 33-39.

1581 Borgerhoff Mulder, M, T M Caro. 1985. The use of quantitative observational techniques in anthropology. *Current Anthropology* 26: 323-335.

1582 Borgerhoff Mulder, M. 1987. Reproductive success in three Kipsigis cohorts. In *Reproductive Success.* Edited by Clutton-Brock, T H. Chicago: University of Chicago Press.

1583 Borgerhoff Mulder, M. 1988. Is the polygyny threshold model relevant to humans? Kipsigis evidence. In *Mating Patterns.* Edited by Boyce, C G N, A J Mascie-Taylor. Pp. 209-230. Cambridge: Cambridge University Press.

1584 Borgerhoff Mulder, M. 1988. Kipsigis brideweath payments. In *Human Reproductive Behavior.* Edited by Betzig, L L, M Borgerhoff Mulder, P Turke. Pp. 65-82. Cambridge: Cambridge University Press.

1585 Borgerhoff Mulder, M. 1989. Early maturing Kipsigis women have higher reproductive success than later maturing women, and cost more to marry. *Behavioral Ecology and Sociobiology* 24: 145-153.

1586 Borgerhoff Mulder, M. 1992. Womens strategies in polygamous marriages: Kipsigis, Datoga, and other east African cases. *Human Nature* 3: 45-70.

1587 Boulton, M J. 1991. A comparison of structural and contextual features of middle school children's playful and aggressive fighting. *Ethology and Sociobiology* 12: 119-146.

1588 Boyd, R, P J Richerson. 1980. Sociobiology, culture and economic theory. *Journal of Economic Behavior and Organization* 1: 97-121.

1589 Boyd, R, P J Richerson. 1981. Culture, biology and the evolution of variation between human groups. In *Science and the Question of Human Inequality. AAAS Selected Symposium 58.* Edited by Collins, M, I Wainer, T Bremmer. Pp. 99-152. Boulder.: Westview Press.

1590 Boyd, R, P J Richerson. 1982. Cultural transmission and the evolution of cooperative behavior. *Human Ecology* 10: 325-351.

1591 Boyd, R, P J Richerson. 1983. Why is culture adaptive? *Quarterly Review of Biology* 58: 209-214.

1592 Boyd, R, J P Lorberbaum. 1987. No pure strategy is evolutionarily stable in the repeated Prisoner's Dilemma game. *Nature* 327: 58.

1593 Bradbury, D W, M B Anderson, eds. 1987. *Sexual Selection: Testing the Alternatives.* Chichester: Wiley.

1594 Bridgeman, D L, ed. 1983. *The Nature of Prosocial Development: Interdisciplinary Theories and Strategies.* New York: Academic Press.

1595 Brodsky, V. 1986. Widows in late Elizabethan London: Remarriage, economic opportunity and family orientations. In *The World We Have Gained: Histories of Population and Social Structure.* Edited by Bonfield, L, R M Smith, K Wrightson. Pp. 122-154. Oxford: Blackwell.

1596 Bronfenbrenner, U. 1979. *The Ecology of Human Nature: Experiments by Nature and Design.* Cambridge: Harvard University Press.

1597 Brooks, A, D E Gelburd, J E Yellen. 1984. Food production and culture change among the !Kung San. In *From Hunters to Farmers: Causes and Consequences of Food Production in Africa.* Edited by Clark, J D, S Brandt. Berkeley: University of California Press.

1598 Burley, N. 1977. Parental investment, mate choice, and mate quality. *Proceedings of the National Academy of Sciences (USA)* 74: 3476-3479.

1599 Burley, N. 1979. The evolution of concealed ovulation. *American Naturalist* 14: 835-858.

1600 Burley, N. 1981. Mate choice by multiple criteria in a monogamous species. *American Naturalist* 117: 515-528.

1601 Burley, N. 1981. The evolution of sexual indistinguishability. In *Natural Selection and Social Behavior: Recent Research and New Theory.* Edited by Alexander, R D, D W Tinkle. Pp. 121-137. New York: Chiron Press.

1602 Buss, D M, M Barnes. 1986. Preferences in human mate selection. *Journal of Personality and Social Psychology* 50: 559-570.

1603 Buss, D. 1989. Sex differences in human mate preferences: Evolutionary hypotheses tested in 37 cultures. *Behavioral and Brain Sciences* 12: 1-49.

1604 Bygott, D J, B C R Bertram, J P Hanby. 1979. Male lions in large coalitions gain reproductive advantages. *Nature* 282: 839-841.

1605 Cahpis, B. 1983. Reproductive activity in relation to male dominance and the likelihood of ovulation in rhesus monkeys. *Behavioral Ecology and Sociobiology* 12: 215-228.

1606 Campbell, D T. 1975. On the conflicts between biological and social evolution and between psychology and moral tradition. *American Psychologist* 30: 1103-1126.

1607 Campbell, J, J Brown, eds. 1990. *Sanctions and Sanctuary: Cross Cultural Perspectives on Wife Abuse.* Boulder.: Westview Press.

1608 Caro, T M, M B Mulder. 1987. The problem of adaptation in the study of human behavior. *Ethology and Sociobiology* 8: 61-72.

1609 Cattell, R. 1982. Inflation and business cycles from the standpoint of psychology and sociobiology. *Journal of Social, Political and Economic Studies* 7: 35-54.

1610 Cela Conde, C J. 1987. *On Genes, Gods, and Tyrants: The Biological Causation of Morality.* Boston: Reidel.

1611 Chagnon, N, R B Hornes. 1979. Protein deficiency and tribal warfare in Amazonia: New data. *Science* 203: 910-913.

1612 Chagnon, N A. 1979. Is reproductive success equal in egalitarian societies? In *Evolutionary Biology and Human Social Behavior: An Anthropological Perspective.* North Scituate, MA: Duxbury.

1613 Chagnon, N A. 1980. Kin selection theory, kinship, marriage and fitness among the Yanomamo Indians. In *Sociobiology: Beyond Nature/Nurture?* Edited by Barlow, G, J Silverberg. Boulder: Westview Press.

1614 Chagnon, N A. 1980. Mate competition, favouring close kin, and village fissioning among the Yanomama indians. In *Evolutionary*

*Biology and Human Social Behavior.* Edited by Chagnon, N A, W Irons. Pp. 86-131. North Scituate, MA.: Duxbury.

1615 Chagnon, N A. 1982. Sociodemographic attributes of nepotism in tribal populations: Man the rule breaker. In *Current Problems in Sociobiology.* Edited by Group, K C S. Cambridge: Cambridge University Press.

1616 Chagnon, N A. 1988. Life histories, blood revenge, and warfare in a tribal society. *Science* 239: 985-992.

1617 Chamie, J. 1981. *Religion and Fertility: Arab-Christian-Muslim Differentials.* Cambridge: Cambridge University Press.

1618 Chapais, B. 1983. Reproductive activity in relation to male dominance and the likelihood of ovulation in rhesus monkeys. *Behavioral Ecology and Sociobiology* 12: 215-228.

1619 Chapais, B. 1983. Male dominance and reproductive activity in rhesus monkeys. In *Primate Social Relationships.* Edited by Hinde, R A. Pp. 267-271. Oxford: Blackwell.

1620 Chapais, B. 1992. The role of alliances in social inheritance of rank among female primates. In *Coalitions and Alliances in Humans and Other Animals.* Edited by Harcourt, A H, F B M de Waal. Pp. 29-59. New York: Oxford University Press.

1621 Charnov, E L. 1982. *Theory of Sex Allocation.* Princeton: Princeton University Press.

1622 Chen, L, et al. 1981. Sex bias and the family allocations of food and health care in rural Bangladesh. *Population and Development Review* 7: 55-70.

1623 Cheney, D L. 1977. The acquisition of rank and the development of reciprocal alliances among free ranging immature baboons. *Behavioral Ecology and Sociobiolology* 2: 303-318.

1624 Cheney, D L, R M Seyfarth. 1986. The recognition of social alliances by vervet monkeys. *Animal Behavior* 34: 1722-1731.

1625 Chepko-Sade, B D, T J Oliver. 1979. Coefficient of genetic relationship and the probability of intragenealogical fission in macaca mulatta. *Behavioral Ecology and Sociobiolology* 5: 263-278.

1626 Chism, J, T Rowell, D Olson. 1984. Life history patterns of female patas monkeys. In *Female Primates: Studies by Women Primatologists.* Edited by Small, M. Pp. 175-190. New York: Alan R. Liss.

1627 Clutton-Brock, T H, P H Harvey, B Rudder. 1977. Sexual dimorphism, socionomic sex ratio and body weight in primates. *Nature* 269: 797-800.

1628 Clutton-Brock, T H, P H Harvey, eds. 1978. *Readings in Sociobiology*. San Francisco: Freeman.

1629 Clutton-Brock, T H, S D Albon. 1982. Parental investment in male and female offspring in mammals. In *Current Problems in Sociobiology*. Edited by Group, K C S. Pp. 223-248. Cambridge: Cambridge University Press.

1630 Clutton-Brock, T H, S D Albon, F E Guinness. 1982. Competition between female relatives in a matrilocal mammal. *Nature* 300: 178-180.

1631 Clutton-Brock, T H. 1988. Reproductive success, selection and adaptation. In *Reproductive Success: Studies of Individual Variation*. Edited by Clutton-Brock, T H. Chicago: University of Chicago Press.

1632 Coleman, D A. 1983. The demography of ethnic minorities. *Journal of Biosocial Science* Supplement No. 8: 43-90.

1633 Connor, R C, K S Norris. 1982. Are dolphins and whales reciprocal altruists? *American Naturalist* 119: 358-374.

1634 Cosmides, L, J Tooby. 1989. Evolutionary psychology and the generation of culture, Part II. Case study: A computational theory of social exchange. *Ethology and Sociobiology* 10: 51-97.

1635 Cowlishaw, G, R I M Dunbar. 1991. Dominance rank and mating success in male primates. *Animal Behaviour* 41: 1045-1056.

1636 Cox, C R, B J LeBoeuf. 1977. Female incitation of male competition: A mechanism in sexual selection. *American Naturalist* 111: 317-335.

1637 Crawford, C, B Galdikas. 1986. Rape in non-human animals: An evolutionary perspective. *Canadian Psychology* 27: 215-230.

1638 Crawford, C. 1987. Sociobiology: Of what value to psychology? In *Sociobiology and Psychology: Ideas, Issues and Applications*. Edited by Crawford, C B, M Smith, D Krebs. Hillsdale, NJ: Erlbaum.

1639 Crawford, C, M Smith, D Krebs, eds. 1987. *Sociobiology and Psychology: Ideas, Issues and Applications*. Hillsdale, NJ: Erlbaum.

1640 Crawford, C B, B E Salter, K L Jang. 1989. Human grief: Is its intensity related to the reproductive value of the deceased? *Ethology and Sociobiology* 10: 297-308.

1641 Cronk, L. 1988. Spontaneous order analysis and anthropology. *Cultural Dynamics* 1: 282-308.

1642 Cronk, L. 1989. From hunters to herders: Subsistence change as a reproductive strategy among the Mukugodo. *Current Anthropology* 30: 224-34.

1643 Cronk, L. 1989. Low socioeconomic status and female-biased parental investment: The Mukugodo example. *American Anthropologist* 91: 414-29.

1644 Crook, J H, S J Crook. 1988. Tibetan polyandry: Problems of adaptation and fitness. In *Human Reproductive Behaviour: A Darwinian Perspective.* Edited by Betzig, L L, M Borgerhoff Mulder, P W Turke. Cambridge: Cambridge University Press.

1645 Daly, M, M Wilson. 1982. Whom are newborn babies said to resemble? *Ethnology and Sociobiology* 3: 69-78.

1646 Daly, M, M Wilson. 1983. *Sex, Evolution, and Behavior.* 2nd ed Boston: Willard Grant Press.

1647 Daly, M, M Wilson. 1988. *Homicide.* New York: Aldine de Gruyter.

1648 Daniels, D. 1983. The evolution of concealed ovulation and self-deception. *Ethology and Sociobiology* 4: 69-87.

1649 Davey, G C, ed. 1983. *Animal Models of Human Behaviour.* Chichester: Wiley.

1650 Davies, N B, A I Houston. 1984. Territory economics. In *Behavioural Ecology: An Evolutionary Approach.* Edited by Krebs, J R, N B Davies. Pp. 148-69. Oxford: Blackwell Scientific.

1651 Davis, B D. 1980. The importance of human individuality for sociobiology. *Zygon* 15: 275-293.

1652 Davis, M. 1983. *Rank and Rivalry: The Politics of Inequality in Rural West Bengal.* Cambridge: Cambridge University Press.

1653 de Montellano, B R O. 1978. Aztec cannibalism: An ecological necessity? *Science* 200: 611-617.

1654 de Waal, F. 1989. *Peacemaking Among Primates.* Cambridge: Harvard University Press.

1655 de Waal, F. 1991. The chimpanzee's sense of social regularity and its relation to the human sense of justice. *American Behavioral Scientist* 34: 335-349.

1656 deCatanzaro, D. 1981. *Suicide and Self-damaging Behavior : A Sociobiological Perspective.* New York: Academic.

1657 Dewsbury, D A. 1981. An exercise in the prediction of monogamy in the field from laboratory data on 42 species of muroid rodents. *Biologist* 63: 138-162.

1658 Dewsbury, D A. 1982. Ejaculate cost and male choice. *American Naturalist* 119: 601-610.

1659 Dewsbury, D A. 1982. Dominance, rank, copulatory behavior, and differential reproduction. *Quarterly Review of Biology* 57: 135-159.

1660 Dickemann, M. 1981. Paternal confidence and dowry competition: A biocultural analysis of purdah. In *Natural Selection and Social Behavior: Recent Research and New Theory*. Edited by Alexander, R D, D Twinkle. Pp. 417-438. New York: Chiron Press.

1661 Dickermann, M. 1979. The ecology of mating systems in hypergynous dowry societies. *Social Science Information* 18: 163-195.

1662 Divale, W T, M Harris. 1976. Population, warfare and the male supremacy complex. *American Anthropologist* 78: 521-538.

1663 Dolhinow, P, M G DeMay. 1982. Adoption: The importance of infant choice. *Journal of Human Evolution* 11: 391-420.

1664 Doolittle, W F, C Sapienza. 1980. Selfish genes, the phenotype paradigm and genome evolution. *Nature* 284: 601-603.

1665 Doust, L L, J L Doust. 1985. Gender chauvinism and the division of labor in humans. *Perspectives in Biology and Medicine* 28: 526-542.

1666 Dow, J. 1984. The genetic basis for affinal cooperation. *American Ethnologist* 11: 380-383.

1667 Draper, P. 1975. !Kung women: Contrasts in sexual egalitarianism in the foraging and sedentary contexts. In *Toward an Anthropology of Women*. Edited by Reiter, R. New York: Monthly Review.

1668 Draper, P, H Harpending. 1982. Father absence and reproductive strategy: An evolutionary perspective. *Journal of Anthropological Research* 38: 255-273.

1669 Duck, S, D Miell. 1983. Mate choice in humans as an interpersonal process. In *Mate Choice*. Edited by Bateson, P. Cambridge: Cambridge University Press.

1670 Dumont, L. 1983. *Affinity as a Value: Marriage Alliance in South India*. London: University of Chicago Press.

1671 Dunbar, R I M. 1984. *Reproductive Decisions: An Economic Analysis of Gelada Baboon Social Strategies*. Princeton: Princeton University Press.

1672 Dunbar, R I M. 1987. Sociobiological explanations and the evolution of ethnocentrism. In *The Sociobiology of Ethnocentrism*. Edited by Reynolds, V, V Falger, I Vine. Beckenham: Croom Helm.

1673 Dupre, J. 1987. Evolution of a mesh between principles of the mind and regularities of the world. In *The Latest on the Best: Essays on Evolution and Optimality*. Edited by Dupre, J. Cambridge: M.I.T. Press.

1674 Dupre, J. 1987. *The Latest on the Best: Essays on Evolution and Optimality*. Cambridge: M.I.T. Press.

1675 Durham, W H. 1976. Resource competition and human aggression. Pt.1 A review of primitive war. *Quarterly Review of Biology* 51: 385-415.

1676 Durham, W H. 1983. Coevolution and law: The New Yam Festivals of West Africa. In *Law, Biology, and Culture: The Evolution of Law*. Edited by Gruter, M, P Bohannon. Santa Barbara: Ross-Erickson.

1677 Durham, W H. 1987. *Coevolution: Genes, Culture, and Human Diversity*. Stanford: Stanford University Press.

1678 Dwyer, P. 1974. The price of protein: Five hundred hours of hunting in the New Guinea Highlands. *Oceania 44* 44: 278-293.

1679 Dyke, B, P G Rivière. 1988. The effect of preference rules on marriage patterns. In *Human Mating Patterns*. Edited by Mascie-Taylor, C G N, A J Boyce. Pp. 183-190. Cambridge: Cambridge University Press.

1680 Dyson, T, M Moore. 1983. On kinship structure, female autonomy, and demographic behaviour in India. *Population and Development Review* 9: 35-60.

1681 Eberhard, M J. 1975. The evolution of social behavior by kin selection. *Quarterly Review of Biology* 50: 1-33.

1682 Eisenberg, J F, N A Muckenhirn, R Rudin. 1972. The relation between ecology and social structure in primates. *Science* 176: 863-874.

1683 Ellis, L. 1985. On the rudiments of possession and property. *Social Science Information* 24: 113-144.

1684 Ellis, L. 1986. Evolution and the nonlegal equivalents of aggressive criminal behavior. *Aggressive Behavior* 12: 57-71.

1685 Emlen, S T. 1980. Ecological determinism and sociobiology. In *Sociobiology: Beyond Nature/Nurture?* Edited by Barlow, G W, J Silverberg. Pp. 125-50. Boulder.: Westview Press.

1686 Emlen, S T. 1982. The evolution of helping. I. An ecological constraints model. *American Naturalist* 119: 29-39.

1687 Emlen, S T. 1982. The evolution of helping. II. The role of behavioral conflict. *American Naturalist* 119: 40-53.

1688 Endler, J, T McLellan. 1988. The processes of evolution: Towards a newer synthesis. *Annual Review of Ecology and Systematics* 19: 395-421.

1689 Enquist, M, O Liemar. 1983. Evolution of fighting behaviour: Decision rules and assessment of relative strength. *Journal of Theoretical Biology* 102: 387-410.

1690 Enquist, M. 1985. Communication during aggressive interactions with particular reference to variation in choice of behaviour. *Animal Behaviour* 33: 1152-61.

1691 Erwin, J, G Mitchell, eds. 1985. *Comparative Primate Biology: Behavior and Ecology.* New York: Alan R. Liss.

1692 Espenshade, R J. 1984. *Investing in Children: New Estimates of Parental Expenditures.* N.p.: Urban Institute Press.

1693 Essock-Vitale, S. 1984. The reproductive success of wealthy Americans. *Ethology and Sociobiology* 5: 45-49.

1694 Etkin, W. 1979. The expendable male animal, with a sociobiological interpretation. *Perspectives in Biology and Medicine* 22: 559-564.

1695 Etkin, W. 1981. A biological critique of sociobiological theory. In *Sociobiology and Politics.* Edited by White, E. Pp. 45-97. Boston: Heath.

1696 Falger, V S E, et al., eds. 1990. *The Sociobiology of Conflict.* London: Chapman Hall.

1697 Faux, S, H Miller. 1984. Evolutionary speculations on the oligarchic development of Mormon polygyny. *Ethology and Sociobiology* 5: 15-31.

1698 Fedigan, L M. 1983. Dominance and reproductive success in primates. *Yearbook of Physical Anthropology* 26: 91-129.

1699 Feldman, M, L L Cavalli-Sforza. 1982. Darwinian selection and behavioral evolution. In *The Fundamental Connection Between Nature and Nurture.* Edited by Grove, W R, G R Carpenter. Pp. 31-39. Lexington, MA.: Heath.

1700 Field, T. 1979. Interaction patterns of preterm and term infants. In *Infants Born at Risk.* Edited by Field, T, A Sostek, S Goldberg, H Shuman. New York: Spectrum.

1701 Field, T, A Sostek, S Goldberg, H Shuman, eds. 1979. *Infants born at risk.* New York: Spectrum.

1702 Field, T. 1980. Interactions of high-risk infants: Quantitative and qualitative differences. In *Current Perspectives on Psychosocial Risks during Pregnancy and Early Infancy.* Edited by Sawin, D, et al. New York: Bruner/Mazel.

1703 Finder, J. 1987. Biological bases of prejudice. *International Political Science Review* 8: 183-192.

1704 Finder, J. 1987. Biological bases of social prejudices. In *The Sociobiology of Ethnocentrism.* Beckenham: Croom Helm.

1705 Flinn, M. 1986. Correlates of reproductive success in a Caribbean village. *Human Ecology* 14: 225-243.

1706 Freedman, D G. 1974. *Human Infancy: An Evolutionary Perspective.* Hillsdale, N.J.: Erlbaum.

1707 Freedman, D G. 1979. *Human Sociobiology: A Holistic Approach.* New York: Free Press.

1708 Fry, D. 1987. What human sociobiology has to offer economic anthropology and vice versa. *Journal of Social and Biological Structures* 10: 37-51.

1709 Galdikas, B M F. 1991. On the comparison of primate social systems. *Current Anthropology* 32: 587.

1710 Gaulin, S J C, M Konner. 1977. On the natural diet of primates including humans. In *Nutrition and the Brain.* Edited by Wurtman, R J, J J Wurtman. Pp. 1-86. New York: Raven.

1711 Gaulin, S, A Schlegel. 1980. Paternal confidence and paternal investment: A cross-cultural test of a sociobiological hypothesis. *Ethology and Sociobiology* 1: 301-309.

1712 Gaulin, S J, J S Boster. 1990. Dowry as female competition. *American Anthropologist* 92: 994-1004.

1713 Geiger, G. 1989. Sociobiology and the structural stability of behavior patterns. *Mathematical Biosciences* 93: 117-145.

1714 Getz, W M, K B Smith. 1983. Genetic kin recognition: Honey bees discriminate between full and half Sisters. *Nature* 302: 147-148.

1715 Gilmore, D D. 1990. Men and women in southern Spain: 'Domestic power' revisited *American Anthropologist* 92: 953-969.

1716 Glassman, R B, E W Packel, D L Brown. 1986. Green beards and kindred spirits: A preliminary mathematical model of altruism toward nonkin who bear similarities to the giver. *Ethology and Sociobiology* 7: 107-115.

1717 Goldsmith, T. 1991. *The Biological Roots of Human Nature: Forging Links between Evolution and Behavior.* New York: Oxford.

1718 Goody, J. 1973. Bridewealth and dowry in Africa and Eurasia. In *Bridewealth and Dowry.* Edited by Goody, J, S J Tambiah. Cambridge: Cambridge University Press.

1719 Goody, J, S J Tambiah, eds. 1973. *Bridewealth and Dowry.* Cambridge: Cambridge University Press.

1720 Granberg, D, B W Granberg. 1985. A search for gender differences on fertility-related attitudes. *Psychology of Women Quarterly* 9: 431-437.

1721 Gray, J P, ed. 1985. *Primate Sociobiology.* New Haven: HRAF Press.

1722 Greene, R, ed. 1987. *Mainstreaming Juvenile Delinquency.* New York: Technomic Publishing Company.

1723 Guttentag, M, P F Secord. 1983. *Too Many Women? The Sex Ratio Question.* Beverly Hills: Sage Publications.

1724 Hajnal, J. 1965. The European marriage pattern in perspective. In *Population in History.* Edited by Glass, D V, D E C Eversley. Chicago: Aldine.

1725 Hajnal, J. 1982. Two kinds of preindustrial household formation system. *Population and Development Review* 8: 449-494.

1726 Halvorson, H O, ed. 1985. *Origin and Evolution of Sex.* New York: Alan R. Liss.

1727 Hamilton, W D. 1964. The genetical evolution of social behavior. *Journal of Theoretical Biology* 7: 1-52.

1728 Hamilton, W D. 1966. The moulding of senescence by natural selection. *Journal of Theoretical Biology* 12: 12-45.

1729 Hamilton, W D. 1967. Extraordinary sex ratios. *Science* 156: 477-488.

1730 Hamilton, W. 1971. The geometry of the selfish herd. *Journal of Theoretical Biology* 31: 295-311.

1731 Hammar, T, ed. 1985. *European Immigration Policy: A Comparative Study.* Cambridge: Cambridge University Press.

1732 Hammerstein, P. 1981. The role of asymmetries in animal conflicts. *Animal Behaviour* 29: 193-205.

1733 Hammerstein, P, G A Parker. 1982. The asymmetric war of attrition. *Journal of Theoretical Biology* 96: 647-82.

1734 Hand, J L. 1986. Resolution of social conflicts: Dominance, egalitarianism, spheres of dominance, and game theory. *Quarterly Review of Biology* 61: 201-220.

1735 Harcourt, A H, P H Harvey, S G Larson, R V Short. 1981. Testis weight, body weight and breeding system in primates. *Nature* 293: 55-57.

1736 Harcourt, A, F B de Waal, eds. 1992. *Coalitions and Alliances in Humans and Other Animals.* Oxford: Oxford University Press.

1737 Harcourt, A H, F B M de Waal, eds. 1992. *Coalitions and Alliances in Humans and Other Animals.* New York: Oxford University Press.

1738 Harcourt, A H, F B M de Waal. 1992. Cooperation in conflict: From ants to anthropoids. In *Coalitions and Alliances in Humans and Other Animals.* Edited by Harcourt, A H, F B M de Waal. Pp. 493-510. New York: Oxford University Press.

1739 Hardin, G. 1986. Cultural carrying capacity: A biological approach to human problems. *BioScience* 36: 599-606.

1740 Harner, M. 1977. The ecological basis for Aztec sacrifice. *American Ethnolgist* 4: 117-135.

1741 Harpending, H, P Draper. 1988. Anticoital behavior and the other side of cultural evolution. In *Biological Contributions to Crime Causation.* Edited by Moffit, T E, S A Mednick. Dordrecht: Nijhoff.

1742 Harris, D R, ed. 1980. *Human Ecology in Savannah Environments.* London: Academic Press.

1743 Harris, M. 1989. *Our Kind: Who We Are, Where We Come From, and Where Are We Going.* New York: Harper & Row.

1744 Hart, K. 1982. *The Political Economy of West African Agriculture.* Cambridge: Cambridge University Press.

1745 Hartung, J. 1976. Natural selection and the inheritance of wealth. *Current Anthropology* 17: 607-622.

1746 Hartung, J. 1981. Genome parliaments and sex with the red queen. In *Natural Selection and Social Behavior: Recent Research and New Theory.* Edited by Alexander, R D, D W Tinkle. New York: Chiron Press.

1747 Hartung, J. 1981. Paternity and inheritance of wealth. *Nature* 291: 652-654.

1748 Hartung, J. 1982. Polygyny and inheritance of wealth. *Current Anthropology* 12: 1-12.

1749 Hartung, J. 1985. Matrilineal inheritance: New theory and analysis. *Behavioral and Brain Sciences* 8: 661-668.

1750 Hartung, J. 1985. Review of Incest: A Biosocial View. *American Journal of Physical Anthropology.* 67: 167-171.

1751 Hartung, J. 1988. Deceiving down: Conjectures on the management of subordinate status. In *Self-Deceit: An Adaptive Mechanism.* Edited by Lockard, J, D Paulhus. Englewood Cliffs, N.J: Prentice-Hall.

1752 Hawkes, K, K Hill, J O'Connell. 1982. Why hunters gather: Optimal foraging and the ache of eastern Paraguay. *American Ethnologist* 9: 379-398.

1753 Hawkes, K, K Hill, J O'Connell. 1985. How much is enough?: Hunters and limited needs. *Ethology and Sociobiology* 6: 3-15.

1754 Heinrich, B. 1979. *Bumblebee Economics.* Cambridge: Harvard University Press.

1755 Heisler, I L. 1981. Offspring quality and the polygyny threshold: A new model for the 'sexy son' hypothesis. *American Naturalist* 117: 316-328.

1756 Hepper, P G, ed. 1991. *Kin Recognition.* Cambridge: Cambridge University Press.

1757 Hewlett, B S. 1988. Sexual selection and parental investment among Aka pygmies. In *Human Reproductive Behavior: A Darwinian Perspective.* Edited by Betzig, L L, M Borgerhoff Mulder, P Turke. Pp. 263-76. Cambridge: Cambridge University Press.

1758 Hiatt, L R. 1980. Polyandry in Sri Lanka: A test case for parental investment theory. *Man* 15: 583-602.

1759 Hill, J. 1984. Human altruism and sociocultural fitness. *Journal of Social and Biological Structures* 4: 17-35.

1760 Hill, J. 1984. Prestige and reproductive success in man. *Ethology and Sociobiology* 5: 77-95.

1761 Hill, K, H Kaplan, K Hawkes, A M Hurtado. 1987. Foraging decisions among Ache hunter-gatherers: New data and implications for optimal foraging models. *Ethology and Sociobiology* 8: 1-36.

1762 Hirshleifer, J. 1977. Economics from a biological viewpoint. *Journal of Law and Economics* 20: 1-52.

1763 Hoenigswald, H M, L F Wiener, eds. 1987. *Biological Metaphor and Cladistic Classification: An Interdisciplinary Perspective.* Philadelphia: University of Pennsylvania Press.

1764 Holy, L. 1986. *Strategies and Norms in a Changing Matrilineal Society: Descent, Succession and Inheritance Among the Toka of Zambia*. Cambridge: Cambridge University Press.

1765 Horn, D J, G R Stairs, R D Mitchell, eds. 1979. *Analysis of Ecological Systems*. Colombus: Ohio State University.

1766 Hölldobler, B, M Lindauer, eds. 1985. *Experimental Behavioral Ecology and Sociobiology*. New York: Springer.

1767 Hrdy, S B. 1981. *The Woman that Never Evolved* Cambridge: Harvard University Press.

1768 Hrdy, S B, G C Williams. 1983. Behavioural biology and the double standard. In *Social Behavior of Female Vertebrates*. Edited by Wasser, S K. Pp. 3-17. New York: Academic Press.

1769 Hughes, A L. 1982. Confidence of paternity and wife-sharing in polygynous and polyandrous societies. *Ethology and Sociobiology* 3: 25-129.

1770 Hughes, A L. 1986. Biological relatedness and social structure. *Journal of Social and Biological Structures* 9: 151-168.

1771 Hughes, A L. 1986. Kin coalitions and social dominance. *Journal of Theoretical Biology* 123: 55-66.

1772 Hughes, A L. 1988. *Evolution and Human Kinship*. New York: Oxford University Press.

1773 Hurtado, A M, K Hawkes, H Kaplan. 1985. Female subsistence strategies among Ache hunter-gatherers of eastern Paraguay. *Human Ecology* 13: 1-28.

1774 Ike, B W. 1987. Man's limited sympathy as a consequence of his evolution in small kin groups. In *The Sociobiology of Ethnocentrism*. Edited by Reynolds, V, V Falger, I Vine. Beckenham/London: Croom Helm.

1775 Ingold, T. 1980. *Hunters, Pastoralists and Ranchers*. Cambridge: Cambridge University Press.

1776 Ingold, T. 1986. *Evolution and Social Life*. Cambridge: Cambridge University Press.

1777 Irons, W. 1979. Cultural and biological success. In *Evolutionary Biology and Human Social Behavior: An Anthropological Perspective*. Edited by Chagnon, N, W Irons. Pp. 257-272. North Scituate, MA.: Duxbury.

1778 Irons, W. 1981. Why lineage exogamy? In *Natural Selection and Social Behavior: Recent Research and New Theory*. Edited by Alexander, R D, D W Tinkle. Pp. 476-489. New York: Chiron Press.

1779 Irons, W. 1983. Human female reproductive strategies. In *Social Behavior of Female Vertebrates*. Edited by Wasser, S K. Pp. 169-213. New York: Academic Press.

1780 Irwin, C J. 1987. A study in the evolution of ethnocentrism. In *The Sociobiology of Ethnocentrism*. Edited by Reynolds, V, V Falger, I Vine. Beckenham: Croom Helm.

1781 Jackson, G B, A K Romney. 1973. Historical inference from cross-cultural data: The case of dowry. *Ethos* 1: 517-520.

1782 Johnson, R C, G P Danko, T J Darvill, S Bochner, J K Bowers, Y-H Huang, J Y Park, V Pecjak, A R A Rahim, D Pennington. 1989. Cross cultural assessment of altruism and its correlates. *Personality and Individual Differences* 10: 855-868.

1783 Johnston, T D. 1982. Selective costs and benefits in the evolution of learning. *Advances in the Study of Behaviour* 12: 65-106.

1784 Kamil, A, J Krebs, H Pulliam. 1987. *Foraging Behavior.* New York: Plenum.

1785 Karylowski, J. 1977. Explaining altruistic behavior: A review. *Polish Psychological Bulletin* 8: 27-34.

1786 Kendrick, D T. 1986. Gender, genes, and the social environment: A biosocial interactionist perspective. In *Sex and Gender: Review of Personality and Social Psychology*. Edited by Shaver, P, C Hendrick. Newbury Park, CA: Sage.

1787 Kenrick, D T, R C Keefe. 1992. Age preferences in mates reflect sex differences in human reproductive strategies. *Behavioral and Brain Sciences* 15: 75-133.

1788 King, B. 1991. Social information transfer in monkeys, apes and hominids. *American Journal of Physical Anthropology* 13: 97-115.

1789 King's College Sociobiology Group, ed. 1982. *Current Problems in Sociobiology*. Cambridge: Cambridge University Press.

1790 Knowlton, N. 1979. Reproductive synchrony, parental investment, and the evolutionary dynamics of sexual selection. *Animal Behavior* 27: 1022-1033.

1791 Kobbenn, J F. 1967. Why exceptions? The logic of cross-cultural analysis. *Current Anthropology* 8: 3-34.

1792 Koenig, W D. 1989. Sex-biased dispersal in the contemporary United States. *Ethology and Sociobiology* 10: 263-278.

1793 Kravitz, D A, J Iwaniszek. 1984. Number of Coalitions and Resources as Sources of Power in Coalition Bargaining. *Journal of Personality and Social Psychology* 47: 534-548.

1794 Krebs, J R, R Dawkins. 1984. Animal signals: Mind reading and manipulation. In *Behavioural Ecology: An Evolutionary Approach.* Edited by Krebs, J R, N B Davies. Pp. 380-402. Oxford: Blackwell Scientific.

1795 Krebs, J R, R H McCleery. 1984. Optimization in behavioural ecology. In *Behavioural Ecology: An Evolutionary Approach.* Edited by Krebs, J R, N B Davies. Pp. 91-121. Oxford: Blackwell Scientific.

1796 Krebs, J R, N B Davis. 1991. *Behavioral Ecology: An Evolutionary Approach.* 3rd ed. Sunderland, MA: Sinauer.

1797 Kummer, H. 1982. Social knowledge in free-ranging primates. In *Animal Mind, Human Mind.* Edited by Griffin, D R. Pp. 113-132. Berlin: Springer.

1798 Kurland, J A. 1979. Paternity, mother's brother, and human sociality. In *Evolutionary Biology and Human Social Behavior.* Edited by Chagnon, N, W Irons. Pp. 145-180. North Scituate, MA: Duxbury.

1799 Lamb, M, B Sutton-Smith, eds. 1982. *Sibling Relationships: Their Nature and Significance Across the Lifespan.* Hillsdale, N.J.: Erlbaum.

1800 Lancaster, J, C S Lancaster. 1983. Parental investment: The hominid adaptation. In *How Humans Adapt: A Biocultural Odyssey.* Edited by Ortner, D. Pp. 33-66. Washington, D.C.: Smithsonian Institution.

1801 Lancaster, J. 1986. Human adolescence and reproduction: An evolutionary perspective. In *School-Age Pregnancy and Parenthood: Biosocial Dimensions.* Edited by Lancaster, J B, B A Hamburg. Pp. 17-38. New York: Aldine.

1802 Lancaster, J, C S Lancaster. 1987. The watershed: Change in parental investment and family formation strategies in the course of human evolution. In *Parenting Across the Life Span: Biosocial Dimensions.* Edited by Lancaster, J, A Rossi, J Altmann, L Sherrod. Pp. 187-205. New York: Aldine.

1803 Lande, R. 1980. Sexual dimorphism, sexual selection, and adaptation in polygenic characters. *Evolution* 34: 292-305.

1804 Laslett, P, K Oosterveen, R M Smith. 1980. *Bastardy and its Comparative History.* Cambridge: Harvard University Press.

1805 Leach, E R, ed. 1960. *Aspects of Caste in South India, Ceylon and North-West Pakistan.* Cambridge: Cambridge University Press.

1806 Leavitt, G C. 1990. Sociobiological explanations of incest avoidance: A critical review of evidential claims. *American Anthropologist* 92: 971-993.

1807 Lee, R. 1992. Art, science or politics? The crisis in hunter-gatherer studies. *American Anthropologist* 94: 31-54.

1808 Lehmann, D, ed. 1982. *Ecology and Exchange in the Andes.* Cambridge: Cambridge University Press.

1809 Leutenegger, W. 1979. Evolution of litter size in primates. *American Naturalist* 114: 525-531.

1810 Levi-Strauss, C. 1949. *Les structures elementaires de la parente.* Paris: Presses Universitaires de France.

1811 Lewin, R. 1984. Practice catches theory in kin recognition. *Science* 223: 1049-51.

1812 Lewontin, R C. 1979. Fitness, survival and optimality. In *Analysis of Ecological Systems.* Edited by Horn, D J, G R Stairs, R D Mitchell. Pp. 3-21. Colombus: Ohio State University.

1813 Lima, S L. 1989. Iterated Prisoner's Dilemma: An appraoch to evolutionary stable cooperation. *American Naturalist* 134: 828-834.

1814 Lindgren, J R, L Pegalis. 1989. Non-kin adoption and sociobiology. *Journal of Social and Biological Structures* 12: 83-86.

1815 Littlefield, C H, J P Rushton. 1989. Levels of explanation in sociobiology and psychology: A rejoinder. *Journal of Personality and Social Psychology* 56: 625-628.

1816 Lopreato, J. 1981. Vilfredo Pareto: Sociobiology, system and revolution. In *The Future of the Sociological Classics.* Edited by Rhea, B. Pp. 81-113. London: Unwin Hyman.

1817 Lopreato, J. 1981. Toward a theory of genuine altruism in Homo sapiens. *Ethology and Sociobiology* 2: 113-126.

1818 Lopreato, J. 1985. Pareto Sociologo: The theory of sentiments in view of behavioral biology. In *Vilfredo Pareto: A 60 Anni dalla Morte.* Edited by Vari, A. Pp. 241-58. Rome: Luigi Sturzo.

1819 Lopreato, J, M-y Yu. 1988. Human fertility and fitness optimization. *Ethology and Sociobiology* 9: 269-89.

1820 Lopreato, J. 1989. The maximization principle: A cause in search of conditions. In *Sociobiology and the Social Sciences.* Edited by Bell, R, N Bell. Pp. 119-30. Lubbock, Texas: Texas Tech University Press.

1821 Lopreato, J. 1990. From social evolutionism to biocultural evolutionism. *Sociological Forum* 5: 187-212.

1822 Lopreato, J, P A Green. 1990. The evolutionary foundations of revolution. In *The Sociobiology of Conflict*. Edited by Falger, V S E, et al. London: Chapman Hall.

1823 Low, B S. 1989. Cross-cultural patterns in the training of children: An evolutionary perspective. *Journal of Comparative Psychology* 103: 311-319.

1824 Lumsden, C J, E O Wilson. 1980. Gene-culture translation in the avoidance of sibling incest. *Proceedings of the National Academy of Sciences USA* 77: 6248-6250.

1825 Lumsden, C J, E O Wilson. 1980. Translation of epigenetic rules of individual behavior into ethnographic patterns. *Proceedings of the National Academy of Sciences USA* 77: 4382-4386.

1826 Lumsden, C J, E O Wilson. 1981. *Genes, Mind and Culture: The Coevolutionary Process*. Cambridge: Harvard University Press.

1827 Lumsden, C. 1989. Does culture need genes? *Ethology and Sociobiology* 10: 11-28.

1828 MacDonald, K B, ed. 1988. *Sociobiological Perspectives on Human Development*. New York: Springer.

1829 MacDonald, K. 1991. A perspective on Darwinian psychology: The importance of domain-general mechanisms, plasticity, and individual differences. *Ethology and Sociobiology* 12: 449-480.

1830 Mainardi, D. 1980. Tradition and the social transmission of behavior in animals. In *Sociobiology: Beyond Nature/Nurture?* Edited by Barlow, G W, J Silverberg. Boulder.: Westview Press.

1831 Mascie-Taylor, C G N, A J Boyce, eds. 1988. *Human Mating Patterns*. Cambridge: Cambridge University Press.

1832 Mascie-Taylor, C G, ed. 1990. *Biosocial Aspects of Social Class*. New York: Oxford University Press.

1833 Maynard Smith, J, G R Price. 1973. The logic of animal conflict. *Nature* 246: 15-18.

1834 Maynard Smith, J, G A Parker. 1976. The logic of asymmetric contests. *Animal Behaviour* 24: 159-175.

1835 Maynard Smith, J. 1979. *Game Theory and the Evolution of Behaviour*. London:

1836 McEachron, D L, D Baer. 1982. A review of selected sociobiological principles: Application to hominid evolution. II. Effects of intergroup conflict. *Journal of Social and Biological Structures* 5: 121-139.

1837 Mealey, L. 1985. The relationship between social status and biological success: A case study of the Mormon religious hierarchy. *Ethology and Sociobiology* 6: 249-257.

1838 Mealey, L, W Mackey. 1990. Variation in offspring sex ratio in women of differing social status. *Ethology and Sociobiology* 11: 83-96.

1839 Meikle, D B, S H Vessey. 1981. Nepotism among monkey brothers. *Nature* 294: 160-161.

1840 Meikle, D B, B L Tilford, S H Vessey. 1984. Dominance rank, secondary sex ratio, and reproduction in polygynous primates. *American Naturalist* 124: 173-88.

1841 Melotti, U. 1987. In-group/out-group relations and the issue of group selection. In *The Sociobiology of Ethnocentrism.* Edited by Reynolds, V, V Falger, I Vine. Beckenham: Croom Helm.

1842 Merkens, H, K Boehnke. 1989. Zum intergenerationales Transfer ethnischer Identität bei Arbeitsmigranten. In *Forschung in den Erziehungswissenschaften.* Edited by Beller, E K. Pp. 74-75. Weinheim: Deutscher Studien Verlag.

1843 Meyer, P. 1987. Ethnocentrism in human social behavior: Some biosociological considerations. In *The Sociobiology of Ethnocentrism.* Edited by Reynolds, V, V Falger, I Vine. Beckenham: Croom Helm.

1844 Michael, R P, J H Crook, eds. 1973. *Comparative Ecology and Behaviour of Primates.* London: Academic Press.

1845 Michod, R. 1982. The theory of kin selection. *Annual Review of Ecology and Systematics* 13: 23-55.

1846 Michod, R E. 1986. On fitness and adaptedness and their role in evolutionary explanation. *Journal of the History of Biology* 19: 289-302.

1847 Moffatt, M. 1979. *An Untouchable Community in South India: Structure and Consensus.* Princeton: Princeton University Press.

1848 Moore, H H. 1990. The reproductive success of Cheyenne war chiefs: A contrary case to Chagnon's Yanomamo. *Current Anthropology* 31: 322-330.

1849 Moran, E F. 1984. *The Ecosystem Concept in Anthropology.* Boulder.: Westview Press.

1850 Murdock, G P, D White. 1969. Standard cross-cultural sample. *Ethnology* 8: 329-369.

1851 Murstein, B I. 1976. *Who will Marry Whom? Theories and Research in Marital Choice.* New York: Springer.

1852 Nelson, S. 1974. Nature/nurture revisited: A review of the biological basis of conflict. *Journal of Conflict Resolution* 18: 285-335.

1853 Nesse, R. 1990. The evolution of psychodynamic mechanisms. In *The Adapted Mind: Evolutionary Psychology and the Generation of Culture*. Edited by Barkow, J, L Cosmides, J Tooby. New York: Oxford University Press.

1854 Newman, K. 1980. Incipient bureaucracy: The development of hierarchies in egalitarian organisations. In *Hierarchy and Society: Anthropological Perspectives on Bureaucracy*. Edited by Britan, G M, R Cohen. Philadelphia: Institute for the Study of Human Issues.

1855 Nöe, R. 1990. A veto game played by baboons: A challenge to the use of the Prisoner's Dilemma as a paradigm for reciprocity and cooperation. *Animal Behaviour* 39: 78-90.

1856 Packer, C, A Pusey. 1985. Asymmetric contests in social mammals: Respect, manipulation and age-specific aspects. In *Evolution: Essays in Honour of John Maynard Smith*. Edited by Greenwood, P J, P H Harvey, M Slatkin. Pp. 173-86. Cambridge: Cambridge Unviersity Press.

1857 Parker, G A. 1974. Assessment strategy and the evolution of fighting behavior. *Journal of Theoretical Biology* 47: 223-243.

1858 Parker, G. 1982. Why are there so many tiny sperm? *Journal of Theoretical Biology* 96: 281-94.

1859 Perper, T. 1989. Theories and observations on sexual selection and female choice. *Medical Anthropology* 11: 409-54.

1860 Peterson, S. 1981. Sociobiology and ideas-become-real: Case study and assessment. *Journal of Social and Biological Structures* 4: 124-143.

1861 Porac, C, S Coren. 1981. *Lateral Preferences and Human Behavior*. New York: Springer.

1862 Pusey, A E. 1980. Inbreeding avoidance in chimpanzees. *Animal Behavior* 28: 543-552.

1863 Raleigh, M J, G L Brammer. 1984. Adaption, selection, and benefit-cost balances: Implications of behavioural physiological studies of social dominance in male vervet monkeys. *Ethology and Sociobiology* 5: 269-277.

1864 Rasa, A E, C Vogel, E Voland, eds. 1989. *The Sociobiology of Sexual and Reproductive Strategies*. London: Chapman and Hall.

1865 Reynolds, V. 1980. Sociobiology and the idea of primordial discrimination. *Ethnic and Racial Studies* 3: 303-315.

1866 Reynolds, V. 1984. Celibacy in biological perspective. *Social Biology and Human Affairs* 49: 110-122.

1867 Reynolds, V. 1986. Biology and race relations. *Ethnic and Racial Studies* 9: 373-381.

1868 Reynolds, V. 1986. Religious rules and reproductive strategies. In *Human Sociobiology.* Edited by Wind, J, V Reynolds. Pp. 110-122. New York: Academic Press.

1869 Reynolds, V, V Floger, I Vine, eds. 1987. *The Sociobiology of Ethnocentrism: Evolutionary Dimensions of Xenophobia, Discrimination, Racism and Nationalism.* London: Croom Helm.

1870 Reynolds, V. 1988. Religious rules, mating patterns, and fertility. In *Human Mating Patterns.* Edited by Boyce, A J, N Mascie-Taylor. Cambridge: Cambridge University Press.

1871 Richerson, P J, R Boyd. 1976. A dual inheritance model of human evolutionary process I: Basic postulates and a simple model. *Journal of Social and Biological Structures* 1: 127-154.

1872 Rindos, D. 1986. The evolution of the capacity for culture: Sociobiology, structuralism, and cultural selectionism. *Current Anthropology* 27: 315-32.

1873 Roberts, D F. 1977. Assortative mating in man: Husband and wife correlations in physical characteristics. *Supplementary Bulletin of the Eugenics Society* 2: 1-45.

1874 Roberts, M. 1981. *Caste Conflict and Elite Formation: The Rise of a Karäva Elite in Sri Lanka, 1500-1931.* Cambridge: Cambridge University Press.

1875 Robertson, R J, G C Bierman. 1979. Parental investment strategies determined by expected benefits. *Zietschrift für Tierpsychologie* 50: 124-8.

1876 Rogers, A R. 1991. Conserving resources for children. *Human Nature* 2: 73-83.

1877 Rosen, S, S Mickler, C Spiers. 1986. The spurned philanthropist. *Humboldt Journal of Social Relations* 13: 145-58.

1878 Rosenberg, A. 1987. Is there really 'juggling' 'artifice' and 'trickery' in Genes, Mind and Culture? *Behavioral and Brain Sciences* 10: 80-82.

1879 Rossi, A S, ed. 1984. *Gender and the Life Course.* New York: Aldine.

1880 Rothstein, S. 1980. Reciprocal altruism and kin selection are not clearly separable phenomena. *Journal of Theoretical Biology* 87: 255-261.

1881 Rothstein, S, R Pierotti. 1988. Distinctions among reciprocal altruism, kin selection, and cooperation and a model for the initial evolution of beneficient behavior. *Ethology and Sociobiology* 9: 189-210.

1882 Rubenstein, D I. 1980. Reproductive value and behavioral strategies: Coming of age in monkeys and horses. In *Perspectives in Ethology*. Edited by Bateson, P P G, P H Klopfer. Pp. 469-487. New York: Plenum Press.

1883 Rushton, J P. 1980. *Altruism, Socialization, and Society*. Englewood Clifs, N.J.: Prentice-Hall.

1884 Russell, R J H, P A Wells. 1987. Estimating paternity confidence. *Ethology and Sociobiology* 8: 215-220.

1885 Saunders, S, J Freedman. 1982. A study of domestic violence: Battered women in Israel. *Jewish Journal of Sociology* 24: 145-147.

1886 Schull, J. 1987. The adaptive-evolutionary point of view in experimental psychology. In *Steven's Handbook of Experimental Psychology*. Edited by Atkinson, R C, R J Herrnstein, G Lindsey, R D Luce. New York: Wiley.

1887 Schulman, S R, B Chapais. 1980. Reproductive value and rank relations among Macaque sisters. *American Naturalist* 115: 580-593.

1888 Shaw, R. 1987. Mankind's propensity to warfare: A sociobiological perspective. *Canadian Review of Sociology and Anthropology* 22: 158-201.

1889 Shaw, R, Y Wong. 1987. Ethnic mobilization and the seeds of warfare: An evolutionary perspective. *International Studies Quarterly* 31: 5-31.

1890 Shepher, J. 1971. Mate selection among second-generation kibbutz adolescents and adults: Incest avoidance and negative imprinting. *Archives of Sexual Behavior* 1: 293-307.

1891 Shepher, J. 1983. *Incest: A Biosocial View*. New York: Academic Press.

1892 Sherman, P. 1977. Nepotism and the evolution of alarm calls. *Science* 197: 1246-1253.

1893 Sherman, P, W Holmes. Kin recognition: Issues and evidence. *Experimental Behavioral Ecology* 31: 437-460.

1894 Silk, J B. 1983. Local resource competition and facultative adjustment of sex ratios in relation to competitive abilities. *American Naturalist* 121: 56-66.

1895 Silk, J, R Boyd. 1983. Cooperation, competition, and mate choice in matrilineal macaque groups. In *Female Vertebrates*. Edited by Wasser, S K. Pp. 316-349. New York: Academic Press.

1896 Silverberg, J, J P Gray. 1992. Violence and peacefulness as behavioral potentialities of primates. In *Aggression and Peacefulness in Humans and Other Primates*. Edited by Silverberg, J, J P Gray. Pp. 1-36. New York: Oxford University Press.

1897 Simon, H A. 1990. A Mechanism for Social Selection and Sucessful Altruism. *Science* 250: 1665-1168.

1898 Smith, R L, ed. 1984. *Sperm Competition and the Evolution of Animal Mating Systems*. Orlando, FL: Academic Press.

1899 Smith, M F, B J Kish, C B Crawford. 1987. Inheritance of wealth as human kin investment. *Ethology and Sociobiology* 8: 171-182.

1900 Sommer, V. 1989. Infant mistreatment in langur monkeys: Sociobiology tackled from the wrong end? In *The Sociobiology of Sexual and Reproductive Strategies*. Edited by Rasa, A E, C Vogel, E Voland. Pp. 110-130. London: Chapman and Hall.

1901 Southwood, T & H, PH, eds. 1991. *The Evolution of Reproductive Strategies*. New York: Cambridge University Press.

1902 Spencer, P. 1973. *Nomads in Alliance*. London: Oxford University Press.

1903 Speth, J D, K A Spielmann. 1983. Energy source, protein metabolism, and hunter-gatherer subsistence strategies. *Journal of Anthropological Archaeology* 2: 1-31.

1904 Standen, V, R Foley, eds. 1989. *Comparative Socioecology of Mammals and Man*. Oxford: Blackwell.

1905 Stein, D M, ed. 1984. *The Sociobiology of Infant and Adult Male Baboons*. Monographs on Infancy. Narwood, N.J.: Ablex.

1906 Stephen, D W, J R Krebs. 1987. *Foraging Theory*. Princeton: Princeton University Press.

1907 Stephens, D, J Krebs. 1986. *Foraging Theory*. Princeton: Princeton University Press.

1908 Stewart, F H. 1977. *Fundamentals of Age-Grouping Systems*. New York: Academic Press.

1909 Strathern, A, ed. 1982. *Inequality in New Guinea Highlands Societies.* Cambridge: Cambridge University Press.

1910 Strum, S & L, B. 1987. Redefining the social link: From baboons to humans. *Social Science Information* 26: 783-802.

1911 Symons, D. 1987. If we're all Darwinians, what's the fuss about? In *Sociobiology and Psychology: Ideas, Issues and Applications.* Edited by Crawford, C, M Smith, D Krebs. Pp. 121-146. Hillsdale, NJ: Erlbaum.

1912 Symons, D. 1989. A critique of Darwinian anthropology. *Ethology and Sociobiology* 10: 131-144.

1913 Taub, D M, ed. 1984. *Primate Paternalism.* New York: Van Nostrand Reinhold.

1914 Taylor, C & M, MT. 1988. Reciprocal altruism: 15 years later. *Ethology and Sociobiology* 9: 67-72.

1915 Thiessen, D D, B Greg. 1980. Human assortative mating and genetic equilibrium: An evolutionary prospective. *Ethology and Sociobiology* 1: 111-140.

1916 Tonnesmann, W. 1987. Group identification and political socialism. In *The Sociobiology of Ethnocentrism.* Edited by Reynolds, V, V Falger, I Vine. Beckenham: Croom Helm.

1917 Tooby, J, L Cosmides. 1989. Evolutionary psychology and the generation of culture, Part I. Theoretical considerations. *Ethology and Sociobiology* 10: 29-49.

1918 Tooby, J, L Cosmides. 1989. Kin selection, genetic selection, and information-dependent strategies. *Behavioral and Brain Sciences* 12: 542-544.

1919 Travis, C B, C P Yeager. 1991. Sexual selection, parental investment, and sexism. *Journal of Social Issues* 47: 117-29.

1920 Trivers, R L. 1971. The evolution of reciprocal altruism. *Quarterly Review of Biology* 14: 35-57.

1921 Trivers, R L. 1974. Parent-offspring conflict. *American Zoologist* 14: 249-264.

1922 Trivers, R L. 1985. *Social Evolution.* Menlo Park, CA: Benjamin-Cummings.

1923 Turke, P W, L L Betzig. 1985. Those who can do: Wealth, status, and reproductive success on Ifaluk. *Ethology and Sociobiology* 6: 79-87.

1924 Turke, P W. 1988. Concealed ovulation, menstrual synchrony, and paternal investment. In *Biosocial Perspectives On the Family*. Edited by Filsinger, E E. Pp. 119-136. Beverly Hills, CA: Sage.

1925 Tuttle, R H, ed. 1975. *Socioecology and Psychology of Primates*. The Hague: Mouton.

1926 van den Berghe, P L, D Barash. 1977. Inclusive fitness and family structure. *American Anthropologist* 79: 809-823.

1927 van den Berghe, P. 1979. *Human Family Systems: An Evolutionary View*. New York: Elsevier.

1928 van den Berghe, P. 1980. Incest and exogamy: A sociobiological reconsideration. *Ethology and Sociobiology* 1: 151-162.

1929 van den Berghe, P L. 1983. Human inbreeding avoidance: Culture in nature. *Behavioral and Brain Sciences* 6: 91-123.

1930 van den Berghe, P L. 1987. Incest taboos and avoidance: Some African evidence. *Sociobiology and Psychology* 353-371.

1931 van den Berghe, P L, K Peter. 1988. Hutterites and Kibbutzniks, A tale of nepotistic communism. *Man* 23: 522-539.

1932 van den Berghe, P L. 1988. The family and the biological base of human sociality. In *Biosocial Perspectives On the Family*. Edited by Filsinger, E E. Pp. 39-60.

1933 van der Dennen, J. 1984. Four fatal fallacies in defense of a myth: The aggression-warfare linkage. In *Essays in Human Sociobiology*. Edited by Wind, J, V Reynolds. Brussels: Free University of Brussels Press.

1934 van der Dennen, J M G. 1987. Ethnocentrism and in-group/out-group differentiation: A review and interpretation of the literature. In *The Sociobiology of Ethnocentrism*. Edited by Reynolds, V, V Falger, I Vine. Beckenham: Croom Helm.

1935 van der Dennen, J. 1988. *The Ethnological Inventory Project*. 3rd ed Groningen: Polemological Institute.

1936 van der Dennen, J, V Falger. 1990. *Sociobiology and Conflict: Evolutionary Perspectives on Competition, Cooperation, Violence and Warfare*. London: Chapman & Hall.

1937 van der Dennen, J. 1990. Biological theories of the genesis and evolution of war. In *Sociobiology and Conflict: Evolutionary Perspectives on Competition, Cooperation, Violence and Warfare*. Edited by van der Dennen, J, V Falger. Pp. 148-188. London: Chapman & Hall.

1938 van der Dennen, J. 1990. The Ethnological Inventory Project: An antidote against some fallacious notions in the study of primitive war. In *Sociobiology and Conflict: Evolutionary Perspectives on Competition, Cooperation, Violence and Warfare*. Edited by van der Dennen, J, V Falger. Pp. 247-269. London: Chapman & Hall.

1939 van Hooff, J A R A M, C P van Schaik. 1992. Cooperation in competition: The ecology of primate bands. In *Coalitions and Alliances in Humans and Other Animals*. Edited by Harcourt, A H, F B M de Waal. Pp. 357-389. New York: Oxford University Press.

1940 Van Rhijn, J G, R Vodegal. 1980. Being honest about one's intentions: An ESS for animal conflicts. *Journal of Theoretical Biology* 85: 623-41.

1941 Vehrencamp, S L, J W Bradbury. 1984. Mating systems and ecology. In *Behavioural Ecology*. Edited by Krebs, J R, N B Davies. Pp. 251-78. Oxford: Blackwell Scientific.

1942 Vincent, T & B, JS. 1988. The evolution of ESS theory. *Annual Review of Ecology and Systematics* 19: 423-443.

1943 Vine, I. 1987. Inclusive fitness and the self-system: The roles of human nature and sociocultural processes. In *The Sociobiology of Ethnocentrism*. Edited by Reynolds, V, V Falger, I Vine. Beckenham: Croom Helm.

1944 Vining, D R. 1986. Social versus reproductive success: The central theoretical problem of human sociobiology. *Behavioral and Brain Sciences* 9: 167-216.

1945 Voland, E. 1984. Human sex-ratio manipulation: Historical data from a German parish. *Journal of Human Evolution* 13: 99-107.

1946 Voland, E. 1991. Cost/benefit oriented parental investment by high status families: The Krummhorn case. *Ethology and Sociobiology* 12: 105-118.

1947 Voorzanger, B. 1984. Altruism in sociobiology: A conceptual analysis. *Journal of Human Evolution* 13: 33-40.

1948 Wade, M J. 1979. Sexual selection and variance in reproductive success. *American Naturalist* 114: 742-747.

1949 Wall, R. 1986. Work, welfare and the family: An illustration of the adaptive family economy. In *The World We Have Gained: Histories of Population and Social Structure*. Edited by Bonfield, L, R M Smith, K Wrightson. Pp. 261-294. Oxford: Blackwell.

1950 Waller, N G, B A Kojetin, T J J Bouchard, D T Lykken, A Tellegen. 1990. Genetic and environmental influences on religious interests, attitudes, and values. *Psychological Science* 1: 138-142.

1951 Washburn, S L. 1978. Human behavior and the behavior of other animals. *American Anthropoligist* 33: 405-418.

1952 Wasser, S K, D P Barash. 1983. Reproductive suppression among female mammals: Implication for biomedicine and sexual selection theory. *Quarterly Review of Biology* 58: 513-538.

1953 Watson, R S. 1985. *Inequality Among Brothers: Class and Kinship in South China.* Cambridge: Cambridge University Press.

1954 Weigel, R M, M M Taylor. 1982. Testing sociobiology theory with respect to human polyandry: A reply to Beall and Goldstein. *American Anthropologist* 84: 406-408.

1955 Weigel, R M, M M Weigel. 1987. Demographic factors affecting the fitness of polyandry for human males: A mathematical model and computer simulation. *Ethology and Sociobiology* 8: 93-134.

1956 Weinrich, J D. 1977. Human sociobiology: Pair-bonding and resource pPredictability (effects of social class and race). *Behavioral Ecology and Sociobiology* 2: 91-118.

1957 Weinrich, J D. 1978. Are humans maximizing reproductive success? The author replies. *Behavioral Ecology and Sociobiology* 3: 97-98.

1958 Weisfeld, G E. 1990. Sociobiological patterns of Arab culture. *Ethology and Sociobiology* 11: 23-49.

1959 Weissner, P. 1982. Risk, reciprocity and social influences in !Kung San economics. In *Politics and History in Band Society.* Edited by Leacock, E, R Lee. Cambridge: Cambridge University Press.

1960 Welden, C W, W L Slauson. 1986. The intensity of competition versus its importance: An overlooked distinction and some implications. *Quarterly Review of Biology* 61: 23-44.

1961 Wenegrat, B. 1989. *The Divine Archetype: The Sociobiology and Psychology of Religion.* Lexington: Lexington Books.

1962 West, D J, D P Farrington. 1977. *The Delinquent Way of Life.* London: Heinemann.

1963 West Eberhard, M J. 1975. The evolution of social behavior by kin selection. *Quarterly Review of Biology* 50: 1-33.

1964 Wickler, W, U Seibt. 1981. Monogamy in crustacea and man. *Zeitschrift für Tierpsychologie* 57: 215-234.

1965 Wiederman, M W, E R Allgeier. 1992. Gender differences in mate selection criteria: Sociobiological or socioeconomic explanation? *Ethology and Sociobiology* 13: 115-124.

1966 Wilson, D S. 1974. A theory of group selection. *Proceedings of the National Academy of Science USA* 72: 143-146.

1967 Wilson, E O. 1975. *Sociobiology: The New Synthesis.* Cambridge: Harvard University Press.

1968 Wilson, E O. 1978. What is sociobiology? In *Sociobiology and Human Nature: An Interdisciplinary Critique and Defense.* Edited by Gregory, M S, A Silvers, D Sutch. Pp. 10-14. San Francisco: Jossey-Bass.

1969 Wilson, D. 1983. The group selection controversy: History and current status. *Annual Review of Ecology and Systematics* 14: 159-187.

1970 Wilson, M, M Daly. 1985. Competitiveness, risk-taking and violence: The young male syndrome. *Ethology and Sociobiology* 6: 59-73.

1971 Wilson, E O, C J Lumsden. 1991. Holism and reduction in sociobiology: Lessons from the ants and human culture. *Biology and Philosophy* 6: 401-412.

1972 Wind, J. 1980. Man's selfish genes, social behavior and ethics. *Journal of Social and Biological Structures* 3:

1973 Wind, J. 1984. Sociobiology and the human sciences. *Journal of Human Evolution* 13: 3-25.

1974 Wind, J, ed. 1984. *Essays in Human Sociobiology.* New York: Academic Press.

1975 Wind, J. 1984. Sociobiology and the human sciences: An introduction. *Journal of Human Evolution* 13: 3-24.

1976 Witt, R, C. Schmidt, J Schmitt. 1981. Social rank and darwinian fitness in a multi-male group of barbary macaques (Macacasylvana Linnaeus, 1758). *Folia Primatologica* 36: 201-221.

1977 Wittenberger, J F, R L Tilson. 1980. The evolution of monogamy: Hypotheses and evidence. *Annual Review of Ecology and Systematics* 11: 197-232.

1978 Wolf, A P. 1968. Adopt a daughter-in-law, marry a sister: A Chinese solution to the problem of the incest taboo. *American Anthropologist* 70: 864-874.

1979 Wozniak, P. 1984. Making sociobiological sense out of sociology. *Sociological Quarterly* 25: 191-204.

1980 Wrangham, R W. 1980. An ecological model of female-bonded primate groups. *Behaviour* 75: 262-300.

1981 Zahn-Walker, C, E M Cummings, R J Iannotti, eds. 1987. *Altruism and Aggression: Social and Biological Origins.* Cambridge: Cambridge University Press.

# 6

# Behavior Genetics

1982 Adams, M S, J V Neel. 1967. Children of incest. *Pediatrics* 40: 55-62.

1983 Ammerman, A J, L L Cavalli-Sforza. 1984. *The Neolithic Transition and the Genetics of Populations in Europe.* Princeton: Princeton University Press.

1984 Ankney, C. 1992. Sex differences in relative brain size: The mismeasure of woman, too? *Intelligence* 16: 329-36.

1985 Annett, M. 1981. The genetics of handedness. *Trends in NeuroSciences* 10: 256-258.

1986 Baer, A S, ed. 1977. *Heredity and Society: Readings in Social Genetics.* 2nd ed New York: Macmillan.

1987 Bajema, C J. 1971. Natural selection in human populations: The measurement of ongoing genetic evolution. In *Contemporary Societies.* Edited by Bajema, C J. New York: Wiley.

1988 Bakan, P. 1971. Handedness and birth order. *Nature* 229: 195.

1989 Bakan, P, G Dibb, P Reed 1973. Handedness and birth stress. *Neuropsychologia* 11: 363-366.

1990 Baker, J R. 1974. *Race.* Oxford: Oxford University Press.

1991 Baker, M C. 1982. Vocal dialect recognition and population genetic consequences. *American Zoology* 22: 561-570.

1992 Ballonoff, P A, ed. 1974. *Genetics and Social Structure.* New York: Halsted Press.

1993 Baron, M, et al. 1987. Genetic linkage between X-chromosome markers and bipolar affective illness. *Nature* 326: 289-92.

1994 Barrai, I, L L Cavalli-Sforza, M Mainardi. 1964. Testing a model of dominant inheritance for metric traits in man. *Heredity* 19: 651-668.

1995 Behrman, J, Z Hrubec, P Taubman, T Wales. 1980. *Socioeconomic Success: A Study of the Effects of Genetic Endowment, Family Environment, and Schooling.* Amsterdam: North-Holland.

1996 Bengtsson, B O. 1978. Avoiding inbreeding: At what cost? *Journal of Theoretical Biology* 73: 439-444.

1997 Benzer, S. 1973. The genetic dissection of behavior. *Scientific American* 224: 24-37.

1998 Bernstein, H, H Byerly, F Hopf, R MIchod, G Vemulapalli. 1983. The Darwinian dynamic. *Quarterly Review of Biology* 58: 185-201.

1999 Bernstein, H, H C Byerly, F A Hopf, R E Michod. 1985. The evolutionary role of recombinational repair and sex. *International Review of Cytology* 96: 1-28.

2000 Bernstein, H, H C Byerly, F A Hopf, R E Michod. 1985. Sex and the emergence of species. *Journal of Theoretical Biolology* 117: 665-690.

2001 Bernstein, H, H C Byerly, F A Hopf, R E Michod. 1985. DNA repair and complementation: The major factors in the origin and maintenance of sex. In *Origin and Evolution of Sex*. Edited by Halvorson, H O. Pp. 29-45. New York: Alan R. Liss.

2002 Bernstein, H, F A Hopf, R E Michod. 1988. Is meiotic recombination an adaptation for repairing DNA, producing genetic variation, or both? In *The Evolution of Sex: An Examination of Current Ideas*. Edited by Levin, B, R Michod. Pp. 139-160. Sunderland, MA: Sinauer.

2003 Bernstein, H, F A Hopf, R E Michod. 1989. The evolution of sex: DNA repair hypothesis. In *The Sociobiology of Sexual and Reproductive Strategies*. Edited by Rasa, A E, C Vogel, E Voland. Pp. 3-18. London: Chapman and Hall.

2004 Bertram, B C R. 1978. Living in groups: Predators and prey. In *Behavioral Ecology*. Edited by Krebs, J R, N B Davies. Pp. 64-96. Oxford: Blackwell.

2005 Billings, P R, J Beckwith, J S Alper. 1992. The genetic analysis of human behavior: A new era. *Social Science & Medicine* 35: 227-238.

2006 Bixler, R H. 1981. Primate mother-son "incest". *Psychological Reports* 48: 531-536.

2007 Bixler, R H. 1981. The incest controversy. *Psychological Reports* 49: 267-283.

2008 Bixler, R H. 1981. Incest avoidance as a function of environment and heredity. *Current Anthropology* 22: 639-654.

2009 Bixler, R H. 1982. Sibling incest in the royal families of Egypt, Peru, and Hawaii. *Journal of Sex Research* 18: 264-281.

2010 Bohman, M, C Cloninger, S Sigvardsson, A von Knorring. 1982. Predisposition to petty criminality in Swedish adoptees 1. Genetic and environmental heterogeneity. *Archives of General Psychiatry* 39: 1233-1241.

2011 Bonne-Tamir, B. 1980. The Samaritans: A living ancient isolate. In *Population Structure and Genetic Disorders.* Edited by Eriksson, A W, H R Forsius, H R Nevanlinna, P L Workman, R K Norio. Pp. 27-41. London: Academic Press.

2012 Boomsma, D I, M B M van den Bree, J F Orlebeke, P C M Molenaar. 1989. Resemblances of parents and twins in sports participation and heart rate. *Behavior Genetics* 19: 123-142.

2013 Boorman, S A, P B Levitt. 1980. *The Genetics of Altruism.* New York: Academic Press.

2014 Bouchard, T J, M McGee. 1981. Familial studies of intelligence: A review. *Science* 212: 1055-1059.

2015 Bouchard, T J. 1983. Do environmental similarities explain the similarity in intelligence of identical twins reared apart? *Intelligence* 7: 175-184.

2016 Bouchard, T J. 1984. Twins reared together and apart: What they tell us about human diversity. In *Individuality and Determinism.* Edited by Fox, S W. Pp. 147-184. New York: Plenum.

2017 Bouchard, T J, D T Lykken, M McGee, N L Segal, A Tellegen. 1990. Sources of human psychological differences: The Minnesota study of twins reared apart. *Science* 250: 223-228.

2018 Bouchard, T J, M McGue. 1990. Genetic and rearing environmental influences on adult personality: An analysis of adopted twins reared apart. *Journal of Personality* 58: 263-92.

2019 Breden, F, M J Wade. 1991. Runaway social evolution: Reinforcing selection for inbreeding and altruism. *Journal of Theoretical Biology* 153: 323-38.

2020 Brennan, P, S A Mednick, E Kandel. 1986. Congenital determinants of violence and property offending. In *The Development and Treatment of Childhood Aggression.* Edited by Pepler, D. New York: Erlbaum.

2021 Briggs, G G, R D Nebes, M Kinsbourne. 1976. Intellectual differences in relation to personal and family handedness. *Quarterly Journal of Experimental Psychology* 28: 591-601.

2022 Buhrich, N, M J Bailey, N G Martin. 1990. Sexual orientation, sexual identity, and sex-dimorphic behaviors in male twins. *Behavior Genetics* 21: 76-96.

2023 Burke, P, J Hoelter. 1988. Identity and sex/race differences in educational and occupational aspirations formation. *Social Science Research* 17: 29-47.

2024 Burnham, J T. 1975. Incest avoidance and social evolution. *Mankind* 10: 93-98.

2025 Buss, A. 1988. *Personality: Evolutionary Heritage and Human Distinctiveness*. Hillsdale, NJ: Erlbaum.

2026 Buss, D. 1990. Towards a biologically informed psychology of personality. *Journal of Personality* 58: 1-17.

2027 Buss, D M, ed. 1990. *Biological Foundations of Personality: Evolution, Behavioral Genetics, and Psychophysiology. Special Issue of The Journal of Personality, vol. 58.*

2028 Cain, D P, C H Vanderwolf. 1990. A critique of Rushton on race, brain size and intelligence. *Personality and Individual Differences* 11: 777-784.

2029 Carey, G. 1991. Evolution and path models in human behavioral genetics. *Behavior Genetics* 21: 433-44.

2030 Carter-Saltzman, L. 1980. Biological and sociocultural effects on handedness: Comparison between biological and adoptive families. *Science* 209: 1263-1265.

2031 Cattel, R B, I H Scheier. 1961. *The Meaning and Measurement of Neuroticism and Anxiety.* New York: Ronald Press.

2032 Cattel, R B. 1965. *The Scientific Analysis of Personality.* Harmondsworth: Penguin.

2033 Cattell, R B. 1950. The fate of national intelligence: Test of a thirteen-year prediction. *Eugenics Review* 42: 136-148.

2034 Cattell, R B, G F Stice, N F Kristy. 1957. A first approximation to nature-nurture ratios for eleven primary personality factors in objective tests. *Journal of Abnormal and Social Psychology* 54: 143-159.

2035 Cattell, R. 1971. *Abilities: Their Structures, Growth and Action.* Boston: Houghton Mifflin.

2036 Cattell, R B. 1982. *The Inheritance of Personality and Ability.* New York: Academic Press.

2037 Cloninger, C R, S Sigvardsson, M Bohman, A von Knorring. 1982. A predisposition to petty criminality in Swedish adoptees II. Cross-fostering analysis of gene-environment interaction. *Archives of General Psychiatry* 39: 1242-1247.

2038 Cloninger, C, I Gottesman. 1987. Genetic and environmental factors in antisocial behavior disorders. In *The Causes of Crime.* Edited by Mednick, S, T Moffitt, S Stock. Cambridge: Cambridge University Press.

2039 Cohen, Y. 1988. The disappearance of the incest taboo. *Human Nature* 1: 72-78.

2040 Colwell, R K, M C King. 1983. Disentangling genetic and cultural influences on human behavior: Problems and prospects. In *Comparing Behavior, Studying Man Studying Animals.* Edited by Rajecki, D W. Hillsdale, N.J.: Erlbaum.

2041 Corne, S, C Porac. 1980. Birth factors in laterality: Effects of birth order, parental age and birth stess on four indices of lateral preference. *Behavior Genetics* 10: 123-138.

2042 Corne, S, A Searleman, C Porac. 1982. The effects of specific birth stressors on four indexes of lateral preference. *Canadian Journal of Psychology* 36: 478-487.

2043 Cortes, J, F Gatti. 1972. *Delinquency and Crime: A Biopsychosocial Approach.* New York: Seminar Press.

2044 Crow, J F. 1979. Genes that violate Mendel's rules. *Scientific American* 240: 134-146.

2045 Daniels, B, R Plomin, G McClearn, R C Johnson. 1982. "Fitness" behavior and anthropometric characters for offspring of first cousin matings. *Behavior Genetics* 12: 527-534.

2046 Darlington, C D. 1958. *The Evolution of Genetic Systems.* London: Oliver and Boyd.

2047 Darlington, C D. 1964. *Genetics and Man.* London: George Allen and Unwin.

2048 DeFries, J C, et al. 1976. Parent-offspring resemblance for specific cognitive abilities in two ethnic groups. *Nature* 261: 131-133.

2049 DeFries, J C, et al. 1979. Family resemblance for specific cognitive abilities. *Behavior Genetics* 9: 23-43.

2050 Demarest, W J. 1977. Incest avoidance among human and nonhuman primates. In *Primate Bio-Social Development.* Edited by Chevalier-Skolnikoff, S, F E Chevalier-Skolnikoff. Pp. 323-342. New York: Garland.

2051 Denno, D. 1988. Human biology and criminal responsibility: Free will or free ride? *University of Pennsylvania Law Review* 137: 615-672.

2052 Detera-Wadleigh, S D, et al. 1987. Close linkage of c-Harvey-ras-1 and insulin gene to affective disorder is ruled out in three North American pedigrees. *Nature* 325: 806-808.

2053 Diamond, M. 1982. Sexual identity: Monozygotic twins reared in discordant sex roles and a BBC follow-up. *Archives of Sexual Behavior* 11: 181-186.

2054 DiLalla, F L, I I Gottesman. 1990. Biological and genetic contributors to violence—Widom's untold tale. *Psychological Bulletin* 109: 125-129.

2055 Dillon, L. 1983. *The Inconstant Gene.* New York: Plenum.

2056 Dobzhansky, T. 1973. *Genetic Diversity and Human Equality.* New York: Basic Books.

2057 Doolittle, W F, C Sapienza. 1980. Selfish genes, the phenotype paradigm and genome evolution. *Nature* 284: 601-603.

2058 Draper, P, J Belskey. 1990. Personality development in evolutionary perspective. *Journal of Personality* 58: 141-62.

2059 Dunn, J, R Polmin. 1990. *Separate Lives: Why Siblings are So Different.* New York: Basic Books.

2060 Eaves, L J, K A Last, P A Young, N G Martin. 1978. Model-Fitting approaches to the analysis of human behavior. *Heredity* 41: 249-320.

2061 Eaves, L J, J H Eysenck, N G Martin. 1989. *Genes, Culture and Personality: An Empirical Approach.* London: Academic Press.

2062 Eaves, L J, N G Martin, A C Heath, J K Hewitt, M C Neale. 1990. Personality and reproductive fitness. *Behavior Genetics* 20: 563-568.

2063 Ehrlich, P, S Felman. 1977. *The Race Bomb.* New York: Quadrangle.

2064 Ehrman, L, P A Parsons. 1976. *The Genetics of Behavior.* Sunderland, MA: Sinauer.

2065 Ehrman, L, P A Parsons. 1981. *Behavior Genetics and Evolution.* New York: McGraw-Hill.

2066 Ellis, L. 1982. Genetics and criminal behavior: Evidence through the end of the 1970s. *Criminology* 20: 43-66.

2067 Ellis, S J, P J Ellis, E Marshall. 1988. Hand preference in a normal population. *Cortex* 24: 157-63.

2068 Ellis, L. 1988. The victimful-victimless crime distinction, and seven universal demographic correlates of victimful criminal behavior. *Personality and Individual Differences* 9: 525-48.

2069 Ellis, L. 1991. A biosocial theory of social stratification derived from the concept of pro/antisociality and r/K selection. *Politics and Life Sciences* 10: 5-23, 39-43.

2070 Erikson, M. 1989. Incest avoidance and familial bonding. *Journal of Anthropological Research* 45: 267-291.

2071 Eriksson, A W, H R Forsius, H R Nevanlinna, P L Workman, R K Norio, eds. 1980. *Population Structure and Genetic Disorders*. London: Academic Press.

2072 Eysenck, H J. 1967. *The Biological Basis of Personality*. Springfield, Illinois: C.C. Thomas.

2073 Eysenck, H. 1971. *Race, Intelligence and Education*. London: Temple Smith.

2074 Eysenck, H. 1973. *The Measurement of Intelligence*. Baltimore: Williams and Wilkins.

2075 Eysenck, H J. 1977. *Crime and Personality*. 3rd ed London: Routledge and Kegan Paul.

2076 Eysenck, H J, ed. 1979. *The Structure and Measurement of Intelligence*. New York: Springer.

2077 Eysenck, H. 1982. *A Model for Intelligence*. Berlin: Springer.

2078 Eysenck, H J, D W Fulker. 1983. The components of Type A behaviour and its genetic determinants. *Personality and Individual Differences* 4: 499-505.

2079 Eysenck, H J, M W Eysenck. 1985. *Personality and Individual Differences: A Natural Science Approach*. New York: Plenum.

2080 Eysenck, H J. 1990. Genetic and environmental contributions to individual differences: The three major dimensions of personality. *Journal of Personality* 58: 245-262.

2081 Faber, S L. 1981. *Identical Twins Reared Apart: A Reanalysis*. New York: Basic Books.

2082 Fagan, J, E Piper, M Moore. 1986. Violent delinquents and urban youths. *Criminology* 24: 439-71.

2083 Fairchild, H. 1991. Scientific racism: The cloak of objectivity. *Journal of Social Issues* 47: 101-115.

2084 Falconer, D. 1966. Genetic consequences of selection pressure. In *Genetic and Environmental Factors in Human Ability.* Edited by Meade, J, A Parkes. Pp. 219-232. Edinburgh: Oliver & Boyd.

2085 Falconer, D S. 1985. The inheritance of liability to certain diseases estimated from the incidence among relatives. *Annals of Human Genetics* 29: 51-76.

2086 Falk, D. 1990. Brain evolution in homo: The radiator theory. *Behavioral and Brain Sciences* 13: 333-343.

2087 Fancher, R. 1985. *The Intelligence Men: Makers of the IQ Controversy.* New York: Norton.

2088 Fishbein, D H. 1990. Biological perspectives in criminology. *Criminology* 28: 27-72.

2089 Fletcher, R. 1991. *Science, Ideology and the Media: The Cyril Burt Scandal.* London: Transaction Books.

2090 Flynn, J. 1980. *Race, IQ, and Jensen.* London: Routledge.

2091 Folstein, S, M Rutter. 1977. Genetic influences and infantile autism. *Nature* 265: 726-728.

2092 Foster, M L. 1983. Solving the insoluble: Language genetics today. In *Glossogenetics: The Origin and Evolution of Language.* Edited by de Grolier, E. Pp. 455-80. Paris: Harwood Academic Publishers.

2093 Fox, S W, ed. 1984. *Individuality and Determinism.* New York: Plenum.

2094 Friedl, J, W S Ellis. 1974. Inbreeding, isonymy, and isolation in a Swiss community. *Human Biology* 46: 699-712.

2095 Fulker, D W, H J Eysenck. 1979. Nature, nurture, and environment. In *The Structure and Measurement of Intelligence.* Edited by Eysenck, H J. Berlin: Springer.

2096 Fuster, V. 1984. Extramarital reproduction and infant mortality in rural Galicia (Spain). *Journal of Human Evolution* 13: 457-465.

2097 Gabrielli, W F J, S A Mednick. 1980. Sinistrality and delinquency. *Journal of Abnormal Psychology* 89: 664-671.

2098 Gabrielli, W F J, S A Mednick. 1983. Genetic correlates of criminal behavior. *American Behavioral Scientist* 27: 59-74.

2099 Gajdusek, D C. 1964. Factors Governing the Genetics of Primitive Human Populations. *Cold Spring Harbor Symposium on Quantitative Biology* 29: 121-135.

2100 Garai, J E, A Scheinfeld. 1968. Sex differneces in mental and behavior traits. *Genetic Psychological Monographs* 77: 169-299.

2101 Gedda, L, P Parisi, W E Nance, eds. 1981. *Twin Research.* New York: Alan R. Liss.

2102 Geschwind, N, P Behan. 1982. Left-handedness: Association with immune disease, migrane and developmental, and learning disorder. *Proceeding of the National Academy of Sciences USA* 79: 5097-5100.

2103 Ghodsian-Carpey, J, L A Baker. 1987. Genetic and environmental influences on aggression in 4- to 7-year-old twins. *Aggressive Behavior* 13: 173-186.

2104 Ghosh, A K, P P Majumder. 1979. Genetic load in an isolated tribal population of South India. *Human Genetics* 51: 203-208.

2105 Giles, E, S Wyber, R J Walsh. 1970. Micro-evolution in New Guinea: Additional evidence for genetic drift. *Archaeology and Physical Anthropology in Oceania* 5: 60-72.

2106 Gill, C E, R Jardine, N G Martin. 1985. Further evidence for genetic influences on educational achievement. *British Journal of Educational Psychology* 55: 240-250.

2107 Goldschmidt, E, T Cohen, N Bloch, L Keleti, S Wartski. 1963. Viability studies in Jews from Kurdistan. In *The Genetics of Migrant and Isolate Populations.* Edited by Goldschmidt, E. Pp. 183-195. New York: Williams and Wilkins.

2108 Goldschmidt, E, ed. 1963. *The Genetics of Migrant and Isolate Populations.* New York: Williams and Wilkins.

2109 Goldschmidt, E, K Fried, A G Steinberg, T Cohen. 1976. The Karaite community of Iraq in Israel: A genetic study. *American Journal of Human Genetics* 28: 243-252.

2110 Goodman, M A, A Koen, J Barnabas, G Moore. 1972. Evolving primate genes and proteins. In *Comparative Genetics in Monkeys, Apes, and Man.* Edited by Chiarelli, A B. Pp. 153-212. New York: Academic Press.

2111 Gottesman, I I. 1968. Biogenetics of race and class. In *Social Class, Race, and Psychological Development.* Edited by Deutsch, M, I Katz, A Jensen. Pp. 11-51. New York: Holt, Rinehart, and Winston.

2112 Gottesman, I I, G Carey. 1983. Extracting meaning and direction from twin data. *Psychiatric Development* 1: 35-50.

2113 Gray, J A. 1981. A critique of Eysencks's theory of personality. In *A Model for Personality.* Edited by Eysenck, H J. Pp. 246-76. Berlin: Springer.

2114 Grayson, D A. 1989. Twins reared together: Minimizing shared environmental effects. *Behavior Genetics* 19: 593-604.

2115 Guttentag, M, P F Secord. 1983. *Too Many Women? The Sex Ratio Question.* Beverly Hills, CA: Sage.

2116 Hahn, M E, et al. 1990. *Developmental Behavior Genetics: Neural, Biometrical, and Evolutionary Approaches.* New York: Oxford University Press.

2117 Haldane, J B S. 1957. The cost of natural selection. *Journal of Genetics* 55: 511-524.

2118 Halliday, T R, P J B Slater, eds. 1983. *Genes, Development and Learning.* New York: Freeman.

2119 Halvorson, H O, ed. 1985. *Origin and Evolution of Sex.* New York: Alan R. Liss.

2120 Hamilton, W D. 1967. Extraordinary sex ratios. *Science* 156: 477-488.

2121 Hardcyk, C, L F Petrinovich, R D Goldman. 1976. Left-handedness and cognitive deficit. *Cortex* 12: 266-279.

2122 Hardin, G. 1972. Genetic consequences of cultural decisions in the realm of population. *Social Biology* 19: 350-361.

2123 Harrison, G A, ed. 1961. *Genetic Variation in Human Populations.* Oxford: Pergamon.

2124 Hartung, J. 1985. Heritable I.Q.—A reason to bother. *Nature* 311: 515-516.

2125 Hassler, M, N Birbaumer. 1988. Handedness, muscial abilities, and dichaptic and dichotic performance in adolescents: A longitudinal study. *Developmental Neurospychology* 4: 129-145.

2126 Hay, D A. 1985. *Essentials of Behaviour Genetics.* Oxford: Blackwell.

2127 Heath, A C, et al. 1985. No decline in assortive mating for educational level. *Behavioral Genetics* 15: 349-370.

2128 Heath, A C, K Berg, L J Eaves, M H Solaas, L A Corey, J Sundet, P Magnus, W E Nancy. 1985. Educational policy and the heritability of educational attainment. *Nature* 314: 734-736.

2129 Heath, A C, M C Neal, J K Hewitt, L J Eaves, D W Fulker. 1989. Testing structural equation models for twin data using LISREL. *Behavior Genetics* 19: 9-36.

2130 Heath, L J, N Martin. 1990. Psychoticism as a dimension of personality: A multivariate genetic test of Eysenck and Eysenck's psychoticism construct. *Journal of Personality and Social Psychology* 58: 111-21.

2131 Henderson, N D. 1982. Human behaviour genetics. *Annual Review of Psychology* 3: 403-440.

2132 Hendrickson, A E. 1982. The biological basis of intellegence. Part I: Theory. In *A Model for Intelligence.* Edited by Eysenck, H J. Berlin: Springer.

2133 Hicks, R E, M Kinsbourne. 1976. Human handedness: A partial cross-fostering study. *Science* 192: 908-910.

2134 Hiese, D R, ed. 1973. *Personality: Biosocial Bases.* Chicago: Rand McNally.

2135 Higgins, J, E Reed, S Reed 1962. Intelligence and family size: A paradox resolved *Eugenics Quarterly* 9: 84-90.

2136 Hioms, R W, G A Harrison, J B Gibson. 1977. Genetic variation in some Oxfordshire villages. *Annals of Human Biology* 4: 197-210.

2137 Hirsch, J, T McGuire. 1982. *Behaviour-Genetic Analysis.* London: Hutchinson Ross.

2138 Hodgkinson, S, et al. 1987. Molecular genetic evidence for heterogeneity in manic depression. *Nature* 325: 805-806.

2139 Hopkins, K. 1980. Brother-sister marriage in Roman Egypt. *Comparative Studies In Society and History* 22: 303-354.

2140 Horn, J M, J C Loehlin, L Willerman. 1982. Aspects of the inheritance of intellectual abilities. *Behavior Genetics* 12: 479-516.

2141 Howell, N. 1982. Components of microevolution in the !Kung. In *Human Genetics and Adaptation, Vol I. Proceedings of the Indian Statistical Institute Golden Jubilee International Conference.* Edited by Malhotra, K C, A Basu. Calcutta: ISI.

2142 Hutchings, B, S A Mednick. 1974. Registered criminality in the adoptive and biological parents of registered male adoptees. In *Genetics, Environment and Psychopathology.* Edited by Mednick, S A, F Schulsinger, J Higgins, B Bell. New York: Elsevier.

2143 Immelmann, K, L Petrinovich, M Main, eds. 1981. *Behavioral Development.* Cambridge: Cambridge University Press.

2144 Itoigawa, N, K Negayama, K Kondo. 1981. Experimental study on sexual behavior between mother and son in Japanese monkeys (Macaca fuscata). *Primates* 22: 494-502.

2145 Itzkoff, S W. 1987. *Why Humans Vary in Intelligence.* Ashfield, MA: Paideia.

2146 Jamieson, J W. 1982. The Samaritans. *Mankind Quarterly* 23: 141-148.

2147 Jardine, R, N Martin. 1983. Spatial ability and throwing accuracy. *Behavior Genetics* 13: 331-40.

2148 Jardine, R, N G Martin, A S Henderson. 1984. Genetic covariation between neuroticism and the symptoms of anxiety and depression. *Genetic Epidemiology* 1: 89-107.

2149 Jencks, C, et al. 1972. *Inequality: A Reassessment of the Effect of Family and Schooling in America.* London: Penguin.

2150 Jenkins, T, P Beighton, A G Steinberg. 1985. Serogenetic studies on the inhabitants of Tristan da Cunha. *Annals of Human Biology* 12: 363-371.

2151 Jensen, A R. 1969. How much can we boost IQ and scholastic achievement? *Harvard Education Review* 39: 1-123.

2152 Jensen, A R. 1972. *Genetics and Education.* London: Methuen.

2153 Jensen, A. 1973. *Educability and Group Difference.* New York: Harper & Row.

2154 Jensen, A. 1975. Race and mental ability. In *Race Variation in Man.* Edited by Ebling, F. London: Blackwell.

2155 Jensen, A. 1979. *Bias in Mental Testing.* New York: Free Press.

2156 Jensen, A R. 1985. The nature of the black-white difference on various psychometric tests: Spearman's hypothesis. *Behavioral and Brain Sciences* 8: 193-263.

2157 Jinks, J L, D W Fulker. 1970. A comparison of the biometrical, genetical, MAVA, and clinical approaches to the analysis of human behavior. *Psychological Bulletin* 73: 311-349.

2158 Johnson, R, G E McClearn, S Y Schwitters, C T Nagoshi, F M Ahern, R E Cole. 1985. Galton's data a century later. *American Psychologist* 40: 875-92.

2159 Johnson, R, et al. 1989. Cross cultural assessment of altruism and its correlates. *Personality and Individual Differences* 10: 855-68.

2160 Jorde, L B. 1985. Human genetic distance studies: Present status and future prospects. *Annual Review of Anthropology* 14: 343-373.

2161 Juel-Nielsen, N. 1980. *Individual and Environment: Monozygotic Twins Reared Apart.* New York: International University Press.

2162 Kamin, L J. 1974. *The Science and Politics of I.Q.* Hillsdale, NJ: Erlbaum.

2163 Kandel, E. 1989. Genetic and perinatal factors in antisocial personality in a birth cohort. *Journal of Crime and Justice* 12: 61-78.

2164 Kandel, E R, P Brennan, S A Mednick. 1989. Minor physical anomalies and recidivistic adult violent offending: Evidence from a birth cohort. *Acta Psychiatrica Scandinavica* 79: 103-107.

2165 Kandel, E. 1991. An examination of the relationship between IQ and delinquency. In *Mainstreaming Juvenile Delinquency.* Edited by Greene, R. New York: Technomic Publishing Company.

2166 Kaplan, A R, ed. 1976. *Human Behavioral Genetics.* Springfield: Charles C. Thomas.

2167 Karlsson, J L. 1978. *The Inheritance of Creative Intelligence.* Chicago: Nelson-Hall.

2168 Kassarjian, H H, M Sheffet. 1982. Personality and consumer behavior: An update. In *Perspectives in Consumer Behavior.* Edited by Kassarjian, J J, T S Roberston. Pp. 160-80. Glenview, IL: Scott Foresman.

2169 Kendler, K S. 1983. Overview: A current perspective on twin studies of schizophrenia. *American Journal of Psychiatry* 140: 1413-1425.

2170 Kendler, K S, R D Robinette. 1983. Schizophrenia in the National Academy of Sciences-National Research Council Twin Registry: A 16 year update. *American Journal of Psychiatry* 140: 1551-63.

2171 Kendler, K, A C Heath, N G Martin, L J Eaves. 1987. Symptoms of anxiety and symptoms of depression: Same genes, different environments? *Archives of General Psychiatry* 44: 451-460.

2172 Kety, S S. 1983. Mental illness in the biological and adoptive relatives of schizophrenic adoptees. Findings relevant to genetic and environmental factors in etiology. *American Journal of Psychiatry* 140: 720-727.

2173 Kimura, D. 1987. Are men's and women's brains really different? *Canadian Psychology* 28: 133-47.

2174 Kolata, G B. 1977. Overlapping genes: More than anomalies? *Science* 196: 1187-1188.

2175 Kovach, J K. 1986. Toward the genetics of an engram: The role of heredity in visual preferences and perceptual imprinting. In *Perspectives in Behavior Genetics*. Edited by Fuller, J L, E C Simmel. Hillsdale, N.J.: Erlbaum.

2176 Lansky, L M, H Feinstein, J M Peterson. 1988. Demography of handedness in two samples of randomly selected adults (n = 2083). *Neuropsychologia* 26: 465-77.

2177 Lasker, G W. 1985. *Surnames and Genetic Structure*. Cambridge: Cambridge University Press.

2178 Layzer, D. 1972. Science or superstition: A physical scientist looks at the IQ controversy. *Cognition* 1: 265-300.

2179 Lederberg, J. 1963. Eugenics and genetics. In *Man and his Future*. Edited by Wolstenholme, G. Pp. 274-298. London: Churchill.

2180 Lederberg, J. 1966. Experimental genetics and human evolution. *Bulletin of Atomic Scientists* 22: 4-11.

2181 Lehrke, R G. 1978. Sex linkage: A biological basis for greater male variability in intelligence. In *Human Variation: The Biopsychology of Age, Race, and Sex*. Edited by Osborne, T R, C E Noble, N Weyl. New York: Academic Press.

2182 Lerner, I. 1969. *Heredity, Evolution, and Society*. San Francisco: Freeman.

2183 Leslie, P W, J W MacCluer, B Dyke. 1978. Consanguinity avoidance and genotype frequencies in human populations. *Human Biology* 50: 281-299.

2184 Leslie, C. 1990. Scientific racism: Reflection on peer review, science and ideology. *Social Science and Medicine* 31: 891-912.

2185 Levin, M. 1992. Responses to race difference in crime. *Journal of Social Philosophy* 23: 5-29.

2186 Lewontin, R. 1974. *The Genetic Basis of Evolutionary Change*. New York: Columbia University Press.

2187 Lewontin, R. 1974. The analysis of variance and the analysis of causes. *American Journal of Human Genetics* 26: 400-411.

2188 Lewontin, R. 1975. Genetic aspects of intelligence. *Annual Review of Genetics* 9: 387-405.

2189 Lewontin, R. 1982. *Human Diversity*. New York: Freeman.

2190 Lieblich, I, ed. 1982. *Genetics of the Brain*. New York: Elsevier Biomedical Press.

2191 Livingston, F B. 1969. Genetics, ecology and the origins of incest and exogamy. *Current Anthropology* 10: 45-61.

2192 Livingston, F B. 1980. Cultural causes of genetic change. In *Sociobiology: Beyond Nature/Nurture?* Edited by Barlow, G, J Silverberg. Pp. 307-329. Washington, DC: American Association for the Advancement of Science.

2193 Livingston, F B. 1980. Natural selection and the origin and maintenance of genetic marker systems. *Year Book of Physical Anthropology* 23: 25-42.

2194 Loeber, R, T Dishion. 1983. Early predictors of male delinquency: A review. *Psychological Bulletin* 94: 68-99.

2195 Loehlin, J C, J M Horn, L Willerman. 1990. Heredity, environment, and personality change: Evidence from the Texas adoption project. *Journal of Personality* 58: 221-44.

2196 Loevinger, J, R Wessler. 1970. *Measuring ego development.* San Francisco: Jossey-Bass.

2197 Lohlin, J C, G Lidzey, J N Spuhler. 1975. *Race Differences in Intelligence.* San Francisco: Foreman.

2198 Lucchetti, E, E Rabino Massa. 1984. Population mobility and biological distances in Bellino (CN, Italy). *Journal of Human Evolution* 13: 357-368.

2199 Lykken, D T. 1982. Research with twins: The concept of emergenesis. *Psychophysiology* 19: 361-373.

2200 Lynn, M. 1989. Race differences in sexual behavior: A critique of Rushton and Bogaert's evolutionary hypothesis. *Journal of Research in Personality* 23: 1-6.

2201 Lynn, R. 1990. The role of nutrition in the secular increases in intelligence. *Personality and Individual Differences* 11: 273-85.

2202 Lynn, R. 1990. New evidence on brain size and intelligence: A comment on Rushton and Cain and Vanderwolf. *Personality and Individual Differences* 11: 795-97.

2203 Malhotra, K C, A Basu, eds. 1982. *Human Genetics and Adaptation: Proceedings of the Indian Statistical Institute Golden Jubilee International Conference1982.* Calcutta: ISI.

2204 Martin, A O, T W Kurczynski, A G Steinberg. 1973. Familial studies of medical and anthropometric variables in a human isolate. *American Journal of Human Genetics* 25: 581-593.

2205 Martin, N G, L J Eaves. 1977. The genetical analysis of covariance structure. *Heredity* 38: 79-95.

2206 Martin, N G, L J Eaves, M J Kearsey, P Davies. 1978. The power of the classical twin study. *Heredity* 40: 97-116.

2207 Martin, N G, R Jardine, L J Eaves. 1984. Is there only one set of genes for different abilities? A reanalysis of the National Merit Scholarship Qualifying Test data. *Behavior Genetics* 14: 355-370.

2208 Martin, N G, J Perl, J G Oakeshott, J G Gibson, G A Starmer, A V Wilks. 1985. A twin study of ethanol metabolism. *Behavior Genetics* 15: 93-109.

2209 Martin, N G, J G Oakeshott, J G Gibson, G A Starmer, J Perl, A V Wilks. 1985. A twin study of psychomotor and physiological responses to an acute dose of alcohol. *Behavior Genetics* 15: 305-347.

2210 Martin, N G, L J Eaves, L J Heath, R Jardine, L M Feingold, J H Eysenck. 1986. Transmission of social attitudes. *Proceedings of the National Academy of Sciences USA* 83: 4364-4368.

2211 Martin, N G, R Jardine, J G Andrews, L J Heath. 1988. Anxiety disorders and neuroticism: Are there genetic factors specific to panic? *Acta Psychiatrica Scandinavica* 77: 698-706.

2212 Martos, G, M Pap, V Hollo-Leleszi. 1982. Frequency of consanguineous marriages and degree of endogamy in the population of Mezokevesd. *Homo* 33: 168-174.

2213 McCartney, K, M Harris, F Bernieri. 1990. Growing up and growing apart: A developmental meta-analysis of twin studies. *Psychological Bulletin* 107: 226-237.

2214 McClearn, G. 1970. Behavioral genetics. *Annual Review of Genetics* 4: 437-468.

2215 McClearn, G E, J C De Fries. 1973. *Introduction to Behavioral Genetics.* San Francisco: Freeman.

2216 McGregor, A, ed. 1986. *Evolution, Creative Intelligence and Intergroup Competition.* Washington, D.C.: Cliveden Press.

2217 McKusick, V A. 1980. Medical genetic studies of the Amish, with comparison to other populations. In *Population Structure and Genetic Disorders.* Edited by Eriksson, A W, H R Forsius, H R Nevanlinna, P L Workman, R K Norio. Pp. 291-300. London: Academic Press.

2218 Meade, J, A Parkes, eds. 1966. *Genetic and environmental factors in human ability.* Edinburgh: Oliver & Boyd.

2219 Mednick, S, K Christiansen, eds. 1977. *Biosocial Bases of Criminal Behavior.* New York: Gardner.

2220 Mednick, S A, W F Gabrielle, B Hutchings. 1984. Genetic influences in criminal convictions: Evidence from an adoption cohort. *Science* 224: 891-894.

2221 Mednick, S A, W F Gabrielli, B Hutchings. 1987. Genetic factors in the etiology of criminal behavior. In *The Causes of Crime.* Edited by Mednick, S A, T E Moffitt, S A Stack. Cambridge: Cambridge University Press.

2222 Mednick, S, T Moffitt, S Stock, eds. 1987. *The Causes of Crime.* Cambridge: Cambridge University Press.

2223 Mednick, S A, E Kandel. 1988. Genetic and perinatal factors in violence. In *Biological Contributions to Crime Causation.* Edited by Moffitt, T E, S A Mednick. Dordrecht: Nijhoff.

2224 Mednick, S A, E Kandel. 1988. Congenital determinants in violence. *Bulletin of the Academy of Psychiatry and Law* 16: 101-110.

2225 Middleton, R. 1962. Brother-sister and father-daughter marriage in Ancient Egypt. *American Sociological Review* 27: 603-611.

2226 Moffitt, T E, S A Mednick, eds. 1988. *Biological Contributions to Crime Causation.* Dordrecht: Nijhoff.

2227 Moore, J, R Ali. 1984. Are dispersal and inbreeding avoidance related? *Animal Behavior* 32: 94-112.

2228 Morton, N E, J F Crow, H J Muller. 1956. An estimate of the mutational damage in man from data on consanguineous marriages. *Proceedings of the National Academy of Sciences USA* 42: 855-863.

2229 Morton, N. 1958. Empirical risks in consanguineous marriages: Birth weight, gestation time, and measurements of infants. *American Journal of Human Genetics* 10: 344-349.

2230 Morton, N E, S S Chin, P M Ming. 1967. *Genetics of Inter-racial Crosses in Hawaii.* Basel: Karger.

2231 Mourant, A E, A C Kopec, K Domaniewska-Sobczak. 1978. *The Genetics of the Jews.* Oxford: Clarendon Press.

2232 Muller, H J, et al. 1939. The geneticists' manifesto. *Eugenical News* 24: 63-64.

2233 Muller, H J. 1963. Genetic progress by voluntarily conducted germinal choice. In *Man and his Future.* Edited by Wolstenholme, G. Pp. 247-262. London: Churchill.

2234 Nagoshi, C T, R C Johnson, F M Ahern, G P Danko, J R Wilson, L S Yamamoto, J Samet-Driver, S G Vandenberg. 1982. Correlations of measures of personality and of cognitive abilities within and across generations. *Behavior Genetics* 12: 327-341.

2235 Nagoshi, C T, R C Johnson. 1986. The ubiquity of g. *Personality and Individual Differences* 7: 201-207.

2236 Nagoshi, C T, R C Johnson, F M Ahern. 1987. Phenotypic assortative mating vs. social homogany among Japanese and Chinese parents in the Hawaii Family Study of Cognition. *Behavioral Genetics* 17: 477-485.

2237 Nagoshi, C T, R C Johnson, G P Danko. 1990. Assortative mating for cultural identification as indicated by language use. *Behavior Genetics* 20: 23-31.

2238 Neel, J, W Schull. 1954. *Human Heredity.* Chicago: University of Chicago Press.

2239 Nei, M. 1987. *Molecular Evolutionary Genetics.* New York: Columbia University Press.

2240 Neubauer, P, A Neubauer. 1990. *Nature's Thumbprint: The New Genetics of Personality.* Reading, MA: Addison-Wesley.

2241 Nurnberger, J I, N S Nadi, W H Berrittini, L R Goldin. 1983. Current status of genetic research in affective disorders. In *The Origins of Depression: Current Concepts and Approaches.* Edited by Angst, J. Pp. 205-220. Berlin: Springer.

2242 Nurnberger, J I, E S Gershon. 1984. Genetics of affective disorders. In *Neurobioloby of Mood Disorders.* Edited by Post, R M, J Ballenger. Pp. 76-101. Baltimore: Williams and Wilkins.

2243 Osborn, F. 1940. *Preface to Eugenics.* New York: Harper & Row.

2244 Osborn, F. 1968. *The Future of Human Heredity: An Introduction to Eugenics in Modern Society.* New York: Weybright and Talley.

2245 Osborn, F, C J Bajema. 1972. The eugenic hypothesis. *Social Biology* 19: 337-345.

2246 Ott, J. 1985. *Analysis of Human Genetic Linkage.* Baltimore: Johns Hopkins.

2247 Parker, S. 1976. The precultural basis of the incest taboo: Toward a biosocial theory. *American Anthropologist* 78: 285-305.

2248 Pearson, R, ed. 1991. *Race, Intelligence and Bias in Academe.* Washington, D.C.: Scott-Townsend.

2249 Plomin, R, D C Rowe. 1977. A twin study of temperament in young children. *Journal of Psychology* 97: 103-13.

2250 Plomin, R, D C Rowe. 1979. Genetic and environmental etiology of social behaviour in infancy. *Development Psychology* 15: 62-72.

2251 Plomin, R, T T Foch. 1980. A twin study of objectively assessed personality in childhood. *Journal of Personality and Social Psychology* 39: 680-688.

2252 Plomin, R, J C DeFries, C E McClearn. 1980. *Behavioral Genetics: A Primer.* San Francisco: Freeman.

2253 Plomin, R. 1981. Hereditary and temperament: A comparison of twin data for self-report questionnaires, peer ratings, and objectively assessed behavior. In *Twin Research.* Edited by Gedda, L, P Parisi, W E Nance. New York: Alan R. Liss.

2254 Plomin, R. 1981. Ethological behavioral genetics and development. In *Behavioral Development.* Edited by Immelmann, K, L Petrinovich, M Main. Cambridge: Cambridge University Press.

2255 Plomin, R, J C Loehlin, J C DeFries. 1985. Genetic and environmental components of "environmental" influences. *Developmental Psychology* 21: 319-402.

2256 Plomin, R, J DeFries. 1985. *Origins of Individual Differences in Infancy: The Colorado Adoption Project.* Orlando, FL: Academic Press.

2257 Plomin, R, J Dunn. 1986. *The Study of Temperament: Changes, Continuities, and Challenges.* Hillsdale, N.J.: Erlbaum.

2258 Plomin, R. 1986. *Development, Genetics, and Psychology.* Hillsdale, NJ: Erlbaum.

2259 Plomin, R, D Daniels. 1987. Why are children in the same family so different from one another? *Behavioral and Brain Sciences* 10: 1-60.

2260 Plomin, R, R Corley, J C DeFries, D W Fulker. 1990. Individual differences in television viewing in early childhood: Nature as well as nurture. *Psychological Science* 1: 371-377.

2261 Plomin, R. 1990. *Nature and Nurture: An Introduction to Human Behavioral Genetics.* Pacific Grove, CA: Brooks-Cole.

2262 Plomin, R, J R Nesselroade. 1990. Behavioral genetics and personality change. *Journal of Personality* 58: 191-220.

2263 Plomin, R, C S Bergeman. 1991. The nature of nurture: Genetic influence on 'environmental' measures. *Behavioral and Brain Sciences* 14: 373-427.

2264 Plomin, R, R Rende. 1991. Human behavioral genetics. *Annual Review of Psychology* 42: 161-190.

2265 Rahim, A R A, C T Nagoshi, R C Johnson, S G Vandenberg. 1988. Familial resemblances for cognitive abilities and personality in an Egyptian sample. *Personality and Individual Differences* 9: 155-163.

2266 Rao, D C, N E Morton, S Yee. 1974. Analysis of family resemblance II. A linear model for familial correlations. *American Journal of Human Genetics* 26: 331-359.

2267 Rao, P S S, S G Inbaraj. 1977. Inbreeding in Tamil Nadu, South India. *Social Biology* 24: 281-288.

2268 Rao, P S S, S G Inbaraj. 1977. Inbreeding effects on human reproduction in Tamil Nadu of South India. *Annals of Human Genetics* 41: 87-98.

2269 Rao, P S S, S G Inbaraj. 1980. Inbreeding effects on fetal growth and development. *Journal of Medical Genetics* 17: 27-33.

2270 Rao, A P, V R Reddy. 1983. Inbreeding among three endogamous groups in a multicaste village of Andhra Pradesh, India. *Social Biology* 30: 109-111.

2271 Rhoads, J G, A Damon. 1973. Some genetic traits of Solomon Island populations. II. Hand clasping, arm folding, and handedness. *American journal of Physical Anthropology* 39: 179-184.

2272 Rice, J, C R Cloninger, T Reich. 1980. Analysis of behavioral traits in the presence of cultural transmission and assortative mating. *Behavioral Genetics* 10: 73-92.

2273 Richerson, P, R Boyd. 1989. The role of evolved predispositions in cultural evolution: Or, human sociobiology meets Pascal's wager. *Ethology and Sociobiology* 10: 195-219.

2274 Ritvo, E R, B J Freeman, A Mason-Brothers, A Mo, A M Ritvo. 1985. Concordance for the syndrome of autism in 40 pairs of afflicted twins. *American Journal of Psychiatry* 142: 74-77.

2275 Roberts, D F, B Bonne. 1973. Reproduction and inbreeding among the Samaritans. *Social Biology* 20: 64-70.

2276 Roberts, D F. 1979. Genetic evolution in an isolated population. *Journal of Anthropological Research* 35: 1-17.

2277 Roberts, D F. 1980. Genetic structure and the pathology of an isolated population. In *Population Structure and Genetic Disorders*. Edited by Eriksson, A W, H R Forsius, H R Nevanlinna, P L Workman, R K Norio. Pp. 7-26. London: Academic Press.

2278 Roberts, D F, G F De Stefano. 1986. *Genetic Variation and its Maintenance*. Cambridge: Cambridge University Press.

2279 Roberts, J V, T Gabor. 1990. Lombrosian wine in a new bottle: Research on crime and race. *Canadian Journal of Criminology* 32: 291-313.

2280 Roche, R, R S Spielman, J V Neel. 1974. A comparison of gene frequency and anthropometric matrices in seven villages of four Indian tribes. *Human Biology* 46: 295-310.

2281 Rowe, H, ed. 1981. *Intelligence: Reconceptualization and Measurement.* Hillsdale, NJ: Erlbaum.

2282 Rowe, D, D Osgood. 1984. Heredity and sociological theories of delinquency: A reconsideration. *American Sociological Review* 49: 526-40.

2283 Rowe, D C. 1986. Genetic and environmental components of antisocial behavior: A study of 265 twin pairs. *Criminology* 24: 513-532.

2284 Rowe, D. 1990. Inherited dispositions toward learning delinquent and criminal behavior: New evidence. In *Crime in Biological, Social, and Moral Contexts.* Edited by Ellis, L, H Hoffman. New York: Praeger.

2285 Roychoudhury, A K. 1984. Genetic relationship between Indian tribes and Australian aboriginals. *Human Heredity* 34: 314-321.

2286 Roychoudhury, A K, M Nei. 1988. *Human Polymorphic Genes: World Distribution.* New York: Oxford University Press.

2287 Rushton, J P, J H Russell, P Wells. 1985. Personality and genetic similarity theory. *Journal of Social and Biological Structures* 8: 63-86.

2288 Rushton, J P. 1985. Differential K theory and race differences in E and N. *Personality and Individual Differences* 6: 769-770.

2289 Rushton, J P. 1985. Differential K theory: The sociobiology of individual and group differences. *Personality and Individual Differences* 6: 441-452.

2290 Rushton, J P, J H Robin, R Wells, P Wells. 1985. Personality and genetic similarity theory. *Journal of Social and Biological Structures* 8: 63-86.

2291 Rushton, J. 1988. Epigenetic rules in moral development: Distal-proximal approaches to altruism and aggression. *Aggressive Behavior* 14: 35-50.

2292 Rushton, J P. 1989. Genetic similarity, human altruism, and group selection. *Behavioral and Brain Sciences* 12: 503-559.

2293 Rushton, J P, A F Bogaert. 1989. Race differences in sexual behavior: Testing an evolutionary hypothesis. *Journal of Research in Personality* 21: 529-51.

2294 Rushton, J P. 1989. Japanese inbreeding depression scores: Predictors of cognitive differences between blacks and whites. *Intelligence* 13: 43-51.

2295 Rushton, J, A Bogaert. 1989. Population differences in susceptiblity to AIDS: An evolutionary analysis. *Social Science and Medicine* 28: 1211-1220.

2296 Rushton, J. 1989. The evolution of racial differences. *Journal of Research in Personality* 23: 7-20.

2297 Rushton, J. 1989. Genetic similarity in male friendships. *Ethology and Sociobiology* 10: 361-374.

2298 Rushton, J P. 1990. AIDS and race: More information. *Social Science and Medicine* 31: 905-909.

2299 Rushton, J P. 1990. Race differences and r/K theory: A reply to Silverman. *Ethology and Sociobiology* 11: 131-40.

2300 Rushton, J P. 1990. Race, brain size and intelligence: A rejoinder to Cain and Vanderwolf. *Personality and Individual Differences* 11: 785-94.

2301 Rushton, J P. 1990. Sir Francis Galton, epigenetic rules, genetic similarity theory, and human life-history analysis. *Journal of Personality* 58: 117-40.

2302 Rushton, J P. 1991. Do r/K strategies underlie human race differences? A reply to Weizmann et al. *Canadian Psychology* 32: 29-42.

2303 Rushton, J. 1992. Cranial capacity related to sex, rank, and race in a stratified random sample of 6,325 U.S. military personnel. *Intelligence* 16: 401-13.

2304 Russell, R, J Rushton, P Wells. 1985. Sociobiology, personality, and genetic similarity detection. *Annals of Theoretical Psychology* 2: 59-65.

2305 Russell, R J H, P A Wells, J P Rushton. 1986. Evidence for genetic similarity detection in human marriage. *Ethology and Sociobiology* 6: 183-187.

2306 Saudino, K J, W O Eaton. 1991. Infant temperament and genetics: An objective twin study of motor activity level. *Child Development* 62: 1167-1174.

2307 Scarr, S, R A Weinberg. 1978. The influence of "family background" on intellectual attainment. *American Sociological Review* 43: 674-692.

2308 Scarr, S, ed. 1981. *Race, Social Class, and Individual Differences.* Hillsdale, N.J.: Erlbaum.

2309 Scarr, S, S Grajek. 1982. Similarities and differences among siblings. In *Sibling Relationships: Their Nature and Significance Across the Lifespan.* Edited by Lamb, M E, B Sutton-Smith. Hillsdale, N.J.: Erlbaum.

2310 Scarr, S, K McCartney. 1983. How people make their own environments: A theory of genotype—environment effects. *Child Development* 54: 424-435.

2311 Schaie, K W, et al, eds. 1975. *Developmental Human Behavior Genetics.* Lexington, MA: Lexington Books.

2312 Scheller, R H, B S Rothman, E Mayeri. 1981. The behavior of organisms, as it is linked to genes and populations. In *Perspectives in Ethology.* Edited by Bateson, P P G, P H Klopfer. New York: Plenum.

2313 Scheller, R H, B S Rothman, E Mayeri. 1983. A single gene encodes multiple peptide-transmitter candidates involved in a stereotyped behavior. *Trends in Neuroscience* 6: 340-45.

2314 Schiff, M, M Duyme, A Dumaret, S Tomkiewicz. 1974. How much could we boost scholastic achievement and IQ scores? A direct answer from a French adoption study. *Cognition* 12: 165-196.

2315 Schmid, W, J Nielsen, eds. 1981. *Human Behavior and Genetics.* Amsterdam: Elsevier.

2316 Schroeder, T. 1915. Incest in Mormonism. *American Journal of Urology and Sexology* 11: 409-416.

2317 Schull, W J, J V Neel. 1965. *The Effects of Inbreeding on Japanese Children.* New York: Harper & Row.

2318 Scott, J P, J L Fuller. 1965. *Genetics and the Social Behavior of the Dog.* Chicago: Univesity of Chicago Press.

2319 Seemanova, E. 1971. A study of children of incestuous matings. *Human Heredity* 21: 108-128.

2320 Serre, J L, M-C Babron. 1985. Polymorphism and genetic evolution in an isolate in the Antilles: Saint-Barthelemy. *Annals of Human Biology* 12: 413-419.

2321 Serre, J L, L Jakobi, M-C Babron. 1985. A genetic isolate in the French Pyrenees: Probabilities of origin of genes and inbreeding. *Journal of Biosocial Science* 17: 405-414.

2322 Shields, J. 1962. *Monozygotic Twins: Brought up Apart and Brought up Together*. London: Oxford University Press.

2323 Sigvardson, S, C R Cloninger, M Bohman, A von Knorring. 1982. Predispositions to petty criminality in Swedish adoptees II. Sex differences and validation of the male typology. *Archives of General Psychiatry* 39: 1248-1253.

2324 Silverman, I. 1990. The r/K theory of human individual differences: Scientific and Social Issues. *Ethology and Sociobiology* 11: 1-9.

2325 Slater, M K. 1959. Ecological factors in the origin of incest. *American Anthropologist* 61: 1042-1059.

2326 Slotkin, J S. 1947. On a possible lack of incest regulations in Old Iran. *American Anthropologist* 61: 612-617.

2327 Smith, R H. 1979. On selection for inbreeding in polygynous animals. *Heredity* 43: 205-211.

2328 Smouse, P E, V J Vitzthum, J V Neel. 1981. The impact of random and lineal fission in the genetic divergence of small human groups: A case study among the Yanomama. *Genetics* 98: 170-197.

2329 Spearman, C E. 1923. *The Nature of Intelligence and the Principles of Cognition*. London: Macmillan.

2330 Spearman, C E. 1927. *Abilities of Man: Their Nature and Measurement*. London: Macmillan.

2331 Spence, A, E R Ritvo, M L Marazita, J Funderbunk, R S Sparkes, B J Freeman. 1985. Gene mapping studies with the syndrome of autism. *Behavior Genetics* 15: 1-14.

2332 Spielman, R S, J V Neel, F H F Li. 1977. Inbreeding estimation from population data: Models, procedures and implications. *Genetics* 85: 355-371.

2333 Stelmack, R M. 1990. Biological bases of extraversion: Psychophysiological evidence. *Journal of Personality* 58: 293-312.

2334 Sternberg, R, ed. 1982. *Handbook of Human Intelligence*. Cambridge: Cambridge University Press.

2335 Sternberg, R J. 1984. Toward a triarchic theory of human intelligence. *Behavioral and Brain Sciences* 7: 269-316.

2336 Sternberg, R, D Detterman, eds. 1986. *What is Intelligence? Contemporary Viewpoints on its Nature and Definition*. Norwood, NJ: Ablex.

2337 Sternberg, R. 1988. *The Triarchic Mind: A New Theory of Human Intelligence.* New York: Viking.

2338 Stime, G J. 1977. *Biosocial Genetics: Human Heredity and Social Issues.* New York: Macmillan.

2339 Susanne, C. 1984. *Genetical and Environmental Factors during the Growth Period.* New York: Plenum.

2340 Talmon, S. 1977. The Samaritans. *Scientific American* 236: 100-108.

2341 Tambs, K, J M Sundet, P Magnus. 1988. Genetic and environmental effects on the convariance structure of the Norwegian army ability tests. *Personality and Individual Differences* 9: 791-799.

2342 Tambs, K, J M Sundet, P Magnus, K Berg. 1989. Genetic and environmental contributions to the covariance between occupation status, educational attainment, and IQ: A study of twins. *Behavior Gentetics* 9: 209-22.

2343 Teasdale, R W, D R Owen. 1984. Heredity and family environment in intelligence and educational level: A sibling study. *Nature* 309: 620-622.

2344 Tellegen, A, D T Lykken, T J Bouchard, K J Wilcox, N L Segal, S Rich. 1988. Personality similarity in twins reared apart and together. *Journal of Personality and Social Psychology* 54: 1031-1039.

2345 Thiessen, D, B Gregg. 1980. Human assortive mating and genetic equilibrium: An evolutionary perspective. *Ethology and Sociobiology* 1: 111-140.

2346 Thiessen, D, M Ross. 1990. The use of a sociobiological questionnaire (SQ) for the assessment of sexual dimorphism. *Behavior Genetics* 20: 297-306.

2347 Thompson, P R. 1980. And who is my neighbor? An answer from evolutionary genetics. *Social Science Information* 19: 733-38.

2348 Thompson, E A. 1986. *Pedigree Analysis in Human Genetics.* Baltimore: Johns Hopkins.

2349 Thornhill, N W. 1990. The evolutionary significance of incest rules. *Ethology and Sociobiology* 11: 113-130.

2350 Travis, O R, C E Noble, N Weyl, eds. 1978. *Human Variation: The Biopsychology of Age, Race and Sex.* New York: Academic Press.

2351 van den Berghe, P L, G Mesher. 1980. Royal incest and inclusive fitness. *American Ethnologist* 7: 330-317.

2352 Vernon, P, ed. 1992. *Biological Approaches to the Study of Human Intelligence.* Norwood, NJ: Ablex.

2353 Vogel, K, K Sperling, eds. 1987. *Human Genetics.* Berlin: Springer Verlag.

2354 Wadsworth, M. 1979. *Roots of Delinquency: Infancy, Adolsecence, and Crime.* Oxford: Robertson.

2355 Waller, N G, B A Kojetin, T J Bouchard, D T Lykken, A Tellegen. 1990. Genetic and environmental influences on religious interests, attitudes, and values: A study of twins reared apart and together. *Psychological Science* 1: 138-42.

2356 Weiss, V. 1980. Inbreeding and genetic distance between hierarchically structured populations measured by surname frequencies. *Mankind Quarterly* 21: 135-149.

2357 Weizmann, F, N I Winer, D L Wisenthal, M Ziegler. 1990. Differential K theory and racial hierarchies. *Canadian Psychology* 31: 1-13.

2358 Welham, C V J. 1990. Incest: An evolutionary model. *Ethology and Sociobiology* 11: 97-112.

2359 Wells, W P. 1980. *Personality and Heredity: An Introduction to Psychogenetics.* London: Longman.

2360 Wiener, L F. 1987. Of phonetics and genetics: A comparison of classification in linguistic and organic systems. In *Biological Metaphor and Cladistic Classification: An Interdisciplinary Perspective.* Edited by Hoenigswald, H M, L F Wiener. Pp. 217-226. Philadelphia: University of Pennsylvania Press.

2361 Willerman, L, J M Horn, J C Loehlin. 1977. The aptitude-achievement test distinction: A study of unrelated children reared together. *Behavioral Genetics* 7: 465-470.

2362 Wilson, J Q, R J Herrnstein. 1985. *Crime and Human Nature.* New York: Simon and Schuster.

2363 Wilson, A, M Stoneking, R Cann, E Prager, S Ferris, L Wrischnik, R G Higuchi. 1987. Mitochondrial clans and the age of our common mother. In *Human Genetics.* Edited by Vogel, K, K Sperling. Pp. 158-64. Berlin: Springer.

2364 Witkin, H, et al. 1976. Criminality in XYY and XXY men. *Science* 193: 547-54.

2365 Wolf, A P. 1968. Adopt a daughter-in-law, marry a sister: A Chinese solution to the problem of the incest taboo. *American Anthropologist* 70: 864-874.

2366 Wolf, A P, C-S Huang. 1980. *Marriage and Adoption in China, 1845-1945.* Stanford: Stanford University Press.

2367 Wolfgang, M E, N A Weiner, eds. 1981. *Criminal Violence.* Beverly Hills, CA: Sage Publications.

2368 Yamaguchi, M, T Yanase, H Nagano, N Nakamoto. 1970. Effects of inbreeding on mortality in Fukuoka population. *American Journal of Human Genetics* 22: 145-155.

2369 Yasuda, N. 1983. Studies of isonymy and inbreeding in Japan. *Human Biology* 55: 263-276.

2370 Yasuda, N, N Saitou. 1984. Random isonymy and inbreeding in Japan. *Human Biology* 1: 75-84.

2371 Zajonc, R, J Bargh. 1980. Birth orders, family size and decline of SAT scores. *American Psychologist* 35: 662-668.

2372 Zuckerman, M, F Bernieri, R Koestner, R Rosenthal. 1989. To predict some of the people some of the time: The search for moderators continues. *Journal of Personality and Social Psychology* 57: 279-93.

# 7

# Ethology

2373 Abramovitch, R, D Pepler, C Corter. 1982. Patterns of sibling interaction among preschool-age children. In *Sibling Relationships, Their Nature and Significance across the Lifespan*. Edited by Lamb, M, B Sutton-Smith. Hillsdale, N.J.: Erlbaum.

2374 Abromovits, R, M M Konstantareas, L Sloman. 1980. An observational assessment of change in two groups of behaviorally disturbed boys. *Journal of Child Psychology and Psychiatry* 21: 133-142.

2375 Adams, G R. 1977. Physical attractiveness research: Toward a developmental social psychology of beauty. *Human Development* 20: 217-239.

2376 Adams, G R. 1989. *Biology of Adolescent Behavior and Development*. Newbury Park, CA: Sage.

2377 Adang, O M J. 1986. Exploring the social environment: A developmental study of teasing in chimpanzees. *Ethology* 73: 136-160.

2378 Ainsworth, M D S, M C Blehar, E Waters, S Wall. 1978. *Patterns of Attachment*. Hillsdale, N.J.: Erlbaum.

2379 Akert, R M, A T Panter. 1988. Extraversion and the ability to decode nonverbal communication. *Personality and Individual Differences* 9: 965-972.

2380 Aldis, O. 1975. *Play Fighting*. New York: Academic Press.

2381 Alexander, T. 1976. Behavioral individuality in childhood. In *Human Behavioral Genetics*. Edited by Kaplan, A R. Pp. 151-163. Springfield: Charles C. Thomas.

2382 Alexander, I E, E W Babad. 1981. Returning the smile of the stranger: Within-culture and cross-cultural comparisons of Israeli and American children. *Genetic Psychology Monographs* 103: 31-77.

2383 Allee, W C. 1942. Social dominance and subordination among vertebrates. *Biological Symposia* 8: 139-62.

2384 Alley, T R. 1983. Infantile head shape as an elicitor of adult protection. *Merrill-Palmer Quarterly* 29: 411-427.

2385 Altmann, J. 1974. Observational study of behavior: Sampling methods. *Behavior* 48: 227-267.

2386 Altmann, J. 1980. *Baboon Mothers and Infants.* Cambridge: Harvard University Press.

2387 Altmann, J. 1990. Primate males go where the females are. *Animal Behavior* 39: 193-194.

2388 Amato, P. 1989. Who cares for children in public places? Naturalistic observation of male and female caretakers. *Journal of Marriage and the Family* 51: 981-990.

2389 Anderson, J L, C B Crawford, J Nadeau, T Lindberg. 1992. Was the Duchess of Windsor right? A cross-cultural review of the socioecology of ideals of female body shape. *Ethology and Sociobiology* 13: 197-227.

2390 Andrew, R J. 1963. The origin and evolution of the calls and facial expressions of the primates. *Behaviour* 20: 1-109.

2391 Andrew, R J. 1963. Evolution of facial expression. *Science* 143: 1034-1041.

2392 Andrew, R J. 1965. The origins of facial expression. *Scientific American* 213: 88-94.

2393 Archer, J. 1970. Effects of population density on behaviour in rodents. In *Social Behaviour of Birds and Mammals.* Edited by Crook, J H. Pp. 169-210. London: Academic Press.

2394 Archer, J, L Birke, eds. 1983. *Exploration in Animals and Humans.* Wokingham: Van Nostrand Reinhold.

2395 Archer, J. 1988. *The Behavioral Biology of Aggression.* Cambridge: Cambridge University Press.

2396 Archer, J, K Browne, eds. 1988. *Human Aggression: Naturalistic Approaches.* New York: Routledge.

2397 Argyle, M, A Kendon. 1967. The experimental analysis of the social performance. In *Advances in Experimental Social Psychology.* Edited by Berkowitz, L. Pp. 55-98. New York: Academic Press.

2398 Argyle, M, ed. 1973. *Social Encounters: Readings in Social Interaction.* Chicago: Aldine.

2399 Argyle, M, L Lefebvre, M Cook. 1974. The meaning of five patterns of gaze. *European Journal of Social Psychology* 4: 125-136.

2400 Argyle, M, M Cook. 1976. *Gaze and Mutual Gaze.* Cambridge: Cambridge University Press.

2401 Argyle, M. 1991. *Cooperation: The Basis of Sociability.* New York: Routledge.

2402 Aries, E J, C Gold, R H Weigel. 1983. Dispositional and situational influences on dominance behavior in small groups. *Journal of Personality and Social Psychology* 44: 779-786.

2403 Attili, G, P C Boggi. 1984. Sex, age and social competence as factors influencing aggression in 3-6 year olds. *Aggressive Behavior* 10: 145-146.

2404 Attili, G. 1985. Concomitants and factors influencing children's aggression. *Aggressive Behavior* 11: 291-301.

2405 Attili, G, B Hold, M Schleidt. 1986. Relationships among peers in kindergardens: A cross-cultural study. In *Current Perspectives in Primate Relationships.* Edited by Taub, M, F A King. New York: Van Nostrand Reinhold.

2406 Attili, G. 1990. Successful and disconfirmed children in the peer group: Indices of social competence within an evolutionary perspective. *Human Development* 33: 238-249.

2407 Bachmann, C, H Kummer. 1980. Male assessment of female choice in hamadryas baboons. *Behavioral Ecology and Sociobiology* 6: 315-321.

2408 Baerends, G, C Beer, A Manning. 1975. *Function and Evolution in Behavior.* Oxford: Clarendon Press.

2409 Bailey, W T, W C Mackey. 1989. Observations of Japanese men and children in public places: A comparative study. *Psychological Reports* 65: 731-734.

2410 Bakeman, R. 1978. Untangling streams of behavior: Sequential analysis of observational data. In *Observing Behavior: Data Collection and Analysis Methods*. Edited by Sackett, G P. Pp. 63-78. Baltimore: University Park Press.

2411 Bakeman, R, J Gottman. 1986. *Observing Interaction: An Introduction to Sequential Analysis*. New York: Cambridge University Press.

2412 Bakeman, R, L Anderson, P Strisik. 1989. Lags and logs: Statistical approaches to interaction. In *Interaction in Human Development*. Edited by Bernstein, M, J Bruner. Hillsdale, N.J.: Erlbaum.

2413 Baker, P M, G G Eaton. 1992. Seniority versus age as causes of dominance in social groups: Macaques and men. *Small Group Research* 23: 322-343.

2414 Bakke, E W. 1965. Concept of the social organization. In *Modern Organization Theory*. Edited by Haire, M. New York: Wiley.

2415 Balandier, G. 1970. *Political Anthropology*. London: Penguin.

2416 Balch, S H. 1986. The neutered civil servant: Eunuchs, celibates, abductees and the maintenance of organizational loyalty. In *Biology and Bureaucracy*. Edited by White, E, J Losco. Pp. 271-303. Lanham, MD: University Press of America.

2417 Balck, M. 1986. *Sheep and Land: The Economics of Power in a Tribal Society*. Cambridge: Cambridge University Press.

2418 Bard, K A. 1992. Orientation to social and nonsocial stimuli in neonatal chimpanzees and humans. *Infant Behavior and Development* 15: 43-56.

2419 Barkow, G. 1968. Ethological units of behavior. In *Central Nervous System and Fish Behavior*. Edited by Ingle, E D. Chicago: University of Chicago Press.

2420 Barkow, J H. 1973. Darwinian psychological anthropology: A biosocial approach. *Current Anthropology* 14: 373-387.

2421 Barkow, J, L Cosmides, J Tooby. 1986. *The Adapted Mind: Evolutionary Psychology and the Generation of Culture*. New York: Oxford University Press.

2422 Barnard, A. 1983. Contemporary hunter-gatherers: Current theoretical issues in ecology and social organisation. *Annual Review of Anthropology* 12: 193-214.

2423 Barner-Barry, C. 1986. Rob: Children's tacit use of peer ostracism to control aggressive behavior. *Ethology and Sociobiology* 7: 281-294.

2424 Barnett, S A. 1972. The ontogeny of behavior and the concept of instinct. In *Brain and Human Behavior.* Edited by Karczmar, A G, J C Eccles. Pp. 377-392. Berlin: Springer.

2425 Barnett, S A. 1977. The instinct to teach: Altruism or aggression? *Aggressive Behavior* 3: 209-229.

2426 Barnett, S A. 1979. Cooperation, conflict, crowding and stress: An essay on method. *Interdisciplinary Science Review* 4: 106-131.

2427 Barnett, S A. 1981. *Modern Ethology: The Science of Animal Behavior.* New York: Oxford University Press.

2428 Baron, M, R L Ball. 1974. The aggression-inhibiting influence of non-hostile humor. *Journal of Experimental Social Psychology* 10: 23-33.

2429 Bastock, M. 1967. *Courtship: An Ethological Study.* Chicago: Aldine.

2430 Bates, B C. 1970. Territorial behavior in primates: A review of recent studies. *Primates* 11: 271-284.

2431 Bateson, P P G, R A Hinde, eds. 1976. *Growing Points in Ethology.* London: Cambridge University Press.

2432 Bateson, P P G. 1979. How do sensitive periods arise and what are they for? *Animal Behavior* 27: 470-486.

2433 Bateson, P P G, P H Klopfer, eds. 1980. *Perspectives in Ethology.* New York: Plenum.

2434 Bateson, P G, ed. 1983. *Mate Choice.* Cambridge: Cambridge University Press.

2435 Bateson, P P G, P H Klopfer, eds. 1985. *Perspectives in Ethology: Mechanisms.* New York: Plenum.

2436 Bateson, P P G, P H Klopfer. 1989. *Perspectives in Ethology: Whither Ethology?* New York: Plenum.

2437 Bateson, P P G, P H Klopfer, eds. 1990. *Perspectives in Ethology: Human Understanding and Animal Awareness.* New York: Plenum.

2438 Beck, B B. 1972. Tool use in captive hamadryas baboons. *Primates* 13: 276-296.

2439 Beck, B B. 1973. Observation learning of tool use by captive guinea baboons (Papio papio). *American Journal of Physical Anthropology* 38: 579-582.

2440 Beck, B B. 1975. Primate tool behavior. In *Primate Socioecology and Psychology.* Edited by Tuttle, R. Pp. 413-447. The Hague: Mouton.

2441 Beck, B B. 1980. *Animal Tool Behavior: The Use and Manufacture of Tools by Animals.* New York: Garland.

2442 Beck, B B. 1982. Chimpocentrism: Bias in cognitive ethology. *Journal of Human Evolution* 11: 3-17.

2443 Beer, C G. 1973. Species-typical behavior and ethology. In *Comparative Psychology: A Modern Survey.* Edited by Dewsbury, D A, D A Rethlingshafer. New York: McGraw Hill.

2444 Beit-Hallahmi, B, A I Rabin. 1977. The kibbutz as a social experiment and as a child-rearing laboratory. *American Psychologist* 32: 532-541.

2445 Bekoff, M. 1977. Quantitative studies of three areas of classical ethology: Social dominance, behavioral taxonomy, and behavioral variability. In *Quantitative Methods in the Study of Animal Behavior.* Edited by Hazlett, B A. Pp. 1-46. New York: Academic Press.

2446 Bekoff, M. 1981. Development of agonistic behaviour: Ethological and ecological aspects. In *Multidisciplinary Approaches to Aggression Research.* Edited by Brain, P F, D Benton. Pp. 161-78. Amsterdam: Elsevier/North Holland.

2447 Bell, S M V, M D S Ainsworth. 1972. Infant crying and maternal responsiveness. *Child Development* 43: 1171-1190.

2448 Bell, R Q, L V Harper. 1977. *The Effect of Children on Parents.* Hillsdale, N.J.: Erlbaum.

2449 Belsky, J. 1979. Mother-father-infant interaction: A naturalistic observational study. *Developmental Psychology* 15: 601-607.

2450 Benirschke, K, ed. 1986. *Primates: The Road to Self-Sustaining Populations.* New York: Springer.

2451 Berlin, B, P Kay. 1973. *Basic Color Terms: Their Universality and Evolution.* Berkeley: University of California Press.

2452 Berman, P. 1980. Are women more responsive than men to the young? A review of developmental and situational variables. *Psychological Bulletin* 88: 668-695.

2453 Berman, C M. 1980. Mother-infant relationships among free-ranging rhesus monkeys on Cayo Santiago: A comparison with captive pairs. *Animal Behavior* 28: 860-873.

2454 Bernardi, B. 1986. *Age Class Systems: Social Institutions and Polities Based on Age.* Cambridge: Cambridge University Press.

2455 Bernieri, F. 1988. Coordinated movement and rapport in teacher-student interactions. *Journal of Nonverbal Behavior* 12: 120-138.

2456 Bernieri, F, R Rosenthal. 1990. Coordinated movement in human interaction. In *Fundamentals of Nonverbal Behavior.* Edited by Feldman, R S, B Rime. New York: Cambridge University Press.

2457 Bernstein, I S. 1970. Primate status hierarchies. In *Primate Behavior.* Edited by Rosenblum, L A. Pp. 71-109. New York: Academic Press.

2458 Bernstein, I S. 1976. Dominance, aggression, and reproduction in primate societies. *Journal of Theoretical Biology* 60: 459-472.

2459 Bernstein, I S. 1991. An empirical comparison of focal and ad libitum scoring with commentary on instantaneous scans, all occurrences and one-zero techniques. *Animal Behaviour* 42: 721-728.

2460 Betzig, L L. 1982. Despotism and differential reproduction: A cross-cultural correlation of conflict asymmetry, hierarchy, and degree of polygyny. *Ethology and Sociobiology* 3: 269-321.

2461 Betzig, L L. 1989. Rethinking evolutionary ethology: A reponse to some recent critiques. *Ethology and Sociobiology* 9: 315-24.

2462 Bicchieri, M G. 1972. *Hunters and Gatherers Today: A Socioeconomic Study of Eleven Such Cultures in the Twentieth Century.* New York: Holt Rinehart and Winston.

2463 Bigelow, R. 1969. *The Dawn Warriors: Man's Evolution toward Peace.* Boston: Little, Brown.

2464 Bigelow, A E. 1992. Locomotion and search behavior in blind infants. *Infant Behavior & Development* 15: 179-189.

2465 Birdswhistell, R L. 1970. *Kinesics and Context: Essays on Body Motion Communication.* Philadelphia: University of Pennsylvania Press.

2466 Bitterman, M. 1965. Phyletic differences in learning. *American Psychologist* 20: 396-410.

2467 Blacking, J, ed. 1978. *The Anthropology of the Body.* New York: Academic Press.

2468 Blanck, P, R Buck, R Rosenthal. 1986. *Nonverbal Communications in the Clinical Context.* University Park, Pa.: Pennsylvania State University Press.

2469 Bloch, M, A Pellegrini. 1969. *The Ecological Context of Children's Play.* Norwood, N.J.: Ablex.

2470 Blurton Jones, N B. 1972. *Ethological Studies of Child Behaviour.* Cambridge: Cambridge University Press.

2471 Blurton Jones, N G. 1972. Non-verbal communication in children. In *Non-Verbal Communication.* Edited by Hinde, R A. Pp. 271-296. Cambridge: Cambridge University Press.

2472 Blurton Jones, N, V Reynolds, eds. 1978. *Human Behaviour and Adaptation.* London: Taylor and Francis.

2473 Blurton Jones, N G. 1990. Three sensible paradigms for research on evolution and human behavior. *Ethology and Sociobiology* 11: 353-360.

2474 Bodenheimer, E. 1986. Individual and organized society from the perspective of philosophical anthropology. *Journal of Social and Biological Structures* 9: 207-226.

2475 Boehm, C. 1982. The evolutionary development of morality as an effect of dominance behavior and conflict interference. *Journal of Social and Biological Structures* 5: 413-422.

2476 Boehm, C. 1985. Execution within the clan as an extreme form of ostracism. *Social Science Information* 24: 309-322.

2477 Boehm, C. 1986. *Blood Revenge: The Enactment and Management of Conflict in Montenegro and Other Tribal Societies.* Philadelphia: University of Pennsylvania Press.

2478 Bohannen, P, ed. 1967. *Law and Warfare: Studies in the Anthropology of Conflict.* New York: Doubleday.

2479 Bolton, F G, R H Laner, S P Kane. 1980. Child maltreatment risk among adolescent mothers: A study of reported cases. *American Journal of Orthopsychiatry* 50: 489-504.

2480 Bonner, J T. 1980. *The Evolution of Culture in Animals.* Princeton: Princeton University Press.

2481 Borgerhoff Mulder, M, T M Caro. 1985. The use of quantitative observational techniques in anthropology. *Current Anthropology* 26: 323-335.

2482 Borgerhoff Mulder, M. 1987. On cultural and reproductive success: Kipsigis evidence. *American Anthropologist* 89: 617-634.

2483 Borgerhoff Mulder, M. 1988. Is the polygyny threshold model relevant to humans? Kipsigis evidence. In *Mating Patterns.* Edited by Boyce, C G N, A J Mascie-Taylor. Pp. 209-230. Cambridge: Cambridge University Press.

2484 Borgerhoff Mulder, M. 1988. Kipsigis brideweath payments. In *Human Reproductive Behavior.* Edited by Betzig, L L, M Borgerhoff Mulder, P Turke. Pp. 65-82. Cambridge: Cambridge University Press.

2485 Borgerhoff Mulder, M. 1989. Early maturing Kipsigis women have higher reproductive success than later maturing women, and cost more to marry. *Behavioral Ecology and Sociobiology* 24: 145-153.

2486 Borgerhoff Mulder, M. 1992. Women's strategies in polygynous marriage: Kipsigis, Datoga, and other East African cases. *Human Nature* 3: 45-70.

2487 Borgia, G. 1980. Human aggression as a biological adaption. In *The Evolution of Human Social Behavior.* Edited by Lockard, J. Pp. 165-191. New York: Elsevier.

2488 Bouissac, P, M Herzfeld, R Posner, eds. 1992. *Iconicity: Essays on the Nature of Culture.* Tubingen: Stauffenburg Verlag.

2489 Boukydis, Z, R Burgess. 1982. Adult physiological responses to infant cries: Effects of temperament of infant, parental status, and gender. *Child Development* 53: 291-298.

2490 Boulton, M, P K Smith. 1982. Issues in the study of children's rough-and-tumble play. In *The Ethological Context of Children's Play.* Edited by Bloch, M, A D Pellegrini. Pp. 57-83. Norwood, N.J.: Ablex.

2491 Bowden, D M, ed. 1979. *Ageing in Non-Human Primates*. New York: Van Nostrand Reinhold.

2492 Bowen, T G. 1971. The object in the world of the infant. *Scientific American* 255: 30-38.

2493 Bowlby, J. 1958. The nature of the child's tie to his mother. *International Journal of Psycho-Analysis* 39: 1-23.

2494 Boyd, R, P J Richerson. 1992. Punishment allows the evolution of cooperation (or anything else) in sizable groups. *Ethology and Sociobiology* 13: 171-195.

2495 Brain, R. 1979. *Rites Black and White*. Melbourne: Penguin.

2496 Brain, P, J Ramirez, eds. 1981. *The Biology of Aggression*. Alphen a/d Rijn: Sythhoff & Noordhoff.

2497 Brain, P, B Olivier, J Mos, D Benton, P Bronstein, eds. 1988. *Multidisciplinary Studies on Aggression*. Swansea: University of Swansea Press.

2498 Bramblett, C A. 1978. Sex differences in the acquisition of play among juvenile vervet monkeys. In *Social Play in Primates*. Edited by Smith, E O. London: Academic Press.

2499 Bremmer, J, H Roodenburg, eds. 1991. *Gestures in History: A Cultural History of Gestures from Antiquity to the Present*. Cambridge: Polity Press.

2500 Brindley, C, P Clarke, C Hutt, I Robinson, E Wethli. 1973. Sex differences in the activities and social interactions of nursury school children. In *Comparative Ecology and Behaviour of Primates*. Edited by Michael, R P, J H Crook. Pp. 799-828. London: Academic Press.

2501 Bronfenbrenner, U. 1979. *The Ecology of Human Development*. Cambridge: Harvard University Press.

2502 Brookfield, H C, P Brown. 1963. *Struggle for Land*. Melbourne: Oxford University Press.

2503 Brown, J K. 1963. A cross-cultural study of female initiation rites. *American Anthropologist* 65: 837-853.

2504 Brown, J K. 1969. Female initiation rites: A review of the current literature. In *Issues in Adolescent Psychology*. Edited by Rogers, D. Pp. 74-87. Monterey, CA: Brooks/Cole.

2505 Brown, R T, A S Hamilton. 1977. Imprinting: Effects of discrepancy from rearing conditions on approach to a familiar imprinting object in a novel situation. *Journal of Comparative and Physiological Psychology* 91: 784-793.

2506 Brown, P, D Tuzin, eds. 1983. *The Ethnography of Cannibalism.* Washington: Society of Physical Anthropology.

2507 Brown, P. 1986. Culture and Aggession. *Anthropological Quarterly. Special issue* 59, no. 4.

2508 Brown, C E, J F Dovidio, S L Ellyson. 1990. Reducing sex differences in visual displays of dominance: Knowledge is power. *Personality and Social Psychology Bulletin* 16: 263-292.

2509 Brown, J C, W Greenhood. 1991. Paternity, jokes, and song: A possible evolutionary scenario for the origin of language and mind. *Journal of Social and Biological Structures* 14: 255-310.

2510 Brown, D. 1991. *Human Universals.* New York: McGraw-Hill.

2511 Bruce, V, A Cowley, A W Ellis, D Perrett, eds. 1992. *Processing the Facial Image.* Oxford: Clarendon Press.

2512 Bruner, J S. 1982. The organization of action and the nature of adult-infant transaction. In *The Analysis of Action: Recent Theoretical and Empirical Advances.* Edited by von Cranach, M, R Harré. Pp. 313-327. Cambridge: Cambridge University Press.

2513 Buck, R. 1979. Individual differences in nonverbal sending accuracy and electrodermal responding: The externalising-internalising dimension. In *Skill in Nonverbal Communication: Individual Differences.* Edited by Rosenthal, R. Cambridge: Oelgeschlager, Gunn & Hain.

2514 Buck, R. 1991. Social factors in facial display and communication: A reply. *Journal of Nonverbal Behavior* 15: 155-62.

2515 Budock, K F R. 1987. Inter-ethnic relations as expressed in name-giving and cultural mimicry. *Namibia* 11: 41-53.

2516 Buirski, P, R Plutchik, H Kellerman. 1978. Sex differences, dominance, and personality in the chimpanzee. *Animal Behaviour* 26: 123-129.

2517 Bull, P. 1987. *Posture and Gesture.* Elmsford, NY: Pergamon.

2518 Buller, D B, J Comstock, R K Aune, K D Strzyewski. 1989. The effect of probing on deceivers and truthtellers. *Journal of Nonverbal Behavior* 13: 155-170.

2519 Bullowa, M. 1975. When infant and adult communicate how do they synchronize their behavior? In *Organization of Behavior in Face-to-face Interaction.* Edited by Kendon, A, R M Harris, M Ritchiekey. Pp. 95-125. The Hague: Mouton.

2520 Burbeck, S. 1978. The dynamics of riot growth: An epidemiological approach. *Journal of Mathematical Sociology* 6: 1-22.

2521 Burgoon, J K, T Birk, M Pfau. 1990. Nonverbal behaviors, persuasion, and credibility. *Human Communications Research* 17: 140-169.

2522 Burhardt, G M, ed. 1985. *Foundations of Comparative Ethology.* New York: Van Nostrand Reinhold.

2523 Buss, D M, A Angleitner. 1989. Mate selection preferences in Germany and the United States. *Individual Differences* 10: 1269-1280.

2524 Buss, D M. 1989. Conflict between the sexes: Strategic interference and the evocation of anger and upset. *Journal of Personality and Social Psychology* 56: 735-747.

2525 Buss, D M, et al. 1990. International preferences in selecting mates: A study of 37 cultures. *Journal of Cross-Cultural Psychology* 21: 5-47.

2526 Buss, D M. 1990. The evolution of anxiety and social exclusion. *Journal of Social and Clinical Psychology* 9: 196-201.

2527 Busse, C, W J Hamilton. 1981. Infant carrying by male chacma baboons. *Science* 212: 1281-1283.

2528 Butler, J. 1979. Maternal deprivation, 1972-1978: New findings, new concepts, new approaches. *Child Development* 50: 283-305.

2529 Butterworth, G, P Bryant. 1990. *Causes of Development: Interdisciplinary Perspectives.* Hillsdale, N.J.: Erlbaum.

2530 Byrne, R W, J M Byrne. 1991. Hand preferences in the skilled gathering tasks of mountain gorillas (Gorilla g. berengei). *Cortex* 27: 521-546.

2531  Cachel, S. 1989. Theory of punctuated equilibria and evolutionary anthropology. *Journal of Social and Biological Structures* 12: 225-240.

2532  Cairns, R B, J L Gariepy, K E Hood. 1990. Development, microevolution, and social behavior. *Psychological Review* 97: 45-65.

2533  Callan, H. 1970. *Ethology and Society: An Anthropolitical View.* New York: Oxford University Press.

2534  Callan, H W, M R A Chance, T K Pitcairn. 1973. Attention and advertance in human groups. *Social Science Information* 12: 27-41.

2535  Campbell, A. 1986. Self-report of fighting by females: A preliminary study. *British Journal of Criminology* 26: 28-46.

2536  Camporesi, P. 1991. *The Body in the Cosmos: Natural Symbols in Medieval and Early Modern Italy.* Cambridge: Polity Press.

2537  Camporesi, P. 1991. *The Fear of Hell: Images of Damnation and Salvation in Early Modern Europe.* Cambridge: Polity Press.

2538  Caporael, L R, R M Dawes, J M Orbell, A J C van de Kragt. 1989. Selfishness examined: Cooperation in the absence of egoistic incentives. *Behavioral and Brain Sciences* 12: 683-740.

2539  Carey, S E, R Diamond, B Woods. 1980. Development of face recognition: A maturational component? *Developmental Psychology* 16: 257-269.

2540  Carey, S E, R Diamond. 1980. Maturational determination of the developmental course of face encoding. In *Biological Studies of Mental Processes.* Edited by Caplan, D. Cambridge: M.I.T. Press.

2541  Carlson, N R. 1980. *Physiology of Behaviour.* Boston: Allyn and Bacon.

2542  Caro, T M, M B Mulder. 1987. The problem of adaptation in the study of human behavior. *Ethology and Sociobiology* 8: 61-72.

2543  Carpenter, C R. 1974. Aggressive behavioral systems. In *Primate Aggression, Territoriality and Xenophobia.* Edited by Holloway, R L. Pp. 459-496. New York: Academic Press.

2544  Carthy, J D, F J Ebling. 1964. *The Natural History of Aggression.* New York: Academic Press.

2545 Cary, M S. 1979. Gaze and facial display in pedestrian passing. *Semiotica* 28: 323-326.

2546 Cashdan, E. 1983. Territoriality among human foragers: Ecological models and applications to four bushman groups. *Current Anthropology* 2: 47-55.

2547 Cashdan, E, ed. 1990. *Risk and Uncertainty in Tribal and Peasant Economies*. Boulder: Westview Press.

2548 Chagnon, N. 1974. *Studying the Yanomamö*. New York: Holt, Rinehart & Winston.

2549 Chagnon, N. 1975. Genealogy, solidarity, and relatedness: Limits to local group size and patterns of fissioning in an expanding population. *Yearbook of Physical Anthropology* 19: 95-110.

2550 Chagnon, N, W Irons, eds. 1979. *Evolutionary Biology and Human Social Behavior: An Anthropological Perspective*. North Scituate, MA: Duxbury.

2551 Chagnon, N. 1979. Is reproductive success equal in egalitarian societies? In *Evolutionary Biology and Human Social Behavior: An Anthropological Perspective*. Edited by Chagnon, N, W Irons. North Scituate, MA: Duxbury.

2552 Chagnon, N. 1983. *Yanomamö, the Fierce People*. 3rd ed New York: Rinehart & Winston.

2553 Chagnon, N. 1988. Life histories, blood revenge, and warfare in tribal population. *Science* 239: 985-992.

2554 Chance, M R A, C Jolly. 1970. *Social Groups of Monkeys, Apes and Men*. London: Jonathon Cape.

2555 Chance, M R A, R R Larsen, eds. 1976. *The Social Structure of Attention*. New York: Wiley.

2556 Chapais, B. 1983. Reproductive activity in relation to male dominance and the likelihood of ovulation in rhesus monkeys. *Behavioral Ecology and Sociobiology* 12: 215-228.

2557 Chapais, B. 1983. Male dominance and reproductive activity in rhesus monkeys. In *Primate Social Relationships*. Edited by Hinde, R A. Pp. 267-271. Oxford: Blackwell.

2558 Chapman, C A, L J Chapman, L Lefebvre. 1990. Spider monkey alarm calls: Honest advertisement or warning kin? *Behaviour* 39: 197-198.

2559 Chapple, E D. 1970. *Culture and Biological Man: Explorations in Behavioral Anthropology.* New York: Holt, Rinehart, and Winston.

2560 Charlesworth, W R. 1992. Darwin and developmental psychology: Past and present. *Developmental Psychology* 28: 5-16.

2561 Chase, I D. 1974. Models of hierarchy formation in animal societies. *Behavioral Science* 19: 374-382.

2562 Chatfield, C, R E Lemon. 1970. Analysing sequences of behavioral events. *Journal of Theoretical Biology* 29: 427-445.

2563 Cheney, D L. 1977. The acquisition of rank and the development of reciprocal alliances among free-ranging immature baboons. *Behavioral Ecology and Sociobiology* 2: 303-318.

2564 Cheney, D L, R M Seyfarth. 1986. The recognition of social alliances by vervet monkeys. *Animal Behavior* 34: 1722-1731.

2565 Cheverud, J M, M M Dow, W Leutenegger. 1986. A phylogenetic autocorrelation analysis of sexual dimorphism in primates. *American Anthropologist* 88: 916-922.

2566 Chivers, D J, B A Wood, A Bilsborough, eds. 1984. *Food Acquisition and Processing in Primates.* New York: Plenum.

2567 Christian, J J. 1970. Social subordination, population density and mammalian evolution. *Science* 168: 84-90.

2568 Ciolek, T M. 1975. Some theoretical and methodological aspects of studies in human communicational behaviour. *Etnografia Polska* 19: 139-148.

2569 Ciolek, T M. 1977. Location of static gatherings in pedestrian areas: An exploratory study. *Man-Environment Systems* 7: 41-54.

2570 Ciolek, T M. 1978. Spatial arrangements in social encounters: An attempt at a taxonomy. *Man-Environment Systems* 8: 52-59.

2571 Ciolek, T M. 1978. Spatial organisation in social interaction. *Canberra Anthropology* 1: 6-26.

2572 Ciolek, T M, A Kendon. 1980. Environment and the spatial arrangement of conversational encounters. *Sociological Inquiry* 50: 237-271.

2573 Ciolek, T M. 1981. Pedestrian behaviour in pedestrian spaces: Some findings of a naturalistic field study. In *Understanding the Built Environment.* Edited by Szokolay, S V. Pp. 95-112. Canberra: Australian and New Zealand Architectural Science Association.

2574 Ciolek, T M. 1982. Zones of co-presence in face-to-face interaction: Some observational data. *Man-Environment Systems* 12: 233-242.

2575 Ciolek, T M. 1983. The proxemics lexicon: A first approximation. *Journal of Nonverbal Behavior* 8: 55-75.

2576 Cloak, F T. 1975. Is a cultural ethology possible? *Human Ecology* 3: 161-182.

2577 Clutton-Brock, T H, P H Harvey. 1976. Evolutionary rules and primate societies. In *Growing Points in Ethology.* Edited by Bateson, P P G, R A Hinde. Pp. 195-237. London: Cambridge University Press.

2578 Cohen, J. 1968. Multiple regression as a general data-analytic system. *Psychological Bulletin* 70: 426-443.

2579 Colgan, P W, ed. 1978. *Quantitative Ethology.* New York: Wiley.

2580 Colgan, P W, J T Smith. 1978. Multidimensional contingency table analysis. In *Quantitative Ethology.* Edited by Colgan, P W. Pp. 145-174. New York: Wiley.

2581 Colson, E. 1974. *Tradition and Contract: The Problem of Order.* Chicago: Aldine Press.

2582 Conroy, G. 1990. *Primate Evolution.* New York: Norton.

2583 Constanzo, M, D Archer. 1989. Interpreting the expressive behavior of others: The interpersonal perception task. *Journal of Nonverbal Behavior* 13: 225-245.

2584 Cook, M, J M C Smith. 1975. The role of gaze in impression formation. *British Journal of Social and Clinical Psychology* 14: 19-25.

2585 Cook, M. 1981. Social skill and human sexual attraction. In *The Bases of Human Sexual Attraction.* Edited by Cook, M. Pp. 145-177. New York: Academic Press.

2586 Cook, M, ed. 1981. *The Bases of Human Sexual Attraction.* New York: Academic Press.

2587 Cooper, W S. 1989. How evolutionary biology challenges the classical theory of rational choice. *Biology and Philosophy* 4: 457-482.

2588 Corson, S A, E O'Leary Corson, J A Alexander, eds. 1980. *Ethology and Nonverbal Communication in Mental Health: An Interdisciplinary Biopsychosocial Exploration.* New York: Pergamon Press.

2589 Cosentino, D J. 1982. *Defiant Maids and Stubborn Farmers: Tradition and Invention in Mende Story Performance.* Cambridge: Cambridge University Press.

2590 Cotterell, J L. 1991. The emergence of adolescent territories in a large urban leisure environment. *Journal of Environmental Psychology* 11: 25-42.

2591 Coult, A D R, R W Habenstein. 1965. *Cross Tabulations of Murdock's World Ethnographic Sample.* Columbia, Mo: University of Missouri.

2592 Count, E W. 1973. *Being and Becoming Human.* New York: Van Nostrand Reinhold.

2593 Creighton, D E. 1984. Sex differences in the visual habituation of 4-, 6-, and 8-month-old infants. *Infant Behavioral Development* 7: 237-49.

2594 Crockenberg, S B. 1981. Infant irritability, mother responsiveness, and social support influences on the security of infant-mother attachment. *Child Development* 52: 857-865.

2595 Crook, J H, ed. 1970. *Social Behaviour of Birds and Mammals.* London: Academic Press.

2596 Crook, J H, ed. 1972. *Sexual Selection, Dimorphism and Social Organization in the Primates.* Sexual Selection and the Descent of Man 1871-1971. Chicago: Aldine.

2597 Curio, E. 1976. *The Ethology of Predation.* New York: Springer.

2598 Curio, E, U Ernst, W Vieth. 1978. Cultural transmission of enemy recognition: One function of mobbing. *Science* 202: 899-901.

2599 Cushing, J M, J Li. 1991. Juvenile versus adult competition. *Journal of Mathematical Biology* 29: 457-474.

2600 Dahlberg, F. 1981. *Woman the Gatherer.* New Haven: Yale University Press.

2601 Datta, S B, G Beauchamp. 1991. Effects of group demography on dominance relationships among female primates. I. Mother-daughter and sister-sister relations. *American Naturalist* 138: 201-226.

2602 Datta, S B. 1992. Effects of availability of allies on female dominance structure. In *Coalitions and Alliances in Humans and Other Animals.* Edited by Harcourt, A H, F B M de Waal. Pp. 61-82. New York: Oxford University Press.

2603 Davies, N B, J R Krebs. 1978. Introduction: Ecology, natural selection and social behavior. In *Behavioural Ecology: An Evolutionary Approach.* Edited by Davies, N B, J R Krebs. Pp. 1-18. Oxford: Blackwell Scientific Publications.

2604 Davis, M. 1983. *Rank and Rivalry: The Politics of Inequality in Rural West Bengal.* Cambridge: Cambridge University Press.

2605 Davis, W. 1986. The origins of image making. *Current Anthropology* 27: 193-215.

2606 Dawkins, R. 1976. Hierarchical organization: A candidate principle for ethology. In *Growing Points in Ethology.* Edited by Bateson, P P G, R A Hinde. Pp. 7-54. London: Cambridge University Press.

2607 Dawkins, R, J R Krebs. 1978. Animal signals: Information or manipulation. In *Behavioural Ecology: An Evolutionary Approach.* Edited by Krebs, J R, N B Davis. Sunderland, M.A.: Sinauer.

2608 Dawkins, R, J R Krebs. 1979. Arms races between and within species. *Proceedings of the Royal Society of London Bulletin* 205: 489-511.

2609 de Casper, A J, W P Fifer. 1980. Of human bonding: Newborns prefer their mother's voices. *Science* 208: 1174-1176.

2610 De Rousseau, C J, ed. 1990. *Primate Life History and Evolution.* New York: Wiley-Liss.

2611 De Vore, I, ed. 1965. *Primate Behaviour: Field Studies of Monkeys and Apes.* New York: Holt, Rinehart & Winston.

2612 de Waal, F B M. 1978. Exploitative and familiarity-dependent support strategies in a colony of semi-free chimpanzees. *Behavior* 66: 268-312.

2613 de Waal, F B M, A van Roosmalen. 1979. Reconciliation and consolation among chimpanzees. *Behavioral Ecology and Sociobiology* 5: 55-66.

2614 de Waal, F B M. 1982. *Chimpanzee Politics: Power and Sex Among Apes.* London: Jonathan Cape.

2615 de Waal, F B M, D Yoshihara. 1983. Reconciliation and re-directed affection in rhesus monkeys. *Behaviour* 85: 224-241.

2616 de Waal, F B M. 1984. Sex differences in the formation of coalitions among chimpanzees. *Ethology and Sociobiology* 5: 239-255.

2617 de Waal, F B M. 1986. The brutal elimination of a rival among captive male chimpanzees. *Ethology and Sociobiology* 7: 237-251.

2618 de Waal, F B M. 1986. The integration of dominance and social bonding in primates. *Quarterly Review of Biology* 61: 459-479.

2619 de Waal, F B M. 1986. Deception in the natural communication of chimpanzees. In *Deception: Perspectives on Human and Nonhuman Deceit.* Edited by Mitchell, R, N Thompson. Albany: SUNY Press.

2620 de Waal, F B M. 1986. Class structure in a Rhesus monkey group: The interplay between dominance and tolerance. *Animal Behaviour* 34: 1033-1040.

2621 de Waal, F B M. 1989. Food sharing and reciprocal obligations among chimpanzees. *Journal of Human Evolution* 18: 433-460.

2622 de Waal, F B M. 1989. Commitments and grudges. *Politics and the Life Sciences* 8: 27-30.

2623 de Waal, F. 1989. *Peacemaking among Primates.* Cambridge: Harvard University Press.

2624 de Waal, F B M. 1991. Complementary methods and convergent evidence in the study of primate social cognition. *Behaviour* 118: 297.

2625 de Waal, F B M, A H Harcourt. 1992. Coalitions and alliances: A history of ethological research. In *Coalitions and Alliances in Humans and Other Animals.* Edited by Harcourt, A H, F B M de Waal. Pp. 1-27. New York: Oxford University Press.

2626 de Waal, F B M. 1992. Aggression as a well-integrated part of primate social relationships: A critique of the Seville Statement on Violence. In *Aggression and Peacefulness in Humans and Other Primates*. Edited by Silverberg, J, J P Gray. Pp. 37-56. New York: Oxford University Press.

2627 Dennett, D C. 1983. Intentional systems in cognitive ethology: The "Panglossian Paradigm" defended *Behavioral and Brain Sciences* 6: 343-390.

2628 Denno, D W. 1990. *Biology and Violence: From Birth to Adulthood*. New York: Cambridge Universtiy Press.

2629 Deutsch, R D. 1979. On the isomorphic quality of endings: An example from everyday face-to-face interaction and Balinese legong dance. *Ethology and Sociobiology* 1: 41-59.

2630 Deutsch, F M. 1990. Status, sex, and smiling: The effect of role on smiling in men and women. *Personality and Social Psychology Bulletin* 16: 531-540.

2631 Dewsburg, D, ed. 1984. *Foundations of Comparative Psychology*. New York: Van Nostrand Reinhold.

2632 Dewsbury, D A, D A Rethlingshafer, eds. 1973. *Comparative Psychology: A Modern Survey*. New York: McGraw Hill.

2633 Dewsbury, D, ed. 1981. *Mammalian Sexual Behavior: Foundations for Contemporary Research*. Stroudsburg, PA: Hutchinson Ross.

2634 Dewsbury, D. 1982. Dominance, rank, copulatory behavior, and differential reproduction. *Quarterly Review of Biology* 57: 135-159.

2635 Diamond, J. 1991. *The Rise and Fall of the Third Chimpanzee*. London: Radius.

2636 Dimberg, U. 1982. Facial reactions to facial expressions. *Psychophysiology* 19: 643-47.

2637 Dimberg, U. 1986. Facial reactions to fear-relevant and fear-irrelevant stimuli. *Biological Psychology* 23: 153-61.

2638 Dissanayake, E. 1988. *What Is Art For?* Seattle: University of Washington Press.

2639 Dodge, K A, J M Price, J D Coie, C Christopoulos. 1990. On the development of aggressive dyadic relationships in boys' peer groups. *Human Development*  33: 260-270.

2640 Douglas, M. 1963. *Purity and Danger: An Analysis of Concepts of Pollution and Taboo.* London: Routledge.

2641 Douglas, J M, R L Tweed 1979. Analysing the patterning of a sequence of discrete behavioral events. *Animal Behavior*  27: 136-152.

2642 Doust, L L, J L Doust. 1985. Gender chauvinism and the division of labor in humans. *Perspectives in Biology and Medicine*  28: 526-542.

2643 Drummond, H. 1981. The nature and description of behavior patterns. In *Perspectives in Ethology.*  Edited by Bateson, P P G, P H Klopfer. New York: Plenum.

2644 Duck, S, D Miell. 1983. Mate choice in humans as an interpersonal process. In *Mate Choice.* Edited by Bateson, P. Pp. 377-386. Cambridge: Cambridge University Press.

2645 Dugatkin, L A. 1992. The evolution of the "con artist". *Ethology and Sociobiology*  13: 3-18.

2646 Dukelow, W R, J Erwin, eds. 1986. *Comparative Primate Biology: Reproduction and Development.* New York: Alan R. Liss.

2647 Dunbar, R I M. 1976. Some aspects of research design and their implications in the observational study of behaviour. *Behaviour*  58: 78-98.

2648 Dunbar, R I M. 1991. Functional significance of social grooming in primates. *Folia Primatologica*  57: 121-31.

2649 Duncan, S D, L J Brunner, D W Fiske. 1979. Strategy signals in face-to-face interaction. *Journal of Personality and Social Psychology* 32: 301-313.

2650 Dunn, J. 1983. Sibling relationships in early childhood. *Child Development*  54: 787-811.

2651 Dunn, J F, R Plomim, M Nettles. 1985. Consistency of mothers' behavior toward infant siblings. *Developmental Psychology* 21: 1188-1195.

2652 Durham, W H. 1976. Resource competition and human aggression, Part I: A review of primitive war. *Quarterly Review of Biology* 51:385-415.

2653 Dyson-Hudson, R, M A Little, eds. 1983. *Rethinking Human Adaptation: Biological and Cultural Models*. Boulder.: Westview Press.

2654 Eaves, L J, K A Last, P A Young, N G Martin. 1978. Model-fitting approaches to the analysis of human behaviour. *Heredity* 41: 249-320.

2655 Eibl-Eibesfeldt, I, H Hass. 1967. Film studies in human ethology. *Current Anthropology* 8: 477-479.

2656 Eibl-Eibesfeldt, I, H Hass. 1967. Neue Wege der Humanethologie. *Homo* 18: 13-23.

2657 Eibl-Eibesfeldt, I. 1967. Concepts of ethology and their significance in the study of human behavior. In *Early Behavior: Comparative and Developmental Approaches*. Edited by Stevenson, H W. Pp. 127-146. New York: Wiley.

2658 Eibl-Eibesfeldt, I. 1968. Zur Ethologie des menschlichen Grußverhaltens. *Zeitschrift für Tierpsychologie* 25: 727-744.

2659 Eibl-Eibesfeldt, I. 1971. Transcultural patterns of ritualized contact behavior. In *The Use of Space by Animals and Men*. Edited by Esser, A H. Pp. 238-246. New York: Plenum.

2660 Eibl-Eibesfeldt, I. 1972. Similarities and differences between cultures in expressive movements. In *Non-verbal Communication*. Edited by Hinde, R. Pp. 297-314. London: Cambridge University Press.

2661 Eibl-Eibesfeldt, I. 1973. The expressive behavior of the deaf-and-blind-born. In *Social Communication and Movement*. Edited by von Cranach, M, I Vine. Pp. 163-94. New York: Academic Press.

2662 Eibl-Eibesfeldt, I. 1974. The myth of the aggression-free hunter and gatherer society. In *Primate Aggression, Territoriality and Xenophobia: A Comparative Perspective*. Edited by Holloway, R L. Pp. 435-457. New York: Academic Press.

2663 Eibl-Eibesfeldt, I. 1975. *Ethology*. 2nd ed New York: Wiley.

2664 Eibl-Eibesfeldt, I. 1975. Aggression in !Ko-Bushmen. In *War, its Causes and Correlates*. Edited by Nettleship, M A, R Dalegivens, A Nettleship. Pp. 281-296. The Hague: Mouton.

2665 Eibl-Eibesfeldt, I. 1978. *Love and Hate*. New York: Basic Books.

2666 Eibl-Eibesfeldt, I. 1979. Human ethology: Concepts and implications for the sciences of man. *Behavioral and Brain Sciences* 2: 1-57.

2667 Eibl-Eibesfeldt, I. 1979. Ritual and ritualization from a biological perspective. In *Human Ethology: Claims and Limits of a New Discipline.* Edited by von Cranach, M, K Foppa, W Lepenies, D Plogg. Pp. 3-55. Cambridge: Cambridge University Press.

2668 Eibl-Eibesfeldt, I. 1979. *The Biology of Peace and War: Men, Animals and Aggression.* London: Thames and Hudson.

2669 Eibl-Eibesfeldt, I. 1982. Kommunikationsstörungen in der Großgesellschaft. *Zeitschrift für Angewandte Sozialwissenschaft* 13: 3-9.

2670 Eibl-Eibesfeldt, I. 1982. Warfare, man's indoctrinability, and group selection. *Zeitschrift für Tierpsychologie* 60: 177-198.

2671 Eibl-Eibesfeldt, I. 1983. The comparative approach in human ethology. In *Comparing Behavior: Studying Man, Studying Animal.* Edited by Rajecki, D W. Pp. 43-65. Hillsdale, NJ: Erlbaum.

2672 Eibl-Eibesfeldt, I. 1984. *Die Biologie des menschlichen Verhaltens: Grundriß der Humanethologie.* Munich: Piper.

2673 Eibl-Eibesfeldt, I. 1984. Ursprung und soziale Funktion des Objekt besitzes. In *Bindungen und Besitzdenken beim Kleinkind.* Edited by Eggers, C. Munich: Urban & Schwarzenberg.

2674 Eibl-Eibesfeldt, I, H Hass, K Freisitzer, E Gehmacher, H Glück. 1985. *Stadt und Lebensqualität.* Stuttgart: DVA.

2675 Eibl-Eibesfeldt, I, C Sütterlin. 1985. Das Bartweisen als apotropäischer Gestus. *Homo* 36: 241-250.

2676 Eibl-Eibesfeldt, I, W Schiefenhövel, V Heeschen. 1989. *Kommunikation bei den Eipo. Eine Humanethologische Bestandsaufnahme.* Berlin: Dietrich Reimer.

2677 Eibl-Eibesfeldt, I. 1989. *Human Ethology.* New York: Aldine de Gruyter.

2678 Eibl-Eibesfeldt, I. 1990. Fear, defence and aggression in animals and man: Some ethological perspectives. In *Fear and Defence.* Edited by Brain, P F, S Parmigiani, R Blanchard, D Mainardi. Pp. 381-408. Chur: Harwood Academic Publishers.

2679 Eibl-Eibesfeldt, I. 1990. Dominance, submission, and love: Sexual pathologies from the perspective of ethology. In *Pedophilia: Biosocial Dimensions.* Edited by Feierman, J R. Pp. 151-175. New York: Springer-Verlag.

2680 Einon, D F. 1980. The purpose of play. In *Not Work Alone.* Edited by Cherfas, J, R Lewin. Pp. 21-32. London: Temple Smith.

2681 Einon, D F. 1983. Play and exploration. In *Exploration in Animals and Humans.* Edited by Archer, J, L I A Birke. Pp. 210-229. Wokingham: Van Nostrand Reinhold.

2682 Eisenberg, J F, D S Wilton, eds. 1971. *Man and Beast: Comparative Social Behavior.* Washington: Smithsonian Institution Press.

2683 Ekman, P, W V Friesen. 1969. The repertoire of nonverbal behavior: Categories, origins, usage and coding. *Semiotica* 1: 50-97.

2684 Ekman, P, W Friesen. 1969. Nonverbal leakage and clues to deception. *Psychiatry* 32: 88-106.

2685 Ekman, P, ed. 1973. *Darwin and Facial Expression: A Century of Research in Review.* New York: Academic Press.

2686 Ekman, P, W V Friesen. 1975. *Unmasking the Face.* Englewood Cliffs, N.J.: Prentice-Hall.

2687 Ekman, P, W V Friesen. 1976. Measuring facial movement. *Journal of Environmental Psychology and Nonverbal Behavior* 1: 56-75.

2688 Ekman, P, W V Friesen. 1977. *Manual for Facial Action Coding System.* Palo Alto: Consulting Psychologists Press.

2689 Ekman, P. 1978. Biological and cultural contributions to body and facial movement. In *The Anthropology of the Body.* Edited by Blacking, J. New York: Academic Press.

2690 Ekman, P, K R Scherer, eds. 1981. *Handbook of Methods in Nonverbal Behavior Research.* New York: Cambridge University Press.

2691 Ekman, P, W V Friesen. 1982. Felt, false, and miserable smiles. *Journal of Nonverbal Behavior* 6: 238-252.

2692 Ekman, P. 1985. *Telling Lies.* New York: Norton.

2693 Elliott, F A. 1983. Biological roots of violence. *Proceedings of the American Philosophy of Science Association* 127: 84-94.

2694 Ellis, L, G J L Scholtz. 1978. *Activity and Play of Children.* Englewood Cliffs, N.J.: Prentice-Hall.

2695 Ellis, L. 1985. On the rudiments of possession and property. *Social Science Information*  24: 113-144.

2696 Ellsworth, P. 1975. Direct gaze as a social stimulus: The example of aggression. In *Nonverbal Communication of Aggression.* Edited by Pliner, P, T Alloway, L Krames. Pp. 53-75. New York: Plenum.

2697 Ellyson, S, J F Dovidio, eds. 1985. *Power, Dominance, and Nonverbal Behavior.* New York: Springer.

2698 Else, J G, P C Lee. 1986. *Primate Ontogeny, Cognition and Social Behaviour.* Cambridge: Cambridge University Press.

2699 Ember, M. 1975. On the origin and extension of the incest taboo. *Behavioral Science Research*  10: 249-281.

2700 Enquist, M, O Leimar. 1990. The evolution of fatal fighting. *Animal Behaviour*  39: 1-9.

2701 Epple, G. 1981. Effect of pair-bonding with adults on the ontogenetic manifestation of aggressive behavior in a primate Saguinus fuscicollis. *Behavioral Ecology and Sociobiology*  8: 117-23.

2702 Ermaine, R, E Gergerian. 1978. *Atlas of Facial Expressions: Album des Expressions du Visage.* Paris: La Pensec Universelle.

2703 Essock-Vitale, S M, M T McGuire. 1985. Women's lives viewed from an evolutionary perspective. I. Sexual histories, reproductive success and demographic characteristics of a random sample of American women. *Ethology and Sociobiology*  6: 137-154.

2704 Exline, R V. 1972. Visual interaction: The glances of power and preference. In *Nebraska Symposium on Motivation.* Edited by Cole, J K. Pp. 162-205. Lincoln: University of Nebraska Press.

2705 Exline, R V, S L Ellyson, L B. 1975. Visual behavior as an aspect of power role relationships. In *Nonverbal Communication of Aggression.* Edited by Pliner, P, L Krames, T Alloway. Pp. 21-52. New York: Plenum.

2706 Fagen, R M, D Y Young. 1978. Temporal patterns of behavior: Durations, intervals, latencies, and sequences. In *Quantitative Ethology.* Edited by Colgan, P W. Pp. 79-114. New York: Wiley.

2707 Fagen, R. 1981. *Animal Play Behavior.*  New York: Oxford University Press.

2708 Farrell, A D. 1991. Computers and behavioral assessment: Current applications, future possibilities, and obstacles to routine use. *Behavioral Assessment* 13: 159-86.

2709 Fedigan, L M. 1982. *Primate Paradigms: Sex Roles and Social Bonds*. Montreal: Eden Press.

2710 Feldman, R, B Rime, eds. 1990. *Fundamentals of Nonverbal Behavior*. New York: Cambridge University Press.

2711 Ferguson, R, ed. 1984. *Warfare, Culture and Environment*. New York: Academic press.

2712 Field, T. 1983. Social interactions between high-risk infants and their mothers, fathers and grandmothers. In *Advances in Clinical Child Psychology*. Edited by Lahey, B B, A Kazdin. New York: Plenum.

2713 Finder, J. 1986. Unsere biokulturelle Natur: Für die Beachtung der Biologie bei der Erklarung menschlichen Sozialverhaltens. In *Menschliches Handeln und Sozialstruktur*. Edited by Elting, A. Leverkusen: Leske.

2714 Fisher, H E. 1982. *The Sexual Contract*. New York: William Morrow.

2715 Fisher, H E. 1989. Evolution of human serial pairbonding. *American Journal of Physical Anthropology* 78: 331-354.

2716 Fogelson, R, R Adams, eds. 1977. *The Anthropology of Power: Ethnographic Studies from Asia, Oceania and the New World*. New York: Academic press.

2717 Foley, R A. 1991. *The Origins of Human Behavior*. New York: Harper Collins.

2718 Fortes, M. 1945. *The Dynamics of Clanship among the Tallensi*. London: Oxford University Press.

2719 Foster, M, R Rubinstein, eds. 1986. *Peace and War: Cross-Cultural Perspectives*. New Brunswick, NJ: Transaction Books.

2720 Fox, R. 1971. The cultural animal. In *Man and Beast: Comparative Social Behavior*. Edited by Eisenberg, J F. Pp. 275-296. Washington: Smithsonian Institute Press.

2721 Fox, M W. 1974. *Concepts in Ethology: Animal and Human Behavior*. Minneapolis: University of Minnesota Press.

2722 Fox, R, ed. 1974. *Biosocial Anthropology.* London: Malaby Press.

2723 Fox, R. 1979. Kinship categories as natural categories. In *Evolutionary Biology and Human Social Behavior: An Anthropological Perspective.* Edited by Chagnon, N, W Irons. North Scituate, MA: Duxbury Press.

2724 Fragaszy, D M, S Boinski, J Whipple. 1992. Behavioral sampling in the field: Comparison of individual and group sampling methods. *American Journal of Primatology* 26: 259-275.

2725 Fray, P. 1976. *Spirits of Protest: Spirit-Mediums and the Articulation of Consensus among the Zezuru of Southern Rhodesia (Zimbabwe).* Cambridge: Cambridge University Press.

2726 Freedman, D G. 1974. *Human Infancy: An Evolutionary Perspective.* Hillsdale, N.J.: Erlbaum.

2727 Freedman, D G. 1984. Village fissioning, human diversity, and ethnocentrism. *Political Psychology* 5: 629-634.

2728 Freeman, D. 1970. Human nature and culture. In *Man and the New Biology.* Pp. 50-75. Canberra: Australian National University Press.

2729 Freeman, D. 1974. Kinship, attachment behaviour and the primary bond. In *The Character of Kinship.* Edited by Goody, J. Pp. 109-119. Cambridge: Cambridge University Press.

2730 Freid, M, M Harris, R Murphy. 1967. *War: The Anthropology of Armed Conflict and Aggression.* New York: Natural History Press.

2731 Freidrich, H, ed. 1968. *Man and Animal.* London: Granada.

2732 Fridlund, A J, J P Sabini, L E Hedlund, J A Schaut, J I Shenker, M J Knauer. 1990. Audience effects on solitary faces during imagery: Displaying to the people in your head. *Journal of Nonverbal Behavior* 14: 113-133.

2733 Friedman, R C, ed. 1974. *Sex Differences in Behavior.* New York: Wiley.

2734 Frodi, A M, M E Lamb, L A Leavitt, W L Donovan. 1978. Fathers' and mothers' responses to infant smiles and cries. *Infant Behaviour and Development* 1: 187-198.

2735 Frodi, A M, M E Lamb. 1978. Sex differences in responsiveness to infants: A developmental study of psychophysiological and behavioral responses. *Child Development* 49:

2736 Fromme, D K, D C Beam. 1974. Dominance and sex differences in nonverbal responses to differential eye contact. *Journal of Research in Personality* 8: 76-87.

2737 Fromme, D K, et al. 1989. Nonverbal behavior and attitudes toward touch. *Journal of Nonverbal Behavior* 13: 3-14.

2738 Fry, D. 1977. *Homo Loquens: Man as a Talking Animal.* Cambridge: Cambridge University Press.

2739 Fukuhara, S. 1990. The effect of eye contact and verbal content about impression on affective reactions of the other partner. *Japanese Journal of Psychology* 61: 177-183.

2740 Galef, B G. 1976. Social transmissions of acquired behaviour: A discussion of tradition and social learning in vertebrates. *Advanced Study of Behaviour* 6: 77-100.

2741 Gangestad, S W, J A Simpson. 1990. Toward an evolutionary history of female sociosexual variation. *Journal of Personality* 58: 69-96.

2742 Gardner, R, K G Heider. 1968. *Gardens of War: Life and Death in the New Guinea Stone Age.* New York: Doubleday.

2743 Gathreaux, S A. 1981. *Animal Migration, Orientation and Navigation.* New York: Academic Press.

2744 Gaulin, S, L Sailer. 1984. Sexual dimorphism in weight among primates: The relative impact of allometry and sexual selection. *International Journal of Primatology* 5: 515-535.

2745 Gaulin, S, J Boster. 1985. Cross-cultural differences in sexual dimorphism: Is there any difference to be explained? *Ethology and Sociobiology* 6: 219-225.

2746 Gauthreaux, S A J. 1978. The ecological significance of behavioral dominance. In *Perspectives in Ethology.* Edited by Bateson, P P G, P K Klopfer. Pp. 17-54. New York: Plenum.

2747 Ginsburg, H, S Miller. 1981. Altruism in children: A naturalistic study of reciprocity and an examination of the relationship between social dominance and aid-giving behavior. *Ethology and Sociobiology* 2: 75-83.

2748 Givens, D. 1978. The non-verbal bases of attraction: Flirtation, courtship and seduction. *Psychiatry* 41: 346-359.

2749 Givens, D. 1981. Greeting a stranger: Some commonly used nonverbal signals of aversiveness. In *Nonverbal Communication. Interaction and Gesture*. Edited by Sebeok, T A, J Umiker-Sebeok. Pp. 219-215. New York: Mouton.

2750 Gladue, B A, H J Belaney. 1990. Gender differences in perception of attractiveness of men and women in bars. *Personality and Social Psychology Bulletin* 16: 378.

2751 Glassman, R B. 1980. An evolutionary hypothesis about teaching and proselytizing behaviors. *Zygon* 15: 133-154.

2752 Godelier, M, F Valjavec. 1983. The creation of great men: Masculine power and domination in the Baruya of New Guinea. *Anthropos* 78:314-316.

2753 Goldberg, M A, B Katz. 1990. The effect of nonreciprocated touch on power dominance perception. *Journal of Social Behavior and Personality* 5: 379-386.

2754 Goldsmith, H H, R N Emde, R J Harmon, eds. 1982. *The Development of Attachment and Affiliative Systems*. New York: Plenum.

2755 Goldsmith, T H. 1992. *The Biological Basis of Human Nature. Forging the Links between Evolution and Behavior*. New York: Oxford University Press.

2756 Goldstein, A G. 1983. Behavioral scientists' fascination with faces. *Journal of Nonverbal Behavior* 7: 223-55.

2757 Goodall, J. 1964. Tool-using and aimed throwing in a community of free-living chimpanzees. *Nature* 201: 1264-1266.

2758 Goodall, J. 1986. Social rejection, exclusion, and shunning among the Gombe chimpanzees. *Ethology and Sociobiology* 7: 227-236.

2759 Goodall, J. 1986. *The Chimpanzees of Gombe: Patterns of Behavior*. Cambridge: Harvard University Press.

2760 Goodman, L A. 1973. The analysis of cross-classified data: Independence, quasi-independence and interactions in contingency tables with or without missing entries. *Journal of the American Statistical Association* 63: 1091-1131.

2761 Goody, E, ed. 1978. *Questions and Politeness: Strategies in Social Interaction.* London: Cambridge University Press.

2762 Gordon, R. 1983. The decline of the Kiapdom and the resurgence of tribal fighting in Enga. *Oceania* 53: 205-223.

2763 Gottman, J M, C Notarius. 1978. Sequential analysis of observational data using Markov chains. In *Single Subject Research: Strategies for Evaluating Change.* Edited by Kratochwill, T R. New York: Academic Press.

2764 Gould, J L. 1982. *Ethology: The Mechanisms and Evolution of Behavior.* New York: Norton.

2765 Graber, R B. 1981. A psychocultural theory of male genital mutilation. *The Journal of Psychoanalytic Anthropology* 4: 413-434.

2766 Grammer, K, R Schropp, H Shibasaka. 1984. Contact, conflict and appeasement—Children's interaction strategies. The use of photography. *International Journal of Visual Sociology* 2: 59-75.

2767 Grammer, K. 1985. Verhaltensforschung am Menschen: Überlegungen zu den biologischen Grundlagen des "Umwegverhaltens". In *Mensch und Tier.* Edited by Svilar, M. Pp. 273-318. Bern: Lang.

2768 Grammer, K. 1988. *Biologische Grundlagen des Sozialverhaltens.* Darmstadt: Wissenschaftliche Buchgesellschaft.

2769 Grammer, K, I Eibl-Eibesfeldt. 1990. The ritualisation of laughter. In *Natürlichkeit der Sprache und der Kultur. Bochumer Beiträge zur Semiotik.* Edited by Koch, W A. Pp. 192-214. Bochum: Brockmeyer.

2770 Grammer, K. 1991. Strangers meet: Laughter and non-verbal signals of interest in opposite sex encounters. *Journal of Nonverbal Behavior* 14: 209-236.

2771 Greenwood, D J, W A Stini. 1977. *Nature, Culture, and Human History: A Biocultural Introduction to Anthropology.* New York: Harper & Row.

2772 Greifeld, K, N Kohnen, E Schröder, eds. 1989. *Schmerz. Interdisziplinäre Perspektiven.* Wiesbaden: Vieweg.

2773 Grennan, S A. 1987. Findings on the role of officer gender in violent encounters with citizens. *Journal of Police Science* 15: 78-85.

2774 Groebel, J. 1989. *Aggression and War: Their Biological and Social Bases*. New York: Cambridge University Press.

2775 Gross, D R. 1975. Protein capture and cultural development in the Amazon basin. *American Anthropologist* 77: 526-549.

2776 Grove, W R, G R Carpenter, eds. 1982. *The Fundamental Connection Between Nature and Nurture: A Review of the Evidence*. Lexington, MA: Heath.

2777 Gruber, A. 1969. A functional definition of primate tool-making. *Man* 4: 573-579.

2778 Gruter, M. 1979. The origins of legal behavior. *Journal of Social and Biological Structures* 2: 43-52.

2779 Gruter, M, R Masters, eds. 1986. *Ostracism: A Social and Biological Phenomenon*. New York: Elsevier.

2780 Gruter, M. 1991. *Law and the Mind: Biological Origins of Human Behavior*. Newbury Park, CA: Sage.

2781 Grzimek, B, ed. 1977. *Grzimek's Encyclopedia of Ethology*. New York: Van Nostrand Reinhold.

2782 Gurevitch, Z D. 1990. The embrace: On the element of non-distance in human relations. *Sociological Quarterly* 31: 187-202.

2783 Guris, D R. 1976. Is society hereditary? *Harvard Magazine* 79: 21-25.

2784 Guthertz, M, T Field. 1989. Lap computer or on-line coding and data analysis for laboratory and field observations. *Journal of Nonverbal Behavior* 12: 305-320.

2785 Guthman, E. 1971. *We Band of Brothers*. New York: Harper & Row.

2786 Haas, J, ed. 1990. *The Anthropology of War*. Cambridge: Cambridge University Press.

2787 Haccou, P, E Meelis. 1990. *Statistical Analysis of Behavioural Data*. Oxford: Oxford University Press.

2788 Hager, J. 1982. Asymmetries in facial expression. In *Emotion in the Human Face*. Edited by Ekman, P. New York: Cambridge University Press.

2789 Halberstadt, A G, C W Hayes, K M Pike. 1989. Gender and gender role differences in smiling and communication consistency. *Sex Roles* 19: 589-604.

2790 Hall, E T. 1969. *The Hidden Dimension.* Garden City, N.Y.: Doubleday.

2791 Hall, J A. 1979. Gender, gender roles, and nonverbal communication skills. In *Skill in Nonverbal Communication: Individual Differences.* Edited by Rosenthal, R. Pp. 32-67. Cambridge, MA: Oelgeschlager, Gunn and Hain.

2792 Halliday, T R, P J B Slater. 1983. *Animal Behaviour: Genes, Development and Learning.* Oxford: Blackwell.

2793 Hallock, M B, J Worobey, P A Self. 1989. Behavioural development in chimpanzee (Pan-Troglodytes) and human newborns across the first month of life. *International Journal of Behavioral Development* 12: 527-540.

2794 Hamburg, D, M Trudeau, eds. 1981. *Biobehavioral Aspects of Aggression.* New York: Alan R. Liss.

2795 Hamilton, W J, R E Buskirk, W H Buskirk. 1975. Defensive stoning by baboons. *Nature* 256: 488-489.

2796 Hand, J L. 1986. Resolution of social conflicts: Dominance, egalitarianism, spheres of dominance, and game theory. *Quarterly Review of Biology* 61: 201-220.

2797 Harcourt, A H, K J Stewart. 1987. The influence of help in contest on dominance rank in primates—Hints from gorillas. *Animal Behavior* 35: 211-217.

2798 Harlow, H F, C Mears. 1979. *The Human Model: Primate Perspectives.* New York: Winston and Sons.

2799 Harper, R, G., A N Wiens, D Matarazza. 1978. *Nonverbal Communication: The State of the Art.* New York: Wiley.

2800 Harré, R, V Reynolds, eds. 1984. *The Meaning of Primate Signals.* Cambridge: Cambridge University Press.

2801 Harris, M. 1975. *Culture, People, Nature: An Introduction to General Anthropology.* 2nd ed New York: Cowell.

2802 Harris, M. 1977. *Cannibals and Kings: The Origins of Cultures.* New York: Random House.

2803 Harris, G G. 1978. *Casting Out Anger: Religion Among the Taita of Kenya.* Cambridge: Cambridge University Press.

2804 Harris, M. 1979. *Cultural Materialism: The Struggle for a Science of Culture.* New York: Random House.

2805 Harrop, A, M Daniels, C Foulkes. 1990. The use of momentary time sampling and partial interval recording in behavioural research. *Behavioural Psychotherapy* 18: 121-128.

2806 Haug, M, C Aron, P F Brain. 1990. *Heterotypical Behaviour in Man and Animals.* London: Chapman & Hall.

2807 Hausfater, G, J Altmann, S A Altmann. 1982. Long-term consistency of dominance relations among female baboons (Papio cynocephalus). *Science* 217: 752-755.

2808 Hawkes, K, J F O'Connell, N B Blurton Jones. 1989. Hardworking Hadza grandmothers. In *Comparative Socioecology of Mammals and Man.* Edited by Standen, V, R Foley. London: Blackwell.

2809 Hay, D F. 1980. Multiple functions of proximity-seeking in infancy. *Child Development* 51: 636-645.

2810 Hayden, B. 1981. Subsistence and ecological adaptations of modern hunter/gatherers. In *Omnivorous Primates: Gathering and Hunting in Human Evolution.* Edited by Harding, R S O, G Teleki. Pp. 344-321. New York: Columbia University Press.

2811 Hazlett, B A, ed. 1977. *Quantitative Methods in the Study of Animal Behavior.* New York: Academic Press.

2812 Heeschen, V, W Schiefenhövel, I Eibl-Eibesfeldt. 1980. Requesting, giving, and taking: The relationship between verbal and nonverbal behavior in the speech community of the Eipo, Irian Jaya (West New Guinea). In *The Relationship of Verbal and Nonverbal Communication. Contributions to the Sociology of Language.* Edited by Key, M R. Pp. 139-166. The Hague: Mouton.

2813 Heeschen, V. 1984. Ästhetische Form und sprachliches Handeln. In *Sprache und Pragmatik. Lunder Symposium 1984.* Edited by Rosengren, I. Pp. 387-411. Stockholm: Almqvist & Wiksell.

2814 Heeschen, V. 1984. Durch Krieg und Brautpreis zur Freundschaft. *Baessler-Archiv* 32: 113-44.

2815 Heeschen, V. 1985. Probleme der rituellen Kommunikation. In *Interkulturelle Kommunikation.* Edited by Rehbein, J. Pp. 150-65. Tübingen: Narr.

2816 Heeschen, V. 1987. Rituelle Kommunikation in verschiedenen Kulturen. *Zeitschrift für Literaturwissenschaft und Linguistik* 65: 82-104.

2817 Heeschen, V. 1990. Human ethology and semiotics. In *Semiotics in the Individual Sciences.* Edited by Koch, W A. Pp. 91-121. Bochum: Borckmeyer.

2818 Heinz, H J. 1972. Territoriality among the Bushmen in general and the !Ko in particular. *Anthropos* 67: 405-416.

2819 Heltne, P G, L A Marquardt. 1989. *Understanding Chimpanzees.* Cambridge: Harvard University Press.

2820 Henley, N M. 1977. *Body Politics: Power, Sex, and Nonverbal Communication.* Englewood Cliffs, N.J.: Prentice Hall.

2821 Herdt, G H. 1982. *Rituals of Manhood: Male Initiation in Papua New Guinea.* Berkeley: University of California Press.

2822 Herzfeld, M. 1985. *The Poetics of Manhood: Contest and Identity in a Cretan Mountain Village.* Princeton: Princeton University Press.

2823 Hess, E H. 1970. The ethological approach to socialization. In *Early Experiences and the Processes of Socialization.* Edited by Hoppe, R A, G A Milton, E C Simmel. New York: Academic Press.

2824 Hess, E H. 1973. *Imprinting: Early Experience and the Developmental Psychology of Attachment.* New York: Van Nostrand Reinhold.

2825 Hinde, R A. 1970. *Animal Behavior: A Synthesis of Ethology and Comparative Psychology.* 2nd ed New York: McGraw-Hill.

2826 Hinde, R A, Y Spencer-Booth. 1971. Effect of brief separation from mother and rhesus monkeys. *Science* 173: 111-118.

2827 Hinde, R A, ed. 1972. *Non-Verbal Communication.* Cambridge: Cambridge University Press.

2828 Hinde, R A. 1974. *Biological Bases of Human Social Behavior.* New York: McGraw-Hill.

2829 Hinde, R A. 1981. Animal signals: Ethological and games-theory approaches are not incompatible. *Animal Behaviour* 29: 535-42.

2830 Hinde, R A. 1982. Attachment: Some conceptual and biological issues. In *The Place of Attachment in Human Behavior.* Edited by Stevenson-Hinde, J, C M Parkes. New York: Basic Books.

2831 Hinde, R A. 1982. *Ethology: Its Nature and Relations to Other Sciences.* London: Fontana.

2832 Hinde, R A, A Tamplin. 1983. Relations between mother-child interaction and behaviour in preschool. *British Journal of Developmental Psychology* 1: 231-257.

2833 Hinde, R A. 1983. *Primate Social Relationships: An Integrated Approach.* Oxford: Blackwell.

2834 Hinde, R A. 1984. Why do the sexes behave differently in close relationships? *Journal of Social and Personal Relationships* 1: 471-510.

2835 Hinde, R A, G Titmus, D Easton, A Tamplin. 1985. Incidence of "friendship" and behavior to strong associates vs. non-associates in preschoolers. *Child Development* 56: 234-245.

2836 Hinde, R A. 1986. Categories of aggression and their motivational heterogeneity. *Ethology and Sociobiology* 7: 17-27.

2837 Hinde, R A. 1990. *Causes of Development in Ethology.* Edited by Butterworth, G, P Bryant. Causes of Development. Hillsdale, N.J.: Erlbaum.

2838 Hinde, R A, P M Miller. 1990. Attachment: Biological, cultural and individual desiderata. *Human Development* 33: 62-72.

2839 Hinde, R A. 1991. Relationships, attachment, and culture: A tribute to John Bowlby. *Infant Mental Health Journal* 12: 154-163.

2840 Hinde, R A. 1991. A biologist looks at anthropology. *Man* 26: 583-609.

2841 Hjortsjö, C H. 1970. *Man's Face and Mimic Language.* Malmö: Nordens Boktryckeri.

2842 Hockett, C F, R Ascher. 1992. The human revolution. *Current Anthropology* 33: 7-46.

2843 Hoebel, E A. 1982. Anthropology, law and genetic inheritance. *Journal of Social and Biological Structures* 5: 335-339.

2844 Hofer, M A. 1983. On the relationship between attachment and separation processes in infancy. In *Emotion: Theory, Research and Experience*. Edited by Plutchik, R, H Kellerman. Pp. 199-219. New York: Academic Press.

2845 Hold, B. 1976. Attention structure and rank-specific behaviour in preschool children. In *The Social Structure of Attention*. Edited by Chance, M R A, R L Larsen. Pp. 177-201. New York: Wiley.

2846 Hold, B, M Schleidt. 1977. The importance of human odour in non-verbal communication. *Zeitschrift für Tierpsychologie* 43: 225-238.

2847 Hold, B. 1980. Attention structure and behavior in G/wi San children. *Ethology and Sociobiology* 1: 285-290.

2848 Hold-Cavell, B C L. 1985. Showing-off and aggression in young children. *Aggressive Behavior* 11: 303-314.

2849 Hold-Cavell, B C L, D Borsutzky. 1986. Strategies to obtain high regard: Longitudinal study of a group of preschool children. *Ethology and Sociobiology* 7: 39-56.

2850 Hold-Cavell, B C L, G Attili, M Schleidt. 1986. A cross-cultural comparison of children's behaviour during their first year in a preschool. *International Journal of Behavioural Development* 9: 471-483.

2851 Holekamp, K E, L Smale. 1991. Dominance acquisition during mammalian social development: The inheritance of maternal rank. *American Zoologist* 31: 306-317.

2852 Hollenbeck, A R. 1978. Problems of reliability in observational research. In *Observing Behavior. Vol. II. Data Collection and Analysis Methods*. Edited by Sackett, G P. Pp. 79-98. Baltimore: University Park Press.

2853 Holloway, R L. 1969. Culture: A human domain. *Current Anthropology* 10: 395-412.

2854 Holloway, R L, ed. 1974. *Primate Aggression, Territoriality and Xenophobia*. New York: Academic Press.

2855 Holy, L. 1986. *Strategies and Norms in a Changing Matrilineal Society: Descent, Succession and Inheritance Among the Toka of Zambia.* Cambridge: Cambridge University Press.

2856 Honeycutt, J M. 1989. Effects of preinteraction expectancies on interaction involvement and behavioral responses in initial interaction. *Journal of Nonverbal Behavior* 13: 25-36.

2857 Howell, S, R Willis, eds. 1989. *Societies at Peace: Anthropological Perspectives.* London: Routledge.

2858 Hoyle, G. 1984. The scope of neuroethology. *Behavioral and Brain Sciences* 7: 367-381.

2859 Humphrey, N K. 1976. The social function of intellect. In *Growing Points in Ethology.* Edited by Bateson, P P G, R A Hinde. Pp. 303-317. Cambridge: Cambridge University Press.

2860 Hunn, E S. 1981. On the relative contribution of men and women to subsistance among hunter gatherers of the Columbian plateau: A comparision with Ethnographic Atlas summaries. *Journal of Ethnobiology* 1: 124-134.

2861 Huntingford, F A. 1984. *The Study of Animal Behaviour.* London: Chapman & Hall.

2862 Huntingford, F A, A Turner. 1987. *Animal Conflict.* London: Chapman & Hall.

2863 Hutt, C. 1966. Exploration and play in children. In *Play, Exploration and Territory in Mammals.* Edited by Jewell, P, C Loizos. Pp. 61-81. London: Academic Press.

2864 Ihobe, H. 1992. Male-male relationships among wild bonobos (Pan paniscus) at Wamba, Republic of Zaire. *Primates* 33: 163-179.

2865 Immelmann, K, G W Barlow, L Petrinovich, M Main. 1981. *Behavioral Development: The Bielefeld Interdisciplinary Project.* Cambridge: Cambridge University Press.

2866 Ingold, T. 1980. *Hunters, Pastoralists and Ranchers.* Cambridge: Cambridge University Press.

2867 Ingold, T, D Riches, J Woodburn, eds. 1988. *Hunters and Gatherers: Property, Power and Ideology.* London: Berg.

2868 Isabella, R A, J Belsky. 1991. Interactional synchrony and the origins of infant-mother attachment: A replication study. *Child Development* 62: 373-384.

2869 Itani, J, A Suzuki. 1967. The social unit of chimpanzees. *Primates* 8: 355-381.

2870 Izard, C E, L Dougherty. 1982. Two complementary systems for measuring facial expressions of emotions in infants and children. In *Measuring Emotions in Infants and Children*. Edited by Izard, C E. New York: Cambridge University Press.

2871 Jankowiak, W R, E M Hill, J M Donovan. 1992. The effects of sex and sexual orientation on attractiveness judgments: An evolutionary interpretation. *Ethology and Sociobiology* 13: 73-85.

2872 Johnson, S M, O D Bolstad. 1973. Methodological issues in naturalistic observation: Some problems and solutions for field research. In *Behaviour Change: Methodology, Concepts and Practice.* Edited by Hamerlynck, L A, L C Handy, E J Mash. Pp. 7-67. Champaign, Ill.: Research Press Company.

2873 Johnson, G R. 1987. In the name of the fatherland: An analysis of kin terms usage in patriotic speech and literature. *International Political Science Review* 8: 165-174.

2874 Johnson, G R, S H Ratwick, T J Sawyer. 1987. The evocative significance of kin terms in patriotic speech. In *The Sociobiology of Ethnocentrism.* Edited by Reynolds, V, V Falger, I Vine. Beckenham: Croom Helm.

2875 Johnson, G R. 1989. The role of kin recognition mechanisms in patriotic socialization: Further reflections. *Politics and the Life Sciences* 8: 62-69.

2876 Johnson, M H, S Dzuirawiec, H Ellis, J Morton. 1991. Newborns' preferential tracking of face-like stimuli and its subsequent decline. *Cognition* 40: 1-20.

2877 Kahn, M. 1986. *Always Hungry Never Greedy: Food and the Expression of Gender in a Melanesian Society.* Cambridge: Cambridge University Press.

2878 Karli, P. 1991. *Animal and Human Aggression.* 2nd ed. Oxford: Oxford University Press.

2879 Kats, A. 1972. An experimental investigation of aimed throwing in some primates (chimpanzees and hamadryas baboons) and its significance in anthropogenesis. *Transactions of Moscow Society Naturalists* 18: 58-76.

2880 Katsikitis, M, I Pilowsky, J M Innes. 1990. The quantification of smiling using a microcomputer-based approach. *Journal of Nonverbal Behavior* 14: 3-18.

2881 Kaufmann, J H. 1983. On the definitions and functions of dominance and territoriality. *Biological Reviews* 58: 1-20.

2882 Kawamura, S. 1959. The process of sub-cultural propagation among Japanese macaques. *Primates* 2: 43-60.

2883 Keating, C F, *et al.* 1981. Culture and the perception of social dominance from facial expression. *Journal of Personality and Social Psychology* 40: 615-626.

2884 Keating, C F, A Mazur, M H Segall. 1981. A cross-cultural exploration of physiognomic traits of dominance and happiness. *Ethology and Sociobiology* 2: 41-48.

2885 Keller, H, A Schölmerich, I Eibl-Eibesfeldt. 1988. Communication patterns in adult-infant interactions in western and non-western cultures. *Journal of Cross-Cultural Psychology* 19: 427-445.

2886 Kendon, A. 1967. Some functions of gaze-direction. *Acta Psychologica* 26: 22-63.

2887 Kendon, A, M Cook. 1969. Consistency of gaze patterns in social interaction. *British Journal of Psychology* 60: 481-494.

2888 Kendon, A. 1970. Movement coordination in social interaction. *Acta Psychologica* 32: 1-25.

2889 Kendon, A. 1972. Some relationships between body motion and speech. In *Studies in Dyadic Communication.* Edited by Seigman, A, B Pope. Pp. 177-216. Elmsford, New York: Pergamon Press.

2890 Kendon, A. 1973. The role of visible behavior in the organization of face-to-face interaction. In *Movement and Communication in Man and Chimpanzee.* Edited by von Cranach, M, I Vine. New York: Academic Press.

2891 Kendon, A, R M Harris, M R Key, eds. 1973. *The Organization of Behavior in Face-to-Face Interaction.* The Hague: Mouton.

2892 Kendon, A, A Ferber. 1973. A description of some human greetings. In *Comparative Behaviour and Ecology of Primates*. Edited by Michael, R P, J H Crook. Pp. 591-668. London: Academic Press.

2893 Kendon, A. 1975. Gesticulation speech and the gesture theory of language origins. *Sign Language Studies* 9: 349-373.

2894 Kendon, A. 1975. Some functions of the face in a kissing round. *Semiotica* 15: 299-334.

2895 Kendon, A. 1977. *Studies in the Behavior of Face-to-Face Interaction*. Lisse, Netherlands: Peter De Ridder Press.

2896 Kendon, A. 1978. Differential perception and attentional frame in face-to-face interaction: Two problems for investigation. *Semiotica* 24: 305-315.

2897 Kendon, A. 1979. Some theoretical and methodological aspects of the use of film in the study of social interaction. In *Emerging Strategies in Social Psychological Research*. Edited by Ginsburg, G P. Pp. 67-91. London and New York: John Wiley.

2898 Kendon, A. 1980. A description of a deaf-mute sign language from the Enga Province of Papua New Guinea with some comparative discussion Part II: The semiotic functioning of Enga signs. *Semiotica* 81-117.

2899 Kendon, A. 1980. A description of a deaf-mute sign language from the Enga Province of Papua New Guinea with some comparative discussion Part I: The formational properties of Enga signs. *Semiotica* 1-34.

2900 Kendon, A. 1980. A description of a deaf-mute sign language from the Enga Province of Papua New Guinea with some comparative discussion Part III: Aspects of utterance construction. *Semiotica* 245-313.

2901 Kendon, A. 1980. The sign language of the women of Yuendumu: A preliminary report on the structure of Warlpiri sign language. *Sign Language Studies* 27: 101-112.

2902 Kendon, A. 1980. Gesture and speech: Two aspects of the process of utterance. In *Nonverbal Communication and Language*. Edited by Key, M R. Pp. 207-227. The Hague: Mouton.

2903 Kendon, A. 1981. Introduction: Current issues in "nonverbal communication". In *Nonverbal Communication, Interaction and*

*Gesture: Selections from Semiotica.* Edited by Kendon, A. Pp. 1-53. The Hague: Mouton.

2904 Kendon, A. 1981. A geography of gesture. *Semiotica* 37: 129-163.

2905 Kendon, A. 1982. The study of gesture: Some observations on its history. *Recherches Semiotique/Semiotic Inquiry* 2: 45-62.

2906 Kendon, A. 1983. Gesture and speech: How they interact. In *Nonverbal Interaction.* Edited by Wiemann, J, R Harrison. Pp. 13-46. Beverley Hills, CA: Sage.

2907 Kendon, A. 1983. Gesture. *Journal of Visual Verbal Languaging* 3: 21-36.

2908 Kendon, A. 1984. Knowledge of sign language in an Australian Aboriginal community. *Journal of Anthropological Research* 40: 556-576.

2909 Kendon, A. 1985. Behavioral foundations for the process of frame attunement in face-to-face interaction. In *Discovery Strategies in the Psychology of Action.* Edited by Ginsburg, G P, M Brenner, M von Cranach. Pp. 229-253. London: Academic Press.

2910 Kenrick, D T, E K Sadalla, G Groth, M R Trost. 1990. Evolution, traits, and the stages of human courtship: Qualifying the parental investment model. *Journal of Personality* 58: 97-116.

2911 Kerlinger, F. 1979. *Behavioral Research: A Conceptual Approach.* New York: Holt, Rinehart and Winston.

2912 Key, M B. 1981. *The Relationship of Verbal and Nonverbal Communication. Contributions to the Sociology of Language.* The Hague: Mouton.

2913 Key, M R. 1982. *Nonverbal Communication Today: Current Research.* Berlin: Mouton.

2914 Kien, J, M Schleidt, B Schöttner. 1991. Temporal segmentation in hand movements of chimpanzees. *Ethology* 89: 297-304.

2915 Killinger, J. 1989. Neuer Ansatz zur metrisch-quantitativen Bewegungsanalyse mimischer Ausdrucksmuster. *Videoinformationen* 2: 28-39.

2916 Killinger, J. 1990. Der Einsatz der metrisch-quantitativen Bewegungsanalyse bein Untersungen zum mimischen

Expressionsverhalten der Menschen. In *Bewegungsabläufe*. Edited by Dewitz, W, I Kaiser. Berlin: ZEAM.

2917 Kimball, S, J Barnett. 1973. *Learning and Culture*. Seattle: University of Washington Press.

2918 Klama, J. 1988. *Aggression: Conflict in Animals and Humans Reconsidered* London: Longmans.

2919 Klaus, M H, et al. 1972. Maternal attachment: Importance of the first post-partum days. *New England Journal of Medicine* 286: 460-463.

2920 Kleck, R E, M Mendolia. 1990. Decoding of profile versus full-face expressions of affect. *Journal of Nonverbal Behavior* 14: 35-50.

2921 Knauft, B. 1987. Reconsidring violence in simple human societies: Homicide among the HGebusi of New Guinea. *Current Anthropology* 28: 457-500.

2922 Knauft, B M. 1991. Violence and sociality in human evolution. *Current Anthropology* 32: 391-428.

2923 Kohl, R M, L J Dowell, G Jessop. 1989. Synergy control of facial expression. *Human Movement Studies* 16: 233-238.

2924 Kohler, W. 1925. *The Mentality of Apes*. New York: Harcourt Brace.

2925 Kohler, F W, C R Greenwood. 1990. Effects of collateral peer supportive behaviors within the classwide peer tutoring program. *Journal of Applied Behavioral Analysis* 23: 307-332.

2926 Konner, M J. 1972. Aspects of the developmental ethology of a foraging people. In *Ethological Studies of Child Behaviour*. Edited by Blurton Jones, N B. Pp. 285-304. Cambridge: Cambridge University Press.

2927 Konstant, M M, S Homatidi. 1985. Dominance hierarchies in normal and conduct-disordered children. *Journal of Abnormal Child Psychology* 13: 259-267.

2928 Koops, W, H Soppe, et al. 1990. *Developmental Psychology behind the Dykes. An Outline of Developmental Psychological Research in the Netherlands*. Delft: Eburon.

2929 Kortlandt, A, M Kooij. 1963. Protohominid behaviour in primates. *Symposium of the Zoological Society of London* 10: 61-88.

2930 Kortlandt, A. 1967. *Handgebrauch bei freilebenden Schimpansen.* Edited by Rensch, B. Handgebrauch und Verständigung bei Affen und Frühmenschen. Bern: Huber.

2931 Kortlandt, A. 1967. Experimentation with chimpanzees in the wild. In *Neue Ergebnisse der Primatologie.* Edited by Stark, D, R Schneider, H-J Kuhn. Pp. 208-224. Stuttgart: Fischer.

2932 Kortlandt, A. 1986. The use of stone tools by wild-living chimpanzees and earliest hominids. *Journal of Human Evolution* 15: 72-132.

2933 Kortmulder, K. 1968. An ethological theory of an incest taboo and exogamy. *Current Anthropology* 9: 437-449.

2934 Kummer, H. 1971. *Primate Societies: Group Techniques of Ethological Adaptions.* Chicago: Aldine.

2935 Kummer, H, V Dasser, P Hoyningen-Huene. 1990. Exploring primate social cognition: Some critical remarks. *Behavior* 112: 84-98.

2936 La Freniere, P, W R Charlesworth. 1983. Dominance, attention, and affiliation in a preschool group: A nine month longitudinal study. *Ethology and Sociobiology* 4: 55-67.

2937 Laird, J D. 1984. The real role of facial response in the experience of emotion: A reply to Tourangeau and Ellsworth, and Others. *Journal of Personality and Social Psychology* 47: 909-917.

2938 Lamb, M E. 1981. *The development of social expectations in the first year of life.* Edited by Lamb, M E, L R Sherrod. Infant Social Cognition: Empirical and Theoretical Considerations. Hillsdale, N.J.: Erlbaum.

2939 Lamb, M E, L R Sherrod. 1981. *Infant Social Cognition: Empirical and Theoretical Considerations.* Hillsdale, N.J.: Erlbaum.

2940 Lamb, M, B Sutton-Smith, eds. 1982. *Sibling Relationships: Their Nature and Significance across the Lifespan.* Hillsdale, N.J.: Erlbaum.

2941 Lamb, M E, C P Hwang, A Frodi, M Frodi. 1982. Security of mother- and father-infant attachment and its relation to sociability with strangers in traditional and non-traditional Swedish families. *International Journal of Behavioral Development* 5: 355-367.

2942 Lamb, M E. 1982. Maternal attachment and mother neonate bonding: A critical review. *Advances in Developmental Psychology* 2: 1-39.

2943 Lamb, M E, R A Thompson, W P Gardner, E L Charnov, D Estes. 1984. Security of infantile attachment as assessed in the "strange situation": Its study and biological interpretation. *Behavioral and Brain Sciences* 7: 127-147.

2944 Lamb, M E, R A Thompson, W Gardner, E L Charnow. 1985. *Infant-Mother Attachment.* Hillsdale, N.J.: Erlbaum.

2945 Lancaster, J B. 1986. Primate social behavior and ostracism. *Ethology and Sociobiology* 7: 215-226.

2946 Landis, C, W A Hunt. 1939. *The Startle Pattern.* New York: Farrar.

2947 Le Camus, J, R Campon, eds. 1986. *Ethologie et Psychologie de l'Enfant.* Toulouse: Privat.

2948 Le Vine, R A, D T Campbell. 1972. *Ethnocentrism: Theories of Conflict, Ethnic Attitudes and Group Behavior.* New York: Wiley.

2949 Leavitt, G D. 1989. Disappearance of the incest taboo: A cross-cultural test of general evolutionary hypotheses. *American Anthropologist* 91: 116-130.

2950 Lederman, R. 1986. *What Gifts Engender: Social Relations and Politics in Mendi, Highland Papua New Guinea.* Cambridge: Cambridge University Press.

2951 Lee, R B. 1968. What hunters do for a living, or, how to make out on scarce resources. In *Man the Hunter.* Edited by Lee, R B, I DeVore. Pp. 30-48. Chicago: Aldine.

2952 Lee, R B, I DeVore. 1976. *Kalahari Hunter-Gatherers.* Cambridge: Harvard University.

2953 Lee, R B. 1979. *!Kung San: Men, Women and Work in a Foraging Society.* New York: Cambridge University Press.

2954 Lee, P C, J A Johnson. 1992. Sex differences in alliances, and the acquisition and maintenance of dominance status among immature primates. In *Coalitions and Alliances in Humans and Other Animals.* Edited by Harcourt, A H, F B M de Waal. Pp. 391-414. New York: Oxford University Press.

2955 Lehmann, A C, L J Mihalyi. 1982. Aggression, bravery, endurance, and drugs: A radical re-evaluation and analysis of the Masai Warrior Complex. *Ethnology* 21: 335-47.

2956 Leinonen, L, I Linnankoski, M-L Laakso, R Aulanko. 1991. Vocal communication between species: Man and macaque. *Language and Communication* 11: 241-262.

2957 Leonard, C M, K S Voeller, J M Kudlau. 1991. When's a smile? Or how to detect a message by digitizing the signal. *Psychological Science* 2: 166-172.

2958 Lester, B M, C F Z Boukydis, eds. 1985. *Infant Crying.* New York: Plenum.

2959 Levi-Strauss, C. 1949. *Les structures elementaires de la parente.* Paris: Presses Universitaires de France.

2960 Levinson, B M. 1980. The child and his pet: A world of non-verbal communication. In *Ethology and Non-Verbal Communication in Mental Health: An Interdisciplinary Biopsychosocial Exploration.* Edited by Corson, S A, E Corson. Pp. 63-82. New York: Pergamon.

2961 Levy, F. 1980. The development of sustained attention (vigilance) and inhibition in children: Some normative data. *Journal of Child Psychology and Psychiatry* 21: 77-84.

2962 Leyhausen, P. 1973. On the function of the relative hierarchy of moods (as exemplified by the phylogenetic and ontogenetic development of prey-catching in carnivores). In *Motivation of Human and Animal Behavior: An Ethological View.* Edited by Lorenz, K, P Leyhausen. Pp. 144-247. New York: Van Nostrand Reinhold.

2963 Leyhausen, P. 1979. Fear and attachment: Complexities and interdependencies. In *Human Ethology: Claims and Limits of a New Discipline.* Edited by von Cranach, M, et al. Pp. 253-264. New York: Cambridge University Press.

2964 Lorenz, K. 1943. Die angeborenen Formen möglicher Erfahrung. *Zeitschrift für Tierpsychologie* 5: 235-409.

2965 Lorenz, K. 1950. The comparative method in studying innate behavior patterns. *Symposia of the Society for Experimental Biology* 4: 221-268.

2966 Lorenz, K. 1965. *Evolution and Modification of Behavior.* Chicago: University of Chicago Press.

2967 Lorenz, K. 1966. *On Aggression.* New York: Harcourt Brace Jovanovich.

2968 Lorenz, K, P Leyhausen. 1973. *Motivation of Human and Animal Behavior: An Ethological View*. New York: Van Ostrand Reinhold.

2969 Lorenz, K. 1977. *Behind the Mirror: A Search for a Natural History of Human Knowledge*. New York: Harcourt Brace Jovanovich.

2970 Lorenz, K. 1981. *The Foundations of Ethology*. Berlin: Springer.

2971 Lorenz, K, F M Wuketits, eds. 1983. *Die Evolution des Denkens*. Munich: Piper.

2972 Lott, D F. 1991. *Intraspecific Variation in the Social Systems of Wild Vertebrates*. New York: Cambridge University Press.

2973 Low, B. 1979. Sexual selection and human ornamentation. In *Evolutionary Biology and Human Social Behavior: An Anthropological Perspective*. Edited by Chagnon, N, W Irons. Pp. 462-487. North Scituate, MA.: Duxbury.

2974 Loy, J D, C B Peters, eds. 1991. *Understanding Behaviour: What Primate Studies Tell Us about Human Behaviour*. Oxford: Oxford University Press.

2975 MacKinnon, J. 1978. *The Ape within Us*. New York: Rinehart and Winston.

2976 Main, M B, D R Weston. 1982. Avoidance of the attachment figure in infancy: Descriptions and interpretations. In *The Place of Attachment in Human Infancy*. Edited by Stevenson-Hinde, J, C M Parkes. New York: Basic Books.

2977 Main, M B. 1990. Cross-cultural studies of attachment organization: Recent studies, changing methodologies, and the concept of conditional strategies. *Human Development* 33: 48-61.

2978 Main, M. 1990. Cross-cultural studies of attachment organization: Recent studies, changing methodologies, and the concept of conditional strategies. *Human Development* 33: 48-61.

2979 Major, B, A M Schmidlin, L Williams. 1990. Gender patterns in social touch: The impact of setting and age. *Journal of Personality and Social Psychology* 58: 634-640.

2980 Malinowski, B. 1922. *Argonauts of the Western Pacific*. New York: Dutton.

2981 Malinowski, B. 1929. *The Sexual Life of Savages in North-Western Melanesia*. New York: P.R. Reynolds.

2982 Mann, J, et al. 1991. Time sampling: A methodological critique. *Child Development*  62: 227-241.

2983 Manusov, V, J Rodriguez. 1989. Intentionality behind nonverbal messages: A perceiver's perspective. *Journal of Nonverbal Behavior*  13: 15-24.

2984 Marler, P, W J Hamilton. 1966. *Mechanisms of Animal Behavior.* New York: Wiley.

2985 Marler, P. 1976. An ethological theory of the origin of vocal learning. *Annals of the New York Academy of Science*  280: 386-396.

2986 Marler, P. 1976. Social organization, communication and graded signals: The chimpanzee and gorilla. In *Growing Points in Ethology.* Edited by Bateson, P P G, R A Hinde. Pp. 239-280. Cambridge: Cambridge University Press.

2987 Marler, P. 1979. The development of auditory perceptions in relation to vocal behaviour. In *Human Ethology: Claims and Limits of a New Discipline,* edited by Von Cranach, M, et al.  Cambridge: Cambridge University Press.

2988 Martin, P, T Caro. 1985. On the functions of play and its role in behavioral development. In *Advances in the Study of Behavior.*  Edited by Rosenblatt, J S, C Beer, M-C Busnel, P J B Slater. Pp. 59-103. New York: Academic Press.

2989 Martin, P, P Bateson. 1986. *Measuring Behaviour: An Introductory Guide.* Cambridge: Cambridge University Press.

2990 Mascie-Taylor, C G N, A J Boyce, eds. 1988. *Human Mating Patterns.* New York: Cambridge University Press.

2991 Mash, E J, J D McElwee. 1974. Situational effects on observer accuracy: Behavioral predictability, prior experience, and complexity of coding categories. *Child Development*  45: 367-377.

2992 Mason, W A. 1979. *Maternal Attributes and Primate Cognitive Development.*  Edited by von Cranach, M, et al. Human Ethology: Claims and Limits of a New Discipline. Cambridge: Cambridge University Press.

2993 Masters, R D. 1976. Exit, voice and loyalty in animal and human behavior. *Social Science Information*  15: 855-878.

2994 Matsumoto, D. 1989. Face, culture, and judgments of anger and fear: Do the eyes have it? *Journal of Nonverbal Behavior*  13: 171-188.

2995 Matsuzawa, T, T Asano, K Kubota. 1986. Acquisition and generalization of numerical labeling by a chimpanzee. In *Current Perspectives in Primate Social Dynamics*. Edited by Taub, D M, F A King. Pp. 416-430. New York: Van Nostrand Reinhold.

2996 Mayo, C, N H Henley. 1981. *Gender and Nonverbal Behavior*. New York: Springer.

2997 Mazur, A, L S Robertson. 1972. *Biology and Social Behavior*. Chicago: Free Press.

2998 Mazur, A, et al. 1980. Physiological aspects of communication via mutual gaze. *American Journal of Sociology* 86: 50-75.

2999 Mazur, A. 1989. Periods and question marks in the punctuated evolution of human social behavior. *Journal of Social and Biological Structures* 12: 241-250.

3000 McCormick, N B. 1979. Come-ons and put-offs: Unmarried students' strategies of having and avoiding sexual intercourse. *Psychology of Women Quarterly* 4: 194-211.

3001 McCormick, N B, J C Jesser. 1983. *The Courtship Game: Power in Sexual Encounter*. Palo Alto: Mayfield.

3002 McFarland, D J. 1977. Decision-making in animals. *Nature* 269: 15-21.

3003 McFarland, D J, A Houston. 1981. *Quantitative Ethology: The State Space Approach*. London: Pitman.

3004 McFarland, D J. 1985. *Animal Behavior: Psychobiology, Ethology, and Evolution*. Menlo Park: Benjamin/Cummings.

3005 McGee, P E. 1979. *Humor: Its Origins and Development*. San Francisco: Freeman.

3006 McGrew, W C. 1972. *On Ethological Study of Children's Behavior*. New York: Academic Press.

3007 McGrew, W C. 1979. Evolutionary implications of sex differences in chimpanzee predation and tool use. In *Perspectives on Human Evolution*. Edited by Hamburg, D, E McCown. Pp. 441-463. Menlo Park, CA: Benjamin-Cummings.

3008 McGrew, W C, C Tutin, P Baldwin. 1979. Chimpanzees, tools, and termites: Cross-cultural comparisons of Senegal, Tanzania, and Rio Muni. *Man* 14: 185-214.

3009 McGrew, W C. 1991. Chimpanzee material culture: What are its limits and why? In *The Origins of Human Behavior*. Edited by Foley, R A. Pp. 13-24. London: Unwin Hyman.

3010 McGrew, W C, L F Marchant. 1992. Chimpanzees, tools, and termites: Hand preference or handedness? *Current Anthropology* 33: 114-119.

3011 McGuire, M T, R H Polsky. 1980. An ethological analysis of behavioral change in hospitalized psychiatric patients. In *Ethology and Nonverbal Communication in Mental Health*. Edited by Corson, S A, et al. Pp. 1-11. New York: Pergamon.

3012 McIntyre, D C, G L Chew. 1983. Relation between social rank, submissive behavior, and brain catecholamine levels in ring-necked pheasants ( Phasians colchicus). *Behavioral Neuroscience* 97: 595-601.

3013 Meaney, M J, J Stewart, W W Beatty. 1985. Sex differences in social play: The socialization of sex roles. *Advances in the Study of Behavior* 15: 1-58.

3014 Meggitt, M. 1977. *Blood is Their Argument: Warfare among the Mae Enga Tribesmen of the New Guinea Highlands*. Palo Alto: Mayfield.

3015 Mehrabian, A. 1972. *Nonverbal Communication*. Chicago: Aldine.

3016 Mellen, S L W. 1981. *The Evolution of Love*. San Francisco: W.H. Freeman.

3017 Menzel, E. 1972. Spontaneous invention of ladders in a group of young chimpanzees. *Folia Primatologica* 17: 87-106.

3018 Menzel, E, S Halperin. 1975. Purposive behavior as a basis for objective communication between chimpanzees. *Science* 189: 652-654.

3019 Merleau-Ponty, M. 1967[1942]. *The Structure of Behavior*. Boston: Beacon.

3020 Michael, R P, D Zumpe. 1978. Potency in male rhesus monkeys: Effects of continuously receptive females. *Science* 200: 451-453.

3021 Middleton, J. 1967. *Magic, Witchcraft and Cursing*. New York: Natural History Press.

3022 Miller, P. 1983. Ethological theory. In *Theories of Developmental Psychology*. Edited by Miller, P. Pp. 301-353. San Francisco: Freeman.

3023 Mitchell, J G. 1980. *The Hunt.* New York: Knopf.

3024 Mitchell, G. 1981. *Human Sex Differences: A Primatologist's Perspective.* New York: Van Nostrand Reinhold.

3025 Mitchell, G, J Erwin. 1986. *Comparative Primate Biology. Vol. 2, Part A: Behavior, Conservation and Ecology.* New York: Alan R. Liss.

3026 Mitchell, R, N Thompson. 1986. *Deception: Perspectives on Human and Nonhuman Deceit.* Albany: SUNY Press.

3027 Moore, S F, B Myerhoff. 1977. *Secular Ritual.* Amsterdam: Van Goreum.

3028 Moore, M M. 1985. Nonverbal courtship patterns in women: Context and consequences. *Ethology and Sociobiology* 6: 237-247.

3029 Morgan, C L. 1970[1900]. *Animal Behavior.* New York: Johnson Reprint.

3030 Morgan, G A, H N Ricciuti. 1973. Infants' response to strangers during the first year. In *The Competent Infant: Research and Commentary.* Edited by Stone, L J, H T Smith, L B Murphy. New York: Basic Books.

3031 Morris, D. 1962. *The Biology of Art.* New York: Knopf.

3032 Morris, D. 1967. *The Naked Ape.* New York: Dell.

3033 Morris, D. 1969. *Primate Ethology.* Chicago: Aldine.

3034 Morris, D. 1977. *Manwatching: A Field Guide to Human Behaviour.* New York: Abrams.

3035 Morris, K, J Goodall. 1977. Competition for meat between chimpanzees and baboons of the Gambe National Park. *Folia Primatologica* 28: 109-121.

3036 Morris, D. 1981. *The Soccer Tribe.* London: Jonathan Cape.

3037 Moynihan, M H. 1976. *The New World Primates: Studies in Adaptive Radiation and the Evolution of Social Behavior, Languages and Intelligence.* Princeton: Princeton University Press.

3038 Mugford, R A. 1980. The social significance of pet ownership. In *Ethology and Nonverbal Communication in Mental Health.* Edited by Corson, S A, et al. Pp. 111-122. New York: Pergamon.

3039 Muller-Schwarze, D. 1978. *Evolution of Play Behavior.* Stroudsburg, Pa.: Dowden, Hutchinson and Ross.

3040 Munroe, R, R L Munroe, B B Whiting. 1981. Male sex-role resolutions. In *Handbook of Cross-cultural Human Development.* Edited by Munroe, R, R L Munroe, B B Whiting. Pp. 611-632. New York: Garland STPM Press.

3041 Murdock, G P. 1949. *Social Structure.* New York: Macmillan.

3042 Murdock, G P. 1967. *Ethnographic Atlas.* Pittsburgh: University of Pittsburgh Press.

3043 Murdock, G P. 1969. Standard cross-cultural sample. *Ethnology* 8: 329-369.

3044 Murdock, G P. 1981. *Atlas of World Cultures.* Pittsburgh: University of Pittsburgh Press.

3045 Musterle, W, O Rossler. 1986. Computer faces: The human Lorenz matrix. *BioSystem* 19: 61-80.

3046 Neel, J. 1980. On being headman. *Perspectives in Biology and Medicine* 23: 277-294.

3047 Nesse, R M, A Silverman, A Bortz. 1990. Sex differences in ability to recognize family resemblance. *Ethology and Sociobiology* 11: 11-21.

3048 Nieburg, H L. 1972. Agonistics: Rituals of conflict. In *Collective Violence.* Edited by Short, J, M Wolfgang. Pp. 82-99. Chicago: Aldine.

3049 Nimon, A J, F R Dalziel. 1992. Cross-species interaction and communication: A study method applied to captive siamang (Hylobates synadactylus) and long-billed corella (Cacatua ternuirostris) contacts with humans. *Applied Animal Behaviour Science* 33: 261-272.

3050 Nishida, T, S Uehara, R Nyundo. 1979. Predatory behavior among wild chimpanzees in the Mahale mountains. *Primates* 20: 1-20.

3051 Nishida, T. 1983. Alpha status and agonistic alliance in wild chimpanzees. *Primates* 24: 318-336.

3052 Nishida, T, M Hiraiwa-Hasgawa, T Hasgawa, Y Takahata. 1985. Group extinction and female transfer in wild chimpanzees in the Mahale National Park, Tanzania. *Zeitschrift für Tierpsychologie* 67: 284-301.

3053 Nitecki, M, D Nitecki, eds. 1986. *The Evolution of Human Hunting.* New York: Plenum.

3054 Noë, R, F B M de Waal, J van Hooff. 1980. Types of dominance in a chimpanzee colony. *Animal Behavior* 34: 90-110.

3055 Noë, R. 1990. A veto game played by baboons: A challenge to the use of the Prisoner's Dilemma as a paradigm for reciprocity and cooperation. *Animal Behavior* 39: 78-90.

3056 Nowicki, S, C Oxenford. 1989. The relation of hostile nonverbal communication styles to popularity in preadolescent children. *Journal of Genetic Psychology* 150: 39-44.

3057 Nurse, G T. 1977. *Health and the Hunter-Gatherer.* Basel: Karger.

3058 Nurse, G T, J S Weiner, T Jenkins. 1985. *The Peoples of Southern Africa and Their Affinities.* Oxford: Clarendon Press.

3059 O'Sullivan, M, P Ekman, W Friesen, K Scherer. 1985. What you say and how you say it: The contribution of speech content and voice quality to judgements of others. *Journal of Personality and Social Psychology* 48: 54-62.

3060 Oakley, K P. 1972. *Man the Tool-Maker.* 6th ed London: British Museum.

3061 Oakley, K P. 1972. *Skill as a human possession.* Edited by Washburn, S, P Dolhinow. Perspectives on Human Evolution. New York: Holt, Rinehart and Winston.

3062 Oettingen, G. 1985. The influence of the kindergarten teacher on sex differences in behavior. *International Journal of Behavioral Development* 8: 3-13.

3063 Oliverio, A, M Zapella. 1983. *The Behavior of Human Infants.* New York: Plenum.

3064 Olivier, B, J Mos, P F Brain, eds. 1987. *Ethopharmacology of Agonistic Behavior in Animals and Humans.* Dordrecht: Nijhoff.

3065 Omark, D R, M S Edelman. 1975. A comparison of status hierarchies in young children: An ethological approach. *Social Science Information* 15: 87-107.

3066 Omark, D R, F F Strayer, D G Freedman. 1980. *Dominance Relations: An Ethological View of Human Conflict and Social Interaction.* New York: Garland.

3067 Owsgley, H H, C M Scotton. 1984. The conversational expression of power by television interviewers. *Journal of Social Psychology* 123: 261-271.

3068 Paige, K E, J M Paige. 1981. *The Politics of Reproductive Ritual.* Berkeley: University of California Press.

3069 Palmer, M T. 1988. Controlling conversations: Turns, topics and interpersonal control. *Communications Monographs* 56: 1-18.

3070 Panksepp, J. 1986. The psychobiology of prosocial behaviors: Separation, distress, play and altruism. In *Altruism and Aggression: Biological and Social Origins.* Edited by Zahn-Waxler, C, E M Cummings, R Iannotti. Cambridge: Cambridge University Press.

3071 Papousek, H, M Papousek. 1979. Early ontogeny of human social interaction: Its biological roots and social dimensions. In *Human Ethology: Claims and Limits of a New Discipline.* Edited by von Cranach, M, et al. Pp. 456-478. Cambridge: Cambridge University Press.

3072 Passingham, R E. 1982. *The Human Primate.* Oxford: Freeman.

3073 Pastor, D L. 1981. The quality of mother-infant attachment and its relationship to toddler's initial sociability with peers. *Developmental Psychology* 17: 326-335.

3074 Pearl, M C, S R Schulman. 1983. Techniques for the analysis of social structure in animal societies. In *Advances in the Study of Behavior.* Edited by Rosenblatt, J S, R A Hinde, C Beer, M C Busnel. New York: Academic Press.

3075 Pereira, M E, J Altmann. 1985. Development of social behavior in free-living nonhuman primates. In *Nonhuman Primate models for growth and development.* Edited by Watts, E S. Pp. 217-309. New York: Alan R. Liss.

3076 Petrovich, S B. 1978. *Extrapolations for Ethological Studies. Dimensions of Behavior.* New York: Butterworth.

3077 Petryszak, N. 1979. The biosociology of the social self. *Sociological Quarterly* 20: 291-303.

3078 Pilowsky, I, M Thornton, B B Stokes. 1986. Towards the quantification of facial expressions with the use of a mathematical model of the face. In *Aspects of Face Processing*. Edited by Ellis, H D, M A Jeeves, F Newcombe, A Young. Pp. 340-348. Dordrecht: Martinus Nijhoff.

3079 Pirta, R S. 1992. Group dynamics and cohesiveness. In *Primates: The New Revolution*. Edited by Seth, P K, S Seth. Pp. 151-161. New Delhi: Today & Tomorrow's.

3080 Pitcairn, T K, I Eibl-Eibesfeldt. 1976. Concerning the evolution of nonverbal communication in man. In *Communicative Behavior and Evolution*. Edited by Simmel, E C, M Hahn. Pp. 81-113. New York: Academic Press.

3081 Pitcher, E G, L H Schultz. 1983. *Boys and Girls at Play: The Development of Sex Roles*. New York: Praeger.

3082 Pitt-Rivers, J. 1977. *The Fate of Shechem or the Politics of Sex*. Cambridge: Cambridge University Press.

3083 Pliner, P, T Alloway, L Krames, eds. 1975. *Nonverbal Communication of Aggression*. New York: Plenum.

3084 Plooij, F X. 1984. *The Behavioral Development of Free-living Chimpanzee Babies and Infants*. Norwood, NJ: Ablex Publishing.

3085 Plooij, F X. 1990. Developmental psychology and education during infancy. In *Developmental Psychology behind the Dykes. An Outline of Developmental Psychological Research in the Netherlands*. Edited by Koops, W, H Soppe, et al. Pp. 211-223. Delft: Eburon.

3086 Plooij, F X. 1990. Developmental psychology: Developmental stages as successive reorganizations of the hierarchy. In *Introduction to Modern Psychology: The Control-Theory View*. Edited by Robertson, R J, W T Powers. Pp. 123-133. Gravel Switch, KY: The Control Systems Group.

3087 Poirer, F E. 1972. *Primate Socialization*. New York: Random House.

3088 Poirer, F E, E O Smith. 1974. Socializing functions of primate play behavior. *American Zoologist* 14: 275-287.

3089 Pomerleau, A, G Malcuit, R Seguin. 1992. Five-month-old girls' and boys' exploratory behaviors in the presence of familiar and unfamiliar toys. *Genetic Psychology* 153: 47-61.

3090 Portman, A. 1953. *Animals as Social Beings.* New York: Viking.

3091 Portman, A. 1956. *Animal Camouflage.* Ann Arbor: University of Michigan Press.

3092 Power, T G, R D Parke. 1982. Play as a context for early learning: Lab and home analyses. In *Families as a Learning Environment for Children.* Edited by Laosa, L M, I E Sigel. New York: Plenum.

3093 Preisler, B. 1986. *Linguistic Sex Roles in Conversation.* Berlin: Walter de Gruyter.

3094 Premack, D, G Woodruff. 1978. Chimpanzee problem-solving: A test for comprehension. *Science* 202: 532-535.

3095 Price-Williams, D R. 1970. *Cross-Cultural Studies.* Baltimore: Penguin.

3096 Provine, R R, K R Fischer. 1989. Laughing, smiling, and talking: Relation to sleeping and social context in humans. *Ethology* 83: 295-305.

3097 Provine, R R. 1989. Contagious yawning and infant imitation. *Bulletin of the Psychonomic Society* 27: 125-127.

3098 Provine, R R, Y L Yong. 1991. Laughter: A stereotyped human vocalization. *Ethology* 89: 115-124.

3099 Pugh, G E. 1977. *The Biological Origin of Human Values.* New York: Basic Books.

3100 Purton, A C. 1978. Ethological categories of behavior and some consequences of their conflation. *Animal Behavior* 26: 653-670.

3101 Pusey, A E. 1983. Mother-offspring relationships in chimpanzees after weaning. *Animal Behavior* 31: 363-377.

3102 Rachkowski, R, K E O'Grady. 1988. Client gender and sex-typed nonverbal behavior: Impact on impression formation. *Sex Roles* 19: 771-784.

3103 Radin, P. 1966. *The Method and Theory of Ethnography.* New York: Basic Books.

3104 Rajecki, D W, M E Lamb, P Obmascher. 1978. Toward a general theory of infantile attachment: A comparative review of aspects of the social bond. *Behavioral and Brain Sciences* 1: 417-464.

3105 Rasa, O A E. 1981. Ethological aspects of aggression in subhuman animals. In *The Biology of Aggression.* Edited by Brain, P F, D Benton. Pp. 585-601. Rockville, Maryland: Sijthoff & Nordhoff.

3106 Redican, W K. 1982. An evolutionary perspective on human facial displays. In *Emotion in the Human Face.* Edited by Ekman, P. Pp. 212-80. Elmsford, NY: Pergamon Press.

3107 Reiss, M, H Sants. 1987. *Behaviour and Social Organisation.* Cambridge: Cambridge University Press.

3108 Reite, M, T Fields, eds. 1985. *The Psychobiology of Attachment and Separation.* New York: Academic Press.

3109 Reiter, R, ed. 1975. *Toward an Anthropology of Women.* New York: Monthly Review Press.

3110 Rentschler, I, B Herzberger, D Epstein, eds. 1988. *Beauty and the Brain.* Basel: Birkhäuser.

3111 Rex, J, D Mason, eds. 1987. *Theories of Race and Ethnic Relations.* Cambridge: Cambridge University Press.

3112 Reynolds, V. 1980. *The Biology of Human Action.* 2nd ed San Francisco: Freeman.

3113 Reynolds, P C. 1982. The primate constructional system: The theory and description of instrumental object use in humans and chimpanzees. In *The Analysis of Action: Recent Theoretical and Empirical Advances.* Edited by von Cranach, M, R Harré. Pp. 343-385. Cambridge: Cambridge University Press.

3114 Reynolds, V. 1982. Behaviour, action and act in relation to strategies and decision making. In *The Analysis of Action.* Edited by von Cranach, M, R Harré. Cambridge: Cambridge University Press.

3115 Reynolds, V. 1984. Social changes in a group of Rhesus monkeys. In *The Meaning of Primate Signals.* Edited by Harré, R, V Reynolds. Cambridge: Cambridge University Press.

3116 Richards, A I. 1969. Characteristics of ethical systems in primitive human society. In *Biology and Ethics.* Edited by Ebling, F J. New York: Academic Press.

3117 Richards, S M. 1974. The concept of dominance and methods of assessment. *Animal Behavior* 22: 914-930.

3118 Ridgeway, C L, J Berger. 1986. Expectations, legitimation, and dominance behavior in task groups. *Sociological Review* 51: 603-617.

3119 Ridley, M. 1986. *Animal Behaviour: A Concise Introduction.* Oxford: Blackwell.

3120 Riopelle, A J, ed. 1967. *Animal Problem Solving.* Baltimore: Penguin.

3121 Riskind, J H. 1984. They stoop to conquer: Guiding and self-regulatory functions of physical posture after success and failure. *Journal of Personality and Social Psychology* 47: 479-493.

3122 Roberts, M. 1981. *Caste Conflict and Elite Formation: The Rise of a Karäva Elite in Sri Lanka, 1500-1931.* Cambridge: Cambridge University Press.

3123 Robinson, L F, H T Reis. 1989. The effects of interruption, gender, and status on interpersonal perceptions. *Journal of Nonverbal Behavior* 13: 141-155.

3124 Romanes, G J. 1969[1884]. *Mental Evolution in Animals.* New York: A.M.S. Press.

3125 Romanes, G J. 1977[1883]. *Animal Intelligence.* Washington, D.C.: University Publications of America.

3126 Rosenblatt, J, C Beer, M-C Busnel, P J B Slater, eds. 1985. *Advances in the Study of Behavior.* New York: Academic Press.

3127 Rosenblum, L A, ed. 1970. *Primate Behavior.* New York: Academic Press.

3128 Rosenblum, L A. 1978. The creation of a behavioral taxonomy. In *Observing Behavior. Vol.II. Data Collection and Analysis Methods.* Edited by Sackett, G P. Pp. 15-24. Baltimore: University Park Press.

3129 Rosenthal, R, ed. 1979. *Skill in Nonverbal Communication: Individual Differences.* Cambridge: Oelgeschlager, Gunn & Hain.

3130 Rowell, T E. 1974. The concept of social dominance. *Behavioral Biology* 11: 131-154.

3131 Russell, W M S, C Russell. 1968. *Violence, Monkeys and Man.* London: Macmillan.

3132 Rutter, M. 1981. *Maternal Deprivation Reassessed* 2nd ed Harmondsworth: Penguin.

3133 Sackett, G P. 1966. Monkeys reared in isolation with pictures as visual imput: Evidence for an innate releasing mechanism. *Science* 154: 1468-1473.

3134 Sackett, G P, ed. 1978. *Observing Behavior: Data Collection and Analysis Methods*. Baltimore: University Park Press.

3135 Sackett, G P. 1978. *Measurement*. Edited by Sackett, G P. Observational Research, Observing Behavior. Vol. II. Data Collection and Analysis Methods. Baltimore: University Park Press.

3136 Sackett, G, P Gould. 1991. What can primate models of human developmental psychopathology model? In *Internalizing and Externalizing Expressions of Dysfunction*. Edited by Chichetti, I D, S Toth. Pp. 265-292. Hillsdale, NJ: Erlbaum.

3137 Sade, D S. 1968. Inhibition of son-mother mating among free-ranging Rhesus monkeys. *Science and Psychoanalysis* 12: 18-38.

3138 Sagi, A. 1990. Attachment theory and research from a cross-cultural perspective. *Human Development* 33: 10-22.

3139 Sahlins, M D. 1968. *Tribesmen*. New York: Prentice-Hall.

3140 Sailer, L, S Gaulin. 1984. Proximity, sociality, and observation: The definition of social groups. *American Anthropologist* 86: 91-98.

3141 Salk, L. 1973. The role of the heartbeat in relations between mother and infant. *Scientific American* 228: 24-29.

3142 Salter, F K. In press. *Command: An Ethological Analysis*. Oxford: Oxford University Press.

3143 Sanday, P R. 1986. *Female Power and Male Dominance: On the Origins of Sexual Inequality*. Cambridge: Cambridge University Press.

3144 Savin-Williams, R C. 1977. Dominance in a human adolescent group. *Animal Behavior* 25: 400-406.

3145 Savin-Williams, R C. 1987. *Adolescence: An Ethological Perspective*. New York: Springer Verlag.

3146 Savin-Williams, R C, G E Weisfeld. 1989. An ethological perspective on adolescence. In *Biology of Adolescent Behavior and Development*. Edited by Adams, G R, et al. Newbury Park, CA: Sage.

3147 Scheller, R H, B S Rothman, E Mayeri. 1974. How "fixed" is the fixed action pattern? *Zeitschrift für Tierpsychologie* 36: 184-211.

3148 Scherer, K. 1975. *Human Aggression and Conflict*. New York: Prentice-Hall.

3149 Scherer, U, K R Scherer. 1980. Psychological factors in bureaucratic encounters: Determinants and effects of interactions between officials and clients. In *The Analysis of Social Skill*. Edited by Singleton, W T, P Spurgen, R B Stammers. New York: Plenum.

3150 Scherer, K R. 1982. Methods of research on vocal communication: Paradigms and parameters. In *Handbook of Methods in Nonverbal Behaviour Research*. Edited by Scherer, K, P Ekman. Pp. 136-98. Cambridge: Cambridge University Press.

3151 Schiefenhövel, W. 1981. "Primitive" childbirth—anachronism or challenge to "modern" obstetrics? In *Proceedings of the 7th European Congress on Perinatal Medicine*. Edited by Ballabriga, A, A Gallart. Pp. 40-49. Barcelona: Sant Vicenc dels Horts.

3152 Schiefenhövel, W. 1984. Preferential female infanticide and other mechanisms regulating population size among the Eipo. In *Population and Biology*. Edited by Keyfitz, N. Pp. 169-192. Liège: Ordina Editions.

3153 Schiefenhövel, W, I Bell-Krannhals. 1986. Wer teilt, hat Teil an der Macht: Systeme der Yams-Vergebe auf den Trobriand-Inseln, Papua Neuguinea. *Mitteilunger der Anthropologischen Gesellschaft (Wein)* 116: 19-39.

3154 Schiefenhövel, W. 1987. Stress factors and stress coping among inhabitants of New Guinea. In *Perspectives on Stress and Related Topics*. Edited by Lolas, F, H Mayer. Pp. 33-43. Berlin: Springer.

3155 Schiefenhövel, W. 1988. *Geburtsverhalten und reproduktive Strategien der Eipo: Ergebnisse humanethologischer und ethnomedizinischer Untersuchungen im zentralen Bergland von Irian Jaya (West-Neuguinea), Indonesien*. Berlin: Reimer.

3156 Schiefenhövel, W. 1989. Reproduction and sex-ratio manipulation through preferential female infanticide among the Eipo, highlands of West-New Guinea. In *Sociobiology of Sexual and Reproductive Strategies*. Edited by Rasa, A, C Vogel, E Voland. Pp. 170-193. New York: Chapman and Hall.

3157 Schiefenhövel, W. 1989. Vom physiologischen Reflex zur Botschaft: Über evolutionsbiologische Zwänge und semiotische Entwicklungslinien in der menschlichen Mimik. In *Katatone und dyskinestische Syndrome*. Edited by Hippius, H, E Rüther, M Schmauß. Pp. 27-39. Berlin: Springer.

3158 Schiefenhövel, W. 1989. Ausdruck, Wahrnehmung und soziale Fun ktion des Schmerzes. Eine humanethologische Synopse. In *Schmerz. Interdisziplinäre Perspektiven.* Edited by Greifeld, K, N Kohnen, E Schröder. Pp. 129-137. Wiesbaden: Vieweg.

3159 Schiefenhövel, W. 1990. Ritualized male homosexuality and other aspects of sexual behavior in Melanesia: An anthropological and ethological approach. In *Pedophilia.* Edited by Feierman, J R, J B Lancaster. New York: Springer.

3160 Schiefenhövel, W. 1992. Zwischen Patriarchat und Matrilinealität: Melanesische Antworten auf ein biologisches und soziokulturelles Problem. In *Interdisziplinäre Aspekte der Geschlechterverhältnisse in einer sich wandelnden Zeit.* Edited by Wessel, K, H Bosinski. Pp. 144-164. Bielefeld: Klein.

3161 Schleidt, M. 1980. Personal odour and nonverbal communication. *Ethology and Sociobiology* 1: 225-231.

3162 Schleidt, M, B Hold. 1982. Human odour and identity. In *Olfaction and Endocrine Regulation.* Edited by Breipohl, W. London: IRL Press.

3163 Schleidt, M, B Hold. 1982. Human axillary odour: Biological and cultural variables. In *Determination of Behaviour by Chemical Stimuli.* London IRL Press.

3164 Schleidt, M. 1988. A universal time constant operating in human short-term behaviour repetitions. *Ethology* 77: 67-75.

3165 Schleidt, M, P Neumann, H Morishita. 1988. Pleasure and disgust: Memories and associations of pleasant and unpleasant odours in Germany and Japan. *Chemical Senses* 13: 279-293.

3166 Schleidt, M, C Genzel. 1990. The significance of mother's perfume for infants in the first weeks of their life. *Ethology and Sociobiology* 11: 145-154.

3167 Schneirla, T C. 1972. *Selected Writings of T.C. Schneirla.* Edited by Aronson, L R, E Tobach, J S Rosenblatt, D S Lehrman. San Francisco: Freeman.

3168 Schoeck, H. 1970. *Envy: A Theory of Social Behavior.* Indianapolis: Liberty Press.

3169 Schropp, R. 1986. Interaction "objectified": The exchange of play-material in a preschool-group. In *Ethology and Psychology.* Edited by Lecamus, J, J Cosnier. Pp. 77-88. Toulouse: University Paul Sabatier.

3170 Schubert, G. 1983. The structure of attention: A critical review. *Journal of Social and Biological Structures* 6: 65-80.

3171 Schuster, I, J Hartzkar. 1986. Kinder, Kueche, Kibbutz: Women's aggression and status quo maintenance in a small-scale community. *Anthropological Quarterly* 59: 191-199.

3172 Scott, J P. 1978. *Critical Periods.* New York: Van Nostrand Reinhold.

3173 Scott, J P. 1989. *The Evolution of Social Systems.* New York: Gordon and Breach.

3174 Scott, J P. 1992. Aggression: Functions and control in social systems. *Aggressive Behavior* 18: 1-20.

3175 Seaford, H W. 1981. Maximizing replicability in describing facial behavior. In *Nonverbal Communication, Interaction and Gesture.* Edited by Kendon, A. Pp. 165-198. The Hague: Mouton.

3176 Sebeok, T A. 1977. *How Animals Communicate.* Bloomington: Indiana University Press.

3177 Sebeok, T A, J Umiker-Sebeok. 1981. *Speaking of Apes: A Critical Anthology of Two-Way Communication with Man.* New York: Plenum.

3178 Seigman, A, S Feldstein, eds. 1987. *Nonverbal Behavior and Communication.* 2nd ed. Hillsdale, NJ: Erlbaum.

3179 Senft, B. 1985. How to tell—and understand—a "dirty" joke in Kilivila. *Journal of Pragmatics* 9: 217-236.

3180 Senft, B. 1987. Kilivila color terms. *Studies in Language* 11: 315-346.

3181 Shapiro, J P, R F Baumeister, J W Kessler. 1991. A three-year component model of children's teasing: Aggression, humor, and ambiguity. *Journal of Social and Clinical Psychology* 10: 459-472.

3182 Shepard, P. 1973. *The Tender Carnivore and the Sacred Game.* New York: Scribner's.

3183 Shepher, J. 1971. Mate selection among second-generation Kibbutz adolescents and adults: Incest avoidance and negative imprinting. *Archives of Sexual Behavior* 1: 293-307.

3184 Shibasaka, H. 1987. Children's access strategies at the entrance to the classroom. *Man Environment Systems* 17: 17-31.

3185 Shibasaka, H. 1988. The function of friends in preschoolers' lives: At the entrance to the classroom. *Journal of Ethology* 6: 21-31.

3186 Short, J F, M E Wolfgang, eds. 1972. *Collective Violence.* Chicago: Aldine and Atherton.

3187 Shostak, M. 1983. *Nisa: The Life and Works of a !Kung San Woman.* New York: Random House.

3188 Siegfried, W. 1988. Dance, the fugitive form of art: Aesthetics as behavior. In *Beauty and the Brain.* Edited by Rentschler, I, B Herzberger, D Epstein. Pp. 117-148. Basel: Birkhäuser.

3189 Siegman, A W, S Feldstein. 1987. *Nonverbal Behavior and Communication.* 2nd ed Hillsdale, N.J.: Erlbaum.

3190 Sigelman, C K, R M Adams. 1990. Family interactions in public: Parent-child distance and touching. *Journal of Nonverbal Behavior* 14: 63-76.

3191 Silberhauer, G B. 1981. *Hunter and Habitat in the Central Kalahari Desert.* Cambridge: Cambridge University Press.

3192 Silk, J B. 1992. The origins of caregiving behavior. *American Journal of Physical Anthropology* 87: 227-30.

3193 Silk, J B. 1992. Patterns of intervention in agonistic contests among male bonnet macaques. In *Coalitions and Alliances in Humans and Other Animals.* Edited by Harcourt, A H, F B M de Waal. Pp. 215-232. New York: Oxford University Press.

3194 Silverberg, J, J P Gray. 1992. *Aggression and Peacefulness in Humans and Other Primates.* New York: Oxford University Press.

3195 Sipes, R. 1973. War, sports and aggression: An empirical test of two rival theories. *American Anthropologist* 75: 64-86.

3196 Slater, P J B. 1973. Describing sequences of behaviour. In *Perspectives in Ethology.* Edited by Bateson, P P G, P H Klopfer. Pp. 131-153. New York: Plenum Press.

3197 Slater, P J B. 1978. Data collection. In *Quantitative Ethology.* Edited by Colgen, P W. Pp. 7-24. New York: Wiley.

3198 Slater, P J B. 1985. *An Introduction to Ethology*.   Cambridge: Cambridge University Press.

3199 Slowman, L. 1977. The role of attractiveness and mate selection in phylogenetics. *Biological Psychiatry* 12: 487-493.

3200 Sluckin, A M, P K Smith. 1977. Two approaches to the concept of dominance in preschool children. *Child Development* 48: 917-923.

3201 Small, M F, ed. 1984. *Female Primates: Studies by Women Primatologists*. New York: Alan R. Liss.

3202 Smith, J, J Chase, A Lieblich. 1974. Tongue showing. *Semiotica* 11: 201-236.

3203 Smith, P K. 1975. Ethological Methods. In *New Perspectives in Child Development*. Edited by Foss, B. Pp. 85-137. Bungay, Suffolk: Penguin.

3204 Smith, E O, ed. 1978. *Social Play in Primates*.   London: Academic Press.

3205 Smith, E O. 1978. A historical view on the study of play: Statement of the problem. In *Social Play in Primates*. Edited by Smith, E O. Pp. 1-32. New York: Academic Press.

3206 Smith, E A, R Dyson-Hudson. 1978. Human territoriality: An ecological reassessment. *American Anthropologist* 80: 21-41.

3207 Smith, P K, K J Connolly. 1980. *The Ecology of Preschool Behaviour*. Cambridge: Cambridge University Press.

3208 Smith, E A. 1981. The application of optimal foraging theory to hunter-gatherer group size. In *Hunter-Gatherer Foraging Strategies: Ethnographic and Archaeological Analyses*. Edited by Winterhalder, B, E A Smith. Pp. 34-65. Chicago: University of Chicago Press.

3209 Smith, P K. 1982. Does play matter? Functional and evolutionary aspects of animal and human play. *Behavioral and Brain Sciences* 5: 139-155.

3210 Smith, P K. 1984. *Play in Animals and Humans*.   Oxford: Blackwell.

3211 Smith, P K, K Lewis. 1985. Rough-and-tumble play, fighting and chasing in nursery school children. *Ethology and Sociobiology* 6: 175-181.

3212 Smith, E A. 1985. *Inujjuamiut Foraging Strategies: Ecology and Economy of Hudson Bay Inuit.* Chicago: Aldine.

3213 Smith, W J. 1985. Consistency and change in communication. In *The Development of Expressive Behavior.* Edited by Zivin, G. Pp. 51-75. Orlando: Academic Press.

3214 Smith, P K, M Boulton. 1990. Rough-and-tumble play, aggression and dominance: Perception and behaviour in children's encounters. *Human Development* 33: 271-282.

3215 Smuts, B. 1985. *Sex and Friendship in Baboons.* New York: Aldine.

3216 Smuts, B B. 1992. Male aggression against women: An evolutionary perspective. *Human Nature* 3: 1-44.

3217 Snow, C. 1989. *Infant Development.* Englewood,Cliffs, NJ: Prentice-Hall.

3218 Snowden, C T. 1982. *Primate Communication.* Cambridge: Cambridge University Press.

3219 Snowdon, C T. 1979. Response of non-human animals to speech and to species-specific sounds. *Brain and Behavioral Evolution* 16: 409-429.

3220 Snowdon, C T. 1983. Ethology, comparative psychology, and animal behavior. *Annual Review of Psychology* 34: 63-94.

3221 Spiro, M. 1979. *Gender and Culture: Kibbutz Women Revisited* Durham: Duke University Press.

3222 Sroufe, L A, E Waters. 1977. Attachment as an organizational construct. *Child Development* 48: 1184-1199.

3223 Sroufe, L A. 1978. Attachment and the roots of competence. *Human Nature* 110: 50-57.

3224 Sroufe, L A, E Waters. 1982. Issues of temperament and attachment. *American Journal of Orthopsychiatry* 52: 743-746.

3225 Sroufe, L A. 1983. Infant-caregiver attachment and patterns of adaptation in preschool. In *The Roots of Maladaption and Competence, Minnesota Symposium on Child Psychology.* Edited by Perlmutter, M. Hillsdale, N.J.: Erlbaum.

3226 Sroufe, L A. 1985. Attachment classification from the perspective of infant-caregiver relationships and infant temperament. *Child Development* 56: 1-14.

3227 Steckler, N A, R Rosenthal. 1985. Sex differences in nonverbal and verbal communication with bosses, peers, and subordinates. *Journal of Applied Psychology* 70: 157-63.

3228 Steinberg, J B. 1977. Information theory as an ethological tool. In *Quantitative Methods in the Study of Animal Behavior.* Edited by Hazlett, B A. New York: Academic Press.

3229 Steiner, J E, ed. 1982. *Determination of Behaviour by Chemical Stimuli.* London: IRL Press.

3230 Steiner, F. 1986. Differentiating smiles. In *FACS in Psychotherapy Research.* Edited by Branniger-Huber, E, F Steiner. Pp. 139-48. Zurich: Department of Clinical Psychology, University Zurich.

3231 Stern, D N. 1974. Mother and infant at play: The dyadic interaction involving facial, vocal, and gaze behaviors. In *The Effect of the Infant on its Caregiver.* Edited by Lewis, M, L A Rosenblum. New York: Wiley.

3232 Sternglanz, S H, A Nash. 1988. *Ethological Contributions to the Study of Human Motherhood.* New York: Plenum.

3233 Stevenson-Hinde, J, C M Parkes. 1982. *The Place of Attachment in Human Infancy.* New York: Basic Books.

3234 Stevenson-Hinde, J. 1990. Attachment within family systems: An overview. *Infant Mental Health Journal* 11: 218-227.

3235 Stoddart, D M. 1990. *The Scented Ape: The Biology and Culture of Human Odour.* Cambridge: Cambridge University Press.

3236 Stone, L J, H T Smith, L B Murphy, eds. 1973. *The Competent Infant: Research and Commentary.* New York: Basic Books.

3237 Storrs, D, C L Kleinke. 1990. Evaluation of high and equal status male and female touchers. *Journal of Nonverbal Behavior* 14: 87-96.

3238 Strathern, A. 1982. *Inequality in New Guinea Highlands Societies.* Cambridge: Cambridge University Press.

3239 Strathern, A. 1988. The aesthetic significance of display: Some examples from Papua New Guinea. In *Beauty and the Brain.* Edited by Rentschler, I, B Herzberger, D Epstein. Basel: Birkhäuser.

3240 Strayer, F F. 1978. Social ecology of the preschool peer group. In *The Proceedings of the Twelfth Minnesota Symposium on Child Psychology*. Edited by Collins, W A. New York: Erlbaum.

3241 Strayer, F F. 1980. Child ethology and the study of preschool social relations. In *Friendship and Social Relations in Children*. Edited by Foot, H C, A J Chapman, J R Smith. New York: Wiley.

3242 Strayer, F F, J M Noel. 1986. The prosocial and antisocial functions of preschool aggression: An ethological study of triadic conflict among young children. In *Altruism and Aggression*. Edited by Zahn-Wazler, C, E M Cummings, R Iannotti. London: Cambridge University Press.

3243 Strum, S C. 1982. Agonistic dominance in male baboons: An alternative view. *International Journal of Primatology* 3: 175-202.

3244 Strum, S. 1990. *Almost Human: A Journey into the World of Baboons*. New York: Norton.

3245 Sugiyama, Y, J Koman. 1979. Tool-using and -making behavior in wild chimpanzees at Bossou, Guinea. *Primates* 20: 513-24.

3246 Sundstrom, E, I Altman. 1974. Field study of territorial behavior and dominance. *Journal of Personality and Social Psychology* 30: 115-124.

3247 Sütterlin, C. 1989. Universals in apotropaic symbolism: A behavioral and comparative approach to some medieval sculptures. *Leonardo* 22: 65-74.

3248 Syme, G J. 1974. Competitive orders as measures of social dominance. *Animal Behaviour* 22: 931-40.

3249 Symonds, D. 1978. *Play and Aggression: A Study of Rhesus Monkeys*. New York: Columbia University Press.

3250 Symonds, D. 1989. Comments on "Distinctions among reciprocal altruism, kin selection, and cooperation and a model for the initial evolution of beneficent behavior". *Ethology and Sociobiology* 10: 449-452.

3251 Takahashi, L K. 1990. Morphological basis of arm-swinging: Multivariate analyses of the forelimbs of Hylobates and Ateles. *Folia Primatologica* 54: 70-85.

3252 Takahasi, K. 1990. Are the key assumptions of the 'Strange Situation' procedure universal? A view from Japanese research. *Human Development* 33: 23-30.

3253 Talmon, Y. 1972. *Family and Community in the Kibbutz.* Cambridge: Harvard University Press.

3254 Tannen, D, M Saville-Troike, eds. 1985. *Perspectives on Silence.* Norwood, NJ: Ablex Publishing Corporation.

3255 Taub, D M. 1980. Testing the agonistic buffering hypothesis 1. The dynamics of participation in the triadic interaction. *Behavioral Ecology and Sociobiology* 6: 187-197.

3256 Taub, D M, F A King, eds. 1986. *Current Perspectives in Primate Relationships.* New York: Van Nostrand Reinhold.

3257 Telecki, G. 1981. The omnivorous diet and eclectic feeding habits of chimpanzees in Gombe National Park, Tanzania. In *Omnivorous Primates.* Edited by Harding, R S O, G Telecki. Pp. 303-343. New York: Columbia University Press.

3258 Teleki, G. 1973. *The Predatory Behavior of Wild Chimpanzees.* Lewisburg: Bucknell University Press.

3259 Teleki, G. 1975. Primate subsistence patterns: Collector-predators and gatherer-hunters. *Journal of Human Evolution* 4: 125-184.

3260 Teleki, G. 1975. Chimpanzee subsistence technology: Material and skills. *journal of Human Evolution* 3: 575-94.

3261 Temerlin, M K. 1975. *Lucy: Growing up Human.* London: Souvenir Press.

3262 Terborgh, J. 1983. *Five New World Primates: A Study in Comparative Ecology.* Princeton: Princeton University Press.

3263 Thierry, B, C Demaria, S Preuschoft, C Desportes. 1989. Structural convergence between silent bared-teeth display and relaxed open-mouth display in the Tonkean macaque (macaca tonkeana). *Folia Primatologica* 52: 178-184.

3264 Thompson, P R. 1978. The evolution of territoriality and society in top carnivores. *Social Science Information* 17: 949-992.

3265 Thompson, R A, M E Lamb, D Estes. 1982. Stability of infant-mother attachment and its relationship to changing life circumstances in an unselected middle class sample. *Child Development* 53: 144-148.

3266 Thompson, R A, M E Lamb. 1983. Security of attachment and stranger sociability in infancy. *Developmental Psychology* 19: 184-191.

3267 Thompson, R A, M E Lamb. 1983. Infants, mothers, families, and strangers. In *Beyond the Dyad*. Edited by Lewis, M, L A Rosenblum. New York: Plenum Press.

3268 Thor, D H, W R Holloway. 1984. Social play in juvenile rats: A decade of methodological and experimental research. *Neuroscience and Biobehavioral Reviews* 8: 455-464.

3269 Thornton, M. 1979. The Mathematical Modelling of Facial Expressions. Dissertation, Adelaide: University of Adelaide.

3270 Tiger, L. 1969. *Men in Groups*. London: Nelson.

3271 Tiger, L, R Fox. 1971. *The Imperial Animal*. New York: Holt, Rinehart and Winston.

3272 Tiger, L, J Shepher. 1975. *Women in the Kibbutz*. New York: Harcourt, Brace, Jovanovich.

3273 Tiger, L, H T Fowler, eds. 1978. *Female Hierarchy: An Evolutionary Perspective*. Chicago: Beresford Book Service.

3274 Tiger, L. 1979. *Optimism: The Biology of Hope*. New York: Simon and Schuster.

3275 Tiger, L. 1987. *The Manufacture of Evil: Ethics Evolution and the Industrial System*. New York: Harper & Row.

3276 Tinbergen, N. 1951. *The Study of Instinct*. Oxford: Oxford University Press.

3277 Tinbergen, N. 1951. The functions of territory. *Bird Study* 4: 14-27.

3278 Tinbergen, N. 1963. On the aims and methods of ethology. *Zeitschrift für Tierpsychologie* 20: 410-33.

3279 Tinbergen, N. 1963. *The Social Behaviour of Animals*. London: Chapman & Hall.

3280 Tinbergen, N. 1972. *The Animal in Its World*. Cambridge: Harvard University Press.

3281 Tinbergen, N. 1972. Functional ethology and the human sciences. *Proceedings of the Royal Society of London* 182: 386-410.

3282 Tizard, B, D Harvey. 1977. *The Biology of Play.* London: Heineman Medical Books.

3283 Todt, D, P Goedeking, D Symmes, eds. 1988. *Primate Vocal Communication.* Berlin: Springer.

3284 Tooke, W, L Camire. 1991. Patterns of deception in intersexual and intrasexual mating strategies. *Ethology and Sociobiology* 12: 345-364.

3285 Townsend, J M. 1989. Mate selection criteria: A pilot study. *Ethology and Sociobiology* 10: 241-254.

3286 Tracy, R L, M D S Ainsworth. 1981. Maternal affectionate behavior and infant-mother attachment patterns. *Child Development* 52: 1341-1343.

3287 Trevarthen, C. 1979. Instincts for human understanding and for cultural cooperation: Their development in infancy. In *Human Ethology: Claims and Limits of a New Discipline.* Edited by von Cranach, M, et al. Pp. 530-571. Cambridge: Cambridge University Press.

3288 Trevathan, W R. 1987. *Human Birth: An Evolutionary Perspective.* Hawthorne, N.Y.: Aldine de Gruyter.

3289 Turke, P W. 1990. Which humans behave adaptively, and why does it matter? *Ethology and Sociobiology* 11: 305-309.

3290 Tuttle, R H. 1986. *Apes of the World: Their Social Behavior, Communication, Mentality, and Ecology.* Park Ridge, N.J.: Noyes Publications.

3291 Unzner, L, K Schneider. 1990. Facial reactions in preschoolers: A descriptive study. *Journal of Nonverbal Behavior* 14: 19-34.

3292 van den Berghe, P L. 1973. *Age and Sex in Human Societies: A Biosocial Perspective.* Belmont, CA: Wadsworth.

3293 van den Berghe, P L. 1978. *Man in Society: A Biosocial View.* 2nd ed New York: Elsevier.

3294 van den Berghe, P L. 1979. *Human Family Systems.* New York: Elsevier.

3295 van den Berghe, P L. 1981. *The Ethnic Phenomenon.* New York: Elsevier.

3296 van Hooff, J. 1973. A structural analysis of the social behavior of a semi-captive group of chimpanzees. In *Expressive Movement and Non-Verbal Communication.* Edited by von Cranach, M, I Vine. London: Academic Press.

3297 van Hooff, J. 1982. Categories and sequences of behavior: Methods of description and analysis. In *Handbook of Methods in Nonverbal Behavior Research.* Edited by Scherer, K R, P Ekman. Pp. 362-439. New York: Cambridge University Press.

3298 van Lawick-Goodall, J. 1971. *In the Shadow of Man.* Boston: Houghton Mifflin.

3299 Vaughn, B, L Crichton, B Egeland. 1982. Individual differences in qualities of caregiving during the first six months of life: Antecedents in maternal and infant behavior during the newborn period. *Infant Behavior and Development* 5: 77-95.

3300 Vessey, S H. 1984. Dominance among Rhesus monkeys. *Political Psychology* 5: 623-628.

3301 von Cranach, M, I Vine, eds. 1973. *Social Communication and Movement: Studies of Interaction and Expression in Man and Chimpanzee.* London: Academic Press.

3302 von Cranach, M, ed. 1976. *Methods of Inference from Animal to Human Behavior.* The Hague: Mouton.

3303 von Cranach, M, U Kalbermatten, K Indermuhle, B Gugler. 1980. *Zielgerichtetes Handeln.* Bern: Huber.

3304 von Cranach, M, R Harré, eds. 1982. *The Analysis of Action: Recent Theoretical and Empirical Advances.* Cambridge: Cambridge University Press.

3305 von Raffler-Engle, W. 1979. *Aspects of Nonverbal Communication.* Amsterdam: Swets & Zeitlinger.

3306 Vrij, A, F W Winkel. 1991. Cultural patterns in Dutch and Surinam nonverbal behavior: An analysis of simulated police-citizen encounters. *Journal of Nonverbal Behavior* 15: 169-84.

3307 Vrugt, A, A Kerkstra. 1984. Sex differences in nonverbal communication. *Semiotica* 50: 1-41.

3308 Vrugt, A J. 1990. When a queen speaks to her nation: A nonverbal analysis. *British Journal of Social Psychology* 29: 367-74.

3309 Vrugt, A. 1990. Negative attitudes, nonverbal behavior and self-fulfilling prophecy in simulated therapy interviews. *Journal of Nonverbal Behavior* 14: 77-86.

3310 Waddington, C H. 1959. Evolutionary adaptations. *Perspectives in Biology and Medicine* 2: 379-401.

3311 Wallace, A F C. 1966. *Religion.* New York: Random House.

3312 Walmsley, D J, G J Lewis. 1989. The pace of pedestrian flows in cities. *Environment and Behavior* 21: 123-150.

3313 Washburn, S L. 1978. Human behavior and the behavior of other animals. *American Anthropologist* 33: 405-418.

3314 Waters, E, D Deane, eds. 1982. *Infant-mother attachment: Theories, models, recent data, and some tasks for comparative developmental analysis.* Parenting: Its Causes and Consequences. Hillsdale, N.J.: Erlbaum.

3315 Watson, R S. 1985. *Inequality among Brothers: Class and Kinship in South China.* Cambridge: Cambridge University Press.

3316 Wawra, M. 1988. Vigilance patterns in humans. *Behavior* 107: 61-71.

3317 Weigel, R M, R P Johnson. 1981. An ethological classification system for verbal behavior. *Ethology and Sociobiology* 2: 55-66.

3318 Weitz, S, ed. 1979. *Nonverbal Communication: Readings with Commentary.* Second ed New York: Oxford University Press.

3319 Wells, G L, R E Petty. 1980. The effects of overt head movements on persuasion: Compatibility and incompatibility of responses. *Basic and Applied Social Psychology* 1: 219-30.

3320 White, N F. 1974. *Ethology and Psychiatry.* Toronto: University of Toronto Press.

3321 Wickler, W. 1973. *The Sexual Code.* Garden City, N.Y.: Anchor/Doubleday.

3322 Wiessner, P. 1981. Measuring the impact of social ties on nutritional status among the !Kung San. *Social Science Information* 20: 641-678.

3323 Wiessner, P. 1982. Risk, reciprocity and social influence on !Kung San economics. In *Politics and History in Band Societies.* Edited by Leacock, E, R B Lee. Pp. 61-84. Cambridge: Cambridge University Press.

3324 Wiessner, P. 1984. Reconsidering the behavioral basis for style: A case study among the Kalahari San. *Journal of Anthropological Archaeology* 3: 190-234.

3325 Wilke, H. 1985. *Coalition Formation.* Amsterdam: Elsevier.

3326 Wilson, M, M Daly. 1985. Competitiveness, risk taking, and violence: The young male syndrome. *Ethology and Sociobiology* 6: 59-73.

3327 Winter, D D N, C Widell, G Truitt, J George-Falvy. 1989. Empirical studies of posture-gesture mergers. *Journal of Nonverbal Behavior* 13: 207-224.

3328 Winterhalder, B, E A Smith. 1981. *Hunter-Gatherer Foraging Strategies: Ethnographic and Archaeological Analyses.* Chicago: University of Chicago Press.

3329 Wirtz, P, M Wawra. 1986. Vigilance and group size in Homo sapiens. *Ethology* 71: 283-286.

3330 Wispe, L G. 1978. *Altruism, Sympathy and Helping.* New York: Academic Press.

3331 Witt, R, C Schmidt, J Schmitt. 1981. Social rank and Darwinian fitness in a multi-male group of Barbary Macaques (Macacasylvana Linnaeus, 1758). *Folia Primatologica* 36: 201-221.

3332 Wolfgang, A, ed. 1979. *Nonverbal Behavior: Perspectives, Applications, Intercultural Insights.* Lewiston, New York and Toronto: C.J. Hogrefe.

3333 Wrangham, R W. 1980. An ecological model of female-bonded primate groups. *Behaviour* 75: 262-299.

3334 Wynn, T, W C McGrew. 1989. An ape's view of the Oldowan. *Man* 24: 383-398.

3335 Wynne Edwards, V C. 1962. *Animal Dispersion in Relation to Social Behavior.* New York: Hafner.

3336 Yerkes, R. 1929. *The Great Apes: A Study of Anthropoid Life.* New Haven: Yale University Press.

3337 Yerkes, R M. 1943. *Chimpanzees*.   New Haven: Yale University Press.

3338 Zahn-Waxler, C, E M Cummings, R Iannotti. 1986. *Altruism and Aggression: Biological and Social Origins*.   Cambridge: Cambridge University Press.

3339 Zivin, G. 1977. Facial gestures predict preschoolers' encounter outcomes. *Social Science Information*   16: 715-730.

3340 Zivin, G, ed. 1985. *The Development of Expressive Behavior: Biology-Environment Interaction*.   Orlando Academic Press.

3341 Zuckerman, M, M Miserandino, F Bernieri. 1983. Civil inattention exists—in elevators. *Personality and Social Psychology Bulletin*   9: 578-586.

# 8

# Parenting

3342 Ainsworth, M D S, S M Bell, D J Stayton. 1974. Infant-mother attachment and social development: "Socialization" as a product of reciprocal responsiveness to signals. In *The Integration of a Child into a Social World*. Edited by Richards, R P M. Cambridge: Cambridge University Press.

3343 Altmann, J. 1987. Life span aspects of reproduction and parental care in anthropoid primates. In *Parenting Across the Life Span—Biosocial Dimensions*. Edited by Lancaster, J B, J Altmann, A S Rossi, L R Sherrod. New York: Aldine De Gruyter.

3344 Aries, P. 1962. *Centuries of Childhood: A Social History of Family Life*. New York: Vintage.

3345 Badinter, E. 1981. *Mother Love: Myth and Reality*. New York: Macmillan.

3346 Beck, N C, L J Siegle, N P Davison, S Kormeier, A Breitenstein, D G Hall. 1980. The prediction of pregnancy outcome: Maternal preparation, anxiety and attitudinal sets. *Journal of Psychosomatic Research* 24: 343-351.

3347 Behlmer, G K. 1982. *Child Abuse and Moral Reform in England, 1870-1908*. Stanford: Stanford University Press.

3348 Bekoff, M. 1981. Mammalian sibling interactions: Genes, facilitate environments, and the coefficient of familiarity. In *Parental Care in Mammals*. Edited by Gubernick, D, P Klopfer. Pp. 307-333. New York: Plenum.

3349 Belsky, J. 1980. A family analysis of parental influence on infant exploratory competence. In *The Father-Infant Relationship: Observational Studies in a Family Context*. Edited by Pedersen, F A. New York: Praeger.

3350 Belsky, J. 1981. Early human experience: A family perspective. *Developmental Psychology* 17: 3-23.

3351 Belsky, J. 1984. The determinants of parenting: A process model. *Child Development* 55: 83-96.

3352 Bengston, V L. 1987. Parenting, grandparenting, and intergenerational continuity. In *Parenting Across the Life Span—Biosocial Dimensions*. Edited by Lancaster, J B, J Altmann, A S Rossi, L R Sherrod. New York: Aldine De Gruyter.

3353 Biller, H B. 1981. Father absence, divorce, and personality development. In *The Role of the Father in Child Development*. Edited by Lamb, M E. New York: Wiley.

3354 Blake, J. 1981. Family size and the quality of children. *Demography* 18: 421-442.

3355 Blake, J. 1982. Demographic revolution and family evolution: Some implications for American women. In *Women: A Developmental Perspective*. Edited by Berman, P W, E R Ramey. Pp. 299-312. Washington, DC: U.S. Department of Health and Human Services.

3356 Blake, J. 1987. Differential parental investment: Its effects on child quality and status attainment. In *Parenting Across the Life Span—Biosocial Dimensions*. Edited by Lancaster, J B, J Altmann, A S Rossi, L R Sherrod. Pp. 351-377. New York: Aldine De Gruyter.

3357 Bridges, R, N Kasnegor, eds. 1990. *Biological and Behavioral Determinants of Parenting in Mammals.* New York: Oxford University Press.

3358 Bronfenbrenner, U. 1971. *The Ecology of Human Development.* Cambridge: Harvard University Press.

3359 Brown, J. 1982. Cross-cultural perspectives on middle-aged women. *Current Anthropology* 23: 143-156.

3360 Brubaker, T H, ed. 1983. *Family Relationships in Later Life.* Beverly Hills, CA: Sage.

3361 Bugos, P E J, L M McCarthy. 1984. Ayoreo infanticide: A case study. In *Infanticide: Comparative and Evolutionary Perspectives.* Edited by Hausfater, G, S B Hrdy. Pp. 503-520. New York: Aldine.

3362 Burgess, R L, J A Kurland, A Pensky. 1988. Ultimate and proximate determinants of child maltreatment: Natural selection, ecological instability and coercive interpersonal contingencies. In *Sociobiological Perspectives on Human Development.* Edited by MacDonald, K. Berlin: Springer.

3363 Cain, M. 1985. Fertility as adjustment to risk. In *Gender and the Life Course*. Edited by Rossi, A S. Pp. 145-160. New York: Aldine.

3364 Calhoun, A. 1960. *A Social History of the American Family*. New York: Barnes & Noble.

3365 Chapman, M. 1980. Infanticide and fertility among Eskimos: A computer simulation. *American Journal of Physical Anthropology* 53: 317-327.

3366 Chisholm, J S. 1983. *Navajo Infancy: An Ethological Study of Child Development*. New York: Aldine.

3367 Clayton, R, J Bokemaier. 1980. Premarital sex in the seventies. *Journal of Marriage and the Family* 42: 750-775.

3368 Coleman, E. 1976. Infanticide in the early Middle Ages. In *Women in Medieval Society*. Edited by Stuard, S. Pp. 47-70. Philadelphia: University of Pennsylvania.

3369 Creighton, S. 1984. *Trends in Child Abuse*. London: National Society for the Prevention of Cruelty to Children.

3370 Daly, M, M Wilson. 1981. Abuse and neglect of children in evolutionary perspective. In *Natural Selection and Social Behavior: Recent Research and New Theory*. Edited by Alexander, R D, D W Tinkle. Pp. 405-416. New York: Chiron Press.

3371 Daly, M, M Wilson. 1981. Child maltreatment from a sociobiological perspective. *New directions for Child Development* 11: 93-112.

3372 Daly, M, M Wilson. 1982. Homicide and kinship. *American Anthropologist* 84: 372-378.

3373 Daly, M, M Wilson. 1987. Evolutionary psychology and family violence. In *Sociobiology and Psychology*. Edited by Crawford, C, M Smith, D Krebs. Hillsdale, NJ: Erlbaum.

3374 Daly, M. 1989. Parent-offspring conflict and violence in evolutionary perspective. In *Sociobiology and the Social Sciences*. Edited by Bell, R, N Bell. Lubbock, TX: Texas Tech University Press.

3375 Daly, M, M Wilson. 1990. Is parent-offspring conflict sex linked? Freudian and Darwinian models. *Journal of Personality* 58: 163-190.

3376 Demos, J. 1982. The changing faces of fatherhood: A new exploration in American family history. In *Father and Child: Developmental and Clinical Perspectives.* Edited by Cath, S H, A R Gurwitt, J M Ross. Pp. 425-450. Boston: Little Brown.

3377 Dickermann, M. 1975. Demographic consequences of infanticide in man. *Annual Review in Ecology and Systematics* 6: 107-137.

3378 Dickermann, M. 1979. Female infanticide, reproductive strategies, and social stratification: A preliminary model. In *Evolutionary Biology and Human Social Behavior.* Edited by Chagnon, N, W Irons. North Scituate, MA.: Duxbury.

3379 Diggory, P. 1981. The long-term effects upon the child of perinatal events. In *Changing Patterns of Child-Bearing and Child Rearing.* Edited by Chester, P, P Diggory, M B Sutherland. Pp. 23-37. London: Academic Press.

3380 Draper, P, H Harpending. 1987. Parent investment and the child's environment. In *Parenting Across the Life Span—Biosocial Dimensions.* Edited by Lancaster, J B, J Altmann, A S Rossi, L R Sherrod. Pp. 207-236. New York: Aldine De Gruyter.

3381 Dryfoos, J G, N Bourque-Scholl. 1981. *Factbook on Teenage Pregnancy.* New York: Guttmacher Institute.

3382 Dunn, J, C Kendrick. 1979. Interaction between young siblings in the context of family relationships. In *The Child and Its Family.* Edited by Lewis, M, L Rosenblum. New York: Plenum.

3383 Dunn, J, C Kendrick. 1982. Siblings and their mothers: Developing relationships within the family. In *Sibling Relationships: Their Nature and Significance Across the Lifespan.* Edited by Lamb, M E, B Sutton-Smith. Pp. 39-60. Hillsdale, N.J.: Erlbaum.

3384 Dunn, J. 1983. Sibling relationships in early childhood. *Child Development* 54: 787-811.

3385 Eiduson, B T, M Kornfein, I L Zimmerman, T S Weisner. 1982. Comparative socialization practices in traditional and alternative families. In *Nontraditional Families: Parenting and Child Development.* Edited by Lamb, M E. Pp. 315-346. Hillsdale, N.J.: Erlbaum.

3386 Elder, G H, A Caspi, G Downey. 1986. Problem behavior and family relationships: A multigenerational analysis. In *Human*

*Development: Multidisciplinary Perspectives.* Edited by Sorensen, A, F Weinert, L Sherrod. Hillsdale, N.J.: Erlbaum.

3387 Elster, A, R Panzanine. 1983. Teenage fathers: Stresses during gestation and early parenthood. *Clinical Pediatrics* 10: 700-703.

3388 Elster, A B, M E Lamb. 1986. Adolescent fathers: The understudied side of adolescent pregnancy. In *School-Age Pregnancy and Parenthood: Biosocial Dimensions.* Edited by Lancaster, J B, B A Hamburg. Pp. 177-190. New York: Aldine De Gruyter.

3389 Feinman, S, M Lewis. 1983. Social referencing at ten months: A second-order effect on infants' responses to strangers. *Child Development* 54: 878-887.

3390 Feldman, S S, S C Nash. 1977. The effect of family formation on sex stereotypic behavior: A study of responsiveness to babies. In *The First Child and Family Formation.* Edited by Miller, W, L Newman. Chapel Hill, N.C.: North Carolina Population Press.

3391 Feldman, S S, S C Nash. 1986. Antecedents of early parenting. In *Origins of Nurturance.* Edited by Fogel, A, G Melson. Pp. 209-32. London: Erlbaum.

3392 Filsinger, E E, L K Lamke. 1983. The lineage transmission of interpersonal competence. *Journal of Marriage and the Family* 45: 75-81.

3393 Filsinger, E E, ed. 1983. *Marriage and Family Assessment: A Sourcebook for Family Therapy.* Beverly Hills, CA: Sage.

3394 Filsinger, E E, ed. 1988. *Biosocial Perspectives on the Family.* Beverly Hills, CA: Sage.

3395 Fox, G, J Inazu. 1980. Patterns and outcomes of mother-daughter communication about sexuality. *Journal of Social Issues* 36: 7-29.

3396 Furstenberg, F. 1976. *Unplanned parenthood: The social consequences of teenage childbearing.* New York: Free Press.

3397 Furstenberg, J, F.F., C W Nord, J L Peterso n, N Zill. 1983. The life course of children of divorce. *American Sociological Review* 48: 656-668.

3398 Garn, S M, P E Cole, S K Bailey. 1979. Living together as a factor in family-line resemblances. *Human Biology* 51: 565-587.

3399 Gelles, R J. 1986. School-age parents and child abuse. In *School-Age Pregnancy and Parenthood: Biosocial Dimensions.* Edited by Lancaster, J B, B A Hamburg. Pp. 347-360. New York: Aldine.

3400 Gelles, R J, J B Lancaster, eds. 1987. *Child Abuse and Neglect: Biosocial Dimensions.* New York: Aldine de Gruyter.

3401 Gelles, R, J B Lancaster. 1987. *Offspring Abuse and Neglect: Biosocial Dimensions.* New York: Aldine.

3402 Gelles, R J. 1991. Physical violence, child abuse, and child homicide: A continuum of violence, or distinct behaviors? *Human Nature* 2: 59-72.

3403 Golinkoff, R M, G J Ames. 1979. A Comparison of fathers' and mothers' speech with their young children. *Child Development* 50: 28-32.

3404 Goodwin, J. 1982. *Sexual Abuse: Incest Victims and Their Families.* Boston: John Wright.

3405 Goody, J, J Thirsk, E P Thompson, eds. 1976. *Family and Inheritance: Rural Society in Western Europe1200-1800.* Cambridge: Cambridge University Press.

3406 Goody, J. 1977. *Production and Reproduction: A Comparative Study of the Domestic Domain.* Cambridge: Cambridge University Press.

3407 Goody, E. 1982. *Parenthood and Social Reproduction: Fostering and Occupational Roles in West Africa.* Cambridge: Cambridge University Press.

3408 Greenberg, M, N Morris. 1974. The newborn's impact upon the father. *American Journal of Orthopsychiatry* 44: 520-531.

3409 Gubernick, D J, P H Klopfer, eds. 1981. *Parental Care in Mammals.* New York: Plenum.

3410 Gubernick, D. 1981. Parent and infant attachment in mammals. In *Parental Care in Mammals.* Edited by Gubernick, D, P Klopfer. New York: Plenum.

3411 Hagestad, G O. 1986. The aging society as a context for family life. *Daedalus* 115: 119-139.

3412 Hagestad, G O. 1987. Parent-child relations in later life: Trends and gaps in past research. In *Parenting Across the Life Span—Biosocial Dimensions*. Edited by Lancaster, J B, J Altmann, A S Rossi, L R Sherrod. Pp. 405-434. New York: Aldine De Gruyter.

3413 Hareven, T K. 1982. *Family Time and Industrial Time: The Relationship Between the Family and Work in a New England Industrial Community*. Cambridge: Cambridge University Press.

3414 Harper, L V. 1981. Offspring effects upon parents. In *Parental Care in Mammals*. Edited by Gubernick, D J, K P H. Pp. 117-117. New York: Plenum.

3415 Harper, L V. 1989. *The Nurture of Human Behavior*. Norwood, NJ: Ablex.

3416 Hatcher, S L M. 1973. The adolescent experience of pregnancy and abortion: A developmental analysis. *Journal of Youth and Adolescence* 2: 53-102.

3417 Hausfater, G, S Hrdy, eds. 1984. *Infanticide: Comparative and Evolutionary Perspectives*. New York: Aldine.

3418 Hausfater, G. 1986. Convergent models: Evidence of a robust theory of infanticide. *Animal Behavior* 34: 617-619.

3419 Held, T. 1984. Generational co-residence and the transfer of authority: Some illustrations from Austrian household listings. In *Intergenerational Relationships*. Edited by Garms-Homolova, V, E M Hoerning, D Schaeffer. Pp. 41-53. Lewiston, New York: C.J. Hogrefe.

3420 Helm, J. 1980. Female infanticide, European diseases, and population levels among the McKenzie Dene. *American Ethnologist* 7: 103-110.

3421 Hendricks, L E, C S Howard, P P Caesar. 1981. Help-seeking behavior among selected populations of black unmarried adolescent fathers. *American Journal of Public Health* 71: 733-735.

3422 Hetherington, M, M Cox, R Cox. 1979. The aftermath of divorce. In *Mother-child, Father-child relations*. Edited by Stevens, J, M Matthews. Washington: National Association for Education of Young Children.

3423 Hewlett, B S. 1992. *Father-Child Relations: Cultural and Biosocial Contexts*. New York: Aldine de Gruyter.

3424 Hill, E M, B S Low. 1992. Contemporary abortion patterns: A life history approach. *Ethology and Sociobiology* 13: 35-48.

3425 Hipgrave, T. 1982. Child-rearing by lone fathers. In *Changing Patterns of Child Bearing and Child Rearing*. Edited by Chester, R, P Diggory, M Sutherland. London: Academic Press.

3426 Hirschfeld, L A, J Howe, B Levin. 1978. Warfare, infanticide, and statistical inference: A comment on Divale and Harris. *American Anthropologist* 80: 110-115.

3427 Hoffer, P C, N E H Hull. 1981. *Murdering Mothers: Infanticide in England and New England, 1558-1803*. New York: New York University Press.

3428 Hoffman, L W, R Gandelman, H R Schiffman, eds. 1982. *Parenting: Its Causes and Consequences*. Hillsdale, N.J.: Erlbaum.

3429 Hogan, D P. 1981. *Transitions and Social Change: The Early Lives of American Men*. New York: Academic Press.

3430 Hotaling, G, D Finkelhor, J Kirkpatrick, M Straus, eds. 1988. *Coping with Family Violence: Research and Policy Perspectives*. Newbury Park, CA: Cage.

3431 Hrdy, S B. 1977. Infanticide as a primate reproduction strategy. *American Scientist* 65: 40-9.

3432 Hrdy, S. 1979. Infanticide among animals: A review, classification, and examination of the implications for the reproductive strategies of females. *Ethology and Sociobiology* 1: 13-40.

3433 Hrdy, S, G Hausfater. 1984. Comparative and evolutionary perspectives on infanticide. In *Infanticide: Comparative and Evolutionary Perspetives*. Edited by Hrdy, S B, G Hausfater. Pp. xiii-xxxv. New York: Aldine.

3434 Hutchins, F L, N Kendall, J Rubino. 1979. Experience with teenage pregnancy. *Obstetrics and Gynecology* 54: 1-5.

3435 Irons, W. 1988. Human parenting: An evolutionary perspective. In *Human Reproductive Behavior: A Darwinian Perspective*. Edited by Betzig, L, M Mulder, P Turke. Cambridge: Cambridge University Press.

3436 Irwin, C. 1989. The sociocultural biology of Netsilingmuit female infanticide. In *The Sociobiology of Sexual and Reproductive*

*Strategies.* Edited by Rasa, A E, C Vogel, E Voland. Pp. 234-264. London: Capman and Hall.

3437 Itani, J. 1959. Paternal Care in the Wild Japanese Monkey (*Macaca fuscata fuscata*). *Primates* 2: 61-93.

3438 Jeffry, R, P Jeffry, A Lyon. 1984. Female infanticide and amniocentesis. *Social Science and Medicine* 19: 1207-12.

3439 Kerckhoff, A C, A A Parrow. 1979. The effect of early marriage on the educational attainment of young men. *Journal of Marriage and the Family* 41: 97-107.

3440 Kinard, E M, L V Klerman. 1980. Teenage parenting and child abuse: Are they related? *American Journal of Orthopsychiatry* 50: 481-488.

3441 Kitson, G C. 1982. Attachment to the spouse in divorce: A scale and its application. *Journal of Marriage and the Family* 44: 379-93.

3442 Klaus, M H, J H Kennell. 1976. *Maternal-Infant Bonding: The Impact of Early Separation or Loss on Family Development.* St Louis: C.V. Mosby.

3443 Kobrin, F E. 1976. The fall in household size and the rise of the primary individual in the United States. *Demography* 13: 127-138.

3444 Kobrin, F E. 1976. The primary individual and the family: Changes in living arrangements in the United States since 1940. *Journal of Marriage and the Family* 38: 233-239.

3445 Kobrin, F E, ed. 1981. *Child Abuse and Neglect: Cross-Cultural Perspectives.* Berkeley: University of California Press.

3446 Konner, H C. 1979. Maternal care, infant behavior, and development amoung the !Kung. In *Kalahari Hunter-Gatherers: Studies of the !Kung San and Their Neighbors.* Edited by Lee, R B, I DeVore. Cambridge: Harvard University Press.

3447 Konner, M, M Shostak. 1986. Adolescent pregnancy and childbearing: An anthropological perspective. In *School-Age Pregnancy and Parenthood: Biosocial Dimensions.* Edited by Lancaster, J B, B A Hamburg. Pp. 325-346. New York: Aldine De Gruyter.

3448 Kraemer, S. 1991. The origins of fatherhood: An ancient family process. *Family Process* 30: 377-392.

3450 Lamb, M E, M A Easterbrooks. 1981. Individual differences in parental sensitivity: Origins, components, and consequences. In *Infant Social Cognition: Empirical and Theoretical Considerations*. Edited by Lamb, M E, L R Sherrod. Hillsdale, N.J.: Erlbaum.

3451 Lamb, M E. 1981. Paternal influences on child development: An overview. In *The Role of the Father in Child Development*. Edited by Lamb, M E. New York: Wiley.

3452 Lamb, M E, ed. 1981. *The Role of the Father in Child Development*. New York: Wiley.

3453 Lamb, M E, W A Goldberg. 1982. The father-child relationship: A synthesis of biological, evolutionary and social perspectives. In *Parenting: Its Causes and Consequences*. Edited by Hoffman, L W, R Gandelman, H R Schiffman. Pp. 55-73. Hillsdale, N.J.: Erlbaum.

3454 Lamb, M E, C P Hwang. 1982. Maternal attachment and mother-neonate bonding: A critical review. In *Advances in Developmental Psychology*. Edited by Lamb, M E, A L Brown. Pp. 1-38. Hillsdale, N.J.: Erlbaum.

3455 Lamb, M E. 1982. Why Swedish fathers aren't liberated *Psychology Today* 18: 74-77.

3456 Lamb, M E, A M Frodi, M Frodi, C P Hwang. 1982. Characteristics of maternal and paternal behavior in traditional and nontraditional Swedish families. *International Journal of Behavioral Development* 5: 131-141.

3457 Lamb, M E, ed. 1982. *Nontraditional Families: Parenting and Child Development*. Hillsdale, N.J.: Erlbaum.

3458 Lamb, M E, R A Thompson, W Gardner, E L Charnov, D Estes. 1984. Security of infantile attactment. Its study and biological interpretation. *Behavioral and Brain Sciences* 7: 127-147.

3459 Lamb, M E, J Pleck, E L Charnov. 1985. Paternal behavior in humans. *American Zoologist* 25: 883-894.

3460 Lamb, M E, ed. 1986. *The Father's Role: Applied Perspectives*. New York: Wiley.

3461 Lamb, M E, ed. 1986. *Fatherhood: A Cross-cultural Perspective.* Hillsdale, N.J.: Erlbaum.

3462 Lamb, M E, J H Pleck, E L Charnov. 1987. A biosocial perspective on paternal behavior and involvement. In *Parenting Across the Life Span—Biosocial Dimensions.* Edited by Lancaster, J B, J Altmann, A S Rossi, L R Sherrod. Pp. 111-142. New York: Aldine De Gruyter.

3463 Lancaster, J B, B A Hamburg. 1986. The biosocial dimensions of school-age pregnance and parenthood: An Introduction. In *School-Age Pregnancy and Parenthood: Biosocial Dimensions.* Edited by Lancaster, J B, B A Hamburg. Pp. 3-16. New York: Aldine De Gruyter.

3464 Lancaster, J B, B A Hamburg, eds. 1986. *School-Age Pregnancy and Parenthood: Biosocial Dimensions.* New York: Aldine De Gruyter.

3465 Lancaster, J B, C S Lancaster. 1987. The watershed: Change in parental-investment and family-formation strategies in the course of human evolution. In *Parenting Across the Life Span—Biosocial Dimensions.* Edited by Lancaster, J B, J Altmann, A S Rossi, L R Sherrod. Pp. 187-206. New York: Aldine De Gruyter.

3466 Lancaster, J B, J Altmann, A Rossi, L Sherrod, eds. 1987. *Parenting Across the Lifespand: Biosocial Dimensions.* New York: Aldine.

3467 Langer, W. 1974. Infanticide: A historical survey. *History of Childhood Quarterly* 1: 353-365.

3468 Laslett, P. 1972. Introduction: The history of the family. In *Household and Family in Past Time.* Edited by Laslett, P, R Wall. Pp. 1-89. Cambridge: Cambridge University press.

3469 Laslett, P, R Wall, eds. 1972. *Household and Family in Past Time.* Cambridge: Cambridge University Press.

3470 Lee, G R. 1980. Kinship in the seventies: A decade review of research and theory. *Journal of Marriage and the Family* 42: 933-954.

3471 Lenerz, K, P L East. 1986. Children and adolescents in their contexts. Tests of a goodness of fit model. In *The Study of Temperament: Changes, Continuities, and Challenges.* Edited by Plomin, R, J Dunn. Hillsdale, N.J.: Erlbaum.

3472 Lenington, S. 1981. Child abuse: The limits of sociobiology. *Ethology and Sociobiology* 2: 17-29.

3473 Leon, M. 1987. Somatic aspects of parent-offspring interactions. In *Parenting Across the Life Span—Biosocial Dimensions.* Edited by Lancaster, J B, J Altmann, A S Rossi, L R Sherrod. Pp. 85-110. New York: Aldine De Gruyter.

3474 Lerner, R M, G B Spanier. 1980. *Adolescent Development: A Life-Span Perspective.* New York: McGraw-Hill.

3475 Lerner, R M, N Busch-Rossnagel. 1981. Individuals as producers of their development: Conceptual and empirical bases. In *Individuals as Producers of Their Development: A Life-Span Perspective.* Edited by Lerner, R M, N A Busch-Rossnagel. New York: Academic Press.

3476 Lerner, R M. 1984. *On the Nature of Human Plasticity.* New York: Cambridge University Press.

3477 Lerner, R, J V Lerner. 1987. Children in their contexts: A goodness-of-fit model. In *Parenting Across the Life Span—Biosocial Dimensions.* Edited by Lancaster, J B, J Altmann, A S Rossi, L R Sherrod. Pp. 377-404. New York: Aldine De Gruyter.

3478 Leventhal, J M. 1981. Risk factors for child abuse: Methodologic standards in case-control studies. *Pediatrics* 68: 684-690.

3479 Levine, J. 1976. *And Who Will Raise the Children? New Options for Fathers and Mothers.* Philadelphia: Lippincott.

3480 Levine, R A. 1980. Influences of women's schooling on maternal behavior in the Third World. *Comparative Education Review* Special Supplement: 75-105.

3481 Levine, R A. 1980. A cross-cultural perspective on parenting. In *Parenting in a Multi-Cultural Society.* Edited by Fantini, M, R Cardenas. New York: Longman.

3482 Lewis, M, L Rosenblum, eds. 1979. *The Child and Its Family.* New York: Plenum.

3483 Lightcap, J L, J A Kurland, R L Burgess. 1982. Child abuse: A test of some predictions from evolutionary theory. *Ethology and Sociobiology* 3: 61-67.

3484 Luker, K. 1975. *Taking Chances: Abortion and the Decision not to Contracept.* Berkeley: University of California Press.

3485 Lystad, M, ed. 1986. *Violence in the Home: Interdisciplinary Perspectives.* New York: Brunner/Mazel.

3486 Maccoby, E E. 1980. *Social Development: Psychological Growth and the Parent-child Relationship.* New York: Harcourt Brace Jovanovich.

3487 Mackey, W C. 1985. *Fathering Behaviors: The Dynamics of the Man-child Bond.* New York: Plenum Press.

3488 Maisch, H. 1972. *Incest.* New York: Stein and Day.

3489 Mangen, D J, W A Peterson, eds. 1982. *Parent-child relations.* Research Instruments in Social Gerontology: Vol 2 Social Roles and Social Participation. Minneapolis: University of Minnesota Press.

3490 Mansick, G, M J Bane. 1980. *The Nation's Families: 1960-1990.* Cambridge, MA: Joint Center for Urban Studies.

3491 McKenna, J J. 1979. Aspects of infant socialization, attachment, and maternal caregiving patterns among primates: A cross-disciplinary review. *Yearbook of Physical Anthropology* 22: 250-286.

3492 McKenna, J J. 1987. Parental supplements and surrogates among primates: Cross-species and cross-cultural comparisons. In *Parenting Across the Life Span—Biosocial Dimensions.* Edited by Lancaster, J B, J Altmann, A S Rossi, L R Sherrod. Pp. 143-186. New York: Aldine De Gruyter.

3493 Miller, B D. 1981. *The Endangered Sex: Neglect of Female Children in Rural North India.* Ithaca, N.Y.: Cornell University Press.

3494 Mohr, J C. 1978. *Abortion in America: The Origins and Evolution of National Policy, 1800-1900.* New York: Oxford University Press.

3495 Morse, C A, L Dennerstein. 1985. Psychological aspects of couples entering an in-vitro fertilisation treatment programme. *Journal of Psychosomatic Obstetrics and Gynaecology* 4: 207-219.

3496 Munroe, R H, R L Munroe. 1980. Infant experience and childhood affect among the Logoli: A longitudinal study. *Ethos* 8: 295-315.

3497 Norbeck, J S, V P Tilden. 1983. Life stress, social support, and emotional disequilibrium in complications of pregnancy: A prospective multivariate study. *Journal of Health and Social Behavior* 24: 3-46.

3498 Ooms, R. 1981. *Adolescent Pregnancy in a Family Context.* Philadelphia: Temple University Press.

3499 Papoz, L, E Eschewege, G Pequignot, J Barrat. 1981. Dietary behaviour during pregnancy. In *Maternal Nutrition in Pregnancy— Eating for Two?* Edited by Dobbing, J. Pp. 41-69. New York: Academic Press.

3500 Parke, R D, T G Power, J Gottman. 1979. Conceptualizing and quantifying influence patterns in the family triad. In *Social Interaction Analysis: Methodological Issues.* Edited by Lamb, M E, S J Suomi, G R Stephenson. Madison: University of Wisconsin Press.

3501 Parke, R D. 1981. *Fathers.* Cambridge: Harvard University Press.

3502 Parker, G, M MacNair. 1979. Models of parent-offspring conflict. IV: Retaliation by the parent. *Animal Behaviour* 27: 1210-35.

3503 Pedersen, F A, ed. 1980. *The Father-Infant Relationship: Observational Studies in a Family Context.* New York: Praeger.

3504 Peristiany, J G. 1976. *Mediterranean Family Structures.* Cambridge: Cambridge University Press.

3505 Plimpton, E, L Rosenblem. 1983. The ecological context of infant maltreatment in primates. In *Child Abuse: The Nonhuman Primate Data.* Edited by Reite, M, N G Caine. New York: Alan R. Liss.

3506 Pollock, L. 1983. *Forgotten Children: Parent-Child Relations— A View from 1500 to 1900.* Cambridge: Cambridge University Press.

3507 Rabin, A I. 1965. *Growing Up in the Kibbutz.* New York: Springer.

3508 Radin, N. 1981. The role of the father in cognitive, academic, and intellectual development. In *The Role of the Father in Child Development.* Edited by Lamb, M E. New York: Wiley.

3509 Reite, M, N Caine, eds. 1983. *Child Abuse: The Nonhuman Primate Data.* New York: Alan R. Liss.

3510 Rendina, I, J D Dickerscheid. 1976. Father involvement with first-born infants. *Family Coordinator* 25: 373-378.

3511 Ripley, S. 1980. Infanticide in Langurs and Man: Adaptive Advantage or Social Pathology? In *Biosocial Mechanisms of Population Regulation.* Edited by Cohen, M N, R S Malpass, H G Klein. Pp. 349-390. New Haven: Yale University Press.

3512 Rite, M, N G Caine. 1983. *Child Abuse: The Nonhuman Primate Data.* New York: Alan R. Liss.

3513 Rockwell, R E C. 1976. Historical trends and variation in educational homogamy. *Journal of Marriage and the Family* 38: 83-95.

3514 Rodholm, M, K Larsson. 1982. The behavior of human male adults at their first contact with a newborn. *Infant Behavior and Development* 5: 121-130.

3515 Rosenberg, K M, G F Sherman. 1975. The role of testosterone in the organization, maintenance and activation of pup-killing behavior in the male rat. *Hormones and Behavior* 6: 173-179.

3516 Rosenblum, L A, G Sunderland. 1982. Feeding ecology and mother-infant relations. In *Parenting: Its Causes and Consequences.* Edited by Hoffman, L W, R Gandelman, H R Schiffman. Pp. 75-110. Hillsdale, N.J.: Erlbaum.

3517 Rosenblum, L A, H Moltz, eds. 1983. *Symbiosis in Parent-Offspring Interactions.* New York: Plenum.

3518 Rossi, A S. 1980. Life span theories and women's lives. *Signs: Journal of Women in Culture and Society* 6: 4-32.

3519 Rossi, A S. 1984. *Gender and the Life Course.* New York: Aldine.

3520 Sagi, A. 1982. Antecedents and consequences of various degrees of paternal involvement in child rearing: The Israeli project. In *Nontraditional Families: Parenting and Child Development.* Edited by Lamb, E M. Hillsdale, N.J.: Erlbaum.

3521 Santrock, J W, R A Warshak, G L Elliot. 1982. Social development and parent-child interaction in father-custody and stepmother families. In *Nontraditional Families: Parenting and Child Development.* Edited by Lamb, M E. Pp. 289-314. Hillsdale, N.J.: Erlbaum.

3522 Schubert, G. 1982. Infanticide by usurper Hanuman Langur males: A sociobiological myth. *Social Science Information* 20: 199-244.

3523 Shinn, M. 1978. Father absence and children's cognitive development. *Psychological Bulletin* 85: 295-324.

3524 Shorter, E. 1975. *The Making of the Modern Family.* New York: Basic Books.

3525 Snowdon, C T, S J Suomi. 1982. Parental behavior in primates. In *Child Nurturance. Vol.3. Primate Behavior and Child Nurturance.* Edited by Mullins, J A, P Gage. New York: Plenum.

3526 Spiro, M E. 1965. *Children of the Kibbutz.* New York: Schocken.

3527 Standley, K, B Soule, S Copans. 1979. Dimensions of prenatal anxiety and their influence on pregnance outcome. *American Journal of Obstetrics and Gynecology* 135: 22-26.

3528 Stevens, J, M Matthews, eds. 1979. *Mother-child, Father-child Relations.* Washington: National Association for Education of Young Children.

3529 Stuart, I R, C F Wells, eds. 1982. *Pregnancy in Adolescence: Needs, Problems, and Management.* New York: Van Nostrand Reinhold.

3530 Susser, M. 1981. Environment and biology in ageing: Some epidemiological notions. In *Aging and Behavior.* Edited by McGaugh, J L, S B Kiesler. Pp. 77-96. New York: Academic Press.

3531 Svare, B B. 1981. Maternal aggression in mammals. In *Parental Care in Mammals.* Edited by Gubernick, D J, P H Klopfer. Pp. 179-210. New York: Plenum.

3532 Svare, B B. 1983. Psychobiological determinants of maternal aggressive behavior. In *Aggressive Behavior: Genetic and Neural Approaches.* Edited by Simmel, E C, M E Hahn, J K Walters. Pp. 129-46. Hillsdale, NJ: Erlbaum.

3533 Svare, B, C Kinsley, M Mann, J Broida. 1984. Infanticide: Accounting for genetic variation in mice. *Physiology and Behavior* 33: 137-152.

3534 Swedlund, A C, R S Meindl, M I Gradie. 1980. Family reconstitution in the Connecticut Valley: Progress on record linkage and the mortality survey. In *Geneological Demography.* Edited by Dyke, B, W Morrill. Pp. 139-145.

3535 Taub, D M, ed. 1984. *Primate Paternalism.* New York: Van Nostrand Reinhold.

3536 Thornton, A, W L Rodgers. 1983. *Changing Patterns of Marriage and Divorce in the United States: Final Report.* Washington, DC: National Institute of Child Health and Human Development.

3537 Vaughn, B, F Gove, B Egeland. 1980. The relationship between out-of-home care and the quality of infant-mother attachment in an economically disadvantaged sample. *Child Development* 51: 1203-1214.

3538 Vinovskis, M A. 1987. Historical perspectives on the development of the family and parent-child interactions. In *Parenting Across the Life Span - Biosocial Dimensions.* Edited by Lancaster, J B, J Altmann, A S Rossi, L R Sherrod. Pp. 295-314. New York: Aldine De Gruyter.

3539 Voland, E. 1989. Differential parental investment: Some ideas on the contact area of European social history and evolutionary biology. In *Comparative Socioecology of Mammals and Man.* Edited by Standen, V, R Foley. London: Blackwell.

3540 Walker, A J, L Thompson. 1983. Intimacy and intergenerational aid and contact among mothers and daughters. *Journal of Marriage and the Family* 45: 841-849.

3541 Wallerstein, J, J Kelly. 1980. *Surviving the Break-up: How Children and Parents Cope with Divorce.* New York: Basic Books.

3542 Walters, J, L H Walters. 1980. Parent-child relationships: A review, 1970-1979. *Journal of Marriage and the Family* 42: 807-822.

3543 Weinberg, S K. 1955. *Incest Behavior.* Secaucus, NJ: Citadel.

3544 Weisner, T S. 1987. Socialization for parenthood in sibling caretaking societies. In *Parenting Across the Life Span - Biosocial Dimensions.* Edited by Lancaster, J B, J Altmann, A S Rossi, L R Sherrod. Pp. 237-270. New York: Aldine De Gruyter.

3545 Werren, J G, M R Gross, R Shine. 1980. Paternity and the evolution of male parental care. *Journal of Theoretical Biology* 82: 619-31.

3546 Westermarck, E. 1926 [1891]. *The History of Human Marriage.* London: Macmillan.

3547 Williams, G, J Money, eds. 1980. *Traumatic Abuse and Neglect of Children at Home.* Baltimore: Johns Hopkins.

3548 Wilson, M I, M Daly, S J Weghorst. 1983. Differential maltreatment of girls and boys. *Victimology* 6: 249-261.

3549 Wilson, M, M Daly. 1987. Risk of maltreatment of children living with stepparents. In *Child Abuse and Neglect: Biosocial Dimensions.* Edited by Gelles, R J, J B Lancaster. New York: Aldine de Gruyter.

3550 Worthman, C M. 1986. Developmental dyssynchrony as normative experience: Kikuyu adolescents. In *School-Age Pregnancy and Parenthood: Biosocial Dimensions.* Edited by Lancaster, J B, B A Hamburg. Pp. 95-114. New York: Aldine De Gruyter.

3551 Wu, D Y H. 1981. Child abuse in Taiwan. In *Child Abuse and Neglect: Cross-Cultural Perspectives.* Edited by Korbin, J E. Pp. 139-165. Berkley: University of California.

3552 Yates, A. 1982. Children eroticized by incest. *American Journal of Psychiatry* 139: 482-485.

3553 Young, F W. 1967. Incest taboos and social solidarity. *American Journal of Sociology* 72: 589-600.

3554 Zelnik, M, J Kantner, K Ford. 1982. *Adolescent Pathways to Pregnancy.* Beverly Hills: Sage.

*Note: Entry 3555 is skipped.*

# 9

# Sexuality

3556 Abramovich, D R, I A Davidson, A Longstaff, C K Pearson. 1987. Sexual differentiation of the human midtrimester brain. *European Journal of Obstetrics, Gynecology and Reproductive Biology* 25: 7-14.

3557 Adelson, E, ed 1975. *Sexuality and Psychoanalysis.* New York: Brunner & Mazel.

3558 Adler, N T, ed 1981. *Neuroendocrinology of Reproduction. Physiology and Behavior.* New York: Plenum.

3559 Ageton, S. 1983. *Sexual Assault Among Adolescents.* Lexington, MA: Lexington Books.

3560 Allen, L S, M Hines, J E Shryne, R A Gorski. 1989. Two sexually dimorphic cell groups in the human brain. *Journal of Neuroscience* 9: 497-506.

3561 Allgeier, E R, N B McCormick. 1983. *Changing Boundaries: Gender Roles and Sexual Behavior.* Palo Alto: Mayfield.

3562 Amir, M. 1971. *Patterns in Forcible Rape.* Chicago: University of Chicago Press.

3563 Arai, Y, A Matsumoto, N Nishizuka. 1986. Synaptogenesis and neuronal plasticity to gonadal steroids: Implications for the development of sexual dimorphism in the neuroendocrine brain. In *Current Topics in Neuroendocrinology.* Edited by Ganten, D, D Pfaff. Pp. 291-307. Berlin: Springer.

3564 Archer, J. 1984. Gender roles as developmental pathways. *British Journal of Social Psychology* 23: 245-256.

3565 Archer, J, B B Lloyd. 1985. *Sex and Gender.* 2nd ed. Cambridge: Cambridge University Press.

3566 Archer, J, N A Pearson, K E Westeman. 1988. Aggressive behaviour of children aged 6 to 11: Gender differences and their magnitude. *British Journal of Social Psycholgoy* 27: 371-384.

3567 Archer, J. 1989. The relationship between gender role measures: A review. *British Journal of Social Psychology* 28: 173-184.

3568 Archer, J. 1989. Childhood gender roles: Structure and development. *The Psychologist* 12: 367-370.

3569 Arnold, A P, R Gorski. 1984. Gonadal steroid induction of structural sex differences in the CNS. *Annual Review of Neuroscience* 7: 413-42.

3570 Arnold, A P, S M Breedlove. 1985. Organizational and activational effects of sex steroids on brain and behavior: A reanalysis. *Hormones and Behavior* 19: 469-98.

3571 Austin, C R, R V Short, eds. 1980. *Reproduction in Mammals: Human Sexuality.* Cambridge: Cambridge University Press.

3572 Austin, C R, R G Edwards. 1981. *Mechanisms of Sex Differentiation in Animals and Man.* New York: Academic Press.

3573 Bailey, K. 1985. Phylogenetic regression-progression and the problem of rape motivation. *New Trends in Experimental and Clinical Psychiatry* 4: 235-51.

3574 Bain, J, R Langevin, R Dickey, M Ben-Aron. 1987. Sex hormones in murderers and assaulters. *Behavioral Science and the Law* 5: 95-101.

3575 Bancroft, J. 1978. The Relationship between hormones and sexual behavior in humans. In *Biological Determinants of Sexual Behavior.* Edited by Hutchinson, J B. Pp. 493-520. New York: Wiley.

3576 Bancroft, J. 1980. Endocrinology of sexual function. *Clinics in Obstetrics and Gynaecology* 7: 253-281.

3577 Bancroft, J. 1983. *Human Sexuality and Its Problems.* Edinburgh: Churchill Livingstone.

3578 Bancroft, J, D Sanders, D Davidson, P Warner. 1983. Mood, sexuality, hormones, and the menstral cycle. III. Sexuality and the role of androgens. *Psychosomatic Medicine* 45: 509-516.

3579 Bancroft, J, J Machover Reinisch. 1991. *Adolescence and Puberty.* Kinsey Institute Series. New York: Oxford University Press.

3580 Barbaree, H E, W L Marshall, R D Lanthier. 1979. Deviant sexual arousal in rapists. *Behaviour Research and Therapy* 17: 215-22.

3581 Baron, R A. 1974. The aggression-inhibiting influence of heightened sexual arousal. *Journal of Personality and Social Psychology* 30: 318-322.

3582 Baron, R A. 1979. Heightened sexual arousal and physical aggression: An extension to females. *Journal of Research in Personality* 13: 91-102.

3583 Baucom, D, P K Besch, S Callahan. 1985. Relation between testosterone concentration, sex role identity, and personality among females. *Journal of Personality and Social Psychology* 48: 1218-26.

3584 Baum, M J, R S Carroll, M S Erskine, S A Tobet. 1985. Neuroendocrine response to estrogen and sexual orientation. *Science* 230: 960-1.

3585 Beatty, W W. 1984. Hormonal organization of sex differences in play fighting and spatial behavior. *Progress in Brain Research* 61: 315-30.

3586 Beckstrom, T, D Sanders, R Leask, D Davidson, P Warner, J Bancroft. 1983. Mood, asexuality, hormones, and the menstral Cycle. II. Hormone levels and their relationship to the premenstral syndrome. *Psychosomatic Medicine* 45: 503-507.

3587 Bell, A P, M S Weinberg. 1978. *Homosexualities: A Study of Diversity Among Men and Women.* New York: Simon and Schuster.

3588 Bell, A P, M S Weinberg, S K Hammersmith. 1981. *Sexual Preference: Its Development in Men and Women.* Bloomington: University of Indiana Press.

3589 Benton, D, P F Brain, M Haug, eds. 1984. *The Aggressive Female.* Montreal: Eden Press.

3590 Bloom, D, A Pebley. 1982. Voluntary childlessness: A review of the evidence and implications. *Population Research and Policy Review* 1: 203-222.

3591 Boles, J, C Tatro. 1982. Androgyny. In *Men in Transition: Theory and Therapy.* Edited by Solomon, K, N B Levy. Pp. 99-130. New York: Plenum.

3592 Boswell, J. 1980. *Christianity, Social Tolerance and Homosexuality: Gay People in Western Europe from the Beginning of the Christian Era to the Fourteenth Century.* Chicago: University of Chicago Press.

3593 Bremer, J. 1959. *Asexualization: A follow-up study of 244 cases.* New York: Macmillian.

3594 Brookes-Gunn, J, A C Peterson, eds. 1981. *Girls at Puberty: Biological and Psychosocial Perspectives.* New York: Plenum.

3595 Brown, H. 1976. *Familiar Faces, Hidden Lives: The Story of Homosexual Men in America Today.* New York: Harcourt Brace Jovanovich.

3596 Buhrich, N, N McConaghy. 1977. The discrete syndromes of transvestism and transsexualism. *Archives of Sexual Behavior* 6: 483-495.

3597 Buhrich, N, N McConaghy. 1979. The tests of gender feelings and behavior in homosexuality, transvestism and transsexualism. *Journal of Clinical Psychology* 35: 187-191.

3598 Byrne, D, K Kelley, eds. 1986. *Alternative Approaches to the Study of Sexual Behavior.* Hillsdale, NJ: Erlbaum.

3599 Caine, M J. 1985. Behavior during puberty and adolescence. In *Comparative Primate Biology: Behavior and Ecology.* Edited by Erwin, J, G Mitchell. New York: Alan R. Liss.

3600 Cantor, J R, D Zillman, E F Einsiedel. 1978. Female responses to provocation after exposure to aggressive and erotic films. *Communication Research* 5: 395-411.

3601 Chappell, D, R Geis, G Geis, eds. 1977. *Forcible Rape.* New York: Columbia University Press.

3602 Chilman, C. 1983. *Adolescent Sexuality in a Changing Society.* New York: Wiley.

3603 Christen, Y. 1991. *Modern Biology and the Unisex Fallacy.* New Brunswick, NJ: Transaction.

3604 Clatterburgh, K C. 1990. *Contemporary Perspectives on Masculinity: Men, Women and Politics in Modern Society.* Oxford: Westview Press.

3605 Cohen, E. 1982. Sexual dimorphism: A tool in the research of brain and behavior. In *Genetics of the Brain.* Edited by Lieblich, I. Pp. 39-57. New York: Elsevier Biomedical Press.

3606 Cohen, A S, R C Rosen, L Goldstein. 1985. EEG hemispheric asymmetry during sexual arousal: Psychophysiological patterns in responsive, unresponsive and dysfunctional males. *Journal of Abnormal Psychology* 94: 580-90.

3607 Constantinople, A. 1979. Sex role acquisition: In search of the elephant. *Sex Roles* 5: 121-133.

3608 Couwenbergs, C, R Knussmann, K Christiansen. 1986. Comparison of intra- and inter-individual variability in sex hormone levels of men. *Annual of Human Biology* 13: 63-72.

3609 Crews, D. 1988. The problem with gender. *Psychobiology* 16: 321-334.

3610 Daly, M, M Wilson, S Weghorst. 1982. Male sexual jealousy. *Ethology and Sociobiology* 3: 11-27.

3611 Davenport-Hines, R. 1990. *Sex, Death and Punishment: Attitudes to Sex and Sexuality in Britain since the Renaissance.* London: Collins.

3612 David, D S, R Bannon, eds. 1976. *The Forty-Nine Percent Majority: The Male Sex Role.* Reading, MA: Addison-Wesley.

3613 David, D S, R Bannon. 1976. The male sex role: Our culture's blueprint of manhood and what it's done for us lately. In *The Forty-Nine Percent Majority: The Male Sex Role.* Pp. 1-45. Reading, MA: Addison-Wesley.

3614 Davidson, J M, C A Camargo, E R Smith. 1979. Effects of androgens on sexual behavior in hypogonadal men. *Journal of Clinical Endocrinology and Metabolism* 48: 955-958.

3615 Dejonge, F H, E M J Eerland, N E Vanepol. 1986. Sex-specific interactions between aggressive and sexual-behavior in the rat: Effects of testosterone and progesterone. *Hormone Behavior* 20: 432-444.

3616 DeLameter, J, M MacCorquodale. 1979. *Premarital Sexuality: Attitudes, Relationships, Behaviors.* Madison: University of Wisconsin Press.

3617 Diamond, M C. 1968. *Perspectives in Reproduction and Sexual Behavior.* Bloomington: Indiana University Press.

3618 Diamond, M. 1979. Sexual identity and sex roles. In *The Frontiers of Sex Research.* Edited by Bullough, V. Pp. 33-56. Buffalo: Prometheus.

3619 Diamond, M C. 1984. Age, sex, and environmental influences. In *Cerebral Dominance: The Biological Foundations*. Edited by Geschwind, N, A M Galaburda. Pp. 134-46. Cambridge: Harvard University Press.

3620 Dittman, R W. 1989. *Pränatal wirksame Hormone und Verhaltensmerkmale von Patientinnen mit den beiden klassischen Varianten des 21-Hydroxylase-Defektes. (Ein Beitrag zur Psychoendokrinologie des Adrenogenitalen Syndroms)*. Frankfurt: Peter Lang.

3621 Dittman, R W, M H Kappes, M E Kappes, D Börger, H F L Meyer-Bahlburg, H Stegner, R H Willig, H Wallis. 1990. Congenital adrenal hyperplasia II: Gender-related behavior and attitudes in female salt-wasting and simple-virilizing patients. *Psychoneuroendocrinology* 15: 421-34.

3622 Dörner, G, F Döcke, G Hinz. 1971. Paradoxical effects of estrogen on brain differentiation. *Neuroendocrinology* 7: 146-55.

3623 Dörner, G, W Rohde, F Stahl, W G Masius. 1975. A neuroendocrine predisposition for homosexuality in men. *Archives of Sexual Behavior* 4: 1-8.

3624 Dörner, G. 1976. *Hormones and Brain Differentiation*. Amsterdam: Elsevier.

3625 Dörner, G, W Rohde, K Siedel, W Haas, G Schott. 1976. On the evocability of a positive estrogen feedback action on LH secretion in transsexual men and women. *Endokrinologie* 67: 20-25.

3626 Dörner, G, T Geier, L Ahrens, L Krell, G Munx, H Sieler, E Kittner, H Muller. 1980. Prenatal stress as possible aetiogenetic factor of homosexuality in males. *Endokrinologie* 75: 365-368.

3627 Dörner, G, B Schenk, B Schmiedel, L Ahrens. 1983. Stressful events in prenatal life of bi- and homosexual men. *Experimental and Clinical Endocrinology* 81: 83-87.

3628 Dörner, G. 1983. Hormone-dependent brain development. *Psychoneuroendocrinology* 8: 205-12.

3629 Dörner, G. 1988. Neuroendocrine response to estrogen and brain differentiation in heterosexuals, homosexuals, and transsexuals. *Archives of Sexual Behavior* 17: 57-75.

3630 Duke, P M, et al. 1982. Educational correlations of early and late sexual maturation in adolescence. *Journal of Pediatrics* 100: 633-637.

3631 Durden-Smith, J, D deSimone. 1983. *Sex and the Brain.* New York: Warney.

3632 Ehrhardt, A A, J Money. 1967. Progestin-induced hermaphroditism: IQ and psychosexual identity in a study of ten girls. *Journal of Sex Research* 3: 83-100.

3633 Ehrhardt, A A, S W Baker. 1974. Fetal androgens, human CNS differentiation and behavior sex differences. In *Sex Differences in Behavior.* Edited by Friedman, R C, R M Richart, R L Van de Wiele. Pp. 33-51. New York: Wiley.

3634 Eibl-Eibesfeldt, I. 1990. Dominance, submission, and love: Sexual pathologies from the perspective of ethology. In *Pedophilia: Biosocial Dimensions.* Edited by Feierman, J R. Pp. 150-175. New York: Springer.

3635 Ellis, L, C Beattie. 1983. The feminist explanation for rape:An empirical test. *Journal of Sex Research* 19: 74-93.

3636 Ellis, L. 1986. Evidence of neuroandrogenic etiology of sex roles from a combined analysis of human, nonhuman primate, and nonprimate mammalian studies. *Personality and Individual Differences* 7: 519-551.

3637 Ellis, L, M A Ames. 1987. Neurohormonal functioning and sexual orientation: A theory of homosexuality-heterosexuality. *Psychological Bulletin* 101: 233-258.

3638 Ellis, L, M A Ames, W Peckham, D Burke. 1988. Sexual orientation of human offspring may be altered by severe maternal stress during pregnancy. *Journal of Sex Research* 25: 152-157.

3639 Ellis, L. 1989. Sex hormones, r/K selection, and victimful criminality. *Mankind Quarterly* 29: 329-340.

3640 Ellis, L. 1989. *Theories of Rape: Inquiries into the Caues of Sexual Aggression.* New York: Hemisphere.

3641 Ellis, L. 1990. Prenatal stress may affect sex-typical behaviors of a child. *The Brown University Child Behavior and Development Letter* 6: 1-3.

3642 Ellis, L, H Hoffman, D M Burke. 1990. Sex, sexual orientation and criminal and violent behavior. *Personality and Individual Differences* 11: 1207-1212.

3643 Ellis, L, H Hoffman, eds. 1990. *Crime in Biological, Social, and Moral Contexts.* Westport, CT: Praeger.

3644 Ember, C R. 1981. A cross-cultural perspective on sex differences. In *Handbook of Cross-Cultural Human Development.* Edited by Munroe, R H, R L Munroe, B B Whiting. New York: Garland.

3645 Feder, H H. 1981. Perinatal hormones and their role in the development of sexually dimorphic behaviors. In *Neuroendocrinology of Reproduction.* Edited by Adler, N T. Pp. 127-158. New York: Plenum.

3646 Feder, H H. 1981. Hormonal action on the sexual differentiation of the genitalia and gonadotropin regulating systems. In *Neuroendocrinology of Reproduction.* Edited by Adler, N T. Pp. 89-126. New York: Plenum.

3647 Feder, H H. 1984. Hormones and sexual behavior. *Annual Review of Psychology* 35: 165-200.

3648 Feierman, J R, ed. 1990. *Pedophilia: Biosocial Dimensions.* New York: Springer.

3649 Field, T, S Widmayer. 1982. Mother-infant interaction among SES Black, Cuba, Puerto Rican and South Americn immigrants. In *Culture and Early Interaction.* Edited by Field, T, A Sostek, P Vietze, A H Liederman. Hillsdale, N.J.: Erlbaum.

3650 Finkelhor, D. 1979. *Sexually Victimized Children.* Riverside, NJ: Free Press.

3651 Finkelhor, D. 1980. Sex among siblings: A survey on prevalence, variety, and effects. *Archives of Sexual Behavior* 9: 171-194.

3652 Finkelhor, D, K Yllo. 1982. Forced sex in marriage: A preliminary research report. *Crime and Delinquency* 28: 459-78.

3653 Ford, C S, F A Beach. 1952. *Patterns of Sexual Behaviour.* London: Methuen.

3654 Forlec, R, W Pasini, eds. 1980. *Medical Sexology.* Amsterdam: Elsevier.

3655 Fox, G L, J K Inazu. 1980. Mother-daughter communication about sex. *Family Relations* 29: 347-352.

3656 Friedman, R C, R M Richart, R L Vande Wiele, eds. 1974. *Sex Differences in Behavior*. New York: Wiley.

3657 Furstenberg, F F, Jr., R Herceg-Baron, J Shea, D Webb. 1986. Family communication and contraceptive use among sexually active adolescents. In *School-Age Pregnancy and Parenthood: Biosocial Dimensions*. Edited by Lancaster, J B, B A Hamburg. Pp. 219-246. New York: Aldine De Gruyter.

3658 Gangestad, S W, J A Simpson. 1990. Toward an evolutionary history of female sociosexual variation. *Journal of Personality* 58: 69-96.

3659 Geer, J H, W T O'Donohue, eds. 1987. *Theories of Human Sexuality*. London: Plenum.

3660 Gilligan, C. 1977. In a different voice: Women's conceptions of the self and of morality. *Harvard Educational Review* 47: 481-517.

3661 Gladue, B. 1983. Hormones, psychosexuality, and reproduction: Biology, brain, and behavior. *Politics and the Life Sciences* 2: 86-88.

3662 Gladue, B. 1984. Neuroendocrine response to estrogen and sexual orientation. *Science* 225: 1496-1499.

3663 Gladue, B. 1987. Psychobiological contributions. In *Male and Female Homosexuality: Psychological spproaches*. Edited by Diamant, L. Pp. 129-154. Washington, D.C.: Hemisphere.

3664 Gladue, B, M Boechler, K D McCaul. 1989. Hormonal response to competition in human males. *Aggressive Behavior* 15: 409-422.

3665 Gladue, B. 1990. Hormones and neuroendocrine factors in atypical human sexual behavior. In *Pedophilia: Biosocial Dimensions*. Edited by Feierman, J. Pp. 274-298. New York: Springer.

3666 Goldman, B D. 1978. Developmental influences of hormones on neuroendocrine mechanisms of sexual behaviour: Comparisons with other sexually dimorphic behaviors. In *Biological Determinants of Sexual Behavior*. Edited by Hutchinson, J B. Pp. 127-152. New York: Wiley.

3667 Gomberg, E S, V Franks. 1979. *Gender and Disordered Behavior: Sex Differences in Psychopathology*. New York: Brummer-Mazel.

3668 Gorski, R. 1979. The neuroendocrinology of reproduction: An overview. *Behvioral Biology* 20: 111-127.

3669 Gorski, R A. 1984. Critical role for the medial preoptic area in the sexual differentiations of the brain. In *Sex Differences in the Brain*. Edited by De Vries, G J, J P C De Bruin, H B M Uylings, M A Corner. Pp. 129-146. New York: Elsevier.

3670 Goy, R W, M Roy. 1991. Heterotypical sexual behaviour in female mammals. In *Heterotypical Behaviour in Man and Animals*. Edited by Haug, M, P F Brain, C Aron. Pp. 71-97. New York: Chapman and Hall.

3671 Green, R. 1987. *The "Sissy Boy Syndrome" and the Development of Homosexuality*. New Haven: Yale University Press.

3672 Gregerson, E. 1983. *Sexual Practices: The Story of Human Sexuality*. New York: Franklin Watts.

3673 Grellert, E A, M D Newcomb, P M Bentler. 1982. Childhood play activities of male and female homosexuals and heterosexuals. *Archives of Sexual Behavior* 11: 451-478.

3674 Groth, A N, H J Birnbaum. 1979. *Men Who Rape: The Psychology of the Offender*. New York: Wiley.

3675 Grumbach, M M, G D Grave, F E Mayer, eds. 1974. *Control of the Onset of Puberty*. New York: Wiley.

3676 Harlan, W R, G P Grillo, J Cornoni-Huntley, P E Leaverton. 1979. Secondary sex characteristics of boys 12 to 17 years of age: The U.S. health examination survey. *Journal of Pediatrics* 95: 293-297.

3677 Harry, J. 1983. Defeminization and adult psychological well-being amoung male homosexuals. *Archives of Sexual Behavior* 12: 1-19.

3678 Herdt, G H. 1980. *Guardians of the Flute: Idioms of Masculinity*. New York: McGraw-Hill.

3679 Herdt, G, ed 1984. *Ritualized Homosexuality in Melanesia*. Berkeley: University of California Press.

3680 Holmes, R M. 1991. *Sex Crimes*. London: Sage.

3681 Holmstrom, L L, A W Burgess. 1980. Sexual behavior of assailants during reported rapes. *Archives of Sexual Behavior* 9: 427-439.

3682 Hrdy, S. 1979. The evolution of human sexuality: The latest word and the last. *Quarterly Review of Biology* 54: 309-314.

3683 Kaffman, M. 1977. Sexual standards and behavior of the kibbutz adolescent. *Americal Journal of Orthopsychiatry* 47: 207-217.

3684 Kalat, J W. 1988. *Biological Psychology.* 3rd ed Belmont, CA.: Wadsworth.

3685 Kaplan, G R, L J Rogers. 1985. Breaking out of a dominant paradigm: A new look at sexual attraction. *Journal of Homosexuality* 10: 71-75.

3686 Katchadourian, H, ed. 1979. *Human Sexuality: A Comparative and Developmental Perspective.* Berkeley: University of California.

3687 Kelley, K, ed. 1987. *Females, Males, and Sexuality: Theory and Research.* Albany: SUNY Press.

3688 Kelly, G F. 1988. *Sexuality Today: The Human Perspective.* Guilford, CT: Duskin.

3689 Kessler, R C, J D McLeod. 1984. Sex differences in vulnerability to undesirable life events. *American Sociological Review* 49: 620-631

3690 Kinsey, A, W Pomeroy, C Martin. 1948. *Sexual Behavior in the Human Male.* Philadelphia: W. B. Saunders.

3691 Kinsey, A C, W B Pomeroy, C E Martin, P H Gebhard. 1953. *Sexual Behavior in the Human Female.* Philadelphia: Saunders.

3692 Komarovsky, M. 1976. *Dilemmas of Masculinity: A Study of College Youth.* New York: Norton.

3693 Langevin, R. 1983. *Sexual Strands: Understanding and Treating Sexual Anomalies in Men.* Hillsdale, NJ: Erlbaum.

3694 Langevin, R, ed. 1985. *Erotic Preference, Gender Identity and Aggression in Men: New Research Studies.* Hillsdale, NJ: Erlbaum.

3695 Langevin, R, et al. 1985. Sexual aggression: Constructing a predictive equation: A controlled pilot study. In *Erotic Preference, Gender Identity and Aggression in Men: New Research Studies.* Edited by Langevin, R. Pp. 39-76. Hillsdale, NJ: Erlbaum.

3696 Laron, Z, J Arad, R Gurewitz, M Grunebaum, Z Dickerman. 1980. Age at first conscious ejaculation: Milestones in male puberty. *Helvetica Paediatrica Acta* 35: 13-20.

3697 Laslett, P, K Oosterveen, R Smith. 1980. *Bastardy and Its Comparative History: Studies in the History of Illegitimacy and Marital*

*Noncomformism in Britain, France, Germany, Sweden, North America, Jamaica and Japan.* Cambridge: Harvard University Press.

3698 Lederer, W. 1970. *The Fear of Women.* New York: Harcourt, Brace & Jovanovitch.

3699 Lederer, W. 1979. The decline of manhood: Adaptive trend or temporary confusion? *Psychiatric Opinion* 16: 14-17.

3700 Lederer, W. 1982. Counterepilogue. In *Men in Transition: Theory and Therapy.* Edited by Solomon, K, N Levy. Pp. 475-92. New York: Plenum.

3701 Liebowitz, M R. 1985. *The Chemistry of Love.* Boston: Little, Brown.

3702 Lips, H M. 1988. *Sex and Gender: An Introduction.* Mountain View, CA: Mayfield.

3703 Loraine, J A, ed. 1974. *Understanding Homosexuality: Its Biological and Psychological Bases.* New York: Elsevier.

3704 Maccoby, E, C Jacklin. 1974. *The Psychology of Sex Differences.* Stanford: Stanford University Press.

3705 Maccoby, E E. 1987. The varied meanings of "masculine" and "feminine". In *Masculinity/Femininity: Basic Perspectives.* Edited by Reinisch, J M, L A Rosenblum, S A Sanders. Pp. 227-239. Oxford: Oxford University Press.

3706 MacDonald, K. 1990. Mechanisms of sexual egalitarianism in Western Europe. *Ethology and Sociobiology* 11: 195-238.

3707 Masters, W, V Johnson. 1966. *Human Sexual Response.* Boston: Little, Brown.

3708 Masters, W, V Johnson. 1969. *Human Sexual Inadequacy.* Boston: Little, Brown.

3709 McGuinness, D, J Sparks. 1983. Cognitive style and cognitive maps: Sex differences inrepresentations of a familiar terrain. *Journal of Mental Imagery* 7: 91-100.

3710 Meaney, M J, J Stewart. 1985. Sex differences in social play: The socialization of sex roles. *Advances in the Study of Behavior* 15: 1-58.

3711 Meiselman, K C. 1978. *Incest: A Psychological Study of Causes and Effects with Treatment Recommendations.* San Francisco: Jossey-Bass.

3712 Meyer-Bahlburg, H F L. 1984. Psychoendocrine research on sexual orientation. Current status and future options. In *Sex Differences in the Brain.* Edited by De Vries, G J, J P C De Bruin, H B M Uylings, M A Corner. Pp. 129-146. New York: Elsevier.

3713 Millon, T. 1990. *Toward a New Personology: An Evolutionary Model.* New York: Wiley.

3714 Money, J. 1955. Hermaphroditism, gender and precocity in hyperandrenocorticism: Psychological findings. *Bulletin of the Johns Hopkins Hospital* 96: 253-264.

3715 Money, J, A A Ehrhardt. 1968. Prenatal hormone exposure: Possible effects on behaviour in man. In *Endocrinology and Human Behaviour.* Edited by Micheal, R P. Pp. 32-48. London: Oxford University Press.

3716 Money, J, A A Ehrhardt. 1972. *Man and Woman, Boy and Girl: The Differentiation and Dimorphism of Gender Identity from Conception to Maturity.* Baltimore: Johns Hopkins.

3717 Money, J. 1975. Nativism versus culturalism in gender-identity differentiation. In *Sexuality and Psychoanalysis.* Edited by Adelson, S. Pp. 48-66. New York: Brunner & Mazel.

3718 Money, J, M Schwartz. 1977. Dating, romantic and nonromantic friendship and sexuality in 17 early-treated androgenital females aged 16-25. In *Congenital Adrenal Hyperplasia,.* Edited by Lee, P H, L P Kowarski, C J Migeon. Baltimore: University Park Press.

3719 Money, J. 1980. *Love and Love Sickness: The Science of Sex, Gender Differences, and Pair Bonding.* Baltimore: Johns Hopkins.

3720 Money, J, D Matthews. 1982. Prenatal exposure to virilizing progestins: An adult follow-up study of twelve women. *Archives of Sexual Behavior* 11: 73-83.

3721 Money, J. 1984. Differentiation of gender identity role. *Delaware Medical Journal* 56: 161-171.

3722 Money, J. 1984. Homosexual genesis, outcome studies, and a nature/nurture paradigm shift. In *Endorphins, Neuroregulators and Behavior in Human Reproduction.* Edited by Pancheri, P, L Zichella, P Falschi. Amsterdam: Excerpta Medica.

3723 Money, J. 1984. Family and gender-identity role. Part I: Childhood-coping and adult follow-up of micropenis syndrome in a case with female sex assignment. *International Journal of Family Psychiatry* 5: 317-339.

3724 Money, J. 1984. Family and gender-identity role. Part II: Transexual versus homosexual coping in micropenis syndrome with male sex assignment. *International Journal of Family Psychiatry* 5: 340-359.

3725 Money, J. 1986. *Venuses Penises: Sexology, Sexosophy, and Exigency Theory.* Buffalo, NY: Prometheus Books.

3726 Money, J. 1988. *Gay, Straight, and In-between: The Sexology of Erotic Orientation.* New York: Oxford University Press.

3727 Money, J, H Musaph, eds. 1988. *Handbook of Sexology: Vol VI The Pharmacology and Endocrinology of Sexual Function.* New York: Elsevier.

3728 Mosher, D L, R D Anderson. 1986. Macho personality, sexual aggression, and reactions to guided imagery of realistic rape. *Journal of Research in Personality* 20: 77-94.

3729 Neely, J C. 1981. *Gender: The Myth of Equality.* New York: Simon & Schuster.

3730 Newcombe, N, N M Bandura, D G Taylor. 1983. Sex differences in spatial ability and spatial activities. *Sex Roles* 9: 377-386.

3731 Norton, J L. 1982. The effect of changing sex roles on male homosexuals. In *Men in Transition: Theory and Therapy.* Edited by Solomon, K, N B Levy. Pp. 151-164. New York: Plenum.

3732 Olweus, D. 1979. Stability of aggressive reaction patterns in males: A review. *Psychological Bulletin* 86: 852-875.

3733 Palmer, C. 1988. Twelve reasons why rape is not sexually motivated: A skeptical examination. *Journal of Sex Research* 25: 512-30.

3734 Palmer, C. 1989. Rape in nonhuman animal societies: Definitions, evidence, and implications. *Journal of Sex Research* 25: 355-75.

3735 Parson, J E, ed. 1980. *The Psychobiology of Sex Differences and Sex Roles.* Washington, D.C.: Hemisphere.

3736 Persky, H, et al. 1982. The relation of plasma androgen levels to sexual behaviors and attitudes of women. *Psychosomatic Medicine* 44: 305-319.

3737 Petersen, A C. 1980. Biopsychosocial processes in the development of sex-related differences. In *The Psychobiology of Sex Differences and Sex Roles*. Edited by Parsons, J E. Washington, D.C.: Hemisphere.

3738 Pitcher, E G, L H Schultz. 1983. *Boys and Girls at Play—The Development of Sex Roles*. New York: Praeger.

3739 Prentky, R A, V L Quinsey, eds. 1988. *Human Sexual Aggression: Current Perspectives*. New York: New York Academy of Sciences.

3740 Purins, J E, R Langevin. 1985. Brain correlates of penile erection. In *Erotic Preference, Gender Identity and Aggression in Men: New Research Studies*. Edited by Langevin, R. Pp. 113-33. Hillsdale, NJ: Erlbaum.

3741 Quinsey, V L, T C Chaplin. 1982. Penile responses to nonsexual violence among rapists. *Criminal Justice and Behavior* 9: 372-81.

3742 Ramirez, J, J Bryant, D Zillmann. 1982. Effects of erotica on retaliatory behavior as a function of level of prior provocation. *Journal of Personality and Social Psychology* 43: 971-78.

3743 Reinisch, J M, L A Rosenblum, S A Sanders, eds. 1987. *Masculinity/Femininity: Basic Perspectives*. Oxford: Oxford University Press.

3744 Reiss, I. 1960. *Premarital Sex Standards in America*. Glencoe, IL: Free Press.

3745 Richmond-Abbott, M. 1983. *Masculine and Feminine: Sex Roles over the Life Cycle*. Reading, MA: Addison-Wesley.

3746 Rogers, L J. 1981. Biology: Gender differentiation and sexual variation. In *Feminist Perspectives: Interdisciplinary Collection of Women's Studies*. Edited by Grieve, N, P Grimshaw. Pp. 44-57. New York: Oxford University Press.

3747 Rogers, L J, J Walsh. 1982. Short-comings of the psychomedical research of John Money and co-workers into sex differences in behaviour. *Sex Roles* 8: 269-281.

3748 Rogers, L J. 1983. Hormonal theories for sex differences—Politics diagnosed as science: A reply to Debold and Luria. *Sex Roles* 9: 1109-1113.

3749 Rogers, L. 1988. Sex differences in cognitive function. In *Crossing Boundaries: Feminisms and the Critique of Knowledges.* Edited by Craine, B. Sydney: Allen and Unwin.

3750 Rubin, R T, J M Reinisch, R F Haskett. 1981. Postnatal gonadal steroid effects on human behavior. *Science* 211: 1318-1324.

3751 Ruse, M. 1988. *Homosexuality.* Oxford: Blackwell.

3752 Salvador, A, V Simon, F Suay, L Llorens. 1987. Testosterone and cortisol responses to competitive fighting in human males: A pilot study. *Aggressive Behavior* 13: 9-13.

3753 Sanday, P R. 1981. The socio-cultural context of rape: A cross-cultural study. *Journal of Social Issues* 37: 5-27.

3754 Sanday, P R. 1990. *Fraternity Gang Rape: Sex, Brotherhood, and Privilege on Campus.* New York: New York University Press.

3755 Sanders, D, P Warner, T Backstrom, J Bancroft. 1983. Mood, sexuality, hormones and the menstrual cycle changes in mood and physical state: Description of subjects and methods. *Psychosomatic Medicine* 45: 487-501.

3756 Scacco, A M, ed. 1982. *Male Rape : A Casebook of Sexual Aggressions.* New York: AMS Press.

3757 Schumacher, M, J J Legros, J Balthazart. 1987. Steroid hormones, behavior and sexual dimorphism in animals and men: The nature-nurture controversy. *Experimental and Clincial Endocrinology* 90: 129-156.

3758 Shatan, C F. 1978. Bogus manhood, bogus honor: Surrender and transfiguration in the United States Marine Corps. In *Psychoanalytic Perspectives on Aggression.* Edited by Goldman, G D, D S Milman. Pp. 77-100. Dubuque, Iowa: Kendall & Hunt.

3759 Shaver, P, C Hendrick, eds. 1986. *Sex and Gender: Review of Personality and Social Psychology.* Newbury Park, CA: Sage.

3760 Shields, W, L Shields. 1983. Forcible rape: An evolutoinary perspective. *Ethology and Sociobiology* 4: 115-36.

3761 Short, R V. 1980. The origins of human sexuality. In *Reproduction in Mammals: Human Sexuality.* Edited by Austin, C R, R V Short. Pp. 1-33. Cambridge: Cambridge University Press.

3762 Sigvardsson, S, C R Cloniger, M Bohman, A Knorring von. 1982. Predispositions to petty criminality in Swedish Adoptees 2. Sex differences and validation of the male typology. *Archives of General Psychiatry* 39: 1248-1253.

3763 Sitsen, J M A. 1988. The Pharmacology and Endocrinology of Sexual Function. In *Handbook of Sexology.* Edited by Money, J, H Musaph. Amsterdam: Elsevier.

3764 Solomon, K, N Levy, eds. 1982. *Men in Transition: Theory and Therapy.* New York: Plenum.

3765 Solomon, K. 1982. The masculine gender role: Description. In *Men in Transition: Theory and Therapy.* Edited by Solomon, K, N Levy. Pp. 45-76. New York: Plenum Press.

3766 Steinmann, A, D J Fox. 1974. *The Male DilemMA* New York: Jason Aronson.

3767 Stoller, R J. 1968. *Sex and Gender.* New York: Science House.

3768 Symonds, D. 1979. *The Evolution of Human Sexuality.* Oxford: Oxford University Press.

3769 Symons, D, B Ellis. 1989. Human male-female differences in sexual desire. In *The Sociobiology of Sexual and Reproductive Strategies.* Edited by Rasa, A E, C Vogel, E Voland. Pp. 131-146. London: Chapman and Hall.

3770 Tauber, E S. 1940. Effects of castration upon the sexuality of the male. *Psychosomatic Medicine* 2: 74-87.

3771 Thornhill, R, N W Thornhill. 1983. Human rape: An evolutionary analysis. *Ethology and Sociobiology* 4: 137-174.

3772 Thornhill, R, N W Thornhill, G Dizinno. 1986. The biology of rape. In *Rape.* Edited by Tomaselli, S, R Porter. Oxford: Blackwell.

3773 Thornhill, N W, R Thornhill. 1990. An evolutionary analysis of psychological pain following rape. 1. The effects of victim's age and marital status. *Ethology and Sociobiology* 11: 155-176.

3774 Thornhill, R, N W Thornhill. 1992. The evolutionary psychology of men's coercive sexuality. *Behavioral and Brain Sciences* 15: 363-421.

3775 Tomaselli, S, R Porter, eds. 1986. *Rape.* Rape. Oxford: Blackwell.

3776 Velle, W. 1982. Sex hormones and behavior in animals and man. *Perspectives in Biology and Medicine* 25: 295-315.

3777 Von Saal, F S, W M Grant, C W McMullen, K S Laves. 1983. High fetal estrogen concentrations: Correlation with increased adult sexual activity and decreased aggression in male mice. *Science* 220: 1306-1309.

3778 Waber, D P. 1977. Sex differences in mental abilities, hemispheric lateralization, and rate of physical growth at adolescence. *Developmental Psychology* 13: 29-38.

3779 Ward, I L. 1972. Prenatal stress feminizes and demasculinizes the behavior of males. *Science* 175: 82-84.

3780 Ward, I. 1978. Sexual behavior differentiation: Prenatal hormonal and environmental control. In *Sex Differences in Behavior.* Edited by Friedman, R C, R M Richart, R L Vande Wiele. Pp. 3-17. New York: Krieger, Huntington.

3781 Ward, I L. 1978. Sexual behavior differentiation: Prenatal hormonal and environmental control. In *Sex Differences in Behavior.* Edited by Friedman, R C, R M Richart, R L Vande Wiele. New York: Krieger, Huntington.

3782 Ward, J L, J Weisz. 1980. Maternal stress alters plasma testosterone in fetal males. *Science* 207: 328-329.

3783 Ward, J L. 1982. Prenatal stress feminizes and demasculinizes the behavior of males. *Science* 175: 82-83.

3784 Ward, I L. 1984. The prenatal stress syndrome: Current status. *Psychoneuroendocrinology* 9: 3-11.

3785 Ward, I L, J Weisz. 1984. Differential effects of maternal stress on circulating levels of corticoterone, progesterone, and testosterone in male and female rat fetuses and their mothers. *Endocrinology* 114: 1635-1644.

3786 Widom, C, ed. 1983. *Sex Roles and Psychopathology.* New York: Plenum.

3787 Wittig, M A, A C Petersen, eds. 1979. *Sex Related Issues in Cognitive Functioning: Developmental Issues.* New York: Academic Press.

3788 Woodbury, J, E Schwartz. 1971. *The Silent Sin.* New York: Signet.

3789 Yalon, I D, R Green, N Fisk. 1973. Prenatal exposure to female hormones: Effect on psychosexual development in boys. *Archives of General Psychiatry* 28: 554-561.

# 10

# Endocrinology

3790 Ader, R. 1975. Early experience and hormones: Emotional behavior and adrenocortical function. In *Hormonal Correlates of Behaviour*. Edited by Eleftheriou, B E, R L Sprott. Pp. 7-33. New York: Plenum.

3791 Andrew, R J, L J Rogers. 1972. Testosterone, search behaviour and persistence. *Nature* 237: 343-346.

3792 Antelman, S M, A R Caggiula. 1977. Norepinephrine-dopamine interactions and behavior. *Science* 195: 646-50.

3793 Apter, A, S-L Brown, M L Korn, H M v Praag. 1991. Serotonergic parameters of aggression and suicide. In *The Role of Serotonin in Psychiatric Disorders*. Edited by Brown, S-L, H M v Praag. Pp. 284-301. New York: Brunner/Mazel.

3794 Axelrod, J, T D Reisine. 1984. Stress hormones: Their interaction and regulation. *Science* 224: 452-59.

3795 Azmitia, E C. 1978. The serotonin producing neurons of the midbrain median and dorsalraphe nuclei. In *Handbook of Psychopharmacology*. Edited by Iversen, L L, S D Iversen, S H Snyder. Pp. 233-314. New York: Plenum.

3796 Bartus, R T, R L Dean, B Beer, A S Lippa. 1982. The cholinergic hypothesis of geriatric memory dysfunction. *Science* 227: 408-417.

3797 Beck-Friis, J, et al. 1984. Melatonin in relation to body measures, sex, age, season, and use of drugs in patients with major affective disorders and healthy subjects. *Psychoneuroendocrinology* 9: 261-77.

3798 Bell, R, P G Hepper. 1987. Catecholamines and aggression in animals. *Behavioural and Brain Research* 23: 1-21.

3799 Benton, D, ed. 1987. *Hormones and Human Behaviour*. London: Longmans.

3800 Bermond, B, et al. 1982. Aggression induced by stimulation of the hypothalamus: Effects of androgens. *Pharmacology, Biochemistry and Behavior* 16: 441-454.

3801 Bernstein, I, T P Gordon, R M Rose. 1983. The interaction of hormones, behavior and social context in nonhuman primates. In *Hormones and Aggressive Behavior.* Edited by Svare, B B. Pp. 535-61. New York: Plenum.

3802 Berrebi, A S, R H Fitch, D L Ralphe, J O Denenberg, V L Friedrich, V H Denenberg. 1988. Corpus callosum: Region-specific effects of sex, early experience, and age. *Brain Research* 438: 216-24.

3803 Besser, G, L Martini, eds. 1982. *Clinical Neuroendocrinology.* New York: Academic Press.

3804 Besson, J-M, ed. 1990. *Serotonin and Pain.* Amsterdam: Excerpta Medica.

3805 Bevan, P, A R Cools, T Archer. 1989. *Behavioral Pharmacology.* Hillsdale, NJ: Erlbaum.

3806 Bleier, R, W Byne, I Siggelkow. 1982. Cytoarchitectonic sexual dimorphisms of the medial preoptic and anterior hypothalamic areas in guinea pig, rat, hamster, and mouse. *Journal of Comparative Neurology* 212: 118-30.

3807 Blundell, J E. 1984. Systems and interactions: An approach to the pharmacology of eating and hunger. In *Eating and Its Disorders.* Edited by Stunkard, A J, E Stellar. Pp. 39-65. New York: Raven Press.

3808 Brandao, M L, G DiScala, M J Bouchet, P Schmitt. 1986. Escape behavior produced by the blockade of glutamic acid decarboxylase (GAD) in the mesencephalic central gray or medial hypothalamus. *Pharmacology, Biochemistry and Behavior* 24: 497-501.

3809 Britton, D R, et al. 1982. Intraventricular corticotropin-releasing factor enhances behavioral effects of novelty. *Life Sciences* 31: 363-7.

3810 Bronson, F H, C Desjardins. 1971. Steroid hormones and aggressive behavior in mammals. In *The Physiology of Aggression and Defeat.* Edited by Eleftheriou, B, J Scott. London: Plenum.

3811 Brown, G L, et al. 1982. Aggression, suicide and serotonin: Relationship to CSF amine metabolites. *American Journal of Psychiatry* 139: 741-746.

3812 Buydens-Branchey, L, M H Branchey. 1992. Cortisol in alcoholics with a disordered aggression control. *Psychoneuroendocrinology* 17:45-54.

3813 Byne, W, R Bleier, L Houston. 1988. Variations in human corpus callosum do not predict gender: A study using magnetic resonance imaging. *Behavioral Neuroscience* 102: 222-227.

3814 Carani, C, J Bancroft, G D Rio, A R M Granata, F Facchinetti, P Marrama. 1990. The endocrine effects of visual erotic stimuli in normal men. *Psychoneuroendocrinology* 15: 207-216.

3815 Carli, G, G L Diprisco, G Martelli, A Viti. 1982. Hormonal changes in soccer players during an agonistic season. *Journal of Sport Medicine* 22: 489-494.

3816 Christian, J J. 1975. Hormonal control of population growth. In *Hormonal Correlates of Behaviour*. Edited by Eleftheriou, B E, R L Sprott. Pp. 205-274. New York: Plenum.

3817 Christian, J J. 1980. Endocrine factors in population regulation. In *Biosocial Mechanisms of Population Regulation*. Edited by Cohen, M N, R S Malpass, H G Klein. Pp. 55-116. New Haven: Yale University Press.

3818 Christiansen, K, R Knussmann. 1987. Sex hormones and cognitive functioning in men. *Neuropsychobiology* 18: 27-36.

3819 Clarke, S, R Kraftsik, H van der Loos, G M Innocenti. 1989. Forms and measures of adult and developing human corpus callosum: Is there sexual dimorphism? *Journal of Comparative Neurology* 280: 213-230.

3820 Clayton, R N, K J Catt. 1981. Gonadotropin-releasing hormone receptors: Characterization, physiologic regulation and relationship to reproductive function. *Endocrine Review* 2: 186-209.

3821 Clodoré, M, J Foret, O Benoit, Y Touitou, A Aguirre, G Bouard, C Touitou. 1990. Psychophysiological effects of early morning bright light exposure in young adults. *Psychoneuroendocrinology* 15: 193-205.

3822 Coe, C L, S Levine. 1983. Biology of aggression. *Bulletin of the American Academy of Psychiatry and the Law* 11: 131-148.

3823 Cohen, M P, P P Foà, eds. 1988. *The Brain as an Endocrine Organ*. New York: Springer.

3824 Comings, D E. 1979. Pel Duarte, a common polymorphism of human brain protein, and its relationship to depressive disease and multiple sclerosis. *Nature* 277: 28-32.

3825 Conner, R L, S Levine, G A Wertheim. 1969. Hormonal determinants of aggressive behavior. *Annals of the New York Academy of Sciences* 159: 760-776.

3826 Conte, F A, M M Grumbach, S L Kaplan, E O Reiter. 1981. Correlation of LRF-induced LH and FSH release from infance to 19 years with the changing pattern of gonadotropin secretion in agonadal patients. *Journal of Clinical Endocrinology and Metabolism* 50: 1163-68.

3827 Costa, E, ed. 1987. *The Benzodiazepines: From Molecular Biology to Clinical Practice.* New York: Raven Press.

3828 Cowley, J J. 1978. Olfaction and the development of sexual behavior. In *Biological Determinants of Sexual Behavior.* Edited by Hutchinson, J B. Pp. 87-126. New York: Wiley.

3829 Cumming, D, M Quigley, S Yen. 1983. Acute suppression of circulating testosterone levels by cortisol in men. *Journal of Clinical Endocrinology and Metabolism* 57: 671-679.

3830 Dabbs, J M, R L Frady, T S Carr, N F Besch. 1987. Saliva testosterone and criminal violence in young adult prison inmates. *Psychosomatic Medicine* 49: 174-182.

3831 Dabbs, J M, R B Ruback, R L Frady, C H Hopper, D S Sgoutas. 1988. Saliva testosterone and criminal violence among women. *Personality and Individual Differences* 9: 269-275.

3832 Dabbs, J, R J Morris. 1990. Testosterone, social class, and antisocial behavior in a sample of 4,462 men. *Psychological Science* 1: 209-211.

3833 Davis, B A, P H Yu, A A Boulton, J S Wormith, D Addington. 1983. Correlative relationship between biochemical activity and aggressive behavior. *Progress in Neuropsychopharmacology and Biological Psychiatry* 7: 529-535.

3834 De Lacoste, M C, R L Holloway, D J Woodward. 1986. Sex differences in the fetal human corpus callosum. *Human Neurobiology* 5: 93-96.

3835 De Vris, G J, J P C De Bruin, H B M Yulings, M A Corner, eds. 1984. *Sex Differences in the Brain: The Relation Between Structure and Function.* Amsterdam: Elsevier.

3836 Delitala, G, M Motta, M Serio, eds. 1984. *Opioid Modulation of Endocrine Function.* New York: Raven Press.

3837 DePaulis, A, M Vergnes. 1985. Elicitation of conspecific attack of defense in the male rat by intraventricular injections of a GABA agonist or antagonist. *Physiology and Behavior* 35: 447-453.

3838 Descarries, L, H H Jasper, eds. 1984. *Monomine Innervation of the Cerebral Cortex.* New York: Alan R. Liss.

3839 Diamond, M C. 1991. Hormonal effects on the development of cerebral lateralization. *Psychoneuroendocrinology* 16: 121-129.

3840 Diaz, J, G Ellison, D Masuoka. 1978. Stages of recovery from central norepinephrine lesions in enriched and impoverished environments: A behavioral and biochemical study. *Experimental Brain Research* 31: 117-130.

3841 Donovan, B T. 1985. *Hormones and Human Behaviour.* Cambridge: Cambridge University Press.

3842 Dunn, A J, N R Kramarcy. 1984. Neurochemical responses in stress: Relationships between the hypothalamic-pituitary-adrenal and catecholamine systems. In *Handbook of Psychopharmacology.* Edited by Iverson, L L, S D Iversen, S H Snyder. Pp. 455-515. New York: Plenum Press.

3843 Edwards, D A. 1969. Early androgen stimulation and aggressive behavior in male and female mice. *Physiology of Behavior* 4: 333-338.

3844 Eleftheriov, B E, S P Nam, eds. 1971. *The Physiology of Aggression and Defeat.* London: Plenum.

3845 Elias, M. 1981. Serum cortisol, testosterone, and testosterone-binding globulin responses to competitive fighting in human males. *Aggressive Behavior* 7: 215-24.

3846 Ellis, L. 1982. Developmental androgen fluctuations and the five dimensions of mammalian sex. *Ethology and Sociobiology* 3: 171-197.

3847 Ellis, L. 1991. Monoamine oxidase and criminality: Identifying an apparent biological marker for antisocial behavior. *Journal of Research in Crime and Delinquency* 28: 227-251.

3848 Elwood, R W. 1986. What makes male mice paternal? *Behavioral and Neural Biology* 46: 54-63.

3849 Essman, W B, ed. 1980. *Neurotransmitters, Receptors and Drug Action.* Lancaster: Spectrum Publications.

3850 Fichter, M M, K M Pirke, F Holsboer. 1986. Weight loss causes neuroendocrine disturbances: Experimental study in healthy starving subjects. *Psychological Research* 17: 61-72.

3851 Floody, O R. 1983. Hormones and aggression in female mammals. In *Hormones and Aggressive Behavior*. Edited by Svare, B B. Pp. 39-90. New York: Plenum.

3852 Frey, H. 1982. The endocrine response to physical exercise. *Scandinavian Journal of Social Medicine* Supplement 1: 71-75.

3853 Fride, E, M Weinstock. 1987. Increased interhemispheric coupling of the dopamine systems induced by prenatal stress. *Brain Research Bulletin* 18: 457-461.

3854 Friedhoff, A J. 1986. A dopamine-dependent restitutive system for the maintenance of mental normalcy. *Annals of the New York Academy of Sciences* 463: 47-52.

3855 Gandelman, R. 1983. Gonadal hormones and sensory function. *Neuroscience and Biobehavioral Reviews* 7: 1-17.

3856 Gandelman, R. 1984. Relative contributions of aggression and reproduction to behavioral endocrinology. *Aggressive Behavior* 10: 120-133.

3857 Ganten, D, D Pfaff, eds. 1988. *Neuroendocrinology of Mood.* Berlin: Springer.

3858 Geen, R G, E I Donnerstein, eds. 1983. *Aggression: Theoretical and Methodological Issues.* New York: Academic Press.

3859 Genazzani, A R, J H Thijssen, P K Siiteri, eds. 1980. *Adrenal Androgens.* New York: Raven Press.

3860 Gerendai, I. 1984. Lateralization of neuroendocrine control. In *Cerebral Dominance: The Biological Foundations.* Edited by Geshwind, N, A M Glaburda. Cambridge: Harvard University Press.

3861 Gerner, R H, B Sharp. 1982. CSF ß-endorphin immunoreactivity in normal, schizophrenic, depressed, manic and anorexic subjects. *Brain Research* 237: 244-47.

3862 Gladue, B A, R Green, R E Hellman. 1984. Neuroendocrine response to estrogen and sexual orientation. *Science* 225: 1496-69.

3863 Gladue, B, M Boechler , K McCaul. 1989. Hormonal response to competition in human males. *Aggressive Behavior* 15: 409-422.

3864 Glincher, P W, A A Giovino, D H Margolin, B G Hoebel. 1984. Endogenous opiate reward induced by enkephalinase inhibitor, thiorphan, injected into the ventral midbrain. *Behavioral Neuroscience* 98: 262-268.

3865 Gooren, L. 1990. The endocrinology of transsexualism: A review and commentary. *Psychoneuroendocrinology* 15: 3-14.

3866 Gouchie, C, D Kimura. 1991. The relationship between testosterone levels and cognitive ability patterns. *Psychoneuroendocrinology* 16:323-34.

3867 Goy, R W, B S McEwen. 1980. *Sexual Differentiation of the Brain.* Cambridge: M.I.T. Press.

3868 Goy, R W, F B Bercovitch, M C McBrair. 1988. Behavioral masculinization is independent of genital masculinization in prenatally androgenized female rhesus macaques. *Hormones and Behavior* 22: 552-71.

3869 Greenough, W T, J M Juraska, eds. 1986. *Developmental Neuropsychobiology.* New York: Academic Press.

3870 Halberg, F. 1982. Biological rhythms, hormones, and aging. In *Hormones in Development and Aging.* Edited by Vernadakis, A, P Timiras. Pp. 451-476. New York: SPMS Books.

3871 Hampson, E. 1990. Estrogen-related variations in human spatial articulatory-motor skills. *Psychoneuroendocrinology* 15: 97-111.

3872 Harvey, P W, P F D Chevins. 1985. Crowding pregnant mice affects attack and threat behavior of male offspring. *Hormones and Behavior* 19: 86-97.

3873 Hassler, M. 1991. Testosterone and artistic talents. *International Journal of Neuroscience* 56: 25-38.

3874 Hassler, M. 1992. Creative musical behavior and sex hormones: Musical talent and spatial ability in the two sexes. *Psychoneuroendocrinology* 17: 55-70.

3875 Henry, J P. 1986. Neuroendocrine response patterns. In *Emotion: Theory, Research, and Experience: Biological Foundations of Emotion.* Edited by Plutchik, R, H Kellerman. Pp. 37-60. New York: Academic Press.

3876 Hier, D V, W F Crowley. 1982. Spatial ability in androgen-deficient men. *New England Journal of Medicine* 306: 1202-1205.

3877 Ho, B T, et al., eds. 1982. *Serotonin in Biological Psychiatry.* New York: Raven Press.

3878 Hoebel, B G. 1984. Neurotransmitters in the control of feeding and its rewards: Monoamines, opiates and brain-gut peptides. In *Eating and Its Disorders.* Edited by Stunkard, A J, E Stellar. Pp. 5-38. New York: Raven Press.

3879 Hosobuchi, Y, F E Bloom. 1983. Analgesia induced by brain stimulation in man: Its effect on release of ß-endorphin and adrenocorticotropin into cerebrospinal fluid. In *Neurobiology of Cerebrospinal Fluid.* Edited by Wood, J H. Pp. 97-105. New York: Plenum.

3880 Hutchinson, J B. 1978. Hypothalamic regulation of male sexual responsiveness to androgen. In *Biological Determinants of Sexual Behavior.* Edited by Hutchinson, J B. Pp. 277-318. New York: Wiley.

3881 Hutchison, J B, ed. 1978. *Biological Determinants of Sexual Behavior.* New York: Wiley.

3882 Hutt, C. 1972. *Males and Females.* London: Penguin.

3883 Hyde, J S. 1984. How large are gender differences in aggression? A developmental meta-analysis. *Developmental Psychobiology* 20: 722-36.

3884 Hyde, J S. 1986. Gender differences in aggression. In *The Psychology of Gender: Advances through Meta-analysis.* Edited by Hyde, J, M Linn. Pp. 51-66. Baltimore: Johns Hopkins.

3885 Hyde, J S, M C Linn. 1988. Gender differences in verbal ability: A meta-analysis. *Psychological Bulletin* 102: 53-69.

3886 Illnerova, H, P Zvokky, J Vanecek. 1985. The circadian rhythm in plasma melatonin concentration of the urbanized man: The effect of summer and winter time. *Brain Research* 328: 186-189.

3887 Immelmann, K, K R Schere, C Vogel, P Schmoock. 1988. *Psychobiologie: Grundlagen des Verhalten.* Munich: Gustav Fischer.

3888 Issacson, R L. 1982. *The Limbic System.* 2nd ed. New York: Plenum.

3889 Iversen, S D, L L Iversen. 1981. *Behavioral Pharmacology.* New York: Oxford University Press.

3890 Iverson, S. 1984. Cortical monamines and behavior. In *Monoamine Innervation of the Cerebral Cortex.* Edited by Descarries, L, H H Jasper. Pp. 321-349. New York: Alan R. Liss.

3891 Jacklin, C N, E E Maccoby. 1983. Issues of gender differentiation. In *Developmental Behavioral Pediatrics.* Edited by Levine, M D, W B Carey, A C Crocker, R T Gross. New York: Saunders.

3892 James, V H T, M Serio, G Giush, L L Martini. 1978. *The Endocrine Function of the Human Adrenal Cortex.* London: Academic Press.

3893 James, W H. 1986. Hormonal control of the sex ratio. *Journal of Theoretical Biology* 118: 427-41.

3894 Juraska, J. 1991. Sex differences in "cognitive" regions of the rat brain. *Psychoneuroendocrinology* 16: 105-19.

3895 Kalin, N H, S E Shelton. 1989. Defensive behaviors in infant rhesus monkeys: Environmental cues and neurochemical regulation. *Science* 243: 1718-21.

3896 Kanarek, R, G H Collier. 1983. Self-starvation: A problem of overriding the satiety signal? *Physiology and Behavior* 30: 307-311.

3897 Kemper, T D. 1991. *Social Structure and Testosterone: Explorations of the Socio-Bio-Social Chain.* New Brunswick, NJ: Rutgers University Press.

3898 Keverne, E B, R E Meller. 1983. Social influences on circulating levels of cortisol and prolactin in male talapoin monkeys. *Physiology and Behaviour* 30: 361-369.

3899 Koob, G F, F E Bloom. 1983. Behavioural effects of opioid peptides. *British Medical Bulletin* 39: 89-94.

3900 Krieger, D T. 1979. *Endocrine Rhythms.* New York: Raven Press.

3901 Larsson, K. 1978. Experiental factors in the development of sexual behavior. In *Biological Determinants of Sexual Behaviour.* Edited by Hutchinson, J B. Pp. 55-86. New York: Wiley.

3902 Leedy, M G, M S Wilson. 1985. Testosterone and cortisol levels in crewmen of United States Air Force fighter and cargo planes. *Psychosomatic Medicine* 47: 333-338.

3903 Leshner, A I. 1978. *An Introduction to Behavioral Endocrinology.* New York: Oxford University Press.

3904 Leshner, A I. 1981. The role of hormones in the control of submissiveness. In *Multidisciplinary Approaches to Aggression Research.* Edited by Brain, P F, D Benton. Pp. 309-22. Amsterdam: Elsevier/North Holland.

3905 Leshner, A I. 1983. Pituitary-adrenocortical effects on intermale agonistic behavior. In *Hormones and Aggressive Behavior.* Edited by Svare, B B. Pp. 27-37. New York: Plenum.

3906 Leshner, A I. 1983. The hormonal responses to competition and their behavioral significance. In *Hormones and Aggressive Behavior.* Edited by Svare, B B. Pp. 393-404. New York: Plenum.

3907 Levi, L. 1965. The urinary output of adrenaline and noradrenaline during different experimentally induced pleasant and unpleasant emotional states. *Psychosomatic Medicine* 27: 80-5.

3908 Lieberman, J, S Cooper. 1989. *The Neuropharmocological Basis of Reward.* London: Oxford University Press.

3909 Lipton, M A, A D Mascio, K F Killam. 1978. *Psychopharmacology: A Generation of Progress.* New York: Raven Press.

3910 Luger, A, et al. 1987. Acute hypothalamic-pituitary-adrenal responses to the stress of treadmill exercise: Physiologic adaptations to physical training. *New England Journal of Medicine* 316: 1309-15.

3911 Maas, J W, J F Leckman. 1983. Relationships between central nervous system noradrenergic function and plasma and urinary MHPS and other norepinephrine metabolites. In *MHPG, Basic Mechanisms and Psychopathology.* Edited by Maas, J W. New York: Academic Press.

3912 MacConnie, S E, et al. 1986. Decreased hypothalamic gonadotropin-releasing hormone secretion in male marathon runners. *New England Journal of Medicine* 315: 411-7.

3913 MacLusky, N J, F Naftolin. 1981. Sexual differentiation of the central nervous system. *Science* 211: 1294-1303.

3914 Madsen, D, M T McGuire. 1984. Whole blood serotonin and Type A behavior pattern. *Psychosomatic Medicine* 46: 546-548.

3915 Marrazzi, M, E Luby, eds. 1988. *The Brain as an Endocrine Organ*. New York: Springer.

3916 Marrazzi, M, E Luby. 1988. The neurobiology of anorexia nervosa: An auto-addiction? In *The Brain as an Endocrine Organ*. Edited by Cohen, M, P Foà. Pp. 46-95. New York: Springer.

3917 Martini, L, W F Gangong, eds. 1971. *Frontiers in Neuroendocrinology*. New York: Oxford University Press.

3918 Mason, S T, S D Iversen. 1978. Reward, attention and dorsal noradrenergic bundle. *Brain Research* 150: 135-148.

3919 Mason, S T, S D Iversen. 1979. Theories of the dorsal bundle extinction effect. *Brain Research Review* 1: 107-137.

3920 Mason, S T. 1981. Noradrenaline in the brain: Progress in theories of behavioural function. *Progress in Neurobiology* 16: 263-303.

3921 Mason, S T. 1983. *Catecholamines and Behaviour*. Cambridge: Cambridge University Press.

3922 Mazur, A, T A Lamb. 1980. Testosterone status and mood in human males. *Hormonal Behavior* 14: 236-246.

3923 McCormick, C M, S F Witelson, E Kingstone. 1990. Left-handedness in homosexual men and women: Neuroendocrine implications. *Psychoneuroendocrinology* 15: 69-76.

3924 McEwen, B S. 1983. Gonadal steroid influences on brain development and sexual differentiation. In *International Review of Psychology*. Edited by Greep, R O. Baltimore: University Park Press.

3925 McGuire, M T, M J Raleigh, C Johnson. 1983. Social dominance in adult male vervet monkeys. II. Behavior-biochemical relationships. *Social Science Information* 22: 265-287.

3926 McKeever, W F, R A Deyo. 1990. Testosterone, dihydrotestosterone, and spatial task performances of males. *Bulletin of the Psychonomic Society* 28: 305-308.

3927 Meites, J. 1984. Effects of opiates on neuroendocrine functions in animals: An overview. In *Opioid Modulation of Endocrine Function*. Edited by Delitala, G, M Motta, M Serio. Pp. 53-63. New York: Raven Press.

3928 Michael, R P, ed. 1968. *Endocrinology and Human Behavior.* New York: Oxford University Press.

3929 Miller, R E. 1974. Social and pharmacological influences on the nonverbal communication of monkeys and of man. In *Nonverbal Communication.* Edited by Krames, L, P Pliner, T Alloway. New York: Plenum.

3930 Moghissi, K. 1988. Gonadotropin Releasing Hormones: Physiopathology and Clinical Applications. In *The Brain as an Endocrine Organ.* Edited by Cohen, M, P Foà. Pp. 1-13. New York: Springer-Verlag.

3931 Montagner, H, et al. 1978. Behavioural profiles and corticosteroid excretion rhythms in young children. In *Human Behaviour and Adaptation.* Edited by Blurton-Jones, N, V Reynolds. London: Taylor & Francis.

3932 Morley, J E, A S Levine. 1985. Pharmacology of eating behavior. *Annual Review of Phrmacological Toxicology* 25: 127-146.

3933 Morris, M, et al. 1990. Endogenous opioids modulate the cardiovascular response to mental stress. *Psychoneuroendocrinology* 15: 185-92.

3934 Morrison, J H, S L Foote, F E Bloom. 1984. Regional, laminar, developmental, and fuctional characteristics of noradrenaline and serotonin innervation patters in monkey coretex. In *Monoamine Innervation of the Cerebral Cortex.* Edited by Descarries, L, H H Jasper. Pp. 61-75. New York: Alan R. Liss.

3935 Nass, R, S Baker. 1991. Androgen effects on cognition: Congenital adrenal hyperplasia. *Psychoneuroendocrinology* 16: 189-201.

3936 Nicholson, A, A Belyavin, P Pascoe. 1989. Modulation of rapid eye movement sleep in humans by drugs that modify monoaminergic and purinergic transmission. *Neuropsychopharmacology* 2: 131-139.

3937 Nyborg, H, J Nielsen. 1981. Sex Hormone Treatment and Spatial Ability in Women with Turner's Syndrome. In *Human Behavior and Genetics.* Edited by Schmid, W, J Nielsen. Amsterdam: Elsevier.

3938 Nyborg, H. 1984. Performance and intelligence in hormonally different groups. In *Sex Differences in the Brain: The Relationship Between Structure and Function. Progress in Brain Research.* Edited by De Vries, G J, J P C DeBruin, H B M Uylings, M A Corner. Amsterdam: Elsevier.

3939 Nyborg, H. 1988. Mathematics, sex hormones, and brain function. *Behavioral and Brain Sciences* 11: 206-207.

3940 Ounsted, C, D C Taylor, eds. 1972. *Gender Differences: Their Ontogeny and Significance.* London: Livingstone.

3941 Palpinger, L, B S McEwen. 1978. Gonadal steroid-brain interactions in sexual differentiation. In *Biological Determinants of Sexual Behavior.* Edited by Hutchinson, J B. Pp. 153-218. New York: Wiley.

3942 Pancheri, P, L Zichella, P Falschi, eds. 1984. *Endorphins, Neuroregulators and Behavior in Human Reproduction.* Amsterdam: Excerpta Medicax.

3943 Panksepp, J. 1981. Brain opioids: A neurochemical substrate for narcotic and social dependence. In *Theory in Psychopharmacology.* Edited by Cooper, S. New York: Academic Press.

3944 Perachio, A A. 1978. Hypothalamic regulations of behavioral and hormonal aspects of aggression and sexual performance. In *Recent Advances in Primatology.* Edited by Chivers, D J, E J Herbert. New York: Academic Press.

3945 Persinger, M. 1987. *Neuropsychological Basis of God Belief.* Westport, CT: Praeger.

3946 Pfaff, D W. 1980. *Estrogens and Brain Function.* Berlin: Springer.

3947 Phillis, J W. 1988. Brain adenosine and purinergic modulation of central nervous system excitability. In *The Brain as an Endocrine Organ.* Edited by Cohen, M P, P P Foà. Pp. 210-250. New York: Springer.

3948 Pirke, K M, G Kockott, F Dittmar. 1974. Psychosexual stimulation and plasma testosterone in man. *Archives of Sexual Behavior* 3: 577-584.

3949 Pirke, K M, et al. 1984. Effect of starvation on central neurotransmitter systems and on endocrine regulation. In *The Psychobiology of Anorexia Nervosa.* Edited by Pirke, K M, D Ploog. Pp. 47-57. Berlin: Springer.

3950 Rakoff, V. 1983. Multiple determinants of family dynamics in anorexia nervosa. In *Anorexia Nervosa: Recent Developments in Research.* Edited by Darby, P L, P E Garfinkel, D M Garner, D V Coscina. Pp. 29-40. New York: Alan R. Liss.

3951 Regestein, Q R, I Schiff, D Tulchinsky, K J Ryan. 1981. Relationships among estrogen-induced psychophysiological changes in hypogonadal women. *Psychosomatic Medicine* 43: 147-155.

3952 Reinisch, J, M Ziemba-Davis, S Sanders. 1991. Hormonal contributions to sexually dimorphic behavioral development in humans. *Psychoneuroendocrinology* 16: 213-78.

3953 Rivier, C, W Vale. 1983. Modulation of stress-induced ACTH release by corticotropin-releasing factor, catecholamines, and vasopressin. *Nature* 305: 325-327.

3954 Rowland, D L, J R Heiman, B A Gladue, J P Hatch, C H Doering, S J Weiler. 1987. Endocrine, psychological and genital responses to sexual arousal in men. *Psychoneuroendocrinology* 12: 149-158.

3955 Salvador, A, V Simon, F Suay, L Llorens. 1987. Testosterone and cortisol responses to competitive fighting in human males: A pilot study. *Aggressive Behavior* 13: 9-13.

3956 Sapolsky, R. 1991. Testicular function, social rank and personality among wild baboons. *Psychoneuroendocrinology* 16: 281-93.

3957 Sassenrath, E N. 1983. Studies in adaptability: Experimental, environmental, and pharmacological influences. In *Hormones, Drugs, and Social Behavior in Primates.* Edited by Steklis, H D, A S Kling. New York: Spectrum.

3958 Sheard, M H. 1984. Clinical-pharmacology of aggressive behavior. *Clinical Neuropathology* 7: 173-183.

3959 Simon, N G, R E Whalen, M P Tate. 1985. Induction of male-typical aggression by androgens but not by estrogens in adult female mice. *Hormones and Behavior* 190: 204-212.

3960 Simon, N, R Whalen. 1986. Hormonal regulation of aggression:Evidence for a relationship among genotype, receptor binding, and behavioral sensitivity to androgen and estrogen. *Aggressive Behavior* 12: 255-266.

3961 Soubrié, P. 1986. Reconciling the role of central serotonin neurons in human and animal Behavior. *Behavioral and Brain Sciences* 9: 319-364.

3962 Steklis, H D, A S Kling. 1983. *Hormones, Drugs, and Social Behavior in Primates.* New York: Spectrum.

3963 Steklis, H D, G L Brammer, M J Raleigh, M T McGuire. 1985. Serum testosterone, male dominance and aggression in captive groups of vervet monkeys (Cercopithecus aethiops sabaeus). *Hormones and Behavior* 19: 154-163.

3964 Svare, B B. 1983. *Hormones and Aggressive Behavior.* New York: Plenum.

3965 Svare, B B, M A Mann. 1983. Hormonal influences on maternal aggression. In *Hormones and Aggressive Behavior.* Edited by Svare, B B. Pp. 91-104. New York: Plenum.

3966 Tallal, P. 1991. Hormonal influences in developmental learning disabilities. *Psychoneuroendocrinology* 16: 203-11.

3967 Thiessen, D D. 1990. Hormone correlates of sexual aggression. In *Crime in Biological, Social and Moral Contexts.* Edited by Ellis, L, H Hoffman. New York: Praeger.

3968 Toates, F. 1985. *Motivational Systems.* Cambridge: Cambridge University Press.

3969 Vernadakis, A, P S Timiras, eds. 1982. *Hormones in Development and Ageing.* New York: Spectrum.

3970 Virkkunen, M. 1983. Serum cholesterol levels in homicidal offenders. *Neuropsychobiology* 10: 65-69.

3971 Virkkunen, M. 1986. Insulin secretion during the glucose tolerance test among habitually violent and impulsive offenders. *Aggressive Behavior* 12: 303-310.

3972 Virkkunen, M, D Horrobin, D Jenkins, M Manku. 1987. Plasma phospholipid essential fatty acids and prostaglandins in alcoholic, habitually violent, and impulsive offenders. *Biological Psychiatry* 22: 1087-96.

3973 Vogel, R B, C A Books, C Ketchum, C W Zauner, F T Murray. 1985. Increase of free and total testosterone during submaximal exercise in normal males. *Medicine and Science in Sports and Exercise* 17: 119-123.

3974 Wakeling, A, V F A DeSouza. 1983. Differential endocrine and menstrual response to weight change in anorexia nervosa. In *Anorexia Nervosa: Recent Developments in Research.* Edited by Darby, P L, P E Garfinkel, D M Garner, D V Coscina. Pp. 271-78. New York: Alan R. Liss.

3975 Watson, N V, D Kimura. 1991. Nontrivial sex differences in throwing and intercepting: Relation to psychometrically-defined spatial functions. *Personality and Individual Differences* 12: 375-85.

3976 Weinder, G, G Sexton, R Mclellar, S L Connor. 1987. The role of type-A behavior and hostility in an elevation of plasma-lipids in adult women and men. *Psychosomatic Medicine* 49: 136-145.

3977 Weiss, S R B, et al. 1986. Corticotropin-releasing factor-induced seizures and behavior: Interaction with amygdala kindling. *Brain Research* 372: 345-351.

3978 Williams, C L, A M Barnett, W H Meck. 1990. Organizational effects of early gonadal secretions on sexual differentiations in spatial memory. *Behavioral Neuroscience* 104: 84-97.

3979 Wilson, J D, J E Griffin, F W George, M Leshin. 1981. The role of gonadal steroids in sexual differentiation. *Recent Progress in Hormone Research* 37: 1-39.

3980 Wilson, J. 1982. Gonadal hormones and sexual behavior. In *Clinical Neuroendocrinology*. Edited by Besser, G, L Martini. New York: Academic Press.

3981 Wise, H A. 1978. Catecholamine theories of reward: A critical review. *Brain Research* 152: 215-247.

3982 Zarrow, M X, V H Denenberg, B D Sachs. 1972. Hormones and Maternal Behavior in Mammals. In *Hormones and Behavior*. Edited by Levine, S. New York: Academic Press.

*Note: Entries 3983-3991 are skipped.*

# 11

# Neurology

3992 Adams, D B. 1979. Brain mechanisms for offense, defense, and submission. *Behavioral and Brain Sciences* 2: 201-241.

3993 Adams, D B. 1980. Motivational systems of agonistic behavior in muroid rodents: A comparative review and neural model. *Aggressive Bahavior* 6: 295-346.

3994 Adelson, G. 1987. *Encyclopedia of Neuroscience.* Boston: Birkhäuser.

3995 Ader, R, ed. 1981. *Psychoneuroimmunology.* New York: Academic Press.

3996 Adler, N T. 1981. The neuroethology of reproduction. In *Advances in Vertebrate Neuroethology.* Edited by Ewert, J. New York: Plenum.

3997 Aggleton, J P, M Mishkin. 1986. The amygdala: Sensory gateway to the emotions. In *Emotion: Theory, Research and Experience.* Edited by Plutchik, R, H Kellerman. Pp. 281-99. New York: Academic Press.

3998 Ahern, G L, G E Schwartz. 1985. Differential lateralization for positive and negative emotion in the human brain: EEG spectral analysis. *Neuropsychologia* 23: 745-55.

3999 Albert, D J, M L Walsh. 1984. Neural systems and the inhibitory modulations of agonistic behaviour: A comparison of mammalian species. *Neuroscience and Biobehavior Review* 8: 5-24.

4000 Alkon, D L. 1988. *Memory Traces in the Brain.* Bethesda: National Institue of Neurological and Communicative Disorder and Stroke and National Institute of Health.

4001 Aram, D M, H A Whitaker. 1988. Cognitive Sequelae of Unilateral Lesions Acquired in Early Childhood. In *Brain Lateralization in Children: Developmental Implications.* Edited by Molfese, D, S Segalowitz. Pp. 417-437. London: Guilford Press.

4002 Arbib, M. 1981. Perceptual structures and distributed motor control. In *Handbook of Physiology: The Nervous System II.* Edited by Brooks, V B. Pp. 1449-1480. Baltimore: Williams and Wilkons.

4003 Armstrong, E. 1991. The limbic system and culture: An allometric analysis of neocortex and limbic nuclei. *Human Nature* 2: 117-136.

4004 Ashton, H. 1992. *Brain Function and Psychotropic Drugs.* 2 ed Oxford: Oxford University Press.

4005 Avoli, M, T Reader, R Dykes, P Gloor, eds. 1988. *Neurotransmitters and Cortical Function: From Molecules to Mind.* New York: Plenum.

4006 Babloyantz, A, ed. 1990. *Self-Organization, Emergent Properties and Learning.* New York: Plenum.

4007 Baerends, G P. 1985. Do the dummy experiments with sticklebacks support the IRM concept? *Behaviour* 93: 258-77.

4008 Bailey, K. 1985. Phylogenetic regression and the problem of extreme aggression. *Journal of Social and Biological Structures* 8: 207-223.

4009 Bairstow, P J, J I Laszlo. 1980. Motor commands and the perception of movement patterns. *Journal of Experimental Psychology* 6: 1-12.

4010 Baker, A B, L D Baker, eds. 1985. *Clinical Neurology.* New York: Harper & Row.

4011 Baldwin, J D, J I Baldwin. 1977. The role of learning phenomena in the ontogeny and Eevolution and play. In *Primate Bio-Social Development: Biological, Social and Ecological Determinants.* Edited by Chevalier-Skolnikops, S, F E Poirer. New York: Garland.

4012 Bandler, R, A DePaulis, M Vergnes. 1985. Identification of midbrain neurones mediating defensive behaviour in the rat by microinjections of excitatory amino acids. *Behavioral and Brain Research* 15: 107-19.

4013 Basbaum, A I, H L Fields. 1978. Endogenous pain control mechanism: Review and hypothesis. *Annals of Neurology* 4: 451-461.

4014 Bear, D M. 1983. Hemispheric specialization and the neurology of emotion. *Archives of Neurology* 40: 195-202.

4015 Beck, H. 1976. Neuropsychological servosystems, consciousness and the problem of embodiment. *Behavioral Science* 21: 139-60.

4016 Begleiter, H, ed. 1979. *Evoked Brain Potentials and Behavior.* New York: Plenum.

4017 Berkinblit, M B, A G Feldman, O I Fukson. 1986. Adaptability of innate motor patterns and motor control mechanism. *Behavioral and Brain Sciences* 9: 585-625.

4018 Berthoz, A, G M Jones, eds. 1985. *Adaptive Mechanisms in Gaze Control.* Amsterdam: Elsevier.

4019 Best, C T. 1988. The emergence of cerebral asymmetries in early human development: A literature review and a neuroembryological model. In *Brain Lateralization in Children Developmental Implications.* Edited by Molfese, D L, S J Segalowitz. Pp. 5-35. London: Guilford Press.

4020 Black, J E, W T Greenough. 1986. Developmental approaches to the memory process. In *Learning and Memory: A Biological View.* Edited by Martinez, J L, R P Kesner. Pp. 55-82. New York: Academic Press.

4021 Blakemore, C. 1977. *Mechanics of the Mind.* New York: Cambrdige University Press.

4022 Blass, E, ed. 1986. *Developmental Psychobiology and Developmental Neurobiology.* New York: Plenum.

4023 Blinkov, S M, I I Gleser. 1968. *The Human Brain in Figures and Tables: A Quantitative Handbook.* New York: Plenum.

4024 Blonder, L X. 1981. Human neuropsychology and the concept of culture. *Human Nature* 2: 83-116.

4025 Boddy, J. 1978. *Brain Systems and Psychological Concepts.* New York: Wiley.

4026 Bond, N W, D A T Siddle, eds. 1989. *Psychobiology: Issues and Applications.* Amsterdam: Elsevier.

4027 Bonica, J J, ed. 1980. *Pain.* New York: Raven Press.

4028 Boulton, A A, G B Baker, W Waltz, eds. 1988. *The Neural Microenvironment.* Clifton, N.J.: Humana Press.

4029 Boulton, A, G Baker, M Hiscock, eds. 1990. *Neuropsychology.* Clifton, N.J.: Humana Press.

4030 Bradshaw, J L, N C Nettleton. 1983. *Human Cerebral Asymmetry.* Englewood Clifs, NJ: Prentice Hall.

4031 Bradshaw, J L, G Nathan, N C Nettleton, J M Pierson, L E Wilson. 1983. Head and body space to left and right III. Vibrotactile stimulation and sensory and motor components. *Perception* 12: 651-661.

4032 Bradshaw, J L. 1986. *Basic Experiments in Neuropsycholgy.* Amsterdam: Elsevier.

4033 Bradshaw, J L, V Burden, N C Nettleton. 1986. Dichotic and dichhaptic techniques. *Neuropsychologia* 24: 79-90.

4034 Bradshaw, J L, N C Nettleton, J M Pierson, L Wilson, G Nathan. 1987. Coordinates of extracorporeal space. In *Neurophysiological and Neuropsychological Aspects of Spatial Neglect.* Edited by Jeannerod, M. Amsterdam: North Holland.

4035 Bradshaw, J L. 1988. The evolution of human lateral asymmetries: New evidence and second thoughts. *Journal of Human Evolution* 17: 615-637.

4036 Bradshaw, J L, J M Pierson-Savage, N C Nettleton. 1988. Hemispace asymmetries. In *Contemporary Reviews in Neuropsychology.* Edited by Whitaker, H A. Pp. 1-35. New York: Springer.

4037 Bradshaw, J L. 1989. *Hemispheric Specialization.* New York: Wiley.

4038 Brodel, A. 1981. *Neurological Anatomy in Relation to Clinical Medicine.* 3rd ed Oxford: Oxford University Press.

4039 Brooks, V B. 1986. *The Neural Basis of Motor Control.* New York: Oxford University Press.

4040 Brown, T S, P M Wallace. 1980. *Physiological Psychology.* New York: Academic Press.

4041 Bryden, M P. 1988. Does laterality make any difference? Thoughts on the relation between cerebral asymmetry and reading. In *Brain Lateralization in Children Developmental Implications.* Edited by Molfese, D L, S J Segalowitz. Pp. 509-527. London: Guilford Press.

4042 Bullock, T H. 1983. Epilogue: Neurobiological roots and neuroethological sprouts. In *Neuroethology and Behavioral Physiology*. Edited by Markl, H. Pp. 403-412. New York: Springer.

4043 Bullock, T H. 1990. Goals of neuroethology: Studying the connections between brain, physiology and behavior. *BioScience* 40: 244-248.

4044 Camhi, J M. 1984. *Neuroethology: Nerve Cells and the Natural Behavior of Animals*. New York: Sinauer.

4045 Changeux, J P. 1985. *Neuronal Man: The Biology of Mind*. New York: Oxford University Press.

4046 Changeux, J P, M Konishi, eds. 1987. *The Neural and Molecular Basis of Learning*. New York: Wiley.

4047 Churchland, P M. 1985. Cognitive neurobiology: A computional hypothesis for laminar cortex. *Biology and Philosophy* 1: 25-52.

4048 Churchland, P. 1986. *Neurophilosophy: Toward a Unified Science of Mind-Brain*. Cambridge: M.I.T. Press.

4049 Clark, A. 1980. *Psychological Models and Neural Mechanisms*. Oxford: Clarendon Press.

4050 Clynes, M, ed. 1982. *Music, Mind and Brain: The Neurobiology of Music*. New York: Plenum.

4051 Clynes, M, N Nettheim. 1982. The living quality of music: Neurobiologic bais of communicating feeling. In *Music, Mind and Brain: The Neurobiology of Music*. Edited by Clynes, M. New York: Plenum.

4052 Cohen, L J. 1981. Can Human Irrationality be Experimentally Demonstrated? *Behavioral and Brain Sciences* 4: 317-370.

4053 Cohen, E. 1982. Sexual dimorphism: A tool in the research of brain and behavior. In *Genetics of the Brain*. Edited by Lieblich, I. Pp. 39-57. New York: Elsevier Biomedical Press.

4054 Coles, M G H, G Gratton, T R Bashore, C W Ericksen, E Donchin. 1985. A psychophysiological investigation of the continuous flow model of human information processing. *Journal of Experimental Psychology: Human Perception and Performance* 11: 529-53.

4055 Coles, M G H, E Donchin, S W Porges, eds. 1986. *Psychophysiology: Systems, Processes, and Applications.* New York: Guilford Press.

4056 Coles, M G H, G Gratton, W J Gehring. 1987. Theory in cognitive psychophysiology. *Journal of Psychophysiology* 1: 13-16.

4057 Cook, N. 1987. *The Brain Code: Mechanisms of Information Transfer and the Role of the Corpus Callosum.* London: Methuen.

4058 Cooke, D. 1959. *The Language of Music.* New York: Oxford University Press.

4059 Cooper, J R, F E Bloom, R H Roth. 1982. *The Biochemical Basis of Neuropharmacology.* New York: Oxford University.

4060 Cooper, S J, C T Dourish, eds. 1990. *Neurobiology of Stereotyped Behaviour.* Oxford: Clarendon Press.

4061 Corballis, M C, M J Morgan. 1978. On the biological basis of human laterality: I. Evidence for a maturational left-right gradient; II. The mechanisms of inheritance. *Behavioral and Brain Sciences* 1: 261-336.

4062 Corina, D P, J Vaid, U Bellugi. 1992. The linguistic basis of left hemisphere specialization. *Science* 255: 1258-1260.

4063 Coslett, H B, K M Heilman. 1986. Male sexual function: Impairment after right hemisphere stroke. *Archives of Neurology* 43: 1036-9.

4064 Coursey, R D, M S Bauchsbaum, D L Murphy. 1979. MAO activity and evoked potentials in the identification of subjects biologically at risk for psychiatric disorders. *British Journal of Psychiatry* 134: 372-381.

4065 Crews, D, ed. 1987. *Psychobiology of Reproductive Behavior: An Evolutionary Perspective.* Englewood Cliffs, NJ: Prentice-Hall.

4066 Critchley, M. 1979. *The Divine Banquet of the Brain and Other Essays.* New York: Raven Press.

4067 Critchley, M. 1986. *The Citadel of the Senses and Other Essays.* New York: Raven Press.

4068 D'Aquili, E G. 1978. The neurobiological bases of myth and concepts of deity. *Zygon* 13: 257-75.

4069 Daniloff, R, G Schuckers, L Feth. 1980. *The Physiology of Speech and Hearing: An Introduction.* Englewood Cliffs, NJ: Prentice-Hall.

4070 Davidson, R J, N A Fox. 1982. Asymmetrical brain activity discriminates between positive and negative affective stimuli in human infants. *Science* 218: 1235-7.

4071 Davidson, R J, N A Fox. 1988. Cerebral asymmetry and emotion: Developmental and individual differences. In *Brain Lateralization in Children Developmental Implications.* Edited by Molfese, D L, S J Segalowitz. Pp. 191-207. London: Guilford Press.

4072 Davis, W. 1986. Memory: Invertebrate Model Systems. In *Learning and Memory: A Biological View.* Edited by Martinez, J, R Kesner. Pp. 267-298. New York: Academic Press.

4073 Dawson, G. 1988. Cerebral Lateralization in Autism: Clues to Its Role in Language and Affective Development. In *Brain Lateralization in Children Developmental Implications.* Edited by Molfese, D, S Segalowitz. Pp. 437-463. London: Guilford Press.

4074 de Kerckhove, D, C Lumsden, eds. 1988. *The Alphabet and the Brain.* New York: Springer.

4075 DeLaCoste-Utamsing, C, R Holloway. 1982. Sexual dimorphism in the human corpus callosum. *Science* 216: 1431-1432.

4076 Denemberg, V H. 1982. Early experience, interactive systems, and brain laterality in rodents. In *Facilitating Infant and Early Childhood Development.* Edited by Bond, L A, J M Joffe. Hanover, Pa.: University Press of New England.

4077 Denenberg, V H. 1988. Laterality in animals: Brain and behavioral asymmetries and the role of early experiences. In *Brain Lateralization in Children Developmental Implications.* Edited by Molfese, D L, S J Segalowitz. Pp. 59-73. London: Guilford Press.

4078 Destexhe, A, A Babloyantz. 1990. Can chaos in the EEG be explained by a simple model? In *Self-Organization, Emergent Properties and Learning.* Edited by Babloyantz, A. New York: Plenum.

4079 Deutsch, J A. 1983. *The Physiological Basis of Memory.* New York: Academic Press.

4080 Diamond, M C. 1988. *Enriching Heredity: The Impact of the Environment on the Anatomy of the Brain.* New York: Free Press.

4081 Dickinson, A. 1980. *Contemporary Animal Learning Theory.* Cambridge: Cambridge University Press.

4082 DiDomenico, R, R Eaton. 1988. Seven principles for command and the neural causation of behavior. *Brain and Behavioral Evolution* 31: 125-140.

4083 Dimberg, U. 1986. Facial expressions as excitory and inhibitory stimuli for conditioned autonomic responses. *Biological Psychology* 22: 37-57.

4084 Dobbing, J, J Sands. 1979. Comparative aspects of the brain spurt. *Early Human Development* 3: 79-83.

4085 Duhamel, J-R, C L Colby, M E Goldberg. 1992. The updating of the representation of visual space in parietal cortex by intended eye movements. *Science* 255: 90-92.

4086 Eaton, R C, ed. 1984. *Neural Mechanisms in Startle Behaviour.* New York: Plenum.

4087 Eaton, R, R DiDomenico. 1985. Command and the neural causation of behavior: A theoretical analysis of the necessity and sufficiency paradigm. *Brain and Behavioral Evolution* 27: 132-164.

4088 Ebbesson, S O E. 1984. Evolution and ontogeny of neural circuits. *Behavioral and Brain Sciences* 7: 321-331.

4089 Eccles, J C. 1980. *The Human Psyche.* Berlin: Springer.

4090 Eccles, J C. 1989. *Evolution of the Brain: Creation of the Self.* New York: Routledge.

4091 Edelman, G, V B Mountcastle. 1978. *The Mindful Brain.* Cambridge: M.I.T. Press.

4092 Edelman, G. 1987. *Neural Darwinism: The Theory of Neuronal Group Selection.* New York: Basic Books.

4093 Epstein, A N, ed. 1983. *Progress in Psychobiology and Physiological Psychology.* New York: Academic Press.

4094 Essman, W B, ed. 1987. *Nutrients and Brain Function.* Basel: Karger.

4095 Ewert, J-P. 1980. *Neuroethology.* Berlin: Springer.

4096 Ewert, J, D Ingle, eds. 1983. *Advances in Vertebrate Neuroethology.* New York: Plenum.

4097 Ewert, J-P. 1985. Concepts in vertebrate neuroethology. *Animal Behaviour* 33: 1-29.

4098 Ewert, J P. 1987. Neuroethology of releasing mechanisms: Prey-catching in toads. *Behavioral and Brain Science* 10: 337-403.

4099 Feldman, R S, L F Quenzer. 1984. *Fundamentals of Neuropsychopharmacology.* Sunderland, MA.: Sinauer.

4100 Fillenz, M. 1990. *The Noradrenergic Neurons.* Cambridge: Cambridge University Press.

4101 Finger, S, T LeVere, C R Almli, D G Stein, eds. 1988. *Brain Injury and Recovery: Theoretical and Controversial Issues.* New York: Plenum.

4102 Fischer, B, L Rogal. 1986. Eye hand coordination in man: A reaction time study. *Biological Cybernetics* 55: 253-261.

4103 Fischer, B. 1989. Visually guided eye and hand movements in man. *Brain and Behavioral Evolution* 33: 109-112.

4104 Fisk, J L, B P Rourke. 1988. Subtypes of learning-disabled children: Implications for a neurodevelopmental model of differential hemispheric processing. In *Brain Lateralization in Children Developmental Implications.* Edited by Molfese, D L, S J Segalowitz. Pp. 547-567. London: Guilford Press.

4105 Flor-Henry, P. 1980. Cerebral aspects of the orgasmic response: Normal and deviational. In *Medical Sexology.* Edited by Forlec, R, W Pasini. Pp. 256-62. Amsterdam: Elsevier.

4106 Foote, S L, F E Bloom, G Aston-Jones. 1983. Nucleus locus coeruleus: New evidence of anatomical and physiological specificity. *Physiological Review* 63: 844-914.

4107 Fox, N A, R J Davidson. 1984. EEG asymmetry in response to sour tastes in newborn infants. *Neuropsychologia* 24: 417-22.

4108 Fox, N A, R J Davidson, eds. 1984. *The Psychobiology of Affective Development.* Hillsdale, N.J.: Erlbaum.

4109 Fox, N A, R J Davidson. 1988. Patterns of brain electrical activity during facial signs of emotion in 10-month-old infants. *Developmental Psychology* 24: 230-6.

4110 Freeman, R L, A M Galaburda, R D Cabal, N Geschwind. 1985. The neurology of depression. *Archives of Neurology* 42: 289-91.

4111 Friedman, L A, ed. 1977. *On the Other Hand.* New York: Academic Press.

4112 Fuster, J M. 1980. *The Prefrontal Cortex: Anatomy, Physiology, and Neuropsychology of the Frontal Lobe.* New York: Raven Press.

4113 Gage, D F, M A Safer. 1985. Hemisphere differences in the mood state-dependent effect for recognition of emotional faces. *Journal of Experimental Psychology: Learning, Memory, and Cognition* 11: 752-63.

4114 Gallez, D, A Babloyantz. 1990. Dynamical silhouttes of chaotic attractors for human brain activity. In *Self-Organization, Emergent Properties and Learning.* Edited by Babloyantz, A. New York: Plenum.

4115 Gazzaniga, M S, D Steen, B T Volpe. 1979. *Functional Neuroscience.* New York: Harper & Row.

4116 Gazzaniga, M. 1985. *The Social Brain: Discovering the Networks of the Mind.* New York: Basic Books.

4117 Gellhorn, E, W R Kiely. 1972. Mystical states of consciousness: Neurophysiological and clinical aspects. *Journal of Nervous and Mental Disease* 154: 399-405.

4118 Gelperin, A. 1986. Complex associative learning in small neuronal networks. *Trends in Neuroscience* 9: 323-28.

4119 Georgopoulos, A P, J Ashe, N Smyrnis, M Taira. 1992. The motor cortex and the coding of force. *Science* 256: 1692-1695.

4120 Gershon, M D. 1981. The enteric nervous system. *Annual Review of Neuroscience* 4: 227-72.

4121 Geschwind, N, A M Galaburda. 1985. Cerebral lateralization. *Archives of Neurology* 42: 428-654.

4122 Geschwind, N, A M Galaburda. 1987. *Cerebral Lateralization: Biological Mechanisms, Associations and Pathology.* Cambridge: M.I.T. Press.

4123 Geshwind, N, A M Glaburda, eds. 1984. *Cerebral Dominance: The Biological Foundations.* Cambridge: Harvard University Press.

4124 Gibson, C. 1988. The Impact of Early Developmental History on Cerebral Asymmetries: Implications for Reading Ability in Deaf Children. In *Brain Lateralization in Children Developmental Implications*. Edited by Molfese, D, S Segalowitz. Pp. 591-605. London: Guilford Press.

4125 Glass, A. 1987. *Individual Differences in Hemispheric Specialization*. New York: Plenum.

4126 Glassman, R B. 1980. An evolutionary hypothesis about teaching and proselytizing behaviors. *Zygon, Journal of Religion and Science* 15: 133-154.

4127 Glassman, R B. 1983. Free will has a neural substrate: Critique of Joseph F. Rychlak's "Discovering free will and personal responsibility". *Zygon, Journal of Religion and Science* 18: 67-82.

4128 Glassman, R B. 1987. An hypothesis about redundancy and reliability in the brains of higher organisms: Analogies with genes, internal organs and engineering systems. *Neuroscience and Biobehavioral Reviews* 11: 275-285.

4129 Glees, P. 1988. *The Human Brain.* Cambridge: Cambridge University Press.

4130 Glick, S D. 1985. *Cerebral Lateralization in Nonhuman Species.* New York: Academic Press.

4131 Globus, G C, G Maxwell, I Savodmik, eds. 1976. *Consciousness and the Brain.* New York: Plenum.

4132 Gold, P E, S F Zornetzer. 1983. The mnemon and its juices: Neuromodulation of memory processes. *Behavioral and Neural Biology* 38: 151-189.

4133 Goldberg, G. 1985. Supplementary motor area structure and function: Review and hypotheses. *Behavioral and Brain Sciences* 8: 567-615.

4134 Goldstein, G, R E Tarter, eds. 1986. *Advances in Clinical Neuropsychology.* New York: Plenum.

4135 Gordon, H. 1983. Music and the right hemisphere. In *Functions of the Right Cerebral Hemisphere.* Edited by Young, A. New York: Academic Press.

4136 Gordon, H W. 1988. The effect of "right brain/left brain" cognitive profiles on school achievement. In *Brain Lateralization in*

*Children Developmental Implications.* Edited by Molfese, D L, S J Segalowitz. Pp. 237-257. London: Guilford Press.

4137 Gorski, R A. 1987. Sex differences in the rodent brain: Their nature and origin. In *Masculinity/Femininity: Basic Perspectives.* Edited by Reinisch, J, L Rosenblum, S Sanders. Pp. 37-67. New York: Oxford University Press.

4138 Gouchie, C, D Kimura. 1991. The relationship between testosterone levels and cognitive ability patterns. *Psychoneuroendocrinology* 16: 323-34.

4139 Goy, R W, B S McEwen. 1980. *Sexual Differentiation of the Brain.* Cambridge: M.I.T. Press.

4140 Graham, F K. 1979. Distinguishing among orienting, defensive, and startle reflexes. In *The Orienting Reflex in Humans.* Edited by Kimmel, H D, E H van Olst, J R Orelebeke. Hillsdale, N.J.: Erlbaum.

4141 Gray, J A. 1964. *Pavlov's Typology.* New York: Pergamon Press.

4142 Gray, J A. 1972. Learning theory, the conceptual nervous system and personality. In *The Biolgical Bases of Individual Behaviour.* Edited by Nebylitsyn, V D, J A Gray. Pp. 372-399. New York: Academic Press.

4143 Gray, J A. 1972. The psychophysiological basis of introversion-extraversion: A modification of Eysenck's theory. In *The Biolgical Bases of Individual Behaviour.* Edited by Nebylitsyn, V D, J A Gray. Pp. 182-205. New York: Academic Press.

4144 Gray, J A. 1976. The behavioural inhibition system: A possible substrate for anxiety. In *Theoretical and Experimental Bases of Behaviour Modification.* Edited by Feldman, M P, A M Broadhurst. Pp. 3-41. London: Wiley.

4145 Gray, J A. 1981. *The Neuropsychology of Anxiety: An Enquiry into the Functions of the Septo-Hippocampal System.* Oxford: Oxford University Press.

4146 Gray, J A. 1982. Précis and multiple peer review of 'The Neuropsychology of Anxiety: An Enquiry into the Functions of the Septo-hippocampal Stystem'. *Behavioral and Brain Sciences* 5: 469-525.

4147 Gray, J A. 1984. The hippocampus as an interface between cognition and emotion. In *Animal Cognition.* Edited by Roitblat, H L, T G Bever, H S Terrace. Pp. 607-626. Hillsdale, NJ: Erlbaum.

4148 Gray, J A. 1987. Interactions between drugs and behaviour therapy. In *Theoretical Foundations of Behaviour Therapy*. Edited by Eysenck, H J, I Martin. New York: Plenum.

4149 Greenough, W T, J M Juraska, eds. 1986. *Developmental Neuropsychobiology*. Orlando, FL: Academic Press.

4150 Grillner, S. 1975. Locomotion in vertebrates: Central mechanism and reflex interaction. *Physiological Review* 55: 247-304.

4151 Grillner, S, P Wallen. 1985. Central pattern generators for locomotion, with special reference to vertebrates. *Annual Review of Neuroscience* 8: 233-61.

4152 Grossberg, S. 1983. Some psychophysiological and pharmacological correlates of a developmental, cognitive, and motivational theory. In *Brain and Information: Event Related Potentials*. Edited by Karrer, R, J Cohen, P Tueting. New York: New York Academy of Sciences.

4153 Gur, R E, R C Gur, N M Sussman, M J O'Connor, M M Vey. 1984. Hemispheric control of the writing hand: The effect of callosotomy in a left-hander. *Neurology* 34: 904-908.

4154 Gur, R E, R C Gur, N M Sussman, M J O'Connor, M M Vey. 1984. Hemispheric control of the writing hand: The effect of callosotomy in a left-hander. *Neurology 34* 34: 904-908.

4155 Hackett, J T, J L Greenfield. 1986. The behavioral role of the Mauthner neuron impulse. *Behavioral and Brain Sciences* 9: 725-764.

4156 Hare, R D, L M McPherson. 1984. Psychopathy and perceptual asymmetry during verbal dichotic listening. *Journal of Abnormal Psychology* 93: 141-149.

4157 Hare, R D, A E Forth. 1985. Psychopathy and lateral preference. *Journal of Abnormal Psychology* 94: 541-546.

4158 Harnad, S, R W Doty, L Goldstein, J Jaynes, G Krauthamer, eds. 1977. *Lateralization in the Nervous System*. New York: Academic Press.

4159 Harris, L J, D F Carlson. 1988. Pathological left-handedness: An analysis of theories and evidence. In *Brain Lateralization in Children Developmental Implications*. Edited by Molfese, D L, S J Segalowitz. Pp. 289-373. London: Guilford Press.

4160 Hassett, J. 1978. *A Primer of Psychophysiology.* San Francisco: W.H. Freeman.

4161 Hecaen, H. 1962. Clinical symptomatology in right and left hemisphere lesions. In *Interhemispheric Relations and Cerebral Dominance.* Edited by Mountcastle, V B. Baltimore: Johns Hopkins.

4162 Hecaen, H, M L Albert. 1978. *Human Neuropsychology.* New York: Wiley.

4163 Hecaen, H, M DeAgostini, A Monson-Montes. 1981. Cerebral orginization in left-handers. *Brain and Language* 12: 261-284.

4164 Heilman, K, T VanDenAbell. 1980. Right hemisphere dominance for attention: The mechanism underlying hemispeheric asymmetry of inattention. *Neurology* 30: 327-330.

4165 Heilman, K M, D Bowers, L Speedie, H B Coslett. 1984. Comprehension of affective and non-affective prosody. *Neurology* 34: 917-30.

4166 Hilgard, E R. 1977. *Divided Consciousness: Multiple Controls in Human Thought and Action.* New York: Wiley.

4167 Hingtgen, J N, D Hallhammer, G Huppmann, eds. 1987. *Advanced Methods in Psychobiology.* Toronto: C.J. Hogrefe.

4168 Hinton, G E, J A Anderson, eds. 1981. *Parallel Models of Associative Memory.* Hillsdale, NJ: Erlbaum.

4169 Hiscock, M. 1988. Behavioral asymmetries in normal children. In *Brain Lateralization in Children Developmental Implications.* Edited by Molfese, D L, S J Segalowitz. Pp. 85-171. London: Guilford Press.

4170 Hoebel, B G, D Novin, eds. 1982. *The Neural Basis of Feeding and Reward.* Brunswick, Maine: Haer Institute.

4171 Hofman, M. 1988. Brain, mind and reality. In *Intelligence and Evolutionary Biology.* Edited by Jerison, H, I Jerison. New York: Springer.

4172 Holloway, R, C d Lacoste. 1986. Sexual dimorphism in the human corpus callosum: An extension and replication study. *Human Neurobiology* 5: 87-91.

4173 Hopfield, J J, D W Tank. 1986. Computing with neural circuits: A model. *Science* 223: 625-33.

4174 Hom, G. 1985. *Memory, Imprinting, and the Brain: An Inquiry into Mechanisms.* New York: Oxford University Press.

4175 Hoyenga, K B, K T Hoyenga. 1984. *Motivational Explanations of Behaviour.* Monterey, CA: Brooks/Cole.

4176 Hoyle, G. 1983. *Muscles and Their Neural Control.* New York: Wiley Interscience.

4177 Huber, F, H Markl, eds. 1983. *Behavioural Physiology and Neuroethology: Roots and Growing Points.* Berlin: Springer.

4178 Hugdahl, K. 1984. Hemispheric asymmetry and bilateral electrodermae recordings: A review of the evidence. *Neuropsychologia* 21: 371-393.

4179 Hugdahl, K, ed. 1988. *Handbook of Dichotic Listening: Theory, Methods and Research.* London: Wiley.

4180 Iacono, R P, B S Nashold. 1982. Mental and behavioural effects of brain stem and hypothalamic stimulation in man. *Human Neurobiology* 1: 273-80.

4181 Immelmann, K, K Schere, C Vogel, P Schmoock. 1988. *Psychobiologie: Grundlagen des Verhalten.* Munich: Gustav Fischer.

4182 Jacobs, B L, ed. 1984. *Hallucinogens: Neurochemical, Behavioral and Clincal Perspectives.* New York: Raven Press.

4183 Jeannerod, M, ed. 1987. *Neurophysiological and Neuropsychological Aspects of Spatial Neglect.* Amsterdam: North Holland.

4184 Jeannerod, M. 1990. *The Neural and Behavioural Organization of Goal-Directed Movements.* Oxford: Oxford University Press.

4185 Jeeves, M A, G Baumgartner, eds. 1986. *Methods in Neuropsychology.* Oxford: Pergamon Press.

4186 Jellestad, F K, R C C Murison. 1987. Stereotactic, electrical and chemical lesions. In *Advanced Methods in Psychobiology.* Edited by Hingtgen, J, D Hellhammer, G Huppmann. Pp. 73-84. Toronto: C.J. Hogrefe.

4187 Jerison, H J, I Jerison. 1988. *Intelligence and Evolutionary Biology.* New York: Springer.

4188 Johnson, L, D Tepas, W Colquhoun, M Colligan, eds. 1981. *Biological Rhythms, Sleep and Shift Work.* New York: MTP Press.

4189 Jorm, A F. 1987. Sex differences in neuroticism: A quantitative synthesis of published research. *Australian & New Zealand Journal of Psychiatry* 21: 501-506.

4190 Kaas, J H. 1982. The segregation of function in the nervous system: Why do sensory systems have so many subdivisions? In *Contributions to Sensory Physiology.* Edited by Neff, W D. New York: Academic Press.

4191 Kalat, J W. 1988. *Biological Psychology.* 3rd ed Belmont, CA: Wadsworth.

4192 Kandel, E R. 1982. Environmental determinants of brain architecture and of behavior: Early experience and learning. In *Principles of Neural Science.* Edited by Kandel, E R, J H Schwartz. Pp. 620-631. London: Edward Arnold.

4193 Kandel, E R, J H Schwartz. 1982. Molecular biology of learning: Modulation of transmitter release. *Science* 218: 433-443.

4194 Kandel, E, D Freed 1989. Frontal lobe dysfunction and antisocial behavior: A review. *Journal of Clinical Psychology* 45: 404-413.

4195 Kapp, B S, J P Pascoe, M A Bixler. 1984. The amygdala: A neuroanatomical systems approach to its contribution to aversive conditioning. In *The Neuropsychology of Memory.* Edited by Squire, L, N Butters. Pp. 473-488. New York: Guilford Press.

4196 Kapp, B, J P Pascoe. 1986. Memory: Vertebrate Model Systems. In *Learning and Memory: A Biological View.* Edited by Martinez, J L, Jr., R P Kesner. Pp. 299-340. New York: Academic Press.

4197 Karczmar, A G, J C Eccles, eds. 1972. *Brain and Human Behavior.* Berlin: Springer.

4198 Kavanau, J L. 1990. Conservative behavioural evolution: The neural substrate. *Animal Behaviour* 39: 758-67.

4199 Kershner, J R. 1988. Dual processing models of learning disability. In *Brain Lateralization in Children Developmental Implications.* Edited by Molfese, D L, S J Segalowitz. Pp. 527-547. London: Guilford Press.

4200 Kesner, R P. 1984. The neurobiology of memory: Implicit and explicit assumptions. In *Neurobiology of Learning and Memory.*

Edited by McGaugh, J L, G Lynch, N M Weinberger. Pp. 111-118. New York: Guilford Press.

4201 Kesner, R P, B V DiMattia. 1984. Posterior parietal association cortex and hippocampus: Equivalency of mnemonic function in animals and humans. In *The Neuropsychology of Memory.* Edited by Squire, L, N Butters. New York: Guilford Press.

4202 Kesner, R P. 1985. Correspondence between humans and animals in coding of temporal attributes: Role of hippocampus and prefontal cortex. *Annals of New York Academy of Sciences* 444: 122-136.

4203 Kesner, R P. 1986. Neurobiological Views of Memory. In *Learning and Memory: A Biological View.* Edited by Martinez, J L, Jr., R P Kesner. Pp. 399-438. New York: Academic Press.

4204 Kety, S S. 1979. Disorders of the human brain. *Scientific American* 241: 202-214.

4205 Kihlstrom, J F, F J Evans, eds. 1979. *Functional Disorders of Memory.* Hillsdale, N.J.: Erlbaum.

4206 Kimura, D. 1983. Sex differences in cerebral organization for speech and praxic functions. *Canadian Journal of Psychology* 37: 19-35.

4207 Kimura, D, R Harshman. 1984. Sex differences in brain organization for verbal and non-verbal functions. In *Progress in Brain Research.* Edited by DeVries, G J, J P C De Bruin, H B M Uylings, M A Corner. Pp. 423-441. Amsterdam: Elsevier.

4208 Kinsbourne, M. 1988. Sinistrality, brain organization, and cognitive deficits. In *Brain Lateralization in Children Developmental Implications.* Edited by Molfese, D L, S J Segalowitz. Pp. 259-281. London: Guilford Press.

4209 Klawans, H. 1990. *Newton's Madness: Further Tales of Clinical Neurology.* New York: Harper & Row.

4210 Kling, A S. 1983. Brain, environment and social behavior. In *Environment and Population: Problems of Adaptation.* Edited by Calhoun, J B. New York: Praeger.

4211 Kling, A. 1986. Neurological correlates of social behavior. *Ethology and Sociobiology* 7: 175-186.

4212 Kolb, B, I Q Whishaw. 1980. *Fundamentals of Human Neuropsychology.* San Francisco: Freeman.

4213 Konishi, M. 1986. Centrally synthesized maps of sensory space. *Trends in Neuroscience* 10: 163-8.

4214 Kreverne, E B. 1988. Central mechanisms underlying the neural and neuroendocrine determinants of maternal behaviour. *Psychoneuroendocrinology* 13: 127-41.

4215 Krieger, D T, J C Hughes, eds. 1980. *Neuroendocrinology*. Sunderland, MA: Sinauer.

4216 Krynicki, V E. 1978. Cerebral dysfunction in repetitively assaultive adolescents. *Journal of Nervous and Mental Disease* 166: 59-67.

4217 Kuffler, S W, J G Nicholls, R A Martin. 1984. *From Neuron to Brain*. 2nd ed Sunderland: Sinauer.

4218 Kugler, P N, M T Turvey. 1987. *Information, Natural Law and the Self-Assembly of Rhythmic Movement*. New York: Erlbaum.

4219 Kupfermann, I, K Weiss. 1978. The command neuron concept. *Behavioral and Brain Sciences* 1: 3-39.

4220 Kupfermann, I. 1982. Learning. In *Principles of Neuroscience*. Edited by Kandel, E R, J H Schwartz. Pp. 570-579. London: Edward Arnold.

4221 Kupfermann, I. 1982. Innate determinants of behavior. In *Principles of Neural Science*. Edited by Kandel, E R, J H Schwartz. Pp. 559-569. London: Edward Arnold.

4222 Lacoste, C d, R Holloway. 1986. Sexual dimorphism in the human corpus callosum. *Science* 216: 1431-1432.

4223 Lacoste, C d, R Holloway, D Woodward. 1986. Sexual differences in the fetal human corpus callosum. *Human Neurobiology* 5: 93-96.

4224 Lansky, L M, H Feinstein, J M Peterson. 1988. Demography of handedness in two samples of randomly selected adults (n = 2083). *Neuropsychologia* 26: 465-77.

4225 Lashley, K S. 1929. *Brain Mechanisms and Intelligence*. Chicago: University of Chicago Press.

4226 Lashley, K S. 1967. The problem of serial order in behavior. In *Cerebral Mechanisms in Behavior: The Hixon Symposium*. Edited by Jeffress, L A. Pp. 112-135. New York: Hafner.

4227 Lee, W A. 1984. Neuromotor synergies as a basis for coordinated intentional action. *Journal of Motor Behavior* 16: 135-170.

4228 Lee, W A. 1984. Neuromotor synergies as a basis for coordinated intentional action. *Journal of Motor Behavior* 16: 135-170.

4229 Lerdahl, F, R Jackendoff. 1983. *A Generative Theory of Tonal Music.* Cambridge: M.I.T. Press.

4230 Levine, S, S G Wiener, C L Coe, F E S Bayart, K T Haysahi. 1987. Primate vocalization: A psychobiological approach. *Child Development* 58: 1408-1419.

4231 Levy, J, W Heller, M T Banich, L A Burton. 1983. Are variations among right-handed individuals in perceptual asymmetries caused by characteristic arousal differences between hemispheres? *Journal of Experimental Psychology: Human Perception and Performance* 9: 329-58.

4232 Lex, B W. 1978. Neurological bases of revitalization movements. *Zygon* 13: 276-312.

4233 Lex, B W. 1979. The neurobiology of ritual trance. In *The Spectrum of Ritual: A Biogenetic Structural Analysis.* Edited by D'Aquili, E G, C D Laughlin, J McManus. New York: Columbia University Press.

4234 Libet, B. 1985. Subjective antedating of a sensory experience and mind-brain theories: Reply to Ted Honderich. *Journal of Theoretical Biology* 114: 563-570.

4235 Libet, B. 1985. Unconscious cerebral initiative and the role of conscious will in voluntary action. *Behavioral and Brain Sciences* 8: 529-566.

4236 Lieblich, I. 1982. Implications for the use of the genetic paradigm for brain research. In *Genetics of the Brain.* Edited by Lieblich, I. Pp. 1-35. New York: Biomedical Press.

4237 Liederman, J. 1988. Misconceptions and new conceptions about early brain damage functional asymmetry, and behavioral outcome. In *Brain Lateralization in Children Developmental Implications.* Edited by Molfese, D L, S J Segalowitz. Pp. 375-401. London: Guilford Press.

4238 Lipsey, J R, R G Robinson, G D Pearlson, K Rao, T R Price. 1983. Mood change following bi-lateral hemisphere brain injury. *British Journal of Psychiatry* 143: 266-273.

4239 Lue, G G. 1971. *Biological Rhythms in Human and Animal Physiology*. New York: Dover.

4240 Luria, A. 1966. *Higher Cortical Functions in Man*. New York: Basic Books.

4241 Luria, A R. 1973. *The Working Brain: An Introduction to Neuropsychology*. London: Penguin.

4242 Lynch, G, M Baudry. 1984. The biochemistry of memory: A new and specific hypothesis. *Science* 224: 1057-1063.

4243 Mackay, W A. 1980. The motor programs: Back to the computer. *Trends in Neurosciences* 3: 97-100.

4244 MacLean, P D, ed. 1973. *A Triune Concept of the Brain and Behaviour*. Toronto: University of Toronto Press.

4245 MacLean, P D. 1984. Evolutionary psychiatry and the triune brain. *Psychological Medicine* 14:

4246 MacLean, P D. 1990. *The Triune Brain in Evolution: Role in Paleocerebral Functions*. New York: Plenum.

4247 MacLusky, N J, F Naftolin. 1981. Sexual differentiation of the central nervous system. *Science* 211: 1294-1303.

4248 Majewski, F. 1981. Alcohol embryopathy: Some facts and speculations about pathogenesis. *Neurobehavioral Toxicology and Teratology* 3: 129-144.

4249 Mandell, A J. 1980. Toward a psychobiology of transcendence: God in the brain. In *The Psychobiology of Consciousness*. Edited by Davidson, J M, R J Davidson. Pp. 379-464. New York: Plenum.

4250 Mark, V H, F Ervin. 1971. *Violence and the Brain*. New York: Harper & Row.

4251 Massion, J, J Paillard, W Schultz, M Wiesendanger. 1983. *Neural Coding of Motor Performance*. Berlin: Springer.

4252 Mateer, C A, S B Polen, G A Ojemann. 1982. Sexual variation in cortical localization of naming as determined by stimulation mapping. *Behavioral and Brain Sciences* 3: 310-11.

4253 McGaugh, J L, G Lynch, N M Weinberger, eds. 1984. *Neurobiology of Learning and Memory*. New York: Guilford Press.

4254 McGrigan, F J, R A Schnoonver. 1973. *The Psychophysiology of Thinking*. New York: Academic Press.

4255 McGuire, M T, R D Masters, eds. 1992. *The Neurotransmitter Revolution*. Carbondale: Southern Illinois University Press.

4256 McNaughton, N, S T Mason. 1980. The neuropsychology and neuropharmacology of the dorsal ascending noradrenergic bundle: A review. *Progress in Neurobiology* 14: 157-219.

4257 Mebert, C J, G F Michel. 1980. Handedness in artists. In *Neuropsychology of Left-handedness*. Edited by Herron, J. New York: Academic Press.

4258 Mesulam, M-M, ed. 1985. *Principles of Behavioral Neurology*. Philadelphia: F.A. Davis.

4259 Miczek, K A, ed. 1983. *Ethnopharmacology: Primate Models in Neuropsychiatric Disorders*. New York: Alan R. Liss.

4260 Miller, L. 1987. Neuropsychology of the aggressive psychopath: An integrative review. *Aggressive Behavior* 13: 119-40.

4261 Minsky, M. 1982. Music, mind and meaning. In *Music, Mind and Brain: The Neurobiology of Music*. Edited by Clynes, M. Pp. 1-20. New York: Plenum.

4262 Morgenson, G. 1977. *The Neurobiology of Behavior: An Introduction*. Hillsdale, N.J.: Erlbaum.

4263 Moscovitch, M, J Olds. 1982. Asymmetries in spontaneous facial expressions and their possible relation to hemispheric specialization. *Neuropsychologia* 20: 71-81.

4264 Moyer, K F. 1976. *The Psychobiology of Aggression*. New York: Harper and Row.

4265 Moyer, K. 1987. *Violence and Aggression: A Physiological Perspective*. New York: Pergamon.

4266 Myrtek, M. 1984. *Constitutional Psychophysiology*. New York: Academic Press.

4267 Nashner, L M, G McCollum. 1985. The organiztion of human postural movements. *Behavioral and Brain Sciences* 8:

4268 Nass, R, et al. 1987. Hormones and handedness: Left-right bias in female congenital adrenal hyperplasia patients. *Neurology* 37: 711-15.

4269 Netley, C, J Rovet. 1988. The development of cognition and personality in X aneuploids and other subject groups. In *Brain Lateralization in Children Developmental Implications.* Edited by Molfese, D, S Segalowitz. Pp. 401-417. London: Guilford Press.

4270 Noback, C R, W Montagna, eds. 1981. *The Primate Brain.* New York: Plenum.

4271 Noback, C R, ed. 1981. *Sensory Systems of Primates.* New York: Plenum.

4272 Nolen, T G, R R Hoy. 1984. Initiation of behavior by single neurons: the role of behavioral context. *Science* 226: 992-994.

4273 Nottebohm, F. 1981. Laterality, seasons and space govern the learning of a motor skill. *Trends in Neuroscience* 4: 104-06.

4274 Numan, R. 1978. Cortical-limbic mechanisms and response control: A theoretical review. *Physiological Psychology* 6: 445-470.

4275 O'Keefe, J, L Nadel. 1978. *The Hippocampus as a Cognitive Map.* Oxford: Clarendon Press.

4276 Oakley, D A, H C Plotkin, eds. 1979. *Brain, Behaviour and Evolution.* London: Methuen.

4277 Oakley, D. 1979. Cerebral cortex and adaptive behavior. In *Brain, Behavior and Evolution.* Edited by Oakley, D A, H C Plotkin. Pp. 154-188. London: Methuen.

4278 Obrzut, J. 1988. Deficient lateralization in learning-disabled children: Developmental lag or abnormal cerebral organization. In *Brain Lateralization in Children Developmental Implications.* Edited by Molfese, D, S Segalowitz. Pp. 567-591. London: Guilford Press.

4279 Ojemann, G A. 1982. Models of brain organization for higher integrative functions derived with electrical stimulation techniques. *Human Neurobiology* 1: 243-249.

4280 Ottoson, D, ed. 1986. *The Dual Brain: Specialization and Unification of the Cerebral Hemispheres.* Stockholm: Wenner-Gren Foundation.

4281 Ottoson, D, ed. 1987. *Duality and Unity of the Brain: Unified Functioning and Specialisation of the Hemispheres.* New York: Plenum.

4282 Paillard, J, ed. 1991. *Brain and Space.* Oxford: Oxford University Press.

4283 Panksepp, J, L Normansell, S Siviy. 1984. The psychobiology of play: Theoretical and methodological perspectives. *Neuroscience and Biobehavioral Reviews* 8: 465-492.

4284 Panksepp, J. 1985. Mood changes. In *Handbook of Clinical Neurology, Revised series.* Edited by Vinken, P J, G W Bruyn, H L Klawans. Pp. 272-285. Amsterdam: Elsevier.

4285 Panksepp, J. 1986. The neurochemistry of behavior. *Annual Review of Psychology* 37: 77-107.

4286 Paredes, J A, M J Hepburn. 1976. The split brain and the culture-and-cognition paradox. *Current Anthropology* 17: 121-127.

4287 Pavlov, I P. 1928. *Lectures on Conditioned Reflexes.* London: Lawrence & Wishart.

4288 Pellionisz, A, R Llinas. 1985. Tensor network theory of the metaorganization of functional geometries in the central nervous system. In *Adaptive Mechanisms in Gaze Control.* Edited by Berthoz, A, G Jones. Pp. 223-232. Amsterdam: Elsevier.

4289 Perrett, D I, et al. 1985. Visual cells in the temporal cortex sensitive to face view and gaze direction. *Philosophical Transactions of the Royal Society London, B* 223: 293-317.

4290 Petrides, M, B Milner. 1982. Deficits on subject-ordered tasks after frontal- and temporal-lobe lesions in man. *Neuropsychologia* 20: 249-262.

4291 Pettigrew, J D, K J Sanderson, W R Levick. 1986. *Visual Neuroscience.* Cambridge: Cambridge University Press.

4292 Pierson-Savage, J M, J L Bradshaw. 1987. Mapping of extracorporeal space by vibrotactile reaction times: A far left side disadvantage. *Perception* 16: 283-290.

4293 Pierson-Savage, J M, J L Bradshaw, J A Bradshaw, N C Nettleton. 1988. Vibrotactile reaction times in unilateral neglect: The effects of hand location, rehabilitation and eyes open/closed *Brain* 111:

4294 Pincus, J H, G J Tucker. 1985. *Behavioral Neurology.* New York: Oxford University Press.

4295 Pisoni, D B. 1979. On the perception of speech sounds as biologically significant signals. *Brain and Behavioral Evolution* 16: 330-350.

4296 Pohl, C R, E Knobil. 1982. The role of the central nervous system in the control of ovarian function in higher primates. *Annual Review of Physiology* 44: 583-594.

4297 Posner, M. 1978. *Chronometric Explorations of Mind.* Hillsdale, NJ: Erlbaum.

4298 Post, R M, J Ballenger, eds. 1984. *Neurobioloby of Mood Disorders.* Baltimore: Williams and Wilkins.

4299 Powell, G E. 1979. *Brain and Personality.* London: Saxon House.

4300 Praag, H M v, M H Lader, O J Rafaelsen, E J Sachar, eds. 1979. *Handbook of Biological Psychiatry Part III: Brain Mechanisms and Abnormal Behavior - Genetics and Neuroendocrinology.* New York and Basel: Marcel Dekker.

4301 Preilowski, B. 1987. Split-brain methods. In *Advanced Methods in Psychobiology.* Edited by Hingtgen, J, D Hellhammer, G Huppmann. Pp. 85-150. Toronto: C.J. Hogrefe.

4302 Pribram, K, ed. 1969. *Brain and Behaviour.* Harmonsworth: Penguin.

4303 Pribram, K H. 1971. *Language of the Brain.* Englewood Cliffs, N.J.: Prentice-Hall.

4304 Pribram, K. 1971. *Languages of the Brain: Experimental Paradoxes and Principles in Neuropsychology.* Englewood Cliffs, NJ: Prentice-Hall.

4305 Pribram, K H, A R Luria, eds. 1973. *Psychophysiology of the Frontal Lobes.* New York: Academic Press.

4306 Pribram, K H. 1979. Holographic memory. *Psychology Today* 12: 70-86.

4307 Rauschecker, J, P Marler, eds. 1987. *Imprinting and Cortical Plasticity: Comparative Aspects of Sensitive Periods.* New York: Wiley.

4308 Rawlins, J N P. 1985. Associations across time: The hippocampus as a temporal memory store. *Behavioral and Brain Sciences* 8: 479-497.

4309 Reinman, E M, M E Raichle, F K Butler, P Hersovitch, E Robins. 1984. A facal brain abnormality in panic disorder, a severe form of anxiety. *Nature* 310: 683-685.

4310 Reite, M, T Field. 1985. *The Psychobiology of Attachment and Separation.* Orlando, Fla: Academic Press.

4311 Renfrew, J W, R R Hutchinson. 1983. The motivation of aggression. In *Handbook of Behavioural Neurobiology. Vol. 6: Motivation.* Edited by Satinoff, E, P Teitelbaum. New York: Plenum.

4312 Restak, R. 1979. *The Brain: The Last Frontier.* New York: Doubleday.

4313 Rinn, W E. 1984. The neuropsychology of facial expression: A review of the neurological and psychological mechanisms for producing facial expressions. *Psychological Bulletin* 95: 52-77.

4314 Roberts, A, B L Roberts. 1983. Neural origin of rhythmic movements. *Symposia of the Society for Experimental Biology* 37:

4315 Robinson, T, ed. 1983. *Behavioral Approaches to Brain Research.* Oxford: Oxford University Press.

4316 Rock, M K, J T Hackett, D L Brown. 1981. Does the Mauthner cell conform to the criteria of the command neuron concept? *Brain Research* 204: 21-27.

4317 Rogal, L, B Fischer. 1986. Eye-hand coordination: A model for computing reaction times in a visually guided reach task. *Biological Cybernetics* 55: 263-273.

4318 Rolls, E T, S J Thorpe, S P Maddison. 1983. Responses of striatal neurons in the behaving monkey. 1. Head of the caudate nucleus. *Behavior and Brain Research* 7: 179-210.

4319 Ross, E D. 1985. Modulation of affect and nonverbal communication by the right hemisphere. In *Principles of Behavioral Neurology.* Edited by Mesulam, M-M. Pp. 239-58. Philadelphia: F.A. Davis.

4320 Routhenbert, A. 1978. The reward system of the brain. *Scientific American* 239: 154-169.

4321 Sanes, J N, V A Jennings. 1984. Centrally programmed patterns of muscle activity in volunatry motor behavior of humans. *Experimental Brain Research* 54: 23-32.

4322 Schmitt, F O, et al, eds. 1981. *The Organization of the Cerebral Cortex.* Cambridge: M.I.T. Press.

4323 Schopler, E, G Mesibov, eds. 1987. *Neurobiological Issues in Autism.* New York: Plenum.

4324 Schull, J. 1988. The adaptive-evolutionary point of view in experimental psychology. In *Steven's Handbook of Experimental Psychology.* New York: Wiley.

4325 Searleman, A, Y-C Tsao, W Balzer. 1980. A re-examination of the relationship between birth stress and handedness. *Clinical Neuropsychology* 2: 124-128.

4326 Searleman, A, T F Cunningham, W Goodwin. 1988. Association between familial sinistrality and pathological left-handedness: A comparison of mentally retarded and nonretarded subjects. *Journal of Clinical and Experimental Neuropsychology* 2: 132-138.

4327 Selverston, A I. 1980. Are central pattern generators understandable? *Behavioral and Brain Sciences* 3: 535-571.

4328 Shagass, C, S Gershon, A J Friedoff, eds. 1977. *Psychopathology and Brain Dysfunction.* New York: Raven Press.

4329 Shair, H, G Barr, M Hofer, eds. 1991. *Developmental Psychobiology: New Methods and Changing Concepts.* New York: Oxford University Press.

4330 Shallice, T. 1989. *From Neuropsychology to Mental Structure.* Cambridge: MRC Applied Psychology Unit.

4331 Sheard, M H. 1984. Clinical-pharmacology of aggressive behavior. *Clinical Neuropathology* 7: 173-183.

4332 Shepherd, G M. 1983. *Neurobiology.* New York: Oxford University Press.

4333 Sherrington, C S. 1906. *The Integrative Action of the Nervous System.* New York: Scribners.

4334 Simmel, E C, M E Hahn, J K Walters, eds. 1983. *Aggressive Behavior: Genetic and Neural Approaches.* Hillsdale, NJ: Erlbaum.

4335 Simonov, P V. 1990. *The Motivated Brain: A Neurophysiological Analysis of Human Behavior.* New York: Gordon and Breach.

4336 Smith, J E, J D Lane, eds. 1982. *Neurobiology of Opiate Reward Mechanisms.* Amsterdam: Elsevier.

4337 Soubrie, P. 1986. Reconciling the role of central serotonin neurons in human and animal behavior. *Behavioral and Brain Sciences* 9: 319-63.

4338 Sperry, R W. 1976. Mental phenomena as causal determinants in brain function. In *Consciousness and the Brain.* Edited by Globus, G C, G Maxwell, I Savodmik. New York: Plenum.

4339 Sperry, R W. 1980. Mind-brain interaction: Mentalism, yes; dualism, no. *Neuroscience* 5: 195-206.

4340 Sprague, J M, A N Epstein, eds. 1980. *Progress in Psychobiology and Physiological Psychology.* New York: Academic Press.

4341 Squire, L, N Butters, eds. 1984. *The Neuropsychology of Memory.* New York: Guilford Press.

4342 Staddon, J E R. 1984. *Adaptive Behavior and Learning.* Cambridge: Cambridge University Press.

4343 Steklis, H D, A R Kling, eds. 1983. *Hormones, Drugs and Social Behavior in Primates.* Jamaica, N.Y.: Spectrum.

4344 Stelkis, H D, A R Kling. 1985. Neurobiology of affiliative behaviour in non-human primates. In *The Psychobiology of Attachment and Separation.* Edited by Reite, M, T Field. Pp. 93-134. New York: Academic Press.

4345 Stokes, P E, C R Sikes. 1988. The hypothalamic-pituitary-adrenocortical axis in major depression. *Neurological Clinics* 6: 1-19.

4346 Sundberg, J. 1982. Speech, song and emotions. In *Music, Mind and Brain: The Neurobiology of Music.* Edited by Clynes, M. Pp. 137-150. New York: Plenum.

4347 Szentagothai, J. 1975. The "module concept" in cerebral architecture. *Brain Research* 95: 475-96.

4348 Taylor, T J. 1975. *A Primer of Psychobiology.* San Francisco: Freeman.

4349 Thelen, E S, G Bradshaw, J A Ward. 1981. Spontaneous kicking in month-old infants: Manifestation of a human central locomotor program. *Behavioral and Neural Biology* 32: 45-53.

4350 Thompson, R F. 1986. The neurobiology of learning and memory. *Science* 233: 941-947.

4351 Thomson, R F. 1983. Neuronal substrates of simple associative learning: Classical conditioning. *Trends in Neuroscience* 6: 270-275.

4352 Thomson, R F, et al. 1983. The engram found? Initial localization of the memory trace for a basic form of associative learning. In *Progress in Psychobiology and Physiological Psychology.* Edited by Epstein, A N. Pp. 167-196. New York: Academic Press.

4353 Thomson, R, N Donegan. 1986. The search for the engram. In *Learning and Memory: A Biological View.* Edited by Martinez, J, R Kesner. Pp. 3-54. New York: Academic Press.

4354 Tiklenberg, J R, J E Thornton. 1983. Neuropeptides in geriatric psychopharmacology. *Psychopharmocology Bulletin* 19: 198-211.

4355 Toran-Allerand, C D. 1986. Sexual differentiation of the brain. In *Developmental Neuropsychobiology.* Edited by Greenough, W T, J M Juraska. Pp. 175-211. Orlando, FL: Academic Press.

4356 Touwen, B. 1976. *Neurological Development in Infancy.* Clinics in Developmental Medicine, no. 58. Spastics International Medical Publications. London: Heinemann.

4357 Towe, A L, E S Luschei. 1981. *Handbook of Behavioural Neurobiology. Vol. 5: Motor Coordination.* New York: Plenum.

4358 Tsunoda, T. 1985. *The Japanese Brain.* Tokyo: Taishukan Publishing Co.

4359 Tucker, D M, C E Stensile, R S Roth, S L Shearer. 1981. Right frontal lobe activation and right hemisphere performance: Decrement during depressed mood. *Archives of General Psychiatry* 38: 169-174.

4360 Tucker, D M, S L Dawson. 1984. Asymmetric EEG power and coherence as method actors generated emotions. *Biological Psychology* 19: 63-75.

4361 Tuckwell, H C, ed. 1988. *Introduction to Theoretical Neurobiology.* Cambridge: Cambridge University Press.

4362 Turkewitz, G. 1988. A prenatal source for the development of hemispheric specialization. In *Brain Lateralization in Children Developmental Implications.* Edited by Molfese, D, S Segalowitz. Pp. 73-83. London: Guilford Press.

4363 Uttal, W. 1978. *The Psychobiology of Mind.* Hillsdale, N.J.: Erlbaum.

4364 Valzelli, L. 1984. Reflections on experimental and human pathology of aggression. *Progress in Neuro-Psychopharmacology and Biological Psychitary* 8: 311-325.

4365 Vinken, P J, G W Bruyn, H L Klawans, eds. 1985. *Handbook of Clinical Neurology, Revised series.* Amsterdam: Elsevier.

4366 Virkkunen, M, M O Huttunen. 1982. Reactive hypoglycemic tendency among habitually violent offenders: A further study by means of the glucose tolerance test. *Neuropsychobiology* 8: 30-34.

4367 von Schilcher, F. 1988. *Vererbung des Verhaltens—eine Einführung für Biologen, Psychologen und Mediziner.* Stuttgart: Georg Thieme Verlag.

4368 Walker, J A, D S Olton. 1984. Fimbria-fornix lesions impair spatial working memory but not cognitive mapping. *Behavior Neuroscience* 98: 226-242.

4369 Walters, E T, J H Byrne. 1983. Associative conditioning of single sensory neurons suggests a cellular mechanism for learning. *Science* 219: 405-408.

4370 Warburton, D M. 1975. *Brain, Behaviour and Drugs: Introduction to the Neurochemistry of Behaviour.* London: Wiley.

4371 Waterhouse, L. 1988. Speculations on the neuroanatomical substrate of special talents. In *The Exceptional Brain.* Edited by Obler, K, D Fein. Pp. 493-512. New York: Guilford Press.

4372 Weis, S, G Weber, E Wenger, M Kimbacher. 1988. The human corpus callosum and the controversy about a sexual dimorphism. *Psychobiology* 16: 411-15.

4373 Weiss, K R, U T Koch, J Koester, D E Mandelbaum, I Kupfermann. 1981. Neural and molecular mechanisms of food-induced arousal in aplysia californica. *Advances in Physiological Sciences* 23: 305-344.

4374 Wetzel, M C, L G Howell. 1981. Properties and mechanisms of locomotion. In *Handbook of Behavioural Neurobiology. Vol. 5, Motor Coordination.* Edited by Towe, A L, E S Luschei. New York: Plenum.

4375 Whitaker, H, ed. 1988. *Phonological Processes and Brain Mechanisms.* New York: Springer.

4376 Wilensky, R. 1983. Story grammars versus story points. *Behavioral and Brain Sciences* 6: 579-623.

4377 Wilson, F R. 1988. Brain mechanisms in highly skilled movements. In *The Biology of Music Making*. Edited by Roehmann, F, F Wilson. St. Louis: MMB Music.

4378 Wine, J J. 1984. The structural basis of an innate behavioral pattern. *Journal of Experimental Biology* 112: 283-319.

4379 Winner, E, G Ettlinger. 1979. Do chimpanzee recognize photographs as representations of objects? *Neuropsychologia* 17: 413-19.

4380 Winston, J. 1985. *Brain and Psyche: The Biology of the Unconscious*. New York: Doubleday.

4381 Wise, S, ed. 1987. *Higher Brain Functions: Recent Explorations of the Brain's Emergent Properties*. New York: Wiley.

4382 Witelson, S, D Kigar. 1988. Anatomical development of the corpus callosum in humans: A review with reference to sex and cognition. In *Brain Lateralization in Children Developmental Implications*. Edited by Molfese, D, S Segalowitz. Pp. 35-59. London: Guilford Press.

4383 Yahr, P. 1988. Sexual differentiation of behavior in the context of developmental psychobiology. In *Developmental Psychobiology and Behavioral Ecology*. Edited by Blass, E M. Pp. 197-243. New York: Plenum.

4384 Yeudall, L T, D Fromm-Ausch, P Davies. 1982. Neuropsychological impairment in persistent delinquency. *Journal of Nervous and Mental Disease* 170: 257-265.

4385 Young, J Z. 1978. *The Programs of the Brain*. London: Oxford University Press.

4386 Young, A. 1983. The development of right hemisphere abilities. In *Functions of the Right Cerebral Hemisphere*. Edited by Young, A. New York: Academic Press.

4387 Young, A, ed. 1983. *Functions of the Right Cerebral Hemisphere*. New York: Academic Press.

4388 Young, D, ed. 1989. *Nerve Cells and Animal Behaviour*. Cambridge: Cambridge University Press.

4389 Young, M P, S Yamane. 1992. Sparse population coding of faces in the inferotemporal cortex. *Science* 256: 1327-1331.

4390 Zatorre, R J, A C Evans, E Meyer, A Gjedde. 1992. Lateralization of phonetic and pitch discrimination in speech processing. *Science* 256: 846-849.

4391 Zornetzer, S F. 1986. Memory: Electrophysiological Analogs. In *Learning and Memory: A Biological View.* Edited by Martinez, J L, Jr., R P Kesner. Pp. 237-266. New York: Academic Press.

4392 Zucker, I. 1983. Motivation, biological clocks and temporal organisation of behaviour. In *Handbook of Behavioural Neurobiology: Motivation.* Edited by Satinoff, E, P Teitelbaum. New York: Plenum.

# 12

# Emotion

4393 Appel, M A, K A Holroyd, L Gorkin. 1983. Anger and the etiology and progression of physical illness. In *Emotions in Health and Illness: Theoretical and Research Foundations.* Edited by Temoshok, L, C Van Dyke, L S Zegans. Pp. 73-87. New York: Grune and Stratton.

4394 Appley, M H, R Trumbull, eds. 1986. *Dynamics of Stress.* New York: Plenum.

4395 Apter, M J. 1982. *The Experience of Motivation.* London: Academic Press.

4396 Averill, J R. 1982. *Anger and Aggression: An Essay on Emotion.* New York: Springer.

4397 Ax, A F, R Lloyd, J C Gorham, A M Lootens, R Robinson. 1978. Autonomic learning: A measure of motivation. *Motivation and Emotion* 2: 213-42.

4398 Babchuk, W A, R B Hames, R A Thompson. 1985. Sex differences in the recognition of infant facial expressions of emotion: The primary caretaker hypothesis. *Ethology and Sociobiology* 6: 89-101.

4399 Badcock, C R. 1988. *Essential Freud.* Oxford: Blackwell.

4400 Bailey, K. 1987. *Human Paleopsychology: Applications to Aggression and Pathological Processes.* London: Erlbaum.

4401 Barfield, R J. 1984. Reproductive hormones and aggressive behavior. In *Biological Perspectives on Aggression.* Edited by Flannelly, K J, R J Blanchard, D C Blanchard. Pp. 105-34. New York: Alan R. Liss.

4402 Berkowitz, L. 1970. Aggressive humor as a stimulus to aggressive responses. *Journal of Personality and Social Psychology* 16: 710-717.

4403 Berkowitz, L. 1983. Aversively-stimulated aggression. *American Psychologist* 38: 1135-44.

4404 Berkowitz, L. 1984. Physical pain and the inclination to aggression. In *Biological Perspectives on Aggression*. Edited by Flanelly, K J, R J Blanchard, D C Blanchard. Pp. 27-47. New York: Alan R. Liss.

4405 Bindra, D. 1969. A unified interpretation of emotion and motivation. *Annals of the New York Academy of Sciences* 159: 1071-83.

4406 Blanchard, R J, D C Blanchard. 1981. The organization and modeling of animal aggression. In *The Biology of Aggression*. Edited by Brain, P F, D Benton. Pp. 529-61. Rockville, MD: Sijthoff & Noordhoff.

4407 Blanchard, D C, R J Blanchard. 1984. Inadequacy of pain-aggression hypothesis revealed in naturalistic settings. *Aggressive Behavior* 10: 33-46.

4408 Blanchard, D C, R J Blanchard. 1984. Affect and aggression: An animal model applied to human behavior. In *Advances in the Study of Aggression*. Edited by Blanchard, R J, D C Blanchard. Pp. 1-62. New York: Academic Press.

4409 Blanchard, R J, D C Blanchard, eds. 1984. *Advances in the Study of Aggression*. New York: Academic Press.

4410 Blankstein, K R, J Polivy, eds. 1982. *Self-Control and Self-Modification of Emotional Behavior*. New York: Plenum.

4411 Bleichfeld, B, B E Moely. 1984. Psychophysiological responses to an infant cry: Comparison of groups of women in different phases of the maternal cycle. *Developmental Psychology* 20: 1082-91.

4412 Bloch, S, P Orthous, G Santibanez. 1987. Effector patterns of basic emotions: A psychophysiological method for training actors. *Journal of Social and Biological Structures* 10: 1-19.

4413 Blumberg, S H, C E Izard. 1991. Patterns of emotion experiences as predictors of facial expressions of emotion. *Merrill-Palmer Quarterly* 37: 183-198.

4414 Booth, M L, D A T Siddle, N W Bond. 1989. Effects of conditioned stimulus fear-relevance and preexposure on expectancy and electrodermal measures of human Pavlovian conditioning. *Psychophysiology* 26: 281-291.

4415 Borod, J C, H S Caron. 1980. Facedness and emotion related to lateral dominance, sex and expression type. *Neuropsychologia* 18: 237-41.

4416 Borod, J C, E Koff, B White. 1983. Facial asymmetry in posed and spontaneous expressions of emotion. *Brain and Cognition* 2: 165-75.

4417 Borod, J C, E Koff, M Perlman-Lorch, M Nicholas. 1986. The expression and perception of facial emotion in patients with focal brain damage. *Neuropsychologia* 24: 169-80.

4418 Brady, J V. 1975. Conditioning and emotion. In *Emotions: Their Parameters and Measurement.* Edited by Levi, L. New York: Raven Press.

4419 Brady, J V. 1975. Toward a behavioral biology of emotion. In *Emotions: Their Parameters and Measurement.* Edited by Levi, L. Pp. 17-45. New York: Raven Press.

4420 Brain, P F, D Benton, eds. 1981. *Multidisciplinary Approaches to Aggression Research.* Amsterdam: Elsevier/North Holland.

4421 Brain, P F, D Benton, eds. 1981. *The Biology of Aggression.* Rockville, Md: Sijthoff & Noordhoff.

4422 Brain, P F, D Benton. 1983. Conditions of housing, hormones, and aggressive behavior. In *Hormones and Aggressive Behavior.* Edited by Svare, B B. Pp. 351-72. New York: Plenum.

4423 Brown, J D, S E Taylor. 1986. Affect and the processing of personal information: Evidence for mood-activated self-schemata. *Journal of Experimental Social Psychology* 22: 436-52.

4424 Bryden, M P, R G Ley, J H Sugarman. 1982. A left-ear advantage for identifying the emotional quality of tonal sequences. *Neuropsychologia* 20: 83-87.

4425 Buck, R. 1980. Nonverbal behavior and the theory of emotion: The facial feedback hypothesis. *Journal of Social Psychology* 38: 811-824.

4426 Buck, R. 1984. *The Communication of Emotion.* New York: Guildford Press.

4427 Buck, R. 1985. Prime theory: An integrated view of motivation and emotion. *Psychological Review* 92: 389-413.

4428 Buck, R, ed. 1986. *The Psychology of Emotion.* New York: Cambridge University Press.

4429 Buck, R. 1988. *Human Motivation and Emotion.* New York: Wiley.

4430 Bugental, D B. 1986. Unmasking the 'polite smile': Situational and personal determinants of managed affect in adult-child interaction. *Social Psychology Bulletin* 12: 7-16.

4431 Cacioppo, J T, R E Petty, M E Losch, H S Kim. 1986. Electromyographic activity over facial muscle regions can differentiate the valence and intensity of affective reactions. *Journal of Social Psychology* 50: 260-8.

4432 Cacioppo, J T, J Martzke, R Petty, L Tassinary. 1988. Specific forms of facial EMG response index emotions during an interview: From Darwin to the continuous flow hypothesis of affect-laden information processing. *Journal of Social Psychology* 54: 592-604.

4433 Campos, J J. 1980/1. Human emotions: Their new importance and their role in social referencing. In *Annual Report, Research and Clinical Center for Child Development.* Sapporo: Faculty of Education, Hokkaido University.

4434 Cannon, W B. 1936. *Bodily Changes in Pain, Hunger, Fear and Rage.* New York: Appleton-Century.

4435 Cassel, R. 1985. Biofeedback for developing self-control of tension and stress in one's hierarchy of psychological states. *Psychology* 22: 50-7.

4436 Castello, C G. 1976. *Anxiety and Depression: The Adaptive Emotion.* Montreal: McGill University Press.

4437 Chance, M R A. 1980. An ethological assessment of emotion. In *Emotion: Theories of Emotion.* Edited by Plutchik, R, H Kellerman. New York: Academic Press.

4438 Cherfas, J, R Lewin, eds. 1980. *Not Work Alone.* London: Temple Smith.

4439 Chesney, M A, R H Rosenman. 1985. *Anger and Hostility in Cardiovascular and Behavioral Disorders.* Washington: Hemisphere.

4440 Chwalisz, K, E Drener, D Gallagher. 1988. Autonomic arousal feedback and emotional experience: Evidence from the spinal cord injured *Journal of Social Psychology* 54: 820-8.

4441 Cialdini, R B, et al. 1987. Empathy bases helping: Is it selflessly or selfishly motivated? *Journal of Social Psychology* 52: 749-58.

4442 Cicone, M, W Wapner, H Gardner. 1980. Sensitivity to emotional expressions and situations in organic patients. *Cortex* 16: 145-58.

4443 Clark, M S. 1982. A role for arousal in the link between feeling states, judgments, and behavior. In *Affect and Cognition: The Seventeenth Annual Carnegie Symposium on Cognition.* Edited by Clark, M S, S T Fiske. Pp. 263-89. Hillsdale, NJ: Erlbaum.

4444 Clark, M S, A M Isen. 1982. Toward understanding the relationship between feeling states and social behavior. In *Cognitive Social Psychology.* Edited by Hastorf, A, A M Isen. Pp. 73-108. New York: Elsevier North-Holland.

4445 Clark, M S, S Milberg, J Ross. 1983. Arousal cues arousal-related material from memory. *Journal of Verbal Learning and Verbal Behavior* 22: 633-49.

4446 Clark, M S, R Ouellette, M Powell, S Milberg. 1987. Recipient's mood, relationship type, and helping. *Journal of Social Psychology* 53: 94-108.

4447 Clynes, M, J Panksepp, eds. 1988. *Emotions and Psychopathology.* New York: Plenum.

4448 Cooper, S, ed. 1981. *Theory in Psychopharmacology.* New York: Academic Press.

4449 Cosmides, L. 1983. Invariances in the acoustic expression of emotion during speech. *Journal of Experimental Psychology: Human Perception and Performance* 9: 864-881.

4450 Cunningham, M. 1988. Does happiness mean friendliness?: induced mood and heterosexual self-disclosure. *Social Psychology Bulletin* 2: 283-97.

4451 Davitz, J R, ed. 1964. *The Communication of Emotional Meaning.* New York: McGraw-Hill.

4452 Denemberg, V H. 1964. Critical periods, stimulation input and emotional reactivity: A theory of infantile stimulation. *Psychological Review* 71: 335-351.

4453 Diamond, R, S Carey, K J Back. 1983. Genetic influences on the development of spatial skills during early adolescence. *Cognition* 13: 167-185.

4454 Dienstbier, R A, D Hillman, J Hillman, J Lehnhoff, M C Valkenaar. 1975. An emotional-attribution approach to moral behavior: Interfacing cognitive and avoidance theories of moral development. *Psychology Review* 82: 299-315.

4455 Dimsdale, J E, C Pierce, D Schoenfeld, A Brown, R Zusman, R Graham. 1986. Suppressed anger and blood pressure: The effects of race, sex, social class, obesity, and age. *Psychosomatic Medicine* 48: 430-6.

4456 Donnerstein, E, M Donnerstein, R Evans. 1975. Erotic stimuli and aggression: Facilitation or inhibition. *Journal of Social Psychology* 32: 227-44.

4457 Doob, A N, L Wood. 1972. Catharsis and aggression: Effects of annoyance and retaliation on aggressive behavior. *Journal of Social Psychology* 22: 156-62.

4458 Dopson, W G, B E Beckwith, D M Tucker, P C Bullard-Bates. 1984. Asymmetry of facial expression in spontaneous emotion. *Cortex* 20: 243-52.

4459 Ebert, P D. 1983. Selection for aggression in a natural population. In *Aggressive Behavior: Genetic and Neural Approaches.* Edited by Himmel, E C, M R Hahn, J K Walterd. Pp. 103-27. Hillsdale, NJ: Erlbaum.

4460 Edmunds, G, D C Kendrick. 1980. *The Measurement of Human Aggressiveness.* Chichester: Ellis Harwood.

4461 Efran, M G, J A Cheyne. 1974. Affective concomitants of the invasion of shared space: Behavioral, physiological, and verbal indicators. *Journal of Social Psychology* 29: 219-226.

4462 Efran, J S, T J Spangler. 1979. Why grown-ups cry: A two factor theory and evidence from the Miracle Worker. *Motivation and Emotion* 3: 63-72.

4463 Eibl-Eibesfeldt, I, C Sütterlin. 1992. *Im Banne der Angst. Zur Natur-und Kunstgeschichte menschlicher Abwehrsymbolik. Mit 335 Abbildungen.* München: Piper.

4464 Ekman, P, W V Friesen. 1969. The repertoire of nonverbal behavior: Categories, origins, usage and coding. *Semiotica* 1: 49-98.

4465 Ekman, P, E R Sorenson, W V Friesen. 1969. Pan-cultural elements in social displays of emotion. *Science* 164: 86-88.

4466 Ekman, P, W V Friesen, P Ellsworth. 1972. *Emotion in the Human Face: Guidelines for Research and an Integration of the Findings.* New York: Pergamon.

4467 Ekman, P, W V Friesen, K R Scherer. 1976. Body movement and voice pitch in deceptive interaction. *Semiotica* 16: 23-7.

4468 Ekman, P, H Oster. 1979. Facial expressions of emotion. *Annual Review of Psychology* 30: 527-554.

4469 Ekman, P, W V Friesen, S Ancoli. 1980. Facial signs of emotional experience. *Journal of Social Psychology* 39: 1125-34.

4470 Ekman, P, G Roper, J C Hager. 1980. Deliberate facial movement. *Child Development* 51: 886-91.

4471 Ekman, P. 1980. *The Face of Man: Expression of Universal Emotions in a New Guinea Village.* New York: Garland.

4472 Ekman, P, W V Friesen, S Ancoli. 1980. Facial signs of emotional expression. *Journal of Social Psychology* 39: 1125-1134.

4473 Ekman, P, R W Levenson, W V Friesen. 1983. Emotions differ in autonomic nervous system activity. *Science* 221: 1208-10.

4474 Ekman, P. 1984. Expression and the nature of emotion. In *Approaches to Emotion.* Edited by Scherer, K, P Ekman. Pp. 319-344. Hillsdale, NJ: Erlbaum.

4475 Ekman, P. 1985. *Telling Lies: Clues to Deceit in the Marketplace, Marriage, and Politics.* New York: Berkeley Books.

4476 Ekman, P, W V Friesen, R C Simons. 1985. Is the startle reaction an emotion? *Journal of Social Psychology* 49: 1416-1426.

4477 Ekman, P. 1986. A new pan-cultural expression of emotion. *Motivation and Emotion* 10: 159-168.

4478 Ekman, P, et al. 1987. Universals and cultural differences in the judgements of facial expressions of emotion. *Journal of Social Psychology* 53: 712-17.

4479 Ekman, P, W V Friesen, M O'Sullivan. 1988. Smiles when lying. *Journal of Social Psychology* 54: 414-420.

4480 Ekman, P, W V Friesen. 1988. Who knows what about contempt: A reply to Izard and Haynes. *Motivation and Emotion* 12: 17-22.

4481 Ekman, P, K Heider. 1988. The universality of a contempt expression: A replication. *Motivation and Emotion* 12: 303-8.

4482 Ekman, P. 1989. The argument and evidence about universals in facial expressions of emotion. In *Handbook of Social Psychophysiology*. Edited by Wagner, H, A Manstead. Pp. 143-164. New York: Wiley.

4483 Ekman, P, R J Davidson, W V Friesen. 1990. Emotional expression and brain physiology II: The Duchenne smile. *Journal of Social Psychology* 58: 342-353.

4484 Eliade, M. 1964. *Shamanism: Archaic Techniques of Ecstasy.* Translated by Trask, W. R. Bollingen Series. Princeton: Princeton University Press.

4485 Ellis, A A, J M Whiteley, eds. 1979. *Theoretical and Empirical Foundations of Rational Emotive Therapy.* San Francisco: Brooks-Cole.

4486 Ellis, H C, R L Thomas, I A Rodriguez. 1984. Emotional mood states and memory: Elaborative encoding, semantic processing, and cognitive effort. *Journal of Experimental Psychology: Learning, Memory, and Cognition* 10: 470-82.

4487 Etcoff, N L. 1984. Selective attention to facial identity and facial emotion. *Neuropsychologia* 22: 281-95.

4488 Etcoff, N. 1986. The neuropsychology of emotional expression. In *Advances in Clinical Neuropsychology*. Edited by Goldstein, G, R Tarter. Pp. 127-79. New York: Plenum.

4489 Fiedler, K, H Pampe, U Scherf. 1986. Mood and memory for tightly organized social information. *European Journal of Social Psychology* 16: 149-64.

4490 Fiedler, K, J Forgas, eds. 1988. *Affect, Cognition and Social Behavior.* Toronto: Hogrefe.

4491 Field, T. 1982. Affective displays of high-risk infants during early interactions. In *Emotion and Interactions*. Edited by Field, T, A Fogel. Hillsdale, N.J.: Erlbaum.

4492 Field, T, A Fogel, eds. 1982. *Emotion and Interactions.* Hillsdale, N.J.: Erlbaum.

4493 Forgas, J, S Moylan. 1988. After the movies: Transient mood and social judgments. *Social Psychology Bulletin* 4: 478-89.

4494 Fox, N A, R J Davidson, eds. 1984. *The Psychobiology of Affective Development*. Hillsdale, N.J.: Erlbaum.

4495 Fox, N A, R J Davidson. 1988. Patterns of brain electrical activity during facial signs of emotion in 10-month-old infants. *Developmental Psychology* 24: 230-236.

4496 Fridlund, A J, C E Izard. 1983. Electromyographic studies of facial expressions of emotions and patterns of emotion. In *Social Psychophysiology: A Sourcebook*. Edited by Cacioppo, J T, R E Petty. Pp. 243-286. New York: Guilford Press.

4497 Fridlund, A J, G E Schwartz, S C Fowler. 1984. Pattern recognition of self-reported emotional state from multiple-site facility EMG activity during affective imagery. *Psychophysiology* 21: 622-37.

4498 Fridlund, A J, J T Cacioppo. 1986. Guidelines for human electromyographic research. *Psychophysiology* 23: 567-89.

4499 Fridlund, A J, P Ekman, H Oster. 1987. Facial expressions of emotion. In *Nonverbal Behavior and Communication*. Edited by Siegman, A, S Feldstein. Pp. 143-223. Hillsdale, NJ: Erlbaum.

4500 Fridlund, A J. 1988. What can asymmetry and laterality in facial EMG tell us about the face and brain? *International Journal of Neuroscience* 39: 53-69.

4501 Friedman, L. 1981. How affiliation affects stress in fear and anxiety situations. *Journal of Social Psychology* 40: 1102-17.

4502 Frijda, N H. 1986. *The Emotions*. Cambridge: Cambridge University Press.

4503 Friswell, R, K M McConkey. 1989. Hypnotically induced mood. *Cognition and Emotion* 3: 1-26.

4504 Frof, S. 1976. *Realms of the Human Unconscious: Observations from L.S.D. Research*. New York: Dutton.

4505 Funkenstein, D H. 1955. The physiology of fear and anger. *Scientific American* 192: 74-80.

4506 Gatchel, R J. 1988. Clinical effectiveness of biofeedback in reducing anxiety. In *Social Psychophysiology and Emotion: Theory and Clinical Applications*. Edited by Wagner, H. Pp. 197-210. Chichester: Wiley.

4507 Gatchel, R J, D Barnes. 1989. Physiological self-control and emotion. In *Handbook of Social Psychophysiology*. Edited by Wagner, H, A Manstead. Pp. 121-138. New York: Wiley.

4508 Geer, J H. 1965. The development of a scale to measure fear. *Behaviour Research and Therapy* 3: 45-53.

4509 Gellhorn, E, G N Loofburrow. 1963. *Emotions and Emotional Disorders: A Neurophysiological Study*. New York: Harper & Row.

4510 Gilbert, P. 1989. *Human Nature and Suffering*. Hillsdale, NJ: Erlbaum.

4511 Goldstein, M L. 1968. Physiological theories of emotion: A critical review from the standpoint of behaviour theory. *Psychological Bulletin* 69: 23-40.

4512 Gray, J A, S Levine. 1964. Effects of induced oestrus on emotional behaviour in selected strains of rats. *Nature* 201: 1198-1200.

4513 Gray, J. 1987. *The Psychology of Fear and Stress*. 2nd ed Cambridge: Cambridge University Press.

4514 Griffiths, P E. 1990. Modularity, and the psychoevolutionary theory of emotion. *Biology and Philosophy* 5: 149-174.

4515 Guidetti, M. 1991. Vocal expression of emotions: A cross-cultural and developmental approach. *Année Psychologique* 91: 383-96.

4516 Hamburg, D, B A Hamburg, J D Barchos. 1975. Anger and depression in perspective of behavioral biology. In *Emotions: Their Parameters and Measurement*. Edited by Levi, L. Pp. 235-273. New York: Raven Press.

4517 Harré, R. 1991. *Physical Being: A Theory for a Corporeal Psychology*. Oxford: Blackwell.

4518 Heilman, K M, P Satz, eds. 1983. *Neuropsychology of Human Emotion*. New York: Guilford Press.

4519 Heller, A. 1980. The emotional division of labor between the sexes. *Social Praxis* 7: 205-218.

4520 Heller, W, J Levy. 1981. Perception and expression of emotion in right-handers and left-handers. *Neuropsychologia* 19: 263-72.

4521 Himmel, E C, M R Hahn, J K Walterd, eds. 1983. *Aggressive Behavior: Genetic and Neural Approaches.* Hillsdale, NJ: Erlbaum.

4522 Hofer, M A. 1984. Relationships as regulators: A psychobiologic perspective on bereavement. *Psychosomatic Medicine* 46: 183-98.

4523 Isen, A M, T E Shalker, M Clark, L Karp. 1978. Affect accessibility of material in memory, and behavior: A cognitive loop? *Journal of Social Psychology* 36: 1-12.

4524 Isen, A M, T E Shalker. 1982. The effect of feeling state on evaluation of positive, neutral, and negative stimuli: When you 'Accentuate the Positive,' do you 'Eliminate the Negative'? *Social Psychology Quarterly* 45: 58-63.

4525 Isen, A M. 1984. Toward understanding the role of affect in cognition. In *Handbook of Social Cognition.* Edited by Wyer, R, T Srull. Pp. 179-236. Hillsdale: Erlbaum.

4526 Isen, A M. 1985. Asymmetry of happiness and sadness in effects on memory in normal college students: Comment on Hasher, Rose, Zacks, Sanft, and Doren. *Journal of Experimental Psychology: General* 11: 388-91.

4527 Isser, N, L Schwartz. 1989. *The History of Conversion and Contemporary Cults.* New York: Peter Lang.

4528 Izard, C E. 1977. *Human Emotions.* New York: Plenum.

4529 Izard, C E, ed. 1979. *Emotions in Personality and Psychopathology.* New York: Plenum.

4530 Izard, C E. 1979. Facial expression, emotion, and motivation. In *Nonverbal Behavior.* Edited by Wolfgang, A. New York: Academic Press.

4531 Izard, C E. 1979. Expression of emotions as a transcultural language in social interaction and theatrical performance. In *Aspects of Nonverbal Communication.* Edited by von Raffler-Engle, W. Amsterdam: Swets & Zeitlinger.

4532 Izard, C E. 1980. The emergence of emotion and the development of consciousness in infancy. In *The Psychobiology of Human Consciousness.* Edited by Davidson, J, R Davidson. New York: Plenum.

4533 Izard, C E, ed. 1982. *Measuring Emotions in Infants and Children.* New York: Cambridge University Press.

4534 Izard, C, E J Kagan, R Zajone. 1984. *Emotions, Cognition, and Behavior*. Cambridge: Cambridge University Press.

4535 Izard, C E, S H Blumberg, C K Oyster. 1985. Age and sex differences in the pattern of emotions in childhood anxiety and depression. In *Motivation, Emotion, and Personality*. Edited by Spence, J T, C E Izard. Pp. 317-324. Amsterdam: Elsevier.

4536 Izard, C E, O M Haynes. 1988. On the form and universality of the contempt expression: A correction for Ekman and Friesen's claim of discovery. *Motivation and Emotion* 12: 1-16.

4537 Izard, C E. 1990. Facial expressions and the regulation of emotions. *Journal of Social Psychology* 58: 487-489.

4538 Izard, C E, O M Haynes, G Chisholm, K Baak. 1991. Emotional determinants of infant-mother attachment. *Child Development* 62: 906-17.

4539 Jacobson, E. 1967. *Biology of Emotions*. Springfield, IL: Charles C. Thomas.

4540 James, G D, L S Yee, G A Harshfield, S G Blanke, T Pickering. 1986. The influence of happiness, anger, and anxiety on the blood pressure of borderline hypertensives. *Psychosomatic Medicine* 48: 502-8.

4541 Jenkins, J H, M Karno. 1992. The meaning of expressed emotion: Theoretical issues raised by cross-cultural research. *American Journal of Psychiatry* 149: 9-21.

4542 Job, R F S. 1987. The effect of mood on helping behavior. *Journal of Social Psychology* 127: 323-328.

4543 Johnson, W F, R N Emde, K R Scherer, M D Klinnert. 1986. Recognition of emotion from vocal cues. *Archives of General Psychiatry* 43: 280-284.

4544 Kaufman, I C, L A Rosenblum. 1969. Effects of separation from mother on the emotional behavior of infant monkeys. *Annals of the New York Academy of Science* 159: 691-695.

4545 Kenrick, D T, R B Cialdini, D E Linder. 1979. Misattribution under fear-producing circumstances: Four failures to replicate. *Social Psychology Bulletin* 5: 329-34.

4546 Kiecolt-Glaser, J K, W Garner, C Speicher, G Penn, J Holiday, R Glaser. 1984. Psychosocial modifiers of immunocompetence in medical students. *Psychosomatic Medicine* 46: 7-13.

4547 King, N J, E Gullone, T H Ollendick. 1992. Manifest anxiety and fearfulness in children and adolescents. *Journal of Genetic Psychology* 153: 63-73.

4548 Kinsbourne, M, B Bemporad. 1984. Lateralization of emotion: A model and the evidence. In *The Psychobiology of Affective Development.* Edited by Fox, N A, R J Davidson. Hillsdale, N.J.: Erlbaum.

4549 Klein, D F. 1981. Anxiety reconceptualized In *Anxiety: New Research and Changing Concepts.* Edited by Klein, D F, J Rabkin. Pp. 235-263. New York: Raven Press.

4550 Kleinginna, P R, A M Kleinginna. 1981. A categorized list of emotion definitions, with suggestions for a consensual definition. *Motivation and Emotion* 5: 348-379.

4551 Klinnert, M D, J J Campos, J F Sorce, R N Emde, M Svejda. 1983. Emotions as behaviour regulators. In *Emotion: Theory, Research and Experience.* Edited by Plutchik, R, H Kellerman. New York: Academic Press.

4552 Knutson, J F, R J Viken. 1982. Animal analogues of human aggression: Studies of social experience and escalation. In *Biological Perspectives on Aggression.* Edited by Flannelly, K J, R J Blanchard, D C Blanchard. Pp. 75-94. New York: Alan R. Liss.

4553 Laird, J D. 1984. The real role of facial response in the experience of emotion: A reply to Tourangeau and Ellsworth, and others. *Journal of Social Psychology* 47: 909-17.

4554 Landauer, T K, J W M Whiting. 1981. Correlates and consequences of stress in infancy. In *Handbook of Cross-Cultural Human Development.* Edited by Munroe, R H, R L Munroe, B B Whiting. New York: Garland.

4555 Langfeld, H S. 1918. The judgment of emotions from facial expressions. *Journal of Abnormal Psychology* 13: 172-184.

4556 LeDoux, J. 1986. A neurobiological view of the psychology of emotion. In *Mind and Brain: Dialogues between Cognitive Psychology and Neuroscience.* Edited by LeDoux, J, W F Hirst. New York: Cambridge University Press.

4557 Levenson, R W. 1988. Emotion and the autonomic nervous system: A prospectus for research on autonomic specificity. In *Social Psychophysiology and Emotion: Theory and Clinical Applications.* Edited by Wagner, H L. Pp. 17-42. Chichester: Wiley.

4558 Levi, L, ed. 1975. *Emotions: Their Paramenters and Measurement.* New York: Raven.

4559 Lewis, M, L A Rosenblum. 1974. The Origins of Fear. In Pp. 76-103. New York: Wiley.

4560 Livesey, P. 1986. *Learning and Emotion: A Biological Synthesis.* Hillsdale, NJ: Erlbaum.

4561 MacLean, P D. 1975. Sensory and perceptive factors in emotional functions of the triune brain. In *Emotions: Their Parameters and Measurement.* Edited by Levi, L. Pp. 71-92. New York: Raven Press.

4562 Mark, V H, F Ervin. 1971. *Violence and the Brain.* New York: Harper & Row.

4563 Maser, J D, ed. 1987. *Depression and Expressive Behavior.* Hillsdale, NJ: Erlbaum.

4564 Maslow, A. 1964. *Religions, Values and Peak-Experiences.* Columbus: Ohio State University Press.

4565 Maudler, G. 1975. The search for emotion. In *Emotions: Their Parameters and Measurement.* Edited by Levi, L. Pp. 1-15. New York: Raven Press.

4566 McClain, E. 1978. Feminists and nonfeminists: Contrasting profiles in independence and affiliation. *Psychological Reports* 43: 435-441.

4567 McClelland, D C. 1982. The need for power, sympathetic activation, and illness. *Motivation and Emotion* 6: 31-41.

4568 McNaughton, N. 1989. *Biology and Emotion.* Cambridge: Cambridge University Press.

4569 Melnechuk, T. 1988. Emotions, brain, immunity, and health: A review. In *Emotions and Psychopathology.* Edited by Clynes, M, J Panksepp. New York: Plenum.

4570 Metzner, R. 1980. Ten classical metaphors of self-transformation. *Journal of Transpersonal Psychology* 12: 47-62.

4571 Meyers, M, B D Smith. 1986. Hemispheric asymmetry and emotions: Effects of nonverbal affective stimuli. *Biological Psychology* 22: 11-20.

4572 Milberg, S, M S Clark. 1988. Moods and compliance. *British Journal of Social Psychology* 27: 79-90.

4573 Mitchell, G, J Erwin, eds. 1987. *Behavior, Cognition, and Motivation.* New York: Alan R. Liss.

4574 Morse, C A, L Dennerstein, K Varnavides, G D Burrows. 1988. Menstrual cycle symptoms: A comparison of a non-clinical sample with a patient group. *Journal of Affective Disorders* 14: 41-50.

4575 Morse, C A. 1989. Menopausal mood disorders. *Contemporary Therapy* 15: 22-27.

4576 Natale, M, R E Gur, R C Gur. 1983. Hemispheric asymmetries in processing emotional expressions. *Neuropsychologia* 21: 555-65.

4577 Nesse, R. 1990. Evolutionary explanations of emotions. *Human Nature* 1: 261-289.

4578 Ney, T, A Gale. 1988. A critique of laboratory studies of emotion with particular reference to psychophysiological aspects. In *Social Psychophysiology and Emotion: Theory and Clinical Applications.* Edited by Wagner, H L. Pp. 65-83. Chichester: Wiley.

4579 Oettingev, G, M E P Seligman. 1990. Pessimism and behavioural signs of depression in east versus west Berlin. *European Journal of Social Psychology* 20: 207-220.

4580 Oken, D. 1960. An experimental study of suppressed anger and blood pressure. *Archives of General Psychology* 2: 441-56.

4581 Olweus, D. 1979. Stability of aggressive reactions in males: A review. *Psychological Bulletin* 86: 852-75.

4582 Olweus, D. 1984. Development of stable aggressive reaction patterns in males. In *Advances in the Study of Aggression.* Edited by Blanchard, R J, D C Blanchard. Pp. 103-37. New York: Plenum.

4583 Orr, S P, J T Lanzetta. 1984. Extinction of an emotional response in the presence of facial expression of emotion. *Motivation and Emotion* 8: 55-66.

4584 Panksepp, J. 1982. Toward a general psychobiological theory of emotions. *Behavioral and Brain Scienes* 5: 407-467.

4585 Panksepp, J, S Siviy, L Normansell. 1985. Brain opioids and social emotions. In *The Psychobiology of Attachment and Separation.* Edited by Reite, M, T Fields. New York: Academic Press.

4586 Panksepp, J. 1986. The anatomy of emotions. In *Emotions: Theory, Research and Experience: Biological Foundations of Emotions.* Edited by Plutchik, R, H Kellerman. Pp. 91-124. New York: Academic Press.

4587 Panksepp, J. 1989. The neurobiology of emotions: Of animal brains and human feelings. In *Handbook of Social Psychophysiology.* Edited by Wagner, H, A Manstead. Pp. 5-26. New York: Wiley.

4588 Plutchik, R, H Kellerman, eds. 1980. *Emotion: Theory, Research and Experience, Vol 1.* New York: Academic Press.

4589 Plutchik, R. 1980. *Emotion: A Psychoevolutionary Synthesis.* New York: Harper & Row.

4590 Plutchik, R, H Kellerman. 1986. *The Origins of Behavior.* Orlando, FL: Academic Press.

4591 Plutchik, R. 1991. *Emotion.* 2nd ed Lanham, Md: University Press of America.

4592 Popp, K, A Baum. 1989. Hormones and emotions: Affective correlates of endocrine activity. In *Handbook of Social Psychophysiology.* Edited by Wagner, H, A Manstead. Pp. 99-120. New York: Wiley.

4593 Pribram, K H, D McGuinness. 1975. Arousal, activation, and effort in the control of attention. *Psychological Review* 82: 116-49.

4594 Pribram, K H. 1981. Emotions. In *Handbook of Clinical Neuropsychology.* Edited by Filskov, S K, T J Boll. Pp. 102-34. New York: Wiley-Interscience.

4595 Ricciuti, H N. 1974. Fear and the development of social attachments in the first year of life. In *The Origins of Fear.* Edited by Lewis, M, L A Rosenblum. Pp. 76-103. New York: Wiley.

4596 Riskind, J H, C C Gotay. 1982. Physical posture: Could it have regulatory or feedback effects on motivation. *Motivation and Emotion* 6: 273-98.

4597 Roberts, R J, T C Weerts. 1982. Cardiovascular responding during anger and fear imagery. *Psychological Reports* 50: 219-30.

4598 Robinson, R G, K L Kubos, K Rao, T R Price. 1984. Mood disorders in stroke patients: Importance of location of lesion. *Brain* 107: 81-93.

4599 Rodgers, R J. 1981. Pain and aggression. In *The Biology of Aggression.* Edited by Brain, P F, D Benton. Pp. 519-27. Rockville, Maryland: Sijthoff & Nordhoff.

4600 Rosenhan, D L, J Karylowski, P Salovey, K Hargis. 1981. Emotion and altrusim. In *Altruism and Helping Behavior.* Edited by Rushton, J P, R M Sorrentino. Pp. 233-48. Hillsdale, NJ: Erlbaum.

4601 Russell, W M S, C Russell. 1968. *Violence, Monkeys and Man.* London: Macmillan.

4602 Russell, J A. 1991. Culture and the categorization of emotions. *Psychological Bulletin* 10: 426-50.

4603 Sackeim, H A, R C Gur. 1982. Facial asymmetry and the communication of emotion. In *Social Psychophysiolog.* Edited by Cacioppo, J T, R E Petty. New York: Guilford Press.

4604 Salovey, P, J Rodin. 1984. Some antecedents and consequences of social comparison jealousy. *Journal of Social Psychology* 47: 780-92.

4605 Salovey, P, D L Rosenhan. 1989. Mood states and prosocial behavior. In *Handbook of Social Psychophysiology.* Edited by Wagner, H L, A S R Manstead. Pp. 369-89. Chichester: Wiley.

4606 Satinoff, E, P Teitelbaum, eds. 1983. *Motivation.* New York: Plenum.

4607 Schachter, J. 1957. Pain, fear, and anger in hypertensives and normotensives: A psychophysiological study. *Psychosomatic Medicine* 19: 17-29.

4608 Schalling, D, B Cronholm, M Asberg. 1975. Components of state and trait anxiety as related to personality and arousal. In *Emotions: Their Parameters and Measurement.* Edited by Levi, L. Pp. 603-617. New York: Raven Press.

4609 Scherer, K R. 1979. Nonlinguistic vocal indicators of emotion and psychopathology. In *Emotions in Personality and Psychopathology.* Edited by Izard, C E. Pp. 493-529. New York: Plenum.

4610 Scherer, K R. 1981. Vocal indicators of stress. In *Speech Evaluation in Psychiatry*. Edited by Darby, J. Pp. 171-87. New York: Grune & Stratton.

4611 Scherer, K R, P Ekman, eds. 1984. *Approaches to emotion.* Hillsdale, NJ: Erlbaum.

4612 Scherer, K R. 1984. On the nature and function of emotion: A component process approach. In *Approaches to Emotion*. Edited by Scherer, K, P Ekman. Pp. 293-318. Hillsdale, NJ: Erlbaum.

4613 Scherer, K R. 1985. Vocal affect signalling: A comparative approach. In *Advances in the Study of Behavior*. Edited by Rosenblatt, J, C Beer, M-C Busnel, P J B Slater. Pp. 189-244. New York: Academic Press.

4614 Scherer, K R, H G Wallbott, F Tolkmitt, G Bergmann. 1985. *Die Stress Reaktion: Physiologie und Verhalten.* Gottingen: Hogrefe.

4615 Scherer, K R. 1986. Voice, stress, and emotion. In *Dynamics of Stress*. Edited by Appley, M H, R Trumbull. Pp. 159-81. New York: Plenum.

4616 Scherer, K R, H G Wallbott, A B Summerfield. 1986. *Experiencing Emotion: A Cross-Cultural Study.* Cambridge: Cambridge University Press.

4617 Scherer, K R, A Kappas. 1988. Vocal affect expression in primates. In *Primate Vocal communication*. Edited by Todt, D, P Goedeking, E Newman. Pp. 171-94. Berlin: Springer.

4618 Scherer, K R. 1989. Vocal correlates of emotional arousal and affective disturbance. In *Handbook of Social Psychophysiology*. Edited by Wagner, H, A Manstead. Pp. 165-198. New York: Wiley.

4619 Schiefenhövel, W, M Schleidt, K Grammer. 1985. Mimik und Emotion: Verhaltensbiologische Aspekte. In *Der Mensch und seine Gefühle*. Edited by Schubert., V. St. Ottilien: E.O.S.

4620 Schwartz, G E, D A Weinberger, J A Singer. 1981. Cardiovascular differentiation of happiness, sadness, anger and fear following images and exercise. *Psychosomatic Medicine* 43: 343-64.

4621 Schwartz, N, G L Clore. 1983. Mood, misattribution, and judgments of well-being: Informative and directive functions of affective states. *Journal of Social Psychology* 45: 513-23.

4622 Schwartz, G M, C Izard, S E Ansul. 1985. The 5-month-old's ability to discriminate facial expressions of emotion. *Infant Behavior and Development* 8: 65-77.

4623 Scott, J P. 1980. The function of emotions in behavioural systems: A systems theory analysis. In *Emotion: Theory, Research and Experience: Theories of Emotion.* Edited by Plutchik, R, H Kellerman. New York: Academic Press.

4624 Shearer, S L, D M Tucker. 1981. Differential cognitive contributions of the cerebral hemispheres in the modulation of emotional arousal. *Cognitive Therapy and Research* 5: 85-93.

4625 Siann, G. 1985. *Accounting for Aggression.* London: Allen & Unwin.

4626 Silberman, E K, H Wwingartner. 1986. Hemispheric lateralization of functions related to emotion. *Brain and Cognition* 5: 322-53.

4627 Sloman, L. 1981. Anxiety and the struggle for power. *International Journal of Family Psychiatry* 2: 13-33.

4628 Smith, C A, G T McHugo, J T Lanzetta. 1986. The facial patterning of posed and imagery induced expressions of emotions by expressive and nonexpressive posers. *Motivation and Emotion* 10: 133-57.

4629 Sorensen, D, J Horii. 1984. Directional perturbation factors for jitter and shimmer. *Journal of Communication Disorders* 12: 143-57.

4630 Spielberger, C D. 1975. The measurement of state and trait anxiety: Conceptual and methodological issues. In *Emotions: Their Parameters and Measurement.* Edited by Levi, L. Pp. 713-725. New York: Raven Press.

4631 Stemmler, G. 1984. *Psychophysiologische Emotionsmuster.* Frankfurt: Lang.

4632 Strauss, E. 1983. Perception of emotional words. *Neuropsychologia* 231: 99-103.

4633 Strauss, E, J Wada, B Kosaka. 1983. Spontaneous facial expressions occurring at onset of focal seizure activity. *Archives of Neurology* 40: 545-7.

4634 Strauss, E. 1986. Cerebral representation of emotion. In *Nonverbal Communication in the Clinical Context.* Edited by Blanck,

P, R Buck, R Rosenthal. Pp. 176-95. University Park, PA: Pennsylvania State Press.

4635 Taylor, G T. 1979. Reinforcement and intraspecific aggressive behavior. *Behavioral and Neural Biology* 27: 1-24.

4636 Tellegen, A, G Atkinson. 1974. Openness to absorbing and self-altering experiences ("absorption"), a trait related to hypnotic susceptibility. *Journal of Abnormal Psychology* 83: 268-277.

4637 Temoshok, L, C Van Dyke, L S Zegans, eds. 1983. *Emotions in Health and Illness: Theoretical and Research Foundations.* New York: Grune and Stratton.

4638 Thayer, R E. 1989. *The Biopsychology of Mood and Arousal.* New York: Oxford University Press.

4639 Thompson, R A, M E Lamb. 1984. Assessing qualitative dimensions of emotional responsiveness. *Infant Behavior and Development* 7: 423-445.

4640 Tolman, E C, ed. 1966. *Behavior and Psychological Man: Essays in Motivation and Learning.* Berkeley: University of California Press.

4641 Tooby, J, L Cosmides. 1990. The past explains the present: Emotional adaptations and the structure of ancestral environments. *Ethology and Sociobiology* 11: 375-424.

4642 Torestad, B. 1990. What is anger provoking? A psychophysical study of perceived causes of anger. *Aggressive Behavior* 16: 9-26.

4643 Tranel, D, A R Damasio. 1985. Knowledge without awareness: An autonomic index of facial recognition by prosopagnosics. *Science* 228: 1453-54.

4644 Trevarthen, C. 1985. Facial expression of emotion in mother-infant interaction. *Human Neurobiology* 4: 21-37.

4645 Truax, S R. 1983. Active search, mediation and the manipulation of cue dimensions: Emotion attribution in the false-feedback paradigm. *Motivation and Emotion* 7: 41-60.

4646 Tucker, D M, J P Newman. 1981. Verbal versus imaginal cognitive strategies in the inhibition of emotional arousal. *Cognitive Therapy and Research* 5: 197-202.

4647 Tucker, D M, C E Stenslie, R S Roth, S Shearer. 1981. Right frontal lobe activation and right hemisphere performance decrement during a depressed mood. *Archives of General Psychiatry* 38: 169-74.

4648 Tucker, D M. 1981. Lateral brain function, emotion, and conceptualization. *Psychological Bulletin* 89: 19-46.

4649 Tucker, D M, S L Dawson. 1984. Asymmetric EEG power and coherence as method actors generated emotions. *Biological Psychology* 19: 63-75.

4650 Tucker, D M, P A Williamson. 1984. Asymmetric neural control systems in human self-regulation. *Psychological Review* 91: 185-215.

4651 Tucker, D M. 1986. Neural control of emotional communication. In *Nonverbal Communication in the Clinical Context.* Edited by Blanck, P, R Buck, R Rosenthal. Cambridge: Cambridge University Press.

4652 Tucker, D M. 1986. Hemisphere specialization: A mechanism for unifying anterior and posterior brain regions. In *The Dual Brain: Specialization and Unification of the Cerebral Hemispheres.* Edited by Ottoson, D. Stockholm: Wenner-Gren Foundation.

4653 Tucker, D, S Frederick. 1989. Emotion and brain lateralization. In *Handbook of Social Psychophysiology.* Edited by Wagner, H, A Manstead. Pp. 27-70. New York: Wiley.

4654 Tyler, S K, D M Tucker. 1982. Anxiety and perceptual structure: Individual differences in neuropsychological function. *Journal of Abnormal Psychology* 91: 210-20.

4655 Van Bezooijec, R. 1984. *The Characteristics and Recognizability of Vocal Expressions of Emotion.* Dordrecht: Foris.

4656 Wagner, H L, ed. 1988. *Social Psychophysiology and Emotion: Theory and Clinical Applications.* Chichester: Wiley.

4657 Wagner, H L. 1988. The theory and application of social psychophysiology. In *Social Psychophysiology and Emotion: Theory and Clinical Applications.* Edited by Wagner, H L. Pp. 1-15. Chichester: Wiley.

4658 Wagner, H. 1989. The peripheral physiological differentiation of emotions. In *Handbook of Social Psychophysiology.* Edited by Wagner, H, A Manstead. Pp. 77-98. New York: Wiley.

4659 Wallbott, H G, K R Scherer. 1986. Cues and channels in emotion recognition. *Journal of Social Psychology* 51: 690-9.

4660 Watson, D, L Clark, A Tellegen. 1984. Cross-cultural convergence in the structure of mood: A Japanese replication and a comparison with U.S. findings. *Journal of Social Psychology* 47: 127-44.

4661 Weinberger, D A, G E Schwartz, R J Davidson. 1979. Low anxious, high anxious, and repressive coping styles: Psychometric patterns and behavioral and physiological response to stress. *Journal of Abnormal Psychology* 88: 368-80.

4662 Weiss, F, G S Blum, L Gleberman. 1987. Anatomically based measurement of facial expressions in simulated versus hypnotically induced affect. *Motivation and Emotion* 11: 67-81.

4663 Weisse, C, L Davidson, A Baum. 1989. Arousal theory and stress. In *Handbook of Social Psychophysiology*. Edited by Wagner, H, A Manstead. Pp. 283-302. New York: Wiley.

4664 White, G L, S Fishbein, J Rutstein. 1981. Passionate love and misattribution of arousal. *Journal of Social Psychology* 41: 56-62.

4665 Wierzbicka, A. 1986. Human emotions: Universals or culture-specific? *American Anthropologist* 88: 584-594.

4666 Wilkinson, G S, C T Nagoshi, R C Johnson, K A M Honbo. 1989. Perinatal mortality and sex ratios in Hawaii. *Ethology and Sociobiology* 10: 435-447.

4667 Winer, H, I Florin, R Murison, D Hellhammer, eds. 1989. *Frontiers of Stress Research*. New York: Hans Huber.

4668 Wispé, L. 1991. *The Psychology of Sympathy*. New York: Plenum.

4669 Wright, R A. 1984. Motivation, Anxiety, and the Difficulty of Avoidance Control. *Journal of Social Psychology* 46: 1376-1388.

4670 Zajonc, R B. 1980. Feeling and thinking: Preferences need no inferences. *American Psychologist* 35: 151-75.

4671 Zivin, G, ed. 1985. *The Development of Expressive Behavior*. Orlando: Academic Press.

4672 Zuckerman, M. 1979. Sensation seeking and risk taking. In *Emotions in Personality and Psychopathology.* Edited by Izard, C E. New York: Plenum.

4673 Zuckerman, M. 1979. *Sensation Seeking: Beyond the Optimal Level of Arousal.* Hillsdale, N.J.: Erlbaum.

4674 Zuckerman, M., ed. 1983. *Biological Bases of Sensation Seeking, Impulsivity and Anxiety.* Hillsdale, N.J.: Erlbaum.

4675 Zuckerman, M, P Como. 1983. Sensation seeking and arousal systems. *Personality and Individual Differences* 4: 381-86.

4676 Zuckerman, M. 1983. A biological theory of sensation seeking. In *Biological Bases of Sensation Seeking, Impulsivity and Anxiety.* Edited by Zuckerman, M. New York: Erlbaum.

4677 Zuckerman, M. 1990. The psychophysiology of sensation seeking. *Journal of Personality* 58: 313-18.

4678 Zuckerman, M. 1991. *Psychobiology of Personality.* Cambridge: Cambridge University Press.

# 13

# Behavior Analysis

4679 Adam, G, E Lang, G Bardos, L Balazs, J Weisz. 1990. Behaviour and visceral functions. In *Behaviour Analysis in Theory and Practice: Contributions and Controversies.* Edited by Blackman, D E, H Lejeune. Pp. 233-242. Hove, England: Erlbaum.

4680 Ader, R, N Cohen. 1985. CNS-immune system interactions: Conditioning phenomena. *Behavioral and Brain Sciences* 8: 379-394.

4681 Allison, J. 1978. Beyond the relational principle of reinforcement. *Journal of the Experimental Analysis of Behavior* 29: 557-560.

4682 Allison, J. 1983. *Behavioral Economics.* New York: Praeger.

4683 Angermeier, W F. 1984. *Evolution of Operant Learning and Memory: A Comparative Etho-Psychology.* New York: Karger.

4684 Axelrod, S, J Apsche, eds. 1983. *The Effects of Punishment on Human Behavior.* New York: Academic Press.

4685 Baer, D M, R F Peterson, J A Sherman. 1967. The development of imitation by reinforcing behavioral similarity to a model. *Journal of the Experimental Analysis of Behavior* 10: 405-416.

4686 Baer, D M. 1986. In application, frequency is not the only estimate of the probability of behavior units. In *Analysis and Integration of Behavioral Units.* Edited by Thompson, T, M D Zeiler. Pp. 117-136. Hillsdale, N.J.: Erlbaum.

4687 Baer, R A. 1987. Effects of caffeine on classroom behavior, sustained attention, and a memory task in pre-school children. *Journal of Applied Behavior Analysis* 20: 225-234.

4688 Baer, R A, R Detrich. 1990. Tacting and manding in correspondence training: Effects of child selection of verbalization. *Journal of the Experimental Analysis of Behavior* 54: 23-30.

4689 Bailey, J, ed. 1990. *Behavior Analysis in Developmental Disabilities.* Rev. ed Lawrence, KS.: Journal of Applied Behavior Analysis.

4690 Barlow, D H, M Hersen. 1984. *Single Case Experimental Designs: Strategies for Studying Behavior Change.* 2nd ed.. New York: Pergamon.

4691 Baron, A, M Perone. 1982. The place of the human subject in the operant laboratory. *The Behavior Analyst* 5: 143-158.

4692 Baron, A, M Galizio. 1983. Instructional control of human operant behavior. *Psychological Record* 33: 495-520.

4693 Baron, A, S R Menich. 1985. Reaction times of younger and older men: Effects of compound samples and a prechoice signal on delayed matching-to-sample performance. *Journal of the Experimental Analysis of Behavior* 44: 1-14.

4694 Baron, A, J Myerson, S Hale. 1988. An integrated analysis of the structure and function of behavior: Aging and the cost of dividing attention. In *Human Operant Conditioning and Behavior Modification.* Edited by Davey, G, C Cullen. Pp. 139-168. Chichester: Wiley.

4695 Baron, A, T M Surdy. 1990. Recognition memory in older adults: Adjustment to changing contingencies. *Journal of the Experimental Analysis of Behavior* 54: 201-212.

4696 Barrett, J E, J M Witkin. 1986. The role of behavioral and pharmacological history in determining the effects of abused drugs. In *Behavioral Analysis of Drug Dependence.* Edited by Goldberg, S R, I P Stolerman. Pp. 195-224. Orlando: Academic Press.

4697 Barrett, J E. 1986. Behavioral history: Residual influences on subsequent behavior and drug effects. In *Developmental Behavioral Pharmacology.* Edited by Krasnegor, N, D B Gray. Pp. 99-114. Hillsdale, N.J.: Erlbaum.

4698 Baum, W M. 1975. Time allocation in human vigilance. *Journal of the Experimental Analysis of Behavior* 23: 45-54.

4699 Baxter, G A, H Schlinger. 1990. Performance of children under a multiple random-ratio random-interval schedule of reinforcement. *Journal of the Experimental Analysis of Behavior* 54: 263-271.

4700 Bayes, R. 1990. The contribution of behavioural medicine to the research and prevention of AIDS. In *Behaviour Analysis in Theory and Practice: Contributions and Controversies.* Edited by Blackman, D E, H Lejeune. Pp. 243-258. Hove, England: Erlbaum.

4701 Belke, T W, W D Pierce, R A Powell. 1989. Determinants of choice for pigeons and humans on concurrent-chains schedules of reinforcement. *Journal of the Experimental Analysis of Behavior* 52: 97-109.

4702 Bellack, A S, M Hersen. 1984. *Research Methods in Clinical Psychology.* New York: Pergamon.

4703 Bentall, R P, C F Lowe, A Beasty. 1985. The role of verbal behavior in human learning: II. Developmental differences. *Journal of the Experimental Analysis of Behavior* 43: 165-181.

4704 Bentall, R P, C F Lowe. 1987. The role of verbal behavior in human learning: III. Instructional effects in children. *Journal of the Experimental Analysis of Behavior* 47: 177-190.

4705 Bernstein, D J, J V Brady. 1986. The utility of continuous programmed environments in the experimental analysis of behavior. In *Behavior Science: Philosophical, Methodological, and Empirical Advances.* Edited by Reese, H W, L J Parrott. Pp. 229-245. Hillsdale, N.J.: Erlbaum.

4706 Bernstein, D J, R L Michael. 1990. The utility of verbal and behavioral assessments of value. *Journal of the Experimental Analysis of Behavior* 54: 173-184.

4707 Bernstein, D J. 1990. Of carrots and sticks: A review of Deci and Ryan's Intrinsic Motivation and Self-Determination in Human Behavior. *Journal of the Experimental Analysis of Behavior* 54: 323-332.

4708 Bickel, W K, B C Etzel. 1985. The quantal nature of controlling stimulus-response relations as measured in tests of generalization. *Journal of the Experimental Analysis of Behavior* 44: 245-270.

4709 Bickel, W K, R J DeGrandpre, J R Highes, S T Higgins. 1991. Behavioral economics of drug self-administration. II. A unit-price analysis of cigarette smoking. *Journal of the Experimental Analysis of Behavior* 55: 145-154.

4710 Biglan, A. 1987. A behavior-analytic critique of Bandura's self-efficacy theory. *The Behavior Analyst* 10: 1-15.

4711 Bijou, S W, D M Baer. 1978. *Behavior Analysis of Child Development.* Englewood Cliffs, N.J.: Prentice-Hall.

4712 Blackman, D E. 1991. B. F. Skinner and G. H. Mead: On biological science and social science. *Journal of the Experimental Analysis of Behavior* 55: 251-265.

4713 Boakes, R A. 1983. Behaviorism and the nature-nurture controversy. In *Animal Models of Human Behavior*. Edited by Davey, G C L. Pp. 15-35. Chichester: Wiley.

4714 Bourgeois, M S. 1990. Enhancing conversational skills in patients with Alzheimer's Disease using a prosthetic memory aid. *Journal of Applied Behavior Analysis* 23: 29-42.

4715 Boyle, M E, R D Greer. 1983. Operant procedures and the comatose patient. *Journal of Applied Behavior Analysis* 16: 3-12.

4716 Bradshaw, C M, H V Ruddle, E Szabadi. 1981. Studies of concurrent performances in humans. In *Quantification of Steady-State Operant Behavior*. Edited by Bradshaw, C M, E Szabadi, C F Lowe. Amsterdam: Elsevier/North-Holland Biomedical Press.

4717 Bradshaw, C M, E Szabadi. 1988. Quantitative analysis of human operant behavior. In *Human Operant Conditioning and Behavior Modification*. Edited by Davey, G, C Cullen. Pp. 225-259. Chichester: Wiley.

4718 Branch, M N. 1977. On the role of "memory" in the analysis of behavior. *Journal of the Experimental Analysis of Behavior* 28: 171-180.

4719 Branch, M N. 1984. Rate dependency, behavioral mechanisms, and behavioral pharmacology. *Journal of the Experimental Analysis of Behavior* 42: 511-522.

4720 Brownstein, A J, ed. 1989. *Progress in Behavioral Studies*. Hillsdale, N.J.: Erlbaum.

4721 Burgio, L D, T J Page, R M Capriotti. 1985. Clinical behavioral pharmacology: Methods for evaluating medications and contingency management. *Journal of Applied Behavior Analysis* 18: 45-59.

4722 Burgio, L D, K A Burgio. 1986. Behavioral gerontology: Application of behavioral methods to the problems of older adults. *Journal of Applied Behavior Analysis* 19: 321-328.

4723 Buskist, W, D Morgan. 1987. Competitive fixed-interval performance in humans. *Journal of the Experimental Analysis of Behavior* 47: 145-158.

4724 Buskist, W, D Morgan. 1988. Method and theory in the study of human competition. In *Human Operant Conditioning and Behavior Modification.* Edited by Davey, G, C Cullen. Pp. 167-196. Chichester: Wiley.

4725 Carroll, M E, G G Carmona, S A May. 1991. Modifying drug-reinforced behavior by altering the economic conditions of the drug and a nondrug reinforcer. *Journal of the Experimental Analysis of Behavior* 56: 361-376.

4726 Case, D A, E Fantino, J Wixted 1985. Human observing: Maintained by negative informative stimuli only if correlated with improvement in response efficiency. *Journal of the Experimental Analysis of Behavior* 43: 289-300.

4727 Case, D A, E Fantino. 1987. Instructions and reinforcement in the observing behavior of adults and children. *Learning and Motivation* 20: 373-412.

4728 Case, D A, B O Ploog, E Fantino. 1990. Observing behavior in a computer game. *Journal of the Experimental Analysis of Behavior* 54: 185-199.

4729 Catania, A C, T A Brigham, eds. 1978. *Handbook of Applied Behavior Analysis: Social and Instructional Processes.* New York: Irvington.

4730 Catania, A C. 1983. Behavior analysis and behavior synthesis in the extrapolation from animal to human behavior. In *Animal Models of Human Behavior.* Edited by Davey, G C L. Pp. 51-69. Chichester: Wiley.

4731 Catania, A C. 1985. Rule-governed behaviour and the origins of language. In *Behaviour Analysis and Contemporary Psychology.* Edited by Lowe, C F, M Richelle, D E Blackman, C M Bradshaw. Pp. 135-156. London: Erlbaum.

4732 Catania, A C, S Harnad, eds. 1988. *The Selection of Behavior: The Operant Behaviorism of B.F. Skinner.* New York: Cambridge University Press.

4733 Catania, A C, B A Matthews, E H Shimoff. 1990. Properties of rule-governed behaviour and their implications. In *Behaviour Analysis in Theory and Practice: Contributions and Controversies.* Edited by Blackman, D E, H Lejeune. Pp. 215-230. Hove, England: Erlbaum.

4734 Catania, A C. 1992. *Learning.* 3rd ed. Englewood Cliffs, N.J.: Prentice-Hall.

4735 Cerutti, D T. 1989. Discrimination theory of rule-governed behavior. *Journal of the Experimental Analysis of Behavior* 51: 259-276.

4736 Chase, P N, K R Johnson, B Sulzer-Azaroff. 1985. Verbal relations with instruction: Are there subclasses of the intraverbal? *Journal of the Experimental Analysis of Behavior* 43: 301-313.

4737 Cherek, D R, R Spiga, J L Steinberg, T H Kelly. 1990. Human aggressive responses maintained by avoidance or escape from point loss. *Journal of the Experimental Analysis of Behavior* 53: 293-303.

4738 Costall, A P. 1984. Are theories of perception necessary? A review of Gibson's The Ecological Approach to Visual Perception. *Journal of the Experimental Analysis of Behavior* 41: 109-115.

4739 Critchfield, T S, M Perone. 1990. Verbal self-reports of delayed matching to sample by humans. *Journal of the Experimental Analysis of Behavior* 53: 321-344.

4740 Czubaroff, J. 1988. Criticism and response in the Skinner controversies. *Journal of the Experimental Analysis of Behavior* 49: 321-329.

4741 Danforth, J S, P N Chase, M Dolan, J H Joyce. 1990. The establishment of stimulus control by instructions and by differential reinforcement. *Journal of the Experimental Analysis of Behavior* 54: 97-112.

4742 Davey, G C L. 1983. An associative view of human classical conditioning. In *Animal Models of Human Behavior.* Edited by Davey, G C L. Pp. 95-114. Chichester: Wiley.

4743 de Freitas Ribeiro, A. 1989. Correspondence in children's self-report: Tacting and manding aspects. *Journal of the Experimental Analysis of Behavior* 51: 361-367.

4744 Deitz, S M, L D Fredrick, P C Quinn, L D Brasher. 1986. Comparing the effects of two correction procedures on human acquisition of sequential behavior patterns. *Journal of the Experimental Analysis of Behavior* 46: 1-14.

4745 Deitz, S M, G R Gaydos, A D Lawrence, P C Quinn, L D Brasher, L D Fredrick. 1987. Feedback effects on sequential ordering in humans. *Journal of the Experimental Analysis of Behavior* 48: 209-220.

4746 Delprato, D J. 1986. Response patterns. In *Behavior Science: Philosophical, Methodological, and Empirical Advances*. Edited by Reese, H W, L J Parrott. Pp. 61-113. Hillsdale, N.J.: Erlbaum.

4747 Devaney, J M, S C Hayes, R O Nelson. 1986. Equivalence class formation in language-able and language-disabled children. *Journal of the Experimental Analysis of Behavior* 46: 243-257.

4748 Dews, P B. 1986. Pharmacological contributions to the experimental analysis of behavior. In *Analysis and Integration of Behavioral Units*. Edited by Thompson, T, M D Zeiler. Pp. 137-159. Hillsdale, N.J.: Erlbaum.

4749 Dickinson, A M. 1989. The detrimental effects of extrinsic reinforcement on "intrinsic motivation". *The Behavior Analyst* 12: 1-15.

4750 Dinsmoor, J A. 1983. Observing and conditioned reinforcement. *Behavioral and Brain Sciences* 6: 693-728.

4751 Dockens, W S. 1984. A biobehavioral approach to treatment of amphetamine addiction: A four-way integration. In *Advances in Behavioral Pharmacology*. Edited by Thompson, T, P B Dews, J E Barrett. Pp. 89-104. Orlando: Academic Press.

4752 Domjan, M, B J Galef. 1983. Biological constraints on instrumental and classical conditioning: Retrospect and prospect. *Animal Learning and Behavior* 11: 151-161.

4753 Donahoe, J W. 1977. Some implications of a relational principle of reinforcement. *Journal of the Experimental Analysis of Behavior* 27: 341-350.

4754 Donahoe, J W, D C Palmer. 1989. The interpretation of complex human behavior: Some reactions to Parallel Distributed Processing, edited by J.L. McClelland, D. E. Rumelhart, and the PDP Research Group. *Journal of the Experimental Analysis of Behavior* 51: 399-416.

4755 Donahoe, J W. 1991. Selectionist approach to verbal behavior: Potential contributions of neuropsychology and computer simulation. In *Dialogues on Verbal Behavior*. Edited by Hayes, L J, P N Chase. Pp. 119-145. Reno: Context Press.

4756 Dugdale, D, C F Lowe. 1990. Naming and stimulus equivalence. In *Behaviour Analysis in Theory and Practice: Contributions and Controversies*. Edited by Blackman, D E, H Lejeune. Pp. 115-137. Hove, England: Erlbaum.

4757 Eisenberger, R, M Mitchell, M McDermitt, F A Masterson. 1984. Accuracy versus speed in the generalizaed effort of learning-disabled children. *Journal of the Experimental Analysis of Behavior* 42: 19-36.

4758 Emley, G E, R R Hutchinson. 1984. Behavioral effects of nicotine. In *Advances in Behavioral Pharmacology*. Edited by Thompson, T, P B Dews, J E Barrett. Pp. 105-131. Orlando: Academic Press.

4759 Emurian, H H, C S Emurian, G E Bigelow, J Brady. 1976. The effects of a cooperation contingency on behavior in a continuous three-person environment. *Journal of the Experimental Analysis of Behavior* 25: 293-302.

4760 Emurian, H H, C S Emurian, J Brady. 1978. Effects of a pairing contingency on behavior in a three-person programmed environment. *Journal of the Experimental Analysis of Behavior* 29: 319-329.

4761 Emurian, H H, C S Emurian, J V Brady. 1985. Positive and negative reinforcement effects on behavior in a three-person microsociety. *Journal of the Experimental Analysis of Behavior* 44: 157-175.

4762 Enright, M K, C K Rovee-Collier, J W Fagan, K Caniglia. 1983. The effects of distributed training of operant conditioning in human infants. *Journal of Experimental Child Psychology* 36: 209-225.

4763 Epling, W F, W D Pierce. 1986. The basic importance of applied behavioral research. *The Behavior Analyst* 9: 89-99.

4764 Epstein, R. 1984. Simulation research in the analysis of behavior. *Behaviorism* 12: 41-59.

4765 Etzel, B C. 1987. Pigeons and people: What are the differences? *The Psychological Record* 37: 17-27.

4766 Falk, J L. 1986. The formation of ritual behavior. In *Analysis and Integration of Behavioral Units*. Edited by Thompson, T, M D Zeiler. Pp. 335-355. Hillsdale, N.J.: Erlbaum.

4767 Fantino, E, D A Case. 1983. Human observing: Maintained by stimuli correlated with reinforcement but not extinction. *Journal of the Experimental Analysis of Behavior* 40: 193-210.

4768 Ferster, C B, B F Skinner. 1957. *Schedules of Reinforcement*. New York: Appleton-Century-Crofts.

4769 Fields, L, T Verhave, S Fath. 1984. Stimulus equivalence and transitive associations: A methodological analysis. *Journal of the Experimental Analysis of Behavior* 42: 143-157.

4770 Fields, L, T Verhave. 1987. The structure of equivalence classes. *Journal of the Experimental Analysis of Behavior* 48: 317-332.

4771 Foltin, R W, M W Fischman, J Brady, D J Bernstein, R M Capriotti, M J Nellis, T H Kelly. 1990. Motivational effects of smoked marijuana: Behavioral contingencies and low-probability activities. *Journal of the Experimental Analysis of Behavior* 53: 5-19.

4772 Furedy, J J, D M Riley, M Fredrickson. 1983. Pavlovian extinction, phobias, and the limits of the cognitive paradigm. *Pavlovian Journal of Biological Science* 18: 126-135.

4773 Gewirtz, J L, E F Boyd. 1977. Experiments on mother-infant interaction underlying mutual attachment acquisition: The infant conditions the mother. In *Attachment Behavior*. Edited by Alloway, T, P Pliner, L Krames. Pp. 109-143. New York: Plenum.

4774 Gewirtz, J L, S B Petrovich. 1982. Early social and attachment learning in the frame of organic and cultural evolution. In *Review of Human Development*. Edited by Field, T M, A Huston, H C Quay, L Troll, G E Finlet. Pp. 3-19. New York: Wiley.

4775 Gewirtz, J L. 1991. Identification, attachment, and their developmental sequencing in a conditioning frame. In *Intersections With Attachment*. Edited by Gewirtz, J L, W M Kurtines. Pp. 247-255. Hillsdale, N.J.: Erlbaum.

4776 Gewirtz, J L. 1991. Social influence on child and parent via stimulation and operant-learning mechanisms. In *Social Influences and Socialization in Infancy*. Edited by Lewis, M, S Feinman. Pp. 137-163. New York: Plenum.

4777 Gewirtz, J L, M Pelaez-Nogueras. 1991. The attachment metaphor and the conditioning of infant separation protests. In *Intersections With Attachment*. Edited by Gewirtz, J L, W M Kurtines. Pp. 123-144. Hillsdale, N.J.: Erlbaum.

4778 Gewirtz, J L. 1991. Identification, attachment, and their developmental sequencing in a conditioning frame. In *Intersections With Attachment*. Edited by Gewirtz, J L, W M Kurtines. Pp. 247-255. Hillsadale, N.J: Erlbaum.

4779 Gewirtz, J L, M Pelaez-Nogueras. 1991. Infant social referencing as a learned process. In *Social Referencing and the Social*

*Construction of Reality in Infancy.* Edited by Feinman, S. Pp. 1-11. New York: Plenum.

4780 Gewirtz, J L, M Pelaez-Nogueras. 1991. Proximal mechanisms underlying the acquisition of moral behavior patterns. In *Handbook of Moral Behavior and Development.* Edited by Kurtines, W M, J L Gewirtz. Pp. 153-182. Hillsdale, N.J: Erlbaum.

4781 Gladstone, B W, J Cooley. 1975. Behavioral similarity as a reinforcer for preschool children. *Journal of the Experimental Analysis of Behavior* 23: 357-368.

4782 Goetz, E M. 1989. The teaching of creativity to preschool children: The behavior analysis approach. In *Handbook of Creativity.* Edited by Glover, J A, R R Ronning, C R Reynolds. Pp. 411-428. New York: Plenum.

4783 Goldberg, S R, R T Kelleher. 1976. Behavior controlled by scheduled injections of cocaine in squirrel and rhesus monkeys. *Journal of the Experimental Analysis of Behavior* 25: 93-104.

4784 Goldstein, H. 1985. Enhancing language generalization using matrix and stimulus equivalence training. In *Teaching Functional Language.* Edited by Warren, S, A Rogers-Warren. Pp. 225-249. Baltimore: University Park Press.

4785 Goudie, A J, C Demellweek. 1986. Conditioning factors in drug tolerance. In *Behavioral Analysis of Drug Dependence.* Edited by Goldberg, S R, I P Stolerman. Pp. 225-286. Orlando: Academic Press.

4786 Gray, J A. 1976. The behavioural inhibition system: A possible substrate for anxiety. In *Theoretical and Experimental Bases of Behaviour Modification.* Edited by Feldman, M P, A M Broadhurst. Pp. 3-41. London: Wiley.

4787 Gray, J A. 1987. Interactions between drugs and behaviour therapy. In *Theoretical Foundations of Behaviour Therapy.* Edited by Eysenck, H J, I Martin. New York: Plenum Press.

4788 Greene, B F, ed. 1987. *Behavior Analysis in the Community.* Lawrence, KA.: Journal of Applied Behavior Analysis.

4789 Griffiths, R R, G E Bigelow, I Liebson. 1976. Facilitation of human tobacco self-administration by ethanol: A behavioral analysis. *Journal of the Experimental Analysis of Behavior* 25: 279-292.

4790 Griffiths, R R, R M Wurster, J V Brady. 1981. Choice between food and heroin: Effects of morphine, naloxone, and secobarbital. *Journal of the Experimental Analysis of Behavior* 35: 335-351.

4791 Griffiths, R R, G E Bigelow, I A Liebson, M O'Keefe, D O'Leary, N Russ. 1986. Human coffee drinking: Manipulation of concentrations and caffeine dose. *Journal of the Experimental Analysis of Behavior* 45: 133-148.

4792 Griffiths, R R, G E Bigelow, I A Liebson. 1989. Reinforcing effects of caffeine in coffee and capsules. *Journal of the Experimental Analysis of Behavior* 52: 127-140.

4793 Hake, D F, R Vukelich, D Olvera. 1975. The measurement of sharing and cooperation as equity effects and some relationships between them. *Journal of the Experimental Analysis of Behavior* 23: 63-79.

4794 Hake, D F, D Olvera, J C Bell. 1975. Switching from competition to sharing or cooperation at large response requirements: Competition requires more responding. *Journal of the Experimental Analysis of Behavior* 24: 343-354.

4795 Hake, D F, D Olvera. 1978. Cooperation, competition, and related social phenomena. In *Handbook of Applied Behavior Analysis: Social and Instructional Processes.* Edited by Catania, A C, T A Brigham. New York: Irvington.

4796 Hake, D F, T L Schmid. 1981. Acquisition and maintenance of trusting behavior. *Journal of the Experimental Analysis of Behavior* 35: 109-124.

4797 Hake, D F, T Donaldson, C Hyten. 1983. Analysis of discriminative control by social behavioral stimuli. *Journal of the Experimental Analysis of Behavior* 39: 7-28.

4798 Hall, G. 1990. Reasoning and associative learning. In *Behaviour Analysis in Theory and Practice: Contributions and Controversies.* Edited by Blackman, D E, H Lejeune. Pp. 159-180. Hove, England: Erlbaum.

4799 Harzem, P, R A Williams. 1983. On searching for a science of human behavior. *Psychological Record* 33: 565-574.

4800 Harzem, P. 1984. Experimental analysis of individual differences and personality. *Journal of the Experimental Analysis of Behavior* 42: 385-398.

4801 Hayes, S C, A J Brownstein. 1986. Mentalism, behavior-behavior relationships, and a behavior-analytic view of the purposes of science. *The Behavior Analyst* 9: 175-190.

4802 Hayes, S C. 1989. *Rule-Governed Behavior: Cognition, Contingencies, and Instructional Control.* New York: Plenum.

4803 Hebb, D O. 1949. *The Organization of Behavior.* New York: Wiley.

4804 Henningfield, J E. 1984. Behavioral pharmacology of cigarette smoking. In *Advances in Behavioral Pharmacology.* Edited by Thompson, T, P B Dews, J E Barrett. Pp. 132-210. Orlando: Academic Press.

4805 Henningfield, J E, S E Lukas, G E Bigelow. 1986. Human studies of drugs as reinforcers. In *Behavioral Analysis of Drug Dependence.* Edited by Goldberg, S R, I P Stolerman. Pp. 69-122. Orlando: Academic Press.

4806 Herrnstein, R J. 1969. Method and theory in the study of avoidance. *Psychological Review* 76: 49-69.

4807 Herrnstein, R J. 1970. On the law of effect. *Journal of the Experimental Analysis of Behavior* 13: 243-266.

4808 Herrnstein, R J, D H Loveland, C Cable. 1976. Natural concepts in pigeons. *Journal of Experimental Psychology: Animal Behavior Processes* 2: 285-311.

4809 Herrnstein, R J. 1984. Objects, categories, and discriminative stimuli. In *Animal Cognition.* Edited by Roitblat, H L, T G Bever, H Terrace. Pp. 233-261. Hillsdale, N.J.: Erlbaum.

4810 Higgins, S T, E K Morris. 1984. A review of the generality of free-operant avoidance conditioning to human behavior. *Psychological Bulletin* 96: 247-272.

4811 Higgins, S T, B M Woodward, J E Henningfield. 1989. Effects of atropine on the repeated acquisition and performance of response sequences in humans. *Journal of the Experimental Analysis of Behavior* 51: 5-15.

4812 Hineline, P N. 1981. The several roles of stimuli in negative reinforcement. In *Predictability, Correlation, and Contiguity.* Edited by Harzem, P, M D Zeiler. New York: Wiley.

4813 Hineline, P N. 1984. Aversive control: A separate domain? *Journal of the Experimental Analysis of Behavior* 42: 495-509.

4814 Hineline, P N. 1990. The origins of environmental-based psychological theory. *Journal of the Experimental Analysis of Behavior* 53: 305-320.

4815 Holland, J G. 1958. Human vigilance. *Science* 128: 61-67.

4816 Hull, C L. 1943. *Principles of Behavior.* New York: Appleton-Century-Crofts.

4817 Hursh, S R. 1980. Economic concepts for the analysis of behavior. *Journal of the Experimental Analysis of Behavior* 34: 219-238.

4818 Hursh, S R. 1984. Behavioral economics. *Journal of the Experimental Analysis of Behavior* 42: 435-452.

4819 Hursh, S R, R A Bauman. 1987. The behavioral analysis of demand. In *Advances in Behavioral Economics.* Edited by Green, L, J H Kagel. Pp. 117-165. Norwood, N.J.: Ablex.

4820 Hursh, S R. 1991. Behavioral economics of drug self-administration and drug abuse policy. *Journal of the Experimental Analysis of Behavior* 56: 377-393.

4821 Iwata, B A, M E Dorsey, K J Slifer, K E Bauman, G S Richman. 1982. Toward a functional analysis of self-injury. *Analysis and Intervention in Developmental Disabilities* 2: 3-20.

4822 Iwata, B A, ed. 1989. *Methodological and Conceptual Issues in Applied Behavior Analysis.* Lawrence, KS.: Journal of Applied Behavior Analysis.

4823 Iwata, B A, G M Pace, M J Kalsher, G E Cowdry, M F Cataldo. 1990. Experimental analysis and extinction of self-injurious escape behavior. *Journal of Applied Behavior Analysis* 23: 11-27.

4824 Johnston, J M, H S Pennypacker. 1980. *Strategies and Tactics of Human Behavioral Research.* Hillsdale, N.J.: Erlbaum.

4825 Johnston, J M, A Wallen, J Partin, E Neu, R Cade, G H Stein, M K Goldstein, H S Pennypacker, E Gfeller. 1983. Human operant laboratory measurement of the effects of chemical variables. *Psychological Record* 33: 457-472.

4826 Kagel, J H, L Green. 1987. Intertemporal choice behavior: Evaluation of economic and psychological models. In *Advances in Behavioral Economics*. Edited by Green, L, J H Kagel. Pp. 166-184. Norwood, N.J.: Ablex.

4827 Kamin, L J. 1969. Predictability, surprise, attention and conditioning. In *Punishment and Aversive Behaviour*. Edited by Campbell, B A, R M Church. Pp. 279-296. Englewood Cliffs, N.J.: Prentice-Hall.

4828 Kazdin, A E. 1988. The token economy: A decade later. In *Human Operant Conditioning and Behavior Modification*. Edited by Davey, G, C Cullen. Pp. 119-128. Chichester: Wiley.

4829 Kehoe, E J. 1989. Connectionist models of conditioning: A tutorial. *Journal of the Experimental Analysis of Behavior* 52: 427-440.

4830 Keller, F S, W N Schoenfeld. 1950. *Principles of Psychology.* New York: Appleton-Century-Crofts.

4831 Kelly, T H, M W Fischman, R W Foltin, J V Brady. 1991. Response patterns and cardiovascular effects during response sequence acquisition by humans. *Journal of the Experimental Analysis of Behavior* 56: 557-574.

4832 King, G R, A W Logue. 1990. Humans' sensitivity to variation in reinforcer amount: Effects of the method of reinforcer delivery. *Journal of the Experimental Analysis of Behavior* 53: 33-45.

4833 Knapp, T. 1987. Perception and action. In *B. F. Skinner: Consensus and Controversy.* Edited by Mogdil, S, C Mogdil. Pp. 283-294. New York: Falmer.

4834 Kohlenberg, B S, S C Hayes, L J Hayes. 1991. The transfer of contextual control over equivalence classes through equivalence classes: A possible model of social stereotyping. *Journal of the Experimental Analysis of Behavior* 56: 505-518.

4835 Konarski, E A, M R Johnson, C R Crowell, T L Whitman. 1981. An alternative approach to reinforcement for applied researchers: Response deprivation. *Behavior Therapy* 12: 653-666.

4836 Krapfl, J E, E A Vargas, eds. 1977. *Behaviorism and Ethics.* Kalamazoo, MI.: Behaviordelia.

4837 Kulig, J W, T J Tighe. 1981. Habituation in children within a behavior suppression paradigm. *Journal of Experimental Child Psychology* 32: 425-442.

4838 Kymissis, E, C L Poulson. 1990. The history of imitation in learning theory: The language acquisition process. *Journal of the Experimental Analysis of Behavior* 54: 113-127.

4839 Lamarre, J, J G Holland. 1985. The functional independence of mands and tacts. *Journal of the Experimental Analysis of Behavior* 43: 5-19.

4840 Lambert, J-L. 1990. The development of thinking in mentally retarded children: Has behaviourism something to offer? In *Behaviour Analysis in Theory and Practice: Contributions and Controversies.* Edited by Blackman, D E, H Lejeune. Pp. 139-157. Hove, England: Erlbaum.

4841 Laurenti-Lions, L, J Gallego, G Vardon, C Jacquemin. 1985. Control of myoelectrical responses through reinforcement. *Journal of the Experimental Analysis of Behavior* 44: 185-193.

4842 Lazar, R M, D Davis-Lang, L Sanchez. 1984. The formation of stimulus equivalences in children. *Journal of the Experimental Analysis of Behavior* 41: 251-266.

4843 Lea, S E G. 1985. Operant psychology and ethology: Failures and successes in interdisciplinary interaction. In *Behaviour Analysis and Contemporary Psychology.* Edited by Lowe, C F, M Richelle, D E Blackman, C M Bradshaw. Pp. 43-51. London: Erlbaum.

4844 Lea, S E G. 1987. Animal experiments in economic psychology. In *Advances in Behavioral Economics.* Edited by Green, L, J H Kagel. Pp. 95-116. Norwood, N.J.: Ablex.

4845 Lee, V L. 1980. Prepositional phrases spoken and heard. *Journal of the Experimental Analysis of Behavior* 35: 227-242.

4846 Lee, V L. 1982. Effects on spelling of training children to read. *Journal of the Experimental Analysis of Behavior* 37: 311-322.

4847 Lee, V L. 1988. *Beyond Behaviorism.* Hillsdale, N.J.: Erlbaum.

4848 Lejeune, H. 1990. Timing: Differences in continuity or generality beyond differences? In *Behaviour Analysis in Theory and Practice: Contributions and Controversies.* Edited by Blackman, D E, H Lejeune. Pp. 53-90. Hove, England: Erlbaum.

4849 Leung, J. 1988. Behavioral vision training for myopia: Stimulus specificity of training effects. *Journal of Applied Behavior Analysis* 21: 217-222.

4850 Leung, J. 1989. Psychological distance to reward: A human replication. *Journal of the Experimental Analysis of Behavior* 51: 343-352.

4851 Lloyd, K E. 1980. Do as I say, not as I do. *New Zealand Psychologist* 9: 1-8.

4852 Lodhi, S, R D Greer. 1989. The speaker as listener. *Journal of the Experimental Analysis of Behavior* 51: 353-359.

4853 Logue, A W, I Ophir, K E Strauss. 1981. The acquisition of taste aversion in humans. *Behaviour Research and Therapy* 19: 319-333.

4854 Logue, A W, T E Pena-Correal, M Rodriguez, E Kabela. 1986. Self-control in adult humans: Variations on positive reinforcer amount and delay. *Journal of the Experimental Analysis of Behavior* 46: 159-173.

4855 Lovaas, O I, R L Koegel. 1979. Stimulus overselectivity in autism: A review of the research. *Psychological Bulletin* 86: 1236-1254.

4856 Lovibond, P F, G C Preston, N J Mackintosh. 1984. Context specificity of conditioning, extinction, and latent inhibition. *Journal of Experimental Psychology: Animal Behaviour Processess* 10: 360-375.

4857 Lowe, C F. 1979. Determinants of human operant behavior. In *Advances in Analysis of Behavior: Reinforcement and the Organization of Behavior*. Edited by Harzem, P, M D Zeiler. Pp. 159-192. New York: Wiley.

4858 Lowe, C F. 1983. Radical behaviorism and human psychology. In *Animal Models of Human Behavior*. Edited by Davey, G C L. Pp. 71-93. Chichester: Wiley.

4859 Lowe, C F, P J Horne. 1985. On the generality of behavioural principles: Human choice and the matching law. In *Behaviour Analysis and Contemporary Psychology*. Edited by Lowe, C F, M Richelle, D E Blackman, C M Bradshaw. Pp. 97-115. London: Erlbaum.

4860 Lowenkeron, B. 1989. Instructional control of generalized relational matching to sample in children. *Journal of the Experimental Analysis of Behavior* 52: 293-309.

4861 Lowenkron, B. 1984. Coding responses and the generalization of matching to sample in children. *Journal of the Experimental Analysis of Behavior* 42: 1-18.

4862 Lowenkron, B. 1988. Generalization of delayed identity matching in retarded children. *Journal of the Experimental Analysis of Behavior* 50: 163-172.

4863 Lubinski, D, T Thompson. 1987. An animal model of the interpersonal communication of interoceptive (private) states. *Journal of the Experimental Analysis of Behavior* 48: 1-15.

4864 Mace, F C, J S Lalli, M C Shea, E P Lalli, B J West, M Roberts, J A Nevin. 1990. The momentum of human behavior in a natural setting. *Journal of the Experimental Analysis of Behavior* 54: 163-172.

4865 MacKenzie-Keating, S E, L McDonald. 1990. Overcorrection: Reviewed, Revisited and Revised *The Behavior Analyst* 13: 39-48.

4866 Mackintosh, N J. 1983. *Conditioning and Associative Learning.* Oxford: Clarendon Press.

4867 Maier, N R F, T C Schneirla. 1935. *Principles of Animal Psychology.* New York: McGraw-Hill.

4868 Maltzman, I, D C Raskin, C Wolff. 1979. Latent inhibition of the GSR conditioned to words. *Physiological Psychology* 7: 193-203.

4869 Maltzman, I. 1979. Orienting reflexes and classical conditioning in humans. In *The Orienting Reflex in Humans.* Edited by Kimmel, H D, E H van Olst, J F Orelbeke. Pp. 323-351. Hillsdale, N.J.: Erlbaum.

4870 Martens, B K, J L Houk. 1989. The application of Herrnstein's law of effect to disruptive and on-task behavior of a retarded adolescent girl. *Journal of the Experimental Analysis of Behavior* 51: 17-27.

4871 Marwell, G, D R Schmitt. 1975. *Cooperation: An Experimental Analysis.* New York: Academic Press.

4872 McDowell, J J. 1988. Matching theory in natural human environments. *The Behavior Analyst* 11: 95-109.

4873 McDowell, J J. 1989. Two modern developments in matching theory. *The Behavior Analyst* 12: 153-166.

4874 Michael, J. 1982. Distinguishing between discriminative and motivational functions of stimuli. *Journal of the Experimental Analysis of Behavior* 37: 149-155.

4875 Michael, J. 1984. Verbal behavior. *Journal of the Experimental Analysis of Behavior* 42: 363-376.

4876 Michael, J. 1985. Fundamental research and behaviour modification. In *Behaviour Analysis and Contemporary Psychology*. Edited by Lowe, C F, M Richelle, D E Blackman, C M Bradshaw. Pp. 159-164. London: Erlbaum.

4877 Miller, N E. 1985. The value of behavioral research on animals. *American Psychologist* 40: 423-440.

4878 Moerk, E L. 1983. A behavioral analysis of controversial topics in first language acquisition: Reinforcements, corrections, modeling, input frequencioes, and the three-term contingency pattern. *Journal of Psycholinguistic Research* 12: 129-155.

4879 Moerk, E L. 1990. Three-term contingency patterns in mother-child verbal interactions during first-language acquisition. *Journal of the Experimental Analysis of Behavior* 54: 293-305.

4880 Morris, E K, D E Hursh, A S Winston, D M Gelfand, D P Hartmann, H W Reese, D M Baer. 1982. Behavior analysis and human development. *Human Development* 25: 340-364.

4881 Myerson, J, S Hale. 1984. Practical implications of the matching law. *Journal of Applied Behavior Analysis* 17: 367-380.

4882 Myerson, J, S Hale, R Hirschman, C Hansen, B Christiansen. 1989. Global increase in response latencies by early middle age: Complexity effects in individual performances. *Journal of the Experimental Analysis of Behavior* 52: 353-362.

4883 Neuringer, A. 1984. Melioration and self-experimentation. *Journal of the Experimental Analysis of Behavior* 42: 397-406.

4884 Neuringer, A. 1986. Can people behave "randomly?": The role of feedback. *Journal of Experimental Psychology: General* 115: 62-75.

4885 Neuringer, A. 1991. Humble behaviorism. *The Behavior Analyst* 14: 1-13.

4886 O'Brien, C P, R N Ehrman, J W Ternes. 1986. Classical conditioning in human opioid dependence. In *Behavioral Analysis of*

*Drug Dependence.* Edited by Goldberg, S R, I P Stolerman. Pp. 329-356. Orlando: Academic Press.

4887 Olds, N E, J C Fobes. 1981. The central basis of motivation: Intracranial self-stimulation studies. *Annual Review of Psychology* 32: 523-574.

4888 Ono, K. 1987. Superstitious behavior in humans. *Journal of the Experimental Analysis of Behavior* 47: 261-271.

4889 Page, S, A Neuringer. 1985. Variability is an operant. *Journal of Experimental Psychology: Animal Behavior Processes* 11: 429-452.

4890 Palmer, D C. 1991. A behavioral interpretation of memory. In *Dialogues on Verbal Behavior.* Edited by Hayes, L J, P N Chase. Pp. 259-279. Reno: Context Press.

4891 Pavlov, I P. 1927. *Conditioned Reflexes.* Translated by Anrep, G.V. London: Oxford University Press.

4892 Pearce, J M, G Hall. 1980. A model for Pavlovian learning: Variations in the effectiveness of conditioned but not unconditioned stimuli. *Psychological Review* 87: 532-552.

4893 Pelham, W E, R W Schnedler, N C Bologna, J A Contreras. 1980. Behavioral and stimulant treatment of hyperactive children: A therapy study with methylphenidate probes in a within-subject design. *Journal of Applied Behavior Analysis* 13: 221-236.

4894 Perone, M, A Baron. 1980. Reinforcement of human observing behavior by a stimulus correlated with extinction or increased effort. *Journal of the Experimental Analysis of Behavior* 34: 239-261.

4895 Perone, M, M Galizio, A Baron. 1988. The relevance of animal-based principles in the laboratory study of human operant conditioning. In *Human Operant Conditioning and Behavior Modification.* Edited by Davey, G, C Cullen. Pp. 59-86. Chichester: Wiley.

4896 Petrovich, S B, J L Gewirtz. 1991. Imprinting and attachment: Proximate and ultimate considerations. In *Intersections With Attachment.* Edited by Gewirtz, J L, W M Kurtines. Pp. 69-93. Hillsdale, N.J.: Erlbaum.

4897 Pierce, W D, W F Epling. 1983. Choice, matching, and human behavior: A review of the literature. *The Behavior Analyst* 6: 57-76.

4898 Poling, A, M Picker, E Hall-Johnson. 1983. Human behavioral pharmacology. *Psychological Record* 33: 473-493.

4899 Poulson, C L, E Kymissis. 1984. Operant theory and methodology in infant vocal conditioning. *Journal of Experimental Child Psychology* 38: 103-113.

4900 Poulson, C L, E Kymissis, K F Reeve, M Andreatos, L Reeve. 1991. Generalized vocal imitation in infants. *Journal of Experimenal Child Psychology* 51: 267-279.

4901 Pouthas, V, S Droit, A-Y Jacquet, J H Wearden. 1990. Temporal differentiation of response duration in children of different ages: Developmental changes in relations between verbal and nonverbal behavior. *Journal of the Experimental Analysis of Behavior* 53: 21-31.

4902 Pouthas, V. 1990. Temporal regulation of behaviour in humans: A developmental approach. In *Behaviour Analysis in Theory and Practice: Contributions and Controversies.* Edited by Blackman, D E, H Legeune. Pp. 33-51. Hove, England: Erlbaum.

4903 Premack, D. 1965. Reinforcement theory. In *Nebraska Symposium of Motivation.* Edited by Levine, D. Pp. 123-180. Lincoln: University of Nebraska Press.

4904 Preston, K L, W K Bigelow, I A Leibson. 1989. Drug discrimination in human post-addicts: Agonist-antagonist opioids. *Journal of Pharmacology and Experimental Therapeutics* 250: 184-196.

4905 Pryor, K W, R Haag, J O'Reilly. 1969. The creative porpoise: Training for novel behavior. *Journal of the Experimental Analysis of Behavior* 12: 653-661.

4906 Rachlin, H. 1974. Self-control. *Behaviorism* 2: 94-107.

4907 Rachlin, H, R Battalio, J Kagel, L Green. 1981. Maximization theory in behavioral psychology. *Behavioral and Brain Sciences* 4: 371-417.

4908 Rachlin, H. 1985. Pain and behavior. *Behavioral and Brain Sciences* 8: 43-83.

4909 Rachlin, H, A Castrogiovanni, D Cross. 1987. Probability and delay in commitment. *Journal of the Experimental Analysis of Behavior* 48: 347-353.

4910 Rachlin, H. 1989. *Judgement, Decision, and Choice: A Cognitive/Behavioral Synthesis.* New York: W.H. Freeman.

4911 Rachlin, H, A Raineri, D Cross. 1991. Subjective probability and delay. *Journal of the Experimental Analysis of Behavior* 55: 233-244.

4912 Rachman, S. 1977. The conditioning theory of fear-acquisition: A critical examination. *Behaviour Research and Therapy* 15: 375-87.

4913 Ragotzy, S P, E Blakely, A Poling. 1988. Self-control in mentally retarded adolescents: Choice as a function of amount and delay of reinforcement. *Journal of the Experimental Analysis of Behavior* 49: 191-199.

4914 Rao, R K, T C Mawhinney. 1991. Superior-subordinate dyads: Dependence of leader effectiveness on mutual reinforcement contingencies. *Journal of the Experimental Analysis of Behavior* 56: 105-118.

4915 Rapport, M D, A Murphy, J S Bailey. 1982. Ritalin vs response cost in the control of hyperactive children: A within-subject comparison. *Journal of Applied Behavior Analysis* 15: 205-216.

4916 Rescorla, R A, A R Wagner. 1972. A theory of Pavlovian conditioning: Variations in effectiveness of reinforcement and nonreinforcement. In *Classical Conditioning II.* Edited by Black, A H, W F Prokasy. Pp. 64-99. New York: Appleton-Century-Crofts.

4917 Rescorla, R A, P C Holland. 1976. Some behavioral approaches to the study of learning. In *Neural Mechanisms of Learning and Memory.* Edited by Rosenzweig, M R, E L Bennet. Pp. 165-192. Cambridge: M.I.T. Press.

4918 Rescorla, R A. 1988. Pavlovian conditioning: It's not what you think it is. *American Psychologist* 43: 151-160.

4919 Ribes, E. 1985. Human behaviour as operant behavior: An empirical or conceptual issue. In *Behaviour Analysis and Contemporary Psychology.* Edited by Lowe, C F, M Richelle, D E Blackman, C M Bradshaw. Pp. 117-133. London: Erlbaum.

4920 Riegler, H C, D M Baer. 1989. A developmental analysis of rule-following. In *Advances in Child Development and Behavior.* Edited by Reese, H W. Pp. 191-219. New York: Academic Press.

4921 Robinson, J K, W R Woodward. 1989. The convergence of behavioral biology and operant psychology: Toward an interlevel and interfield science. *The Behavior Analyst* 12: 131-141.

4922 Rovee-Collier, C K, M J Gekoski. 1979. The economics of infancy: A review of conjugate reinforcement. In *Advances in Child Development and Behavior*. Edited by Reese, H W, L P Lipsitt. Pp. 195-255. New York: Academic Press.

4923 Rovee-Collier, C K, L P Lipsitt. 1982. Learning, adaptation, and memory in the newborn. In *Psychobiology of the Human Newborn*. Edited by Stratton, P. Pp. 147-190. London: Wiley.

4924 Rovee-Collier, C K. 1983. Infants as problem-solvers: A psychobiological perspective. In *Biological Factors in Learning*. Edited by Zeiler, M D, P Harzem. Chichester: Wiley.

4925 Rovee-Collier, C. 1987. Learning and memory in infancy. In *Handbook of Infant Development*. Edited by Osofsky, J D. Pp. 98-148. New York: Wiley.

4926 Sampson, H H. 1987. Initiation of ethanol-maintained behavior: A comparison of animal models and their implication to human drinking. In *Neurobehavioral Pharmacology*. Edited by Thompson, T, P B Dews, J E Barrett. Pp. 221-248. Hillsdale, N.J.: Erlbaum.

4927 Savage-Rumbaugh, E S. 1984. Verbal behavior at a procedural level in the chimpanzee. *Journal of the Experimental Analysis of Behavior* 41: 223-250.

4928 Schlinger, H, E Blakely. 1987. Function-altering effects of contingency-specifying stimuli. *The Behavior Analyst* 10: 41-45.

4929 Schmid, T L, D F Hake. 1983. Fast acquisition of cooperation and trust: A two-stage view of trusting behavior. *Journal of the Experimental Analysis of Behavior* 40: 179-192.

4930 Schmitt, D R. 1976. Some conditions affecting the choice to cooperate or compete. *Journal of the Experimental Analysis of Behavior* 25: 165-178.

4931 Schmitt, D R. 1981. Performance under cooperation or competition. *American Behavioral Scientist* 24: 649-679.

4932 Schmitt, D R. 1984. Interpersonal relations: Cooperation and competition. *Journal of the Experimental Analysis of Behavior* 42: 377-383.

4933 Schmitt, D R. 1986. Competition: Some behavior issues. *The Behavior Analyst* 9: 27-34.

4934 Schmitt, D R. 1987. Interpersonal contingencies: Performance differences and cost-effectiveness. *Journal of the Experimental Analysis of Behavior* 48: 221-234.

4935 Schuster, C R. 1986. Implications of laboratory research for the treatment of drug dependence. In *Behavioral Analysis of Drug Dependence*. Edited by Goldberg, S R, I P Stolerman. Pp. 357-385. Orlando: Academic Press.

4936 Schwartz, B, H Lacey. 1988. What applied studies of human operant conditioning tell us about humans and about operant conditioning. In *Human Operant Conditioning and Behavior Modification*. Edited by Davey, G, C Cullen. Pp. 27-42. Chichester: Wiley.

4937 Schweitzer, J B, B Sulzer-Azaroff. 1988. Self-control: Teaching tolerance for delay in impulsive children. *Journal of the Experimental Analysis of Behavior* 50: 173-186.

4938 Segal, E F. 1975. Psycholinguistics discovers the operant: A review of Roger Brown's A First Language: The Early Years. *Journal of the Experimental Analysis of Behavior* 23: 149-158.

4939 Segal, E F. 1987. Walden Two: The morality of anarchy. *The Behavior Analyst* 10: 147-160.

4940 Seron, X. 1985. Behaviour modification and neuropsychology. In *Behaviour Analysis and Contemporary Psychology*. Edited by Lowe, C F, M Richelle, D E Blackman, C M Bradshaw. Pp. 171-183. London: Erlbaum.

4941 Sidman, M. 1971. Reading and auditory-visual equivalences. *Journal of Speech and Reading Research* 14: 5-13.

4942 Sidman, M, W Tailby. 1982. Conditional discrimination versus matching to sample: An expansion of the testing paradigm. *Journal of the Experimental Analysis of Behavior* 37: 5-22.

4943 Sidman, M, et al. 1982. A search for symmetry in the conditional discriminations of rhesus monkeys, baboons, and children. *Journal of the Experimental Analysis of Behavior* 37: 23-44.

4944 Sidman, M, B Kirk, M Wilson-Morris. 1985. Six-member stimulus classes generated by conditional-discrimination procedures. *Journal of the Experimental Analysis of Behavior* 43: 21-42.

4945 Sidman, M. 1986. Functional analysis of emergent verbal classes. In *Analysis and Integration of Behavioral Units*. Edited by Thompson, T, M D Zeiler. Pp. 213-245. Hillsdale, N.J.: Erlbaum.

4946 Sidman, M. 1990. Equivalence relations: Where do they come from? In *Behaviour Analysis in Theory and Practice: Contributions and Controversies*. Edited by Blackman, D E, H Lejeune. Pp. 93-114. Hove, England: Erlbaum.

4947 Siegel, S. 1975. Evidence from rats that morphine tolerance is a learned response. *Comparative and Physiological Psychology* 89: 489-506.

4948 Siegel, S. 1977. Morphine tolerance acquisition as an associative process. *Journal of Experimental Psychology: Animal Behavior Processes* 3: 1-13.

4949 Siegel, S, R E Hinson, M D Krank, J McCully. 1982. Heroin "overdose" death: The contribution of drug-associated environmental cues. *Science* 216: 436-437.

4950 Sigurdardottir, Z G, G Green, R R Saunders. 1990. Equivalence classes generated by sequence training. *Journal of the Experimental Analysis of Behavior* 53: 47-63.

4951 Silberberg, A, P Murray, J Christenson, T Asano. 1988. Choice in the repeated-gambles experiment. *Journal of the Experimental Analysis of Behavior* 50: 187-195.

4952 Skinner, B F. 1938. *The Behavior of Organisms*. Englewood Cliffs, N.J.: Prentice-Hall.

4953 Skinner, B F. 1953. *Science and Human Behavior*. New York: Macmillan.

4954 Skinner, B F. 1957. *Verbal Behavior*. Englewood Cliffs, N.J.: Prentice-Hall.

4955 Skinner, B F. 1969. *Contingencies of Reinforcement: A Theoretical Analysis*. New York: Appleton-Century-Crofts.

4956 Skinner, B F. 1974. *About Behaviorism*. New York: Knopf.

4957 Skinner, B F. 1978. *Reflections on Behaviorism and Society*. Englewood Cliffs, N.J.: Prentice Hall.

4958 Skinner, B F. 1984. The evolution of behavior. *Journal of the Experimental Analysis of Behavior* 41: 217-221.

4959 Skinner, B F. 1986. The evolution of verbal behavior. *Journal of the Experimental Analysis of Behavior* 45: 115-122.

4960 Skinner, B F. 1987. *Upon Further Reflection.* Englewood Cliffs, N.J.: Prentice Hall.

4961 Skinner, B F. 1989. *Recent Issues in the Analysis of Behavior.* Columbus: Bobbs-Merrill.

4962 Smith, L D. 1986. *Behaviorism and Logical Positivism: A Reassessment of the alliance.* Stanford: Stanford University Press.

4963 Sonuga-Barke, E J S, S E Lea G., P Webley. 1989. The development of adaptive choice in a self-control paradigm. *Journal of the Experimental Analysis of Behavior* 51: 77-85.

4964 Sonuga-Barke, E J S, S E Lea G., P Webley. 1989. Children's choice: Sensitivity to changes in reinforcer density. *Journal of the Experimental Analysis of Behavior* 51: 185-197.

4965 Staddon, J E R. 1985. The comparative psychology of operant behavior. In *Behavior Analysis and Contemporary Psychology.* Edited by Lowe, C F, M Richelle, D E Blackman, C M Bradshaw. Pp. 83-94. London: Erlbaum.

4966 Stampfl, T G. 1987. Theoretical implications of the neurotic paradox as a problem in behavior theory: An experimental resolution. *The Behavior Analyst* 10: 161-173.

4967 Stemmer, N. 1990. Skinner's Verbal Behavior, Chomsky's review, and mentalism. *Journal of the Experimental Analysis of Behavior* 54: 307-315.

4968 Sulzer-Azaroff, B, ed. 1988. *Behavior Analysis in Education.* Lawrence, KS.: Journal of Applied Behavior Analysis.

4969 Takahashi, M, T Iwamoto. 1986. Human concurrent performances: The effects of experience, instructions, and schedule-correlated stimuli. *Journal of the Experimental Analysis of Behavior* 45: 257-267.

4970 Terrace, H S. 1963. Discrimination learning with and without "errors". *Journal of the Experimental Analysis of Behavior* 6: 1-27.

4971 Thompson, T, C E Johanson, eds. 1981. *Behavioral pharmacology of human drug dependence.* Rockville, MD.: National Institute on Drug Abuse.

4972 Thompson, R F, et al. 1984. Neuronal substrates of associative learning in the mammalian brain. In *Primary Neural Substrates of Learning and Behavioral Change*. Edited by Alkon, D, J Farley. Pp. 71-77. Cambridge: Cambridge University Press.

4973 Thompson, T. 1984. The examining magistrate for nature: A retrospective review of Claude Bernard's An Introduction to the Study of Experimental Medicine. *Journal of the Experimental Analysis of Behavior* 41: 211-216.

4974 Tighe, T J, R N Leaton, eds. 1976. *Habituation: Perspectives from Child Development, Animal Behavior, and Neurosphysiology.* Hillsdale, N.J.: Erlbaum.

4975 Timberlake, W. 1980. A molar equilibrium theory of learned performance. In *The Psychology of Learning and Motivation*. Edited by Bower, G H. New York: Academic Press.

4976 Torgrud, L J, S W Holbom. 1989. Effectiveness and persistence of precurrent mediating behavior in delayed matching to sample and oddity matching with children. *Journal of the Experimental Analysis of Behavior* 52: 181-191.

4977 Van Houten, R. 1983. Punishment: From animal laboratory to the applied setting. In *The Effects of Punishment on Human Behavior*. Edited by Axelrod, S, J Apsche. Pp. 13-44. New York: Academic Press.

4978 Vaughan, M E, J L Michael. 1982. Automatic reinforcement: An important but ignored concept. *Behaviorism* 10: 217-227.

4979 Vaughan, J, W., R J Herrnstein. 1987. Stability, melioration, and natural selection. In *Advances in Behavioral Economics*. Edited by Green, L, J H Kagel. Pp. 185-215. Norwood, N.J.: Ablex.

4980 Vaughan, M. 1989. Rule-governed behavior in behavior analysis: A theoretical and experimental history. In *Rule-Governed Behavior: Cognition, Contingencies, and Instructional Control*. Edited by Hayes, S C. Pp. 325-357. New York: Plenum.

4981 Wasserman, E A, D J Neunaber. 1986. College students' responding to and rating of contingency relations: The role of temporal contiguity. *Journal of the Experimental Analysis of Behavior* 46: 15-35.

4982 Watson, J B. 1924. *Behaviorism.* New York: Norton.

4983 Wearden, J H. 1988. Some neglected problems in the analysis of human operant behavior. In *Human Operant Conditioning and Behavior Modification.* Edited by Davey, G, C Cullen. Pp. 197-224. Chichester: Wiley.

4984 Weiner, H. 1981. Contribution of reinforcement schedule histories to our understanding of drug effects in human subjects. In *Behavioral Pharmacology of Human Drug Dependence.* Edited by Thompson, T, C E Johnason. Rockville, MD.: National Institute on Drug Abuse.

4985 Weiner, H. 1983. Some thoughts on discrepant human-animal performances under schedules of reinforcement. *Psychological Record* 33: 521-532.

4986 Weiss, B. 1983. Behavioral toxicology and environmental science: Opportunity and challenge for psychology. *American Psychologist* 1174-1187.

4987 Whitehurst, G J, M C Valdez-Menchaca. 1988. What is the role of reinforcement in early language acquisition? *Child Development* 59: 430-440.

4988 Whitehurst, G J, B D De Baryshe. 1989. Observational learning and language acquisition. In *The Many Faces of Imitation in Language Learning.* Edited by Speidel, G E, K E Nelson. Pp. 251-276. New York: Springer-Verlag.

4989 Williams, B A. 1983. Revising the principle of reinforcement. *Behaviorism* 11: 63-88.

4990 Wilson, J F, M B Cantor. 1987. An animal model of excessive eating: Schedule-induced hyperphagia in food-satiated rats. *Journal of the Experimental Analysis of Behavior* 47: 335-346.

4991 Winston, A S, J E Baker. 1985. Behavior analytic studies of creativity: A critical review. *The Behavior Analyst* 8: 191-205.

4992 Wood, R L. 1988. Clinical constraints affecting human conditioning. In *Human Operant Conditioning and Behavior Modification.* Edited by Davey, G, C Cullen. Pp. 87-118. Chichester: Wiley.

4993 Woody, C D. 1983. *Conditioning: Representation of Involved Neural Functions.* New York: Plenum Press.

4994 Wulfert, E, S C Hayes. 1988. Transfer of a conditional ordering response through conditional equivalence classes. *Journal of the Experimental Analysis of Behavior* 50: 113-123.

4995 Wulfert, E, M J Dougher, D E Greenway. 1991. Protocol analysis of the correspondence of verbal behavior and equivalence class formation. *Journal of the Experimental Analysis of Behavior* 56: 489-504.

4996 Yulevich, L, S Axelrod. 1983. Punishment: A concept that is no longer necessary. In *Progress in Behavior Modification.* Pp. 355-382. New York: Academic Press.

4997 Zeiler, M D. 1984. The sleeping giant: Reinforcement schedules. *Journal of the Experimental Analysis of Behavior* 42: 485-493.

4998 Zeiler, M D. 1986. Behavioral units and optimality. In *Analysis and Integration of Behavioral Units.* Edited by Thompson, T, M D Zeiler. Pp. 81-116. Hillsdale, N.J.: Erlbaum.

4999 Zellner, D A, P Rozin, M Aron, C Kulish. 1983. Conditioned enhancement of human's liking for flavor by pairing with sweetness. *Learning and Motivation* 14: 338-350.

5000 Zuriff, G E. 1985. *Behaviorism: A Conceptual Reconstruction.* New York: Columbia University Press.

# 14

# Cognition

5001 Abraham, R H. 1985. Dynamic models for thought. *Journal of Social and Biological Structures* 8: 13-26.

5002 Albury, W R, P Slezak, eds. 1987. *Mind Matters.* Sydney: University of New South Wales Press.

5003 Allen, J F, C R Perrault. 1980. Analyzing intention in utterances. *Artificial Intelligence* 15: 143-178.

5004 Allman, J. 1987. Maps in context: Some analogies between visual cortical and genetic maps. In *Matters of Intelligence.* Edited by Vaina, L M. Pp. 369-393. Dortrecht: Riedel.

5005 Allport, D A, B Antonis, P Reynolds. 1972. On the division of attention: A disproof of the single-channel hypothesis. *Quarterly Journal of Experimental Psychology* 24: 225-35.

5006 Anderson, J R. 1980. *Cognitive Psychology and Its Implications.* San Francisco: Freeman.

5007 Anderson, J R. 1983. *The Architecture of Cognition.* Cambridge: Harvard University Press.

5008 Annett, M, D Kilshaw. 1982. Mathmatical ability and lateral asymmetry. *Cortex* 18: 547-568.

5009 Apter, M J, K C P Smith. 1976. Humour and the theory of psychological reversals. In *It's a Funny Thing: Humour.* Edited by Chapman, A J, H C Fast. Oxford: Pergamon Press.

5010 Apter, M J. 1982. *The Experience of Motivation: A Theory of Psychological Reversals.* London: Academic Press.

5011 Apter, M J, D Fontana, S Murgatroyd, eds. 1985. *Reversal Theory: Applications and Developments.* Cardiff: University College Cardiff Press.

5012 Arnoff, J, R Oehrle, eds. 1984. *Language Sound Structure.* Cambridge: M.I.T. Press.

5013 Asquith, P J. 1984. The inevitability and utility of anthropomorphism in description of primate behaviour. In *The Meaning of Primate Signals*. Edited by Harré, R, V Reynolds. Pp. 138-76. Cambridge: Cambridge University Press.

5014 Baars, B J. 1989. *A Cognitive Theory of Consciousness*. Berkeley: The Wright Institute.

5015 Bach-y-Rita, P. 1984. The relationship between motor processes and cognition in tactile visual substitution. In *Cognition and Motor Processes*. Edited by Prinz, W, A F Sanders. Pp. 149-160. Berlin: Springer.

5016 Bachevalier, J, C Hagger. 1991. Sex differences in the development of learning abilities in primates. *Psychoneuroendocrinology* 16: 177-88.

5017 Barnes, C A, B L McNaughton. 1983. Where is the cognitive map? *Neuroscience Abstracts* 9: 191-6.

5018 Barratt, E S, J H Patton. 1983. Impulsivity: Cognitive, behavioral, and psychophysiological correlates. In *Biological Bases of Sensation Seeking, Impulsivity and Anxiety*. Edited by Zuckerman, M. Hillsdale, N.J.: Erlbaum.

5019 Benbow, C P. 1988. Sex differences in mathematical reasoning ability in intellectually talented preadolescents: Their nature, effects, and possible causes. *Behavioral and Brain Sciences* 11: 169-83.

5020 Beninger, R J. 1983. The role of dopamine in locomotor activity and learning. *Brain Research Reviews* 6: 173-196.

5021 Bergland, R. 1985. *The Fabric of Mind*. Melbourne: Penguin.

5022 Berthenthal, B I, J J Campos, K C Barett. 1984. Self-produced locomotion: An organizer of emotional, cognitive and social development in infancy. In *Continuities and Discontinuities in Development*. Edited by Erride, R N, R J Harmon. Pp. 175-210. New York: Plenum.

5023 Bickerton, D. 1984. Creole is still king. *Behavioral and Brain Sciences* 7: 212-218.

5024 Bickerton, D. 1984. The language bioprogram hypothesis. *Behavioral and Brain Sciences* 7: 173-187.

5025 Birhle, A M, H H Brownell, J A Powelson, H Gardner. 1986. Comprehension of humorous and non-humorous materials by left and right brain-damaged patients. *Brain and Cognition* 5: 399-411.

5026 Blackman, D E. 1983. On cognitive theories of animal learning: Extrapolation from humans to animals. In *Animal Models of Human Behaviour.* Edited by Davey, G C L. New York: Wiley.

5027 Blakemore, C. 1977. *Mechanics of the Mind.* New York: Cambrdige University Press.

5028 Boden, M. 1981. *Minds and Mechanisms.* Ithaca: Cornell University Press.

5029 Boden, M A. 1982. Implications of language studies for human nature. In *Language, Mind, and Brain.* Edited by Scholes, R J, T W Simon. Pp. 129-144. Hillsdale, NJ: Erlbaum.

5030 Boden, M A. 1988. *Computer Models of Mind: Computational Approaches in Theoretical Psychology.* Cambridge: Cambridge University Press.

5031 Bolwig, N. 1964. Observations on the mental and manipulative abilities of a captive baboon (Papio doguera). *Behaviour* 22: 24-40.

5032 Brand, M, R M Harnish. 1986. *The Representation of Knowledge and Belief.* Tucson: University of Arizona Press.

5033 Brown, R, ed. 1970. *Psycholinguistics.* New York: Macmillan.

5034 Brown, R. 1970. The first sentences of child and chimpanzee. In *Psycholinguistics.* Edited by Brown, R. Pp. 208-231. New York: Macmillan.

5035 Brown, R. 1973. *A First Language: The Early Stages.* Cambridge: Harvard University Press.

5036 Brown, P, S Levinson. 1978. Universals in language: Politeness phenomena. In *Questions and Politeness: Strategies in Social Interaction.* Edited by Goody, E. Pp. 56-310. London: Cambridge University Press.

5037 Buffery, A W H, J A Gray. 1972. Sex differences in the development of spatial and linguistic skills. In *Gender Differences, Their Onotgeny and Significance.* Edited by Ounsted, C, D C Taylor. Pp. 123-157. London: Churchill.

5038 Bunder, S. 1962. Intolerance of ambiguity as a personality variable. *Journal of Personality* 30: 29-50.

5039 Bundy, A M. 1983. *The Computer Modelling of Mathematical Reasoning*. London: Academic Press.

5040 Buser, P. 1992. *Audition*. Cambridge: M.I.T. Press.

5041 Byrne, R W, A Whiten. 1988. *Machiavellian Intelligence: Social Expertise and the Evolution of Intelligence in Monkeys, Apes and Man*. London: Oxford University Press.

5042 Cacioppo, J T, L G Tassinary. 1989. The concept of attitudes: A psychophysiological analysis. In *Handbook of Social Psychophysiology*. Edited by Wagner, H, A Manstead. Pp. 309-346. New York: Wiley.

5043 Calvin, W H. 1960. *Conscious Machines*. New York: Bantam.

5044 Calvin, W H. 1983. A stone's throw and its launch window: Timing precision and its implications for language and hominid brains. *Journal of Theoretical Biology* 104: 121-135.

5045 Calvin, W H. 1983. *The Throwing Madonna: Essays on the Brain*. New York: McGraw-Hill.

5046 Calvin, W H. 1987. The brain as a Darwin machine. *Nature* 330: 33-34.

5047 Calvin, W H. 1991. *A Brain For All Seasons: Climate and Intelligence from the Ice Age to the Greenhouse Era*. New York: Bantam Books.

5048 Campbell, R, P Smith, eds. 1978. *Recent Advances in the Psychology of Language*. New York: Plenum.

5049 Campbell, J. 1984. *Historical Atlas of World Mythology: The Way of the Animal Powers*. San Francisco: Alfred van der Marck Editions.

5050 Caplan, D, ed. 1980. *Biological Studies of Mental Processes*. Boston: M.I.T. Press.

5051 Chamberlain, D B. 1987. The cognitive newborn: A scientific update. *British Journal of Psychotherapy* 4: 30-71.

5052 Chance, M R A. 1977. The infrastructure of mentality. In *Ethological Psychiatry*. Edited by McGuire, M T, L A Fairbanks. London: Grune & Stratten.

5053 Chapman, A J, H C Fast, eds. 1976. *It's a Funny Thing: Humour.* Oxford: Pergamon Press.

5054 Cheney, D L, R M Seyfarth. 1990. *How Monkeys See the World: Inside the Mind of Another Species.* Chicago: University of Chicago Press.

5055 Chomsky, N. 1964. *Language and Mind.* New York: Harcourt, Brace.

5056 Christiansen, K, R Knussmann. 1987. Sex hormones and cognitive functioning in men. *Neuropsychobiology* 18: 27-36.

5057 Clark, M S, S T Fiske, eds. 1982. *Affect and Cognition: The Seventeenth Annual Carnegie Symposium on Cognition.* Hillsdale, NJ: Erlbaum.

5058 Clark, J H. 1983. *A Map of Mental States.* London: Routledge.

5059 Clynes, M, ed. 1982. *Music, Mind and Brain.* New York: Plenum.

5060 Cohen, G. 1977. *The Psychology of Cognition.* London: Academic Press.

5061 Cohen, L J. 1981. Can human irrationality be experimentally demonstrated? *Behavioral and Brain Sciences* 4: 317-70.

5062 Cole, D, J Fetzer, eds. 1990. *Philosophy, Mind, and Cognitive Inquiry: Resources for Understanding Mental Processes.* Dordrecht: Reidel.

5063 Coltheart, M, E Hull, D Slater. 1975. Sex differences in imagery and reading. *Nature* 253: 438-440.

5064 Corballis, M. 1983. *Human Laterality.* New York: Academic Press.

5065 Cosmides, L, J Tooby. 1987. Reasoning and natural selection. In *Encyclopedia of Human Biology.* San Diego: Academic Press.

5066 Cosmides, L, J Tooby. 1987. From evolution to behavior: Evolutionary psychology as the missing link. In *The Latest on the Best: Essays on Evolution and Optimality.* Edited by Dupre, J. Cambridge: M.I.T. Press.

5067 Cosmides, L. 1989. The logic of social exchange: Has natural selection shaped how humans reason? Studies with the Wason selection task. *Cognition* 31: 187-276.

5068 Costall, A, A Still, eds. 1987. *Cognitive Psychology in Question.* Brighton: Harvester Press.

5069 Coulter, J. 1983. *Rethinking Cognitive Theory.* London: Macmillan.

5070 Crawford, C B. 1989. The theory of evolution: Of what value to psychology? *Journal of Comparative Psychology* 103: 4-22.

5071 Crick, F H C, C Asanuma. 1986. Certain aspects of the anatomy and physiology of the cerebral cortex. In *Parallel Distributed Processing: Explorations in the Microstructure of Cognition.* Edited by Rumelhart, D E, J L McClelland. Pp. 333-71. Cambridge: M.I.T. Press.

5072 Cutler, A. 1982. *Slips of the Tongue and Language Production.* Amsterdam: Mouton.

5073 Davey, G, ed. 1987. *Cognitive Processes and Pavlovian Conditioning in Humans.* Chichester: Wiley.

5074 Davidson, J, R Davidson, eds. 1980. *The Psychobiology of Human Consciousness.* New York: Plenum.

5075 Davis, H, J Memmott. 1982. Counting behavior in animals: A critical evaluation. *Psychological Bulletin* 92: 547-71.

5076 de Grolier, E, ed. 1983. *Glossogenetics: The Origin and Evolution of Language.* Paris: Harwood Academic Publishers.

5077 de Matteo, A. 1977. Visual imagery and visual analogues in American Sign Language. In *On the Other Hand.* Edited by Friedman, L A. Pp. 109-36. New York: Academic.

5078 de Renzi, E. 1982. *Disorders of Space Exploration and Cognition.* New York: Wiley.

5079 Delgado, J M R. 1969. *Physical Control of the Mind.* New York: Harper and Row.

5080 Delis, D C, W Wapner, H Gardner, J A Moses. 1983. The contribution of the right hemisphere to the organization of paragraphs. *Cortex* 19: 43-50.

5081 Dember, W N, J S Warm. 1979. *Psychology of Perception.* 2nd ed New York: Holt, Rinehart, and Winston.

5082 Denenberg, V H. 1983. Animal studies of laterality. In *Neuropsychology of Human Emotion.* Edited by Heilman, K M, P Satz. New York: Guilford Press.

5083 Dennett, D C. 1983. Intentional systems in cognitive ethology: The "Panglossian paradigm" defended *Behavioral and Brain Sciences* 6: 343-390.

5084 Diamond, R, S Carey, K J Back. 1983. Genetic influences on the development of spatial skills during early adolescence. *Cognition* 13: 167-185.

5085 Diamond, A, ed. 1990. *The Development and Neural Bases of Higher Cognitive Functions.* Chicago: University of Chicago Press.

5086 Donovan, B T. 1988. *Humors, Hormones, and the Mind.* New York: Stockton Press.

5087 Dooley, G N, T V Gill. 1977. Acquisition and use of mathematical skills by a linguistic chimpanzee. In *Language Learning by a Chimpanzee.* Edited by Rumbough, D M. Pp. 247-260. New York: Academic Press.

5088 Dunn, A J. 1986. Biochemical correlates of learning and memory. In *Learning and Memory: A Biological View.* Edited by Martinez, J L, Jr., R P Kesner. Pp. 165-202. New York: Academic Press.

5089 Duval, S, R A Wicklund. 1972. *A Theory of Objective Self Awareness.* New York: Academic Press.

5090 Ekman, P. 1985. *Telling Lies.* New York: Norton.

5091 Farrer, D N. 1967. Picture memory in the chimpanzee. *Perception and Motor Skills* 25: 305-315.

5092 Feldman, H, S Goldin-Meadow, L Gleitman. 1978. Beyond Herodotus: The creation of language by linguistically deprived deaf children. In *Action, Gesture and Symbol.* Edited by Lock, A. Pp. 351-414. New York: Academic Press.

5093 Ferster, C B. 1964. Arithmetic behavior in chimpanzees. *Scientific American* 210: 98-106.

5094 Festinger, L. 1957. *A Theory of Cognitive Dissonance.* Evanston, IL.: Row, Peterson and Cy.

5095 Fetzer, J, ed. 1991. *Epistemology and Cognition.* Dordrecht: Reidel.

5096 Fillmore, C J, D Kempler, W S Y Wang, eds. 1979. *Individual Differences in Language Ability and Language Behavior.* New York: Academic Press.

5097 Fischer, R. 1961. Biological time. In *The Voices of Time.* Edited by Frazer, J T. Pp. 351-384. New York: George Braziller.

5098 Fischer, R. 1987. On fact and fiction: The structure of stories that the brain tells it itself about itself. *Journal of Social and Biological Structures* 10: 343-52.

5099 Flin, R H. 1980. Age effects in children's memory for unfamiliar faces. *Developmental Psychology* 16: 373-374.

5100 Fodor, J A. 1983. *The Modularity of Mind: An Essay on Faculty Psychology.* Cambridge: MIT Press.

5101 Foster, M L, S H Brandes, eds. 1980. *Symbol as Sense: New Approaches to the Analysis of Meaning.* New York: Academic Press.

5102 Frazer, J T, ed. 1961. *The Voices of Time.* New York: George Braziller.

5103 Frisby, J P. 1979. *Seeing.* Oxford: Oxford University Press.

5104 Fritsch, V. 1968. *Left and Right in Science and Life.* London: Barrie & Rockliff.

5105 Frost, G T. 1980. Tool behavior and the origins of laterality. *Journal of Human Evolution* 9: 447-459.

5106 Funt, B V. 1983. A parallel-process model of mental rotation. *Cognitive Science* 7: 67-93.

5107 Gallup, G G. 1975. Towards an operational definition of self-awareness. In *Socioecology and Psychology of Primates.* Edited by Tuttle, R H. Pp. 309-341. The Hague: Mouton.

5108 Gallup, G G. 1977. Self-recognition in primates: A comparative approach to the bidirectional properties of consciousness. *American Psychologist* 32: 329-338.

5109 Gardner, H A. 1983. *Frames of Mind: The Theory of Multiple Intelligences*. New York: Basic Books.

5110 Gardner, H A, B T Gardner. 1985. Signs of intelligence in chimpanzees. *Philosophical Transactions of the Royal Society (London)* B308: 159-76.

5111 Gaulin, S, R Fitzgerald. 1986. Sex differences in spatial ability: An evolutionary hypothesis and test. *American Naturalist* 127: 74-88.

5112 Gay, P. 1983. *The Education of the Senses*. New York: Oxford University Press.

5113 Gelman, R. 1978. *The Child's Understanding of Number*. Cambridge: Harvard University Press.

5114 Geschwind, N. 1984. The biology of cerebral dominance: Implications for cognition. *Cognition* 17: 193-208.

5115 Gessinger, I, W v Rahden, eds. 1989. *Theorien vom Ursprung der Sprache*. Berlin: de Gruyter.

5116 Getzels, J W, P W Jackson. 1962. *Creativity and Intelligence: Expolorations with Gifted Students*. New York: Wiley.

5117 Gibson, J J. 1966. *The Senses Considered as Perceptual Systems*. Boston: Houghton-Mifflin.

5118 Gibson, J J. 1979. *An Ecological Approach to Visual Perception*. Boston: Houghton-Mifflin.

5119 Gibson, K R, A C Peterson. 1991. *Brain Maturation and Cognitive Development: Comparative and Cross-Cultural Perspectives*. Hawthorne, NY: Aldine de Gruyter.

5120 Giles, H, P Robinson, P Smith. 1980. *Language: Social Psychological Perspectives*. Oxford: Pergamon.

5121 Gillan, D J, D Premack, G Woodrugg. 1981. Reasoning in the chimpanzee: I. Analogical reasoning. *Journal of Experimental Psychology* 7: 1-17.

5122 Ginsburg, B. 1980. The misperception of signals in abnormal social behavior. In *Ethology and Nonverbal Communication in Mental Health*. Edited by Corson, S A, et al. Pp. 167-178. New York: Pergamon.

5123 Goldfield, E. 1983. The ecological approach to perceiving as a foundation for understanding the development of knowing in infancy. *Developmental Review* 3: 371-404.

5124 Goldin-Meadow, S, C Mylander. 1983. Gestural communication in deaf children: Noneffect of parental input on language development. *Science* 221: 372-4.

5125 Goldman, A. 1986. *Epistemology and Cognition.* Cambridge: Harvard University Press.

5126 Goldman-Rakic, P S. 1987. Development of cortical circuitry and cognitive function. *Child Development* 58: 610-22.

5127 Goldsmith, R E, T A Matherly. 1986. Seeking simple solutions: Assimilators and explorers, adaptors and innovators. *Journal of Psychology* 120: 149-55.

5128 Goldstein, K M, S Blackman. 1978. *Cognitive Style: Five Approaches and Relevant Research.* New York: Wiley.

5129 Goodenough, W H. 1990. Evolution of the human capacity for beliefs. *American Anthropologist* 92: 597-612.

5130 Goodnow, J J. 1976. The nature of intelligent behavior: Questions raised by cross-cultural studies. In *The Nature of Intelligence.* Edited by Resnick, L. Hillsdale, NJ: Erlbaum.

5131 Gottfried, A. 1984. *Home Environment and Early Cognitive Development.* New York: Academic Press.

5132 Gould, S J. 1991. Exaptation: A crucial tool for an evolutionary psychology. *Journal of Social Issues* 47: 43-66.

5133 Gray, J A. 1975. *Elements of a Two-process Theory of Learning.* London: Academic Press.

5134 Green, S. 1975. Dialects in Japanese monkeys: Vocal learning and cultural transmission of locale-specific vocal behavior. *Zeitschrift für Tierpsychologie* 38: 304-14.

5135 Greenberg, J H. 1966. *Language Universals, with Special Reference to Feature Hierarchies.* The Hague: Mouton.

5136 Greenfield, P, E S Savage-Rumbaugh. 1990. Grammatical combination in Pan paniscus: Processes of learning and invention in the evolution and development of language. In *Language and*

*Intelligence in Monkeys and Apes.* Edited by Parker, S, K Gibson. Cambridge: Cambridge University Press.

5137 Greenfield, P M. 1991. Language, tools, and brain: The ontogeny and phylogeny of hierarchically organized sequential behavior. *Behavioral and Brain Sciences* 14: 531-550.

5138 Gregory, R L. 1987. *The Oxford Companion to the Mind.* New York: Oxford University Press.

5139 Gregson, R A M. 1983. *Time Series in Psychology.* Hillsdale, NJ: Erlbaum.

5140 Gregson, R A M. 1988. *Nonlinear Psychophysical Dynamics.* Hillsdale, NJ: Erlbaum.

5141 Griffin, D R. 1976. *The Question of Animal Awareness: Evolutionary Continuity of Mental Experience.* New York: Rockefeller University Press.

5142 Griffin, D R. 1976. A possible window on the minds of animals. *American Scientist* 64: 530-35.

5143 Griffin, D R. 1978. Prospects for a cognitive ethology. *Behavioral and Brain Sciences* 1: 527-538.

5144 Griffin, D R. 1982. Animal communication as evidence of thinking. In *Language, Mind and Brain.* Edited by Simon, T W, R J Scholes. Pp. 241-50. London: Erlbaum.

5145 Griffin, D R. 1982. Animal Mind, Human Mind. In  Berlin: Springer.

5146 Griffin, D R. 1984. *Animal Thinking.* Cambridge: Harvard University Press.

5147 Griffin, D R. 1985. Cognitive dimensions of animal communication. In *Experimental Behavioral Ecology and Sociobiology.* Edited by Hölldobler, B, M Lindauer. New York: Springer.

5148 Grossberg, S. 1982. Processing of expected and unexpected events during conditioning and attention: A psychophysiological theory. *Psychological Review* 89: 529-572.

5149 Guilford, J P. 1967. *The Nature of Human Intelligence.* New York: McGraw-Hill.

5150 Hadamard, J. 1954. *The Psychology of Invention in the Mathematical Field.* New York: Dover.

5151 Hallpike, C R. 1979. *The Foundations of Primitive Thought.* New York: Oxford University Press.

5152 Halpern, D F. 1986. *Sex Differences in Cognitive Abilities.* Hillsdale, NJ: Erlbaum.

5153 Hamilton, D L. 1981. Cognitive representations of persons. In *Social Cognition: The Ontario Symposium.* Edited by Higgins, E T, C P Herman, M P Zanna. Pp. 135-159. Hillsdale, N.J.: Erlbaum.

5154 Harnad, S, H Steklis, J Lancaster, eds. 1976. *Origins and Evolution of Language and Speech.* New York: New York Academy of Sciences.

5155 Harnad, S, ed. 1986. *Categorical Perception.* New York: Cambridge University Press.

5156 Harré, R, V Reynolds, eds. 1984. *The Meaning of Primate Signals.* Cambridge: Cambridge University Press.

5157 Hassler, M. 1990. Functional cerebral asymmetries and cognitive abilities in musicians, painters, and controls. *Brain and Cognition* 13: 1-17.

5158 Heeschen, V. 1989. Humanethologische Aspekte der Sprachevolution. In *Theorien vom Ursprung der Sprache.* Edited by Gessinger, I, W v Rahden. Pp. 196-249. Berlin: de Gruyter.

5159 Henderson, B, L Dias. 1987. An exploratory study of infant problem solving in natural environments. *Ethology and Sociobiology* 8: 205-214.

5160 Herrnstein, R J. 1984. Objects, categories, and discriminative stimuli. In *Animal Cognition.* Edited by Roitblat, H L, T G Bever, H S Terrace. Pp. 233-61. Hillsdale, N.J.: Erlbaum.

5161 Hess, W. 1983. *Pitch Determination of Speech Signals.* Berlin: Springer.

5162 Hewes, G W. 1977. Language origin theories. In *Language Learning by a Chimpanzee.* Edited by Rumbaugh, D M. Pp. 3-53. New York: Academic Press.

5163 Hilgard, E R, G H Bower. 1975. *Theories of Learning.* Engelwood Cliffs, NJ: Prenctice Hall.

5164 Hilgard, E R. 1977. *Divided Consciousness: Multiple Controls in Human Thought and Action.* New York: Wiley.

5165 Hilgard, E R. 1980. Consciousness in contemporary psychology. *Annual Review of Psychology* 31: 1-26.

5166 Hill, J H. 1972. On the Evolutionary Foundation of Language. *American Anthropologist* 74: 308-317.

5167 Hinton, G E, J A Anderson, eds. 1981. *Parallel Models of Associative Memory.* Hillsdale, NJ: Erlbaum.

5168 Hiroto, D S, M E P Seligman. 1975. Generality of learned helplessness in man. *Journal of Personality and Social Psychology* 31: 311-327.

5169 Hoenigswald, H, L Wiener, eds. 1987. *Biological Metaphor and Cladistic Classification: An Interdisciplinary Perspective.* Philadelphia: University of Pennsylvania Press.

5170 Hoenigswald, H. 1987. Language family trees: Topological and metrical. In *Biological Metaphor and Cladistic Classification: An Interdisciplinary Perspective.* Edited by Hoenigswald, H, L Wiener. Pp. 257-68. Philadelphia: University of Pennsylvania Press.

5171 Holender, D. 1986. Semantic activation without conscious identification in dichotic listening, parafoveal vision, and visual masking: A survey and appraisal. *Behavioral and Brain Sciences* 9: 1-66.

5172 Holland, J, K Holyoak, R E Nisbett, P Thagard. 1986. *Induction: Processes of Inference, Learning, and Discovery.* Cambridge: M.I.T. Press.

5173 Hookway, C. 1984. *Minds, Machines, and Evolution.* Cambridge: Cambridge University Press.

5174 Hulse, S H, H Fowler, W K Honig, eds. 1978. *Cognitive Processes in Animal Behaviour.* Hillsdale, N.J.: Erlbaum.

5175 Hurford, J R. 1991. The evolution of the critical period for language acquisition. *Cognition* 40: 159-202.

5176 Illingworth, R S. 1980. *The Development of the Infant and the Young Child, Abnormal and Normal.* 7th ed Edinburgh: Churchill Livingstone.

5177 Inhelder, B, J Piaget. 1958. *The Growth of Logical Thinking from Childhood to Adolescence.* New York: Basic Books.

5178 Jaffe, J, S Feldstein. 1970. *Rhythms of Dialogue.* New York: Academic Press.

5179 Jaynes, J. 1977. *The Origin of Consciousness in the Breakdown of the Bicameral Mind.* Boston: Houghton Mifflin.

5180 Jenkins, P. 1977. Cultural transmission of song patterns and dialect development in a free-living bird population. *Animal Behavior* 26: 50-78.

5181 Jervis, R. 1976. *Perception and Misperception in International Politics.* Princeton: Princeton University Press.

5182 Jervis, R. 1989. *The Logic of Images in International Politics.* New York: Columbia University Press.

5183 Johnson, R, J K Bowers, M Gamble, F M Lyons, T W Presbrey, R Vetter. 1977. Ability to transcribe music and ear superiority for tone sequences. *Cortex* 13: 295-299.

5184 Johnson, R, C T Nagoshi. 1985. Parental ability, education, and occupation as influences on offspring cognition in Hawaii and Korea. *Personality and Individual Differences* 6: 413-23.

5185 Johnson, E S, A C Meade. 1987. Developmental patterns of spatial ability: An early sex difference. *Child Development* 58: 725-40.

5186 Jones, E E, R E Nisbett. 1971. *The Actor and the Observer: Divergent Perceptions of the Causes of Behavior.* New York: General Learning Press.

5187 Jorm, A F. 1983. Specific reading retardation and working memory: A review. *British Journal of Psychology* 74: 311-342.

5188 Jorm, A F. 1983. *The Psychology of Reading and Spelling Disabilities.* London: Routledge.

5189 Jouventin, P, P Pasteur, J Cambefort. 1977. Observational learning of baboons and avoidance of mimics: Exploratory texts. *Evolution* 31: 214-18.

5190 Kahneman, D, A Tversky. 1982. The psychology of preferences. *Scientific American* 246: 160-173.

5191 Kaplan, S. 1987. Aesthetics, affect and cognition: Environmental preference from an evolutionary perspective. *Environment and Behavior* 19: 3-32.

5192 Kaufman, L. 1974. *Sight and Mind*. Oxford: Oxford University Press.

5193 Keating, D P, V Clark. 1980. Development of physical and social reasoning in adolescence. *Developmental Psychology* 16: 23-30.

5194 Khatena, J, E P Torrance. 1976. *Manual for Khatena-Torrance Creative Perception Inventory*. Chicago: Steolting.

5195 Kien, J. 1991. The need for data reduction may have paved the way for evolution of language ability in hominids. *Journal of Human Evolution* 20: 157-165.

5196 Kintsch, W, A Flammer, eds. 1982. *Discourse Processing*. New York: North-Holland.

5197 Kirton, M, S de Ciantis. 1989. Cognitive style in organisational climate. In *Adaptors and Innovators: Styles of Creativity and Problem Solving*. Edited by Kirton, M. London: Routledge.

5198 Kirton, M. 1989. Adaptors and innovators at work. In *Adaptors and Innovators: Styles of Creativity and Problem Solving*. Edited by Kirton, M. London: Routledge.

5199 Kirton, M. 1989. A theory of cognitive style. In *Adaptors and Innovators: Styles of Creativity and Problem Solving*. Edited by Kirton, M. London: Routledge.

5200 Kirton, M, ed. 1989. *Adaptors and Innovators: Styles of Creativity and Problem Solving*. London: Routledge.

5201 Klein, S B, R R Mowrer. 1989. *Contemporary Learning Theories: Instrumental Conditioning Theory and the Impact of Biological Constraints on Learning*. Hillsdale, NJ: Erlbaum.

5202 Klinger, E. 1978. Modes of normal conscious flow. In *The Stream of Consciousness*. Edited by Pope, K S, J L Singer. New York: Plenum.

5203 Kogan, N. 1976. Sex differences in creativity and cognitive styles. In *Individuality in Learning*. Edited by Messic, S. San Francisco: Jossey-Bass.

5204 Kreitler, H, S Kreitler. 1976. *Cognitive Orientation and Behavior.* New York: Springer.

5205 Kuhl, P, A Meltzoff. 1982. The bimodal perception of speech in infancy. *Science* 218: 1138-41.

5206 Kuhl, P K, K A Williams, F Lacerda, K N Stevens, B Lindblom. 1992. Linguistic experience alters phonetic perception in infants by 6 months of age. *Science* 255: 606-608.

5207 Kupfermann, I. 1982. Learning. In *Principles of Neuroscience.* Edited by Kandel, E R, J H Schwartz. Pp. 570-579. London: Edward Arnold.

5208 Lau, R, D Sears, eds. 1986. *Cogniton and Political Behavior.* Hillsdale, NJ: Erlbaum.

5209 Laver, J. 1980. *The Phonetic Description of Voice Quality.* Cambridge: Cambridge Unviersity Press.

5210 Le May, M. 1975. The language capacity of Neanderthal man. *American Journal of Physical Anthropology* 42: 9-14.

5211 LeDoux, J, W F Hirst, eds. 1986. *Mind and Brain: Dialogues between Cognitive Psychology and Neuroscience.* New York: Cambridge University Press.

5212 Leet-Pellegrine, H. 1980. Conversational dominance as a function of gender and expertise. In *Language: Social Psychological Perspectives.* Edited by Giles, H, P Robinson, P Smith. Pp. 97-104. Oxford: Pergamon.

5213 Lefebvre, V. 1987. The fundamental structures of human reflexion. *Journal of Social and Biological Structures* 10: 129-175.

5214 Leger, D W, ed. 1988. *Comparative Perspectives in Modern Psychology. Nebraska Symposium on Motivation.* Lincoln: University of Nebraska Press.

5215 Lehman, D R, R O Lempert, R E Nisbett. 1988. The effects of graduate training on reasoning: Formal discipline and thinking about everyday life events. *American Psychologist* 43: 431-443.

5216 Lenneberg, E. 1967. *The Biological Foundation of Language.* New York: Wiley.

5217 Levine, D N, R Calvanio, A Popovics. 1982. Language in the absence of inner speech. *Neuropsychophysiology* 20: 391-409.

5218 Levy, F. 1980. The development of sustained attention (vigilance) and inhibition in children: Some normative data. *Journal of Child Psychology and Psychiatry* 21: 77-84.

5219 Libet, B. 1985. Unconscious cerebral initiative and the role of conscious will in voluntary action. *Behavioral and Brain Science* 8: 529-566.

5220 Lieberman, P. 1975. *On the Origins of Language: An Introduction to the Evolution of Human Speech.* New York: Macmillan.

5221 Lieberman, P. 1984. *The Biology and Evolution of Language.* Cambridge: Harvard University Press.

5222 Lieberman, P. 1985. On the evolution of human syntactic ability: Its pre-adaptive bases - motor control and speech. *Journal of Human Evolution* 14: 657-668.

5223 Lightfoot, D. 1982. *The Language Lottery: Toward a Biology of Grammars.* Cambridge: M.I.T. Press.

5224 Lock, A. 1978. *Action, Gesture and Symbol: The Emergence of Language.* New York: Academic Press.

5225 Lock, A, E Fisher. 1984. *Language Development.* London: Croom Helm.

5226 Lockard, J. 1980. Speculations on the adaptive significance of self-deception. In *The Evolution of Human Social Behavior.* Edited by Lockard, J. New York: Elisevier.

5227 Lockard, J, D Paulhus. 1988. *Self-Deceit: An Adaptive Mechanism.* Englewood Cliffs, N.J.: Prentice-Hall.

5228 Loftus, G R, E F Loftus. 1976. *Human Memory: The Processing of Information.* Hillsdale, N.J.: Erlbaum.

5229 Lorenz, K. 1977. *Behind the Mirror: A Search for a Natural History of Knowledge.* New York: Harcourt Brace.

5230 Lynch, M P, R E Eilers, D K Oller, R C Urbano. 1990. Innateness, experience, and music perception. *Psychological Science* 1: 272-276.

5231 Mandler, G. 1984. *Mind and Body.* New York: Norton.

5232 Mandler, G. 1985. *Cognitive Psychology: An Essay in Cognitive Science.* Hillsdale, N.J.: Erlbaum.

5233 Marcus, M. 1980. *A Theory of Syntactic Recognition for Natural Language.* Cambridge: M.I.T. Press.

5234 Marken, R S. 1986. Perceptual organization of behavior: A hierarchical control model of coordinated action. *Journal of Experimental Psychology: Human Perception and Performance* 12: 267-76.

5235 Marken, R S. 1988. The nature of behavior: Control as fact and theory. *Behavioral Science* 33: 196-206.

5236 Marler, P. 1984. Animal communication: Affect or cognition? In *Approaches to Emotion.* Edited by Scherer, K, P Ekman. Pp. 345-68. Hillsdale, NJ: Erlbaum.

5237 Marr, D. 1982. *Vision: A Computational Investigation into the Human Representation and Processing of Visual Information.* San Francisco: Freeman.

5238 Martinez, J, R Kesner, eds. 1986. *Learning and Memory: A Biological View.* New York: Academic Press.

5239 Martinez, J. 1986. Memory: Drugs and hormones. In *Learning and Memory: A Biological View.* Edited by Martinez, J, R Kesner. Pp. 127-64. New York: Academic Press.

5240 Maslow, A H. 1954. *Motivation and Personality.* New York: Harper & Row.

5241 Maslow, A H. 1968. The need to know and the fear of knowing. *Journal of General Psychology* 68: 111-125.

5242 Matlin, M, D Stang. 1978. *The Pollyanna Principle: Selectivity in Language, Memory, and Thought.* Cambridge: Schenkman.

5243 Matsuzawa, T. 1985. Use of numbers by a chimpanzee. *Nature* 315: 57-59.

5244 Matsuzawa, T. 1989. Spontaneous pattern construction in a chimpanzee. In *Understanding Chimpanzees.* Edited by Heltne, P, L Marquardt. Cambridge: Harvard University Press.

5245 McCrone, J. 1991. *The Ape That Spoke: Language and the Evolution of the Human Mind.* New York: William Morrow.

5246 McGuinness, D. 1976. Away from a unisex psychology: Individual differences in visual, sensory and perceptual processes. *Perception* 5: 279-94.

5247 McKeever, W F. 1986. The influence of handedness, sex, familial sinitrality and androgeny on language laterality, verbal ability, and spatial ability. *Cortex* 22: 521-37.

5248 Medin, D L, W A Roberts, R T Davis, eds. 1976. *Processes of Animal Memory.* Hillsdale, NJ: Erlbaum.

5249 Meltzoff, A. 1988. Imitation, objects, tools, and the rudiments of language in human ontogeny. *Human Evolution* 3: 45-64.

5250 Meltzoff, A. 1990. Foundations for developing a concept of self. In *The Development and Neural Bases of Higher Cognitive Functions.* Edited by Diamond, A. Chicago: University of Chicago Press.

5251 Menzel, E W. 1978. Cognitive mapping in chimpanzees. In *Cognitive Processes in Animal Behavior.* Edited by Hulse, S H, H Fowler, W K Honig. Pp. 375-422. Hillsdale, N.J.: Elbraum.

5252 Menzel, E W, E S Savage-Rumbaugh. 1985. Chimpanzee (Pan troglodytes) spatial problem solving with the use of mirrors and televised equivalents of mirrors. *Journal of Comparative Psychology* 99: 211-17.

5253 Metlzoff, A, M Moore. 1977. Imitation of facial and manual gestures by human neonates. *Science* 198: 75-78.

5254 Michaels, C F, C Carello. 1981. *Direct Perception.* Englewood Cliffs, NJ: Prentice-Hall.

5255 Miller, G A, E H Galanter, K H Pribram. 1960. *Plans and Structure of Behavior.* New York: Holt.

5256 Miller, G A. 1981. *Language and Speech.* San Francisco: Freeman.

5257 Mithen, S. 1988. Looking and learning: Upper Paleolithic art and information gathering. *World Archaeology* 19: 297-327.

5258 Needham, R, ed. 1973. *Right and Left—Essays on Dual Symbolic Classification.* Chicago: Universtiy of Chicago Press.

5259 Nevatia, R. 1982. *Machine Perception.* Englewood Cliffs, N.J.: Prentice-Hall.

5260 Nicholas, J M, ed. 1977. *Images, Perception, and Knowledge.* Dordrecht: Reidel.

5261 Nisbett, R E, T D Wilson. 1977. Telling more than we can know: Verbal reports on mental processes. *Psychological Review* 84: 231-259.

5262 Nisbett, R E, L Ross. 1980. *Human Inference: Strategies and Shortcomings of Informal Judgment.* Englewood Cliffs, N.J.: Prentice-Hall.

5263 Nisbett, R E, D H Krantz, C Jepson, Z Kunda. 1983. The use of statistical heuristics in everyday reasoning. *Psychological Review* 90: 339-363.

5264 Nisbett, R E, G T Fong, D R Lehman, P W Cheng. 1987. Teaching reasoning. *Science* 238: 625-631.

5265 Nishihara, H K. 1978. Visual information processing: Artificial intelligence and the sensorium of sight. *Technology Review (Oct)* 28-49.

5266 Noble, W. 1987. Perception and language: Towards a complete ecological psychology. In *Cognitive Psychology in Question.* Edited by Costall, A, A Still. Pp. 128-41. Brighton: Harvester Press.

5267 Norman, D A. 1976. *Memory and Attention: An Introduction to Information Processing.* New York: Wiley.

5268 Norman, D A. 1986. Reflections on cognition and PDP. In *Parallel Distributed Processing.* Edited by Rumelhart, D E, J L McClelland. Pp. 531-546. Cambridge: M.I.T. Press.

5269 O'Keefe, J, L Nadel. 1979. Precis of O'Keefe and Nadel's 'The hippocampus as a cognitive map'. *The Behavioral and Brain Sciences* 2: 487-533.

5270 O'Neill, M. 1991. A biologically based model of spatial cognition and wayfinding. *Journal of Environmental Psychology* 11: 299-320.

5271 Oden, D L, R K R Thompson, D Premack. 1990. Infant chimpanzees spontaneously perceive both concrete and abstract same/different relations. *Child Development* 61: 621-630.

5272 Olson, D, E Bialystok. 1983. *Spatial Cognition: The Structure and Development of Mental Representations of Spatial Relations.* Hillsdale, N.J.: Erlbaum.

5273 Olson, D R. 1986. The cognitive consequences of literacy. *Canadian Psychology* 27: 109-21.

5274 Olton, D S. 1978. Characteristics of spatial memory. In *Cognitive Processes in Animal Behaviour.* Edited by Hulse, S H, H Fowler, W K Honig. Pp. 341-73. Hillsdale, N.J.: Erlbaum.

5275 Orme, J E. 1969. *Time, Experience, and Behavior.* London: Iliffe Books.

5276 Ornstein, R E. 1977. *The Psychology of Consciousness.* New York: Harcourt, Brace & World.

5277 Paredes, J A, M J Hepburn. 1976. The split brain and the culture-and-cognition paradox. *Current Anthropology* 17: 121-127.

5278 Parker, S, K Gibson, eds. 1990. *Language and Intelligence in Monkeys and Apes.* Cambridge: Cambridge University Press.

5279 Pekala, R J, R L Levine. 1981-1982. Mapping consciousness: Development of an empirical-phenomenological approach. *Imagination, Cognition and Personality* 1: 29-47.

5280 Pekala, R J, R L Levine. 1982-1983. Quantifying states of consciousness via an empirical-phenomenological approach. *Imagination, Cognition and Personality* 2: 51-71.

5281 Perry, F. 1978. *Sign Language and Language Acquisition in Man and Ape. AAAS Symposium.* Boulder.: Westview Press.

5282 Peters, R, L Mech. 1975. *Behavioral and intellectual adaptations of selected mammalian predators to the problems of hunting large animals.* Edited by Tuttle, R. Socioecology and Psychology of Primates. The Hague: Mouton.

5283 Peters, R. 1978. Communication, cognitive mapping and strategy in wolves and hominids. In *Wolves and Men.* Edited by Hal, R, H Sharp. Pp. 95-107. New York: Academic Press.

5284 Petersen, A C. 1983. Pubertal change and cognition. In *Girls at Puberty: Biological and Psychosocial Perspectives.* Edited by Brooks-Gunn, J, A C Petersen. New York: Plenum.

5285 Piaget, J. 1952. *The Origins of Intelligence in Children.* New York: Norton.

5286 Piaget, J. 1954. *The Construction of Reality in the Child.* New York: Ballantine Books.

5287 Piaget, J. 1965[1932]. *The Moral Judgement of the Child.* New York: Free Press.

5288 Piaget, J. 1972[1947]. *The Psychology of Intelligence.* Totowa, N.J.: Littlefield, Adams.

5289 Platt, J R. 1964. Strong inference. *Science* 146: 347-53.

5290 Plotkin, H C, F J Odling-Smee. 1979. Learning, change and evolution: An enquiry into the teleonomy of learning. In *Advances in the Study of Behavior.* Edited by Rosenblatt, J S, R A Hinde, C Beer, M-C Busnel. Pp. 1-42. New York: Academic Press.

5291 Pope, K S, J L Singer, eds. 1978. *The Stream of Consciousness.* New York: Plenum.

5292 Posner, M. 1978. *Chronometric Explorations of Mind.* Hillsdale, NJ: Erlbaum.

5293 Powers, W T. 1973. *Behavior: The Control of Perception.* New York: Aldine.

5294 Powers, W T. 1976. Control-system theory and performance objectives. *Journal of Psycholinguistic Research* 5: 285-97.

5295 Powers, W T. 1978. Quantitative analysis of purposive systems: Some spadework at the foundations of scientific psychology. *Psychological Review* 85: 417-35.

5296 Powers, W T. 1979. Degrees of freedom in social interaction. In *Communication and Control in Society.* Edited by Krippendorf, K. Pp. 267-78. New York: Gordon and Breach.

5297 Powers, W T. 1980. A systems approach to consciousness. In *The Psychobiology of Consciousness.* Edited by Davidson, J M, R J Davidson. Pp. 217-42. New York: Plenum.

5298 Pöppel, E. 1985. *Grenzen des Bewusstseins.* Stuttgart: Deutsche Verlagsanstalt.

5299 Premack, D, G Woodruff. 1978. Does the chimpanzee have a theory of mind? *Behavioral and Brain Sciences* 1: 515-26.

5300 Premack, D, J Premack. 1983. *The Mind of an Ape.* New York: Norton.

5301 Premack, D. 1983. The codes of man and beasts. *Behavioral and Brain Sciences* 6: 125-167.

5302 Pribram, K H. 1980. Brain, mind, and consciousness: The organization of competence and conduct. In *The Psychobiology of Consciousnes*. Edited by Davidson, J M, R J Davidson. New York: Plenum Press.

5303 Prinz, W, A F Sanders, eds. 1984. *Cognition and Motor Processes*. Berlin: Springer.

5304 Pylyshyn, Z. 1980. Computation and cognition: Issues in the foundation of cognitive science. *Behavioral and Brain Sciences* 3: 111-69.

5305 Ratner, H H, L J Stettner. 1991. Thinking and feeling: Putting Humpty Dumpty together again. *Merrill-Palmer Quarterly* 37: 1-26.

5306 Ricben, R W, ed. 1976. *The Neuropsychology of Languages: Essays in Honor of Eric Lenneberg*. New York: Plenum Press.

5307 Rieber, R W. 1980. *Body and Mind: Past, Present, and Future*. New York: Academic Press.

5308 Riedl, R. 1984. *Biology of Knowledge: The Evolutionary Basis of Reason*. New York: Wiley.

5309 Ristau, C A. 1991. *Cognitive Ethology: The Minds of Other Animals*. Hillsdale, NJ: Erlbraum.

5310 Robertson, R J, W T Powers. 1990. *Introduction to Modern Psychology. The Control-Theory View*. Gravel Switch, KY: The Control Systems Group.

5311 Roitblat, H L, T G Bever, H S Terrace. 1984. *Animal Cognition*. Hillsdale, N.J.: Erlbaum.

5312 Rolls, E T. 1987. Information pepresentation, processing, and storage in the brain: Analysis at the single neuron level. In *The Neural and Molecular Bases of Learning*. Edited by Changeux, J-P, M Konishi. Pp. 503-539. New York: Wiley.

5313 Rosch, E, B B Lloyd, eds. 1978. *Cognition and Categorization*. Hillsdale, N.J.: Erlbaum.

5314 Rozin, P. 1976. The evolution of intelligence and access to the cognitive unconcious. In *Progress in Psychobiology and Physiological Psychology*. Edited by Sprague, J M, A N Epstein. New York: Academic Press.

5315 Rumbough, D, E von Glasersfeld. 1973. Reading and sentence completion by a chimpanzee. *Science* 182: 731-733.

5316 Rumbough, D M. 1977. *Language Learning by a Chimpanzee.* New York: Academic Press.

5317 Rumelhart, D E, J L McClelland, eds. 1986. *Parallel Distributed Processing: Explorations in the Microstructure of Cognition.* Cambridge: M.I.T. Press.

5318 Sackheim, H, R Gur. 1978. Self-deception, self-confrontation, and consciousness. In *Consciousness and Self-Regulation: Advances in Research.* Edited by Scwartz, G, D Shapiro. New York: Plenum.

5319 Sackheim, H. 1983. Self-deception, self-esteem, and depression: The adaptive value of lying to oneself. In *Empirical Studies of Psychoanalytic Theories.* Edited by Masling, J. Pp. 101-157. London: Analytic Press.

5320 Sanders, G, L Ross-Field. 1986. Sexual orientation, cognitive abilities and cerebral asymmetry: A review and a hypothesis tested *Italian Journal of Zoology* 20: 459-65.

5321 Savage-Rumbaugh, E S, D M Rumbaugh. 1985. The capacity of chimpanzees to acquire language. *Philosophical Transactions of the Royal Society (London)* B308: 177-86.

5322 Savage-Rumbaugh, E S. 1986. *Ape Language: From Conditioned Response to Symbol.* New York: Columbia Unversity Press.

5323 Savage-Rumbough, E S, D M Rumbough, S Boysen. 1980. Do apes use language? *American Scientist* 68: 49-61.

5324 Scholes, R J, T W Simon, eds. 1982. *Language, Mind, and Brain.* Hillsdale, N.J.: Erlbaum.

5325 Schroder, H M. 1989. Managerial competence and style. In *Adaptors and Innovators: Styles of Creativity and Problem Solving.* Edited by Kirton, M J. London: Routledge.

5326 Seidenberg, M S, L A Petitto. 1979. Signing behavior in apes: A critical review. *Cognition* 7: 177-215.

5327 Shafton, A. 1976. *Conditions of Awareness: Subjective Factors in the Social Adaptations of Man and other Primates.* Portland, Oregon: Riverstone Press.

5328 Shagass, C, S Gershon, A Friedoff, eds. 1977. *Psychopathology and Brain Dysfunction.* New York: Raven Press.

5329 Shepard, P. 1978. *Thinking Animals: Animals and the Development of Human Intelligence.* New York: Viking Press.

5330 Shepard, R N. 1984. Ecological constraints on internal representation: Resonant kinematics of perceiving, imagining, thinking, and dreaming. *Psychological Review* 91: 417-447.

5331 Siddle, D A T, ed. 1983. *Orienting and Habituation: Perspectives in Human Research.* Chichester: Wiley.

5332 Singer, J L. 1975. *The Inner World of Daydreaming.* New York: Harper & Row.

5333 Skarda, C, W Freeman. 1987. How brains make chaos in order to make sense of the world. *Behavioral and Brain Sciences* 10: 161-95.

5334 Slobin, D I. 1982. Universal and particular in the acquisition of language. In *Language Acquisition: The State of the Art.* Edited by Wanner, E, L Gleitman. Cambridge: Cambridge University Press.

5335 Slobin, D I. 1984. Cross-linguistic evidence for the language-making capacity. In *The Cross-Linguistic Study of Language Acquisition.* Edited by Slobin, D I. Hillsdale, N.J.: Erlbaum.

5336 Smail, B, A Kelly. 1984. Sex differences in science and technology among 11-year-old school children. I. Cognitive. *Research in Science and Technological Education* 2: 61-76.

5337 Snyder, M, S Gangestad. 1986. On the nature of self-monitoring: Matters of assessment, matters of validity. *Journal of Personality and Social Psychology* 51: 125-39.

5338 Sperber, D, D Wilson. 1986. *Relevance: Cognition and Communication.* Cambridge: Harvard University Press.

5339 Squires, L R. 1986. Mechanisms of memory. *Science* 232: 1612-19.

5340 Staddon, J E R. 1984. *Adaptive Behavior and Learning.* New York: Cambridge Unviersity Press.

5341 Stark, R E, ed. 1981. *Language Behavior in Infancy and Early Childhood.* North Holland: Elsevier.

5342 Stein, E, P Lipton. 1989. Where guesses come from: Evolutionary epistemology and the anomaly of guided variation. *Biology and Philosophy* 4: 33-56.

5343 Stent, G. 1981. Cerebral hermeneutics. *Journal of Social and Biological Structures* 4: 107-124.

5344 Stevens, A. 1983. *Archetypes.* London: Routledge.

5345 Stiff, J B, G R Miller, C Sleight, P Mongeau, R Garlick, R Rogan. 1989. Explanations for visual cue primacy in judgements of honesty and deceit. *Journal of Personality and Social Psychology* 56: 555-564.

5346 Studdert-Kennedy, M G. 1977. Universals in phonetic structure and their role in linguistic communication. In *Recognition of Complex Acoustical Signals.* Edited by Bullock, T H. Berlin: Dahlem.

5347 Synder, M. 1987. *Public Appearances/Private Realities: The Psychology of Self-monitoring.* New York: Freeman.

5348 Tellegen, A, G Atkinson. 1974. Openness to absorbing and self-altering experiences ("absorption"), a trait related to hypnotic susceptibility. *Journal of Abnormal Psychology* 83: 268-277.

5349 Terrace, H S. 1988. The Neanderthals and the human capacity for symbolic thought: Cognitive and problem-solving aspects of Mousterian symbols. In *L'homme de Néandertal: Actes du Colloque International, 1986.* Edited by Otte, M. Pp. 57-91. Liège: Editions Ordina.

5350 Terrance, H S. 1979. *Nim: A Chimp Who Learned Sign Language.* New York: Washington Square Press.

5351 Thatcher, R W, E R John. 1977. *Foundations of Cognitive Processes.* Hillsdale, N.J.: Erlbaum.

5352 Tiger, L. 1985. Ideology as brain disease. *Zygon* 20: 31-39.

5353 Tolman, E C. 1966. Operational behaviorism and current trends in psychology. In *Behavior and Psychological Man: Essays in Motivation and Learning.* Edited by Tolman, E C. Berkeley: University of California Press.

5354 Tolman, E C, ed. 1966. *Behavior and Psychological Man: Essays in Motivation and Learning.* Berkeley: University of California Press.

5355 Tooby, J. 1985. The emergence of evolutionary psychology. In *Emerging Syntheses in Science.* Edited by Pines, D. Santa Fe: Santa Fe Institute.

5356 Tooby, J, L Cosmides. 1990. On the universality of human nature and the uniqueness of the individual: The role of genetics and adaptation. *Journal of Personality* 58: 17-67.

5357 Totman, R. 1985. *Social and Biological Roles of Language: The Psychology of Justification.* London: Academic Press.

5358 Tucker, D M, J P Newmann. 1981. Verbal versus imagined cognitive strategies in the inhibition of emotional arousal. *Cognitive Therapy and Research* 5: 197-202.

5359 Tversky, A, D Kahneman. 1974. Judgments under uncertainty: Heuristics and biases. *Science* 185: 1124-31.

5360 Tye, M. 1991. *The Imagery Debate.* Cambridge: M.I.T. Press.

5361 Upmeyer, A, ed. 1989. *Attitudes and Behavioral Decisions.* New York: Springer.

5362 van der Molen, P P. 1989. K.A.I. and changes in social structures: On the anatomy of catastrophe. In *Adaptors and Innovators: Styles of Creativity and Problem Solving.* Edited by Kirton, M. London: Routledge.

5363 Vygotsky, L S. 1986. *Thought and Language.* London: M.I.T. Press.

5364 Waber, D P. 1976. Sex differences in cognition: A function of maturation rate? *Science* 192: 572-574.

5365 Waber, D. 1979. Cognitive abilities and sex-related variations in the maturation of the cerebral cortical functions. In *Sex-Related Differences in Cognitive Functioning: Developmental Issues.* Edited by Wittig, M, A Petersen. Pp. 161-186. New York: Academic Press.

5366 Walker, S F. 1983. *Animal Thought.* London: Routledge.

5367 Wang, W S-Y. 1983. Variation and selection in language change. *Bulletin of the Institute of History and Philology* 53: 467-91.

5368 Wang, W S-Y. 1987. Representing language relationships. In *Biological Metaphor and Cladistic Classification: An Interdisciplinary Perspective.* Edited by Hoenigswald, H M, L F Wiener. Pp. 243-256. Philadelphia: University of Pennsylvania Press.

5369 Wang, W S-Y, ed. 1987. *Language Transmission and Change.* Oxford: Blackwell.

5370 Watt, R J, M J Morgan. 1985. A theory of the primitive spatial code in human vision. *Vision Research* 25: 1661-74.

5371 Wheeler, H. 1987. A constructional biology of hermeneutics. *Journal of Social and Biological Structures* 10: 103-123.

5372 Wicklynd, R A. 1979. The influence of self-awareness on human behavior. *American Scientist* 67: 187-193.

5373 Wilber, K. 1977. *The Spectrum of Consciousness.* London: Theosophical Publishing House.

5374 Wilensky, R. 1983. Story grammars versus story points. *Behavioral and Brain Sciences* 6: 579-623.

5375 Williams, C L, A M Barnett, W H Meck. 1990. Organizational effects of early gonadal secretions on sexual differentiations in spatial memory. *Behavioral Neuroscience* 104: 84-97.

5376 Winner, E, G Ehlinger. 1979. Do chimpanzees recognize photographs as representations of objects? *Neuropsychologica* 17: 413-420.

5377 Woodruff, G, D Premack. 1979. Intentional communication in the chimpanzee: The development of deception. *Cognition* 7: 333-62.

5378 Woodruff, G, D Premack. 1981. Primitive mathematical concepts in the chimpanzee: Proportionality and numerosity. *Nature* 293: 568-70.

5379 Yerkes, R M, B W Learned 1925. *Chimpanzee Intelligence and Its Vocal Expressions.* Baltimore: Williams and Wilkins.

5380 Yville, J C, ed. 1983. *Imagery, Memory and Cognition: Essays in Honor of Allan Paivio.* Hillsdale, N.J.: Erlbaum.

5381 Zivin, G, ed. 1979. *The Development of Self-regulation through Private Speech.* New York: Wiley.

# 15

# Altered Consciousness

5382 Al-Issa, I. 1977. Social and cultural aspects of hallucination. *Psychological Bulletin* 84: 570-587.

5383 Albers, P, S Parker. 1971. The plains vision experience: A study of power and privilege. *Southwestern Journal of Anthropology* 27: 203-233.

5384 Anon. 1986. *Transe, chamanisme, possession: de la fête a l'extase: Actes des deuxièmes rencontres internationales sur la fête et la communication, Nice Acropolis 24-28 avril 1985.* Nice: Editions Serré.

5385 Barnett, H G. 1953. *Indian Shakers: A Messianic Cult of the Pacific Northwest.* Carbondale, IL: Southern Illinois University Press.

5386 Berrios, G E. 1981. Stupor revisited. *Comprehensive Psychiatry* 22: 466-478.

5387 Bourguignon, E, ed. 1973. *Religion, Altered States of Consiousness and Social Change.* Columbus: Ohio State University Press.

5388 Bourguignon, E. 1974. *Culture and the Varieties of Consciousness.* Reading, MA: Addison-Wesley.

5389 Bourguignon, E. 1976. *Possession.* San Francisco: Chandler and Sharp.

5390 Bourguignon, E, T L Evanscu. 1977. Altered states of consiousness within a general evolutionary perspective: A holocultural analysis. *Behavior Science Research* 12: 197-216.

5391 Bourguinon, E. 1970. Hallucination and trance: An anthropologist's perspective. In *Origin and Mechanisms of Hallucination.* Edited by Keup, W. Pp. 183-189. New York: Plenum.

5392 Bowers, K S. 1966. Hypnotic behavior: The differentiation of trance and demand characteristic variables. *Journal of Abnormal Psychology* 71: 42-51.

5393 D'Aquili, E G, C Laughlin. 1975. Biopsychological determinants of religious ritual behaviour. *Zygon* 10: 32-58.

5394 D'Aquili, E G. 1978. The neurobiological bases of myth and concepts of deity. *Zygon* 13: 257-275.

5395 D'Aquili, E G. 1982. Senses of reality in science and religion: A neuroepistemological perspective. *Zygon* 17: 361-364.

5396 D'Aquili, E G. 1983. The myth-ritual complex: A biogenetic structural analysis. *Zygon* 18: 247-269.

5397 D'Aquili, E G. 1985. Human ceremonial ritual and the modulation of aggression. *Zygon* 20: 21-30.

5398 D'Aquili, E G. 1986. Myth, ritual, and the archetypal hypothesis. *Zygon* 21: 141-160.

5399 Davidson, J M. 1984. The physiology of meditation and mystical states of consciousness. In *Meditation: Classic and Contemporary Perspectives.* Edited by Shapiro, D H, R N Walsh. Pp. 376-395. New York: Aldine.

5400 Du Toit, B, ed. 1977. *Drugs, Rituals and Altered States of Consciousness.* Rotterdam: A. A. Balkema.

5401 Eliade, M. 1964. *Shamanism: Archaic Techniques of Ecstasy.* Translated by Trask, W.R. Princeton: Princeton University Press.

5402 Ervin, F R, R M Palmourn, B P Murphy, R H Prince. 1988. The psychobiology of trance: II. Physiological and endocrine correlates. *Transcultural Psychiatric Research Review* 25: 267-284.

5403 Farthing, G. 1992. *The Psychology of Consciousness.* Englewood Cliffs, N.J.: Prentice Hall.

5404 Fischer, R. 1969. On creative, psychotic and ecstatic states. In *Psychiatry and Art: Art Interpretation and Art Therapy.* Edited by Jakab, S. Basel: Karger.

5405 Fischer, R. 1970. Prediction and measurement of perceptual-behavioral change in drug-induced hallucinations. In *Origin and Mechanisms of Hallucinations.* Edited by Keup, W. Pp. 303-332. New York: Plenum.

5406 Fischer, R. 1971. A cartography of the ecstatic and meditative states. *Science* 174: 897-904.

5407 Fischer, R. 1975. Cartography of inner space. In *Hallucinations: Behavior, Experience and Theory.* Edited by Siegel, R K, L J West. Pp. 197-239. New York: Wiley.

5408 Fischer, R. 1975. *The Sociology of the Paranormal: A Reconnaissance.* Beverly Hills, CA: Sage.

5409 Fischer, R. 1978. A cartography of conscious states: Integration of East and West. In *Expanding Dimensions of Consciousnss.* Edited by Sugerman, A A, R E Tarter. New York: Springer.

5410 Foulks, E F. 1972. *The Arctic Hysterias of the North Alaskan Eskimo.* Washington, D.C.: American Anthropological Association.

5411 Fray, P. 1976. *Spirits of Protest: Spirit-Mediums and the Articulation of Consensus among the Zezuru of Southern Rhodesia (Zimbabwe).* Cambridge: Cambridge University Press.

5412 Frof, S. 1976. *Realms of the Human Unconscious: Observations from L.S.D. Research.* New York: Dutton.

5413 Gellhorn, E, W R Kiely. 1972. Mystical states of consciousness: Neurophysiological and clinical aspects. *Journal of Nervous and Mental Disease* 154: 399-405.

5414 Goodman, F D. 1981. States of consciousness: A study of soundtracks. *Journal of Mind & Behavior* 2: 209-219.

5415 Goodman, F. 1990. *Where the Spirits Ride the Wind: Trance Journeys and other Ecstatic Experiences.* Bloomington: Indiana University Press.

5416 Greeley, A. 1974. *Ecstasy: A Way of Knowing.* Englewood Cliffs: Prentice-Hall.

5417 Greenbaum, L. 1973. Societal correlates of possession trance in sub-Saharan Africa. In *Religion, Altered States of Consiousness and Social Change.* Edited by Bourguignon, E. Pp. 39-87. Columbus: Ohio State University Press.

5418 Gruber, E. 1982. *Tranceformation: Schamanismus und die Auflosung der Ordnung.* Basel: Sphinx Verlag.

5419 Hanley, D L, A P Kerr, eds. 1989. *May '68: Coming of Age.* New York: Macmillan.

5420 Harris, G G. 1978. *Casting Out Anger: Religion Among the Taita of Kenya.* Cambridge: Cambridge University Press.

5421 Hay, D, A Morisy. 1977. *Reports of Ecstatic. Paranormal or Religious Experience in Great Britain and the United States: A Comparison of Trends.* Oxford: Religious Experience Unit, Manchester College.

5422 Hayden, B. 1987. Alliances and ritual ecstasy: Human responses to resource stress. *Journal for the Scientific Study of Religion* 26: 81-91.

5423 Henry, J L. 1982. Possible involvement of endorphins in altered states of consciousness. *Ethos* 10: 398-408.

5424 Hilgard, E R. 1977. *Divided Consciousness: Multiple Controls in Human Thought and Action.* New York: Wiley.

5425 Jacobs, B L, ed. 1984. *Hallucinogens: Neurochemical, Behavioral and Clincial Perspectives.* New York: Raven Press.

5426 Keup, W, ed. 1970. *Origin and Mechanisms of Hallunications.* New York: Plenum.

5427 Kiely, W F. 1974. From the symbolic stimulus to the pathophysiological response. *International Journal of Psychiatry in Medicine* 5: 517-529.

5428 Kokoszka, A. 1987-88. An intergrated model of the main states of consciousness. *Imagination, Cognition & Personality* 7: 285-294.

5429 La Barre, W. 1971. Material for a history of studies of crisis cults: A bibliographic essay. *Current Anthropology* 12: 3-44.

5430 La Barre, W. 1972. *The Ghost Dance: The Origins of Religion.* New York: Dell.

5431 Lapassade, G. 1976. *Essai sur la transe: Le materialisme hysterique.* Paris: J. P. Delarge.

5432 Lex, B W. 1978. Neurological basis of revitalization movements. *Zygon* 13: 276-312.

5433 Lex, B W. 1979. The neurobiology of ritual trance. In *The Spectrum of Ritual: A Biogenetic Structural Analysis.* Edited by d'Aquili, E G, C D Laughlin, J McManus. New York: Columbia University Press.

5434 Mandell, A J. 1980. Toward a psychobiology of transendence: God in the brain. In *The Psychobiology of Consciousness.* Edited by Davidson, J M, R J Davidson. Pp. 379-464. New York: Plenum Press.

5435 Marsh, C. 1977. A framework for describing subjective states of consciousness. In *Alternate States of Consciousness.* Edited by Zinberg, N E. New York: Free Press.

5436 Maslow, A. 1964. *Religions, Values and Peak-Experiences.* Columbus: Ohio State University Press.

5437 Metzner, R. 1980. Ten classical metaphors of self-transformation. *Journal of Transpersonal Psychology* 12: 47-62.

5438 Moore, P. 1978. Mystical experience, mystical doctrine, mystical technique. In *Mysticism and Philosophical Analysis*. Edited by Katz, S T. Pp. 101-131. London: Sheldon Press.

5439 Narajo, C, R E Ornstein. 1972. *On the Psychology of Meditation*. New York: Viking.

5440 Natsoulas, T. 1986. On the radical behaviorist conception of consciousness. *Journal of Mind and Behavior* 7: 87-115.

5441 Ozouf, M. 1976. *La fête révolutionnaire 1789-1799*. Paris: Gallimard.

5442 Pekala, R J, R L Levine. 1981-1982. Mapping consciousness: development of an empirical-phenomenological approach. *Imagination, Cognition and Personality* 1: 29-47.

5443 Pekala, R J, R L Levine. 1982-1983. Quantifying states of consciousness via an empirical-phenomenological approach. *Imagination, Cognition and Personality* 2: 51-71.

5444 Pope, K S, J L Singer, eds. 1978. *The Stream of Consciousness*. New York: Plenum.

5445 Prince, R, ed. 1968. *Trance and Possession States*. Montreal: R.M. Bucke Memorial Society.

5446 Rouget, G. 1985. *Music and Trance: A Theory of the Relations between Music and Possession*. Chicago: University of Chicago Press.

5447 Schwartz, T. 1962. The Paliau movement of the Admirality Islands, 1946-54. In *Anthropological Papers of the Museum of Natural History, Part 2*. Pp. 207-422. New York: Museum of Natural History.

5448 Sharpiro, D H, R N Walsh, eds. 1984. *Meditation: Classic and Contemporary Approaches*. New York: Aldine.

5449 Siegel, R K, L J West, eds. 1975. *Hallucinations: Behavior, Experience and Theory*. New York: Wiley.

5450 Sugerman, A A, R E Tarter, eds. 1978. *Expanding Dimensions of Consciousness*. New York: Springer.

5451 Swanson, G E. 1960. *The Birth of the Gods: The Origin of Primitive Beliefs*. Ann Arbor: University of Michigan Press.

5452 Swanson, G E. 1973. The search for a guardian spirit: A process of empowerment in simple societies. *Ethnology* 12: 359-378.

5453 Swanson, G. 1987. Trance and possession: Studies of charismatic influence. *Review of Religious Research* 19: 253-278.

5454 Tambiah, S J. 1984. *The Buddhist Saints of the Forest and the Cult of Amulets: A Study in Charisma, Hagiography, Sectarianism and Millennial Buddhism.* Cambridge: Cambridge University Press.

5455 Tart, C T. 1975. *States of Consciousness.* New York: Dutton.

5456 Tart, C T, ed. 1975. *Transpersonal Psychologies.* New York: Harper & Row.

5457 Tart, C, ed. 1990. *Altered States of Consciousness.* 3rd ed. San Francisco: Harper.

5458 Thornton, R. 1986. *We Shall Live Again: The 1870 and 1890 Ghost Dance Movements as Demographic Revitalization.* Cambridge: Cambridge University Press.

5459 Tiryakian, E. 1981. The Elementary Forms as 'revelation '. In *The Future of the Sociological Classics.* Edited by Rhea, B. Pp. 114-135. London: Allen & Unwin.

5460 Walker, S. 1972. *Ceremonial Spirit Possession in Africa and Afro-America: Forms, Meanings, and Functional Significance for Individuals and Social Groups.* Leiden: Brill.

5461 West, M A, ed. 1990. *The Psychology of Meditation.* Oxford: Clarendon Press.

5462 White, J, ed. 1972. *The Highest State of Consciousness.* New York: Doubleday.

5463 Wilber, K. 1977. *The Spectrum of Consciousness.* London: Theosophical Publishing House.

5464 Wilber, K, J Engler, DP Brown. 1986. Transformations of Consciousness: Conventional and Contemplative Perspectives on Development. New York: New Science Library.

5465 Williams, F E. 1976. The Valilala madness. In *The Valilala Madness and Other Essays.* Edited by Schwimmer, E. London: Hurst.

5466 Winkelman, M. 1986. Trance states: A theoretical model and cross-cultural analysis. *Ethos* 14: 174-203.

5467 Wolmanol, B, M Ullman, eds. 1986. *Handbook of States of Consciousness*. New York: Van Nostrand Rinehold.

5468 Zinberg, N E, ed. 1977. *Alternate States of Consciousness*. New York: Free Press.

# Psychiatry

5469 Amenson, C S, P M Lewinsohn. 1981. An investigation into the observed sex differences in prevalance of unipolar depression. *Journal of Abnormal Psychology* 90: 1-13.

5470 Andreasen, N C. 1985. *The Broken Brain: The Biological Revolution in Psychiatry.* New York: Harper & Row.

5471 Angst, J, ed. 1983. *The Origins of Depression: Current Concepts and Approaches.* Berlin: Springer.

5472 Antelmon, S M, A R Caggiula. 1980. Stress-Induced Behavior: Chemotherapy without Drugs. In *The Psychobiology of Consciousness.* Edited by Davidson, J M, R J Davidson. Pp. 65-104. New York: Plenum.

5473 Avison, W R, D D McAlpine. 1992. Gender differences in symptoms of depression among adolescents. *Journal of Health and Social Behavior* 33: 77-96.

5474 Bailey, K G. 1991. Human paleopsychopathology: Implications for the paraphilias. *New Trends in Experimental and Clinical Psychiatry* 7: 5-16.

5475 Baranowska, B. 1990. Are disturbances in opioid and adrenergic systems involved in the hormonal dysfunction of anorexia nervosa? *Psychoneuroendocrinology* 15: 371-9.

5476 Barratt, E S, J H Patton. 1983. Impulsivity: Cognitive, behavioral, and psychophysiological correlates. In *Biological Bases of Sensation Seeking, Impulsivity and Anxiety.* Edited by Zuckerman, M. Hillsdale, N.J.: Erbaum.

5477 Bauer, R M. 1984. Autonomic recognition of names and faces in prosopagnosia: A neuropsychological application of the guilty knowledge test. *Neuropsychologia* 22: 456-69.

5478 Baum, A, N E Grunber, J E Singer. 1982. The use of psychological and neuroendocrinological measurements in the study of stress. *Health Psychology* 1: 217-36.

5479 Baumgartner, A, K-J Graff, I Kurten. 1988. Prolactin in patients with major depressive disorder and in healthy subjects. Parts 1-3. *Biological Psychiatry* 24: 249-98.

5480 Baxter, L R, M E Phelps, J C Mazziotta, et al. 1987. Local cerebral glucose metabolic rates in obsessive-compulsive disorder. *Archives of General Psychiatry* 44: 211-218.

5481 Beckham, E E, W R Leber. 1985. *Handbook of Depression: Treatment, Assessment, and Research.* Homewood, Illinois: Dorsey Press.

5482 Benson, D F, N Geschwind. 1985. The aphasias and related disturbances. In *Clinical Neurology.* Edited by Baker, A B, L D Baker. New York: Harper & Row.

5483 Bernstein, I L, S Borson. 1986. Learned food aversion: A component of anorexia syndromes. *Psychological Review* 93: 462-72.

5484 Bettelheim, B. 1955. *Symbolic Wounds.* London: Thames and Hudson.

5485 Blanchard, E B, L C Kolb, T P Pallmeyer, R J Gerardi. 1982. A psychophysiological study of post-traumatic stress disorder in Vietnam veterans. *Psychiatry Quarterly* 54: 220-227.

5486 Blanck, P, R Buck, R Rosenthal, eds. 1986. *Nonverbal Communication in the Clinical Context.* University Park, PA: Pennsylvania State Press.

5487 Blumenthal, J, D McKee, eds. 1987. *Applications in Behavioral Medicine and Health Psychology: A Clinician's Source Book.* Sarasota, FL: Professional Resource Exchange.

5488 Boehnke, K, M Meador, M J Macpherson. 1989. Zur jugendpsychiatrischen Bedeutsamkeit von Atomkriegsangsten bei 8-bis 13jahrigen. In *Forschung in den Erziehungswissenschaften.* Edited by Beller, E K. Pp. 60-62. Weinheim: Deutscher Studien Verlag.

5489 Bond, N, ed. 1984. *Animal Models in Psychopathology.* Melbourne: Academic Press.

5490 Borod, J C, E Koff, R Buck. 1980. The neuropsychology of facial expression: data from normal and brain-damaged adults. In *Nonverbal Communication in the Clinical Context.* Edited by Blanck, P, R Buck, R Rosenthal. University Park, PA: Penn State Press.

5491 Borysenko, M, J Borysenko. 1982. Stress, behavior and immunity: Animal models and mediating mechanisms. *General Hospital Psychiatry* 4: 69-74.

5492 Bouhuys, A L, D G M Beersman, R H van den Hoofdakker, A Rossien. 1987. The prediction of short and long-term improvement in depressive patients: Ethological methods of observing behavior versus clinical ratings. *Ethology and Sociobiology* 8: 1175-1205.

5493 Bouhuys, A L, et al. 1990. Relations between depressed mood and vocal parameters before, during and after sleep deprivation: A circadian rhythm study. *Journal of Affective Disorders* 19: 249-58.

5494 Bouhuys, A L, C J Jansen, R H van den Hoofdakker. 1991. Analysis of observed behaviors displayed by depressed patrients during clinical interview: Relationships between behavioral factors and clinical concepts of activation. *Journal of Affective Disorders* 21: 79-88.

5495 Boulton, A, G Baker, M Martin-Iverson. 1991. *Animal Models in Psychiatry*. Clifton, N.J.: Humana Press.

5496 Bowlby, J. 1980. *Loss, Sadness, and Depression*. London: Hogarth Press.

5497 Bowlby, J. 1982. *Attachment and Loss*. 2nd ed. London: Hogarth Press.

5498 Branniger-Huber, E, F Steiner, eds. 1986. *FACS in Psychotherapy Research*. Zurich: Department of Clinical Psychology, Universitat Zurich.

5499 Breier, A, D S Charney, G R Heninger. 1985. The diagnostic validity of anxiety disorders and their relationship to depressive illness. *American Journal of Psychiatry* 142: 787-97.

5500 Breslau, N, G C Davis. 1986. Chronic stress and major depression. *Archives of General Psychiatry* 43: 309-314.

5501 Broadhurst, P L. 1978. *Drugs and the Inheritance of Behavior: A Survey of Comparative Psychopharmacogenetics*. New York: Plenum.

5502 Brown, G W, T O Harris. 1978. *Social Origins of Depression: A Study of Psychiatric Disorder in Women*. New York: Free Press.

5503 Brown, G, et al. 1982. Aggression, suicide and serotonin: Relationships to CSF amine metabolites. *American Journal of Psychiatry* 139: 741-746.

5504 Brown, G M, S H Koslow, S Reichlin, eds. 1984. *Neuroendocrinology and Psychiatric Disorders*. New York: Raven Press.

5505 Brown, S-L, H M v Praag, eds. 1991. *The Role of Serotonin in Psychiatric Disorders.* New York: Brunner/Mazel.

5506 Bucher, K D, et al. 1981. The transmission of manic depressive illness - II: Segregation analysis of three sets of family data. *Journal of Psychiatric Research* 16: 65-78.

5507 Buchsbaum, M S, R J Haier. 1983. Psychopathology: Biological approaches. *Annual Review of Psychology* 34: 401-30.

5508 Buck, R. 1980. Nonverbal communication of affect in brain-damaged patients. *Cortex* 16: 351-62.

5509 Burrows, G D, ed. 1977. *Handbook of Studies on Depression.* New York: Excerpta Medica.

5510 Burrows, C D, T R Norman, K P Maguire, eds. 1984. *Biological Psychiatry: New Prospects.* New York: J. Libbey.

5511 Carey, G. 1987. Big genes, little genes, affective disorder, and anxiety. *Archives of General Psychiatry* 44: 486-492.

5512 Castellani, S, et al. 1988. TSH and catecholamine response to TRH in panic disorder. *Biological Psychiatry* 24: 87-90.

5513 Castello, C G. 1976. *Anxiety and Depression: The Adaptive Emotion.* Montreal: McGill University Press.

5514 Caton, H. 1986. Pascal's Syndrome: Positivism as a symptom of depression and mania. *Zygon* 21: 319-351.

5515 Charney, D, G Heninger, D Sternberg. 1982. Adrenergic receptor sensitivity in depression: Effects of clonidine in depressed patients and healthy controls. *Archives of General Psychiatry* 39: 200-204.

5516 Charney, D, D E Redmond. 1983. Neruobiological mechanisms in human anxiety: Evidence supporting central noradrenergic hyperactivity. *Neuropharmacology* 22: 1531-1536.

5517 Charney, D, G Heninger, A Brier. 1984. Noradrenergic function in panic anxiety. *Archives of General Psychiatry* 91: 751-63.

5518 Checkley, S. 1982. Endocrine changes in psychiatric illness. In *Clinical Neuroendocrinology.* Edited by Besser, G, L Martini. New York: Academic Press.

5519 Chess, S, A Thomas. 1982. Infant bonding: Mystique and reality. *American Journal of Orthopsychiatry* 52: 213-22.

5520 Clark, D C, S Cavanaugh, R Gibbons. 1983. The core symptoms of depression in medical and psychiatric patients. *Journal of Nervous and Mental Disease* 171: 705-713.

5521 Cloninger, C R, C Lavis, J Rice, T Reich. 1981. Strategies for resolution of cultural and biological inheritance. In *Genetic Research Strategies in Psychobiology and Psychiatry*. Edited by Gershon, E S, S Matthysse, X O Breakefield, R D Ciaranello. Pp. 319-332. Pacific Grove, CA: Boxwood Press.

5522 Cloninger, C R. 1992. *Personality and Psychopathology: A Unified Biosocial Theory*. New York: Oxford University Press.

5523 Cohen, S. 1980. Aftereffects of stress on human performance and social behavior: A review of research and theory. *Psychological Bulletin* 88: 82-108.

5524 Cohen, S, G W Evans, D Stokols, D S Krantz. 1986. *Behavior, Health, and Environmental Stress*. New York: Plenum.

5525 Colligan, M J, J W Pennebaker, L R Murphy, eds. 1982. *Mass Psychogenic Illness: A Social Psychological Analysis*. Hillsdale, N.J.: Erlbaum.

5526 Cookson, J, T Silverstone, S Williams, G Besser. 1985. Plasma cortisol levels in mania: Associated with clinical ratings and changes during treatment with haloperidol. *British Journal of Psychiatry* 146: 498-502.

5527 Cooper, A M. 1985. Will neurobiology influence psychoanalysis? *American Journal of Psychiatry* 142: 1395-1402.

5528 Coursey, R D, M S Bauchsbaum, D L Murphy. 1979. MAO activity and evoked potentials in the identification of subjects biologically at risk for Psychiatric disorders. *British Journal of Psychiatry* 134: 372-81.

5529 Crider, A. 1979. *Schizophrenia. A Biopsychological Perspective*. Hillsdale, N.J.: Erlbaum.

5530 Cummings, J L, M F Mendez. 1984. Secondary mania with focal cerebrovascular lesions. *American Journal of Psychiatry* 141: 1084-7.

5531 Curran, D. 1987. *Adolescent Suicidal Behavior*. New York: Hemisphere.

5532 Curtis, G C, B A Thyer, D McCann, M J Huber-Smiith. 1985. Endocrine and cardiovascular responses during phobic anxiety. *Psychosomatic Medicine* 47: 320-332.

5533 Damasio, A R, H Damasio, G W Van Hoesen. 1982. Prosopagnosia: anatomic basis and behavioral mechanisms. *Neurology* 32: 331-41.

5534 Darby, J, ed. 1981. *Speech Evaluation in Psychiatry.* New York: Grune & Stratton.

5535 Darby, P L, P E Garfinkel, D M Garner, D V Coscina, eds. 1983. *Anorexia Nervosa: Recent Developments in Research.* New York: Alan R. Liss.

5536 Davidson, L M, A Baum. 1986. Chronic stress and posttraumatic stress disorders. *Journal of Consulting and Clinical Psychology* 54: 303-8.

5537 Davis, D P, S R Dunlap, P Shear, H Brittain, H Hendrie. 1985. Biological stress response in high and low trait anxious students. *Biological Psychiatry* 20: 843-51.

5538 de Villiers, A, V Russell, M Carstens, C Aalbers, C Gagiano, D Chalton, J Toljaard. 1987. Noradrenergic function and hypothalamic-pituitary adrenal axis activity in primary unipolar major depressive disorder. *Psychiatry Research* 22: 127-40.

5539 Demisch, L, K Georgi, B Patzke, K Demisch, J Bochnik. 1982. Correlation of blood platelet MAO activity with introversion: A study on a German rural population. *Psychiatry Research* 6: 303-311.

5540 Depue, R A. 1979. *The Psychobiology of the Depressive Disorders: Implications for the Effects of Stress.* New York: Academic Press.

5541 Depue, R A, R M Kleinman. 1979. Free Cortisol as a peripheral index of central vulnerability to major forms of polar depressive disorders: Examining stress-biology interactions in subsyndromal high-risk persons. In *The Psychobiology of the Depressive Disorders: Implications for the Effects of Stress.* Edited by Depue, R A. New York: Academic Press.

5542 Dienske, H, J Sanders-Woudstra, G de Jonge. 1987. A biologically meaningful classification in child psychiatry that is based upon ethological methods. *Ethology and Sociobiology* 8: 27S-46S.

5543 Doane, B K, K E Livingstone, eds. 1986. *The Limbic System: Functional Organization and Clinical Disorders.* New York: Raven Press.

5544 Dorus, E. 1980. Variability in the Y chromosome and variability of human behavior. *Archives of General Psychiatry* 37: 587-594.

5545 Drugan, R, S Maier, P Skolnick, S Paul, J Crawley. 1985. An anxiogenic benzodiazepine receptor ligand induces learned helplessness. *European Journal of Pharmacology* 113: 453-7.

5546 DuPont, R L. 1982. *Phobia: A Comprehensive Summary of Modern Treatments.* New York: Brunner-Mazel.

5547 Egeland, B, M Breitenbucher, M Dodds, D Pastor, D Rosenberg. 1979. *Life Stress Scale and Scoring Manual.* Minneapolis: University of Minnesota Press.

5548 Egeland, J A, et al. 1987. Bipolar affective disorders linked to DNA markers on chromosome 11. *Nature* 325: 783-787.

5549 Eitinger, L, A Strom. 1973. *Mortality and Morbidity after Excessive Stress.* New York: Humanities Press.

5550 Ellgring, H. 1989. *Nonverbal Communication in Depression.* Paris: Maison des Sciences de l'Homme.

5551 Ellis, H C, P W Ashbrook. 1988. Resource allocation model of the effects of depressed mood states on memory. In *Affect, Cognition and Social Behavior.* Edited by Fiedler, K, J Forgas. Pp. 25-43. Toronto: Hogrefe.

5552 Engel, G L. 1980. The clinical application of the biopsychosocial model. *American Journal of Psychiatry* 17: 535-544.

5553 Estes, W K, B F Skinner. 1941. Some quantitative properties of anxiety. *Journal of Experimental Psychology* 29: 390-400.

5554 Fann, W E, A D Pokorny, I Koracau, R Williams, eds. 1979. *Phenomenology and Treatment of Anxiety.* New York: Spectrum.

5555 Favazza, A. 1987. *Bodies Under Siege: Self Mutilation in Culture and Psychiatry.* Baltimore: Johns Hopkins.

5556 Fedio, P. 1986. Behavioral characteristics of patients with temporal lobe epilepsy. *Psychiatric Clinics of North America* 9: 267-81.

5557 Fedora, O, et al. 1992. Sadism and other paraphilias in normal controls and aggressive and nonaggressive sex offenders. *Archives of Sexual Behavior* 21: 1-15.

5558 Feierman, J R. 1987. The ethology of psychiatric population: An introduction. *Ethology and Sociobiology* 8: 1S-8S.

5559 Fichter, M M, K M Pirke. 1984. Hypothalamic pituitary function in starving healthy subjects. In *The Psychobiology of Anorexia Nervosa*. Edited by Pirke, K M, D Ploog. Berlin: Springer.

5560 Field, T, D Sandberg, R Garcia, N Vega-Lahr, S Goldstein, L Guy. 1985. Pregnancy problems: postpartum depression and early mother-infant interaction. *Developmental Psychology* 21: 1152-56.

5561 Figley, C R, ed. 1985. *Trauma and Its Wake*. New York: Brunner/Mazel.

5562 Filskov, S K, T J Boll, eds. 1981. *Handbook of Clinical Neuropsychology*. New York: Wiley-Interscience.

5563 Fleming, A S, H Krieger, P Wong. 1987. Affect and nurturance in first-time mothers: Role of psychobiological influences. In *New Directions in Affective Disorders*. Edited by Lerer, B, S Gershon. New York: Springer.

5564 Fleming, I, A Baum, L M Davisdon, E Rectanus, S McArdle. 1987. Chronic stress as a factor in physiologic reactivity to challenge. *Health Psychology* 6: 221-37.

5565 Fowles, D C, F S Gersh. 1979. Neurotic depression: The concept of anxious depression. In *The Psychobiology of the Depressive Disorders: Implications for the Effects of Stress*. Edited by Depue, R A. New York: Academic Press.

5566 Freud, A. 1937. *The Ego and the Mechanisms of Defense*. London: Hogarth Press.

5567 Fridlund, A J, M E Hatfield, G L Cottom, S C Fowler. 1986. Anxiety and striate-muscle activation: evidence from electromyographic pattern analysis. *Psychophysiology* 17: 47-55.

5568 Garber, J, S D Hollon. 1980. Universal versus personal helplessness in depression: Belief in uncontrollability or incompetence. *Journal of Abnormal Psychology* 89: 56-66.

5569 Garmezy, N, A Tellegen. 1984. Studies of stress-resistant children: Methods, variables and preliminary findings. In *Advances in Applied Development Psychology*. Edited by Morrison, F, C Lord, D Keating. New York: Academic Press.

5570 Gellhorn, E, W R Kiely. 1973. Autonomic nervous system in psychiatric disorder. In *Biological Psychiatry*. Edited by Mendels, J. New York: Wiley.

5571 George, D T, J A Ladenheim, D J Nutt. 1987. Effect of pregnancy on panic attacks. *American Journal of Psychiatry* 14: 1078-9.

5572 Gershon, E S, S Matthysse, X O Breakefield, R D Ciaranello, eds. 1981. *Genetic Research Strategies in Psychobiology and Psychiatry.* Pacific Grove, CA: Boxwood Press.

5573 Gessler, S, J Cutting, C D Frith, J Weinman. 1989. Schizophrenic inability to judge facial emotion: A controlled study. *British Journal of Clinical Psychology* 28: 19-30.

5574 Gilbert, P. 1984. *Depression: From Psychology to Brain State.* Hillsdale, N.J.: Erlbaum.

5575 Glantz, K, J K Pearce. 1989. *Exiles from Eden: Psychotherapy from an Evolutionary Perspective.* New York: Norton.

5576 Glaser, R, J K Kiecolt-Glaser, C E Speicher, J E Holliday. 1984. Stress, loneliness and changes in herpes virus latency. *Journal of Behavioral Medicine* 8: 249-60.

5577 Goldman, G D, D S Milman, eds. 1978. *Psychoanalytic Perspectives on Aggression.* Dubuque, Iowa: Kendall & Hunt.

5578 Goodwin, F K, K R Jamison. 1990. *Manic-Depressive Illness.* New York: Oxford University Press.

5579 Gottesman, I I, J Shields. 1982. *Schizophrenia: The Epigenetic Puzzle.* Cambridge: Cambridge University Press.

5580 Gray, J A, et al. 1982. Multiple book review of The Neuropsychology of Anxiety: An enquiry into the functions of the septo-hippocampal system. *Behavioral and Brain Sciences* 5: 469-534.

5581 Gray, J A. 1982. The Neuropsychology of Anxiety: An Enquiry into the Functions of the Septo-Hippocampal System. *Behavioral and Brain Sciences* 5: 469-484.

5582 Guttmacher, L, D Murphy, T Insel. 1983. Pharmacologic models of anxiety. *Comprehensive Psychiatry* 24: 312-26.

5583 Hahlweg, K, L Reisner, G Kohli, M Vollmer, L Schindler, D Revenstorf. 1984. Development and validity of a new system to analyze interpersonal communication. In *Marital Interaction: Analysis and Modification.* Edited by Hahlweg, K, N Jacobson. New York: Guilford Press.

5584 Hahlweg, K, N Jacobson, eds. 1984. *Marital Interaction: Analysis and Modification.* New York: Guilford Press.

5585 Halaris, A. 1987. *Chronobiology and Psychiatric Disorders.* New York: Elsevier.

5586 Halbreich, U, J Vitalher, S Goldstein, K Zander. 1984. Can Gender Differences in Prevalence of Depression be Attributed to Biological Differences? *Psychopharmocology Bulletin* 20: 472-474.

5587 Hamburg, D, B A Hamburg, J D Barchos. 1975. Anger and depression in perspective of behavioral biology. In *Emotions: Their Parameters and Measurement.* Edited by Levi, L. Pp. 235-273. New York: Raven Press.

5588 Hamburg, D, G Elliott, D Perron, eds. 1982. *Health and Behavior: Frontiers of Research in the Biobehavioral Sciences.* Washington: National Academy Press.

5589 Hare, R D, D Schalling, eds. 1978. *Psychopathic Behaviour: Approaches to Research.* Chichester: Wiley.

5590 Hare, R D, J F Connolly. 1987. Perceptual asymmetries and information processing in psychopaths. In *The Causes of Crime.* Edited by Mednick, S A, T E Moffit, S A Stack. Pp. 218-238. Cambridge: Cambridge University Press.

5591 Harpending, H C, J Sobus. 1987. Sociopathy as an Adaptation. *Ethology and Sociobiology* 8: 63S-72S.

5592 Harvey, N S. 1987. Neurological factors in obsessive compulsive disorder. *British Journal of Psychiatry* 150: 567-568.

5593 Hebb, D O. 1947. Spontaneous neurosis in chimpanzees. *Psychosomatic Medicine* 9: 3-19.

5594 Hellekson, C J. 1989. Phenomenology of Seasonal Affective Disorder. In *Seasonal Affective Disorders and Phototherapy.* Edited by Rosenthal, N E, M Blehar. New York: Guilford Press.

5595 Hofer, M A. 1984. Relationships as regulators: A psychobiologic perspective on bereavement. *Psychosomatic Medicine* 46: 183-197.

5596 Hollon, S D, A T Beck. 1979. Cognitive therapy of depression. In *Cognitive-Behavioral Interventions: Theory, Research and Procedures.* Edited by Kendall, P C, S D Hollon. New York: Academic Press.

5597 Holmes, D S. 1981. Existence of classical projection and the stress-reducing function of attributive projection: A reply to Sherwood. *Psychological Bulletin* 90: 460-66.

5598 Holsboer, F, M Philipp, U v Bardeleben, K Wiedemann. 1987. Endocrine methods in affective disorders. In *Advanced Methods in Psychobiology.* Edited by Hingtgen, J N, D Hellhammer, G Huppmann. Pp. 53-66. Toronto: C.J. Hogrefe.

5599 Honma, K, S Honma, T Wada. 1987. Phase-dependent shift of free-running human circadian rhythms in response to a single bright light pulse. *Experientia* 43: 1205-1207.

5600 Hsu, L K G. 1980. Outcome of anorexia nervosa: A review of the literature (1954-1978). *Archives of General Psychiatry* 37: 1041-46.

5601 Hutt, S J. 1975. An ethological analysis of autistic behavior. In *On the Origin of Schizophrenia Psychosis.* Edited by Van Pragg, H M. Amsterdam: De Erven Bohn.

5602 Illingworth, R S. 1980. *The Development of the Infant and the Young Child, Abnormal and Normal.* 7th ed. Edinburgh: Churchill Livingstone.

5603 Issacs, C, D S Strainer, T E Sensky, S Moor, C Thompson. 1988. Phototherapy and its mechanisms of action in seasonal affective disorder. *Journal of Affective Disorders* 14: 13-19.

5604 Izard, C E, S H Blumberg, C K Oyster. 1985. Age and sex differences in the pattern of emotions in childhood anxiety and depression. In *Motivation, Emotion, and Personality.* Edited by Spence, J T, C E Izard. Pp. 317-324. Amsterdam: Elsevier.

5605 Jacob, T, ed. 1987. *Family Interaction and Psychopathology: Theories, Methods and Findings.* New York: Plenum.

5606 Jacobsen, F M, N E Rosenthal. 1986. Seasonal affective disorder and the use of light as an antidepressant. *Directions in Psychiatry* 6: 1-8.

5607 James, S P, T A Wehr, D A Sack, B L Parry, N E Rosenthal. 1985. Treatment of seasonal affective disorder with evening light. *British Journal of Psychiatry* 147: 424-428.

5608 Jenike, M A, L Baer, W E Minichiello, eds. 1986. *Obsessive-Compulsive Disorder: Theory and Management.* Littleton, MA: PSG Inc.

5609 Jimerson, D C, R M Post. 1984. Psychomotor stimulants and dopamine agonists in depression. In *Neurobiology of Mood Disorders*. Edited by Post, R M, J C Ballenger. New York: Williams and Wilkins.

5610 Johansson, G, A Collins, V P Collins. 1983. Male and female psychoneuroendocrine response to examination stress: A case report. *Motivation and Emotion* 7: 1-9.

5611 Jorm, A F. 1987. Sex and age differences in depression: A quantitative syntheses of published research. *Australian & New Zealand Journal of Psychiatry* 21: 46-53.

5612 Jorm, A F, A E Korten, A S Henderson. 1987. The prevalence of dementia: A quantitative integration of the literature. *Acta Psychiatrica Scandinavica* 76: 465-479.

5613 Joyce, P, R Donald, P Elder. 1987. Individual differences in plasma cortisol changes during mania and depression. *Journal of Affective Disorders* 12: 1-5.

5614 Kalin, N, G Dawson. 1986. Neuroendocrine dysfunction in depression: Hypothalamic-anterior pituitary systems. *Trends in Neuroscience* 9: 261-6.

5615 Kalin, N, G Dawson, P Tariot, S Shelton, C Barksdale, S Weiler, M Thienemann. 1987. Function of the adrenal cortex in patients with major depression. *Psychiatry Research* 22: 117-25.

5616 Kandel, D, M Davies. 1982. Epidemiology of adolescent depressive mood: an empirical study. *Archives of General Psychiatry* 39: 1209-1212.

5617 Kandel, E R. 1983. From metapsychology to molecular biology: Exploration into the nature of anxiety. *American Journal of Psychiatry* 140: 1277-1293.

5618 Kaplan, H. 1987. *Sexual Aversion, Sexual Phobias, and Panic Disorder*. New York: Brunner/Mazel.

5619 Kaufman, I C, A J Stynes. 1978. Depression can be induced in a bonnett macaque. *Psychosomatic Medicine* 40: 71-75.

5620 Keane, T M, J A Fairbank, J M Caddell, R T Zimering, M E Bender. 1985. A behavioral approach to assessing and treating post-traumatic stress disorder in Vietnam veterans. In *Trauma and its Wake*. Edited by Figley, C R. Pp. 257-94. New York: Brunner/Mazel.

5621 Keehn, J D. 1986. *Animal Models for Psychiatry*. London: Routledge & Kegan Paul.

5622 Kemali, D, P V Morozov, G Toffano, eds. 1984. *New Research Strategies in Biological Psychiatry*. London: John Libbey.

5623 Kiecolt-Glaser, J K, D Ricker, J George, G Messick, C E Speicher, W Garner, R Glaser. 1984. Urinary cortisol levels, cellular immunocompetency and loneliness in psychiatric inpatients. *Psychomatic Medicine* 46: 15-23.

5624 Kiecolt-Glaser, J K, L D Fisher, P Ogrocki, J Stout, C E Speicher, R Glaser. 1987. Marital quality, marital disruption and immune function. *Psychomatic Medicine* 49: 13-34.

5625 Klein, D F, J Rabkin, eds. 1981. *Anxiety: New Research and Changing Perspectives*. New York: Raven Press.

5626 Kofoed, L. 1988. Selective Dimensions of Personality: Psychiatry and Sociobiolgy in Collision. *Perspectives in Biology and Medicine* 31: 228-242.

5627 Konstantareas, M M, S Homatidi. 1984. Aggressive and pro-social behaviors before and after treatment in conduct-disordered children and in matched control. *Journal of Child Psychiatry* 25: 607-20.

5628 Koslow, N, et al. 1983. CSF and urinary biogenic amines and metabolites in depression and mania: A controlled univariate analysis. *Archives of General Psychiatry* 40: 999-1010.

5629 Kosten, R T, J W Mason, E L Giller, R B Ostroff, L Harkness. 1987. Sustained urinary norepinephrine and epinephrine elevation in post-traumatic stress disorder. *Psychoneuroendocrinology* 12: 13-20.

5630 Kraemer, G W, W T McKinney. 1979. Interactions of pharmacological agents which alter biogenic amine metabolism and depression: An analysis of contributing factors within a primate model of depression. *Journal of Affective Disorders* 1: 33-54.

5631 Kraemer, G W. 1986. Developmental theories of depression in nonhuman primates. *Psycholparmacological Bulletin* 22: 587-92.

5632 Kraemer, G W. 1988. Speculations on the developmental neurobiology of protest and despair. In *Inquiry into Schizophrenia and Depression: Animal Models of Psychiatric Disorders*. Pp. 101-139. Basel: Karger.

5633 Krantz, D S, A Baum, J E Singer, eds. 1983. *Handbook of Psychology and Health: Cardiovascular Disorders and Behavior*. Hillsdale, NJ: Erlbaum.

5634 Kronfol, Z, J Silva, J Greden, S Dembinski, R Gardner, B Carroll. 1983. Impaired lymphocyte function in depressive illness. *Life Sciences* 33: 241-7.

5635 Lader, M M. 1975. *The Psychophysiology of Mental Illness.* London: Routledge.

5636 Laudenslager, M L, M L Reite. 1984. Losses and separations: Immunological consequences and health implications. In *Review of Personality and Social Psychology: Emotions, Relationships, and Health.* Edited by Shaver, P. Beverly Hills, CA: Sage.

5637 LeFave, M K, R Neufeld. 1980. Anticpatory threat and physical danger trait anxiety: A signal-detection analysis of effects on automatic responding. *Journal of Research in Personality* 14: 283-306.

5638 Leighton, D C, J S Harding, D B Macklin, A M Macmillan, A H Leighton. 1963. *The Character of Danger : Psychiatric Symptoms in Selected Communities.* New York: Basic Books.

5639 Levenson, R W, J M Gottman. 1983. Marital interaction: Physiological linkage and affective exchange. *Journal of Personality and Social Psychology* 45: 587-97.

5640 Levi, L, ed. 1971. *Society, Stress and Disease: The Psychological Environment and Psychosomatic Diseases.* New York: Oxford University Press.

5641 Lewinsohn, P M, W Mischel, W Chaplin, R Barton. 1980. Social competence and depression: The role of illusory self-perceptions. *Journal of Abnormal Psychology* 89: 203-212.

5642 Lewinsohn, P M, J L Steinmetz, D W Larson, J Franklin. 1981. Depression related cognitions: Antecedent or consequence? *Journal of Abnormal Psychology* 90: 213-219.

5643 Lewis, M, C Feiring, C McGuffog, J Jaskir. 1984. Predicting psychopathology in six-year-olds from early social relations. *Child Development* 55: 123-136.

5644 Lewy, A J, H E Kern, N E Rosenthal, T A Wehr. 1982. Bright artificial light treatment of a manic-depressive patient with a seasonal mood cycle. *American Journal of Psychiatry* 139: 1496-1498.

5645 Lewy, A J, R L Sack, S Miller, T M Slaban. 1987. Antidepressant and circadian phase-shifting effects of light. *Science* 235: 352-354.

5646 Lewy, A J. 1987. Treating chronobiological sleep and mood disorders disorders with bright light. *Psychiatric Annals* 17: 664-669.

5647 Liebowitz, M R, et al. 1985. Lactate provocation of panic attacks. II. Biochemical and physiological findings. *Archives of General Psychiatry* 42: 709-19.

5648 Lishman, W A. 1987. *Organic Psychiatry: The Psychological Consequences of Cerebral Disorder.* 2nd ed.. Oxford: Blackwell Scientific Publications.

5649 Macdonald, K. 1986. Civilization and its discontents revisited: Freud as an evolutionary biologist. *Journal of Social and Biological Structures* 9: 307-318.

5650 Malloy, P F, J A Fairbank, T M Keane. 1983. Validation of a multi-method assessment of posttraumatic stress disorder in Vietnam veterans. *Journal of Consulting and Clinical Psychology* 51: 488-94.

5651 Mannuzza, S, A J Fyer, D F Klein. 1985. *Schedule for Affective Disorders and Schizophrenia: Lifetime Version (modified for the study of anxiety disorders).* New York: Anxiety Disorders Clinic, New York State Psychiatric Institute.

5652 Mansky, P, D Deveines. 1984. Major psychiatric illness related to endogenous and exogenous opiates. In *Psychiatric Medicine Update: Massachusetts General Hospital Reviews.* New York: Elsevier.

5653 Margolin, G, B Wampold. 1981. Sequential analysis of conflict and accord in distressed and nondistressed marital partners. *Journal of Consulting and Clinical Psychology* 49: 554-67.

5654 Markman, H, C Notarius. 1987. Coding marital and family interaction: Current status. In *Family Interaction and Psychopathology: Theories, Methods and Findings.* Edited by Jacob, T. New York: Plenum.

5655 Marks, I. 1987. *Fears, Phobias and Rituals.* New York: Oxford University Press.

5656 Marrazzi, M, E Luby. 1986. An auto-addiction opioid model of chronic anorexia nervosa. *International Journal of Eating Disorders* 5: 191-208.

5657 Marselle, A J, R M A Hirschfeld, M M Katz. 1987. *The Measurement of Depression.* New York: The Guilford Press.

5658 Mason, S T, D C S Roberts, H C Fibiger. 1978. Noradrealine and neophobia. *Physiology and Behavior* 21: 353-61.

5659 Mathews, A M, M G Gelder, D W Johnston. 1981. *Agoraphobia: Nature and Treatment.* New York: Guilford Press.

5660 McGuffin, P, S Hodgson. 1984. *Scientific Principles of Psychopathology.* London: Grune and Stratton.

5661 McGuire, M T, L A Fairbanks. 1977. *Ethological Psychiatry: Psychopathology in Context of Evolutionary Biology.* New York: Grune and Stratton.

5662 McGuire, M T, S Essock-Vitale, R H Polsky. 1981. Psychiatric disorders in the context of evolutionary biology: An ethological model of behavioral changes associated with psychiatric disorders. *Journal of Nervous and Mental Disease* 169: 687-704.

5663 McGuire, M T, A Troisi. 1987. Physiological regulation-deregulation and psychiatric disorders. *Ethology and Sociobiology* 8: 9S-26S.

5664 McNeal, E, P Cimbolic. 1986. Antidepressants and biochemical theories of depression. *Psychological Bulletin* 90: 361-74.

5665 Mednick, S A, K M Finello. 1983. Biological factors and crime: Implications for forensic psychiatry. *International Journal of Law and Psychiatry* 6: 1-15.

5666 Mendels, J, ed. 1973. *Biological Psychiatry.* New York: Wiley.

5667 Mendels, J, J L Stinnet. 1973. Biogenic amine metabolism, depression, and mania. In *Biological Psychiatry.* Edited by Mendels, J. Pp. 65-87. New York: Wiley.

5668 Mendels, J. 1975. *The Psychobiology of Depression.* New York: Spectrum.

5669 Michelson, L, L Ascher, eds. 1987. *Anxiety and Stress Disorders: Cognitive-Behavioral Assessment and Treatment.* New York: Guilford Press.

5670 Miczek, K A, ed. 1983. *Ethnopharmacology: Primate Models of Neuropsychiatric Disorders.* New York: Alan Liss.

5671 Mindlewicz, J, R Van Canter. 1979. Circadian changes in plasma enzymes and hormone activity in manic-depressive illness. In *Biological Psychiatry Today.* Edited by Obiols, J, et al. Pp. 271-278. Amsterdam: Elsevier.

5672 Monroe, R R. 1986. Episodic behavioral disorders and the limbic ictus. In *The Limbic System: Functional Organization and Clinical Disorders*. Edited by Doane, B, K Livingstone. Pp. 251-66. New York: Raven Press.

5673 Montagner, H, et al. 1978. Behavioural profiles and corticosteroid excretion rhythms in young children. In *Human Behaviour and Adaptation*. Edited by Blurton-Jones, N, V Reynolds. London: Taylor & Francis.

5674 Morgan, C S, M Affleck, L R Riggs. 1986. Gender, personality traits, and depression. *Social Science Quarterly* 67: 69-78.

5675 Murphy, D L. 1977. Animal models for mania. In *Animal Models in Psychiatry and Neurology*. Edited by Hanin, I, E Usdin. New York: Pergamon Press.

5676 Mühlbauer, H D, B Müller-Oerlinghausen. 1985. Fenfluramine stimulation of serum cortisol in patients with major affective disorders and healthy controls: Further evidence for central serontonergic action of lithium in man. *Journal of Neural Transmission* 61: 81-94.

5677 Nesse, R M, G C Curtis, B A Thyer, D McCann, M J Huber-Smith. 1984. Adrenergic function in panic anxiety patients. *Archives of General Psychiatry* 41: 771-776.

5678 Nesse, R M. 1984. An evolutionary perspective on psychiatry. *Comparative Psychiatry* 25: 575-80.

5679 Nesse, R M. 1987. An evolutionary perspective on panic disorder and agoraphobia. *Ethology and Sociobiology* 8: 735-45.

5680 Nesse, R M. 1990. The evolutionary functions of repression and the ego defenses. *Journal of the American Academy of Psychoanalysis* 18: 260-85.

5681 Noller, P. 1984. *Nonverbal Communication and Marital Interaction*. Oxford: Pergamon.

5682 Notarius, C, J Johnson. 1982. Emotional expression in husbands and wives. *Journal of Marriage and the Family* 44: 483-9.

5683 Notarius, C, C Wemple, L Ingraham, T Burns, E Kollar. 1982. Multichannel responses to an interpersonal stressor: Interrelationships among facial display, heart rate, self-report of emotion, and threat appraisal. *Journal of Personality and Social Psychology* 43: 400-8.

5684 Notarius, C, H Markman, J Gottman. 1983. Couples interaction scoring system: Clinical implications. In *Marriage and Family*

*Assessment: A Sourcebook for Family Therapy.* Edited by Filsinger, E E. Beverly Hills, CA: Sage.

5685 Notarius, C, L Herrick. 1988. Listener response strategies to a distressed other. *Journal of Social and Personal Relationships* 5: 97-108.

5686 Nurnberger, J I, E Gershon. 1984. Genetics of affective disorders. In *Neurobiology of Mood Disorders.* Edited by Post, R M, J C Ballenger. Pp. 76-101. Baltimore: Williams and Wilkins.

5687 Panksepp, J, T Sahley. 1987. Possible brain opioid involvement in disrupted social intent and language development in autism. In *Neurobiological Issues in Autism.* Edited by Schopler, E, G Mesibov. New York: Plenum.

5688 Parkes, C M. 1972. *Bereavement: Studies of Grief in Adult Life.* London: Travistock.

5689 Peabody, C, H Whiteford, D Warner, K Faull, J Barchas, P Berger. 1987. TRH stimulation test and depression. *Psychiatry Research* 22: 21-8.

5690 Perris, H. 1984. Life events and depression. 1. Effects of sex, age and civil Status. *Journal of Affective Disorders* 7: 11-24.

5691 Phillips, D P. 1985. The Werther effect: Suicide, and other forms of violence are contagious. *The Sciences* 25: 32-39.

5692 Pitman, R K. 1984. Obsessions and Psychasthenia: A synopsis. *Psychiatric Quarterly* 56: 291-314.

5693 Pitman, R, S P Orr. 1986. Test of the conditioning model of neurosis: Differential aversive conditioning of angry and neutral facial expressions. *Journal of Abnormal Psychology* 95: 208-213.

5694 Pitman, R K, B Kolb, S P Orr, M M Singh. 1987. Ethological study of facial behavior in nonparanoid and paranoid schizophrenics. *American Journal of Psychiatry* 144: 99-102.

5695 Pitman, R K, B Kolb, S Orr, J DeJong, S Yadati, M Singh. 1987. On the utility of ethological data in psychiatric research: The example of facial behavior in schizophrenia. *Ethology and Sociobiology* 8: 111S-116S.

5696 Ploog, D. 1992. Ethological foundations of biological psychiatry. In *Integrative Biological Psychiatry.* Edited by Emrich, H M, M Wiegand. Pp. 30-35. New York: Springer.

5697 Praag, H M v, M H Lader, O J Rafaelsen, E J Sachar, eds. 1979. *Handbook of Biological Psychiatry Part II: Brain Mechanisms and Abnormal Behavior - Psychophysiology.* New York: Marcel Dekker.

5698 Praag, H M v, M H Lader, O J Rafaelsen, E J Sachar, eds. 1979. *Handbook of Biological Psychiatry Part I: Disciplines Relevant to Biological Psychiatry.* New York: Marcel Dekker.

5699 Praag, H M v, M H Lader, O J Rafaelsen, E J Sachar, eds. 1979. *Handbook of Biological Psychiatry Part III: Brain Mechanisms and Abnormal Behavior: Genetics and Neuroendocrinology.* New York: Marcel Dekker.

5700 Praag, H M v, M H Lader, O J Rafaelsen, E J Sachar, eds. 1981. *Handbook of Biological Psychiatry: Chemsitry.* New York: Marcel Dekker.

5701 Price, J S, L Sloman. 1987. Depression as yielding behavior: An animal model based on Schjelderup-Ebbe's peeking order. *Ethology and Sociobiology* 8: 85S-98S.

5702 Prosen, M, D C Clark, M Harrow, J Fawcett. 1983. Guilt and conscience in major depressive disorders. *American Journal of Psychiatry* 140: 839-844.

5703 Purcell, E. 1980. *Psychopathology of Children and Youth: A Cross Cultural Perspective.* New York: Josia Macy, Jr. Foundation.

5704 Rachman, S J. 1968. *Phobias: Their Nature and Control.* Springfield, IL: C.C. Thomas.

5705 Rachman, S, R Hodgson. 1978. *Obsessions and Compulsions.* New York: Prentice Hall.

5706 Rapoport, J. 1989. The biology of obsessions and compulsions. *Scientific American* 260: 82-89.

5707 Raskin, M, H V S Peeke, W Dickman, H Pinkster. 1982. Panic and generalised anxiety disorders: Devlopmental antecedents and precipitants. *Archives of General Psychiatry* 39: 687-689.

5708 Rasmussen, K L R, M Reite. 1982. Loss-induced depression in an adult Macaque monkey. *American Journal of Psychiatry* 139: 679-681.

5709 Roessler, R, J W Lester. 1979. Vocal patterns in anxiety. In *Phenomenology and Treatment of Anxiety.* Edited by Fann, W E, A D Pokorny, I Koracau, R Williams. New York: Spectrum.

5710 Rosenthal, N E, R G Skwerer, D A Sack, C C Duncan, F M Jacobsen, L Tamarkin, T A Wehr. 1987. Biological effects of morning-plus-evening bright light treatment of seasonal affective disorder. *Psychopharmol Bull.* 23: 364-369.

5711 Rosenthal, N E, F M Jacobsen, D A Sack, J Arendt, S P James, B L Parry, T A Wehr. 1988. Atenolol in seasonal affective disorder: A test of the melatonin hypothesis. *American Journal of Psychiatry* 145: 52-56.

5712 Roth, M. 1979. A classification of affective disorders based on a synthesis of new and old concepts. In *Research in the Psychobiology of Human Behavior.* Edited by Meyer, E, J V Brady. Pp. 75-114. Baltimore: John Hopkins.

5713 Roy, A. 1985. Early parental separation and adult depression. *Archives of General Psychiatry* 42: 987-995.

5714 Roy-Byrne, P P, T W Uhde. 1985. Panic disorder and major depression: Biological relationship. *Psychopharmacology Bulletin* 3: 546-50.

5715 Rush, A J, K Z Altshaler. 1986. *Depression: Basic Mechanisms, Diagnosis, and Treatment.* New York: Guilford Press.

5716 Rutter, M, C E Izard, P B Read, eds. 1986. *Depression in Young People: Developmental and Clinical Perspectives.* New York: Guilford Press.

5717 Rutter, M, P Casaer, eds. 1991. *Biological Risk Factors for Psychosocial Disorders.* Cambridge: Cambridge University Press.

5718 Sachar, E J. 1981. Psychobiology of schizophrenia. In *Principles of Neural Science.* Edited by Kandel, E R, J H Schwartz. New York: Elsevier.

5719 Sachar, E J. 1981. Psychobiology of affective disorders. In *Principles of Neural Science.* Edited by Kandel, E R, J H Schwartz. New York: Elsevier.

5720 Schaap, C. 1982. *Communication and Adjustment in Marriage.* Amsterdam: Swets and Zeitlinger B.U.

5721 Schaffer, C E, R J Davidson, C Saron. 1983. Frontal and parietal electroencephalogram asymmetry in depressed and nondepressed subjects. *Biological Psychiatry* 18: 753-62.

5722 Scherer, K R. 1987. Vocal assessment of affective disorders. In *Depression and Expressive Bahavior.* Edited by Maser, J D. Pp. 57-82. Hillsdale, NJ: Erlbaum.

5723 Schmidt-Degenhard, M. 1983. *Meloncholie und Depression.* Stuttgart: Kohlhammer.

5724 Schneiderman, N. 1983. Animal behavior models of coronary heart disease. In *Handbook of Psychology and Health: Cardiovascular Disorders and Behavior.* Edited by Krantz, D S, A Baum, J E Singer. Pp. 19-56. Hillsdale, NJ: Erlbaum.

5725 Schwartz, G E, P L Fair, P Salt, M R Mandel, G L Klerman. 1976. Facial muscle patterning to affective imagery in depressed and nondepressed subjects. *Science* 192: 489-491.

5726 Schwartz, G, P L Fair, P Salt, M R Mandel, G L Klerman. 1976. Facial expression and imagery in depression: An electromyographic study. *Psychosomatic Medicine* 38: 337-346.

5727 Schwarzer, R. 1984. *The Self in Anxiety, Stress and Depression.* Amsterdam: North-Holland.

5728 Seligman, M E P. 1975. *Helplessness: On Depression Development and Death.* San Francisco: Freeman.

5729 Shagass, C, R A Roemer, J J Straumanis, R C Josiassen. 1984. Distinctive somatosensory evoked potential features in obsessive compulsive disorder. *Biological Psychiatry* 19: 1507-1524.

5730 Shapiro, D. 1965. *Neurotic Styles.* New York: Basic Books.

5731 Shaver, P. 1984. Review of Personality and Social Psychology: Emotions, Relationships, and Health. In Beverly Hills: Sage.

5732 Shwerdlow, N R, G F Koob. 1987. Dopamine, schizophrenia, mania & depression. *Behavioral and Brain Sciences* 10: 197-245.

5733 Siever, L, K Davis. 1984. Dysregulation of the noradrenergic system in depression. *Psychopharmacology Bulletin* 20: 500-4.

5734 Siever, L, et al. 1984. Differential inhibitory responses to clonidine in 25 depressed patients and 25 normal control subjects. *American Journal of Psychiatry* 141: 733-41.

5735 Siever, L, et al. 1984. Plasma cortisol responses to clonidine in depressed patients and controls: Evidence for a possible alteration in noradregergic-neuroendocrine relationships. *Archives of General Psychiatry* 41: 63-8.

5736 Siever, L J, K L Davis. 1985. Overview: Toward a dysregulation hypothesis of depression. *American Journal of Psychiatry* 142: 1017-31.

5737 Simon, P, P Soubrie, D Widlocher, eds. 1988. *Inquiry into Schizophrenia and Depression: Animal Models of Psychiatric Disorders.* Basel: Karger.

5738 Singh, M M, S R Kay, R K Pitman. 1981. Territorial behavior of schizophrenics: A phylogenetic approach. *Journal of Nervous and Mental Disease* 169: 503-12.

5739 Singh, M M, S R Kay, R K Pitman. 1981. Aggression control and structuring of social relations among recently admitted schizophrenics. *Psychiatry Research* 5: 157-69.

5740 Skinner, E R. 1935. A calibrated recording and analysis of the pitch, force and quality of vocal tones expressing happiness and sadness. *Speech Monographs* 2: 81-137.

5741 Skwerer, R G, C C Duncan, D A Sack, F M Jacobsen, L Tamarkin, T A Wehr, N E Rosenthal. 1988. Neurobiology of seasonal affective disorder and phototherapy. *Journal of Biological Rhythms* 3: 135-154.

5742 Sloman, L, M Konstamtareas, D W Dunham. 1979. The adaptive role of maladaptive neurosis. *Biological Psychiatry* 14: 961-71.

5743 Sloman, L. 1981. Anxiety and the struggle for power. *International Journal of Family Psychiatry* 2: 13-33.

5744 Sloman, L, J S Price. 1987. Losing behavior (yielding subroutine) and human depression: Proximate and selective mechanisms. *Ethology and Sociobiology* 8: 99S-110S.

5745 Snaith, P. 1991. *Clinical Neurosis.* 2nd ed. Oxford: Oxford University Press.

5746 Snyder, S H. 1980. *Biological Aspects of Mental Disorder.* New York: Oxford University Press.

5747 Soulairac, A, H Lambinet. 1984. Biological and pharmacological data on aggressive behavior. *Annals of Medical Psychiatry* 142: 542-55.

5748 Spielberger, C. 1975. The measurement of state and trait anxiety: Conceptual and methodological issues. In *Emotions: Their Parameters and Measurement.* Edited by Levi, L. Pp. 713-725. New York: Raven Press.

5749 Stein, D J, N Shoulberg, K Helton, E Hollander. 1992. The neuroethological approach to obsessive-compulsive disorder. *Comprehensive Psychiatry* 33: 274-281.

5750 Stone, E A. 1983. Problems with the current catecholamine hypothesis of antidepressant agents: Speculations leading to a new hypothesis. *Behavioral and Brain Sciences* 6: 535-577.

5751 Stunkard, A J, E Stellar, eds. 1984. *Eating and Its Disorders.* New York: Raven.

5752 Stunkard, A, A Baum, eds. 1989. *Perspectives in Behavioral Medicine: Eating, Sleeping, and Sex.* Nillsdale, NJ: Erlbaum.

5753 Sturt, E, P McGuffin. 1985. Can linkage and marker association resolve the genetic aetiology of psychiatric disorders?: Review and argument. *Psychological Medicine* 15: 455-462.

5754 Suarez, S D, G G Gallup. 1985. Depression as a response to reproductive failure. *Journal of Social and Biological Structures* 8: 279-287.

5755 Tallal, P, R E Stark, E D Mellitis. 1985. Identification of language-impaired children on the basis of rapid perception and production skills. *Brain and Language* 25: 314-322.

5756 Tallal, P, R Ross, S Curtis. 1989. Familial aggregation in specific language impairment. *Journal of Speech and Hearing Disorders* 54: 167-173.

5757 Terman, M. 1988. Light therapy. In *Principles and Practice of Sleep Medicine.* Edited by Kryger, M. Pp. 717-722. Philadelphia: Saunders.

5758 Terman, M, et al. 1988. Response of the melatonin cycle to phototherapy for seasonal affective disorder. *Journal of Neural Transmission* 72: 147-165.

5759 Tolkmitt, F J, H Helfrich, R Standke, K R Scherer. 1982. Vocal indicators of psychiatric treatment effects in depressives and schizophrenics. *Journal of Communication Disorders* 15: 209-22.

5760 Trimble, M R. 1988. *Biological Psychiatry.* Chichester: Wiley.

5761 Tucker, D M, C E Stensile, R S Roth, S L Shearer. 1981. Right frontal lobe activation and right hemisphere performance: Decrement during depressed mood. *Archives of General Psychiatry* 38: 169-74.

5762 Tuma, H, J Maser, eds. 1985. *Anxiety and Anxiety Disorders.* Hillsdale, N.J.: Erlbaum.

5763 Uhde, T, J Boulinger, L Siever, R DuPont, R Post. 1982. Animal models of anxiety: Implications for research in humans. *Psychopharmacology Bulletin* 18: 47-52.

5764 Ursin, R. 1987. Sleep Recording and Scoring. In *Advanced Methods in Psychobiology*. Edited by Hingtgen, J N, D Hellhammer, G Huppmann. Pp. 203-220. Toronto: C.J. Hogrefe.

5765 Usdin, E, M Asberg, L Bertilsson, F Sjöqvist, eds. 1984. *Frontiers in Biochemical and Pharmacological Research in Depression*. New York: Raven Press.

5766 van der Kolk, B, eds. 1984. *Post-Traumatic Stress Disorder: Psychological and Biological Sequelae.* Washington: American Psychiatric Press.

5767 Verebey, K. 1982. *Opioids in Mental Illness: Theories, Clinical Observations and Treatment Possibilities.* New York: New York Academy of Sciences.

5768 Voland, E, R Voland. 1989. Evolutionary biology and psychiatry: The case of anorexia nervosa. *Ethology and Sociobiology* 10: 223-240.

5769 Walsh, B, P Rosen. 1988. *Self-Mutilation: Theory, Research, and Treatment*. New York: Guilford Press.

5770 Wampold, B, G Margolin. 1982. Nonparametric strategies to test the independence of behavioral states ion sequential data. *Psychological Bulletin* 92: 755-65.

5771 Wehr, T A, F M Jacobsen, D A Sack, J Arendt, L Tamarkin, N E Rosenthal. 1986. Phototherapy of seasonal affective disdorder: Time of day and suppression of melatonin are not critical for antidepressant effects. *Archives of General Psychiatry* 43: 870-875.

5772 Weinberger, D A, G E Schwartz, R J Davidson. 1979. Low-anxious, high-anxious, and repressive coping styles: Psychosomatic patterns and behavioral and physiological responses to stress. *Journal of Abnormal Psychology* 88: 369-80.

5773 Weiss, B, U Laties, eds. 1975. *Behavioral Toxicology*. New York: Plenum.

5774 Weiss, J M, H I Glazer, L A Pohorecky, W H Bailey, I H Schneider. 1979. Coping Behavior and Stress-induced Behavioral Depression. In *Studies of the Role of Brain Catecholamines: The Psychobiology of the Depressive Disorders*. Edited by Depue, R A. New York: Academic Press.

5775 Weiss, R L, K J Summers. 1983. Marital interaction coding system. III. In *Marriage and Family Assessment: A Sourcebook for Family Therapy*. Edited by Filsinger, E E. Beverly Hills, CA: Sage.

5776 Weiss, J M, P G Simson. 1986. Depression in an animal model: Focus on the locus coeruleus. In *CIBA Foundation Sypmposium 123, Antidepressants and Receptor Function.* Pp. 191-209. Chichester: Wiley.

5777 Wender, P, D Klein. 1981. *Mind, Mood and Medicine: A Guide to the New Biopsychiatry.* New York: Farrar-Strauss.

5778 Wenegrat, B. 1984. *Sociobiology and Mental Disorders.* Menlo Park, CA: Addison-Wesley.

5779 Wenegrat, B. 1990. *Sociobiological Psychiatry: Normal Behavior and Psychopathology.* Lexington, MA: Lexington.

5780 Wessinger, W D. 1986. Approaches to the study of drug interactions in behavioral pharmacology. *Neuroscience and Behavioral Reviews* 10: 103-113.

5781 Westenberg, H G, H M van Praag, J T De Jong, J H Thijssen. 1982. Postsynaptic serotonergic activity in depressive patients: Evaluation of the neuroendocrine strategy. *Psychiatric Research* 7: 361-371.

5782 Westenberg, H, J den Boer, R Kahn. 1987. Psychopharmacology of anxiety disorders: On the role of serotonin in the treatment of anxiety states and phobic disorders. *Psychopharmacology Bulletin* 23: 1063-67.

5783 Whybrow, P C, H S Akiskal, W T McKinney. 1984. *Mood Disorders: Toward a New Psychology.* New York: Plenum.

5784 Williams, G, R Nesse. 1990. The dawn of Darwinian medicine. *Quarterly Review of Biology* 66: 1-22.

5785 Willner, P. 1984. The validity of animal models of depression. *Psychopharmacology* 83: 1-16.

5786 Willner, P. 1985. *Depression: A Psychobiological Synthesis.* New York: Wiley.

5787 Windle, M, K Hooker, K Lenerz, P L East, J V Lerner, R M Lerner. 1986. Temperament, perceived competence, and depression in early- and late-adolescents. *Developmental Psychology* 22: 384-392.

5788 Wing, J K, J E Cooper, N Sartorius. 1974. *Measurement and Classification of Psychiatric Symptoms: An Instruction Manual for the PSE and Catego Program.* Cambridge: Cambridge University Press.

5789 Winokur, G. 1983. The validity of familial subtypes in unipolar depression. *McLean Hospital Journal* 8: 17-37.

5790 Witkin, H A, S A Mednick, F Schulsinger, E Bakkestrom, F O Christiansen, D R Goodenough, K Hirschhorn, C Lundsteen, D R Owen, J Philip, D B Rubin, M Stocking. 1976. Criminality in XYY and XXY men. *Science* 193: 547-554.

5791 Woods, S W, D S Charney, C A McPherson, A H Gradman, G R Heninger. 1987. Situational panic attacks. *Archives of General Psychiatry* 44: 365-75.

5792 Wright, R A. 1984. Motivation, Anxiety, and the Difficulty of Avoidance Control. *Journal of Personality and Social Psychology* 46: 1376-1388.

5793 Wurtman, R J, J J Wurtman. 1989. Carbohydrates and depression. *Scientific American* Jan.: 68-75.

5794 Yeragani, U K, R Pohl, R Balon, P Weinberg, R Berchou, J M Rainey. 1987. Preinfusion anxiety predicts lactate-induced panic attacks in normal controls. *Psychosomatic Medicine* 49: 383-89.

5795 Zohar, Y, T Insel. 1987. Obsessive-compulsive disorder: Psychobiological approaches to diagnosis, treatment, and pathophysiology. *Biological Psychiatry* 22: 667-687.

5796 Zuckermann, M. 1983. A biological theory of sensation seeking. In *Biological Bases of Sensation Seeking, Impulsivity and Anxiety*. Edited by Zuckermann, M. New York: Erlbaum.

# 17

# Social Psychology

5797 Abelson, R P. 1976. Script processing in attitude formation and decision making. In *Cognition and Social Behavior.* Edited by Carroll, J S, J W Payne. New York: Erlbaum.

5798 Abramson, L Y, M E P Seligman, J D Teasdale. 1978. Learned helplessness in humans: Critique and reformulation. *Journal of Abnormal Psychology* 87: 49-74.

5799 Abramson, L, ed. 1988. *Social Cognition and Clinical Psychology: A Synthesis.* London: Guilford Press.

5800 Aiello, J R, A Baum, eds. 1979. *Residential Crowding and Design.* New York: Plenum.

5801 Aiello, J R, D E Thompson, D M Bridzinsky. 1983. How funny is crowding, anyway? Effects of room size, group size, and the introduction of humor. *Basic and Applied Social Psychology* 4: 193-207.

5802 Allison, P D, J K Liker. 1982. Analyzing sequential categorical data on dyadic interaction: A comment on Gottman. *Psychological Bulletin* 91: 393-403.

5803 Antkai, C, ed. 1981. *The Psychology of Ordinary Explanations of Social Behaviour.* London: Academic Press.

5804 Argyle, M. 1964. Introjection: A form of social learning. *British Journal of Psychology* 55: 391-412.

5805 Argyle, M. 1983. *The Psychology of Interpersonal Behaviour.* 4th ed. Harmondsworth: Penguin.

5806 Aronfreed, J. 1969. The problem of imitiation. In *Advances in Child Development and Behavior.* Edited by Lippsitt, L P, H W Reese. Pp. 209-19. New York: Academic Press.

5807 Baldassare, M, C S Fischer. 1977. The relevance of crowding experiments to urban studies. In *Perspectives on Environment and Behavior: Theory, Research and Applications.* Edited by Stokols, D. Pp. 273-286. New York: Plenum.

5808 Baldassare, M. 1978. Human spatial behavior. *Annual Review of Sociology* 4: 29-56.

5809 Bales, R F. 1950. *Interaction Process Analysis: A Method for the Study of Small Groups*. Chicago: University of Chicago Press.

5810 Bales, R. 1970. *Personality and Interpersonal Behavior*. New York: Rinehart & Winston.

5811 Bandura, A. 1977. Self-efficacy: Toward a unifying theory of behavioral change. *Psychological Review* 84: 191-215.

5812 Bar-Tal, D, A Kruglanski, eds. 1984. *The Social Psychology of Knowledge*. New York: Cambridge University Press.

5813 Barnett, M A. 1982. Empathy and prosocial behavior in children. In *Review of Human Development*. Edited by Field, T M, A Huston, H C Quay, L Troll, G E Finley. Pp. 316-26. New York: Wiley.

5814 Baron, R A, D Byrne. 1987. *Social Psychology: Understanding Human Interaction*. 5th ed. Boston: Allyn and Bacon.

5815 Baum, A, J E Singer, S Valins, eds. 1978. *Advances in Environmental Psychology*. Hillsdale, NJ: Erlbaum.

5816 Baum, A, Y M Epstein, eds. 1978. *Human Response to Crowding*. Hillsdale, NJ: Erlbaum.

5817 Baumann, D J, R B Cialdini, D T Kenrick. 1981. Altruism as hedonism: Helping and self-gratification as equivalent responses. *Journal of Personality and Social Psychology* 40: 1039-46.

5818 Bell, P A, R J Loomis, J C Cervone. 1982. Effects of heat, social facilitation, sex differences, and task difficulty on reaction time. *Human Factors* 24: 19-24.

5819 Bennett, A, K McConkey, eds. 1989. *Cognition in Individual and Social Contexts*. Amsterdam: North Holland.

5820 Bensman, J, M Givant. 1975. Charisma and modernity: The use and abuse of a concept. *Social Research* 69: 571-580.

5821 Berger, S M. 1962. Conditioning through vicarious instigation. *Psychological Review* 69: 450-66.

5822 Blasovich, J, E S Katkin. 1983. Visceral perception and social behavior. In *Social Psychophysiology: A Sourcebook*. Edited by Cacioppo, J T, R E Petty. Pp. 493-509. New York: Guilford Press.

5823 Boehnke, K. 1988. *Prosoziale Motivation, Selbstkonzept und politische Orientierung: Entwicklungsbedingungen und Veranderungen im Jugendalter*. Frankfurt: Peter Lang.

5824 Boehnke, K, M J Macpherson, M Meador, J Petri. 1989. How West German adolescents experience the nuclear threat. *Political Psychology* 10: 419-443.

5825 Boehnke, K, M J Macpherson, F Schmidt, eds. 1989. *Leben unter atomarer Bedrohung. Ergebnisse internationaler psychologischer Forschung.* Heidelberg: Asanger.

5826 Bond, C F, L J Titus. 1983. Social facilitation: A meta-analysis of 241 studies. *Psychological Bulletin* 94: 265-92.

5827 Breckler, S J. 1984. Empirical validation of affect, behavior, and cognition as distinct components of attitude. *Journal of Personality and Social Psychology* 47: 1191-1205.

5828 Brock, T C, S Shavitt, eds. 1990. *Psychology of Persuasion.* San Francisco: W.H. Freeman.

5829 Brown, G W, T Harris. 1978. *Social Origins of Depression: A Study of Psychiatric Disorder in Women.* New York: Free Press.

5830 Brown, J D, S E Taylor. 1986. Affect and the processing of personal information: Evidence for mood-activated self-schemata. *Journal of Experimental Social Psychology* 22: 436-52.

5831 Burns, T R, H Flam. 1988. *The Shaping of Social Organization: Social Rule System Theory with Applications.* Beverly Hills: Sage.

5832 Byrne, D, K Kelley, ed. 1986. *Alternative Approaches to the Study of Sexual Behavior.* Hillsdale, NJ: Erlbaum.

5833 Cacioppo, J T, R E Petty. 1981. Electromyograms as measures of extent affectivity of information processing. *American Psychologist* 36: 441-56.

5834 Cacioppo, J T, R E Petty. 1982. A biosocial model of attitude change: Signs, symptoms, and undetected physiological responses. In *Perspectives in Cardiovascular Psychophysiology.* Edited by Cacioppo, J T, R E Petty. New York: Guilford Press.

5835 Cacioppo, J T, R E Petty, eds. 1983. *Social Psychophysiology: A Sourcebook.* New York: Guilford Press.

5836 Cacioppo, J T, R E Petty, L Tassinary. 1989. Social psychophysiology: A new look. *Advances in Experimental Social Psychology* 22: 39-91.

5837 Cacioppo, J T, L G Tassinary, eds. 1990. *Principles of Psychophysiology: Physical, Social, and Inferential Elements.* New York: Cambridge University Press.

5838 Cacioppo, J T, R E Petty, M E Losch. 1990. Psychophysiological approaches to attitudes: Detecting opinions when people won't say, can't say, or don't even know. In *Psychology of Persuasion*. Edited by Brock, T C, S Shavitt. San Francisco: W.H. Freeman.

5839 Campbell, D T. 1967. Stereotypes and the perception of group differences. *American Psychologist* 22: 817-829.

5840 Carlestram, G, L Levi. 1971. *Urban Conglomerates as Psychosocial Human Stressors. General Aspects, Swedish Trends, and Psychological and Medical Implications.* Stockholm: Royal Ministery for Foreign Affairs.

5841 Carlson, M, N Miller. 1987. Explanations of the relationship between negative mood and helping. *Psychological Bulletin* 102: 91-108.

5842 Cartwright, D, A Zander, eds. 1968. *Group Dynamics: Research and Theory.* 3rd ed. New York: Harper & Row.

5843 Carver, C S, M F Scheier. 1981. *Attention and Self-Regulation: A Control-Theory Approach to Human Behavior.* New York: Springer.

5844 Carver, C S, M F Scheier. 1981. The self-attention-induced feedback loop and social facilitation. *Journal of Experimental Social Psychology* 17: 545-68.

5845 Carver, C, M Scheier. 1988. *Perspectives on Personality.* Boston: Allyn and Bacon.

5846 Cawte, J. 1978. Gross Stress in Small Islands: A Study in Micropsychiatry. In *Extinction and Survival in Human Populations.* Edited by Laughlin, C, I Brady. New York: Columbia University Press.

5847 Chase, I D. 1980. Social process and hierarchy formation in small groups: A comparative perspective. *American Sociological Review* 45: 905-24.

5848 Cialdini, R B, B L Darby, J E Vincent. 1973. Transgression and altruism: A case for hedonism. *Journal of Experimental Social Psychology* 9: 502-16.

5849 Cialdini, R B, D T Kenrick. 1976. Altruism as hedonism: A social development perspective on the relationship of negative mood state and helping. *Journal of Personality and Social Psychology* 34: 907-14.

5850 Cialdini, R B, D J Baumann, D T Kenrick. 1981. Insights from sadness: A three step model of the development of altruism as hedonism. *Development Review* 1: 207-23.

5851 Clark, M S, A M Isen. 1982. Toward understanding the relationship between feeling states and social behavior. In *Cognitive Social Psychology*. Edited by Hastorf, A, A M Isen. Pp. 73-108. New York: Elsevier/North Holland.

5852 Clark, M S, G M Williamson. 1989. Moods and social judgments. In *Handbook of Social Psychophysiology*. Edited by Wagner, H, A Manstead. Pp. 347-370. New York: Wiley.

5853 Cohen, J L. 1980. Social facilitation: Audience versus evaluation apprehension effects. *Motivation and Emotion* 4: 21-33.

5854 Coleman, J C. 1980. Friendship and the peer group in adolescence. In *Handbook of Adolescent Psychology*. Edited by Adelson, J. New York: Wiley.

5855 Colligan, M J, J W Pennebaker, L R Murphy, eds. 1982. *Mass Psychogenic Illness: A Social Psychological Analysis*. Hillsdale, NJ: Erlbaum.

5856 Cottrell, N B, S W Epley. 1977. Affiliation, social comparison, and socially mediated stress reduction. In *Social Comparison Processes: Theoretical and Empirical Perspectives*. Edited by Suls, J M, R L Miller. Washington: Hemisphere.

5857 Cox, V C, P B Paulus, G McCain, J K Schkade. 1979. Field research on the effects of crowding in prisons and on offshore drilling platforms. In *Residential Crowding and Design*. Edited by Aiello, J R, A Baum. New York: Plenum.

5858 Crano, W D, M B Brewer. 1973. *Principles of Research in Social Psychology*. New York: McGraw-Hill.

5859 D'Atri, D A, A M Ostfeld. 1975. Crowding: Its effect on the elevation of blood pressure in a prison setting. *Preventive Medicine* 4: 550-66.

5860 D'Atri, D A, E F Fitzgerald, S V Kasl, A M Ostfeld. 1981. Crowding in prison: The relationship between changes in housing mode and blood pressure. *Psychomatic Medicine* 43: 95-105.

5861 Deutsch, M, R M Kraus. 1965. *Theories in Social Psychology*. New York: Basic Books.

5862 Diener, E. 1980. Deindividuation: The absence of self-awareness and self-regulation in group members. In *Psychology of

*Group Influence*. Edited by Paulus, P. Pp. 209-44. Hillsdale, NJ: Erlbaum.

5863 Dion, K L, R S Baron, N Miller. 1970. Why do groups make riskier decisions than individuals? In *Advances in experimental social psychology*. Pp. 306-377. New York: Academic Press.

5864 Doise, W. 1978. *Groups and Individuals: Explanations in Social Psychology*. Cambridge: Cambridge University Press.

5865 Douglas, M, A Wildavsky. 1982. *Risk and Culture: An Essay on the Selection of Technical and Environmental Dangers*. Berkeley: University of California Press.

5866 Eagly, A, V Steffen. 1986. Gender and aggressive behavior: A meta-analytic review of the social psychological literature. *Psychological Bulletin* 100: 309-330.

5867 Eiser, J R. 1986. *Social Psychology: Attitudes, Cognition, and Social Behavior*. Cambridge: Cambridge University Press.

5868 Elliott, E S, J L Cohen. 1981. Social facilitation effects via interpersonal distance. *Journal of Social Psychology* 114: 237-49.

5869 Epstein, Y M, R A Karlin. 1975. Effects of acute experimental crowding. *Journal of Applied Social Psychology* 5: 34-53.

5870 Epstein, Y M, R L Woolfolk, P M Lehrer. 1981. Physiological, cognitive, and nonverbal responses to repeated exposure to crowding. *Journal of Applied Social Psychology* 11: 1-13.

5871 Evans, G W. 1979. Behavioral and physiological consequences of crowding in humans. *Journal of Applied Social Psychology* 9: 27-46.

5872 Evans, G W, ed. 1982. *Environmental Stress*. Cambridge: Cambridge University Press.

5873 Faust, M S. 1960. Developmental maturity as a determinant of prestige in adolescent girls. *Child Development* 31: 173-184.

5874 Field, T M, A Huston, H C Quay, L Troll, G E Finley, eds. 1982. *Review of Human Development*. New York: Wiley.

5875 Fielder, K, J Forgas, eds. 1988. *Affect, Cognition and Social Behavior: New Evidence and Integrative Attempts*. Toronto: C.J. Hogrefe.

5876 Fishbein, M, I Ajzen. 1975. *Belief, Attitude, Intention, and Behavior: An Introduction to Theory and Research.* Reading, MA: Addison-Wesley.

5877 Fisher, J D, P A Bell, A Baum. 1984. *Environmental Psychology.* 2nd ed. New York: Holt, Rinehart & Winston.

5878 Fiske, S T, S E Taylor. 1984. *Social Cognition.* Reading, MA: Addison-Wesley.

5879 Flowers, M L. 1977. A laboratory test of some implications of Janis's groupthink hypothesis. *Journal of Personality and Social Psychology* 35: 888-896.

5880 Forsyth, D R. 1987. *Social Psychology.* Monterey, CA: Brooks/Cole.

5881 Freedman, J L. 1970. Transgression, compliance, and guilt. In *Altruism and Helping Behavior.* Edited by Maccaulay, J R, L Berkowitz. New York: Academic.

5882 Freedman, J L, S Klevansky, P I Ehrlich. 1971. Crowding and human aggressiveness. *Journal of Experimental Social Psychology* 8: 528-548.

5883 Freedman, J. 1975. *Crowding and Behavior.* New York: Viking.

5884 Freud, S. 1921. *Group Psychology and Analysis of the Ego.* London: International Psychoanalytic Press.

5885 Friedman, L. 1981. How affiliation affects stress in fear and anxiety situations. *Journal of Personality and Social Psychology* 40: 1102-17.

5886 Froming, W J, L Allen, R Jensen. 1985. Altruism, role-taking, and self-awareness: The acquisition of norms governing altruistic behavior. *Child Development* 56: 1223-38.

5887 Gamson, W, B Fireman, S Rytina. 1982. *Encounters with Unjust Authority.* Homewood, IL: Dorsey.

5888 Gangestad, S W, J A Simpson. 1990. Toward an evolutionary history of female sociosexual variation. *Journal of Personality* 58: 69-96.

5889 Geen, R, E O'Neal, eds. 1976. *Perspectives on Aggression.* New York: Academic Press.

5890 Geen, R G, J J Gange. 1977. Drive theory of social facilitation: Twelve years of theory and research. *Psychological Bulletin* 84: 1267-88.

5891 Geen, R G. 1979. Effects of being observed on learning following success and failure experiences. *Motivation and Emotion* 3: 355-71.

5892 Geen, R G. 1979. Evaluation apprehension and social facilitation: A reply to Sanders. *Journal of Experimental Social Psychology* 17: 252-6.

5893 Geen, R G, E I Donnerstein, eds. 1983. *Aggression: Theoretical and Methodological Issues*. New York: Academic Press.

5894 Geen, R G, B J Bushman. 1987. Drive theory: The effects of socially engendered arousal. In *Theories of Group Behavior*. Edited by Mullen, B, G Goethals. New York: Springer.

5895 Geen, R G. 1989. Alternative conceptions of social facilitation. In *Psychology of Group Influence*. Edited by Paulus, P. Hillsdale, NJ: Erlbaum.

5896 Geen, R G, B J Bushman. 1989. The arousing effects of social presence. In *Handbook of Social Psychophysiology*. Edited by Wagner, H, A Manstead. Pp. 261-282. New York: Wiley.

5897 Glass, D C, J E Singer. 1972. *Urban Stress*. New York: Academic Press.

5898 Glassman, R B. 1980. An evolutionary hypothesis about teaching and proselytizing behaviors. *Zygon* 15: 133-154.

5899 Goffman, E. 1959. *The Presentation of Self in Everyday Life*. New York: Doubleday.

5900 Goffman, E. 1966. *Behavior in Public Places: Notes on the Social Organization of Gatherings*. New York: Free Press.

5901 Goffman, E. 1971. *Relations in Public: Microstudies of the Public Order*. New York: Basic Books.

5902 Goldstein, J, ed. 1979. *Sports, Games and Play*. Hillsdale, NJ: Erlbaum.

5903 Graumann, C F, ed. 1986. *Changing Conceptions of Crowd Mind and Behavior*. New York: Springer.

5904 Groff, B D, R S Baron, D L Moore. 1983. Distraction, attentional conflict, and drivelike behavior. *Journal of Experimental Social Psychology* 19: 359-80.

5905 Guerin, B, J M Innes. 1982. Social facilitation and social monitoring: A new look at Zajonc's "mere presence" hypothesis. *British Journal of Social Psychology* 21: 7-18.

5906 Gurvitch, G. 1964. *The Spectrum of Social Time.* Dordrecht: Reidel.

5907 Hackman, J R, C G Morris. 1975. Group tasks, group interaction process, and group performance effectiveness: A review and proposed integration. In *Advances in Experimental Social Psychology.* Edited by Berkowitz, L. New York: Academci Press.

5908 Hackworth, J R. 1976. Relationship between spatial density and sensory overload, personal space, and systolic and diastolic blood pressure. *Perceptual and Motor Skills* 43: 867-72.

5909 Hamilton, D. 1976. Cognitive biases in perception of social groups. In *Cognition and Social Behavior.* Edited by Carroll, J S, J W Payne. New York: Lawrence Erlbaum Associates.

5910 Hamilton, D. 1981. *Cognitive Processes in Stereotyping and Intergroup Behavior.* Hillsdale, N.J: Erlbaum.

5911 Hannaway, J. 1985. Managerial behaviour, uncertainty and hierarchy: A prelude to synthesis. *Human Relations* 38: 1085-1100.

5912 Hare, A P, E F Borgatta, R F Bales, eds. 1965. *Small Groups: Studies in Social Interaction.* Rev. Ed. New York: Knopf.

5913 Hare, A P. 1976. *Handbook of Small Group Research.* 2nd ed. New York: Free Press.

5914 Hartup, W W. 1978. Peer relations and the growth of social competence. In *The Primary Prevention of Psychopathology Vol 3: Promoting Social Competence and Coping in Children.* Edited by Kent, M W, J E Rolf. Hanover, PA: University Press of New England.

5915 Hastorf, A, A M Isen, eds. 1982. *Cognitive Social Psychology.* New York: Elsevier/North Holland.

5916 Hershberger, W A, ed. 1989. *Volitional Action: Conation and Control.* Amsterdam: Elsevier/North Holland.

5917 Hoffman, M. 1981. Is altruism part of human nature? *Journal of Personality and Social Psychology* 40: 121-37.

5918 Hogg, M A, J C Turner. 1985. When liking begets solidarity: An experiment on the role of interpersonal attraction in psychological group formation. *British Journal of Social Psychology* 24: 267-281.

5919 Hogg, M A. 1987. Social identity and group cohesiveness. In *Rediscovering the Social Group: A Self-Categorization Theory.* Edited by Turner, J C, M A Hogg, P J Oakes, S D Reicher, M S Wetherell. Pp. 89-116. Oxford: Blackwell.

5920 Hogg, M A, D Abrams. 1988. *Social Identifications: A Social Psychology of Intergroup Relations and Group Processes.* London: Routledge.

5921 Horowitz, I L. 1970. Deterrence games: From academic casebook to military codebook. In *The Structure of Conflict.* Edited by Swingle, P. Pp. 277-296. New York: Academic Press.

5922 Isen, A M. 1970. Success, failure, attention and reaction to others: The warm glow of success. *Journal of Personality and Social Psychology* 15: 294-301.

5923 Isen, A M, R Patrick. 1983. The effects of positive feelings on risk-taking: When the chips are down. *Organizational Behavior and Human Performance* 31: 194-202.

5924 Isen, A M, K A Daubman, G P Nowicki. 1987. Positive affect facilitates creative problem solving. *Journal of Personality and Social Psychology* 52: 1122-31.

5925 Janis, I L. 1945. Psychodynamic aspects of adjustment to army life. *Psychiatry* 8: 159-176.

5926 Janis, I L. 1958. *Psychological Stress.* New York: Wiley.

5927 Janis, I L. 1968. Group identification under conditions of external danger. In *Group Dynamics: Research and Theory.* Edited by Cartwright, D, A Zander. Pp. 80-90. New York: Harper & Row.

5928 Janis, I L, L Mann. 1977. *Decision Making: A Psychological Analysis of Conflict and Choice, and Commitment.* New York: Free Press.

5929 Janis, I L. 1982. *Groupthink: Psychological Studies of Policy Decisions and Fiascoes.* 2nd rev. ed. Boston: Houghton Mifflin.

5930 Janis, I L. 1982. Counteracting the adverse effects of concurrence-seeking in policy-planning groups: Theory and research perspectives. In *Group Decision Making.* Edited by Brandstatter, H, J H Davis, G Stocker-Kreichgauer. London: Academic Press.

5931 Jessor, S, R Jessor. 1975. Transition from virginity to nonvirginity among youth: A social-psychological study over time. *Developmental Psychology* 11: 473-484.

5932 Jessor, R, S L Jessor. 1977. *Problem Behavior and Psychosocial Development*. New York: Academic Press.

5933 Johnson, N. 1987. Panic and the breakdown of social order: Popular myth, social theory, empirical evidence. *Sociological Focus* 20: 171-83.

5934 Johnson, N. 1987. Panic and the breakdown of social order: Popular myth, social theory, empirical evidence. *Sociological Focus* 20: 171-83.

5935 Kadish, M, S Kadish. 1973. *Discretion to Disobey: A Study of Lawful Departures from Legal Rules*. Stanford: Stanford University Press.

5936 Kalb, L, J Keating. 1081. The measurement of perceived crowding. *Personality and Social Psychology Bulletin* 7: 650-54.

5937 Karlin, R A, Y Epstein, J Aiello. 1978. Strategies for the investigation of crowding. In *Design for Communality and Privacy*. Edited by Esser, A, B Greenbie. New York: Plenum.

5938 Karlin, R A, S Katz, Y M Epstein, R L Woolfold. 1979. The use of therapeutic interventions to reduce crowding-related arousal: A preliminary investigation. *Environmental Psychology and Nonverbal Behavior* 3: 219-27.

5939 Katz, D, R Kahn. 1978. *The Social Psychology of Organizations*. 2nd ed. New York: Wiley.

5940 Kelman, H C, V L Hamilton. 1989. *Crimes of Obedience: Toward a Social Psychology of Authority and Responsibility*. New Haven: Yale University Press.

5941 Kissel, S. 1965. Stress-reducing properties of social stimuli. *Journal of Personality and Social Psychology* 2: 378-84.

5942 Knight, M L, R J Borden. 1979. Autonomic and affective reactions of high and low socially anxious individuals awaiting public performance. *Psychophysiology* 16: 209-13.

5943 Krippendorf, K. 1979. Communication and Control in Society. In New York: Gordon and Breach.

5944 Lamb, M E, S J Suomi, G R Stephenson, eds. 1979. *Social Interaction Analysis: Methodological Issues*. Madison: University of Wisconsin Press.

5945 Landis, C, W A Hunt. 1939. *The Startle Pattern*. New York: Farrar.

5946 Langer, E J. 1975. The illusion of control. *Journal of Personality and Social Psychology* 32: 311-328.

5947 Latane, B, S Nida. 1980. Social impact theory and group influence: A social engineering perspective. In *Psychology of Group Influence*. Edited by Paulus, P. Pp. 3-34. Hillsdale, NJ: Erlbaum.

5948 Lawrence, P R, J W Lorsch. 1969. *Organization and Environment: Managing Differentiation and Intergration*. Homewood, Ill.: Irwin.

5949 Le Bon, G. 1960 [1895]. *The Crowd*. New York: Viking.

5950 Lepper, M R, D Greene, R E Nisbett. 1973. Undermining children's intrinsic interest with extrinsic reward: A test of the overjustification hypothesis. *Journal of Personality and Social Psychology* 28: 129-137.

5951 Lerner, M. 1980. *The Belief in a Just World: A Fundamental Delusion*. New York: Plenum.

5952 Leventhal, G, M Marrurro. 1980. Differential effects of spatial crowding and sex on behavior. *Perception and Motor Skills* 51: 111-120.

5953 Levine, S, N Scotch, eds. 1970. *Social Stress*. Chicago: Aldine.

5954 Lewin, K. 1952. *Field Theory in Social Science*. London: Tavistock Publications.

5955 Lindbolm, E. 1969. The science of "muddling through". In *Readings on Modern Organizations*. Pp. 154-165. Englewood Cliffs, NJ: Prentice-Hall.

5956 Lipp, W. 1986. Geschlechtsrollenwechsel. Formen und Funktionen, am Beispiel ethonographischer Materialien. *Kölner Zeitschrift für Soziologie und Sozialpsychologie* 38: 529-559.

5957 Lipp, W. 1990. Männerbünde, Frauen und Charisma. Geschlechterdrama in Kulturprozeß. In *Männerbünde. Zur Rolle des Mannes im Kulturvergleich*. Edited by Völger, G, K v Welck. Pp. 31-40. Köln: Gesellschaft für Völkerkunde.

5958 Long, S. 1992. *A Structural Analysis of Small Groups*. New York: Routledge.

5959 Longley, J, D G Pruitt. 1980. Groupthink: A critique of Janis's theory. *Review of Personality and Social Psychology* 1: 74-93.

5960 Lorr, T, R P Youniss. 1985. *The Interpersonal Style Inventory Manual*. Los Angeles: Western Psychological Services.

5961 Lundberg, U. 1976. Urban commuting: Crowdedness and catecholamine excretion. *Journal of Human Stress* 2: 26-32.

5962 MacAloon, J. 1984. *Rite, Drama, Festival, Spectacle*. Philadelphia: Institute for Human Issues.

5963 Maccaulay, J R, L Berkowitz, eds. 1970. *Altruism and Helping Behavior*. New York: Academic.

5964 Maccoby, E E, T M Newcomb, E L Hartley, eds. 1958. *Readings in Social Psychology*. New York: Henry Holt.

5965 Maccoby, E E. 1987. The Varied meanings of "masculine" and "feminine". In *Masculinity/Femininity: Basic Perspectives*. Edited by Reinisch, J M, L A Rosenblum, S A Sanders. Pp. 227-239. Oxford: Oxford University Press.

5966 MacDonald, K. 1990. Mechanisms of sexual egalitarianism in Western Europe. *Ethology and Sociobiology* 11: 195-238.

5967 Manucia, G K, D J Baumann, R B Cialdini. 1984. Mood influences on helping: Direct effects or side effects? *Journal of Personality and Social Psychology* 46: 357-64.

5968 Marsh, P. 1978. *The Illusion of Violence*. London: J.M. Dent.

5969 Martin, S E, L B Sechrest, R Redner, eds. 1981. *New Directions in the Rehabilitation of Criminal Offenders*. Washington: National Academic Press.

5970 Maynard, D W. 1984. *Inside Plea Bargaining: The Language of Negotiation*. New York: Plenum.

5971 McGrath, J E, I Altman. 1966. *Small Group Research: A Synthesis and Critique of the Field*. New York: Holt, Rinehart, and Winston.

5972 McKinnery, M E, R J Gatchel, P B Paulus. 1983. The effects of audience size on high and low speech-anxious subjects during an actual speaking task. *Basic and Applied Social Psychology* 4: 73-87.

5973 McPhail, C. 1983. Individual and collective behaviors within gatherings, demonstrations, and riots. *Annual Review of Sociology* 1983: 579-600.

5974 McPhail, C. 1989. Blumer's theory of collective behavior: The development of a non-symbolic interaction explanation. *Sociological Quarterly* 30: 401-23.

5975 McPhail, C, C Tucker. 1990. Purposive collective action. *American Behavior Scientist* 34: 81-94.

5976 McPhail, C. 1990. *The Myth of the Madding Crowd.* New York: Aldine.

5977 McPhee, W N. 1963. *Formal Theories of Mass Behavior.* New York: Free Press.

5978 Mead, G H. 1974[1934]. *Mind, Self, and Society.* Chicago: University of Chicago Press.

5979 Meuller, D J. 1986. *Measuring Social Attitudes: A Handbook for Researchers and Practitioners.* New York: Teachers College Press.

5980 Milgram, S, H Toch. 1969. Collective behavior: The crowd and social movements. In *Handbook of Social Psychology.* Edited by Lindzey, G. Pp. 507-610. Reading, MA: Addison-Wesley.

5981 Milgram, S. 1974. *Obedience to Authority.* London: Tavistock.

5982 Moore, D L, R S Baron. 1983. Social facilitation: A psychophysiological analysis. In *Social Psychophysiology: A Sourcebook.* Edited by Cacioppo, J, R Petty. New York: Guilford Press.

5983 Morris, S J, F H Kanfer. 1983. Altruism and depression. *Personality and Social Psychology Bulletin* 9: 567-77.

5984 Moscovici, S. 1985. *The Age of the Crowd: A Historical Treatise on Mass Psychology.* Cambridge: Cambridge University Press.

5985 Mullen, B, G Goethals, eds. 1987. *Theories of Group Behavior.* New York: Springer.

5986 Myers, D G, H Lamm. 1977. The polarizing effect of group discussion. In *Current Trends in Pychology: Readings from the American Scientist.* Edited by Janis, I L. Los Altos, Calif.: Kaufmann.

5987 Newton, J, L Mann. 1980. Crowd size as a factor in the persuasion process: A Study of religious crusade meetings. *Journal of Personality and Social Psychology* 39: 874-83.

5988 Nicosia, G J, D Hyman, R A Karlin, Y M Epstein, J R Aiello. 1979. Effects of bodily contact on reactions to crowding. *Journal of Applied Social Psychology* 9: 508-23.

5989 Nuttin, J. 1975. *The Illusion of Attitude Change: Towards a Response Contagion Theory of Persuasion*. London: Academic Press.

5990 Nye, R. 1975. *The Origins of Crowd Psychology*. Beverly Hills, CA: Sage.

5991 Ohman, A, U Dimberg. 1984. An evolutionary perspective on human social behavior. In *Sociophysiology*. Edited by Waid, W. Pp. 47-86. New York: Springer.

5992 Paulus, P. 1989. *Psychology of Group Influence*. Hillsdale, NJ: Erlbaum.

5993 Pratkanis, A R, S J Breckler, A G Greenwald, eds. 1989. *Attitude Structure and Function*. Hillsdale, NJ: Erlbaum.

5994 Pratkanis, A R. 1992. *Age of Propaganda : The Everyday Use and Abuse of Persuasion*. New York: Freeman.

5995 Quarantelli, E. 1954. The nature and conditions of panic. *American Journal of Sociology* 60: 267-75.

5996 Quarantelli, E. 1957. The behavior of panic participants. *Sociology and Social Research* 41: 187-94.

5997 Quarantelli, E, R Dynes. 1968. Looting in civil disorders: An index of social change. In *Riots and Rebellion*. Edited by Masotti, L, D Bowen. Pp. 131-41. Beverly Hills, CA: Sage.

5998 Quarantelli, E, J Hundley. 1969. A test of some propositions about crowd formation and behavior. In *Readings in Collective Behavior*. Edited by Evans, R. Pp. 538-54. Chicago: Rand McNally.

5999 Rajecki, D W. 1982. *Attitudes: Themes and Advances*. Sunderland, MA: Sinauer Associates.

6000 Rogoff, B. 1990. *Apprenticeship in Thinking: Cognitive Development in Social Context*. New York: Oxford University Press.

6001 Rosen, G. 1968. *Madness in Society*. New York: Harper.

6002 Rosenblatt, J S, C Beer, M-C Busnel, P J B Slater. 1985. Advances in the Study of Behavior. In New York: Academic Press.

6003 Rosenhan, D L, J Karylowski, P Salovey, K Hargis. 1981. Emotion and altrusim. In *Altruism and Helping Behavior.* Edited by Rushton, J P, R M Sorrentino. Pp. 233-48. Hillsdale, NJ: Erlbaum.

6004 Rosenhan, D L, P Salovey, K Hargis. 1981. The joys of helping. *Journal of Personality and Social Psychology* 40: 899-905.

6005 Rosenthal, R. 1967. *Experimenter Effects in Behavioral Research.* New York: Appleton-Century-Crofts.

6006 Rushton, J P, R M Sorrentino, eds. 1981. *Altruism and Helping Behavior.* Hillsdale, NJ: Erlbaum.

6007 Savin-Williams, R C. 1987. *Adolescence: An Ethological Perspective.* New York: Springer.

6008 Schachter, S. 1959. *The Psychology of Affiliation.* Stanford: Stanford University Press.

6009 Schmidt, D E, J P Keating. 1979. Human crowding and personal control: An integration of the research. *Psychological Bulletin* 86: 680-700.

6010 Shaver, K G, ed. 1985. *Self, Situations, and Social Behavior: Review of Personality and Social Psychology.* Beverly Hills: Sage.

6011 Shaver, K G. 1987. *Principles of Social Psychology.* 3 ed. Hillsdale, NJ: Erlbaum.

6012 Sighele, C. 1894. *La Foule Criminelle.* Paris: Alcan.

6013 Simmel, E C, R A Hoppe, G A Milton, eds. 1968. *Social Facilitation and Initiative Behavior.* Boston: Allyn and Bacon.

6014 Singer, J E, U Lundberg, M Frankenhaueser. 1978. Stress of the train: A study of urban commuting. In *Advances in Environmental Psychology.* Edited by Baum, A, J E Singer, S Valins. Hillsdale, NJ: Erlbaum.

6015 Singerman, K J, T D Borkovec, R S Baron. 1976. Failure of 'misattribution therapy' manipulation with a clinically relevant target behavior. *Behavior Therapy* 7: 306-13.

6016 Smith, W J. 1977. *The Behavior of Communicating.* Cambridge: Harvard University Press.

6017 Smith, P K, K J Connolly. 1977. Social and aggressive behaviour in preschool children as a function of crowding. *Social Science Information* 16: 601-620.

6018 Smith, M. 1983. *Violence and Sport.* Toronto: Butterworth.

6019 Smith-Lovin, L, D Heise, eds. 1988. *Analyzing Social Interaction: Advances in Affect Control Theory.* New York: Gordon and Breach.

6020 Snow, D, L Zurcher, R Peters. 1981. Victory celebrations as theater: A dramaturgical approach to crowd behavior. *Symbolic Interaction* 4: 21-42.

6021 Staub, E, et al., eds. 1984. *Development and Maintenance of Prosocial Behavior: International Perspectives on Positive Morality.* New York: Plenum.

6022 Staub, E. 1989. *The Roots of Evil: The Psychological and Cultural Origins of Genocide and Other Group Violence.* New York: Cambridge University Press.

6023 Stokols, D. 1978. A typology of crowding experience. In *Human Response to Crowding.* Edited by Baum, A, Y Epstein. Hillsdale, NJ: Erlbaum.

6024 Stouffer, S. 1949. *The American Soldier.* Princeton: Princeton University Press.

6025 Stroebe, W, M Hewstone, eds. 1990. *The European Review of Social Psychology.* Chichester: Wiley.

6026 Suls, J M, R L Miller. 1977. *Social Comparison Processes: Theoretical and Empirical Perspectives.* Washington,D.C.: Hemisphere.

6027 Suls, J, ed. 1982. *Psychological Perspectives on the Self.* Hillsdale, NJ: Erlbaum.

6028 Sundstrom, E. 1975. An experimental study of crowding: Effects of room size, intrusion, and goal-blocking on nonverbal behavior, self-disclosure, and reported stress. *Journal of Personality and Social Psychology* 32: 645-654.

6029 Tajfel, H. 1981. *Human Groups and Social Categories.* New York: Cambridge University Press.

6030 Tajfel, H, ed. 1982. *Social Identity and Intergroup Relations.* Cambridge: Cambridge University Press.

6031 Tajfel, H, J C Turner. 1986. The social identity theory of intergroup behaviour. In *Psychology of Intergroup Relations.* Edited by Worchel, S, W G Austin. Pp. 7-24. Chicago: Nelson-Hall.

6032 Tannenbaum, P H, ed. 1980. *The Entertainment Function of Television.* Hillsdale, NJ: Erlbaum.

6033 Tarde, G. 1890. *The Laws of Imitation.* New York: Henry Holt.

6034 Tarde, G. 1969. *On Communication and Social Influence.* Translated by Clark, T.N. Chicago: University of Chicago Press.

6035 Taylor, R B. 1978. Human territoriality: A review and a model for future research. *Cornell Jounal of Social Relations* 13: 125-151.

6036 Tetlock, P E. 1979. Identifying victims of groupthink from public statements of decision makers. *Journal of Personality and Social Psychology* 37: 1314-1324.

6037 Tilly, C, R Tilly. 1975. *The Rebellious Century, 1830-1930.* Cambridge: Harvard University Press.

6038 Tilly, C. 1978. *From Mobilization to Revolution.* Reading, MA: Addison-Wesley.

6039 Toi, M, C D Batson. 1982. More evidence that empathy is a source of altruistic motivation. *Journal of Personality and Social Psychology* 18: 281-92.

6040 Tranel, D, D C Fowles, A R Damasion. 1985. Electrodermal discrimination of familiar and unfamiliar faces: A methodology. *Psychophysiology* 22: 403-8.

6041 Triandis, H C. 1971. *Attitude and Attitude Change.* New York: John Wiley.

6042 Trotter, W. 1916. *Instincts of the Herd in Peace and War.* London: Fisher Unwin.

6043 Tuckman, B W. 1965. Developmental sequence in small groups. *Psychological Bulletin* 63: 384-399.

6044 Turner, R. 1964. Collective behavior. In *Handbook of Modern Sociology.* Edited by Faris, R. Pp. 382-425. Chicago: Rand McNally.

6045 Turner, V. 1969. *The Ritual Process: Structure and Anti-Structure.* New York: Aldine.

6046 Turner, V. 1974. *Dramas, Fields, and Metaphors: Symbolic Action in Human Society.* Ithaca: Cornell University Press.

6047 Turner, J C, H Giles, eds. 1981. *Intergroup Behaviour.* Chicago: University of Chicago Press.

6048 Turner, J C. 1981. Some considerations in generalizing experimental social psychology. In *Progress in Applied Social Psychology*. Edited by Stephenson, G M, J H Davis. Pp. 3-34. New York: Wiley.

6049 Turner, J C. 1981. The experimental social psychology of intergroup behaviour. In *Intergroup Behaviour*. Edited by Turner, J C, H Giles. Pp. 66-101. Chicago: University of Chicago Press.

6050 Turner, V. 1982. *From Ritual to Theater: The Human Seriousness of Play*. New York: Performing Arts Journals Publications.

6051 Turner, V. 1982. *Celebration: Studies in Festivity and Ritual*. Washington: Smithsonian Institution Press.

6052 Turner, J C. 1982. Towards a cognitive redefinition of the social group. In *Social Identity and Intergroup Relations*. Edited by Tajfel, H. Pp. 15-40. Cambridge: Cambridge University Press.

6053 Turner, V. 1983. Body, brain, and culture. *Zygon: Journal of Religion and Science* 18: 221-245.

6054 Turner, J C, P J Oakes. 1986. The significance of the social identity concept for social psychology with reference to individualism, interactionism and social influence. *British Journal of Social Psychology* 25: 237-252.

6055 Turner, J C, M A Hogg, P J Oakes, S D Reicher, M S Wetherell, eds. 1987. *Rediscovering the Social Group: A Self-Categorization Theory*. Oxford: Blackwell.

6056 Turner, J C. 1991. *Social Influence*. Milton Keynes: Open University Press.

6057 Valsiner, J, ed. 1986. *The Individual Subject and Scientific Psychology*. New York: Plenum.

6058 Wagner, H, ed. 1988. *Social Psychophysiology and Emotion: Theory and Clinical Applications*. Chichester: Wiley.

6059 Waid, W, ed. 1984. *Sociophysiology*. New York: Springer.

6060 Webb, E J, et al. 1966. *Unobtrusive Measures: Nonreactive Research in the Social Sciences*. Chicago: Rand McNally.

6061 Weimann, G, K Boehnke, P Noack. 1989. Jugendsymbole: Funktionen des Buttontragens. In *Forschung in den Erziehungswissenschaften*. Edited by Beller, E K. Pp. 57-60. Weinheim: Deutscher Studien Verlag.

6062 Wheeler, D D, I L Janis. 1980. *A Practical Guide for Making Decisions.* New York: Free Press.

6063 Wilensky, H. 1967. *Organizational Intelligence: Knowledge and Policy in Government and Industry.* New York: Basic Books.

6064 Wilson, J Q, R J Herrnstein. 1985. *Crime and Human Nature.* New York: Simon and Schuster.

6065 Worchel, S, J Cooper, R Goethals. 1988. *Understanding Social Psychology.* 4th ed. Chicago: Dorsey Press.

6066 Wright, S. 1978. *Crowds and Riots.* Beverly Hills, CA: Sage.

6067 Wyer, R, T Srull, eds. 1984. *Handbook of Social Cognition.* Hillsdale, NJ: Erlbaum.

6068 Zahn-Waxler, C, E M Cummings, R Iannotti, eds. 1986. *Altruism and Aggression: Biological and Social Origins.* Cambridge: Cambridge University Press.

6069 Zanna, M P, J K Rempel. 1984. A new look at an old concept. In *The Social Psychology of Knowledge.* Edited by Bar-Tal, D, A Kruglanski. New York: Cambridge University Press.

6070 Zillmann, D. 1980. Anatomy of suspense. In *The Entertainment Function of Television.* Edited by Tannenbaum, P H. Pp. 133-63. Hillsdale, NJ: Erlbaum.

# 18

# Politics

6071 Anderson, W. 1976. *A Place of Power: The American Episode in Human Evolution.* Santa Monica, CA: Goodyear.

6072 Anderson, W. 1987. *To Govern Evolution.* Cambridge, MA: Harcourt Brace Jovanovich.

6073 Arnhart, L. 1988. Aristotle's biopolitics: A defense of biological teleology against biological nihilism. *Politics and the Life Sciences* 6: 173-229.

6074 Arnhart, L. 1990. Aristotle, chimpanzees and other political animals. *Social Science Information* 29: 479-559.

6075 Arnhart, L. 1992. Feminism, primatology, and ethical naturalism. *Politics and the Life Sciences* 11: 157-78.

6076 Axelrod, R. 1981. The emergence of cooperation among egoists. *American Political Science Review* 75: 306-318.

6077 Axelrod, R, D A Bositis. 1983. Biology, gender, and politics: An assessment and critique. *Women and Politics* 3: 29-66.

6078 Axelrod, R. 1984. *The Evolution of Cooperation.* New York: Basic Books.

6079 Axelrod, R, D Dion. 1988. The further evolution of cooperation. *Science* 242: 1385-1390.

6080 Azar, E E, J W Burton. 1986. *International Conflict Resolution: Theory and Practice.* Boulderlo.: Lynne Rienner.

6081 Baer, D. 1983. The political socialization of gender: What contribution biology? *Politics and the Life Sciences* 1: 125-134.

6082 Bagehot, W. 1872. *Physics and Politics; Or Thoughts on the Application of the Principles of Natural Selection and Inheritance to Political Society.* New York: Appleton-Century-Crofts.

6083 Barner-Barry, C. 1977. An observational study of authority in a preschool peer group. *Political Methodology* 4: 415-449.

6084 Barner-Barry, C. 1978. The structure of young children's authority relationships. In *Power Relationships*. Edited by Omark, D R, et al. New York: Garland.

6085 Barner-Barry, C. 1981. Longitudinal observational research and the study of basic forms of political socialization. In *Biopolitics*. Edited by Watts, M W. San Francisco: Jossey-Bass.

6086 Barner-Barry, C. 1982. An ethological study of a leadership succession. *Ethology and Sociobiology* 3: 199-207.

6087 Barner-Barry, C. 1983. Zum Verhaltnis zwischen Ethologie und Politik. In *Politik und Biologie*. Edited by Flohr, H, W Tonnesmann. Berlin: Verlag Paul Parey.

6088 Barner-Barry, C. 1986. Informal organization and the study of bureaucratic behavior: A research agenda. In *Biology and Bureaucracy*. Edited by White, E, J Losco. Lanham, MD: University Press of America.

6089 Barner-Barry, C. 1986. An introduction to nonparticipant observational research techniques. *Politics and the Life Sciences* 5: 139-146.

6090 Barnett, S A. 1990. Evolutionary science or misguided metaphor? Repetition-compulsion in political biology. *Australian Journal of Politics and History* 36: 327-342.

6091 Beck, H. 1976. Attentional struggles and silencing strategies in a human political conflict: The case of the Vietnam moratoria. In *The Social Structure of Attention*. Edited by Chance, M R A, R D Larson. New York: Wiley.

6092 Beck, H. 1979. The Ocean-Hill Brownsville and Cambodian-Kent State crises: A biobehavioral approach to human sociobiology. *Behavioral Science* 24: 25-36.

6093 Beer, F A. 1979. The epidemiology of peace and war. *International Studies Quarterly* 23: 45-86.

6094 Brittan, A. 1989. *Masculinity and Power*. New York: Blackwell.

6095 Corning, P, C H Corning. 1972. Toward a general theory of violent aggression. *Social Science Information* 11: 7-35.

6096 Corning, P. 1983. Politik und evolution. In *Politik und Biologie*. Edited by Flohr, H, W Tonnesmann. Berlin: Verlag Paul Parey.

6097 Corning, P, S Corning. 1986. *Winning With Synergy*. New York: Harper & Row.

6098 Corning, P, S M Hines. 1988. Political development and political evolution. *Politics and the Life Sciences* 6: 141-155, 164-168.

6099 Crow, W J, R C Noel. 1975. An experiment in simulated historical decision-making. In *A Psychological Examination of Political Leaders*. Edited by Hermann, M G, T W Milburn. New York: Free Press.

6100 Darrough, M, R H Blank, eds. 1983. *Biological Differences and Social Equality*. Boulderlo.: Greenwood Press.

6101 Davis, J C. 1986. Surface and depth in political biology. *Journal of Social and Biological Structures* 9: 94-103.

6102 Davis, J C. 1986. Roots of political behavior. In *Political Psychology*. Edited by Hermann, M. San Fransisco: Jossey-Bass.

6103 Davis, J C. 1986. Biology, Darwinism, and political science. *Journal of Social and Biological Structures* 9: 227-240.

6104 Davis, K, M Leijenaar, J Oldersma, eds. 1991. *The Gender of Power*. London: Sage Publications.

6105 de Vree, J. 1982. *Foundations of the Social and Political Process: The Dynamics of Human Behaviour, Politics and Society*. Bilthoven: Prime Press.

6106 Deutsch, K W. 1963. *The Nerves of Government*. New York: Free Press.

6107 Di Stefano, C. 1991. *Configurations of Masculinity: A Feminist Perspective on Modern Political Theory*. Ithaca: Cornell University Press.

6108 Eagly, A H, S J Karau. 1991. Gender and the emergence of leaders: A meta-analysis. *Journal of Personality and Social Psychology* 60: 685-710.

6109 Eagly, A H, M G Makhijani, B G Klonsky. 1992. Gender and the evaluation of leaders: A meta-analysis. *Psychological Bulletin* 111: 3-22.

6110 Eltung, A. 1986. What is biopolitics? In *Essays in Human Sociobiology*. Edited by Wind, J, V Reynolds. Brussels: Free University of Brussels.

6111 Eltung, A, ed. 1986. *Menschliches Handeln und Sozialstruktur.* Leverkusen: Leske.

6112 Eltung, A. 1987. Biological bases of political prejudices. In *The Sociobiology of Ethnocentrism.* Edited by Reynolds, V, et al. Kent: Croom Helm.

6113 Ferguson, R B, ed. 1984. *Warfare, Culture and Environment.* New York: Academic press.

6114 Finder, J. 1987. Biological bases of prejudice. *International Political Science Review* 8: 183-192.

6115 Fischer, F. 1989. *Technocracy and the Politics of Expertise: Managerial and Policy Perspectives.* Newbury Park, CA: Sage.

6116 Fleming, T. 1988. *The Politics of Human Nature.* New Brunswick, NJ: Transaction Books.

6117 Flohr, H. 1979. Evolution-Politik-Wissenschaft. In *Sozialforschung und Soziale Demokratie.* Edited by Neuman, L F. Bonn: Verlag Neue Gesellschaft.

6118 Flohr, H, W Tonnesmann, eds. 1983. *Politik und Biologie.* Berlin: Verlag Paul Parey.

6119 Flohr, H. 1984. Darwin und die Politik. Vom Wert der biosozialen Perspektive. In *Idee und Pragmatik in der politischen Entscheidung.* Edited by Rebe, B, et al. Bonn: Verlag Neue Gesellschaft.

6120 Foster, M L, R A Rubemstein, eds. 1986. *Peace and War: Cross-cultural Perspectives.* New Brunswick, NJ: Transaction Books.

6121 Frank, R S. 1973. *Linguistic Analysis of Political Elites: A Theory of Verbal Kinesics.* Beverly Hills, CA: Sage.

6122 Frank, R S. 1977. Nonverbal and paralinguistic analysis of political behavior: The first McGovern-Humphrey California primary debate. In *A Psychological Examination of Political Leaders.* Edited by Hermann, M G, T W Milbum. New York: Free Press.

6123 Gay, P. 1983. *The Education of the Senses.* New York: Oxford University Press.

6124 George, A. 1974. Adaptation to stress in political decision making: The individual, small group, and organizational context. In *Coping and Adaptation.* Edited by Coelho, G V, D A Hamburg, J E Adams. New York: Basic Books.

6125 Gilder, G. 1981. *Men and Marriage*. Gretna, LA: Pelican.

6126 Goldschmidt, W. 1990. *The Human Career*. Cambridge, MA: Blackwell.

6127 Goode, W J. 1970. *World Revolution and Family Patterns*. New York: Free Press.

6128 Goody, J. 1971. *Technology, Tradition, and the State in Africa*. London: Oxford University Press.

6129 Gurr, T R, ed. 1980. *Handbook of Political Conflict*. New York: Free Press.

6130 Gwartney-Gibbs, P, D Lach. 1991. Sex differences in nuclear war attitudes. *Journal of Peace Research* 28: 161-174.

6131 Hammar, T, ed. 1985. *European Immigration Policy: A Comparative Study*. Cambridge: Cambridge University Press.

6132 Handwerker, W, ed. 1989. *Births and Power: The Politics of Reproduction*. Boulderlo: Westview Press.

6133 Hartigan, R S. 1988. *The Future Remembered: An Essay in Biopolitics*. Notre Dame: Notre Dame University Press.

6134 Herrnstein, R J. 1973. *I.Q. in the Meritocracy*. Boston: Little Brown.

6135 Heyer, P. 1982. *Nature, Human Nature, and Society*. Westport, CT: Greenwood.

6136 Hinchman, L, S Hinchman. 1989. 'Deep ecology' and the revival of natural right. *Western Political Quarterly* 42: 201-228.

6137 Hinde, R, ed. 1992. *The Institution of War*. New York: St Martin's Press.

6138 Hirsch, L P, T C Wiegele. 1981. Methodological aspects of voice stress analysis. In *Biopolitics*. Edited by Watts, M W. San Francisco: Jossey-Bass.

6139 Hopple, G. 1980. *Political Psychology and Biopolitics*. Boulderlo: Westview Press.

6140 Hormann, W. 1984. *Biologie und Politik*. Der Staat am Steuer der Evolution. Tübingen: Hohenrain.

6141 Hughes, A. 1988. Kin networks and political leadership in a stateless society. *Journal of Social and Biological Structures* 9: 29-44.

6142 Itzkoff, S W. 1991. *Human Intelligence and National Power: A Political Essay in Sociobiology.* New York: Peter Lang.

6143 Jaggar, A. 1983. *Feminist Politics and Human Nature.* Totowa, NJ: Rowman and Allanheld.

6144 Jaros, D, E S White. 1983. Sex, endocrines, and political behavior. *Women and Politics* 3: 129-146.

6145 Johnson, G R. 1986. Kin selection, socialization, and patriotism. *Politics and the Life Sciences* 4: 127-140.

6146 Johnson, G R. 1986. Some thoughts on human extinction, kin recognition, and the impact of patriotism on inclusive fitness. *Politics and the Life Sciences* 4: 149-154.

6147 Johnson, G R. 1987. In the name of the fatherland. *International Political Science Review* 8: 165-174.

6148 Johnson, G R, S H Ratwik, T Sawyer. 1987. The evocative significance of kin terms in patriotic speech. In *The Sociobiology of Ethnocentrism.* Edited by Reynolds, V, et al. Kent: Croom Helm.

6149 Jones, D C. 1983. Power structures and perceptions of power holders in same-sex groups of young children. *Women and Politics* 3: 147-164.

6150 Kaufman, H. 1975. The natural history of human organizations. *Administration and Society* 7: 131-149.

6151 Kay, S A, D B Meikle. 1983. Political ideology, sociobiology, and the U. S. women's rights movement. *Women and Politics* 3: 67-96.

6152 Kisiel, S V. 1984. Voice stress analysis as a methodology for the study of international crises. In *Foreign Policy Decision Making.* Edited by Sylvan, D A, S Chan. New York: Praeger.

6153 Kleck, G, K McElrath. 1991. The effects of weaponry on human violence. *Social Forces* 69: 669-692.

6154 Korda, M. 1986. Symbols of power. In *Organizational Reality: Reports from the Firing Line.* Edited by Frost, P J, et al. Pp. 145-57. Glenview, IL: Scott, Foresman.

6155 Kort, F. 1986. Considerations for a biological basis of civil rights and liberties. *Journal of Social and Biological Structures* 9: 37-52.

6156 Kort, F. 1987. Developments in the ethology of law. *Politics and the Life Sciences* 6: 81-85.

6157 Kuper, L. 1989. The prevention of genocide: Cultural and structural indicators of genocidal threat. *Ethnic and Racial Studies* 12: 157-174.

6158 Laponce, J A. 1981. *Left and Right: The Topography of Political Perceptions.* Toronto: University of Toronto Press.

6159 Laponce, J A. 1987. Relating physiological, physical, and political phenomena: Center and centrality. *International Political Science Review* 8: 175-182.

6160 Laponce, J A. 1987. *Languages and Their Territories.* Toronto: University of Toronto Press.

6161 Leacock, E, R B Lee. 1982. *Politics and History in Band Societies.* Cambridge: Cambridge University Press.

6162 Lefebvre, V. 1982. *The Algebra of Conscience: A Comparative Analysis of Western and Soviet Ethical Systems.* Boston: Reidel.

6163 Lerner, G. 1986. *The Creation of Patriarchy.* New York: Oxford University Press.

6164 Levy, J. 1982. The contagion of great power war behavior, 1495-1975. *American Journal of Political Science* 26: 562-584.

6165 Lopreato, J, P A Green. 1990. *The evolutionary foundations of revolution.* Edited by van der Dennen, J, V Falger. Sociobiology and Conflict. London: Chapman & Hall.

6166 Losco, J. 1985. Evolution, consciousness, and political thinking. *Political Behavior* 7: 223-247.

6167 Losco, J. 1987. On the notion of rule: A construct for integrating the behavioral and life sciences. *International Political Science Review* 8: 155-164.

6168 Madson, D. 1985. A biochemical property related to power-seeking in humans. *American Political Science Review* 79: 448-457.

6169 Masters, R D. 1983. The biological nature of the state. *World Politics* 25: 161-193.

6170 Masters, R D. 1986. Why bureaucracy? In *Biology and Bureaucracy*. Edited by White, E, J Losco. Pp. 149-192. Lanham, MD: University Press of America.

6171 Masters, R D. 1986. Ostracism, voice and exit: The biology of social participation. In *Ostracism: A Social and Biological Phenomenon*. Edited by Gruter, M, R D Masters. Pp. 231-47. New York: Elsevier.

6172 Masters, R D. 1987. Evolutionary biology and natural right. In *The Crisis of Liberal Democracy*. Edited by Soffer, W, K Deutsch. Albany, NY: SUNY.

6173 Masters, R D. 1989. Obligation and the new naturalism. *Biology and Philosophy* 4: 17-32.

6174 Masters, R D. 1989. Gender and political cognition: Integrating evolutionary biology and political science response. *Politics and the Life Sciences* 8: 31-40.

6175 Masters, R D. 1989. *The Nature of Politics*. New Haven: Yale University Press.

6176 Masters, R D. 1991. Individual and cultural differences in response to leaders' nonverbal displays. *Journal of Social Issues* 47: 151-166.

6177 Masters, R D, M Gruter, eds. 1992. *The Sense of Justice: An Inquiry into the Biological Foundations of Law*. Newbury Park, CA: Sage.

6178 Maxwell, M. 1990. *Morality among Nations. An Evolutionary View*. Albany, NY: SUNY.

6179 McHugo, G, J T Lanzatta, D G Sullivan, R D Masters, B Englis. 1985. Emotional reactions to a political leaders' expressive displays. *Journal of Personality and Social Psychology* 49: 1513-29.

6180 Modelski, G. 1990. Is world politics evolutionary learning? *International Organization* 44: 1-24.

6181 Neely, J C. 1981. *Gender: The Myth of Equality*. New York: Simon & Schuster.

6182 O'Manique, J. 1990. Universal and inalienable rights: A search for foundations. *Human Rights Quarterly* 12: 465-485.

6183 Ohman, A, U Dimberg. 1984. An evolutionary perspective on human social behavior. In *Sociophysiology.* Edited by Waid, W. Pp. 47-86. New York: Springer.

6184 Ophuls, W. 1977. *Ecology and the Politics of Scarcity: Prologue to a Political Theory of the Steady State.* San Francisco: Freeman.

6185 Palgi, M, J R Blasi, M Rosner, M Safir, eds. 1983. *Sexual Equality: The Israeli Kibbutz Tests the Theories.* Norwood, PA: Norwood Editions.

6186 Peterson, S A. 1981. Psychophysiological arousal as a predictor of student protest. *Journal of Political Science* 8: 108-113.

6187 Peterson, S A. 1985. Death, experience and politics. *Political Psychology* 6: 19-27.

6188 Peterson, S A. 1990. *Political Behavior: Patterns in Everyday Life.* Newbury Park, CA: Sage.

6189 Pettman, R. 1975. *Human Behavior and World Politics.* New York: St. Martin's Press.

6190 Pettman, R. 1981. *Biopolitics and International Values.* New York: Pergamon Press.

6191 Pettman, R. 1987. Politics: An aspect of cultural evolution. *Politics and the Life Sciences* 5: 234-237.

6192 Platt, J R. 1964. Strong inference. *Science* 146: 347-53.

6193 Potter, V R. 1990. Getting to the Year 3000: Can global bioethics overcome evolution's fatal flaw? *Perspectives in Biology and Medicine* 34: 89-98.

6194 Re, R N. 1986. *Bioburst: The Impact of Modern Biology on the Affairs of Man.* Baton Rouge: Louisiana State University Press.

6195 Rieber, R W, ed. 1991. *The Psychology of War and Peace: The Image of the Enemy.* New York: Plenum.

6196 Ritchie, D G. 1891. *Darwinism and Politics.* London: Swan Sonnenschein.

6197 Rota, F P. 1986. *Menschen-Staaten-Umwelt.* Munich: Minerva Press.

6198 Schubert, G. 1982. Political ethology. *Micropolitics* 2: 51-86.

6199 Schubert, G. 1985. Sexual differences in political behavior. *Political Science Review* 15: 1-68.

6200 Schubert, G. 1989. *Evolutionary Politics.* Carbondale, IL: Southern Illinois University Press.

6201 Schubert, G, R D Masters, eds. 1991. *Primate Politics.* Carbondale: Southern Illinois University Press.

6202 Schultz, V. 1990. Telling stories about women and work: Judicial interpretations of sex segregation in the workplace in title VII cases raising the lack of interest argument. *Harvard Law Review* 103: 1749-1843.

6203 Shaw, R P, Y Wong. 1989. *Genetic Seeds of Warfare: Evolution, Nationalism, and Patriotism.* Boston: Unwin Hyman.

6204 Somit, A. 1990. Human, chimps, and bonobos: The biological bases of aggression, war, and peacemaking. *Journal of Conflict Resolution* 34: 553-582.

6205 Stagdill, R M, A E Coons, eds. 1957. *Leader Behavior: Its Description and Measurement.* Columbus: Ohio State University.

6206 Steklis, H D, A Walter. 1991. Culture, biology, and behavior: A mechanistic approach. *Human Nature* 2: 137-169.

6207 Vanhanen, T. 1990. *The Process of Democratization: A Comparative Study of 147 States 1980-1988.* Bristol, PA: Crane Russak.

6208 Volkan, V, J Montville, D Julius, eds. 1990. *The Psychodynamics of International Relationships.* Lexington, MA: Lexington Books.

6209 Waddell, C. 1990. The role of pathos in the decision making process: A study in the rhetoric of science policy. *Quarterly Journal of Speech* 76: 381-400.

6210 Watts, M W. 1984. *Biopolitics and Gender.* New York: Haworth Press.

6211 White, E, ed. 1981. *Human Sociobiology and Politics.* Lexington, MA: Lexington Books.

6212 White, E, J Losco, eds. 1986. *Biology and Bureaucracy.* Lanham, Md: University Press of America.

6213 Wickler, W. 1972. *The Biology of the Ten Commandments.* New York: McGraw-Hill.

6214 Wiegel, T C, ed. 1982. *Biology and the Social Sciences.* Boulder: Westview Press.

6215 Wiegele, T C. 1979. *Biopolitics.* Boulder: Westview Press.

6216 Wiegele, T, G Hilton, K Oots, S Kisiel. 1985. *Leaders Under Stress: A Psychobiological Analysis of International Crisis.* Durham, NC: Duke University Press.

6217 Willhoite, F H. 1981. Rank and reciprocity: Speculations on human emotions and political life. In *Human Sociobiology and Politics.* Edited by White, E. Lexington, MA: Lexington Books.

# 19

# History and Philosophy

6218 Albury, W R. 1980. Politics and rhetoric in the sociobiology debate. *Social Studies of Science* 10: 519-36.

6219 Alexander, R. 1980. Evolution, social behavior and ethics. In *Knowing and Valuing: The Search for Common Roots.* Edited by Engelhardt, H T. Pp. 124-155. Hastings on Hudson: Hastings Center.

6220 Archer, J. 1991. Human sociobiology: Basic concepts and limitations. *Journal of Social Issues* 47: 11-26.

6221 Aronoff, J, ed. 1987. *The Emergence of Personality.* New York: Springer.

6222 Ayala, F J, T Dobzhanky, eds. 1974. *Studies in the Philosophy of Biology.* Berkeley: University of California Press.

6223 Ayala, F J. 1982. Beyond Darwinism? The challenge of macroevolution to the synthetic theory of evolution. In *Philosophy of Science Association, 1982.* Edited by Asquith, P, T Nickles. Pp. 275-291. East Lansing, MI: Philosophy of Science Association.

6224 Ayala, F J. 1987. The biological roots of morality. *Biology and Philosophy* 2: 235-252.

6225 Babloyantz, A. 1986. *Molecules, Dynamics, and Life: An Introduction to Self-organization of Matter.* New York: Wiley.

6226 Baldwin, J M. 1896. A new factor in evolution. *American Naturalist* 30: 441-451, 536-553.

6227 Bannister, R C. 1979. *Social Darwinism: Science and Myth in Anglo-American Thought.* Philadelphia: Temple University Press.

6228 Barash, D P, J E Lipton. 1985. *The Caveman and the Bomb: Human Nature, Evolution and Nuclear War.* New York: McGraw-Hill.

6229 Barash, D P. 1986. *The Hare and the Tortise: Culture, Biology and Human Nature.* New York: Penguin.

6230 Barlow, G, J Silverberg, eds. 1980. *Sociobiology: Beyond Nature/Nurture?* Washington, DC: American Association for the Advancement of Science.

6231 Barlow, G. 1991. Nature-nurture and the debates surrounding ethology and sociobiology. *American Zoologist* 31: 286-296.

6232 Barnett, S A. 1983. Humanity and natural selection. *Ethology and Sociobiology* 4: 35-51.

6233 Barnett, S A. 1990. The reductionist imperative and the nature of humanity. *Interdisciplinary Science Reviews* 15: 119-132.

6234 Barrett, P H. 1980. *Metaphysics, Materialism, and the Evolution of Mind: Early Writings of Charles Darwin.* Chicago: University of Chicago Press.

6235 Barthelemy-Madaule, M. 1982. *Lamarck: The Mythical Precursor.* Cambridge: M.I.T. Press.

6236 Bateson, P P G. 1989. Evolution and ethics. In *Evolutionary Studies.* Edited by Keynes, M, G A Harrison. London: Macmillan.

6237 Bateson, P G. 1989. Does evolutionary biology contribute to ethics? *Biology and Philosophy* 4: 287-302.

6238 Beatty, J. 1981. What's wrong with the received view of evolutionary theory? In *Philosophy of Science Association 1980.* Edited by Asquith, P, R M Giere. Pp. 397-426. East Lansing, MI: Philosophy of Science Association.

6239 Beatty, J. 1982. What's in a word? Coming to terms in the Darwinian revolution. *Journal of the History of Biology* 15: 215-239.

6240 Beatty, J. 1987. Chance and natural selection. *Philosophy of Science* 51: 183-211.

6241 Beatty, J. 1987. Dobzhansky and drift: Facts, values, and chance in evolutionary biology. In *The Probabilistic Revolution.* Edited by Kruger, L. Cambridge: M.I.T. Press.

6242 Bell, R W, N J Bell, eds. 1989. *Sociobiology and the Social Sciences.* Lubbock: Texas Tech University Press.

6243 Berry, T. 1989. *The Dream of the Earth.* San Francisco: Sierra Club.

6244 Biervliet, H, et al. 1980. Biologism, racism and eugenics in the anthropology and sociology of the 1930s. *Netherlands Journal of Sociology* 16: 69-92.

6245 Bixler, R H. 1980. Nature versus nurture: The timeless anachronism. *Merrill-Palmer Quarterly* 26: 153-159.

6246 Blinderman, C. 1986. *The Piltdown Inquest.* New York: Prometheus.

6247 Boakes, R. 1984. *From Darwin to Behaviourism: Psychology and the Minds of Animals.* Cambridge: Cambridge University Press.

6248 Bock, K. 1980. *Human Nature and History: A Response to Sociobiology.* New York: Columbia University Press.

6249 Bodenheimer, E. 1986. Individual and organized society from the perspective of a philosophical anthropology. *Journal of Social and Biological Structures* 9: 207-226.

6250 Bonner, J T. 1974. *On Development: The Biology of Form.* Cambridge: Harvard University Press.

6251 Bonner, J. 1988. *The Evolution of Complexity.* Princeton: Princeton University Press.

6252 Bowlby, J. 1991. *Charles Darwin: A Biography.* New York: Norton.

6253 Bowler, P. 1976. Malthus, Darwin and the concept of struggle. *Journal of the History of Ideas* 38: 631-650.

6254 Bowler, P. 1983. *The Eclipse of Darwinism: Anti-Darwinian Evolution Theories in the Decades around 1900.* Baltimore: Johns Hopkins.

6255 Bowler, P. 1984. *Evolution: The History of an Idea.* Berkeley: University of California Press.

6256 Bowler, P. 1987. *Theories of Human Evolution: A Century of Debate 1844-1944.* Oxford: Blackwell.

6257 Bowler, P. 1988. *The Non-Darwinian Revolution: Reinterpreting a Historical Myth.* Baltimore: Johns Hopkins.

6258 Bowler, P. 1989. *The Invention of Progress: The Victorians and the Past.* Oxford: Blackwell.

6259 Bowler, P. 1990. *Charles Darwin: The Man and His Influence.* Oxford: Blackwell.

6260 Bradie, M. 1986. Assessing evolutionary epistemology. *Biology and Philosophy* 1: 401-459.

6261 Brandon, R N, N Hornstein. 1986. From icons to symbols: Some speculations on the origins of language. *Biology and Philosophy* 1:169-190.

6262 Brooks, D, E Wiley. 1986. *Evolution as Entropy: Toward a United Theory of Biology.* Chicago: University of Chicago Press.

6263 Brown, F. 1986. The evolution of Darwin's theism. *Journal of the History of Biology* 19: 1-45.

6264 Burkhardt, R W. 1977. *The Spirit of System: Lamarck and Evolutionary Biology.* Cambridge: Harvard University Press.

6265 Burstein, Z. 1991. A new concept of developmental and evolutionary adaptation. *Journal of Social and Biological Structures* 14: 15-34.

6266 Buss, L. 1987. *The Evolution of Individuality.* Princeton: Princeton University Press.

6267 Callebaut, W. 1986. Current issues in the philosophy of biology. *Philosophica* 37: 1-162.

6268 Callebaut, W, R Pinxten, eds. 1986. *Evolutionary Epistemology: A Multiparadigm Program.* Dordrecht: Reidl.

6269 Calvin, W H. 1986. *The River that Flows Uphill: A Journey from the Big Bang to the Big Brain.* New York: Macmillan.

6270 Calvin, W. 1990. *The Cerebral Symphony.* New York: Bantam.

6271 Campbell, D T. 1974. Evolutionary epistemology. In *The Philosophy of Karl Popper.* Edited by Schilpp, P A. Pp. 413-463. LaSalle, Ill.: Open Court Publishing.

6272 Campbell, D T. 1982. Evolutionary epistemology. In *Learning, Development, and Culture: Essays in Evolutionary Epistemology.* Edited by Plotkin, H C. Pp. 78-108. Chichester: Wiley.

6273 Campbell, J. 1982. *Grammatical Man: Information, Entropy, Language and Life.* New York: Simon & Schuster.

6274 Campbell, C, W Hodes. 1991. The scala naturae revisited: Evolutionary scales and anagenesis in comparative psychology. *Journal of Comparative Psychology* 105: 211-221.

6275 Canguilhem, G. 1989. *The Normal and the Pathological.* Cambridge: M.I.T. Press.

6276 Caporael, L R, M B Brewer. 1991. The quest for human nature: Social and scientific issues in evolutionary psychology. *Journal of Social Issues* 47: 1-22.

6277 Capra, F. 1982. *The Turning Point.* New York: Simon & Schuster.

6278 Caton, H. 1973. Objectivity: Man as a Machine. In *The Origin of Subjectivity: An Essay on Descartes.* Pp. 74-100. New Haven: Yale University Press.

6279 Caton, H, ed. 1990. *The Samoa Reader: Anthropologists Take Stock.* Lanham, MD: University Press of America.

6280 Cattell, R. 1972. *A New Morality from Science: Beyondism.* New York: Pergamon Press.

6281 Chaisson, E. 1987. *The Life Era.* Boston: Atlantic Monthly Press.

6282 Chardin, P T d. 1964. *The Future of Man.* New York: Harper & Row.

6283 Charlesworth, W R. 1992. Darwin and developmental psychology: Past and present. *Developmental Psychology* 28: 5-16.

6284 Christen, Y. 1979. *L'Heure de la sociobiologie.* Paris: Albin Michel.

6285 Christen, Y. 1981. *Le grand affrontement: Marx et Darwin.* Paris: Albin Michel.

6286 Christen, Y. 1982. *Le dossier Darwin: La selection naturelle, l'eugenisme, la sociobiologie, le darwinisme social.* Paris: Editions Copernic.

6287 Clarke, A. 1986. Evolutionary epistemology and the scientific method. *Philosophica* 37: 151-162.

6288 Cliquet, R L. 1984. The relevance of sociobiological theory to emancipatory feminism. *Journal of Human Evolution* 13: 117-128.

6289 Collias, N E. 1991. The role of American zoologists and behavioural ecologists in the development of animal sociology. *Animal Behaviour* 41: 613-632.

6290 Colp, R. 1982. The myth of the Darwin-Marx letter. *History of Political Economy* 14: 461-482.

6291 Corsi, P. 1988. *The Age of Lamarck: Evolutionary Theories in France 1970-1830.* Berkeley: University of California Press.

6292 Cracraft, J. 1987. Species concept and the ontology of evolution. *Biology and Philosophy* 2: 329-346.

6293 Cravens, H. 1978. *The Triumph of Evolution: American Scientists and the Heredity-Environment Controversy.* Philadelphia: University of Pennsylvania Press.

6294 Cronin, H. 1991. *The Ant and the Peacock: Altruism and Sexual Selection from Darwin to Today.* New York: Cambridge University Press.

6295 Crook, D P. 1989. 'Man—the fighting animal': Belligerent images of humankind in the Anglo-American world, 1914-1918. *Australiasian Journal of American Studies* 8: 25-39.

6296 Cullis, C A. 1984. Environmentally induced DNA changes. In *Evolutionary Theory: Paths into the Future.* Edited by Pollard, J. Pp. 203-216. New York: Wiley.

6297 Daly, M, M Wilson. 1991. Anti-science and the pre-darwinian image of mankind. *American Anthropologist* 93: 162-165.

6298 Danielli, J, M Danielli, D McGiuiness, B Goodwin, K Pribram, R Rosen, H Wheeler. 1982. Constructional biology: A new paradigm. *Journal of Social and Biological Structures* 15: 15-47.

6299 Darlington, C D. 1948. *The Conflict of Science and Society.* London: Watts.

6300 Davies, P. 1988. *The Cosmic Blueprint.* New York: Simon & Schuster.

6301 Davis, B. 1976. Novel pressure on the advance of science. *Annals of the New York Academy of Sciences* 265: 193-205.

6302 Davis, B. 1986. *Storm Over Biology: Essays on Science, Sentiment and Public Policy.* Buffalo: Prometheus.

6303 Dawkins, R. 1978. Replicator selection and the extended phenotype. *Zeitschrift für Tierpsychologie* 47: 61-76.

6304 Dawkins, R. 1982. *The Extended Phenotype: The Gene as the Unit of Selection*. San Francisco: Freeman.

6305 de Vree, J K. 1989. *Order and Disorder in the Human Universe: The Foundations of Behavioral and Social Science*. Bilthoven: Prime Press.

6306 Delbrück, M. 1985. *Mind from Matter?: An Essay on Evolutionary Epistemology*. London: Blackwell.

6307 Delger, C N. 1991. *In Search of Human Nature: The Decline and Revival of Darwinism in American Social Thought*. New York: Oxford University Press.

6308 Denton, M. 1985. *Evolution: A Theory in Crisis*. New York: Adler and Adler.

6309 Depew, D, B Weber, eds. 1985. *Evolution at a Crossroads: The New Biology and the New Philosophy of Science*. Cambridge: M.I.T. Press.

6310 Desmond, A. 1989. *The Politics of Evolution: Morphology, Medicine, and Reform in Radical London*. Chicago: University of Chicago Press.

6311 Desmond, A, J Moore. 1991. *Darwin*. London: Michael Joseph.

6312 Devereux, P. 1989. *Earthmind*. New York: Harper & Row.

6313 Dewsbury, D A. 1984. *Comparative Psychology in the Twentieth Century*. Stroudsburg, PA: Hutchinson Ross.

6314 Dewsbury, D A, ed. 1985. *Leaders in the Study of Animal Behavior*. Lewisburg: Bucknell University Press.

6315 Di Gregorio, M A. 1984. *T.H. Huxley's Place in Natural Science*. New Haven: Yale University Press.

6316 Dover, G A. 1982. Molecular drive: A cohesive mode of species formation. *Nature* 299: 338-347.

6317 Dretske, F. 1988. *Explaining Behavior: Reasons in a World of Causes*. Cambridge: M.I.T. Press.

6318 du Bois-Raymond, E. 1886. Kulturgeschichte and Naturgeschichte. In *Reden von Emil de Bois-Raymond*. Pp. 240-306. Leipzig: Verlag von Veit.

6319 Dubos, R. 1965. *Man Adapting.* New Haven: Yale University Press.

6320 Dubos, R. 1974. *Beast or Angel?* New York: Scribner's.

6321 Dunn, L C, ed. 1951. *Genetics in the 20th Century: Essays on the Progress of Genetics during its First Fifty Years.* New York: Macmillan.

6322 Dyson, F. 1981. *Disturbing the Universe.* New York: Harper Colophon.

6323 Dyson, F. 1985. *Infinite in All Directions.* New York: Harper & Row.

6324 Dyson, F. 1986. *Origins of Life.* Cambridge: Cambridge University Press.

6325 Dyson, F. 1992. *From Eros to Gaia.* New York: Pantheon.

6326 Eldredge, N. 1980. *Phylogenetic Patterns and the Evolutionary Process.* New York: Columbia University Press.

6327 Eldredge, N. 1985. *Time Frames: The Rethinking of Dawinian Evolution and the Theory of Punctuated Equilibria.* New York: Columbia University Press.

6328 Eldredge, N. 1985. *Unfinished Sythnesis: Biological Hierarchies and Modern Evolutionary Thought.* New York: Oxford University Press.

6329 Ellegard, A. 1990. *Darwin and the General Reader: The Reception of Darwin's Theory of Evolution in the British Periodical Press, 1859-1872.* Chicago: University of Chicago Press.

6330 Ereshefsky, M, ed. 1992. *The Units of Evolution: Essays on the Nature of Species.* Cambridge: M.I.T. Press.

6331 Erhlich, P. 1976. *Biology and Society.* New York: McGraw-Hill.

6332 Fabel, A. 1991. The phenomenon of discovery: The unity of a new science and the perennial wisdom. *Journal of Social and Biological Structures* 14: 1-14.

6333 Fales, E. 1982. Natural kinds and freaks of nature. *Philosophy of Science* 49: 67-90.

6334 Falk, A E. 1981. Purpose, feedback and evolution. *Philosophy of Science* 48: 198-217.

6335 Fay, M. 1978. Did Marx offer to dedicate Capital to Darwin? *Journal of the History of Ideas* 39: 133-146.

6336 Fetzer, J H, ed. 1985. *Sociobiology and Epistemology.* Dordrecht: Reidel.

6337 Feuer, L S. 1977. Marx and Engels as sociobiologists. *Survey* 23: 109-136.

6338 Feuer, L S. 1978. The case of the Marx-Darwin letter. *Encounter* October: 62-78.

6339 Feuer, L. 1978. Marx and Engels as sociobiologists. *Survey* 23: 109-136.

6340 Flanagan, O J. 1981. Is morality epiphenomenal? The failure of the sociobiological reduction of ethics. *Philosophical Forum* 13: 207-225.

6341 Fleming, D. 1967. Attitude: A history of a concept. *Perspectives in American History* 1: 287-365.

6342 Fox, R. 1983. *The Red Lamp of Incest: An Inquiry into the Origins of Mind and Society.* Notre Dame: University of Notre Dame Press.

6343 Fox, R. 1987. The disunity of anthropology and the unity of mankind: An introduction to the concept of the ethosystem. In *Waymarks: The Notre Dame Inaugural Lectures in Anthropology.* Edited by Moore, K. Pp. 17-41. South Bend: University of Notre Dame Press.

6344 Fox, R. 1989. *The Search for Society: Quest for a Biosocial Science and Morality.* New Brunswick: Rutgers University Press.

6345 Fox, R. 1989. *The Violent Imagination.* New Brunswick: Rutgers University Press.

6346 Freeman, D. 1974. The evolutionary theories of Charles Darwin and Herbert Spencer. *Current Anthropology* 15: 211-236.

6347 Freeman, D. 1980. Sociobiology: The "antidiscipline" of anthropology. In *Sociobiology Examined.* Edited by Montagu, A. Pp. 198-219. New York: Oxford University Press.

6348 Freeman, D. 1983. *Margaret Mead and Samoa: The Making and Unmaking of an Anthropological Myth.*  Cambridge: Harvard University Press.

6349 Freeman, D. 1983. Inductivism and the test of truth: A rejoinder to Lowell D. Holmes and others. *Canberra Anthropology*  6: 101-192.

6350 Frisch, K v. 1974. *Animal Architecture.*  New York: Harcourt Brace Jovanovich.

6351 Frolov, I. 1977. Genes or culture? A Marxist perspective on humankind. *Biology and Philosophy*  1: 89-108.

6352 Frolov, I. 1986. *Man-Science-Humanism: A New Synthesis.*  Moscow: Progress Publishers.

6353 Fuller, W, ed. 1971. *The Social Impact of Modern Biology.*  London: Routledge.

6354 Futuyma, D J. 1983. *Science on Trial: The Case for Evolution.*  New York: Pantheon Books.

6355 Geissler, E, W Scheler. 1983. *Darwin Today.*  Berlin: Akademie-Verlag.

6356 Gillespie, N C. 1979. *Charles Darwin and the Problem of Creation.*  Chicago: University of Chicago Press.

6357 Gillispie, C C. 1959. *Genesis and Geology.*  New York: Harper & Row.

6358 Glass, B. 1959. *Forerunnrs of Darwin, 1745-1859.*  Baltimore: Johns Hopkins.

6359 Glass, B. 1970. *The Timely and the Timeless: The Interrelationships of Science, Education, and Society.*  New York: Basic Books.

6360 Glass, B. 1985. *Progress or Catastrophe? The Nature of Biological Science and Its Impact on Human Society.*  New York: Praeger.

6361 Gleick, J. 1988. *Chaos: Making a New Science.*  New York: Penguin.

6362 Goodall, J. 1990. *Through a Window: My Thirty years with the Chimpanzees of Gombe.*  Boston: Houghton Mifflin.

6363 Goodwin, B, et al, eds. 1989. *Dynamic Structures in Biology.* Edinburgh: Edinburgh University Press.

6364 Gould, S. 1977. *Ever Since Darwin: Reflections in Natural History.* New York: Norton.

6365 Gould, S, R C Lewontin. 1979. The spandrels of San Marco and the Panglossian paradigm: A critique of the adaptationist programme. *Proceedings of the Royal Society (London)* 205: 581-598.

6366 Gould, S. 1980. Is a new and general theory of evolution emerging? *Paleobiology* 6: 119-130.

6367 Gould, S. 1980. *The Panda's Thumb: More Reflections in Natural History.* New York: Norton.

6368 Gould, S. 1983. *Hen's Teeth and Horse's Toes: Further Reflections in Natural History.* New York: Norton.

6369 Gould, S. 1987. *Time's Arrow, Time's Cycle.* Cambridge: Harvard University Press.

6370 Gould, S. 1991. *Bully for Brontosaurus: Reflections in Natural History.* New York: Norton.

6371 Gould, S. 1991. Exaptation: A crucial tool for evolutionary psychology. *Journal of Social Issues* 47: 43-65.

6372 Graham, L R. 1981. *Between Science and Values.* New York: Columbia University Press.

6373 Greene, J C. 1959. *The Death of Adam: Evolution and Its Impact on Western Thought.* Des Moines: Iowa State University Press.

6374 Greenwood, D. 1984. *The Taming of Evolution: The Persistence of Nonevolutionary Views in the Study of Humans.* Ithaca: Cornell University Press.

6375 Gregory, M S, A Silvers, D Sutch, eds. 1978. *Sociobiology and Human Nature: An Interdisciplinary Critique and Defence.* San Francisco: Jossey-Bass.

6376 Gregory, R L. 1981. *Mind in Science.* London: Weidenfeld.

6377 Grene, M, E Mandelsohn, eds. 1974. *Topics in the Philosophy of Biology.* Dordrecht: Reidel.

6378 Grene, M. 1986. *Dimensions of Darwinism: Themes and Counterthemes in Twentieth-Century Evolutionary Theory.* Cambridge: Cambridge University Press.

6379 Griffin, D, ed. 1988. *The Reenchantment of Science.* New York: SUNY Press.

6380 Haldane, J B S. 1924. *Daedelus, or the Science of the Future.* London: Kegan Paul.

6381 Haldane, J B S. 1963. Biological possibilities for the human species in the next ten thousand years. In *Man and his Future.* Edited by Wolstenholme, G. Pp. 337-361. London: Churchill.

6382 Haraway, D. 1989. *Primate Visions: Gender, Race, and Nature in the World of Modern Science.* New York: Routledge.

6383 Hardin, G. 1980. *Promethean Ethics: Living with Death, Competition, and Triage.* Seattle: University of Washington Press.

6384 Hardin, G. 1991. Paramount positions in ecological economics. In *Ecological Economics: The Science and Management of Sustainability.* Edited by Costanza, R. New York: Columbia University Press.

6385 Hardy, A. 1984. *Darwin and the Spirit of Man.* London: Collins.

6386 Harris, E. 1990. The universe in the light of contemporary scientific developments. In *Bell's Theorem, Quantum Theory and Conceptions of the Universe.* Edited by Kafatos, M. Boston: Kluwer.

6387 Harvey, P H, M D Pagel. 1991. *The Comparative Method in Evolutionary Biology.* New York: Oxford University Press.

6388 Hatfield, G. 1991. *The Natural and the Normative: Theories of Spatial Perception from Kant to Helmholtz.* Cambridge: M.I.T. Press.

6389 Haycraft, J B. 1895. *Darwinism and Race Progress.* London: Swann Sonnenschein.

6390 Himmelfarb, G. 1962. *Darwin and the Darwinian Revolution.* New York: Anchor.

6391 Ho, M W, P T Saunders, eds. 1984. *Beyond Neo-Darwinism.* New York: Academic.

6392 Hodge, M J S. 1983. The development of Darwin's general biological theorizing. In *Evolution from Molecules to Men*. Edited by Bendall, D S. Pp. 43-62. Cambridge: Cambridge University Press.

6393 Hoebel, E, R Currier, S Kaiser, eds. 1982. *Crisis in Anthropology. View from Spring Hill*. New York: Garland.

6394 Hoffman, A. 1983. Paleobiology at the crossroads: A critique of some modern paleobiological research programs. In *Dimensions of Dawinism*. Edited by Greene, M. Pp. 241-272. Cambridge: Cambridge University Press.

6395 Holcomb, H. 1992. *Sociobiology, Sex and Science*. Albany, NY: SUNY Press.

6396 Hrdy, S B. 1990. Raising Darwin's consciousness: Females and evolutionary theory. *Zygon* 25: 129-138.

6397 Hull, D L. 1973. *Darwin and His Critics: The Reception of Darwin's Theory of Evolution by the Scientific Community*. Cambridge: Harvard University Press.

6398 Humphrey, N. 1983. *Consciousness Regained: Chapters in the Development of Mind*. Oxford: Oxford University Press.

6399 Huxley, J. 1947. *Evolution and Ethics*. London: Pilot.

6400 Huxley, J. 1963. The future of man—Evolutionary aspects. In *Man and His Future*. Edited by Wolstenholme, G. Pp. 1-22. London: Churchill.

6401 Jackobs, J. 1984. Teleology and reduction in biology. *Biology and Philosophy* 1: 389-400.

6402 Janck, J R. 1982. Is the neodarwinian synthesis robust enough to withstand the challenge of recent discoveries in molecular biology and molecular evolution? In *Philosophy of Science Association Proceedings*. Edited by Asquith, P, T Nickles. Pp. 322-330. East Lansing, MI: Philosophy of Science Association.

6403 Jantsch, E, C Waddington, eds. 1976. *Evolution and Consciousness: Human Systems in Transition*. Reading, MA: Addison-Wesley.

6404 Jantsch, E. 1980. *The Self-Organizing Universe: Scientific and Human Implications of the Emerging Paradigm of Evolution*. Oxford: Pergamon Press.

6405 Jensen, J J, R Harré. 1981. *The Philosophy of Evolution.* New York: St Martin's.

6406 Jones, G. 1980. *Social Darwinism and English Thought.* Brighton: Harvester.

6407 Jordan, W. 1991. *Divorce Among the Gulls: An Uncommon Look at Human Nature.* Berkeley, CA: North Point Press.

6408 Jordanova, L J. 1984. *Lamarck.* Oxford: Oxford University Press.

6409 Judson, H F. 1979. *The Eighth Day of Creation: Makers of the Revolution in Biology.* New York: Simon & Schuster.

6410 Kammerer, P. 1924. *The Inheritance of Acquired Characteristics.* New York: Boni and Liveright.

6411 Kauffman, S. 1992. *Origins of order: Self-organization and Selection in Evolution.* New York: Oxford University Press.

6412 Kayes, H L. 1986. *The Social Meaning of Modern Biology: From Social Darwinism to Sociobiology.* New Haven: Yale University Press.

6413 Kitahara, M. 1991. *The Tragedy of Evolution: The Human Animal Confronts Modern Society.* New York: Praeger.

6414 Kitcher, P. 1985. *Vaulting Ambition: Sociobiology and the Search for Human Nature.* Cambridge: M.I.T. Press.

6415 Kitcher, P. 1990. Developmental decomposition and the future of human behavioral ecology. *Philosophy of Science* 57: 96-117.

6416 Kleiner, S A. 1985. Darwin's and Wallace's revolutionary research programme. *British Journal of Philosophy of Science* 36: 367-392.

6417 Kohn, D. 1980. Theories to work by: Rejected theories, reproduction, and Darwin's path to natural selection. *Studies in the History of Biology* 4: 67-170.

6418 Kohn, D, ed. 1985. *The Darwinian Heritage: A Centennial Retrospect.* Princeton: Princeton University Press.

6419 Konner, M J. 1980. Human behavioral biology: Preparations for the birth of a paradigm in anthropology. In *Crisis in Anthropology.* Edited by Hoebel, E. New York: Garland Press.

6420 Konner, M J. 1982. *The Tangled Wing: Biological Constraints on the Human Spirit.* New York: Holt, Rinehart, and Winston.

6421 Krementsov, N, D Todes. 1991. On metaphors, animals, and us. *Journal of Social Issues* 47: 67-81.

6422 Kropotkin, P A. 1902. *Mutual Aid, A Factor in Evolution.* London: Heinemann.

6423 Kuper, A. 1988. *The Invention of Primitive Society: Transformations of an Illusion.* London: Routledge.

6424 Kushner, H I. 1985. Biochemistry, suicide and history: Possibilities and problems. *Journal of Inter-disciplinary History* 16: 69-86.

6425 Küppers, B. 1990. *Information and the Origin of Life.* Cambridge: M.I.T. Press.

6426 Laszlo, E. 1987. *Evolution: The Grand Synthesis.* Boston, MA: Shambhala.

6427 Layzer, D. 1990. *Cosmogenesis.* New York: Oxford University Press.

6428 Leith, B. 1982. *The Descent of Darwin.* London: Collins.

6429 Levins, R, R C Lewontin. 1985. *The Dialectical Biologist.* Cambridge: Harvard University Press.

6430 Levinson, P. 1988. *Mind at Large: Knowing in the Technological Age.* Greenwich, CT: JAI Press.

6431 Lewontin, R C. 1969. The bases of conflict in biological explanation. *Journal of the History of Biology* 2: 35-46.

6432 Lewontin, R. 1972. Testing the theory of natural selection. *Nature* 236: 181-182.

6433 Lewontin, R C. 1974. Biological determinism as a social weapon. In *Biology as a Social Weapon.* Edited by Anon. Pp. 6-20. Minneapolis: Burgess Publishing.

6434 Lewontin, R C, R Levins. 1976. The problem of Lysenkoism. In *The Radicalisation of Science.* Edited by Rose, H, S Rose. Pp. 32-64. London: Macmillan.

6435 Lewontin, R C. 1982. Sociobiology as an adaptationist program. In *Biology and the Social Sciences: An Emerging Revolution.* Edited by Wiegele, T C. Pp. 335-348. Boulderlo.: Westview.

6436 Lewontin, R C, S Rose, L Kamin. 1984. *Not in Our Genes.* New York: Pantheon Books.

6437 Lloyd, L. 1983. The nature of Darwin's support for the theory of natural selection. *Philosophy of Science* 1: 483-493.

6438 Lopreato, J. 1981. Vilfredo Pareto: Sociobiology, system, and revolution. In *The Future of the Sociological Classics.* Edited by Rhea, B. Pp. 81-113. Boston: Allen and Unwin.

6439 Lorenz, K. 1973. *Civilized Man's Eight Deadly Sins.* New York: Harcourt, Brace Jovanovich.

6440 Lumsden, C, E O Wilson. 1981. Letter to the Editor. *New York Review of Books* Sept. 24: 73-74.

6441 Luria, S, S Gould, S Singer. 1981. *A View of Life.* Menlo Park, CA: Benjamin/Cummings.

6442 MacDonald, K. 1986. Civilization and Its Discontents revisited: Freud as an evolutionary biologist. *Journal of Social and Biological Structures* 9: 307-318.

6443 Mackenzie, B D. 1977. *Behaviourism and the Limits of Scientific Method.* London: Routledge.

6444 Magoun, H W. 1960. Evolutionary concepts of brain function following Darwin and Spencer. In *Evolution after Darwin.* Edited by Tax, S. Chicago: University of Chicago Press.

6445 Makepeace, J. 1991. 'Anti-hereditarianism' in the groves of academe. *Journal of Social, Political and Economic Studies* 16: 369-384.

6446 Mallove, E. 1987. *The Quickening Universe.* New York: St Martins.

6447 Manghi, S. 1984. Two biological paradigms compared: Sociobiology and the self-organization of life. *Journal of Human Evolution* 13: 49-60.

6448 Marsh, G P. 1874. *The Earth as Modified by Human Action.* New York: Scribner's.

6449 Masters, R D. 1982. Is sociobiology reactionary? The political implications of inclusive-fitness theory. *Quarterly Review of Biology* 57: 275-292.

6450 Masters, R D. 1985. Biology, ideology, and human social behavior. *Quarterly Review of Biology* 60: 309-315.

6451 Masters, R D. 1985. Evolutionary biology, human nature, and knowledge. In *Sociobiology and Epistemology*. Edited by Fetzer, J H. Pp. 97-113. Dordrecht: Reidel.

6452 Maturana, H, F Varela. 1980. *Autopoiesis and Cognition: The Realization of the Living*. Boston: Reidel.

6453 Maxwell, M. 1984. *Human Evolution: A Philosophical Anthropology*. London: Croom Helm.

6454 Maynard Smith, J. 1984. Group selection. In *Genes, Organisms and Populations*. Edited by Brandon, R N, R M Burian. Pp. 238-249. Cambridge: M.I.T. Press.

6455 Maynard Smith, J. 1989. *Did Darwin Get it Right? Essays on Games, Sex and Evolution*. New York: Chapman and Hall.

6456 Maynard-Smith, J. 1982. *Evolution and the Theory of Games*. Cambridge, UK: Cambridge University Press.

6457 Mayr, E. 1974. Teleological and teleonomic: A new analysis. In *Boston Studies in the Philosophy of Science*. Edited by Cohen, R S, M Wartofsky. Boston: Reidel.

6458 Mayr, E. 1982. *The Growth of Biological Thought: Diversity, Evolution and Inheritance*. Cambridge: Harvard University Press.

6459 Mayr, E. 1991. The ideological resistance to Darwin's theory of natural selection. *Proceedings of the Natural Philosophical Society* 135: 123-139.

6460 Medawar, P. 1982. *Pluto's Republic*. Oxford: Oxford University Press.

6461 Menzies, R J. 1985. Genetic ideology: Observations on the biologicalization of sociology. *Canadian Review of Sociology and Anthropology* 22: 202-226.

6462 Merchant, C. 1980. *The Death of Nature*. New York: Harper & Row.

6463 Meyerson, E. 1930. *Identity and Reality*. London: George Allen & Unwin.

6464 Michod, R E. 1986. On fitness and adaptedness and their role in evolutionary expansion. *Journal of the History of Biology* 19: 289-302.

6465 Midgley, M. 1978. *Beast and Man: The Roots of Human Behavior*. Ithaca: Cornell University Press.

6466 Midgley, M. 1983. *Animals and Why They Matter*. Harmondsworth: Penguin.

6467 Midgley, M. 1985. *Evolution as a Religion: Strange Hopes and Stranger Fears*. New York: Methuen.

6468 Milkman, R, ed. 1982. *Perspectives on Evolution*. Sunderland, MA: Sinauer.

6469 Mills, S K, J H Beatty. 1979. The propensity interpretation of fitness. *Philosophy of Science* 46: 263-286.

6470 Monod, J. 1971. *Chance and Necessity: An Essay on the Natural Philosophy of Modern Biology*. New York: Knopf.

6471 Montagu, A. 1961. *Man in Process*. New York: Mentor.

6472 Montagu, A, ed. 1980. *Sociobiology Examined*. New York: Oxford University Press.

6473 Montgomery, C. 1991. *Walking with the Great Apes: Jane Goodall, Dian Fossey, Birute Galdikas*. Boston: Houghton Mifflin.

6474 Moorhead, P S, M M Kaplan, eds. 1967. *Mathematical Challenges to the Neo-Darwinian Interpretation of Evolution*. Philadelphia: Wistar Institute Press.

6475 Morowitz, H. 1987. The mind-body problem and the second law of thermodynamics. *Biology and Philosophy* 2: 271-276.

6476 Morowitz, H. 1987. *Cosmic Joy and Local Pain*. New York: Scribners.

6477 Mortessen, V. 1987. *Determinism*. Aarhus, Denmark: Aarhus University Press.

6478 Murdoch, G. 1971. Anthropology's mythology. *[T.H. Huxley Memorial Lecture]*. *Proceedings of the Royal Anthropological Institute of Great Britain and Ireland* 17-24.

6479 Murphy, J G. 1982. *Evolution, Morality, and the Meaning of Life.* Totowa, NJ: Rowman and Littlefield.

6480 Musschenga, A W. 1984. Can sociobiology contribute to moral science and ethics? *Journal of Human Evolution* 13: 137-148.

6481 Nasmyth, G. 1916. *Social Progress and the Darwinian Theory: A Study of Force as a Factor in Human Relations.* New York: Garland.

6482 Nicholson, S, ed. 1989. *The Goddess Reawakening.* New York: Quest.

6483 Nicolis, G. 1989. Physics of far-from-equilibrium systems and self-organization. In *The New Physics.* Edited by Davies, P. Cambridge: Cambridge University Press.

6484 Nitecki, M, ed. 1989. *Evolutionary Progress.* Chicago: University of Chicago Press.

6485 Novikoff, A B. 1945. The concept of integrative levels in biology. *Science* 101: 209-215.

6486 O'Grady, R T. 1986. Historical process, evolutionary explanations, and problems with teleology. *Canadian Journal of Zoology* 64: 1010-1020.

6487 Offerman-Zuckerberg, J, ed. 1991. *Politics and Psychology: Contemporary Psychodynamic Perspectives.* New York: Plenum.

6488 Oldroyd, D, I Langham, eds. 1983. *The Wider Domain of Evolutionary Thought.* Dordrecht: Reidel.

6489 Oldroyd, D. 1983. *Darwinian Impacts: An Introduction to the Darwinian Revolution.* 2nd ed. Sydney: University of New South Wales Press.

6490 Oldroyd, D. 1984. How did Darwin arrive at his theory? The secondary literature to 1982. *History of Science* 22: 325-374.

6491 Oldroyd, D. 1986. Charles Darwin's theory of evolution: A review of our present understanding. *Biology and Philosophy* 1: 133-168.

6492 Orel, V. 1984. *Mendel.* New York: Oxford University Press.

6493 Ospovat, D. 1981. *The Development of Darwin's Theory.* Cambridge: Cambridge University Press.

6494 Outram, D. 1984. *Georges Cuvier: Vocation, Science and Authority in Post-Revolutionary France.* Manchester: Manchester University Press.

6495 Oyama, S. 1986. *The Ontogeny of Information: Developmental Systems and Evolution.* Cambridge: Cambridge University Press.

6496 Oyama, S. 1991. Bodies and minds: Dualism in evolutionary theory. *Journal of Social Issues* 47: 27-42.

6497 Pagels, H. 1982. *The Cosmic Code.* New York: Simon & Schuster.

6498 Pagels, H. 1988. *The Dreams of Reason.* New York: Simon & Schuster.

6499 Paradis, J G. 1978. *T.H. Huxley: Man's Place in Nature.* Omaha: University of Nebraska Press.

6500 Pasmau, R O. 1990. Darwin's illness: A biopsychosocial perspective. *Psychosomatics* 31: 121-128.

6501 Passmore, J. 1971. *Man's Responsibility for Nature.* London: Duckwork.

6502 Paterson, H E H. 1985. The recognition concept of species. In *Species and Speciation.* Edited by Vrba, E S. Pp. 21-29. Pretoria: Transvaal Museum Monograph.

6503 Paul, C R C. 1982. The adequacy of the fossil record. In *Problems of Phylogenetic Reconstruction.* Edited by Joysey, K A, A E Friday. London: Academic Press.

6504 Paul, D. 1984. Eugenics and the Left. *Journal of the History of Ideas* 46: 567-590.

6505 Peacocke, A R. 1986. *God and the New Biology.* New York: Harper & Row.

6506 Piaget, J, R Garcia. 1989. *Psychogenesis and the History of Science.* New York: Columbia University Press.

6507 Pines, D, ed. 1988. *Emerging Syntheses in Science.* Reading, MA: Addison-Wesley.

6508 Plotkin, H C. 1982. Evolutionary epistemology and evolutionary theory. In *Learning, Development, and Culture: Essays in Evolutionary Epistemology.* Edited by Plotkin, H C. Pp. 3-16. Chichester: Wiley.

6509 Plotkin, H C, ed. 1982. *Learning, Development and Culture: Essays in Evolutionary Epistemology.* New York: Wiley.

6510 Plotkin, H C. 1987. Evolutionary epistemology as science. *Biology and Philosophy* 2: 295-314.

6511 Pollard, J, ed. 1984. *Evolutionary Theory: Paths into the Future.* New York: Wiley.

6512 Potter, V R. 1990. Getting to the Year 3000: Can global bioethics overcome evolution's fatal flaw? *Perspectives in Biology and Medicine* 34: 89-98.

6513 Prigogine, I. 1976. Order through fluctuation: Self-organization and social system. In *Evolution and Consciousness.* Edited by Jontach, E, C H Waddington. Reading, MA: Addison-Wesley.

6514 Prigogine, I, I Stengers. 1984. *Order Out of Chaos.* New York: Bantam.

6515 Qumsiyeh, M B. 1990. On the nature of controversies in evolutionary biology. *Perspectives in Biology and Medicine* 33: 241-230.

6516 Rachels, J. 1990. *Created from Animals: The Moral Implications of Darwinism.* New York: Oxford University Press.

6517 Radniszsky, G, W Bartley. 1987. *Evolutionary Epistemology, Theory of Rationality, and the Sociology of Knowledge.* La Salle, Ill.: Open Court.

6518 Radnitzsky, G, W W Bartley, eds. 1984. *Evolutionary Epistemology, Rationality, and the Sociology of Knowledge.* La Salle, Ill: Open Court.

6519 Rappoport, A. 1991. Ideological commitments in evolutionary theories. *Journal of Social Issues* 47: 83-100.

6520 Raup, D M. 1986. *The Nemesis Affair: The Story of the Death of Dinosaurs and the Ways of Science.* New York: Norton.

6521 Reanney, D. 1991. *The Death of Forever: A New Future for Human Consciousness.* London: Longman Cheshire.

6522 Rehbock, P F. 1983. *The Philosophical Naturalist.* Madison: University of Wisconsin Press.

6523 Rensch, B. 1972. *Homo Sapiens: From Man to DemiGod.* New York: Columbia University Press.

6524 Rescher, N, ed. 1990. *Evolution, Cognition, and Realism: Studies in Evolutionary Epistemology.* Lanham, MD: University Press of America.

6525 Reusch, B. 1978. *Biophilosophy.* New York: Columbia University Press.

6526 Rhea, B, ed. 1981. *The Future of the Sociological Classics.* Boston: Allen and Unwin.

6527 Richards, R J. 1977. Discussion: The natural selection model of conceptual evolution. *Philosophy of Science* 44: 494-501.

6528 Richards, R J. 1986. A defense of evolutionary ethics. *Biology and Philosophy* 1: 265-292.

6529 Richards, R J. 1986. Justification through biological faith: A rejoinder. *Biology and Philosophy* 1: 337-354.

6530 Richards, R J. 1987. *Darwin and the Emergence of Evolutionary Theory of Mind and Behavior.* Chicago: University of Chicago Press.

6531 Riddiford, A, D Penny. 1984. The scientific status of modern evolutionary theory. In *Evolutionary Theory: Paths into the Future.* Edited by Pollard, J. Pp. 1-38. New York: Wiley.

6532 Rieber, R W, ed. 1980. *Wilhelm Wundt and the Making of a Scientific Psychology.* New York: Plenum.

6533 Riedl, R. 1980. *Biology of Knowledge.* Chichester: Wiley.

6534 Roades, F H T. 1986. Darwinian gradualism and its limits: The development of Darwin's views on the rate and pattern of evolutionary change. *Journal of the History of Biology* 20: 139-158.

6535 Romanes, G. 1892. *Animal Intelligence.* New York: Appleton.

6536 Romanes, G. 1970 [1888]. *Mental Evolution in Man: Origin of Human Faculty.* New York: Gregg International.

6537 Rose, S. 1982. *Towards a Liberatory Biology.* London: Allison and Busby.

6538 Rose, S, ed. 1982. *Against Biological Determinism.* New York: Schocken.

6539 Rosenberg, A. 1980. *Sociobiology and the Preëmption of Social Science.* Baltimore: Johns Hopkins.

6540 Rosenberg, A. 1985. *The Structure of Biological Science*. New York: Cambridge University Press.

6541 Rosenberg, A. 1986. Ignorance and disinformation in the philosophy of biology: A reply to Stent. *Biology and Philosophy* 1: 461-471.

6542 Rottschaefer, W A, D Martinsen. 1990. Really taking Darwin seriously: An alternative to Michael Ruse's Darwinian metaethics. *Biology and Philosophy* 5: 175-196.

6543 Runkel, P J. 1990. *Casting Nets and Testing Specimens: Two Grand Methods of Psychology*. Westport, CT: Praeger.

6544 Ruse, M. 1979. *Sociobiology: Sense or Nonsense?* London: Reidel.

6545 Ruse, M. 1981. *The Darwinian Revolution: Science Red in Tooth and Claw*. Chicago: University of Chicago Press.

6546 Ruse, M. 1982. Is human sociobiology a new paradigm? *Philosophical Forum* 13: 119-143.

6547 Ruse, M. 1982. *Darwinism Defended : A Guide to the Evolution Controversies*. Reading, MA: Addison-Wesley.

6548 Ruse, M, ed. 1983. *Nature Animated: Historical and Philosophical Studies in Greek Medicine, 19th Century and Recent Biology, Psychiatry, and Psychoanalysis*. Dortrecht: Reidel.

6549 Ruse, M. 1984. Is there a limit to our knowledge of evolution? *Biological Science* 34: 100-104.

6550 Ruse, M. 1986. Evolutionary ethics: A phoenix arisen. *Zygon* 21: 95-112.

6551 Ruse, M, E O Wilson. 1986. Moral philosophy as applied science. *Philosophy* 61: 173-192.

6552 Ruse, M. 1989. *The Philosophy of Biology Today*. Albany: SUNY Press.

6553 Ruse, M, ed. 1989. *What the Philosophy of Biology Is : Essays Dedicated to David Hull*. Boston: Kluwer Academic.

6554 Ruvolo, M. 1987. Reconstructing genetic and linguistic trees: Phonetic and cladistic approaches. In *Biological Metaphor and Cladistic Classification: An Interdisciplinary Perspective*. Edited by

Hoenigswald, H M, L F Wiener. Pp. 193-216. Philadelphia: University of Pennsylvania Press.

6555 Sahlins, M. 1976. *The Use and Abuse of Biology.* Ann Arbor: University of Michigan Press.

6556 Sahtouris, E. 1989. *Gaia.* New York: Bantam.

6557 Salk, J. 1983. *Anatomy of Reality.* New York: Columbia University Press.

6558 Sapp, J. 1987. *Beyond the Gene: Cytoplasmic Inheritance and the Struggle for Authority in Genetics.* New York: Oxford University Press.

6559 Schallmeyer, F, N Tennant. 1984. *Philosophy, Evolution and Human Nature.* London: Routledge.

6560 Schleidt, W M, ed. 1988. *Der Kreis um Konrad Lorenz. Ideen, Hypothesen, Ansichten.* Berlin: Paul Parey.

6561 Schmid, M, F M Wuketis, eds. 1987. *Evolutionary Theory in Social Science.* Dortrecht: Kluwer.

6562 Schubert, G. 1985. Review essay: Epigenetic evolutionary theory - Waddington in retrospect. *Journal of Social and Biological Structures* 8: 233-253.

6563 Schwartz, G. 1987. The unification of psychology and modern physics. In *The Emergence of Personality.* Edited by Aronoff, J, et al. New York: Springer.

6564 Schwemmler, W. 1989. *Symbiogenesis: A Macro-Mechanism of Evolution.* New York: de Gruyter.

6565 Segerstråle, U. 1986. Colleagues in conflict: An in vitro analysis of the sociobiology controversy. *Biology and Philosophy* 1: 53-87.

6566 Segerstråle, U. 1987. Scientific controversy as moral-political discourse. *Contemporary Sociology* 16: 544-547.

6567 Segerstråle, U. 1990. Social taboos and the distortion of academic discourse: A meta-critique of critical reasoning. In *In Science We Trust? Moral and Political Issues in Science and Society.* Edited by Elzinga, A, J Nolin, R Pranger, S Sunesson. Lund: Lund University Press.

6568 Segerstråle, U. 1990. The sociobiology of conflict and the conflict about sociobiology. In *Sociobiology and Conflict:*

*Evolutionary Perspectives on Competition, Cooperation, Violence and Warfare.* Edited by van der Dennen, J, V Falger. London: Chapman and Hall.

6569 Segerstråle, U. 1990. Negotiating 'sound science': Expert disagreement about release of genetically engineered organisms. *Politics and the Life Sciences* 8: 221-231.

6570 Segerstråle, U. 1992. Critique of anti-reductionist reasoning. *Politics and the Life Sciences* 11: 199-214.

6571 Seielstad, G. 1989. *At the Heart of the Web.* San Diego: Harcourt, Brace, Jovanovich.

6572 Shanahan, T. 1990. Evolution, phenotypic selection, and the units of selection. *Philosophy of Science* 57: 210-226.

6573 Sheldrake, C. 1981. *A New Science of Life: The Hypothesis of Formative Causation.* London: Bond.

6574 Simpson, G G. 1971. *The Meaning of Evolution.* New York: Bantam Books.

6575 Simpson, G G. 1978. *Concession to the Improbable.* New Haven: Yale University Press.

6576 Simpson, G G. 1980. *Splendid Isolation.* New Haven: Yale University Press.

6577 Singer, P. 1981. *The Expanding Circle: Ethics and Sociobiology.* New York: Farrar, Straus and Giroux.

6578 Sintonen, M. 1990. Darwin's long and short arguments. *Philosophy of Science* 57: 677-89.

6579 Sirks, M, C Zirkle. 1964. *The Evolution of Biology.* New York: Ronald Press.

6580 Skinner, B F. 1971. *Beyond Freedom and Dignity.* New York: Knopf.

6581 Sloan, P R. 1986. Darwin, vital matter, and the transformation of species. *Journal of the History of Biology* 19: 369-445.

6582 Smith, C U M. 1976. *The Problem of Life: An Essay in the Origins of Biological Thought.* London: Macmillan.

6583 Smith, C U M. 1978. Charles Darwin, the origin of consciousness, and panpsychism. *Journal of the History of Biology* 11: 245-67.

6584 Smith, C U M. 1982. Evolution and the problem of mind: Part 1, Herbert Spencer. *Journal of the History of Biology* 5: 55-88.

6585 Smith, C U M. 1983. Herbert Spencer's epigenetic epistemology. *Studies in the History and Philosophy of Science* 14: 1-22.

6586 Smith, C U M. 1986. Friedrich Nietzsche's biological epistemics. *Journal of Social and Biological Structures* 9: 375-88.

6587 Smith, C U M. 1987. 'Clever beasts who invented knowing': Nietzsche's evolutionary biology of knowledge. *Biology and Philosophy* 2: 1-27.

6588 Smith, J. 1988. Eugenics and Utopia. *Daedalus* 117: 73-92.

6589 Smith, C U M. 1989. Evolution, epistemology and visual science. In *Issues in Evolutionary Epistemology*. Edited by Hahlweg, K, C Hooker. Pp. 527-44. Albany, NY: SUNY Press.

6590 Smith, C U M. 1991. *The Problem of Mind: Evolution, Neuroscience, Philosophy*. London: Athlone.

6591 Smolensky, P. 1986. Information processing in dynamical systems: Foundations of harmony theory. In *Parallel Distributed Processing*. Edited by Rumelhart, D E, J L McClelland. Pp. 194-281. Cambridge: MIT Press.

6592 Sober, E. 1984. *The Nature of Selection: Evolutionary Theory in Philosophical Focus*. Cambridge: M.I.T. Press.

6593 Somit, A, S Peterson, eds. 1992. *The Dynamics of Evolution: The Punctuated Evolution Debate in the Natural and Social Sciences*. Ithaca: Cornell University Press.

6594 Spencer, F, ed. 1982. *A History of American Physical Anthropology 1930-1980*. New York: Academic Press.

6595 Sperry, R W. 1983. *Science and Moral Priority*. New York: Columbia University Press.

6596 Stamps, J A. 1991. Why evolutionary issues are reviving interest in proximate behavioral mechanisms. *American Zoologist* 31: 338-348.

6597 Stanley, S M. 1979. *Macroevolution: Pattern and Process.* San Francisco: W.H. Freeman.

6598 Stebbins, G L, F Ayala. 1985. The evolution of Darwinism. *Scientific American* 253: 72-82.

6599 Steele, E J. 1981. *Somatic Selection and Adaptive Evolution: On the Inheritance of Acquired Characters.* 2nd ed. Chicago: University of Chicago.

6600 Steele, E, R M Gorczynski, J W Pollard. 1984. The somatic selection of acquired characters. In *Evolutionary Theory: Paths into the Future.* Edited by Pollard, J W. Pp. 217-237. New York: Wiley.

6601 Steele, E J, J W Pollard. 1987. Hypothesis: Somatic hypermutation by gene conversion via the error prone DNA-RNA-DNA information loop. *Molecular Immunology* 24: 667-673.

6602 Steele, E J, L Tayler, G Both. 1990. Somatic mutation in antibody genes. *Today's Life Science* 2: 28-36.

6603 Steele, E J, ed. 1991. *Somatic Hypermutation in V-Regions.* Boston: CRC Press.

6604 Stocking, G. 1982. *A Franz Boas Reader: The Shaping of American Anthropology1883-1911.* Chicago: University of Chicago Press.

6605 Stocking, G W. 1987. *Victorian Anthropology.* New York: Free Press.

6606 Stocking, G, ed. 1988. *Bones, Bodies, Behavior: Essays on Biological Anthropology.* Madison: University of Wisconsin Press.

6607 Sulloway, F. 1979. *Freud, Biologist of the Mind: Beyond the Psychoanalytic Legend.* New York: Basic Books.

6608 Sulloway, F. 1982. Darwin and his finches: The evolution of a legend. *Journal of the History of Biology* 15: 1-53.

6609 Thomas, K. 1983. *Man and the Natural World: Charting Attitudes in England 1500-1800.* London: Allen Lane.

6610 Thompson, P. 1987. A defense of the semantic conception of evolutionary theory. *Biology and Philosophy* 2: 26-32.

6611 Thompson, P. 1989. *The Structure of Biological Theories.* Albany: SUNY Press.

6612 Thornton, E M. 1984. *The Freudian Fallacy: An Alternative View of Freudian Theory*. New York: Dial Press.

6613 Thorpe, W. 1974. *Animal Nature and Human Nature*. London: Methuen.

6614 Thorpe, W H. 1979. *The Origins and Rise of Ethology*. New York: Praeger.

6615 Tinbergen, N. 1974. *Curious Naturalists*. New York: Anchor.

6616 Trigg, R. 1986. Evolutionary ethics. *Biology and Philosphy* 1: 325-336.

6617 van den Berghe, P L. 1990. Why most sociologists don't (and won't) think evolutionarily. *Sociological Forum* 5: 173-186.

6618 van Parijs, P. 1981. *Evolutionary Explanation in the Social Sciences: An Emerging Paradigm*. Totowa, NJ: Roman and Littlefield.

6619 von Schilcher, F, N Tennant. 1984. *Philosophy, Evolution and Human Nature*. London: Routledge and Kegan Paul.

6620 Wachbroit, R. 1986. Progress: Metaphysical and otherwise. *Philosophy of Science* 53: 354-371.

6621 Waddington, C H. 1957. *The Strategy of the Genes*. London: Allen and Unwin.

6622 Waddington, C H. 1961. *The Ethical Animal*. New York: Atheneum.

6623 Waddington, C H. 1975. *The Evolution of an Evolutionist*. Ithaca: Cornell University Press.

6624 Waddington, C H. 1978. *The Man-made Future*. London: Croom Helm.

6625 Waddinton, C, ed. 1968. *Toward a Theoretical Biology. An IUBS Symposium*. Chicago: Aldine.

6626 Wallace, A R. 1913. *Social Environment and Moral Progress*. New York: Cassell.

6627 Wallace, R A. 1980. *The Genesis Factor*. New York: William Morrow.

6628 Walton, D. 1991. The units of selection and the bases of selection. *Philosophy of Science* 58: 417-435.

6629 Wasserman, G. 1981. On the nature of the theory of evolution. *Philosophy of Science* 48: 416-437.

6630 Waters, C K. 1986. Natural selection without survival of the fittest. *Biology and Philosophy* 1: 207-225.

6631 Webster, G, B C Goodwin. 1982. The origin of species: A structuralist approach. *Journal of Social and Biological Structures* 5: 15-47.

6632 Weigele, T C, ed. 1982. *Biology and the Social Sciences: An Emerging Revolution.* Boulderlo.: Westview Press.

6633 Wiley, E O, D R Brooks. 1982. Victims of history: A nonequilibrium approach to evolution. *Systematic Zoology* 31: 1-24.

6634 Wills, C. 1991. *Exons, Introns, and Talking Genes: The Science Behind the Human Genome Project.* New York: Basic Books.

6635 Wilson, E O. 1976. The social instinct. *Bulletin of the American Academy of Arts and Sciences* 30: 11-25.

6636 Wilson, E O. 1977. Biology and the social sciences. *Daedalus* 106: 127-140.

6637 Wilson, E O. 1978. *On Human Nature.* Cambridge: Harvard University Press.

6638 Wilson, E O. 1980. *Comparative Social Theory.* Ann Arbor: Tanner Foundation.

6639 Wilson, E O. 1980. The relation of science to theology. *Zygon* 15: 425-434.

6640 Wilson, E O. 1984. *Biophilia: The Human Bond with Other Species.* Cambridge: Harvard University Press.

6641 Woodcock, A, M Davis. 1978. *Catastrophe Theory.* New York: Avon.

6642 Wuketis, F. 1990. *Evolutionary Epistemology and Its Implications for Humankind.* Albany, NY: SUNY.

6643 Wuketits, F M, ed. 1986. *Concepts and Approaches in Evolutionary Epistemology.* Dordrect: Reidel.

6644 Wuketits, F M. 1986. Evolution as a cognition process: Towards an evolutionary epistemology. *Biology and Philosophy* 1: 191-202.

6645 Yates, F, ed. 1987. *Self-Organizing Systems.* New York: Plenum.

6646 Yerkes, R. 1925. *Almost Human.* New York: Century.

6647 Young, R M. 1969. Malthus and the evolutionists: The common context of biological and social theory. *Past and Present* 43: 109-145.

6648 Young, R M. 1970. *Mind, Brain and Adaptation in the Nineteenth Century.* Oxford: Clarendon Press.

6649 Young, R M. 1971. Evolutionary biology and ideology: Then and now. In *The Social Impact of Modern Biology.* Edited by Fuller, W. Pp. 178-189. London: Routledge.

6650 Young, R M. 1985. *Darwin's Metaphor: Nature's Place in Victorian Culture.* Cambridge: Cambridge University Press.

6651 Zirkle, C. 1946. The early history of the idea of the inheritance of acquired characters and of pangenesis. *Transactions of the American Philosophical Society, N.S.* 5: 91-151.

6652 Zirkle, C, ed. 1949. *Death of a Science in Russia: The Fate of Genetics as Described in Pravda and Elsewhere.* Philadelphia: University of Pennsylvania Press.

6653 Zirkle, C. 1951. The knowledge of heredity before 1900. In *Genetics in the 20th Century: Essays on the Progress of Genetics during its First Fifty Years.* Edited by Dunn, L C. New York: Macmillan.

6654 Zirkle, C. 1959. *Evolution, Marxian Biology, and the Social Scene.* Philadelphia: University of Pennsylvania Press.

# 20

# Bibliography and Reference

6655 Akins, F R, et al., eds. 1981. *Behavioral Development of Nonhuman Primates: An Abstracted Bibliography.* New York: Plenum.

6656 Anon. 1982. *Learning and Communication. An Abstracted Bibliography 1971-1980. Psychological Abstracts, Supplement 2.* Washington: American Psychological Association.

6657 Anon. 1984. Infanticide. In *Infanticide.* Edited by Hausfater, G, S B Hrdy. Pp. 521-587. New York: Aldine.

6658 Anon. 1988. Bibliography [of Eurasia Prehistory]. In *Upper Pleistocene Prehistory of Western Eurasia.* Edited by Dibble, H L, A Montet-White. Pp. 431-461. Philadelphia: University Museum, University of Pennsylvania.

6659 Anon. 1990. Bibliography of recent literature in sleep research. *Sleep* 13: 286-295.

6660 Arnold, C, J W Bowers, eds. 1984. *Handbook of Rhetorical and Communication Theory.* Boston: Allyn & Bacon.

6661 Atkinson, R C, R J Herrnstein, G Lindsey, R D Luce, eds. 1988. *Steven's Handbook of Experimental Psychology.* 2nd ed. New York: Wiley.

6662 Ausubel, D, E V Sullivan, S W Ives, eds. 1980. *Theory and Problems of Child Development.* New York: Grune and Stratton [Bibliography pp. 484-596].

6663 Bahn, P G, J Vertut. 1988. Bibliography [of Ice Age Art]. In *Images of the Ice Age.* Edited by Bahn, P G, J Vertut. Pp. 216-234. Leicester: Windward.

6664 Baker, J R. 1974. *Race.* London: Oxford University Press [Bibliography of 1200 titles].

6665 Barnett, S A. 1979. Cooperation, conflict, crowding and stress: An essay on method. *Interdisciplinary Science Review* 4: 106-131 [Bibliography of 300 titles].

6666 Beach, F A. 1974. A review of physiological and psychological studies of sexual behaviour in mammals. *Psychological Reviews* 27: 240-307.

6667 Beaton, A. 1985. *Left Side, Right Side: A Review of Laterality Research*. London: Batsford.

6668 Binstock, R H, E Shanas, eds. 1976. *Handbook of Aging and the Social Sciences*. New York: Van Nostrand Reinhold.

6669 Bjorklund, A, T Hokfeld. 1985. *Handbook of Chemical Neuroanatomy: GABA and Neuropeptides in the CNS, Part 1*. Amsterdam: Elsevier.

6670 Brooks, V B, ed. 1981. *Handbook of Physiology: The Nervous System II*. Bethesda, Md.: American Physiological Society.

6671 Carver, C, M Scheier. 1988. *Perspectives on Personality*. Boston: Allyn and Bacon [Bibliography pp. 529-580].

6672 Ciolek, T M. 1974. Human communicational behaviour: A bibliography. *Sign Language Studies* 6: 1-64.

6673 Ciolek, T M, R Elzinga, A McHoul. 1979. Selected references to coenetics (the study of behavioural organization of face-to-face interaction). *Sign Language Studies* 22: 1-74.

6674 Crabtree, J M, K E Moyer. 1981. *Bibliography of Aggressive Behavior: A Reader's Guide to the Research Literature. 2 vols.* New York: Alan R. Liss.

6675 Cziko, G, D Campbell. 1990. Comprehensive bibliography: Evolutionary epistemology. *Journal of Social and Biological Structures* 13:

6676 Davis, E B. 1981. *Using the Biological Literature.* New York/Basel: Mercel Dekker.

6677 Davis, M, J Skupien, eds. 1982. *Body Movement and Non-Verbal Communication: An Annotated Bibliography 1971-1981*. Bloomington: University of Indiana Press.

6678 Divale, W T. 1973. *Warfare in Primitive Societies: A Bibliography*. Santa Barbara: Clio.

6679 Estes, R D. 1991. *The Behavior Guide to African Mammals*. Los Angeles: University of California Press.

6680 Ferguson, R B, L Farragher. 1988. *The Anthropology of War: A Bibliography*. H.F. Guggenheim Occasional Paper. NTIS, 1.

6681 Fielder, K, J Forgas, eds. 1988. *Affect, Cognition and Social Behavior: New Evidence and Integrative Attempts*. Toronto: C.J. Hogrefe [Bibliography pp. 241-288].

6682 Freedman, R. 1975. *The Sociology of Human Fertility: An Annotated Bibliography*. New York: Irvington Publishers.

6683 Galle, H-K. 1980-. *Publikationen zu Wissenschaftlichen Film ISSN 0073-8417*. Göttingen: Institut für Wissenschaftlichen Film.

6684 Goshen, D A. 1969. *Handbook of Socialization Theory and Research*. Chicago: Rand-McNally.

6685 Grzimek, B, ed. 1976. *Grzimek's Encyclopedia of Evolution*. New York: Van Nostrand Reinhold.

6686 Harré, R, R Lamb, eds. 1986. *The Dictionary of Ethology and Animal Learning*. Cambridge: M.I.T. Press.

6687 Hewes, G W. 1975. *Language Origins: A Bibliography*. 2nd ed. The Hague: Mouton.

6688 Honigmann, J. 1973. *Handbook of Social and Cultural Anthropology*. Chicago: Rand McNally.

6689 Issacs, H. 1981. *A Biosociocultural Bibliography for Interdisciplinary Graduate Research*. Monticello, IL: Vance Bibliographies.

6690 Iverson, L L, S D Iverson, S H Snyder, eds. 1984. *Handbook of Psychopharmacology*. New York: Plenum.

6691 Jackson, D N. 1976. *Jackson Personality Inventory Manual*. Goshen, New York: Research Psychologists' Press.

6692 Jensen, A R. 1972. *Genetics and Education*. London: Methuen [Bibliography pp. 336-369].

6693 Kemmer, E. 1977. *Rape and Rape-related Issues: An Annotated Bibliography*. New York: Garland.

6694 Keppel, G. 1982. *Design and Analysis: A Researcher's Handbook*. Englewood Cliffs: Prentice-Hall.

6695 Kuper, J, ed. 1988. *A Lexicon of Psychology, Psychiatry, and Psychoanalysis*. London: Routledge.

6696 Kurland, J. 1980. Kin selection theory: A review and selective bibliography. *Ethology and Sociobiology* 1: 255-274.

6697 La Barre, W. 1971. Material for a history of studies of crisis cults: A bibliographic essay. *Current Anthropology* 12: 3-44.

6698 Lehner, P N. 1979. *Handbook of Ethological Methods.* New York: Garland.

6699 Macdonald, D, ed. 1984. *The Encyclopaedia of Mammals.* London: Allen & Unwin.

6700 March, J G, ed. 1965. *Handbook of Organization.* Chicago: Rand McNally.

6701 Marler, P, J G van den Bergh, eds. 1980. *Handbook of Behavioral Neurobiology.* New York: Plenum.

6702 McFarland, D, ed. 1981. *The Oxford Companion to Animal Behaviour.* Oxford: Oxford University Press.

6703 Miletich, J J. 1988. *States of Awareness: An Annotated Bibliography.* Westport, CT: Greenwood Press.

6704 Money, J. 1990. *Venuses Penises: Sexology, Sexosophy, and Exigency Theory.* Buffalo, N.Y.: Prometheus Books [Bibliography of sexology, 1948-1985, pp. 613-659].

6705 Munroe, R H, R L Munroe, B Whiting, eds. 1981. *Handbook of Cross-cultural Human Development.* New York: Garland.

6706 Murdock, G. 1967. *Enthographic Atlas.* Pittsburgh: University of Pittsburgh Press.

6707 Napier, J R, P H Napier, eds. 1967. *Handbook of Living Primates.* New York: Academic Press.

6708 Neu, J, ed. 1980. *Isis Cumulative Bibliography, 1966-1975: A Bibliography of the History of Science Formed from the Isis Critical Bibliographies 91-100, 1965-1974.* London: Mansell.

6709 O'Leary, T. 1963. *Bibliography of South American Indians.* New Haven: Human Relations Area File.

6710 Oetzel, R M. 1966. Annotated Bibliography. In *The Development of Sex Differences.* Edited by Maccoby, E E. Stanford: Stanford University Press.

6711 Oldroyd, D. 1984. How did Darwin arrive at his theory? The secondary literature to 1982. *History of Science* 22: 325-374.

6712 Powell, F C. 1982. *Statistical Tables for the Social, Biological and Physical Sciences.* Cambridge: Cambridge University Press.

6713 Pritchard, J L. 1991. *Pan Paniscus Bibliography: Anatomy, Behavior, Colony Management, Conservation/Ecology, Field Studies, Genetics & Taxonomy. A Selective Bibliography, 1970-1991.* Seattle: Primate Inormation Centre.

6714 Renshon, S A, ed. 1977. *Handbook of Political Socialization.* New York: Free Press.

6715 Rogoff, B. 1990. *Apprenticeship in Thinking: Cognitive Development in Social Context.* New York: Oxford University Press [Bibliography pp. 211-32].

6716 Runkel, P, J E McGrath. 1972. *Research on Human Behavior: A Systematic Guide to Method.* New York: Holt, Rinehart, and Winston.

6717 Sargent, F. 1983. *Human Ecology: A Guide to Information Sources.* Detroit: Gale Research Co.

6718 Satinoff, E, P Teitelbaum, eds. 1983. *Handbook of Behavioral Neurobiology: Motivation.* New York: Plenum Press.

6719 Scherer, K R, P Ekmann, eds. 1982. *Handbook of Methods in Nonverbal Behavior Research.* New York: Cambridge University Press.

6720 Selye, H, ed. 1984. *Selye's Guide to Stress Research.* New York: Van Nostrand Reinhold.

6721 Shea, J. 1983. *An Annotated Bibliography of Family Involvement.* Washington: Prepared for the Office of Adolescent Family Life Program.

6722 Somit, A, et al. 1980. *The Literature of Biopolitics.* DeKalb, IL: Northern Illinois University.

6723 Somit, A, S Peterson. 1990. *Biopolitics and Mainstream Political Science: A Master Bibliography.* DeKalb, IL: Northern Illinois University.

6724 Sommer, B, R Sommer. 1991. *A Practical Guide to Behavioral Research. Tools and Techniques.* 3rd ed. New York: Oxford University Press.

6725 Sorenson, E, C Gajdusek. 1966. *The Study of Child Behavior and Development in Primitive Cultures. A Research Archive for Ethnopediatric Film Investigations of Styles in the Patterning of the Nervous System. Pediatrics* 37 Supplement.

6726 Trivers, R. 1985. *Social Evolution.* Menlo Park, Ca: Benjamin-Cummings [Bibliography of 700 titles].

6727 van der Dennen, J. 1981. On war: Concepts, definitions, research data: A literature review and bibliography. In *UNESCO Yearbook on Peace and Conflict Studies 1980.* Westport, CT: Greenwood Press.

6728 van der Dennen, J, ed. 1984. *Source Materials for the Study of 'Primitive' War: A Bibliography Containing Some 5,500 Enteries on Warfare, Feuding and Intratribal Violence in Preliterate Societies.* Groningen: Polemological Institute, Groningen.

6729 van der Dennen, J. 1985. Psychological approaches to war and macro-level violence: A critical review of the literature. In *Multidisciplinary Approaches to Conflict and Appeasement in Animals and Man.* Edited by LeMoli, F. Parma: Instituto de Zoologia.

6730 von Emmett, K, P K Machamer. 1976. *Perception: An Annotated Bibliography.* New York: Garland.

6731 von Key, M. 1977. *Nonverbal Communication: A Research Guide and Bibliography.* Metuchen, NJ: Scarecrow Press.

6732 von Peuser, G. 1977. *Sprache und Gehirn: Eine Bibliographie zur Neurolinguistik.* Munich: Fink.

6733 Wagner, H L, A S R Manstead, eds. 1989. *Handbook of Social Psychophysiology.* New York: Wiley.

6734 Walker, P, ed. 1989. *Chambers Biology Dictionary.* Edinburgh: Chambers.

6735 Wassersug, R, M Rose. 1984. A reader's guide and retrospective to the 1982 Darwin centennial. *Quarterly Review of Biology* 59: 417-434.

6736 Weinrich, J D. 1978. Nonreproduction, homosexuality, transsexualism, and intelligence: 1. A systematic literature search. *Journal of Homosexuality* 3: 275-289.

6737 Whitaker, H A, ed. 1988. *Contemporary Reviews in Neuropsychology.* New York: Springer.

# Author Index

Andreasen, NC 5470
Andrew, RJ 2390, 2391, 2392, 3791
Andrews, P 8
Angel, JL 9
Angermeier, WF 4683
Angst, J 5471
Ankney, CD 1984
Annett, M 1985, 5008
Antelman, SM 3792, 5472
Antkai, C 5803
Aoki, K 1531, 1532, 1533, 1534,
    1535, 1536, 1537, 1538
Appadurai, A 771
Appel, MA 4393
Appley, MH 4394
Apter, A 3793
Apter, D 772
Apter, MJ 4395, 5009, 5010, 5011
Arai, Y 3563
Aram, DM 4001
Arambourou, R 429
Arbib, M 4002
Archer, JE 1539,1540, 2393, 2394,
    2395, 2396, 3564, 3565, 3566,
    3567, 3568, 6220
Argyle, M 2397, 2398, 2399, 2400,
    2401, 5804, 5805
Aries, EJ 2402
Aries, P 3344
Armstrong, E 10, 4003
Arnhart, L 6073, 6074, 6075
Arnoff, J 5012
Arnold, AP 3569
Arnold, C 6660
Aronfreed, J 5806
Aronoff, J 6221
Aschoff, J 773
Ashton, H 4004
Asquith, PJ 5013
Atchley, WR 11
Attili, G 2403, 2404, 2405, 2406
Atkinson, RC 6661
Austin, CR 3571, 3572
Ausubel, DP 6652
Averill, JR 4396
Avison, WR 5473
Avoli, M 4005

Ax, AF 4397
Axelrod, J 774
Axelrod, R 1541, 1542, 1543, 1544,
    6078, 6079
Axelrod, S 4684
Ayala, FJ 6222, 6223, 6224
Azar, EE 6080
Azmitia, EC 3795
Babchuk, WA 4398
Babloyantz, A 4006, 6225
Bach-y-Rita, P 5015
Bachevalier, J 5016
Bachmann, C 1545, 2407
Backstrom, T 3586
Badcock, CR 1546, 4399
Badinter, E 3345
Baer, AS 1986
Baer, DM 1547, 4685, 4686 6081
Baer, RA 4687, 4688
Baerends, G 2408, 4007
Bagehot, W 6082
Bahn, PG 430, 431, 6663
Bailey, GN 432, 433
Bailey, J 4689
Bailey, KG 3573, 4008, 4400, 5474
Bailey, SM 775
Bailey, WT 2409
Bain, J 3574
Bairstow, PJ 4009
Bajema, CJ 1987
Bakan, P 1988, 1989
Bakeman, R 2410, 2411, 2412
Baker, AB 4010
Baker, H 434
Baker, JR 1990, 6664
Baker, MC 1991
Baker, PM 2413
Baker, PT 776
Bakke, EW 2414
Balandier, G 2415
Balch, SH 2416
Balck, M 2417
Baldassare, M 5807, 5808
Baldwin, JD 4011
Baldwin, JM 6226
Baldwin, W 777
Bales, RF 5809, 5810

Foote, SL 4106
Ford, CS 3653
Ford, K 862
Forde, CD 526
Forgas, J 4493
Forlec, R 3654
Forsyth, DR 5880
Fortes, M 2718
Foster, A 863
Foster, ML 2092, 2719, 5101, 6120
Foulks, EF 5410
Fowles, DC 5565
Fox, G 3395, 3655
Fox, MW 2721
Fox, NA 4107, 4108, 4109, 4494, 4495
Fox, R 2720, 2722, 2723, 6342, 6343, 6344, 6345
Fox, SW 2093
Fragaszy, DM 2724
Frank, RS 6121, 6122
Frankenhaeuser, M 864
Fray, P 2725, 5411
Frayer, DW 527
Frazer, JT 5102
Freedman, D 6347
Freedman, DG 1706, 1707, 2726, 2727
Freedman, JC 867
Freedman, JL 865, 5881, 5882
Freedman, R 866, 868, 6682
Freeman, D 2728, 2729, 6346, 6348, 6349
Freeman, LG, Jr 528
Freeman, RL 4110
Freid, M 2730
Freidman, RC 2733
Freidrich, H 2731
Freud, A 5566
Freud, S 5884
Frey, H 3852
Fride, E 3853
Fridlund, AJ 2732, 4496, 4497, 4498, 4499, 4500, 5567
Friedhoff, AJ 3854
Friedl, J 2094
Friedlaender, SJ 869

Friedman, L 4501, 5885
Friedman, LA 4111
Friedman, RC 3656
Frijda, NH 4502
Frisancho, AR 870, 871, 872
Frisby, JP 5103
Frisch, K 6350
Frisch, RE 873, 874, 875, 876, 877, 878, 879, 880, 881, 882
Frison, GC 529, 530, 531, 532, 533, 534, 535, 536, 537
Friswell, R 4503
Fritsch, V 5104
Fritz, MA 883
Frodi, AM 2734, 2735
Frof, S 4504, 5412
Frolov, I 6351, 6352
Froming, WJ 5886
Fromme, DK 2736, 2737
Frost, GT 5105
Fry, DP 1708, 2738
Fukuhara, S 2739
Fulker, DW 2095
Fuller, W 6353
Funkenstein, DH 4505
Funt, BV 5106
Furedy, JJ 4772
Furstenberg, F 3657, 3396, 3397
Fuster, JM 4112
Fuster, V 2096
Futuyma, DJ 6354
Gabrielli, WF 2097, 2098
Gage, DF 4113
Gajdusek, DC 2099
Galdikas, BMF 1709
Galef, BG 2740
Gallagher, JP 538
Gallez, D 4114
Gallup, GG 5107, 5108
Gamble, C 96, 540, 541, 542
Gamble, GC 539
Gamson, W 5887
Gandelman, R 3855, 3856
Gangestad, SW 2741, 3658, 5888
Ganten, D 3857
Garai, JE 2100
Garber, J 5568

# Subject Index

cargo 1220, 1604, 573
castration 3770
catatonia 5386
chance 6240, 6241
chaos theory 5333, 5362, 6361
charisma 5454, 5820
cheating 2645
chiefdom 1184, 1236, 1568, 1620
child abuse 3362, 3371, 3399, 3400, 3401, 3402, 3440, 3445, 3472, 3493, 3512, 3549, 3551, 3650; history of 3347
childhood, history 3344
children 995, 1022, 2470, 2849, 2850, 3006, 4925, 6084; childlessness 3590
chimpanzees 106, 129, 187, 242, 295, 409, 2377, 2613, 2614, 2635, 2819, 2869, 2924, 2930, 2931, 2995, 3007, 3009, 3050, 3051, 3052, 3101, 3258, 3337, 4379, 5110, 5121, 5243, 6362; cognition 5278, 5299, 5378; language learning of 5034, 5315, 5316, 5321, 5322, 5323, 5377, 5379; space perception of 5252
China 1190, 1574
choice 2587, 4911, 4913, 4969
chronomedicine 840
circadian rhythms 3821, 3886, 5585
circumscription theory 1181, 1183, 1186, 1273, 1336, 1351, 1443, 1458, 1501, 1565, 1567, 1570, 1657, 1720, 1735, 1827, 1842, 1885
cities 1385, 1392, 1470, 1472, 1508, 1769, 1776, 1854, 1856, 1892, 1902
civilization 621, 677, 726, 746, 794, 1008, 1172, 1187, 1241, 1243, 1247, 1253, 1272, 1313, 1314, 1371, 1451, 1481, 1488, 1556, 1571, 1625, 1627, 1631, 1637, 1656, 1697, 1698, 1755, 1835, 1865, 1872
climate 417, 614, 1148, 1532
coalitions 2616, 2625, 3325

cognition 1284, 1668, 2698, 2859, 2964, 2969, 2971, 4443, 5007, 5057, 5069, 5229, 5338, 5915; animal 5309; chimpanzee 3017, 3018, 3094, 5301; cognitive bias 5909; cognitive development 5119; cognitive map 5004, 5251, 5283; cognitive style 5197, 5199; nonlinear cognition 5140; social 5799, 5878, 6067; spatial 3709, 5078, 5272, 5370
color terms 2451, 3180
command 3142
command neuron 4082, 4087, 4316
communication 2676, 2956, 2986, 3049, 3079, 3283, 4051, 5236, 5283, 6016, 6650
competition 388, 1254, 1638, 3035, 3906, 4723, 4724, 4931, 4932, 4933; intergroup 6, 2216
complexity 6251
computation 5304
computer modelling 5030
concepts 1304,1688
conceptual behavior 4808, 4809
concurrent performances 4716
conditional discrimination 4693, 4769, 4834, 4943, 4942, 4944, 4950, 4976, 4994, 4995
conditioning 4750, 4866, 4867, 4993, 5073, 5821
conflict 2862, 3148, 6049; conflict resolution 6080
conformity 6056
connectionist model 4829
consciousness 55, 173, 4015, 4131, 4380, 4570, 5074, 5164, 5165, 5179, 5202, 5261, 5276, 5279, 5280, 5297, 5298, 5348, 5373, 5395, 5398, 5402, 5407, 5409, 5414, 5424, 5435, 5437, 5438, 5440, 5442, 5443, 5444, 5450, 5455, 5456, 5462, 5463, 5466, 6166, 6345, 6398, 6403; animal awareness 2437, 5141
conservatism 1346, 1730
constructional biology 6298

## About the Editor

HIRAM CATON is Professor of Politics and History, Griffith University, Brisbane, Australia.